Patent Protection for Second Medical Uses

AIPPI Law Series

VOLUME 2

Series Editors

AIPPI

Introduction & Contents/Subjects

Books in this series are developed within the framework of the International Association for the Protection of Intellectual Property (AIPPI), a non-affiliated non-profit organization dedicated to the development and improvement of legal regimes for the protection of intellectual property at both national and international levels.

Objective & Readership

The aim is to publish innovative work appealing to practitioners, other users of IP systems and academics.

The titles in this series are listed at the back of this volume.

Patent Protection for Second Medical Uses

Edited by

Jochen Bühling

Wolters Kluwer

Published by:
Kluwer Law International B.V.
PO Box 316
2400 AH Alphen aan den Rijn
The Netherlands
Website: www.wklawbusiness.com

Sold and distributed in North, Central and South America by:
Wolters Kluwer Legal & Regulatory U.S.
7201 McKinney Circle
Frederick, MD 21704
United States of America
Email: customer.service@wolterskluwer.com

Sold and distributed in all other countries by:
Turpin Distribution Services Ltd
Stratton Business Park
Pegasus Drive, Biggleswade
Bedfordshire SG18 8TQ
United Kingdom
Email: kluwerlaw@turpin-distribution.com

Printed on acid-free paper.

ISBN 978-90-411-8253-1

AIPPI Law Series ISBN 98-888-8020-8

Printed in the United Kingdom.

List of Contributors

Dan Altman

Dan Altman is a partner in the Orange County California office of Knobbe Martens. He specializes in patent protection and related licensing issues for the biotechnology, pharmaceutical and chemical industries. During law school, Mr. Altman was an editor for the Berkeley Technology Law Journal. He completed an externship with the former chief judge of the U.S. District Court for the Central District of California, and was an adjunct professor for 11 years at the University of San Diego School of Law, where he initiated a course entitled "Biotechnology Law."

Tal Band

Tal Band is a member of the Executive Board of S. Horowitz & Co. and Chair of the firm's Intellectual Property Practice Group. Tal represents leading players in the pharmaceuticals and life sciences industry in complex litigation on all matters relating to patents, trademarks and copyright issues. Tal serves as President of the Israel Chapter of AIPPI (since 2004) and is a regular speaker in conferences and contributor to practitioner reference books on IP.

Nicolaj Bording

Nicolaj Bording is an attorney-at-law with the Danish law firm Kromann Reumert. His practice primarily focuses on Danish and international patent litigation, but his expertise also includes licence agreements, technology transfer and research cooperation agreements, as well as trademark and other IP litigation. Nicolaj frequently gives lectures on patent related issues and has authored a number of articles within this area and is a co-author of *The Unified Patent Court – the administration of justice at Europe's new patent court*.

Jochen Bühling

Dr. jur., attorney-at-law, is a partner at the IP law firm Krieger Mes & Graf v. der Groeben specializing in patent and trademark matters with a strong focus on IP litigation. He advises national and international clients in all aspects of IP and has distinct experience, among others, in the field of pharmaceutical and biotechnological inventions, chemistry, medical engineering and electronics. He teaches IP law at the University of Münster (WWU) and publishes and lectures regularly about IP topics. In AIPPI, he held the office of Reporter General from 2006-2010.

Thierry Calame

Dr. iur., Attorney at Law, Partner at Lenz & Staehelin, Dipl. nat. sc. ETH (Chemistry). Thierry is an expert in intellectual property matters, with a particular emphasis in patent law and life sciences. He has over 20 years of experience as counsel in patent, trademark, copyright and unfair competition litigation as well as IP related arbitration. Thierry also sits as arbitrator in IP related arbitration and advises on licensing, the intellectual property aspects of a wide range of other transactions as well as pharmaceutical law, including regulatory and advertising issues.

An Chen

Mr. An Chen is a patent attorney and attorney at law at Wu, Feng & Zhang, who focuses his practice in chemical and pharmaceutical fields. He has over 13 years of extensive experience in the area of patent prosecution and client counseling concerning infringement, validity and FTO. He has a bachelor degree in organic synthesis and a master degree in chemical engineering and also obtained a LLM degree in intellectual property from a US law school.

Dan Davies

Daniel Davies practices litigation at Smart & Biggar. He represents clients in court proceedings involving patents, trademarks, copyrights and trade secrets. He also advises clients on intellectual property enforcement matters, and represents clients in trademark oppositions, trademark expungement proceedings, patent appeal board proceedings and domain name disputes. Daniel works with clients in a wide variety of fields, including high-tech, Internet, manufacturing, retail, pharmaceuticals, and oil and gas.

Maria Carmen de Souza Brito

Chemical engineer graduated from the State University of Rio de Janeiro. A patent specialist in the areas of chemistry. pharmaceutical, cosmetics, agribusiness, biotechnology and traditional knowledge, amongst others. Partner at the Dannemann Siemsen firm where she started her career in 1988. President of the Brazilian Intellectual Property Association (ABPI) for the 2016-2017 term and member of International Association for the Protection of Intellectual Property (AIPPI), Inter-American

Association of Intellectual Property (ASIPI) and Brazilian Association of Industrial Property Agents (ABAPI).

Amy Feng

Ms. Amy Feng has been practicing Patent law in the fields of Chemistry, Pharmaceuticals and Biotech for over 20 years. She is the founding partner of Wu, Feng & Zhang. She is a Chinese attorney at law and a patent attorney. She has a master degree in Organic Chemistry and she got LLM from the John Marshall Law Scholl of the U.S.A. She is the co-chair of Biotech/Pharma committee of AIPPI and the vice director of the patent law committee of Beijing Lawyers Association.

Steven Garland

Steven Garland is a partner at Smart & Biggar. He has 25 years of experience in intellectual property litigation of all types and regularly acts on behalf of innovator pharmaceutical and biopharmaceutical companies in respect of patent related matters. He has also mediated intellectual property disputes. Steven is a Past President of the International Association for the Protection of Intellectual Property (AIPPI) Canadian Group, Past President of the Intellectual Property Institute of Canada, and an adjunct professor of patent law.

Penny Gilbert

Dr. Penny Gilbert is a founding Partner of Powell Gilbert LLP. She has an MA in Biochemistry and DPhil in Molecular Biology from Oxford University and is a solicitor advocate and qualified mediator. Penny specialises in patent litigation, particularly in the life sciences. She represents clients before the UK Patents Courts, including acting in the first patent case to be heard by the UK Supreme Court, and has acted in referrals on the SPC Regulation to the CJEU and to the EFTA Court. Penny is a member of AIPPI and is President of the European Patent Lawyers Association (EPLAW).

Bianca Manuela Gutierrez

IP Law Firm Gutierrez. Practising as a lawyer in the industrial and intellectual property field for over thirty years. Founder in 1997 of the Law Firm Gutierrez in Milan, specialized and currently operating in litigation and counsel work in patent, trade-mark, unfair competition, copyright and related contractual matters. Author of several publications in the field of intellectual and industrial property and competition. Among these, *La Tutela del Diritto di Autore* (first edition: 2000; second edition: 2008).

Seong-Ki Kim

Co-Chair of Lee & Ko IP. Areas of practice: Chemical/Bio/Pharmaceutical; IP litigation, license & transaction, prosecution outside Korea. Work experience: Lee & Ko IP: 2015-Present; AIPPI KOREA, President: 2011-Present; Ministry of Food and Drug Safety, Expert: 2014-Present; Organizing Committee for AIPPI Congress 2012 Seoul, Chairman: 2011-2013; Korean Intellectual Property Office, Patent Examiner:

1985-1991; WIPO, EPO, USPTO, and JPO, Liaison Officer: 1981-1982. Awards: AIPPI Award of Merits (2013).

Gertjan Kuipers

Gertjan Kuipers is an attorney-at-law and partner at De Brauw Blackstone Westbroek. He studied law and physics at Utrecht University, and is a Fulbright alumnus of Franklin Pierce Law Center, Concord N.H. Gertjan advises and litigates for various international companies. He works mainly in cross-border projects, and has a vast experience in conducting and coordinating multi-jurisdictional litigation. His dual background in science and law serves him well in patent cases. Gertjan lectures on patent law at universities and to IP practitioners-in-training and is a country respondent for Bio Science Law Rèview.

Nicolai Lindgreen

Nicolai Lindgreen is an attorney-at-law and a partner of the Danish law firm Kromann Reumert. He has for many years predominantly been engaged with Danish and international patent litigation, but his practice also includes trademark and other IP litigation. He also advises on technology transfer, licensing, R&D and similar agreements. Nicolai is a frequent lecturer on patent-related topics and has authored a long list of articles, in particular within the patent area, and is a co-author of *The Annotated Danish Patents Act* and *The Unified Patent Court – the administration of justice at Europe's new patent court*.

Lei Liu

Dr. Lei Liu's practice at Smart & Biggar focusses on obtaining patent protection in Canada and around the world for pharmaceutical and biotechnology companies, universities, and research institutions. Lei has also been involved in numerous intellectual property transactional projects. Lei's educational background is in the fields of biotechnology, biological science and chemistry. His doctoral studies focused on cardiovascular, obesity and atherosclerosis research.

Lamberto Liuzzo

IP Law Firm Liuzzo. Founder in 1990 of the Law Firm Liuzzo, specialized in the field of Intellectual Property Law. Former Professor of Intellectual Property Law at Lumsa University in Rome. Lecturer of Intellectual Property Law at "Qualifying Course for the legal professions" at Law faculty of Tor Vergata and Lumsa Universities of Rome. For many years Research Fellow at Max Planck Institute for Foreign and International Patent, Copyright and Competition Law – Munich, Germany. Author of numerous publications in Italian and international Industrial Law journals. Invited speaker at numerous national and international conferences in the field of Intellectual Property. Associated to: AIPPI, LES, LIDC, EPLAW, GRUR e UAE.

Simon Tianle Luo

Mr. Simon Tianle Luo is a patent attorney and attorney at law at Wu, Feng & Zhang. He has been practicing Patent law in the fields of biotech and biopharmaceuticals for over 11 years. He has a bachelor degree in biological engineering from Beijing Institute of Technology and a master degree in biochemical engineering from the University of the Chinese Academy of Sciences. He did scientific research in Institute of Biophysics of the CAS before becoming a patent attorney.

Sarah Matheson

Sarah Matheson BA LLB is an attorney-at-law and a partner at Allens. She advises in contentious and non-contentious IP matters. She is an experienced patent litigator with a focus on acting for multinationals, and is also a registered Trade Marks Attorney. Sarah is the Reporter General of the International Association for the Protection of Intellectual Property (AIPPI), and a member of the Intellectual Property Society of Australia and New Zealand (IPSANZ), and the Licensing Executives Society of Australia and New Zealand (LESANZ).

Jürgen Meier

Dr. Meier is a European and German Patent Attorney, and a partner at Vossius & Partner, Munich. He has extensive experience representing clients before both national courts and the EPO in all phases of patent prosecution and litigation, including opposition, appeals, infringement actions and nullity suits. He primarily focuses on the fields of biotechnology, pharmaceuticals and medical uses. His legal expertise is supported by his technical background, having previously obtained a doctorate in molecular biology.

Shoichi Okuyama

Shoichi Okuyama is a registered Japanese Patent Attorney, Principal of Okuyama & Sasajima. He is the Vice-President of AIPPI Japan and a former President of the Japan Patent Attorneys Association. He holds a Ph.D. in chemistry from the University of Chicago and a bachelor's degree in E.E. from Waseda University in Tokyo. He serves as an expert member of the Intellectual Property Strategy Headquarters organized by the Prime Minister of Japan since 2013.

Tim Powell

Tim Powell is a founding Partner of Powell Gilbert LLP. He is a solicitor advocate and has represented clients as an advocate in the UK and European Patent Offices the English Courts and the European Court of Justice. Tim specialises in multi-jurisdictional litigation, particularly in the patents field where he has experience in coordinating litigation taking place simultaneously across Europe, North America and beyond. He also advises clients on healthcare regulatory issues. He is a member of the Intellectual Property Advisory Committee of the UK Bioindustry Association and a board member of IPLA.

Justyna Rasiewicz

Attorney at law, Partner in LDS Łazewski Depo & Partners. Litigator with wide experience in intellectual property cases. Extensive experience in patent litigation, in particular pharmaceutical and biotech. Recommended by IP Star, Chambers and Partners, The Legal 500, The World's Leading Trademark Professionals. Co-author of *Commentary to the Law on Combating Unfair Competition* (ed. 2011, 2016); of *Commentary to the Industrial Property Law* (ed. 2016); and *International Design Protection a Global Handbook* (2012).

Isabelle Romet

Isabelle Romet (1964) was admitted to the Bar in 1988. She is a partner with the French firm Véron & Associés that she co-founded, whose motto is 100 % patent litigation. She studied law at the Universities in Grenoble and Montpellier and at the Franklin Pierce Law center, USA. Like the other lawyers of the firm, she is active in all technical fields. However, she has developed a special expertise in life sciences and chemistry. Her experience in the field of pharmaceuticals goes with a focus on supplementary protection certificates. She extensively lectures on patent litigation including at Sciences Po Paris. She is a co-author of the book *Saisie-Contrefaçon*, published by French publisher Dalloz and edited by Pierre Véron (3rd edition, 2012).

Yoon Suk Shin

Yoon Suk Shin is a senior patent attorney at Lee International IP & Law Group with extensive experience of prosecuting patent applications before the Korean Intellectual Property Office in the fields of Chemistry, Biotechnology, Biochemistry and Pharmaceuticals. She has experience in handling patent litigation matters before the Korean Courts in the fields of pharmaceuticals and OLED materials. She has represented various clients in pharmaceutical regulatory matters with administrative bodies including the Patent-Marketing Approval Linkage System.

Hari Subramaniam

Hari Subramaniam is a leading IPR Attorney in practice for 35 years. He has been involved in over 40,000 cases including many landmark cases. He is a regular speaker at IPR fora worldwide including AIPPI, APAA, IPO, ABA and WIPO. He has authored several articles on IPR for leading international journals. He is a member of AIPPI Pharma and Biotech committees. Voted as "Leading Asia IPR Lawyer" by Asia Law for thirteen consecutive years and top tier Attorney by several magazines, he was featured in "50 IP Lawyers one must know in Asia and Oceania" in *Asia Law*.

Matthew Swinn

Matthew Swinn is a partner of King & Wood Mallesons, based in Melbourne. He is an intellectual property litigator recognised in particular for his patent litigation expertise in the manufacturing industries and life sciences sector, in which he also acts on other aspects of therapeutic goods regulation and marketing. Matt is a member of the Law Council of Australia's Intellectual Property Committee and convenes its patents sub-committee.

Marta Sznajder

Attorney-at-law trainee, PhD candidate in the Department of Intellectual Property Law, Faculty of Law of Warsaw University, preparing doctoral dissertation concerning prior user rights in the industrial property law. Specializes in litigations in the field of patent law including pharmaceutical and biotech patents, as well as in the field of industrial design infringement and unfair competition. Author of the articles focused on patent infringement under the doctrine of equivalents and its application in Polish jurisprudence.

Dora Talvard

Dora Talvard (1986) has been a member of the Paris Bar since 2013. She is an associate at French patent law firm Véron & Associés, whose activity is entirely devoted to patent litigation. She obtained a Master 2 degree in intellectual property law at the Centre for International Intellectual Property Studies (CEIPI), University of Strasbourg, after a Master 1 degree in international law at University Paris I Panthéon-Sorbonne. Like the other lawyers of the firm, she is active in all technical fields, with a focus on pharmaceutical cases and supplementary protection certificates. She lectures about patent litigation in the Intellectual Property Master 2 at the University of Lyon III.

Javier Uhthoff-Orive

As a senior partner in the patent department at Uhthoff, Gomez Vega & Uhthoff, he has had substantial experience representing numerous clients, mostly in advising multinational companies, protecting different types of innovations. He has advised an extensive variety of industries of Europe, North America, Asia and Latin America. Javier Uhthoff-Orive has established a leading international reputation for IP matters.

Jonas Westerberg

Jonas Westerberg, Partner and Head of IP at Lindahl, has more than 20 years' experience of patent litigation and currently spends 80 percent of his time on such matters. In addition he mainly represents clients in litigation concerning trade secrets and copyright, primarily in the context of disputes over right to technology. Most of the patent cases have concerned pharma patents (or SPCs). Jonas is a member of ICC Sweden's IP group and since long on the boards of the Swedish AIPPI group and the European Patent Lawyers Association (EPLAW).

Yair Ziv

Yair Ziv is an associate in the Intellectual Property Practice Group of S. Horowitz & Co., where he assists in the representation of clients in the pharmaceuticals and life sciences industry on various IP issues.

Table of Contents

Foreword

Felipe Claro

AIPPI, the International Association for the Protection of Intellectual Property, was founded in 1897 and is dedicated to the development, improvement, and legal protection of intellectual property. AIPPI is a non-affiliated, non-profit organization headquartered in Switzerland, having approximately 9,000 members representing over 100 countries. The members of AIPPI include lawyers, attorneys, and agents working across all fields of intellectual property in corporate and private practice throughout the world, as well as academics, judges, government officials and other persons interested in intellectual property. AIPPI is organized into 68 National and Regional Groups.

The objective of AIPPI is to improve and promote the protection of intellectual property at both national and international levels. It does this by studying and comparing existing and proposed laws and policies relating to intellectual property, and working with both government and non-government organisations for the development, expansion and improvement of international and regional treaties and agreements, and national laws.

As Series Editor, AIPPI is proud to continue working with Wolter Kluwer to produce the AIPPI Law Series, which introduces to a broader audience the substantial studies carried out by AIPPI's members in preparation for the Resolutions adopted by its Executive Committee.

The present volume was inspired by AIPPI's Resolution Q 238 – "Second medical use and other second indication claims" adopted at the AIPPI Congress in Toronto in 2014. The granting of patent protection for second medical uses encourages the development of solutions for unmet medical needs. Key to that incentive is the availability of enforceable patent rights of effective scope. This volume is a valuable tool for those working in or with the life sciences sector to navigate the key jurisdictional differences and challenges in protecting and enforcing second medical use claims.

AIPPI would particularly like to thank Jochen Bühling – Volume Editor, member of AIPPI and a past Reporter General. AIPPI is pleased to partner with him in an area which continues to see important legal developments. The chapter authors are also primarily AIPPI members. AIPPI sincerely thanks all contributors for their work on this timely and topical volume.

Felipe Claro
President of AIPPI
July 2016

Introduction

Dr. Jochen Bühling

The importance of inventions in the medical field continues to increase. Article 27 of TRIPS expressly states that patents must be granted for inventions in all fields of technology. However, it also allows the exclusion from patentability for diagnostic, therapeutic and surgical methods for the treatment of humans or animals.

The discussions around the patent protection for pharmaceuticals which led to the Doha Declaration on TRIPS and Public Health in 2001 and further decisions by the WTO remain very relevant today.

Besides the controversies about patent protection for pharmaceuticals and the related public health issues, the legal questions in this field concerning the availability of protection, the conditions for protection and the scope of protection for pharmaceutical patents are of much more than academic interest. They are of tremendous practical importance for the pharmaceutical industry, governments and the broader public. The underlying public health issues are often based on political, social, ethical, and maybe even religious considerations. These considerations are necessarily reflected in the legal problems to which they are linked.

One of the central topics is patent protection for so-called second medical uses. In general, this concerns the use of a known pharmaceutical substance or compound for a new medical indication (the "second medical use"). To the extent there is controversy as to whether patent protection for second medical uses should be allowed at all, the focus is again mainly on non-legal considerations. Once the decision has been made to allow such protection, rather than prohibit it in general, there are a number of questions around practical implementation.

There are significant differences between jurisdictions around the world in this regard, although they may share common approaches in patent law in general. It is the purpose of this volume to give an insight into the legal issues and the practical implications of second medical use claims in various jurisdictions. It serves as a thorough comparative law study and a compendium of contributions from around the world.

It should be noted that this volume is not intended to give an overview of patent law in general. Rather, it focusses on particular issues around second medical use claims based on the general principles of patent law which are assumed to be well-known to the readers, and so are not explained in detail.

The topic has been broken down into a number of sections in each chapter. The analysis starts with the availability of the protection for second medical use claims and the legal basis. We have chosen almost exclusively jurisdictions where this protection is available, with the exception of India. India is not the only country in the world which does not allow patent protection for second medical uses. However, India is particularly interesting because the approach taken there is to find ways that provide some protection moving in the direction of second medical use claims.

The first step is to determine how claims can or must be worded to meet the patentability requirements of, in particular, novelty and inventive step. The claim wording will inevitably have an impact on the scope of protection and therefore the ability to enforce the granted patent. In Europe, the abandoning of traditional "Swiss-type claims" by the EPO in its landmark decision of the Enlarged Board of Appeal in 2010 (G 2/08) under the regime of the EPC 2000 has brought about significant changes. The consequences of these changes for enforcement, and for national patents, are still open and have not yet fully been explored in practice.

The analysis then continues with the scope of protection and infringement of second medical use claims. One of the focal issues is how these claims differ from "usual" patent claims and the consequences for the assessment of direct and indirect infringement. This includes questions of the acts considered to be infringing, who can be held liable, the specific conditions for a finding of infringement of these claims and what remedies are available.

Finally, each chapter contains some procedural aspects and tactical recommendations for the parties involved.

Due to the limitations of volume for the printed version of this compendium, only a selection of countries could be included. The goal therefore is to give a representative overview of the situation worldwide. Hence, we included contributions from Europe, the Americas, Asia and Australia. The listing of countries is by no means an exhaustive list of jurisdictions that provide protection for second medical use claims. It serves as an exemplary selection based on the relevance of the case law in the various jurisdictions.

There is inevitably a strong focus on Europe. Since all profiled countries from this area are members of the European Patent Convention, we have included a general chapter on the EPO practice to avoid duplication in the other European chapters. Therefore, these other chapters deal with the local situation and point out differences from the EPO practice on the national prosecution side. Relevantly, infringement and litigation in any event follow national rules. The European patent package which aims at a Unified Patent Court (UPC) and a European patent with unitary effect will change this only in parts (despite the consequences – yet to be fully determined – created by the recent Brexit vote in the UK).

The chapters for the non-European countries follow the same format as the European chapters, and also explain the national prosecution situation for second medical use claims. They comprise common law countries (USA, Canada and

Australia) and countries from the Americas (Brazil and Mexico), as well as Asia (Japan, China, Republic of Korea and India) and Israel.

The chapters in this volume demonstrate many similarities between the various systems. However, they also reveal the specifics which must be observed in the respective jurisdictions. It is very clear that a case-by-case analysis is required to assess whether a second medical use of a known medicament will merit patent protection and how a granted patent may be infringed. The possible variations and options are manifold. In a given case for the same invention and on the same facts, the results may differ from jurisdiction to jurisdiction – a situation common to patent cases generally.

This is the second volume published by Wolters Kluwer in cooperation with the International Association for the Protection of Intellectual Property (AIPPI) in its AIPPI Law Series. AIPPI is world renowned as an excellent source of comparative law studies. The authors from the various jurisdictions have been carefully selected in close consultation with AIPPI on the basis of their broad experience and in-depth knowledge about this topic.

AIPPI studied certain aspects of second medical use claims on the occasion of its Congress in Toronto in 2014. This led to its Resolution Q 238 – "Second medical use and other second indication claims", a copy of which is found at the end of this volume. This statement by AIPPI, based on reports from 41 of its national and regional groups, also revealed the need for a broader and more detailed exposition in order to allow more detailed comparison between jurisdictions, and to give practical guidance for patent applicants, third parties and the public. Therefore, it seemed natural to continue the exercise started by AIPPI. The result is this compendium.

I would especially like to express my thanks and gratitude to Sarah Matheson (Reporter General of AIPPI) and Matthew Swinn (Chair of the AIPPI Communications Committee) for their continuous support and efforts in making this volume possible. Our discussions have been elementary in the realization of this project.

Likewise, I thank all authors and co-authors for their highly interesting and valuable contributions. Their hard work has formed the core of this volume.

Jochen Bühling
Volume Editor
July 2016

European Patent Office

Dr. Jürgen Meier

A. AVAILABILITY OF PROTECTION

I. Legal framework

1. National statutory laws

The European Patent Convention 1973/2000 and its stipulations on "medical uses"

European patents are granted by the European Patent Office ("EPO"). The European patent system was created in 1973 by the European Patent Convention ("EPC") and currently has 38 "Contracting States" (Albania, Austria, Belgium, Bulgaria, Switzerland, Cyprus, Czech Republic, Germany, Denmark, Estonia, Spain, Finland, France, United Kingdom, Greece, Croatia, Hungary, Ireland, Iceland, Italy, Liechtenstein, Lithuania, Luxembourg, Latvia, Monaco, Former Yugoslav Republic of Macedonia, Malta, Netherlands, Norway, Poland, Portugal, Romania, Serbia, Sweden, Slovenia, Slovakia, San Marino, Turkey), and allows for extension/validation in four additional states (Bosnia-Herzegovina, Montenegro, Morocco, Republic of Moldova). An additional validation agreement has been signed with Tunisia.

Once granted, a European Patent ("EP") has to be validated in the designated contracting/extension states in form of "national patents". Here, the planned United Patent System and the planned "Unitary Patent", i.e. a truly "European Patent with Unitary Effect" will be another option for users of the EP system. The "Unitary Patent" will be granted by the EPO under the provisions of the EPC and has unitary effect after grant at patentee's request in the territory of all participating EU member states. The regulations on the Unitary Patent will only apply from the date of entry into force of the Agreement on a Unified Patent Court.

The stipulations of the EPC are to be interpreted in light of the case law of the Boards of Appeal of the European Patent Office. In addition, the "Guidelines for Examination in the European Patent Office" (last edition: November 2015) provide guidance for applicants.

Selected Technical Boards of Appeal decisions (T decisions) of general interest were previously published in the Official Journal of the EPO (OJ EPO). Now, all T decisions are published online. The important decisions of the Enlarged Board of Appeals ("EBA"), G decisions, are still published in the OJ EPO. All T or G decisions can be retrieved directly from the EPO website (https://www.epo.org/law-practice/case-law-appeals/advanced-search.html). Some of these decisions are briefly discussed in the periodically published EPO book *Case Law of the Boards of Appeal of the EPO* (last amended version: 7th edition, 2013).

The original European Patent Convention of 1973 was revised by the Act revising Article 63 EPC of 17 December 1991 and the Act revising the EPC of 29 November 2000. The revised EPC (known as "EPC2000") entered into force in all contracting states on 13 December 2007. EPC2000 also amended Article 53(c) and Article 54(4)/(5) EPC which are relevant for the "second medical uses" discussed herein.

The general requirements for patentability under the EPC are set forth in Article 52(1) EPC:

> "European patents shall *be granted for any inventions* which are susceptible of industrial application, which are new and which involve an inventive step." [emphasis added]

Article 53(c) EPC explicitly excludes the patentability of "surgical/therapeutic methods of treatment" and "in vivo" diagnostics:

> "European patents *shall not* be granted in respect of: ...
>
> (c) *methods for treatment of the human or animal body by surgery or therapy* and *diagnostic methods practiced on the human or animal body*; this provision shall not apply to products, in particular substances or compositions, for use in any of these methods." [emphasis added]

Article 54(4)/(5) EPC provides the legal basis for the grant of (first, second and further) medical use claims under EPC2000 by codifying an exception to the "absolute novelty" requirement defined in Article 54(1) to (3) EPC. Article 54 EPC reads:

> "(1) An invention shall be considered to be new if it does not form part of the state of the art.
>
> (2) The state of the art shall be held to comprise everything made available to the public by means of a written or oral description, by use, or in any other way, before the date of filing of the European patent application.
>
> (3) Additionally, the content of European patent applications as filed, the dates of filing of which are prior to the date referred to in paragraph 2 and which were published on or after that date, shall be considered as comprised in the state of the art.
>
> (4) Paragraphs 2 and 3 shall *not exclude the patentability of any substance or composition*, comprised in the state of the art, *for use in a method referred to in Article 53(c)*, provided that its use for any such method is *not comprised in the state of the art*.
>
> (5) Paragraphs 2 and 3 *shall also not exclude the patentability of any substance or composition* referred to in paragraph 4 for *any specific use in a method referred*

to in Article 53(c), provided that such use is not comprised in the state of the art." [emphasis added]

"First medical uses"

Under the "old" EPC of 1973, Article 52(4) EPC1973 excluded "methods for treatment of the human or animal body by surgery or therapy" and "diagnostic methods practiced on the human or animal body" from patentability as lacking "industrial applicability". The legislation intended that physicians were to be left free to act unfettered in their medical art. Consequently, and in contrast to other jurisdictions, such as the US, claims covering "methods of treatment" or diagnostic methods practiced on the human or animal body were considered as inventions "excluded from patent protection under the EPC". This exclusion of patentability is also supported by Article 27(3)(a) TRIPS that allows legislators to exclude such subject matter from patentability.

Nevertheless, legislators and the European Patent System recognised the clear need for the protection of pharmaceuticals. Accordingly, Article 54(5) EPC1973 clarified that the *use of* substances/compositions *in* any of the non-patentable methods of treatment or diagnostic methods practiced on the human/animal body were patent eligible before the EPO as long as such *use* for any of these method is novel (and inventive).

Thus, Article 54(5) EPC1973 established that there would still be novelty *for first medical use inventions* even if the compound that is used for the 'first medical use' was already known in the art *per se*. An allowable claim language for the *first medical use* before the EPO (under EPC1973) was:

> "Compound X *for use* as an active pharmaceutical substance".

Under EPC1973 and the corresponding Guidelines for Examination before the EPO, the EPO indeed accepted such "first medical use claims" even without the explicit indication or recitation of the term "for use". It was sufficient to indicate in the corresponding claim that the composition to be employed in a medical setting is, e.g., a "pharmaceutical composition". Accordingly, claims in the form of

> "Pharmaceutical composition comprising compound X and, optionally, a pharmaceutically acceptable carrier"

were readily granted and also accepted by the Boards of Appeal. Yet, the composition needs to be novel and inventive *per se*. Nowadays, Examining Divisions are of the opinion that the "first medical use" of a known compound should be expressed in a form that specifically recites said use (see examples below).

While there have been multiple decisions dealing with the patentability of first medical use inventions, T 128/82 (*Pyrrolidine derivatives/HOFFMANN-LA ROCHE*), is considered pivotal. Specifically, it was held that the inventor of a first medical use is entitled to a claim scope covering *all therapeutic uses*, i.e., it is not required to limit such claims to the actual first medical use that was discovered and described in the patent application.

When the EPC2000 came into force on 13 December 2007, the exclusion of methods of treatment was transferred from Article 52(4) EPC1973 to Article 53(c) EPC2000 without substantive change.

Therefore, EPC2000 did not leave applicants from the medical/pharmaceutical world without European protection for pharmaceuticals. Under EPC2000, Article 54(5) EPC1973 was editorially, yet importantly, amended to become Article 54(4) EPC2000. This Article clarifies that "*any substance or composition*, comprised in the state of the art, for use in a method referred to in Article 53(c)" can be patentable, "provided that its use for *any* such method is not comprised in the state of the art". The implementation of Article 54(4) EPC, as explained in the Guidelines for Examination before the EPO, November 2015 Part G-II 4.2., now requires that a claim to a known substance or composition for the first medical use in surgical, therapeutic and/or diagnostic methods should be in a form that stresses the indication "for use". Non-limiting examples of the recommended (new) format for a first medical use claim are:

> "Composition X *for use as* a medicament"

or

> "Composition X *for use in* therapy/in vivo diagnostics/surgery"

or

> "Substance X *for use as* a medicament, wherein said medicament optionally comprises a pharmaceutically acceptable carrier and/or diluents".

It is the position of some Examining Divisions of the EPO that without the term "for use" it is not evident if the claim is directed to the substance/composition suitable for the specified use or if the claim is limited by the medical use. The same considerations are also evident in the assessment of "second or further medical use claims" discussed below.

It should be noted that the Guidelines for Examination before the EPO make clear that methods of treatment are not allowable before the EPO under Article 53(c) EPC if these claims comprise *at least one feature* defining a physical activity or action that constitutes a "method step for treatment of the human or animal body by surgery or therapy". This prompted several discussions before the Boards of Appeal regarding claims that comprised as a mandatory feature a dosage regime or that contained language such as "wherein substance/compound X *is administered* to a subject in need of treatment". However, since the advent of EPC2000 (Article 54(4)/(5) EPC) and corresponding relevant case law (e.g. G 2/08 (*Dosage regime/ ABBOTT RESPIRATORY*)) it was clarified that inventions relating to, for example, dosage regimes can be protected in the "second medical use format". Accordingly, not only are new indications for known drugs now available for patent protection, but also the "uses" of such drugs in new patient groups, new administration regimes, new technical effects, etc. are patent accessible as long as these technical features lead to a truly novel medical or clinical situation. Some of these "second medical use" categories will be discussed herein below.

"Second medical uses" in EPC 1973 and EPC2000: "purpose-limited process claims" versus "purpose-limited product claims"

EPC1973 did not contain any notional acknowledgement of novelty of a claim directed to a further medical use of a known pharmaceutical compound/medicament nor did it include any specific stipulation that would have provided guidance for the circumstances under which second (or further) medical uses might be patentable and how corresponding claims should be worded. However, as early as 1983, three parallel (published) decisions of the EBA of the EPO dealt with patentability of second medical use inventions: G 1/83 (*Second medical indication/BAYER*), G 5/83 (*Second medical indication/EISAI*) and G 6/83 (*Second medical indication/ PHARMUKA*). G 5/83 explicitly states:

> "No intention to exclude second (and further) medical indications generally from patent protection can be deduced from the terms of the European Patent Convention: nor can it be deduced from the legislative history of the articles in question". (Reason 22)

The result of the sophisticated legal debates (also in national jurisdictions and in the proceedings of G 5/83, G 1/83 and G 6/83) was that, under EPC1973 second medical use contributions were patentable, but only when claimed by a so-called Swiss-type claim. In Reason 23 of G 5/83, the EBA followed the then already implemented practice of the Swiss Federal Intellectual Property Office (see Swiss legal advice of 30 May 1984) and considered it

> "legitimate in principle to allow claims directed to the use of a substance or composition for the manufacture of a medicament for a specified new and inventive therapeutic application, even in a case in which the process of manufacture as such does not differ from known processes using the same active ingredient".

Accordingly, the

> "[u]*se of* substance/compound X *in the manufacture of a medicament* for the therapeutic application or disease Y" [emphasis added]

became the standard wording for a Swiss-type claim in the second (or further medical use) format before the EPO and in European patents.

On the basis of these early decisions, it was clear that a valid claim in a "second medical use" or Swiss-type format must comprise two decisive features: (1) the specified novel (and inventive) medical indication/therapeutic application/ diagnostic application, and (2) the use of the substance/composition in manufacturing a medicament/pharmaceutical composition, whereby this manufacturing step does not need to be novel and invention. The invention is still based on the novel and non-obvious medical indication/therapeutic application/diagnostic application. In light of G 5/83, both features are needed to establish novelty and to define the scope of protection of these claims. Therefore, the Swiss-type claim is formally directed to a process, namely the "manufacturing of a medicament", and not to the use of the medically active substance *per se*. Technical Boards of Appeal ("TBAs") also confirmed in several decisions that the expression "for the manufacture of a medicament" was considered by the EBA in G 5/83 as a way to remove from the exclusion from patentability for lack of industrial application the sort of claims that the EBA basically intended to allow, *namely the use of a substance or composition* (and not devices!) for any of the methods recited in Article 52(4) EPC1973 (now Article 53(c) EPC); see, e.g. T 2003/08 (*Dilated cardiomyopathy/EDWARDS LIFESCIENCES CORPORATION ET AL.*) (discussed below). In light of G 5/83, it is the *medical treatment* of the human or animal body *per se* (and not the use in the manufacture of a medicament) that is not patent-eligible under the European Patent Convention.

Even though the above recited EBA decisions, in particular G 5/83, were issued as early as end of 1984, for decades afterwards legal uncertainty existed in relation to the patentability of further medical use(s). Certain European national courts raised concerns as to the validity of the corresponding "purpose-limited process/use"/Swiss-type claims; see. e.g. *Bristol-Myers-Squibb v Baker Norton Pharmaceuticals,* [1999] RPC 253. As a matter of fact, the Institute of Professional Representatives (epi) in its "Final Comments" to the revision of the EPC during the Diplomatic Conference in Munich (November 2000; Info 9 /MR2000e) stated in light of the Swiss-type claims:

> "The position of the Enlarged Board of Appeal, now accepted by examiners and the Boards of Appeal of the EPO has led to the grant of a great number of European patents. Unfortunately, the national courts of certain Member States [of the EPC] have difficulties understanding clearly the decision of the Enlarged Board of Appeal and the validity of the claims granted in accordance with this decision. The epi considers that this unclear situation is highly detrimental to European industry and to the development of new means for curing diseases".

Last but not least, these positions and the uncertainty for users of the European Patent System, prompted the revision of Article 54(4) EPC (reflecting Article 54(5) of EPC1973 and providing for patent protection as a "first medical use") and the introduction of Article 54(5) in the EPC2000. Revised Article 54(5) EPC provided a shift from "purpose-limited *process* claims" as provided by the Swiss-type format to "purpose-limited *product* claims". In particular, Article 54(5) EPC now makes clear that the EPC does not exclude the patentability of any substance or composition for *any specific use* in any method referred to in Article 53(c) EPC (i.e. a "method of treatment" or "diagnosis on the human or animal body"), provided that such use is not comprised in the state of the art.

As confirmed in G 2/08 (*loc. cit.* and also discussed below), Article 54(5) EPC allows the additional avenue to medical use claims that protect further specific uses of a given (known) compound/medicament in the medical intervention of the same illness. The headnotes of G 2/08 clarified that where it is already known to use a medicament to treat an illness, Article 54(5) EPC does not exclude that this medicament can also be patented for use in a different treatment of the same illness. Such patenting is also not excluded where, e.g., a dosage regime or a novel patient group is the only (technical) feature claimed which is not in the state of the art.

Accordingly, "second (and further) medical uses" have now become established in the European Patent Convention codifying the previous case law, e.g. G 5/83. Decision G 2/08 confirmed the patentability of these additional medical uses, as long as they are novel, inventive and lead to novel medical/clinical situations.

Article 54(5) EPC also provides legal certainty in countries where courts previously doubted the validity of Swiss-type claims. The EBA and TBAs also support this notion: G 2/08 held that:

> "Swiss-type claims could be (and have been) considered objectable as regards the question as to whether they fulfil the patentability requirements, due to absence of any functional relationship of features (belonging to therapy)

conferring to novelty and inventiveness, if any, and the claimed manufacturing process" (Reason 7.1.3).

With G 2/08 and the advent of "purpose-limited product claims" supported by Article 54(5) EPC, the specifically restricted medical use claims should not longer be questioned by national courts. This is because national revocation proceedings of patents granted by the EPO can only apply the nullity grounds pursuant to Article 138 EPC, i.e., for such proceedings the patenting options created by Article 54(5) EPC have to be respected.

The "specifically restricted use" now recited in Article 54(5) EPC also allows a simple format for second (and further) medical use claims. In accordance with the latest Guidelines for Examination before the EPO, November 2015, Part G-VI 7.1.2., an independent claim directed to a further therapeutic use of a substance/ composition which is based on the use of said product in the treatment of a different disease should be formulated as provided in the following table:

Table 1

Substance X	for use	in a method for the treatment of Y, or
or		in the therapy of Y, or
Composition comprising X		in a method of treating Y, or
		in a method of therapy of Y, or
		as a medicament defined by its function, (e.g. as an anti-inflammatory medicament)

The Guidelines for Examination before the EPO make it clear that the presence of the term "for use" is *mandatory*, to closely adhere to the wording of Article 54(5) EPC. However, and in contrast to Swiss-type claims, the term for "manufacture of a medicament" must be avoided in second medical use claims in EPC2000 format. This is a consequence of G 2/08 wherein it is stated that "where the subject matter of a claim is rendered novel only by a new therapeutic use of a medicament, the claim may no longer have the format of the Swiss-type claim as instituted by decision G 5/83". Accordingly, for any application having a filing date (or an earliest priority date) after 28 January 2011 (three months after publication of G 2/08 in the OJ) only second medical use claims in the above recited format are allowable.

G 2/08 clarified that claims directed to therapeutic uses of a known substance/ composition may be based not only on the treatment of a different disease but also on the treatment of the same disease by a different therapeutic method, e.g., different dosage regimens, different administration modes, different modes or mechanisms of action, or patient/subject selection. All that is required is that the distinction from the known treatment is novel and inventive.

Also in the context of further technical features of medical use claims (administration schemes, dosages, patient groups, etc.), the most recent Guidelines for Examination before the EPO propose formulations of the independent claims; see G-VI, section 7.1.2:

Table 2

Substance X for use or Composition comprising X for use	in a method for the treatment of Y, or in the therapy of Y, or in a method of treating Y, or in a method of therapy of Y, or as a medicament defined by its function (e.g. as an anti-inflammatory medicament)	characterised in that/ wherein	other features (e.g. the substance/ composition is administered topically, three times daily ...)

Scope of second medical use claims according to the EPO

As soon as Article 54(5) EPC was introduced in EPC2000, practitioners and applicants wondered whether new Article 54(5) EPC format claims ("EPC claims") were identical in scope to Swiss-type claims. While it is clear that Swiss-type claims are *process claims* and EPC claims are *product claims* (with a specifically restricted use) the explanatory notes to the Swiss delegates' proposal to Article 54(5) EPC2000 suggested that the protection offered by new Article 54(5) 'is equivalent, as far as the further uses are concerned, to that offered by the Swiss type claim'. Nevertheless, the Federal Supreme Court of Switzerland confirming G 2/08 has cautioned:

> "It is to be expected that the new claim category according to Article 54(5) EPC2000, that of purpose-limited claim, will result in *broader protection* for the patentee than was previously the case" Swiss Federal Supreme Court, BGE 137 III 170 (Alendronate); [emphasis added]

Because EPC claims would potentially provide broader protection than the established Swiss-type claims, practitioners tried in applications filed before 29 January 2011 to obtain both type of claims, or to shift Swiss-type claims to purpose-limited product EPC claims. In the decision T 250/05 (*Use of nitric oxide for systemic treatment/ THE BRIGHAM AND WOMEN HOSPITAL*), a request to amend a European Patent post-grant at opposition/appeal proceedings by changing a Swiss-type claim to second medical use (product) EPC claim was found unallowable. It was held that this change of claim wording would have extended the protection conferred by the patent, in contravention of Article 123(3) EPC. This conclusion of the TBA would not have been reached if the two claim types had provided the same scope of protection.

The question of "scope of protection" of second medical use claims is in particular relevant for European applications granted after 13 December 2007 (entry into force of ECP2000) and filed on or before 28 January 2011 (publication of G 2/08). During this time period, applicants are entitled to *both formats of second medical use claims*. Many currently pending European applications in the life science/pharmaceutical field date from before 29 January 2011 and, there are legitimate reasons to retain both types of claims where possible, either together in one patent or in two separate patents (for example in form of a parental and a divisional application). This situation has recently provoked decisions from the TBA since certain Examining Divisions have refused divisional applications merely on an alleged "double patenting ground". These Examining Divisions based their assessment on the preparatory documents for EPC2000, which were published in a Special Edition (4/2007) of the OJ EPO. Indeed, in this Special Edition, it was held that the scope of protection of a Swiss-type claim and an EPC claim "are considered equivalent" (see OJ EPO, Special Edition 4/2007, EN version, p. 27). However, in T 1780/12 (*Cancer treatment/BOARD OF REGENTS, THE UNIVERSITY OF TEXAS SYSTEM*) it was made clear that both medical use claims belong to different categories and, accordingly, have a different scope of protection. Furthermore, it was held that the scope of protection conferred by a "Swiss-type claim and a claim pursuant to Article 54(5) EPC *is notionally different* whereby the protection conferred by an EPC claim is considered larger. Accordingly, double-patenting was denied in this case. Recent decisions T 809/12 (APO-*2 ligand/ GENENTECH*), T 13/14 (*Agent for treatment of schizophrenia/SUMITOMO DAINIPPON*), and T 15/14 (*Immunemodulating oligosaccharides/N.V.NUTRICIA*) concur with the findings of T 1780/12: purpose-limited EPC claims are "restricted product claims", whereas the category of Swiss-type claims are "restricted process claims". Both claims are "notionally different" in the eyes of the EPO.

1.1 Pharmaceuticals

The patenting of "first", "second" or even "later" medical uses of chemical "small molecules" is admissible before the EPO. If the chemical compounds are new they can, obviously, be protected via absolute product protection. Within the framework of chemical pharmaceuticals, certain novelty discussions took place before the Technical Boards when specific chemical purities, modifications and/or, for example, isomeric structures had to be assessed.

For example, in T 990/96 (*Erythro-compounds/NOVARTIS*) or T 728/98 (*Pure terfenadine/ALBANY*) it was held that a *higher degree of purity* of a chemical compound that is obtainable by *conventional purification* methods *cannot establish novelty*. T 100/00 (*–/AKZO NOBEL B.V.*) made clear that the "qualification 'conventional' can only mean 'conventional in view of the concrete technical context concerned'" and novelty of the claimed purified resin as obtained by a "non-conventional ion-exchange post-treatment" was acknowledged.

As already established in T 296/87 (*Enantiomere/HOECHST*) a chemical substance is held to be new if it differs from a known substance in a reliable parameter. Configuration may be such a parameter. Also T 1046/97 (*Enantiomer/ZENECA*) confirmed that a specifically claimed enantiomer is not directly and unambiguously disclosed when said enantiomer belongs *conceptually* to a possible group of optically active forms mentioned in the prior art.

Similarly, also diastereomers may be novel when the prior art does not provide for this very compound in form of a clear technical teaching, or a clear pointing to the claimed individual member, see, inter alia, T 940/98 (*Diastereomere/HOECHST*) or T 1048/92 (*Penem derivatives/PFIZER*).

However, to simply claim a tautomer of a known chemical compound is not sufficient to establish patentability; see, e.g. T 133/01, "Dopamine agonist/WYETH", in light of keto-enol tautomerism.

Interestingly, a specific not disclosed salt (for example a hydrochloride) of a chemical compound of the prior art can establish novelty; see, e.g., T 1194/06 (*Arylalkylamine carbamates/LABORATORIOS S.A.L.V.A.T.*); Reason 6.5.

Very recent decisions of the TBA dealt with novelty of "polymorphs" and their medical use(s). A chemical substance was repeatedly held to be new if it differs from a known one in a reliable manner; see, e.g. T 296/87. Accordingly, in T 1753/06 (*Tert-butylamine du perindopril/LABORATOIRES SERVIER*) novelty of a polymorph characterised by X-ray powder diffraction peaks was ultimately denied since as long as the position of the peaks in an XRPD diagram were substantially identical to the prior art, a deviation in intensity of the peaks could not be seen as indicative of a different crystalline form. Yet, in T 777/08 (*Atorvastatin polymorph/WARNER-LAMBERT*), it was held that "the mere provision of a crystalline form of a known pharmaceutically active compound cannot be regarded as involving an inventive step". In T 2397/11 (*Erlotinib hydrochloride polymorph/HOFFMANN-LA ROCHE*) a polymorph was considered novel since the polymorph was additionally defined by a characterising melting point. Decisions T 205/14 and T 517/14 (*Crystalline form of Ibandronate/TEVA*) relate to two different polymorphs disclosed in one application. Whereas a specific polymorph as claimed in the parent application leading to T 205/14 was considered obvious over the prior art, a specific polymorph in the divisional application (see T 517/14) was inventive since the methods disclosed in prior art did not suggest how the specific polymorph can be obtained and the skilled artisan "would have no cause to expect to be able to obtain a further crystalline form with similarly favourable properties" (Reason 5.5.4).

1.2 Biologics

Biotherapeutics make it routinely into the best-seller charts and list of "blockbusters" since recombinant technology and antibody engineering has revolutionised the pharmaceutical world. The top 25 best-selling drugs of 2014 are discussed in Philippidis, "The Top 25 Best-Selling Drugs of 2014", *Genetic Engineering & Biotechnology News*, 2015. Ten biologics were on the list and seven of the top eight best-selling drugs were biologics. Examples of such successful drugs include (genetically engineered) antibodies, protein fragments, hormones, but also nucleic acid molecules, such as inhibiting RNAs. The unprecedented success of biologics in the pharmaceutical world also stirs desires, for example in form of now approaching "biosimilars" and their medical uses.

Like small molecules, biologics are also patentable in the EPO and accessible to protection in second (and further) medical use formats. However, apparently due to stronger surveillance from the general public, in biotechnology only 27% of applications in the biotech field led to granted EPO patents – very few in the form originally requested by the applicant. In other fields, the granting ratio in 2012 was about 47%; see "Biotechnology blog of the EPO President" of 26 November 2012 at www.epo.org.

The EPO has adopted the EU biotech directive 98/44/EC in form of Rules 26 to 29 EPC. Accordingly, biological material which is isolated from its natural environment or produced by means of a technical process may be patentable even if it previously occurred in nature (Rule 27(a) EPC). Whereas the discovery of the sequence or partial sequence of a gene or a corresponding protein cannot constitute a patentable invention in the EPO, an element isolated from the human body or otherwise produced by means of a technical process, which is susceptible of industrial application, including the sequence or partial sequence of a gene, may constitute a patentable invention; see also Rule 29(1) and (2) EPC and Guidelines for Examination before the EPO, G-II 3.1, G-II 5.2 and G-II 5.3. For industrial application of biotechnological inventions (and their medical use), Rule 29(3) EPC needs to be taken into account and claimed use of these "elements of nature" needs to be plausibly and credibly disclosed in the patent/patent application. Rule 29(3) EPC requires in particular that the patent application must provide evidence for the (claimed) biological function.

2. *International treaties*

The case law and jurisdiction of the European Patent Office is based on the European Patent Convention. The EPC constitutes a special agreement within Article 19 of the Paris Convention for the Protection of Industrial Property and a regional patent treaty within the meaning of Article 45(1) PCT. In context of the interpretation of the EPC, since G 5/83 it has been established that even though the principles of Articles 31 and 32 of the Vienna Convention do not apply *ex lege*, the European Patent Office and the Boards of Appeal in fact should apply Articles 31 and 32 of the Vienna Convention on the Law of Treaties.

Accordingly, the provisions of the EPC must first be construed according to the ordinary meaning of the terms in their context and in light of the object and purpose of the respective provision; see Article 31 Vienna Convention. As the case law of the Boards of Appeal has shown, this principle was often applied in cases relating to "second medical uses". For example, the question of whether "devices" such as stents would be accessible to second medical use claims under Article 54(4)/(5) EPC has often been denied under the interpretation of the term "substance or composition" as laid down in Article 54(4) EPC; see also Guidelines for Examination before the EPO, G-VI, 7.1.1. Article 32 Vienna Convention provides the legal basis that the Boards of Appeal and the EBA can take preparatory documents (such as the *travaux préparatoires*) into consideration in order to confirm a meaning or to determine a meaning if the first and ordinary means of construction would lead to ambiguity or to an absurd result; see also G 1/07 (Reasons 3.1) and the "Case Law of the Boards of Appeal", 7th edition, 2013, III, H, 1.1.3. Especially in G 2/08 (the "dosage regime" decision) the EBA applied Articles 31 and 32 Vienna Convention.

2.1 TRIPS

The European Patent Office is not a party to the WTO/TRIPS Agreement. Yet, in G 2/02 and G 3/02 (OJ 2004, 483), it was held that although the EPO is not bound by TRIPS, the national legal systems of the EPC contracting states might be affected by TRIPS and they may be under an obligation to see to it that the EPC is in conformity with TRIPS; see "Case Law of the Board of Appeal"; 7th edition, 2013, III, H, 2.1.. For example, during the revision of the EPC (EPC2000), the stipulation on recognition of priority rights, Article 87 (1) EPC, was amended to align it with Article 2 of the TRIPS Agreement, which requires that priority rights be extended to first filings made in any WTO member state (and not only to states which are party of the Paris Convention). Accordingly, TRIPS provisions, such as decisions of the European and International Courts of Justice and national decisions, are elements to be taken into consideration by the Boards of Appeal but are not binding on them; see "Case Law of the Board of Appeal"; 7th edition, 2013, III, H, 7 and T 154/04.

2.2 FTAs

None with the EPO.

3. Availability through case law

As evident herein, there is ample case law in the EPO that deals with medical and diagnostic uses. This case law is not limited to decisions of the TBAs (T decisions) but also includes very prominent decisions of the EBA (G decisions). These include G 1/83, G 5/83 and 6/83 ("second medical uses"), G 1/04 ("diagnostic methods"), G 1/07 ("method of treatment by surgery") as well as G 2/08 ("dosage regime").

The case law of the EBA is binding for other boards and divisions of the EPO. The same holds true for TBA decisions to a certain degree. Article 111(2) EPC stipulates that if the Board of Appeal remits the case for further prosecution to the department whose decision was appealed, that department shall be bound by the *ratio decidendi* of the Board of Appeal, in so far as the facts are the same. As confirmed by the established jurisprudence of the TBAs, the same binding effect applies to a subsequent appeal in respect of an earlier decision; see e.g. T 365/09 or T 1545/08 (as discussed herein below).

As far as the consideration of decisions/opinions given by national courts is concerned, the *Case Law of the Boards of Appeal*, 7th edition, (2013) refers to G 5/83 in section III.H.7 and emphasises that TBAs may take these decisions/opinions into consideration.

4. Patent term extension/SPCs

As regards Supplementary Protection Certificates (SPCs) for "second medical uses", in July 2012 the Court of Justice of the European Union (CJEU) delivered its clarifying decision, C-130/11 (Neurim Pharmaceuticals), wherein it was held that an SPC can also be obtained for "further medical uses".

In C-130/11, it was held that the mere existence of an earlier marketing authority obtained for a veterinary medicinal product does not preclude the grant of an SPC for a different application of the same product, provided that the application is within the scope of protection conferred by the basic patent relied upon for the purpose of the application for the SPC.

Before the *Neurim* decision, and based on older CJEU jurisprudence (e.g. C-202/05 *Yissum*; C-195/09 *Synthon*, or C-427/09 *Generics*), it was the general assumption that SPCs in Europe are not available if the active ingredient in question had been authorised in any earlier marketing authority with the European Union, even if the earlier authorisation was based on a different use (or a different species).

After C-130/11 *Neurim*, originators can apply for SPCs on new and inventive "further" uses of earlier known active ingredients.

It should be noted that currently only *national* SPCs are available. Nevertheless, it may very well be that things may change in the very near future. Thus, the currently discussed 'patent package' that lays the ground for the creation of unitary patent protection in the EU does not explicitly provide for a 'unitary SPC'. In order to overcome this shortcoming the European Commission is working on the articulation of unitary patent protection and SPC legislation. The EU is tendering a project to review the fundamentals of the SPC regime. Thus, the EU communication (Call for Tender; 479/PP/GRO/IMA/15/15153) stated that:

> "[t]he study shall evaluate whether a new European SPC title, in its current scope, or broadened with improved provisions, is required to meet the requirements of current and expected innovative market developments in the EU.
>
> With this primary purpose, the study shall evaluate the current SPC framework in terms of its legal efficiency in meeting its stated objectives given the development of directly affected and related product markets. The study shall also evaluate some economic aspects of the current SPC framework.
>
> With this primary purpose, the study shall evaluate the current SPC framework in terms of its legal efficiency in meeting its stated objectives given the development of directly affected and related product markets. The study shall also evaluate some economic aspects of the current SPC framework.
>
> The results could serve as a basis for an impact assessment for a future proposal by the Commission to create a European SPC title, and complement the recalibration of the existing EU SPC rules".

II. Policy considerations

1. Health and social issues

The EPO's patenting of further medical uses, such as dosage regimes, has controversially been discussed. Such patents/patent applications have been alleged to be an "evergreening strategy" allowing pharmaceutical companies to extend their drug product patents once they expire. This strategy is popularly known as "life-cycle management" of drugs. However, improvements on the basic invention are often insignificant (and inventive) improvements of a basic drug. According to critics of second medical use claims the end result of "life-cycle" scenario is an alleged monopolisation of the market and ousting of generics/biosimilars.

2. Legal issues

Where a substance or composition is already known to have been used in a "first medical use", it may still be patentable under Article 54(5) EPC for a second or further medical use, provided that said use is novel and inventive; see Guidelines for Examination before the EPO, Part G, VI, 7.1. Indeed, product claims for a first, second or further medical use need to fulfil *all requirements of patentability* especially those of novelty and inventive step; see, e.g. G 2/08. This principle alone should prevent pharmaceutical companies from extending the patent life of drugs with insignificant improvements of the basic invention without legal ground.

B. VALIDITY

I. Allowable claim wording

1. Product claims

In accordance with the Guidelines for Examination before the EPO (November 2015), a claim to a known substance or composition for the first medical use in surgical, therapeutic and/or diagnostic methods should be of the form "substance/composition X" followed by the indication of the use such as "*for use* as a medicament" or "*for use* in therapy/in vivo diagnostics/in surgery"; see Guidelines for Examination before the EPO, Part G, II 4.2.

2. Method claims

"Methods of treatment" claims are not allowable under the EPC due to the exception to patentability laid down in Article 53(c) EPC. However, there is a large body of case law of the TBAs and also of the EBA that supports the notion that, especially under the wording of Article 54(4)/(5) EPC, different new and inventive treatments of an illness can be patentable under the EPC. Significantly, it has also been accepted that the treatment of the same disease with the same substance/compound in a novel method of administration, a new class of patients, a new dosage regime, etc. is patentable as long as inventive step is also to be acknowledged over the claimed subject matter which also needs to be plausibly and concretely disclosed in the patent application as filed. In decision G 2/08 it was held that:

> "By virtue of a legal fiction Article 54(4) and (5) EPC acknowledges the notional novelty of substances or compositions even when they are as such already comprised in the state of the art, provided they are claimed for a new use in a method which Article 53(c) EPC excludes as such from patent protection.

In such cases the notional novelty and following it the non-obviousness, if any, is not derived from the substance or composition as such but from the purpose the claimed substance or composition is related to, namely from its intended therapeutic use." (Reason 5.10.9)

Consequently, decision G 2/08, by referring to previous decision T 1020/03 (*Method of administration of IGF-1/GENENTECH INC.*), stresses that:

> "there is a seamless fit, either a method of using a composition is not a treatment by therapy and therefore falls outside the provision of Article 52(4) EPC [1973] first sentence, and so is patentable subject to compliance with the other provisions of the EPC, or else a method is a treatment by therapy and therefore inside the provision of Article 52(4) EPC [1973] first sentence, and

> so not itself patentable, but use of a composition for making a medicament for use in such treatment by therapy is patentable for unspecified therapy as a first medical indication or for a specified therapy as a further medical indication, again subject to compliance with the other provisions of the EPC, in particular novelty and inventive step."

G 2/08, accordingly, opened the door and provided legal certainty for, inter alia, the patentability of dosage regimens or modes of administration, which were previously considered by some TBAs as "instructions to the physician how to deal with regard to patient handling", and as such, a classical *method of treatment* excluded from patentability under Article 53(c) EPC.

3. *Use claims*

Since the EPO does not allow "method of treatment" claims medical use claims are the way of protection for pharmaceutical inventions. Accordingly, it is well established EPO practice to grant patents for novel and inventive (second and further) medical uses under Article 54(5) EPC. In these "use claims", novelty may be derived from the new therapeutic purpose, but also from a new patient group to be treated or a novel treatment or (drug) administration regime, etc.

Allowable claim formats for "second medical uses" in accordance with Article 54(5) EPC are provided in Tables 1 and 2 above and as also laid down in the Guidelines for Examination before the EPO, Part G, VI 7.12.

The simplest wording would be "substance X *for use in the treatment of [specific] disease Y*". As the Guidelines for Examination before the EPO further point out, purpose-limited product claims in the EPC format which *do not* exclusively define a *medical use* excluded from patentability under Article 53(c) EPC are to be construed as a claim to a product *per se* which is *suitable* for the claimed use. Such a claim would raise novelty objections in case the substance/compound *per se* is known in the prior art *in a form* which could be considered *suitable* for the claimed use.

4. *System claims*

The EPO is routinely faced with the question of whether medical devices and corresponding "medical systems" would also be covered by the stipulations as laid down in Article 54(4)/(5) EPC2000 and could be protected in a "medical use" format. The TBAs have up to now always denied that medical devices/medical systems or medical instruments are accessible to the protection under the second medical use claims format.

In T 1096/11 (*Hyperplasia plaque-preventing stent/CARDIATIS S.A.*) a claim relating to a

> "[s]tent for use in prevention of restenoses of a wall ... of a blood vessel having atheromatous plaque consisting of a multilayer braided framework."

was rejected by the Examining Division as lacking novelty. The appellant stated that novelty of the subject matter of claim 1 should be also acknowledged on basis of a specific medical indication, i.e. that the claimed stent is supposed to be used in the prevention of restenoses or in a blood vessel having atheromatous plaque. However, the TBA confirmed that *a device*, like a stent, is not accessible to the protection under Article 54(4)/(5) EPC. It is held that according to Article 54(4) EPC, it is possible to acknowledge the novelty of a "*substance or composition*, comprised in the state of the art, for use in a method referred to in Article 53(c)" but not for a device (emphasis added by the Board). The Board was furthermore of the opinion that the legislator deliberately made a distinction between products that can qualify as substances or compositions, and which are patentable within the framework of Article 54(4)/(5) EPC, and other products, which do not fall under the exceptions provided by those provisions. In this respect, the Board confirmed the older decision T 1099/09 (*–/ CARDIATIS S.A.*).

The Board also pointed out that the *travaux préparatoires* of the EPC 1973 (BR/ 219 e/72 ico/PA/gc, §30, second paragraph) do not suggest a different interpretation of the provisions of Article 54(4)/(5) EPC. Whereas this passage of the *travaux préparatoires* stated that the patentability of medical equipment should not be prejudged, the Board held that the *travaux* do not stipulate that said patentability can be acknowledged on the basis of the medical indication of those devices.

Finally, the Board was of the opinion that the claimed product is a stent consisting of a multilayer braided framework devoid of any cover layer. Accordingly, *it is a finished product having a certain shape and certain dimensions and which does not comprise any active ingredient*. Hence, the claimed stent did not qualify as a "substance or a composition" in the sense of Article 54(4)/(5) EPC. Novelty was denied.

In T 2369/10 (*Cranial nerve stimulation /CYBERONICS, INC.*) a claim was amended to the

> "[*u*]*se of an electrode* configured for directly coupling to a cranial nerve of a patient and applying an electrical signal to said cranial nerve *for the manufacture of a neurostimulator system for treating a patient having a substance addiction* to alleviate a symptom of the substance addiction."

Also here, the TBA denied novelty. The Board acknowledged that a difference exists between protection for pharmaceuticals and protection for devices and by referring to the older decision T 773/10 (*–/GAMBRO LUNDIA AB et al.*), it held that "it is neither the Board's duty nor its competence to evaluate the arguments about how desirable or equitable patent protection for any medical product may or may not be". The Board assumed that the restriction to "substances and compositions" is deliberate and was of the opinion that "the terminology employed in Article 54(4)/(5) EPC betrays a deliberate intention to restrict the special provisions on novelty to first and further medical uses of substances and compositions only".

T 2003/08 (*–/FRESENIUS MEDICAL CARE*) is an interesting case on immunoapheresis which achieves the therapeutic effect extracorporally. The claim under question relates to the

> "[*u*]*se of a specific ligand for human immunoglobulin in the manufacture of a column having said ligand coupled thereto for the treatment of a patient suffering from dilated cardiomyopathy* (DCM), said treatment comprising passing plasma of the patient over the column under conditions which effect the binding of said specific ligand to immunoglobulin in the patient's plasma, thereby removing

a significant portion of the immunoglobulin from the patient's plasma, and reinfusing the plasma to the patient." (emphasis added)

The TBA held that in the present case the therapeutic effect on which the treatment according to claim 1 is based is the removal of immunoglobulin from the plasma of patients suffering from DCM. This effect is achieved by the "specific ligand for human immunoglobulin" which is undisputedly a chemical entity. The "column" serves as a carrier for the ligand and is not instrumental in achieving the therapeutic effect. In fact, the ligand could also bind immunoglobulin, if it was not bound to the column, i.e. if it was free in solution. Accordingly, the Board judged that the means used for the treatment in accordance with claim 1 is to be considered as *a "substance" or "composition"* in the sense of decision G 5/83. The Board also considered the treatment defined in the claims under revision as a treatment by therapy in accordance with Article 53(c) EPC and judged that the claims are to be interpreted as claims to a second medical use in the sense of decision G 5/83.

Accordingly, the indication of the purpose *"for the treatment of a patient suffering from dilated cardiomyopathy"* was considered by the Board as not merely descriptive. In a final decision of October 2012, novelty and inventive step of the subject matter as recited above was established.

Claim wording in potential system claims should follow the recommendations provided herein above for "product" or "(second medical) use", whereby it should be clarified that the substance/compound to be used is not a "device".

5. *Dosage regimes*

An important milestone in second medical uses before the EPO was the indication that claims relating to treatment/dosage regimes are not merely an instruction to the attending physicians as to how to perform their art and are not excluded from patentability by Article 53(c) EPC (former Article 52(4) EPC1973). In particular, it was intensively discussed whether such treatment regimes could even confer patentability where the medical use of a given compound was already known.

In the early landmark decision T 1020/03, it was held that "any use to which Article 52(4) EPC first sentence applies in circumstances where the composition has already been suggested for some therapeutic use, allows a second medical use claim to the preparation of the composition for that second medical use, irrespective of in what detail that use was specified, subject to the use being novel and inventive. For the purposes of novelty also under Article 54(5) EPC this depends on whether use for therapy is novel, irrespective of the detail with which the therapy is stated in the claim." (Headnote). Accordingly, this decision and also T 36/04 from the same TBA indicated that claim features relating to a "treatment or dosage regimen" can establish patentability and claims that are based on these features are not excluded from patentability. However, T 1319/04 (*Dosage regimen/KOS LIFE SCIENCES*) was reluctant to share this view and referred corresponding questions to the EBA. G 2/08 (*Dosage regime/ABBOTT RESPIRATORY*) confirmed patentability of a treatment regimen. In particular, it was confirmed that dosage regimes may relate to a different technical teaching and may lead to a truly new (medical) situation.

Potential claim language for a "dosage second medical use claim" as proposed in the Guidelines for Examination before the EPO, Part G, VI 7.12. may be:

> "Substance X for use in the treatment of [specific] disease Y, *whereby X is administered by the dosage regime Z.*"

6. Patient groups

The TBAs of the EPO have found medical inventions in which a new group of subjects or a new sub-group of patients have been identified for medical intervention of a given disease with a known compound to be patentable as long as the treatment of this new (sub-) group of patients is novel and inventive. The new patient group to be treated should be clearly distinct from subjects treated in the prior art and the two groups must not overlap. However, a new "mechanism of action" which identifies a truly new clinical situation may lead to a granted EP patent in which patient groups overlap; see e.g. T 1229/03 or T 1955/09 discussed herein below. Furthermore, it was routinely held by the TBAs that the distinction in the patient groups must not be arbitrary and must be based on a (plausible/creditable) functional relationship between the physiological or pathological characteristics of the novel patient group to be treated and the obtained therapeutic effect.

The first positive decision on "patient groups" was T 19/86 (*Pigs/DUPHAR*) in which the TBA had to decide whether the use of a known vaccine in a new class of pigs, namely sero-positive piglets that were still maternally immune, constituted a patentable use of the known vaccine. It was held that the intranasal vaccination of piglets with the known vaccine against Aujeszky's disease (pseudo-rabies in pigs) was not disclosed or hinted at in the prior art (vaccination of older sero-negative pigs) and provided for a novel and inventive therapeutic intervention in accordance with G 5/83.

A further, yet negative, decision in "patient groups" was T 233/96 (*Adrenaline/MEDCO RESEARCH*) wherein it was decided that if the decisive group chosen overlaps with the group previously treated (or diagnosed) or the choice of the novel group is arbitrary (e.g. no functional relationship exists between the particular physiological or pathological status of this group of subjects and the therapeutic or pharmacological effect achieved), novelty of the therapeutic (or diagnostic) use was denied.

It is recommended that the second medical use claim before the EPO clearly and unambiguously *defines the patient group to be treated* and that the defined patient group cannot be considered as arbitrary.

An interesting special case is a second medical use on specific genetic sub-populations of individuals to be treated in accordance with the invention. Here, a method for the selection of the individualised patient group should be claims and, furthermore, the genetic definition/molecular markers should be contained in a corresponding "use" claim. Such a claim could, for example, read:

> "Substance X *for use* in the treatment/therapy of [specific] disease Y in a subgroup of *patients carrying allele/genetic marker Z.*"

However, it has to be noted that certain Examining Divisions of the EPO have raised novelty objections against such a claim.

II. Novelty

1. General definition of novelty and prior art

Article 54 EPC requires "absolute novelty" and, accordingly, the prior art comprises anything that was made available to the public before the priority (or filing) date of the invention. It is irrelevant how and where the disclosure took place and even oral public disclosures and public prior uses are taken into account. For example, in T 1399/04 (*loc. cit.* and discussed below) the second medical use claim under dispute comprises a specific treatment regime ("administering for 40 to 50 weeks") and a specific defined patient group ("naive chronic HCV genotype 1 patients"). It was alleged by the opponent that there was prior public use which took place at the Charité in Berlin. However, a corresponding declaration showed that the patient at the Charité had been treated for 200 weeks and it was not clear whether the patient was antiviral treatment naive. Accordingly, novelty was acknowledged.

Certain second medical use claims are considered novel in the EPO since the EPC does consider an "inherent", yet not publically available feature as not novelty destroying; see also T 1955/09 (*Antimicrobial peptides/OCTOPLUS SCIENCES*) (discussed below). The term "photographic novelty" is often employed in order to describe the EPO's novelty approach.

Furthermore, the EPO allows for "selection inventions" and thereby modulates the concept of "absolute novelty". Such "selection inventions" relate to, for example, narrower ranges from already disclosed ranges with additional previously unknown technical effects. Also the concept of "selection inventions" may be the basis of further medical use claims in the EPO. Selection inventions in the EPO are often considered when it comes to second medical uses relating to dosage regimes and/or (sub-)patient groups.

In order to establish novelty, the EPO also allows for "disclaimers" over "accidental disclosures" in the prior art; see also G 1/03, G 2/03 and G 2/10.

2. Definition of skilled person

The EPC does not define the "person skilled in the art" in the context of novelty assessment (in contrast to the assessment under "inventive step"). However, Article 54 EPC states that the subject matter is considered as novel when it was not "public" or "available to the public". Whereas the EPC does not provide for a clear definition of "public", the TBA case law over the years has clarified that subject matter is "available to the public" as soon as at least one person could gain access to the corresponding information, understands it and/or could reproduce it without undue burden.

3. Scope of disclosure

3.1 General rules

Article 83 EPC stipulates that the application shall disclose the invention in a manner sufficiently clear and complete to be carried out by a person skilled in the art. The subject matter of an application must be sufficiently disclosed at the effective date of the application, based on the application as a whole and taking into account the common general knowledge of the skilled person; see *Case Law of the Boards of Appeal*, 7th edition, 2013, II.C6. At least one way of enabling the person skilled in the art to carry out the invention must be disclosed, but this is sufficient only if it allows the invention to be performed in the whole range claimed and if the invention is reproducible without undue burden. In T 1150/09 (*–/Vlaams Interuniversitair Instituut voor Biotechnologie*), the patent in suit did not indicate which criteria the skilled person should apply for identifying a cancer which can be treated with the claimed angiogenesis inhibitor. The TBA concluded that the skilled person was not in a position to predict, on the basis of the information contained in the specification and taking into account the relevant common general knowledge, which cancers can be treated, and the requirements of Article 83 EPC were not fulfilled.

3.2 *First medical use*

In T 609/02, the Board pointed out that where a therapeutic application is claimed in the form allowed by the EBA in G 5/83, i.e. in the form of the use of a substance or composition for the manufacture of a medicament for a defined therapeutic application, attaining the claimed therapeutic effect is a functional technical feature of the claim. As a consequence, under Article 83 EPC, the application must disclose the suitability of the product recited in the claims for the claimed therapeutic application; see also T 433/05 (*Fusion peptide inhibitors/ CONJCHEM*).

3.3 *New subject matter*

For providing sufficient disclosure of a first, second or further medical use claim the "novel" subject matter (i.e. the therapeutic effect) must be disclosed in the application as filed. Following T 609/02, the Board in T 801/06 recalled that a claimed therapeutic effect may be proven by any kind of data in the specification as long as they clearly and unambiguously reflect the therapeutic effect; see *Case Law of the Boards of Appeal*, 7th edition, 2013, II.C.6.2. For example, showing a pharmaceutical effect in vitro has been considered to be sufficient if for the skilled person this observed effect directly and unambiguously reflects the claimed therapeutic application; see T 609/02.

3.4 *New data*

In order to comply with the requirement of sufficiency of disclosure, the application as filed must provide some information showing that the claimed compound or composition has a direct effect on a (metabolic) mechanism specifically involved in the disease. Once this evidence is available from the application as filed, post-published evidence may be taken into account to support the disclosure in the patent application; see *Case Law of the Boards of Appeal*, 7th edition, 2013, II.C.; see also T 433/05 (*loc. cit.* and below). However, such documents can only be used to support the findings in the patent application in relation to the use of the ingredient/composition as a pharmaceutical, and not to establish sufficiency of disclosure on their own; see also T 604/04, T 699/06 and T 1396/06. Post-filed data are considered before the Examining Division as "secondary indicia" for inventive step. Such secondary indicia must be taken into account by the Examining Division. However, as Rainer Moufang in the "Commentary" in Rainer Schulte, *Patentgesetz mit Europäischem Patentübereinkommen* (9th edition, Heymanns Verlag) points out, there must be "a nexus between the merits of the invention and the secondary factor".

4. *Requirements for second medical use*

It has been established by the case law relating to sufficiency of disclosure with regard to claims to a second medical use, that a claimed therapeutic effect may be proven by any kind of data as long as they directly and unambiguously reflect the therapeutic application; *Case Law of the Boards of Appeal*, 7th edition, 2013, section II.C.6.2, T 609/02 and T 801/06. Furthermore, the patent specification should include plausible and credible teaching as to why the claimed second medical use should work and the specification must disclose the suitability of the product to be manufactured for the claimed therapeutic application; see also T 1150/09.

4.1 *Distinction from first medical use*

Whereas the claims on first medical uses protect *any* therapeutic use of a given compound, second and further medical uses are limited in their scope of protection to specific medical settings, like specific disorders, specific patient groups and/or specific treatment regimes.

4.2 *Sub-species of second medical use*

With the new medical use format as provided by Article 54(5) EPC and the positive EBA decision G 2/08, the avenue for additional second or further medical uses was opened. These include second medical uses of a known compound in a novel disease. Also novel dosage/treatment regimes of a known compound in a known disease may be patentable, see (besides G 2/08) T 1020/03, T 36/04 or T 1074/06. A different route of administration in second medical use format was considered allowable, inter alia, in T 51/93 or T 906/10. Examples for second medical uses on novel patient groups include decisions T 734/12 or T 1107/11 (discussed below). Also novel technical effects may provide for claims in second medical use format in the EPO, see e.g. T 1229/03 or T 1955/09 (both discussed below). Also the avoidance of undesired side effects (as for example elucidated in clinical trials) may be claimed in the second medical use format; see as an example EP-B1 2 324 831.

4.3 *Dosage regimes*

The EBA confirmed in G 2/08 the basic findings of earlier landmark decision T 1020/03. In T 1020/03, the TBA decided in favour of a treatment/dosage regimen contribution.

Claims that include dosage regimens are often considered novel, however the hurdle of inventive step is quite high. In this respect, the patent specification should provide for a credible teaching that the proposed dosage/treatment regimes provide for unexpected technical advantages or that a surprising technical effect can be obtained. For example, in T 1074/06 (*Infertility/ARS*) the TBA considered the technical problem to be to provide a more user-friendly regimen while maintaining good follicle growth. Eventually, the Board acknowledged inventive step since neither the closest state of the art, nor any other prior art document on file, disclosed or even suggested modifying the different treatment regimens compared in the art with three groups of patients with quiescent ovaries, by further spacing the time interval between two consecutive doses of FSH or a biologically active analogue, and to apply the proposed and claimed treatment regimen.

The subject matter of the request under dispute in T 1409/06 (*Use of granisetron for the treatment of PONV/F. HOFFMANN-LA ROCHE AG*) concerned the use of granisetron for the manufacture of a medicament for the treatment and prophylaxis of post-operative nausea and vomiting (PONV) in a dosage of 1 mg to 3 mg. The closest prior art was a scientific article in which the physiology of nausea and vomiting and in particular of PONV is discussed. It contains the teaching that 5-HT3 receptor antagonists such as ondansetron and granisetron are successful in treating emesis caused by anticancer chemotherapy. The TBA was of the opinion that the even determination of the dosage which yields the best effect does not involve an inventive step when the effect as such is already known or obvious. In the TBA's opinion the person skilled in the art was aware that the intensity of a pharmacological effect depends, inter alia, on the concentration of the active agent. Finding the optimum dosage was considered as a matter of routine experimentation and was of the opinion that there was no evidence for any additional non-obvious effects in the application as filed that might be attributed to the claimed dosage.

4.4 *Special patient groups*

The TBAs of the EPO have routinely accepted that the selection of a new group of patients to be treated can confer novelty and inventive step to a second medical use claim. Accordingly, established case law of the Boards of Appeal accepted new therapeutic applications in specific patient groups as long as these novel patient groups to be treated are distinguishable by their physiological and pathological status from the patients treated in the prior art; see e.g. T 19/86 or T 893/90.

In T 1399/04 (*Combination therapy HCV/SCHERING*) the question at stake was whether a second medical use of ribavirin in combination with interferon alpha in chronic hepatitis C infection is novel when this treatment regime is characterised in that ribavirin in association with the interferon alpha is administered for a time period of 40-50 weeks and the patient to be treated is an antiviral treatment naive patient having a HCV genotype type 1 infection and the viral load is greater than 2 million copies per ml of serum. The TBA held (Reason 35) that the patient group to be treated in accordance with the claims under dispute

> "is defined as being infected by a specific genotype of HCV, genotype 1, which is a pathological characteristic allowing to differentiate members of this group

from all other HCV patients, and it is further defined by a viral load of greater than 2 million copies per ml of serum, which is a physiologically characterising feature."

Since this selection of a new group of subjects was not disclosed in the prior art, novelty was acknowledged. In a following decision (necessary due to a remittal of the case to the Opposition Division), inventive step was also accepted; see T 1545/08 (*Combination therapy HCV/SCHERING*).

The combination of a novel patient group with a novel specific technical effect may also contribute to novelty. For example in T 1107/11 (*Prebiotic for decreasing inflammatory process in elderly/NESTLE*) the use of a prebiotic for decreasing the inflammatory process in an elderly human, wherein the medicament decreases expression of interleukin-6 mRNA in peripheral blood monocytes was considered novel (and inventive) since the prior art did not mention any decrease of IL-6 after administration of a prebiotic and there was no hint of decreasing the age-associated rise of IL-6 involved in the inflammatory process in elderly patients.

New patient groups to be treated with a known compound may also be novel and inventive when this treatment is linked to a novel clinical situation or a novel clinical/medical effect. For example, in T 509/04 (*Cerebral palsy/ALLERGAN*) a claim relating to the use of botulinum toxin for the promotion of normal muscle growth in a juvenile patient suffering from contractures due to cerebral palsy before the patient had completed its growing period was considered novel and inventive over the prior art that disclosed the treatment of cerebral palsy in children with botulinum toxin wherein an improvement in muscle control and a decrease in muscle spasticity was observed.

Also a prophylactic treatment may confer novelty and inventiveness over a curative treatment provided for in the prior art. A distinction in the groups receiving medical treatment may here been seen as the prophylactic treatment of (still) healthy subjects versus medical intervention in diseased individuals. For example in T 433/11 (*Erkältungskrankheiten/PANDALIS*), the use of a Cystus composition in the prophylactic treatment of colds and sneezes caused by rhinoviruses was considered novel and inventive over the prior art disclosure that Cystus syrup is employed in the treatment of cold-associated symptoms such as sneezing/coryza and sore throat. The TBA was of the opinion that the term "prophylaxis" as used in the claim under dispute limits the claimed use to an administration of the known compound before disease breakout.

4.5 Special technical effect or mechanism leading to a truly novel clinical/medical situation

T 1229/03 (*Estrogen compositions for neuroprotection/UNI FLORIDA*) concerned the use of estrogen compounds for treating a neurodegenerative disorder by protecting a population of nerve cells from death. The specific technical effect "protecting nerve cells from death" was considered a novel feature. This "protection" was shown in the patent application as being directly linked to the claimed therapeutic use as well as to the estrogen compound(s). The TBA was satisfied that the intended technical effect was credibly disclosed in the application in suit in a meaningful and plausible manner and had been proven by technical data obtained from several in vitro and in vivo tests.

In T 1955/09 (*Antimicrobial peptides/OCTOPLUS SCIENCES*), the discussed claim related to the use of a specific peptidic compound for the manufacture of a medicament for the prophylactic or therapeutic treatment of a bacterial or fungal infection of a mammal *by killing said bacteria or fungi*. The cited closest prior art document disclosed that the very same peptidic compound may be used to "*neutralize toxins produced by bacteria or fungi*". Yet, the attained therapeutic effect of the use of the compounds defined in claim 1, namely the "killing of bacteria or fungi", was not described in the prior art. The TBA held (Reason 6) that the attaining of a *new technical effect* ("killing of bacteria or fungi") is considered *as a functional technical feature* of a claim, referring to the new *use of a known substance*. Since this technical feature had not been previously made available to the public, the claim was considered novel even though such technical effect *may have inherently taken place in the course of carrying out what was previously made available to the public*.

This principle has been provided previously in the case law of the Boards of Appeal relating to second or further medical uses of a known substance. For example, T 290/86 (*Cleaning plaque/ICI*), T 542/96 (*Xylitol-Fluoride/COLGATE-PALMOLIVE*), T 509/04 (*Cerebral palsy/ALLERGAN, INC.*) or T 1229/03 (*Estrogen compounds for treating neurodegenerative disorders/UNIVERSITY OF FLORIDA*), acknowledged novelty on the basis of *a new technical effect*. Yet, novelty was also denied for "technical effects or mechanisms", see, e.g., T 486/01 (*IGF-1/GENENTECH, INC. et al.*), T 384/03 (*Use of a carbonic anhydrase inhibitors/ADVANCED RESEARCH*) or T 1805/09 (*Polyunsaturated fatty acids/PRO*). In T 1805/09, it was noted that the patent under dispute does not disclose any new mechanism of action nor any other effect associated with the use of the same composition in the same disease. Here, polyunsaturated fatty acids of the omega-3 series in a specific ratio are claimed in the prevention of death from a cardiological cause in subjects who have not undergone previous infarct episodes. The patent under dispute referred very generally to the prevention of death by a cardiological cause, and no underlying effect is disclosed.

Accordingly, the novel technical effect must lead to a truly novel clinical/medical situation such as the healing of a different pathology or the treatment of the same disease with the same compound in a new group of subjects distinguishable from the previously treated patients; see also T 836/01 (*Interferon-beta2/YEDA RESEARCH AND DEVELOPMENT CO. LTD.*), T 1642/06 (*Sigma receptor/SPRUCE/BARBARA, et al.*). Also the combination of "patient groups" and specific treatment regimes are patentable as seen, inter alia, in T 1074/06 (i) wherein different treatment regimens of the prior art were modified in different groups of patients leading to the proposed treatment regimens.

5. *Timing issues*

5.1 Relevant time of development of second use

Second medical uses are often developed after a drug was developed and is tested in vitro and/or in vivo. This might involve early experimental laboratory data as well as clinical trials. Since the case law of the EPO has repeatedly confirmed that an invention needs to be plausibly and credibly disclosed in the specification, most medical use patents are filed when corresponding data are available.

Decision T 1545/08, (as discussed herein) is a further example, how important credible data in the patent are. In this case, data obtained from clinical trials and not available to the public from the prior art showed an beneficial, unexpected effect of a combination treatment in specific Hepatitis C patients. In view of the results reported in the patent, the TBA was satisfied that the specific patient group profits most from the claimed combination therapy.

5.2 *Role of new data*

In T 433/05, a second medical use claim reciting the use of particular modified peptides for preventing or treating viral infection was discussed. There was no experimental evidence in the application as filed. However, the TBA based its finding of "plausibility" under Article 56 EPC on what was known in the art about the unmodified peptides as well as the detailed information given in the application concerning preparation of the modified peptides, their use, and the measurement of the extended presence of the modified peptides. The TBA considered evidence of the in vivo stability based solely on the post-published data to determine that the application did indeed solve the problem it purported to solve. Similarly, in T 866/08, T 578/06 and T 1642/07, the claimed medical uses were considered sufficiently disclosed even though the specifications did not contain experimental data.

5.3 *Use of old data*

In T 734/12 it was confirmed that the provisions of Article 83 EPC are met, in relation to claims to a second medical use, if (i) the disclosure content of the application or the common general knowledge at the relevant date enables the skilled person to produce the compounds as claimed and (ii) the claimed treatment can be achieved in a reliable and reproducible manner. It follows from this that either the application must provide suitable evidence for the claimed therapeutic effect or it must be derivable from the prior art (see also T 609/02). Here, old data may be of relevance. According to T 433/04, for acceptance of sufficient disclosure of a therapeutic application in a patent, it is not always necessary that results of clinical trials are provided at the relevant date. However, it is required that the patent provides some information that the claimed compound has a direct effect on a metabolic mechanism specifically involved in the disease. This mechanism can be either known from the prior art or demonstrated in the patent.

III. Inventive step/non-obviousness

1. *Definition of inventive step/non-obviousness*

Article 56 EPC stipulates that "an invention is considered as involving an inventive step if, having regard to the state of the art, it is not obvious to a person skilled in the art". Whereas the assessment of inventive step is considered to be more subjective than the "novelty test" in the EPO, the case law of the EPO has developed the so-called "problem-solution approach" as a guidance tool. Here, the closest prior art is determined, the technical problem solved by the invention is established and it is assessed whether or not the claimed invention, starting from the closest prior art, would have been obvious. In this assessment, structural or functional differences between the invention and the closest prior art are taken into account and it is determined whether these differences would provide a non-obvious technical effect or not. For this assessment one additional prior art document or general public knowledge may be taken into account.

2. *Same scope of disclosure as for novelty?*

The patent/patent application needs to include plausible teaching that a technical problem has been solved by the features recited in the claims. In this respect, the concept of the person skilled in the art is even more important in the assessment of inventive step than in the novelty assessment.

3. *Assessment of inventive step/non-obviousness*

The assessment of inventive step very often involves rather scientific discussions since it needs to be determined whether a distinct technical problem is plausibly and credibly solved over the full range as claimed. Furthermore, it needs to be determined whether the teachings in the prior art would (not simply could) have prompted the skilled artisan to modify/adapt the closest prior art.

The main claim of T 1805/09 (*Polyunsaturated fatty acids/PRO APARTS – INVESTIMENTOS E CONSULTARIA LDA*) reads:

> "1. *Use of* specifically defined *polyunsaturated fatty acids of the omega-3 series in a given ratio*, for the preparation of a drug, to be administered orally, *in the primary prevention of death from a cardiological cause in subjects affected by cardiac decompensation*, who have not undergone previous infarct episodes." (emphasis added)

As none of the other documents on file disclosed the full set of features of claim 1 of the main request, the claims were considered as novel over the prior art (Article 54(2) and (3) EPC).

The *closest prior art* disclosed the therapeutical use of omega-3 fatty acids in the context of treating patients with congestive heart failure. The prior art also taught that administration of the omega-3 fatty acids decreases the risk of arrhythmia and of myocardial infarction. The TBA held that there *is no evidence in the patent or elsewhere on file* supporting any improvement linked to the differences between the claims and the closest prior art. Thus, the *technical problem* was formulated as the provision of a further formulation of polyunsaturated fatty acids of the omega-3 series, enriched to a content of > 50% omega-3, for the preparation of a drug for use in the prevention of death from a cardiological cause in patients with cardiac decompensation. While the TBA was satisfied that the technical problem, as formulated above, is plausibly solved, it however held that *the patent does not provide any data or information* on any specific effect linked to the differences over the closest prior art. Accordingly, the novel features of the main claim *could not* per se justify an inventive step. The Board thus concluded that the claimed subject matter lacks inventive step.

In elaboration of this case law it becomes apparent that the TBAs require that a technical feature relied on in prosecution or in oppositions before the EPO needs to be *plausibly* and *enablingly* disclosed in the originally filed patent application. This is also confirmed in decisions such as T 1545/08 (*Combination therapy HCV/MERCK SHARP & DOME*) (a continuation of T 1399/04, discussed under "Novelty", *supra*). The TBA's assessment of inventive step of *a combination therapy of ribavirin and interferon alpha (IFN) for a time period of 40-50 weeks in a novel, physiological and pathologically distinct hepatitis patient group of naive chronic HCV genotype 1 patients* with a virus load greater than 2 million copies/ml focused on the technical problem of identifying "that patient sub-group among all antiviral treatment naive patients having chronic HCV infection that profits most from prolonged treatment with IFN and ribarivin"; see Reason 61 of T 1545/08. In view of the results reported in the patent, the TBA was satisfied that the given patient group profits most from an extension of the combination therapy from 24 weeks to 48 weeks and considered that solving said technical problem required inventive effort. It was held that the results of the 48-week clinical trials mentioned in the prior art were not available to the public at the priority date. Thus, no conclusion could be drawn as regards any beneficial effect of the combination treatment for 48 weeks for any particular patient group, even if that patient group was included in the trial. A major point was that one of the experts executing a declaration on behalf of the opponents stated in an article published shortly before the priority date that "[i]t is impossible to predict accurately who will eliminate the virus if given interferon". Based on this statement, the TBA concluded that at the priority date even the response to IFN monotherapy was not predictable. Also due to the data provided in the patent under dispute, the granted claims were considered inventive.

Where therapeutic outcome cannot, plausibly, be predicted, inventive step cannot be prejudiced; see, e.g., T 385/07 (*Aplidine/PHARMA MAR*). In that case, the claims related to the medical use of aplidine for the treatment of pancreatic cancer. A prior art document disclosed that patients suffering from gastric adenocarcinoma, kidney carcinoma, non-Hodgkin lymphoma and renal carcinoma could benefit from aplidine treatment. This prior art document also disclosed that aplidine was undergoing a clinical phase evaluation for pancreatic cancer, however, no data had been released. According to the TBA the test that has to be performed in order to evaluate inventive activity of the claims is the question whether in the light of the (non-pancreatic) results of the prior art, the anti-tumour activity of a drug against a certain cancer type is predictive of its anti-tumour activity in another cancer type; T 385/07 (Reason 16). Since the data of the prior art was not predictive for the results of the clinical trial in pancreatic cancer, inventive step was acknowledged.

It is evident from the EPO case law on "first or further medical use claims" that clear, plausible and credible teaching in the patent/patent application helps in the argumentation of inventive step.

IV. Amendment of claims after grant

1. *Admissibility of post-grant amendments in general*

Amendments to a granted EP patent are admissible during opposition and opposition appeal proceedings as well as during limitation proceedings (centralised *ex parte* procedures at the level of the EPO which allow the patent proprietor to have the claims of its granted patent limited). Any amendments are formally assessed under Article 123 EPC ("impermissible broadening") and, accordingly, whereas a change of category of claims to, for example, product claims and first medical use to second medical use is formally allowable, a clear and unambiguous disclosure of the claimed subject matter in the patent specification is required.

2. *Procedural issues*

2.1 *Independent limitation proceedings*

Under Article 105 (a)-(c) EPC, the EP may be limited at the request of the patent proprietor by amendment of the claims. The proprietor may also limit the claims by changing the claim category, for example from a product claim to a more limiting second medical use claim.

2.2 *Opposition proceedings*

In oppositions (Article 100 EPC) before the EPO, the patentee is allowed file new claim requests which take the objections of the opponent of the Opposition Division into account. Yet, these amended claims cannot go beyond the content of the patent as granted since this would interfere with Article 123(3) EPC ("impermissible broadening of the granted patent").

3. *Added matter*

In opposition proceedings as well as during limitations, a very strict assessment of Article 123 EPC by the deciding body takes place.

4. *Sufficiency*

In light of Article 83 EPC, also during second instance proceedings such as oppositions or limitations, it is assessed whether the claims under discussion are sufficiently clear and complete to be carried out by a person skilled in the art. This also applies for second medical use claims and in particular for the parameters in the claim which render the subject matter novel and inventive. In particular, the suitability of the product recited in the claims for the claimed (second) therapeutic application is also assessed; see also T 433/05.

5. *Multiple indications*

According to Rule 43(2) EPC the number of independent claims is limited to one independent claim in each category. Exceptions to this rule can only be admitted in the specific circumstances defined in sub-paragraphs (a), (b) or (c) of this Rule, provided the requirement of Article 82 EPC ("unity") is met. Separate claims that are directed to different medical uses are generally allowed under Rule 43(2)(b) EPC, if they are different inventive uses of a product or composition; see Guidelines for Examination before the EPO, F, VI 3.2. In G 1/91 the EBA held that unity of invention did not come under the requirements which an EP and the invention to which it related had to meet under Article 102(3) EPC1973 (Article 101(3)(a) EPC2000) when the patent was maintained in an amended form. It is consequently irrelevant in opposition proceedings whether a patent as granted or amended meets the requirement of unity. Indeed, the requirement of unity under Article 82 EPC has to be satisfied only until grant of the patent; see *Case Law of the Boards of Appeal*, II.B.3.3. Accordingly, multiple therapeutic indications can be introduced into the claims after grant, provided that the requirements of Article 123(2) and (3) EPC are satisfied.

V. Change of patent category

1. *General admissibility*

The EPO allows amendments to claims of a patent application during examination or of a granted patent, for example during opposition proceedings, under the strict observation of the "impermissible broadening stipulations" of Article 123 EPC. However, a medical use that is clearly and unambiguously disclosed in a patent specification can certainly provide the basis for a change in patent category.

G 2/88 established that the change of category from product to (medical) use claims does not broaden the scope of protection. Similarly, a "limitation" from a first medical use claim to a (disclosed!) second medical use claim is generally allowed under the EPC and EPO case law.

On the basis of Article 53(c) EPC "methods for treatment of the human or animal body by surgery or therapy and diagnostic methods practised on the human or animal body" are not allowable in the EPO. Accordingly, a category change form a "medical use" claim in accordance with Article 54(4)/(5) EPC to a "method of treatment claim" is not allowable in the EPO. For example, in T 1075/09 (*Treatment of anovulatory women/LABORATOIRE SERONO SA*), the patentee encountered a "method of treatment problem" because of the mixed nature of the claim which included the words "wherein the medicament [comprising LH] is to be administered" and "wherein folliculogenesis is induced by the administration of FSH". Here the TBA held that the contested claim "can be read as a sequence of two separate activities, the induction of folliculogenesis by the administration of FSH which is not drafted in Swiss-type format followed by the administration of LH drafted in the Swiss-type format and is therefore excluded from patentability pursuant to Article 53(c) EPC". However, since G 2/08 and other case law of the EPO already established that "any method claim containing even a single step pertaining by nature to a treatment by therapy is not allowable", the patentee had to amend the claims further to a truly second medical use format.

2. *Use claim as a category*

In the EPO, the question of category change within "use claims" occurred during the transition period from EPC1973 to EPC2000. Applicants in particular desired to modify Swiss-type claims to EPC claims or to obtain protection for two independent claims. In T 1570/09 (*Alpha-ketoglutaric acid/PROTISTA*), this was denied by reasoning that "G 2/08 does not give applicants an absolute right to draft two independent claims in one single set of claims for one and the same medical indication of one and the same substance, one claim following the praetorian rule introduced in view of the old provisions of EPC 1973, and the other claim following the new provisions in Article 54(5) EPC 2000"; see Reason 4.4. This is in contrast to T 879/12, wherein both "use claims" were allowable since the scope of protection is not the same.

3. *From product to method claim*

Due to the stipulation of Article 53(c) EPC, the EPO does not allow "method of treatment" claims.

4. *From method to product claim*

As discussed above, the change form a "method of treatment claim" to a product claim such as "substance X for use as a medicament" is allowable in the EPO.

5. *System claims*

Second medical use claims for systems/devices are not allowable in the EPO as discussed in detail in section B.I.4 (*supra*).

6. *Use claims*

In proceedings before the EPO, applicants/patentees may revert to "medical use" claims as long as the specification of the patent (patent application) provides for clear and unambiguous support for such claims. Also "method of treatment claims" as drafted in US-PCT applications may be redrafted into medical use claims, which are acceptable under the EPC, when entering the regional phase before the EPO.

Germany

Dr. Jochen Bühling

A. AVAILABILITY OF PROTECTION

I. Legal framework

Germany has traditionally allowed use claims and in particular claims for second medical use in patent law for a long time.

As a Member of the European Patent Convention and the European Union Germany adheres to the legal provisions of the EPC and other European law. Germany is also expected to ratify the European Patent Package which may eventually also influence German law and in particular German case law.

1. National statutory laws

The main provisions can be found in the German Patent Act of 1981 ("GPA") and the German Utility Model Act of 1986 ("UMA") following a long tradition of more than a hundred years. German law is in conformity with the EPC and other European legal instruments.

Use claims are not mentioned in the statutory provisions. They have been developed by case law in the existing legal framework which states in general that patents are granted for inventions in all fields of technology, provided that they are new, involve an inventive step and are susceptible of industrial application (Sec. 1 para. 1 German Patent Act[1]). In the context of Sec. 9 GPA which concerns the exclusive right of the patentee, a distinction is made between products and processes which are the subject of the patent.

Claims which cover the use of a product for a specific purpose are not explicitly mentioned in the Patent Act. The same applies to second medical use claims. The

1. Patentgesetz; translated as German Patent Act ("GPA").

only indication dealing with such claims can be found in Sec. 3 GPA which concerns requirements for novelty. It has a similar wording as Art. 54 EPC.

A peculiarity of German law is the utility model. It is sometimes described as "a small patent". It basically follows the same rules with some exceptions and some significant differences. One may obtain a utility model for an invention provided it is new, involves an inventive step and is susceptible of industrial application (Sec. 1 para. 1 Utility Model Act[2]). In contrast to the Patent Act a utility model may not be registered for an invention comprising a process. It is limited to products. This may have consequences for the availability of utility model protection for use claims. Besides the limitation to a maximum term of 10 years the Utility Model Act also contains some other provisions which differ significantly from the Patent Act. These concern mainly the definition of novelty, prior art and inventive step. Where this becomes important for the purposes of this chapter, reference is made to the specific sections below.

1.1 Pharmaceuticals

Patent protection for chemical substances and in particular pharmaceuticals has been available under German law since 1968 when the prohibition to grant product patents for inventions which were achieved by way of chemical reactions and for pharmaceuticals was abolished. Today, a patent can generally be obtained for any product in this field.

Sec. 2a GPA contains a number of exclusions for which patents are not granted. This section was introduced in 2005 when the EU Biotech Directive (98/44/EC) was transformed into German law. Sec. 2a para. 2 GPA specifically mentions methods for surgical or therapeutic treatment of the human or animal body and diagnostic methods performed on the human or animal body. Until then, such methods were considered not to be industrially applicable. At the same time, this exception does not apply to products for use in such methods, in particular to substances and compositions. Although the method of treatment as such cannot be the subject matter of a patent, pharmaceuticals and chemical substances may be patented, even when they are intended for a use in those methods.

In this regard, the term "substance or composition" should be understood in a broad sense. It is not limited to medicaments which require a marketing authorization but also includes other preparations which can be used as nutrition or for other purposes.[3] This also applies to combination products or products which have been obtained from body fluids (e.g. from blood or blood cells).

1.2 Biologics

Following the EU Biotech Directive, German law has also introduced the protection of certain inventions which comprise biological material. This relates to elements isolated from the human body or otherwise produced by means of a technical

2. Gebrauchsmustergesetz; translated as Utility Model Act ("UMA").
3. OLG Düsseldorf, 07/08/2014, I-2 U 8/14 – *Ubichinon.*

process and includes gene sequences and the products made using the genes, such as antibodies (Sec. 1a para. 2 GPA). Also the exception from patentability mentioned before concerning therapeutic or diagnostic methods does not apply to these products.

2. *International treaties*

Most international treaties relating to IP have been ratified by the German parliament. They usually require a transformation into national law. An immediate effect would be limited to so-called self-executing provisions which can be applied directly to a specific case.

2.1 TRIPS

Art. 27 (1) TRIPS obligates the member states to provide for protection of inventions, whether products or processes, in all fields of technology. German law is in full compliance with TRIPS including the allowed exceptions from patentability as explained above.

2.2 FTAs

Germany is bound to a number of FTAs mainly through its membership of the EU which has the prerogative for concluding such agreements. However, with regard to patents, these agreements have no additional effect beyond the existing German law. Currently discussions are going on with the USA (TTIP), Canada (CETA), Japan and a number of other countries. It is not to be expected that those agreements will impact IP in this context.

3. *Availability through case law*

As mentioned earlier, the statutory law in Germany does not specifically address claims for a second medical use. The main source for this type of claim is therefore the case law as it has been established in particular by the Federal Patent Court (FPC) and the civil courts, i.e. the District Courts and Courts of Appeal in the first and second instance and the Federal Court of Justice (*Bundesgerichtshof*, "BGH"). which is the highest German court both for cases from the civil courts and patent cases coming from the FPC.

4. *Patent term extension/SPCs*

German law complements European Regulations No. 469/2009 concerning the Supplementary Protection Certificate for Medicinal Products and No. 1901/06 concerning Medicinal Products for Pediatric Use with Sec. 16a and 49a GPA. They comprise the provisions for the application of the national law to the SPCs and the procedural rules to obtain SPC protection.

II. Policy considerations

1. *Health and social issues*

The health system is highly regulated in Germany. There are basically two corresponding and to some extent also competing systems for the health insurance. In a nutshell on the one hand employees have a mandatory health insurance. They pay monthly fees (shared with the employers) and receive a certain standard of free healthcare which includes physicians' treatments, hospital stays and medicaments. The services are charged directly to the insurers. On the other hand, non-employees (such as self-employed people, freelancers, independent contractors, public servants, etc.) find their own private health insurance. Typically, they receive an invoice from their doctors, hospitals or pharmacists and will get reimbursed by their insurer. In both systems, the prices for services and medicaments are not left to the free market but are highly regulated and also limited. They are usually based on fixed schedules which are negotiated between the main associations of insurers, physicians and patients. Besides this, extra expenses are normally not reimbursable.

This leads to competition not only among the originators but in particular between originators and generics manufacturers. Mainly for economic reasons, physicians and pharmacists are obligated to choose the most cost effective treatment where possible. This primarily applies to the prescription of medicaments. In principle, physicians enjoy freedom of treatment, i.e. they determine what they believe is best for the patient in a given situation. Nevertheless, they face pressure from the insurers to keep budgets low.

The patentability of second medical use claims is in line with considerations known from other jurisdictions. There is a clear need for research and development of new pharmaceuticals and of new treatments in areas which are not yet fully satisfied. One of the incentives is the patent protection which will allow a company to recover the investment connected to R&D in these fields. In order to promote this both the first and second medical use claims have been allowed to expand the available protection.

2. *Legal issues*

As mentioned the highly regulated market follows strict principles in the domain of public and administrative law provisions. Their influence on the patent situation shall not be investigated further here.

Legal policy considerations have their basis mainly in the fact that Germany is part of the EU and also of the EPC. Much of the law has been harmonized. Therefore, the legal considerations have to bring the national law in line with EU law and the EPC. This is clearly reflected in many provisions of the GPA and – to a lesser extent – in the UMA which run in parallel with the EPC provisions.[4]

4. The law for utility models is not harmonized internationally.

B. VALIDITY

I. Allowable claim wording

The GPA does not specify the claim wording for which protection should be allowable.

1. *Product claims*

According to Sec. 9 para. 1 GPA the subject matter of a patent can be a product. Product claims may be worded as comprising a device or also a substance or composition. The product must then be described by its characteristic structural elements. This is possible by using chemical formulas of various formats (e.g. the Markush formula). Another option is to describe in the claim specific physical features, such as the melting point, the weight or the proportions of the individual compounds.

2. *Method claims*

Sec. 9 para. 2 GPA mentions as the subject matter of a claim a method or process. This may be any kind of method or process in any technical field.[5] The subject matter of a method claim may be a process to manufacture a product, to work on a product, to treat a product or any other kind of method which is applied in the technical field.

The purpose of the method is not limiting, unless the method is specified in that it can only be used for a specific product or purpose. One has to interpret on a case by case basis whether that purpose is meant to limit the subject matter or just serves as an example.

3. *Use claims*

Use claims are not limited to the medical use. On the contrary, they originate from situations where a known device is used for a specific purpose for which it had not been used before and which is considered to be an invention and therefore should merit patent protection.[6] Here, the applicant could not obtain protection for the product itself but only for the specific use. The claim wording would then read "use of ABC for XYZ".

This format of a use claim needs modification for the medical use when the medical use is a treatment of the human body or a diagnostic for the human body. Since the treatment and the diagnostic method per se are excluded from patent protection also the use or the device for that method would in principle not be patentable. In line with the EPO case law also the German Patent and Trademark Office (GPTO) has allowed Swiss-type claims in the format "use of ABC for the manufacture of a

5. German law does not allow patents for business methods. This is not discussed further here.
6. BGH 14/03/1972, X ZB 33/70, GRUR 1972, 638 – *Aufhellungsmittel*; BGH 16/06/1987, X ZR 51/86, GRUR 1987, 794 – *Antivirusmittel*; BGH 20/12/2011, X ZR 53/11, GRUR 2012, 373 – *Glasfasern*.

medicament for treatment of XYZ". This had been standard practice for a number of years and was fully in line with the EPO practice.[7]

Following the new practice under the EPC 2000 the GPTO also requires claims with the format "use of ABC for the treatment of patients suffering from XYZ".[8]

4. *System claims*

System claims are also allowed under German law. In particular, they refer to a system which consists of several independent components.

In the field of the medical use as a general rule a system claim in combination with a use claim should also be feasible provided that the system is defined (e.g. as a system comprising several chemical substances).

5. *Dosage regimes*

In principle, it is also possible to formulate a claim which is directed at a specific dosage regime to be administered to a patient. This dosage may either be contained in a product claim or in a use claim.[9]

6. *Patient groups*

In the same way a claim wording is allowed which specifically concerns the use of a substance/compound/medicament for a specific patient group. Again, this may give rise to novelty issues but does not exclude such a wording from the outset.

II. Novelty

1. *General definition of novelty and prior art*

According to the general definition in Sec. 3 GPA an invention is considered novel if it is not part of the prior art. Prior art is defined as all information which has been made publicly available prior to the relevant date which may be either the priority date or the application date. All means of making the information publicly available are included. It is not necessary that the public in fact noted the information. The possibility that an indefinite number of people could have seen the information is sufficient.

For novelty purposes certain documents which have been published after the application date or the priority date are also considered prior art (Sec. 3 para. 2 GPA).

For utility models the UMA shows significant differences in the definition of prior art. As far as a use is concerned it only forms part of the prior art if it occurred in Germany. Outside Germany only written descriptions constitute prior art.

---

7. BGH 20/09/1983, X ZB 4/83, GRUR 1983,729 – *Hydropyridin*; BGH 20/01/1977, X ZB 13/75, GRUR 1977, 652 – *Benzolsulfonylharnstoff.*
8. BGH 25/02/2014, X ZB 5/13, GRUR 2014, 461 – *Kollagenase I*; BGH 25/02/2014, X ZB 6/13, GRUR 2014, 464 – *Kollagenase II.*
9. As regards the novelty issues see below II.

Furthermore, there is a grace period of six months for utility models (Sec. 3 UMA). Documents published after the relevant date are not prior art.

2. *Definition of skilled person*

The skilled person is a fictitious person. It is a person who has obtained a general knowledge and possesses all information which is relevant in the respective technical field. In particular in the field of medicines and biotechnology the single person is more and more replaced by an interdisciplinary team which then determines what the skilled person would read from a specific disclosure.[10]

3. *Scope of disclosure*

3.1 *General rules*

As a general rule everything which can be derived clearly and unambiguously from a document is disclosed. This takes into consideration the entire document, irrespective of its nature.

A patent application comprises the specification, claims and the figures. A scientific article will comprise the text as well as tables or also figures.

Furthermore, according to German practice, the disclosure also includes what the skilled person will naturally understand and read from the document based on their general knowledge in that specific field without supplementing the disclosed content.[11] It goes further than a simply photographic approach. The boundaries are to be set where the skilled person involved draws conclusions in connection with other documents or sources of information.

3.2 *First medical use*

Sec. 3 (3) GPA concerns the first medical use. Patent protection for a product (composition or compound or substance) conveys absolute protection irrespective of the purpose for which the product is used or intended to be used. Consequently, the use of a known product for a new purpose should not be considered novel under these principles. However, in order to allow the protection for such medical uses Sec. 3 para. 3 GPA makes an exception. The patentability of a substance or composition is not excluded by the general definition of prior art if the product is intended to be used in a method for the treatment or diagnostic of the human body and if the use for such a method was not known in the prior art. This allows protection for the first medical use and covers situations where a known compound is used as a medicament for the first time.

It must be noted that this exception only covers substances and compounds but no other products. It is therefore not applicable to medical devices or other systems.

10. See e.g. BGH 19/12/1985, X ZR 53/83, GRUR 1986, 372 – *Thrombozyten-Zählung*.
11. See e.g. BGH 16/12/2008, X ZR 89/07, GRUR 2009, 382 – *Olanzapin*.

3.3 *New subject matter*

Compounds and substances which were not known from the prior art will generally not face issues of novelty.

This does not allow the inclusion of new subject matter after an application has been filed. The principles of added matter apply in the same way as in other patent cases.

3.4 *New data*

In principle new data which are not available in the prior art can also support a patent for a medical use. However, there is a fine line of distinction. Where the new data only confirm the use which occurred in the prior art or where the data provide an explanation as to the physiological effect of a medicament this will not be considered as novel. An application based on those data would at least lack inventive step.[12]

4. ***Requirements for second medical use***

4.1 *Distinction from first medical use*

Sec. 3 (4) GPA also allows patent protection for the second medical use if that specific medical use was not known from the prior art even where the compounds or substances were already used in another medical field.[13] It is therefore important to clearly distinguish the second medical use and the therapeutic effect from the uses which were known before. This must be based on a technical (medical and physiological) assessment which allows the conclusion that the contemplated medical use is not encompassed by any earlier medical use (indication).[14]

4.2 *Subspecies of first medical use*

Problems arise where the second medical use seems to be a subspecies (or more concrete form) of the first medical use. In principle, a general description or term does not necessarily anticipate a specific example or embodiment which would be covered by that general term. Again, it should be allowable to formulate a use claim which is directed to a new subspecies of the first use which was not known even though the more general term was used. In practice, this will nevertheless very likely raise issues of the inventive step.

The BGH also held that the mere discovery of the biological connections on which a therapeutic effect is based does not provide a new technical teaching if the ingredient, the indication, the dosage and the way the ingredient is administered remain the same as has been described in an earlier use for treatment of a specific

12. BGH 30/03/1993, X ZB 13/90, GRUR 1993, 651 – *Tetraploide Kamille.*
13. BGH 14/03/1972, X ZB 2/71, GRUR 1972, 541 – *Imidazoline*; BGH 20/09/1983, X ZB 4/83, GRUR 1983, 729 – *Hydropyridin.*
14. BGH 19/12/2006, X ZR 236/01, GRUR 2007, 404 – *Carvedilol II.*

illness.[15] In a very recent decision concerning nucleic acids and antibodies and a pharmaceutical composition comprising the nucleic acid the BGH has, however, also ruled that a teaching may be patentable if it comprises the use of a discovery for a specific effect even if it does not contain any exceeding invention which goes beyond the finding of the biological connections.[16]

4.3 *Dosage regimes*

The same principles apply to dosage regimes. According to the older case law the mere development of a specific dosage regime does not change the general medical use described in the prior art.[17] On the other hand, one can also assess the administration of a medicament to a patient in a specific dosage regime as a specific medical use which was not known from the prior art. Latest case law suggests that there might be a more tolerant view in the future.[18]

4.4 *Special patient groups*

Also with regard to special patient groups the same principles apply. An invention can be considered novel if that specific patient group is clearly distinguished from earlier patient groups and shows characteristics which were not described in the prior art.

5. ***Timing issues***

5.1 *Relevant time of development of second use*

The second medical use must have been developed at the time of the application (or the priority date if applicable), but may not have been comprised by the prior art. A medical use which is developed after the application date or priority date can in principle not lead to a patent with that application or priority date.

5.2 *Role of new data*

New data, i.e. data which have been established after the priority/application date and during the prosecution of the application may be considered if they contribute to the examples and descriptions disclosed in the application and if they support the statements contained in the application. They are not admissible if the disclosure has been insufficient and if the new data serve to enable the skilled person to work the invention for the first time.[19]

---

15. BGH 19/06/2011, X ZR 68/08, GRUR 2011, 999 – *Memantin*; BGH 24/09/2013, X ZR 40/12, GRUR 2014, 54 – *Fettsäuren.*
16. BGH 19/01/2016, X ZR 141/13, GRUR 2016, 475 – *Rezeptortyrosinkinase.*
17. BGH 19/12/2006, X ZR 236/01, GRUR 2007, 404 – *Carvedilol II.*
18. BGH; 25/02/2014, X ZB 6/13, GRUR 2014, 464 – *Kollagenase II.*
19. BGH 30/03/1993, X ZB 13/90, GRUR 1993, 651 – *Tetraploide Kamille.*

5.3 Use of old data

Old data which were known in the prior art may nevertheless be used if the second medical use which is based on those old data is a new invention and was not disclosed to the skilled person earlier. In fact, it is not uncommon that the new use originates from old data which are then supported by additional new data.

III. Non-obviousness

According to German law an invention must involve an inventive step. It should be noted that the English translation does not properly show the subtle distinction between the German wording used in Sec. 1 para. 1 GPA for patents ("*erfinderische Tätigkeit*") on the one hand and in the corresponding provision for utility models in Sec. 1 para. 1 UMA ("*erfinderischer Schritt*") on the other hand. The former term used in the Patent Act should literally be translated as "inventive activity". However, it has become customary to use the same English wording for patents and utility models. The common theory in the past was that there should be a different standard in that the "inventive activity" for patents requires more than the mere inventive step which would be sufficient for a utility model. This has led to an important decision of the Federal Court of Justice which ruled that in fact the same standard should apply to both rights.[20] However, this issue has not been pursued further and since then has not been the subject of another decision of the BGH.

1. Definition of inventive step

Sec. 4 GPA states that an invention is considered to involve an inventive step if it is not obvious to the skilled person from the prior art. Here the term "obvious" is the key element. The UMA does not contain a similar legal definition for utility models. That is one of the reasons why the discussion described above could take place.

2. Same scope of disclosure as for novelty?

The standard and the scope of disclosure remain the same irrespective of the purpose for which it is needed. Consequently, all issues which relate to a disclosure either of the patent or of a document from the prior art, i.e. novelty, inventive step, enablement and sufficiency and scope of protection should lead to the same content and scope of the disclosure based on what the skilled person derives from the document.

3. Assessment of inventive step

The assessment of the inventive step requires a general comparison with the entire prior art in contrast to novelty where the comparison is made one to one with a single document at a time.

The standard is the same as for European patents (Art. 56 EPC).

---

20. BGH 20/06/2006, X ZB 27/05, GRUR 2006, 842 – *Demonstrationsschrank*.

Although German case law also seems to slowly adopt a problem/solution approach, similar to the EPO, the starting point is somewhat different. Under German case law the problem is determined objectively through the eyes of the skilled person from the specification of the patent. The next step then is to interpret what the solution is according to the claims and the understanding of the skilled person. Finally, it must be determined whether the step from the prior art to the patented solution involves an inventive step.

With regard to second medical use claims the assessment of the inventive step follows the same rules as for other patents. The statutory law does not provide for any privilege for second use claims as it does for novelty.

IV. Amendment of claims after grant

1. Admissibility of post-grant amendments in general

For German patents and utility models post-grant amendments of the claims are in general allowed under certain circumstances.

The utility model is peculiar in that it has a set of claims which are registered upon application without examination (apart from certain minimum formal requirements). It is allowed under German law to amend the registered claims. Another option is to use different claims in infringement proceedings even when these claims are not registered.[21] This offers a great flexibility to the right holder and opens up a variety of options which the proprietor can use when needed, in particular in light of new prior art of which the proprietor was not aware.

2. Procedural issues

2.1 Independent limitation proceedings

Sec. 64 GPA allows a request of the patentee to have the patent revoked or restricted by amending the claims. This is done with retroactive effect. The amended claims are only examined as to certain formal aspects and whether they extend the scope of protection and properly limit the claims.

It has to be noted that with regard to the German part of European patents the limitation proceedings according to Sec. 64 GPA as well as the centralized limitation (Art. 105a EPC) are permissible and can be done in parallel. Theoretically this may lead to different decisions of the GPTO and the EPO. In that case the subject matter of the patent will only comprise what has been protected according to both decisions.[22]

21. BGH 19/06/2011, X ZR 68/08, GRUR 2011, 999 – *Memantin*.
22. BGH 20/03/2001, X ZR 177/98, GRUR 2001, 730 – *Trigomelin*; this decision concerned the parallelism of national limitation proceedings and opposition proceedings but should apply also to parallel EPO limitation proceedings.

2.2 *Opposition proceedings*

Sec. 59 GPA allows any third party to file an opposition against the granted patent. The opposition may be based on the grounds for revocation listed in Sec. 21 GPA which is lack of patentability, insufficient disclosure, usurpation by third party or added matter.

During the opposition proceedings claims may be limited. In this case they are fully examined as to patentability, sufficiency and added matter.

2.3 *Nullity actions*

Nullity actions are brought before the Federal Patent Court. They concern either national German patents or the German parts of European patents.

During the nullity proceedings the patent proprietor may file a request to maintain the patent in amended form. Those amendments must limit the claims and are examined with regard to patentability, sufficiency and added matter.

3. *Added matter*

Added matter is also a ground for a revocation of the patent. Amendments made to the claims may not lead to this objection. Otherwise, the amendment would have to be rejected.

It should be noted that the so-called "inescapable trap" which has been established by the case law of the EPO is not applied under German law. The German case law allows such amendments, whereby the added feature which was not disclosed originally will remain in the claim and thus affect the scope of protection. For the purposes of determining patentability this added feature is not considered.[23]

4. *Sufficiency*

Sec. 34 para. 4 GPA requires that the invention is sufficiently disclosed so that a skilled person can work the invention. There are also no specific issues related to use claims in this regard.

5. *Multiple indications*

Amendments to the claims can also comprise the addition of one or more additional medical indications for which the product could be used.

In this situation, the same principles as described before are applicable. This means in particular that the medical indication must have been disclosed in the application before. It may not contain any added matter and it must be novel and inventive. Furthermore, the scope of protection of the granted patent may not be expanded. This means that replacing one medical indication by another where this additional indication was not originally comprised by the claim should not be

---

23. BGH 17/02/2015, X ZR 16112, GRUR 2015, 573 – *Wundbehandlungsvorrichtung.*

admissible. If the claim already comprised several alternative indications as a choice the limitation to only one of those indications would lead to an allowable limitation of the claim. If the original claim prescribed that the product must be suitable for both indications the omission of one of the indications would expand the scope of protection and would therefore not be admissible.

V. Change of patent category

1. General admissibility

As mentioned earlier, German law knows two patent categories, namely product patents and process patents. A change from one category to the other is not generally excluded. However, one has to strictly observe the conditions which prevent an expansion of the scope of protection and also the issues of added matter.

2. Use claim as a category

Use claims do not constitute a category of their own, but are rather encompassed by one of the two existing categories. Depending on the specific wording of the claim the patent may be seen as a product patent or as a method patent.

3. From product to method claim

In principle a change from a product claim to a method claim always raises issues of expanding the scope of protection. While a product is characterized by certain structural features the method claim looks at various steps in the process which are in principle irrespective of the structural elements of the finished product. Generally this relates to something different and cannot be considered a limitation of the original product claim. However, a change from a product claim to the manufacture of that very specific product or the change from a product by process claim to a claim for a manufacturing process may be allowable if the manufacturing process does not cover other products.

4. From method to product claim

A change from a method to a product claim is generally not admissible. Although the scope of protection of a method claim also covers a product which has been directly obtained by the respective method (Sec. 9 no. 3 GPA), this requires that the patented steps have been used to obtain the product and that no further steps were necessary. Otherwise the criterion of "directly obtained" would not be fulfilled.

A mere product claim covers the product in its structural elements irrespective of the way of manufacturing and irrespective of whether it was directly obtained or only by way of additional steps. Therefore, the scope of protection of a product claim is generally broader. An exception may be made where the product claim is worded as a product by process claim which then incorporates all of the steps of the original method claim. However, the scope still changes from the manufacturing process to an absolute product protection which is generally an inadmissible amendment.

5. System claims

Claims which are directed at a system do not form a separate category. It remains to be decided on a case by case basis subject to the specific circumstances, the claim wording and the specification of the patent whether the system claim must be regarded as a product claim or a process claim. Amendments must be assessed in consideration of the explanations above.

6. Use claims

The same principles also apply to use claims. Since use claims do not form a separate category, the admissibility of amendments must be checked against the existing categories of product claims and method claims.

It is generally allowed to amend a general product claim to a specific use of a product for a specific purpose. This comprises a limitation, since a product claim usually covers every possible use while the use claim should then only comprise one specific use. The change from the general product claim to a specific use claim implies that the applicant waives protection for all other possible uses of the product.[24]

For the second medical use this means that a patent application which was originally directed at the substance (product) may be limited to the use of the substance for the specific purpose. This applies also to the claim format according to the EPC 2000.

The change from a use claim to a claim to manufacture a medicament (similar to the old Swiss-type format) would not be admissible. It would contain a change of the scope of protection. In the same way it would not be possible to switch from the use claim to a general product claim.

C. INFRINGEMENT AND LITIGATION

I. Legal framework

Infringement is governed almost entirely by national law. Even under the new regime of the UPC national law will be applicable to a great extent. This concerns the conditions for infringement as well as the remedies.

1. National statutory laws

Secs. 9-13 GPA provide the exclusive rights of the patentee. Sec. 9 concerns direct infringement, Sec. 10 deals with indirect infringement. As mentioned above Sec. 9 distinguishes between product and process claims. It does not specifically address

24. BGH 16/01/1990, X ZB 24/87, GRUR 1990 ,508 – *Spreizdübel.*

use claims. One will therefore have to fit such claims and an infringement of such claims into one of the appropriate claim categories.

Similar provisions can be found in the Utility Model Act. Both Acts also comprise detailed provisions on the remedies available (Sec. 139 et seq. GPA, Sec. 24 et seq. UMA).

2. *Case law*

Case law has played a vital role in providing the legal basis for use claims and in determining the scope of protection against the background of the statutory law.

II. Claim construction

1. *General rules*

The interpretation of claims follows Sec. 14 GPA. This provision reads that the scope of the patent is determined by the claims and that the specification and the drawings are used to interpret the claims. This is fully in line with Art. 69 EPC and the Protocol on the Interpretation of Art. 69. Sec. 14 GPA is the fundamental rule for claim construction which allows a reasonable balance to be achieved between the interest of the applicant in obtaining adequate protection for the invention and the interest of third parties and the public in legal certainty.

The BGH has repeatedly decided that the claim construction is the vital task of the courts when they are confronted with issues of validity and infringement cases. The courts have to determine in the first step what the invention according to the patent is before they move on to issues of novelty or inventive step or other questions in a specific case.[25]

The claim construction should come to a reasonable result of what the applicant intended and shall not be biased by potential invalidity arguments. The courts may not omit that task, simply because they may find it too difficult or even impossible to come to a decision in this regard.[26]

2. *Specific issues for use claims*

Use claims are also to be interpreted in the same way as other patent claims taking into account the functionality of the claimed features.

Since the wording of the claim is decisive in this context, one may have to carefully assess if differences in the wording also lead to differences in the determination of the scope of protection. An old Swiss-type claim such as "Use of X in the manufacture of a medicament for the treatment of ..." may be considered differently from today's EPC 2000 claims such as "Substance X for use in the treatment of Y..." or the like.

25. BGH 12/05/2015, X ZR 43/13, GRUR 2015, 875 – *Rotorelemente.*
26. See e.g. BGH 09/06/2015, X ZR 101/13, GRUR 2015, 868 – *Polymerschaum II.*

Other issues arise with regard to the scope of protection and the infringing acts. When is a certain act considered a "use" in the meaning of the patent claim and what other acts are to be encompassed in the scope of protection?

III. Scope of protection

The scope of protection can be determined only after the invention has been clearly identified. Rather than describing the abstract boundaries of the scope of protection one may find certain guidelines. A concrete determination will assess whether a specific allegedly infringing embodiment or act is still covered by the scope of protection.

1. Scope of the use

Since the wording of the claim is the starting point for the interpretation and determination of the scope of protection, first and foremost the term "use" in the claim and the specific conditions for that use must be taken into consideration.

1.1 General definition of the term "use"

The German Patent Act employs the term "use" in various contexts. Hence, German legal language uses several similar terms which may also translate differently.

Sec. 9 GPA mentions the term "use" for all patent claims in the context of the exclusive right conveyed by the patent. It states that the patent has the effect that only the patent holder is authorized to use the patented invention under the applicable law. The same can be found in Sec. 139 para. 1 GPA which deals with remedies in cases of infringement. Here the law talks about a "use of the invention contrary to Sec. 9-13".

Sec. 9 then distinguishes between product and process claims and sets up an exhaustive list of acts which are prohibited to third parties without the consent of the patent holder. Where the subject matter of the patent (i.e. the claimed invention) is a product, these acts comprise the manufacture, the offer for sale, the marketing and the utilization of the product as well as the import or possession for those purposes. In the case of a process patent the utilization of the patented process and the offer of the process for utilization in Germany are prohibited.

This should not be confused with the term "use" as in the title of this book. "Medical use" is a use of the substance or composition in a method referred to as a method for treatment of the human or animal body or a diagnostic method practiced on the human or animal body (cf. Sec. 3 para. 3 and sec 2a para. 1 no. 2 GPA).

1.2 Manufacture of the pharmaceutical

The manufacture of the medicament comprises the acts necessary to obtain the final product (the medicament). In general, the preparation of only parts of the medicament (e.g. as one of the raw materials) will not be sufficient to be considered a manufacture. However, it may nevertheless contribute to the manufacture and thus make the acting person liable for supporting the infringement or under the provisions of contributory infringement.

1.3 *Sale of the product*

The sale of a product (putting the product on the market, marketing) is another exclusive right of the patentee for which a third party needs the consent. The terms of the sale are usually irrelevant. However, the specific use as claimed in the patent must also be reflected in the way the product is put on the market. In particular, the medical indication for which patent protection has been granted must be clearly communicated to the customer.

1.4 *Offer for sale*

The same applies to the offer for sale. It only differs from the actual sale in that there is not (yet) a transaction with regard to the product. Acts which are made in the context e.g. of negotiations between the pharmaceutical manufacturers and the insurers about listings and prices, the refund to patients and the inclusion of generics into the medicaments which a doctor is allowed to prescribe can already be seen as offering the medicament for sale.

1.5 *Application to the patient*

The application of a medicament to the patient may also be considered a use of the invention. One has to be aware of the fact that, under German law, there is no general exception for the physician from patent infringement. In other words, a doctor who treats a patient may theoretically also be held liable for patent infringement.

Sec. 11 GPA which concerns the limitations to patent protection lists a number of acts to which the effect of a patent does not extend. These include private acts (Sec. 11 no. 1 GPA), the use for clinical trials (Sec. 11 no. 2 GPA) or the Bolar exception (Sec. 11 no. 2b GPA). Another exception is made for the extemporaneous preparation of an individual medicine in pharmacies due to a medical prescription and for acts related to the medicines thus prepared (Sec.11 no. 3 GPA). This provision is mainly directed at the preparation of a medicament in a hospital for an individual patient and does not cover pre-fabricated medicaments. It is limited to extemporaneous mixtures. Only in these cases would the physician also enjoy exemption from patent protection.

In practice, claims for patent infringement brought against an individual physician or against a hospital or other organization which employs the physician are naturally rare. A general exception from patent protection of physicians' acts in treatment is an issue of general policy and would require the legislators to change the existing laws.

1.6 *Combination products*

Where the patent protects two or more substances to be administered in combination to the patient, the scope of protection usually requires that all components which form part of the combination are offered. The protection cannot be extended to one of the components alone. German law does not allow so-called partial protection even where one of the parts is more significant compared to the remaining parts or where that part far outweighs the remaining parts. However, the sale or offer of one component may still be covered under the principle of indirect (contributory) infringement.

2. *Absolute product protection*

Absolute protection has been available under German law also for chemical substances and pharmaceuticals since 1968. The term "absolute protection" describes the fact that the product is protected simply due to its composition or ingredients. The claimed composition alone determines the subject matter of the patent and the scope of protection and is not limited by the intended use.

On the contrary, a process patent cannot convey such absolute product protection.

In this case the acts which can be prohibited and which are reserved exclusively to the patentee are the offering for sale, marketing and utilization of the product in Germany.

2.1 Limitation through the term "use"

A "second medical use" claim is characterized in that it protects the use of a certain substance or composition for a specific purpose. For a long time such claims – like other claims which protect the use of a known product for a specific purpose – were considered a special form of process claims. This automatically led to the conclusion that no absolute protection for the product could be conveyed by the use claim.

On the other hand, the protection of the medical use justifies limited product protection. This applies to the first medical use as well as to the second medical use. When the patentee has provided an invention which brings a known substance/composition into the medical field (first medical use or indication) or to a new medical use (second medical indication) this should be awarded with protection which on the one hand acknowledges the inventive contribution to technical progress for the public in general and on the other hand also takes into consideration that the substance or composition as such is not new. This leads to a so-called purpose-limited protection of the product.

The limitation lies in that the manufacture of the substance or composition as such cannot be prohibited. It remains free and in the public domain. The protection only covers the use as a medicament.

However, as far as the medical indication is concerned, this is again absolute protection in this field. Any third party would be prevented from using the substance or composition for the production of a medicament for the same indication. Absolute protection in this context means that not only the specific therapeutic use is covered by the patent, but also the preparation of the substance or composition for that indication. In this regard there is no difference between the first and the second medical use (indication).

In conclusion one can state that the use claim for the (second) medical indication conveys protection which comes very close to the generally known product claims. It is not to be interpreted as a traditional process claim. This also has consequences for the protection by way of a utility model. In its decision *Arzneimittelgebrauchsmuster* the BGH held that the claim which was directed to the "use of serin/threonine proteinphosphatase inhibitors for a medicament for the therapeutic and preventive treatment of arterosclerotic diseases" did not concern a method in the sense of Sec. 2 no. 3 UMA which would be excluded from protection through a utility model.[27] Instead, the Court held that the use of a known substance for a specific therapeutic or preventive effect on the human body cannot be interpreted as a manufacturing process with the aim of obtaining a substance or other product. The use is directed to the effect of the application of the medicament. The core of the claim is the ability of the substance for the specific medical use. That is an inherent property of the substance. Consequently, such use claims show elements of the commonly known product claims. In essence, the Court described the claim as a limitation of the comprehensive uses allowed for a product under the product claim for a specific use. This limitation does not change the overall gist of the claim and does not alter the protection in general. Henceforth, the BGH also allows utility model protection for second medical use claims.

2.2 Off-label use

The term "off-label use" designates a situation where a medicament is used in a way which is not covered by the marketing authorization granted for that medicament. This may be a different medical indication, different dosage regime, different way of application or a different patient group. The term "cross-label use" typically means that the medical indication, dosage regime, way of application or patient group has been approved and is covered by a patent, but is not mentioned on the label instructions. Both may be considered here as off-label use in a broader and more general sense.

The off-label use may also be seen as a "use" in the meaning of the patent claim which is encompassed by the scope of protection of a second medical use claim. Again, one should emphasize that the protection is limited to the use for the specific indication. It cannot cover the use for another indication, since this would extend the scope to a more general product protection and would be contrary to the granted claims. However, as long as an off-label use is also covered by the patented indication, it may also be assessed as falling within the scope of protection.

3. Dosage regimes

The scope of protection of the use claim in principle covers all dosages, unless a specific dosage forms an element of the granted claim. In this case, the protection is limited to the specific dosage.

---

27. BGH 05/10/2005, X ZB 7/03, GRUR 2006, 135 – *Arzneimittelgebrauchsmuster.*

As explained earlier, the German situation with regard to patent claims which are solely based on the dosage regime is somewhat open. The latest case law seems to suggest that in Germany one may also see a convergence with EPO practice. That would mean that a patent could be based solely on the dosage of the medicament to be applied to the patient. In any event, the dosage will form a limitation to the claim irrespective of standing alone or together with other elements which describe the use of a substance or composition.

4. Patient groups

If a patent claim is granted defining use for a specific patient group the scope of protection is limited to use for that specific group only and in principle does not give protection for any use outside that group. The patient group is then to be considered as part of the relevant indication (use) and therefore has to be observed when determining the scope of protection.

5. Extension under the doctrine of equivalents

Sec. 14 GPA is silent as to the extension of the scope of protection to embodiments which do not literally realize all features of the relevant patent claim. German law does not have a statutory provision which would be comparable to the Protocol on the Interpretation of Art. 69 EPC. Nevertheless, it is a long established practice of German case law and jurisprudence that the scope of protection of a patent not only covers the literal infringement but also equivalent embodiments.[28]

According to the BGH an equivalent requires that the embodiment to be assessed replaces at least one of the claimed features by a variant. The variant is considered an equivalent infringement when three main conditions are fulfilled. These are:

- the variant solves the problem underlying the patented invention with means which have essentially the same technical effect as the replaced feature;
- a skilled person would have been able to recognize the variant based on their general knowledge as having the same technical effect at the priority date of the patent;
- the considerations of the skilled person are oriented at the patented solution such that the skilled person would consider the variant as an equivalent to the patented solution and not as an "aliud".[29]

Apart from these conditions, case law has established several exceptions to equivalence. The first one is the so-called Formstein defence (similar to the Gillette defence under English law).[30]

Further exceptions concern situations where the patent specification discloses several different technical solutions but does not address all of them in the claim

28. See e.g. BGH 12/03/2002, X ZR 168/00, GRUR 2002, 515 – *Schneidmesser I.*
29. BGH 14/12/2010, X ZR 193/03, GRUR 2011, 313 – *Crimpwerkzeug IV*; BGH 13/01/2015, X ZR 81/13, GRUR 2015, 361 – *Kochgefäß.*
30. BGH 29/04/1986, X ZR 28/85, GRUR 1986, 803 – *Formstein.*

wording. There is currently a tendency in case law to follow a somewhat stricter line in that the wording is to be interpreted so that certain embodiments which are described in the specification but not addressed in the claims should not be covered by the scope of protection at all and therefore should also not be included by way of equivalence.[31]

In general, the doctrine of equivalents is also applicable to second medical use claims. In this regard it must be distinguished where the variant lies. As far as the substance or composition which is used for the medicament or the treatment is concerned, the same rules as described above for all other inventions have to be observed.[32]

On the other hand, it would most likely not be possible to argue that a different use than the one for which the patent was granted could also be captured by way of equivalence. At first glance one might consider this situation no different from any of the other features of the claim. Also the specific use (the medical indication) is part of the combination of claimed features and could therefore be replaced by a variant. However, in most cases it seems doubtful whether a different medical indication could be seen as having the same technical effect. Unless the indications are very close to each other, this criterion could not reasonably be fulfilled. In general an indication cannot simply be substituted with another without losing the technical effect. The second criterion of obviousness for the skilled person to replace the indication might be possible, but for the same reasons also seems highly unlikely. Finally, it seems almost impossible that the skilled person would come to the conclusion that, in light of the patented solution (and the underlying problem to be solved), the substitution of the indication would be equivalent. Consequently, the claimed medical indication, i.e. the second medical use, clearly limits the scope of protection to that specific purpose and can generally not be extended by way of equivalence to other indications. This is in line with the legal assessment that a use claim conveys a limited product protection which is determined by the specific purpose. This purpose cannot be altered or extended and must be strictly observed for the scope of protection.

IV. Infringing acts

The possible infringing acts mirror the exclusive rights of the patentee explained above. This is in principle no different from cases relating to other patents. However, also in this context the specific use and the function of such claims must be taken into consideration. All acts which are linked to the specific use of the substance or composition are covered by the scope of protection and therefore considered infringing. At the same time it is not only the use itself that is the first infringing act. The protection also covers certain acts which precede the concrete use of the substance, provided that these acts are still sufficiently linked to the specific medical use (indication). This requires a so-called "manifest preparation" of the substance

31. BGH 10/05/2011, X ZR 16/09, GRUR 2011, 701 – *Okklusionsvorrichtung*; BGH 13/09/2011, X ZR 69/10, GRUR 2012, 45 – *Diglycidverbindung*.
32. See e.g. BGH 12/03/2002, X ZB 12/00 and X ZR 73/01, GRUR 2002, 523/527 – *Custodiol I/II*; OLG Düsseldorf, 13/09/2013, I-2 U 26/13.

or composition for the specific treatment.[33] On the other hand, certain acts which might usually be considered infringing may be exempt if the manifest preparation is lacking. This again reflects purpose-limited product protection.

1. *Infringing person or entity*

Every person and every entity which is involved in the preparation, the manufacture, the marketing and the use of the medicament may be liable, provided however that the circumstances of the case fulfil all requirements of such liability. It was already mentioned that under German law the physician does not enjoy general exemption from patent law. Therefore, at least in theory, the entire chain from the preparation to the final application of the medicament may be encompassed.

2. *Direct infringement*

Direct infringement according to Sec. 9 GPA requires that the acting person/entity fully realizes one of the acts which establish a use of the invention. In contrast, indirect infringement (Sec. 10 GPA) concerns the case where the infringer only offers or supplies means relating to an essential element of the invention to a third party.

2.1 *Manufacture of the pharmaceutical*

a) The manufacture is one of the main acts which are reserved exclusively for the patent holder of a product patent.

The first issue in this context concerns the limited scope of protection which is linked to the use for a specific indication rather than for any purpose as would be the case for a normal product claim. One might therefore argue that the manufacture itself does not infringe the use claim, since it is the use of the product which constitutes the invention and thus the patent protection. However, one must take into consideration that the manufacture is essential for any further act and also part of Swiss-type claims. Only where the substance or composition itself is prepared without any further instructions or indications for the intended use and where it may be used also for other purposes than the patented ones, could one argue that the manufacture does not yet constitute an infringement of the exclusive rights conveyed by the patent.

b) German case law has therefore also shifted the decisive moment when infringement begins. It is the "manifest preparation" which makes the act an infringement. The use of a substance for the manufacture of the medicament for a therapeutic use is considered as the beginning of the use for this purpose if there is a manifest preparation.[34] Nevertheless, it remains to be determined in each case independently and taking into account all the circumstances what encompasses such manifest preparation. Regarding a medicament, all acts and means which specifically relate to the relevant medical use or indication are usually considered preparation as such.

33. The relevant German wording is "*sinnfällige Herrichtung*" and sometimes also translated as "manifestly arranged".
34. BGH 20/03/2001, X ZR 177/98, GRUR 2001, 730 – *Trigonellin*.

That includes: preparation of the substance itself if this reveals the intended purpose; the formulation, dosage and packaging; specific instructions for the therapy or dosage regimes; the patient information leaflet; the branding which indicates the specific use or the designation of the product in invoices or shipping documents. In any event it must be clear from those means that the intended use of the medicament is for the patented indication and must be made in direct connection with the product.[35]

Consequently, mere general statements, such as advertising, which only explain the general effect of a medicament and which do not relate specifically to the patented use are not considered as sufficient manifest preparation.[36]

c) A user who is in contact with those means is decisive for the point of view of whether manifest preparation can be established. In most cases the user is the consumer or patient. Here the point of view is mainly formed by the materials provided to the end user (packaging, advertising etc.). Other materials and in particular documents which are used for obtaining the marketing authorization are usually not looked at by the consumer and therefore not relevant in this context.

On the contrary, a physician who prescribes a medicament is not to be considered as the relevant user even where the medicament requires a prescription (no OTC medicament) and the physician gathers their information from a public database, such as the AMIS database in Germany (Pharmaceutical Information System).[37]

d) In the same way the courts have held that the application for a marketing authorization is not to be seen as the beginning of the manufacture.[38] Although the request for the marketing authorization is a necessary step for marketing the product, the courts have been reluctant in assuming that this request and the proceedings which lead to the authorization are sufficient to assume that an infringing act will follow. The main reason is that these proceedings do not determine the final properties or fields of use of the medicament. Both may be altered after obtaining the authorization which then requires another approval.

e) Another question concerns the distinction between traditional Swiss-type claims and EPC 2000 claims. While Swiss-type claims expressly require the use of a substance or composition for the manufacture of a medicament this is no longer true for an EPC 2000 claim. The wording of EPC 2000 claims is directed at the use of the substance or composition for the treatment of a specific illness.

As regards Swiss-type claims the German courts have repeatedly held that the claims comprise the act of manufacturing a medicament. Consequently, the use of a substance or composition can only be covered by the scope of protection of the patent if it is used for the manufacture of a medicament. A use without manufacturing the medicament is not covered and cannot be considered as infringing.[39]

---

35. LG Düsseldorf, 24/02/2004, 4a O 12/03 – *Ribavirin*.
36. OLG Düsseldorf, 31/01/2013, I-2 U 53/11 – *Cistus incanus II*; OLG Düsseldorf, 07/08/2014, I-2 U 8/14 – *Ubichinon*.
37. LG Düsseldorf, 14/03/2013, 4a O 145/12 – *Chronische Hepatitis-C-Behandlung*.
38. LG Düsseldorf 30/03/2010, 4a O 13/10 – *Oxycodonhydrochlorid*.
39. OLG Düsseldorf, 05/03/2015, I-2 U 16/14 – *Pemetrexed*; upon further appeal the BGH has reversed this judgment with its decision of 14 June 2016 and sent the case back to the OLG Düsseldorf for further consideration.

One might now argue that EPC 2000 claims provide a broader protection. This would mean that the patented use of a substance or composition for the treatment of a specific illness also covers cases where no medicament is manufactured from the substance or composition.[40] The future will tell what the courts make of this situation. In any event one will still have to adhere to the requirement of the "manifest preparation" for the use in order to distinguish absolute product protection from purpose-limited protection of the product for the specific use.

2.2 Offer for sale

An express offer for sale infringes the exclusive rights of the patent holder. The same should be acknowledged for general offers through the usual channels. A distinction has to be made for OTC products and prescription medicaments where the advertising means are very often regulated. An offer in a general advertisement can already be seen as an offer for sale irrespective of whether it is a prescription medicament or an OTC product.

Regulation of the markets and in particular the refund from insurers provides another set of acts offering the product for sale. Courts have dealt with listings in public databases (cf. above) where an offer for sale was denied[41] and also in the standard German database which contains information about all available products, their prices, and other detailed information, the so-called Lauer-Taxe. In this case the listing is usually considered as an offer for sale.[42] In the cited case of the Court of Appeal Düsseldorf, a generic was listed in the Lauer-Taxe. In general, the Court of Appeal considered this an offer for sale. Only due to the specific circumstances of that case did the Court not find a concrete intention for such a listing and therefore denied an infringing offer for sale.

The District Court Hamburg had to deal with a number of cases in which the manufacturer of a generic entered into negotiations with insurers about discount agreements in a public tender. Here the Court issued an injunction against the generics company and held that the participation in the tender was already sufficient indication that the company would be willing and able to supply the medicament.[43]

2.3 Sale

The sale of the medicament to users follows the same rules as for other product claims provided there is manifest preparation regarding the specific patented use.

---

40. Cf. also EBA of EPO, G2/08 – *Dosage regime/ABBOTT RESPIRATORY.*
41. LG Düsseldorf, 14/03/2013, 4a O 145/12 – *Chronische Hepatitis-C-Behandlung.*
42. OLG Düsseldorf, 29/03/2006, I-2 W 43/05, Mitteilungen 2006, 426– *Aufnahme eines Generikums in die Lauer-Taxe vor Ablauf der Schutzfrist.*
43. LG Hamburg, 02/04/2015, 327 O 67/15 – *Uneingeschränkter Beitritt des Generika-Herstellers mit seinem pharmazeutischem Präparat zu einem nicht indikationsbeschränkten Rabattvertrag im Open-House-Verfahren.*

2.4 *Export*

The use according to a use claim only infringes the German patent or the German part of a European patent if it occurs in Germany. The territorial scope of the patent limits the protection to Germany and only a use within that territory can interfere with the exclusive rights of the patentee. Consequently, export of the product for use outside Germany is not in conflict with the patent and cannot be prohibited.

2.5 *Import*

On the contrary, import of a product for further sale or use in Germany is covered by the patent provided again there are clear indications which allow the conclusion of the manifest preparation for a use according to the patent.

2.6 *Combination products*

Direct infringement of a claim which comprises the use of a combination product or the use of a product in combination with another product occurs when all elements of the combination are offered or marketed by the respective party. This does not necessarily require that the elements are offered in a package together. It is sufficient if the patient prepares the combination which is offered to them even where this happens over time. An example is the combination of a product in which one component has to be administered to the patient in short intervals with the second component to be administered only in larger intervals and where the therapeutic effect is achieved in this specific routine.

3. *Indirect infringement*

Sec. 10 GPA deals with indirect infringement of a patent. A third party is liable for indirect infringement if it offers for sale or sells to a person who is not entitled to use the invention means relating to an essential element of the invention, provided that the third party knew or that it was obvious that the means are suitable and intended for use of the invention in Germany.

A means relates to an essential element not only if it incorporates the invention itself. Moreover, this condition is already fulfilled if the means contributes to putting the invention into effect. The means must not be new or inventive itself. This may also be the case if the means are just ordinary staple goods. It is also irrelevant if the means can be used only for the invention or also in a manner which is not covered by the scope of the patent.[44]

One has to distinguish objective acts of the party offering/selling the means and the subjective elements of this provision.

44. BGH 04/05/2004, X ZR 48/03, GRUR 2004, 758 – *Flügelradzähler*; BGH 27/02/2007, X ZR 38/06, GRUR 2007, 769 – *Pipettensystem*; BGH 03/02/2015, X ZR 69/13, GRUR 2015, 467 – *Audiosignalcodierung*.

3.1 *Objective acts*

Sec. 10 GPA exhaustively lists the acts which are exclusively reserved to the patent holder. They are limited to the offer and the supply of the means. In contrast to Sec. 9 GPA (direct infringement) in particular, the manufacture of the means is not mentioned.

The reason for this is that the absolute product protection conveyed by a product patent or – in limited form – by a patent with a second medical use claim only covers the entire product and does not cover a part of the product. The acts of offering and supplying are moreover limited to Germany and a means may – depending on the specific circumstances of the case – also be exported or used in a patent-free way.

3.2 *Subjective conditions*

An offer or sale of a means can only be considered indirect infringement if certain subjective elements are fulfilled. These concern the third party offering/selling the means (the potential infringer) and also the recipient of the offer or the supply.

First, there must be an intention of the recipient to use the invention and to make use of the means for this purpose. This does not raise doubts if the means are only suitable to be used for the invention and cannot be used in a patent-free manner. Otherwise, there must be specific circumstances which allow the conclusion to be drawn that the means (the product) will be used for the patented invention. This may be difficult to assess in particular in cases of cross-label use (see below).

Secondly, on the side of the infringer this requires either positive knowledge or the obviousness of that intention. In other words, the infringer must assume that the product or medicament will be used to realize the invention. In cases where the medicament is only suitable for this purpose, it becomes obvious and no further indications are needed to establish indirect infringement. Where this is not the case, other circumstances must be taken into consideration, particularly the manifest preparation of the medicament. Where the medicament is manifestly prepared for the invention it is clear to the infringer that the recipient will use the medicament accordingly and thus infringe the patent.

3.3 *Export*

Indirect infringement requires a double relation to the domestic territory (Germany). The third party must offer or supply the medicament in Germany and the recipient must also use the medicament in Germany.

Export is generally not covered, provided that the use of the medicament does not occur in Germany (e.g. by way of a re-import).

3.4 *Import*

Similar rules apply to the import of a medicament. It will again be decisive if there is manifest preparation for the patented use or not. The pure transit of goods is usually not considered to have a sufficiently close link to the German market and is therefore not an infringement of the German patent.

3.5 *Combination products*

A particular situation occurs where the patented use consists of two or more components which are to be used in combination. This leads to various scenarios with different results.

a) If the combination of medicaments is offered together in one set, this does not differ from any other case with only one medicament which may contain one or more active ingredients. The same rules then also apply to the combination.
b) If the components are offered separately by two parties one will have to assess if the offers can be considered as manifest preparation of the medicament for use in combination with the other component. Indirect infringement can be established if it becomes sufficiently clear to the user that both components belong together in the use. Again, a mere general statement in this regard will most likely not be sufficient. On the other hand, infringement may also occur if the advertising or similar statements suggest the combination as only one possible option for the user.
c) Another scenario depicts the situation where the user is already in possession of one component and the third party offers the missing component independently from another product or medicament. The decisive factor is again the manifest preparation. If it is obvious or known to the third party that the user will supplement the medicament to form the combination product, the sale of the second component will lead to an indirect infringement. However, if the intention of the user is not clear and the third party does not give any indication directed at the patented use, indirect infringement would likely be difficult to argue. A neutral offer of the second component which can also be used in a patent-free manner (similar to "staple goods") will usually not constitute an indirect infringement.

4. *Off-label use*

Issues of infringement through off-label use arise in particular in the context of the manifest preparation of the medicament which has been described earlier and which is a requirement for the determination of infringement of the use claim.

4.1 *General admissibility of off-label use*

Off-label use is generally permitted under German regulatory rules. In particular, the fact that a medicament has received the marketing authorization for one or more indications does not exclude the use for other indications. Neither ethical rules for the physician nor other regulatory provisions prohibit the physician from using a medicament for a patient if the physician believes that this is a proper way of treatment. In principle, physicians have the freedom to choose what they believe is best for the patient. This not only applies to the method of treatment as such, but also to the choice of pharmaceuticals for the selected treatment. At the same time this freedom is not unlimited. In particular, economic considerations have brought about several limitations in that – although the physician remains in principle free – there are limits of reimbursement for the patient and possibly additional issues for malpractice liability and product liability.

4.2 Liable persons

Liable persons are the acting parties involved in the supply chain of the medicament. This mainly concerns the manufacturer or distributor of the medicament, but could theoretically also include the physician or the pharmacist who sells or otherwise disposes of the medicament to the patient.

4.3 Objective requirements for infringement

The key element is again the manifest preparation of the medicament, including the medical indications for which the medicament should be used. If the patented indication is mentioned, there is no doubt about infringement (see above). Problems may occur in situations where the patented indication is not mentioned, either because the medicament has no marketing authorization for it (off-label use) or because the manufacturer has omitted that indication from the labelling instructions although it has also obtained a marketing authorization for that indication (cross-label use). The concrete assessment will in any case depend on the specific circumstances. The following scenarios may serve as examples from current case law, but are by no means exhaustive.

a) The first scenario concerns a situation where the manufacturer has no marketing authorization for the patented use (the relevant indication). As explained above the physician would still be in a position to prescribe the medicament for a treatment which may concern the patented indication. If it nevertheless becomes sufficiently clear from the advertising or other information materials about the medicament that it would be suitable for the patented indication one may establish sufficient manifest preparation so that there is indirect infringement. If that specific indication is not mentioned or only in a very general sense without a sufficient link to the medicament, one may deny infringement.
b) The same applies in principle also to the situation where there is an authorization for that specific indication, but the manufacturer has deliberately omitted any reference. This so-called "skinny labelling" or "carving out" is typically done where the manufacturer would otherwise fear that they would be held liable for direct infringement. One has to assess again if the information given otherwise about the medicament can lead to the conclusion that there is nevertheless (also) manifest preparation for that indication or whether the information is too general.
c) Another aspect concerns the common practice which has been agreed by the German Association of Pharmacists and the umbrella organization of

the insurers more than ten years ago. It is now the general requirement according to Sec. 129 of the Social Law Code V [45] that a prescription issued by a physician contains the indication "*aut idem*" (in English: "or the same"). Unless the physician specifically excludes such an "*aut idem*" prescription and if the prescription is for the active ingredient only without specific indication, the pharmacist is required to dispense to the patient another medicament with the same active ingredient which is listed in the discount agreements between the insurers and the manufacturers, which also include manufacturers of generics. The pharmacist is required to select a medicament with the same ingredient and concentration, the same package size and a comparable way of application and with (at least) the same indications.[46] In this regard the District Court Hamburg has rendered a preliminary injunction against a manufacturer of generics ordering the manufacturer to cease and desist from further participating in a tender by public insurers for such a discount agreement with a specific medicament which did not list the patented indication, unless the manufacturer explicitly mentions to the insurer that the medicament is not to be used for the patented indication. The reason was that in more than 90% of all treatments the specific medicament was used for the patented indication even without any specific prescription.[47] This may go further than other decisions, since the manifest preparation for the patented indication was not entirely clear. However, the Court took its reasoning from the fact that only 1% of the prescriptions were made for patent-free indications while the vast majority of prescriptions concerned the patented indication.

d) The situation may be different if the physician also mentions the specific indication for which the active ingredient is intended. In that case, the pharmacist would not be obligated to dispense another medicament and it would be solely their choice if they decided to do so anyway. In that case, it would be doubtful if the unconditional participation of the manufacturer in the tender could be held against them or if not other circumstances would have to be present which would allow establishing the manifest preparation.

e) With regard to EPC 2000 claims issues may arise if one argues that the manufacture of the medicament is no longer an essential element of the claims and that the use (and effect) is the core of the claim. So far German case law has not yet decided this constellation. The Federal Court of Justice seems to take the position that there is no significant difference in the scope of protection of a traditional "Swiss-type" claim and an EPC 2000 claim.[48] It remains to be seen if this will become the predominant opinion or if the

45. § 129 SGB V.
46. The substitution is not required for certain medicaments which are contained in a specific listing of exclusions.
47. LG Hamburg 02/04/2015, 327 O 67/15.
48. BGH 25/02/2014, X ZB 6/13, GRUR 2014, 464 – *Kollagenase II.*

Court will turn more towards the EPO opinion expressed in G 2/08 suggesting that the new claims may have in fact a broader scope.[49]

If one accepts such a broader scope this might mean that the prescription and administration of a substance which then has the patented therapeutic effect in the patient's body due to e.g. metabolic or other reactions could be considered as realizing the patented use and therefore as an indirect infringement of the use claim concerning the specific medicament which is formed only in the body and is not manufactured prior to administration to the patient.

4.4 *Subjective requirements for infringement*

The subjective requirements are the same as explained above. Concerning carving out and skinny labelling it has to be assessed if the intention of the recipient to use the medicament for the patented indication is still there and if it is known or obvious to the third party (e.g. the manufacturer of the generic). In its decision referenced above the District Court Hamburg held that the fact that the tender was not limited to a specific indication made it evident that the patented indication could also be included, irrespective of the carving out and the skinny labelling.[50]

5. *Dosage regimes*

A similar situation occurs when the patented use is not only a medical indication but (also) includes a specific dosage regime. Here it would be even more difficult to conclude that the general offer of an active ingredient (generic) constitutes manifest preparation for that specific regime, unless there are clear indications for the user to also apply that dosage.

6. *Patient groups*

If the patented use concerns a specific patient group the same rules apply as described for the other scenarios.

V. Remedies

For use claims the same remedies are in principle available as for other patent infringement cases. The civil sanctions follow Sec. 139 et seq. GPA. Criminal sanctions are also foreseen in the law (Sec. 142 GPA), but shall not be discussed further here.

1. *Injunctions*

According to Sec. 139 (1) GPA the patentee has the right to obtain an injunction in cases of infringement. This injunction has to specify the concrete infringing act. It

49. One may gather some more information from the latest decision of the FCJ in the *Pemetrexed* case (see footnote 39 above).
50. See LG Hamburg 02/04/2015, 327 O 67/15.

will not be sufficient for the court to issue an order along the lines "not to infringe patent xyz". It must list the features of the patent claim or the embodiment to be able to identify the infringing product. Furthermore, the act which was incriminated and from which the defendant shall refrain in the future must also be named.

The injunction will be directed at refraining from the manifest preparation of the product. This comprises the sale of the product and other acts which specifically address the patented use (see above), but not acts which have no sufficient link and therefore are not covered by the scope of the use claim.

2. *Damages*

Sec. 139 (2) GPA provides a claim for damages in cases of willful or negligent infringement. While the claim for an injunction in cases of indirect infringement does not require a direct infringement to be committed afterwards, this is different for damage claims. An indirect infringer is only liable for damages for those acts which have been succeeded by a direct infringement.[51] The reason for this is that the protection against indirect infringement begins at an early stage in order to provide protection also against a potential further use of the invention. However, damages shall compensate an actual use and therefore in principle require a direct infringement.

3. *Information*

3.1 *Names of manufacturer, distributors etc.*

According to Sec. 140b GPA the patentee has the right to obtain detailed information about the names and addresses of the manufacturer, the distributor and other third parties involved in the supply chain. This allows the proprietor to close up further supply and to find the original source of the infringement.

If the manufacture itself is not to be prohibited due to lacking the manifest preparation, the claim for information will generally not encompass the manufacturer.

3.2 *Names of customers*

The information also comprises the names and addresses of commercial customers. Private customers who are exempt from patent protection do not have to be disclosed.

3.3 *Information about infringing sales*

In order to prepare the concrete claims for damages it is important to obtain detailed information about the sales. This includes the numbers of sales, prices, amounts, shipments and the like. The information must be accompanied by copies of the relevant documents (usually the commercial invoices or documents for the shipments).

---

51. BGH 07/06/2005, X ZR 247/02, GRUR 2005, 848 – *Antriebsscheibenaufzug*; BGH 07/05/2013, X ZR 69/11, GRUR 2013, 713 – *Fräsverfahren*.

3.4 *Account of profits*

According to German case law the patent proprietor has a choice of three different ways of calculating damages. These are based on (1) reasonable royalties, (2) the infringer's profits and (3) the lost profits of the patent proprietor. Hence, the information must also comprise a detailed statement about the profits, e.g. the various cost factors which can be deducted from the total infringing sales.

The determination of what portion of the profits can be allocated to the infringement requires an assessment of what can be seen as fair compensation for the unlawful use of the patent.

4. *Recall of products and destruction*

Sec. 140a GPA allows a claim for the recall of products from the supply chain and also the destruction of the infringing products. In principle, this is also applicable in cases of claims protecting the second medical use.

However, this has the proviso that it may not be inappropriate in a given case taking into account all circumstances (Sec. 140a para. 4). If in a case where the manufacture itself cannot be prohibited as the manifest preparation is not a result of the manufacture but rather of the packaging, instructions for use, patients leaflet etc., it may be justified to recall the products. Destruction of the product (the medicament) itself could be seen as inappropriate if it can be exported to patent-free countries or used for other indications which are not covered by the patent.

5. *Recovery of legal costs*

The remuneration of legal costs is usually also ordered by the court. German law has a rather strict system as to what can be recovered. These costs are usually based on the value of litigation and are determined by a statutory table of fees which list the amounts to be reimbursed as a maximum.

VI. Exceptions from patent protection

The general exceptions from patent protection are also applicable for use claims.

1. *Exhaustion of rights*

The exhaustion of patent rights is a generally acknowledged and accepted principle under German law.[52] Unlike for other intellectual property rights[53] there is only a limited statutory provision in the GPA. Only Sec. 9b GPA mentions the exhaustion of rights in connection with biological material. Regarding other patents and situations the same principle has been adopted by case law. In accordance with the decisions of the CJEU Germany also adheres to the EU-wide exhaustion.

---

52. BGH 14/12/1999, X ZR 61/98, GRUR 2000, 299 — *Karate*.
53. Cf. e.g. sec. 24 German Trademark Act for trademarks.

With regard to the expansion of the EU and the accession of a number of countries over the last years, such as the Baltics, the Czech Republic, Hungary, Poland, Slovenia and Slovakia, certain additional limitations to the parallel import of pharmaceuticals from those countries into other countries of the EU were introduced. As part of the Accession Agreements the so-called Specific Mechanism applies. As an exception from the general principle of exhaustion of rights it prohibits the parallel import of an original product covered by patent protection from those countries if it was put on the market there with the consent of the patentee and if no patent protection was available in the respective country at the time the protection was obtained in one of the older member states of the EU.[54]

2. *Patient welfare*

Patient welfare plays a role for the policy considerations explained in the beginning. There is no specific mentioning of patient welfare in the GPA. Voices have been raised which criticize the way that the court finding infringement of a valid patent automatically leads to an injunction. However, the courts have means to take extraordinary circumstances into consideration, such as patient welfare. Where the injunction would for example leave patients without proper and sufficient treatment of their illnesses with serious consequences, the courts can take steps to prohibit the enforcement of the injunction at least temporarily.

3. *Others specific to second medical use claims*

There are no further specific issues or provisions regarding exceptions or limitations to patent protection for second medical use claims.

VII. Procedural issues

Claims resulting from patent infringement can be pursued by way of a case on the merits or by way of preliminary injunction proceedings. The latter basically follow the same rules of a case on the merits with certain specifics to bear in mind.

1. *Preliminary injunction cases*

1.1 *Availability for second medical use claims*

Motions for a preliminary injunction are also available for cases where the patent comprises second medical use claims. In principle, these cases do not differ from other patent infringement cases, provided that the rather high standards for evidence are met. This concerns the infringement and the validity of the patent as well as a general weighing up of the interests of the parties involved (balance of convenience). In particular, the patentee has to show that the interest in obtaining a preliminary injunction in summary proceedings – potentially even without an oral hearing before

54. OLG Düsseldorf, 06/08/2015, 2 U 21/ 15 – *Ezetimib*; LG Düsseldorf, 26/08/2014, 4c 116/13.

the decision (*ex parte*) – outweighs the interests of the defendants in continuing to sell the infringing products until a decision has been rendered by the court in an ordinary case on the merits. This will very often be the case where the patent is coming to the end of its maximum term and generics are already launched prior to the end of the term.

Unlike in cases on the merits, the court will not appoint an expert and all evidence must be brought by the parties. The standard differs from cases on the merit and no full evidence is required. Instead of hearing witnesses it is very common to submit affidavits of witness statements.

1.2 Specific requirements

The specific requirements for such cases have to be oriented again to the main issue of the manifest preparation. Besides the evidence mentioned above it is important for the patentee to show that the offers or sales by the defendant have been made such that there is manifest preparation with regard to the patented use. A rather general offer without specifying the use would not be sufficient.

In cases of indirect infringement the evidence must also cover the subjective elements and in particular the intention of the customer of the infringer to use the product in the patented way. In cases where the patented indication has been carved out (skinny labelling) this may put an additional burden on the patentee and certainly requires a careful and thorough investigation of the facts.

2. Cases on the merits

In general, the majority of cases are better suited for proceedings on the merits. This is mainly linked to issues of validity. In Germany, the validity of a patent is not assessed by the infringement court, but before the FPC. A civil court will therefore be hesitant to issue a preliminary injunction when there are doubts about the validity.

Furthermore, if there are problems of evidence, they may be cured more easily in a case on the merits. Here, the court may hear witnesses where needed and also appoint a technical expert besides party experts when this is necessary to confirm the infringement.

For cases involving second medical use claims the same procedural rules apply and no further specific aspects have to be observed here.

3. Enforcement of judgments

Judgments of courts in first instance (District Courts) are provisionally enforceable even when they are appealed. The difference is that a judgment in a case on the merits can only be enforced against a security (bond) which must be deposited by the enforcing party and which covers potential damages resulting from the enforcement. Judgments ordering a preliminary injunction are generally enforceable without such a security. However, depending on the circumstances of the case and in particular in situations where the court is not entirely sure about the case but still feels that a preliminary injunction should be granted, such a security can also be ordered by the court.

VIII. Validity

1. *Relevance for infringement cases*

German law separates infringement cases from invalidation actions. In cases on the merits the infringement court has the discretion to stay the proceedings pending the outcome of the invalidation action, whereas in preliminary injunction cases the assessment of the validity is part of the balance of interests.

2. *Specifics for second medical use claims*

There are no additional specific issues regarding second medical use claims.

IX. Tactical considerations

1. *Plaintiff*

As explained above, the patentee will have a choice between proceedings on the merits and preliminary injunction proceedings. In certain situations it will be necessary for the patentee to act swiftly in order to defend a position on the market and to prevent the defendant from entering the market e.g. with a generic or otherwise infringing drug. The preference for one or the other option will mainly depend on the circumstances and the facts of the specific case.

While a preliminary injunction may be desirable, one will also have to assess the risk associated with such a motion. The risk of bearing the cost of litigation in case of a negative decision will usually not play a decisive role. Rather, one has to take into account that a negative decision may have an impact as a precedent on a subsequent case on the merits. Although the decision is technically not a binding precedent it will nevertheless influence the thinking of the same judges who will often hear the case on the merits as well. It may therefore be wise to take the somewhat slower route of a case on the merits if timing allows it. Naturally, there may also be situations where urgent action is inevitable. One example was shown above where the defendant was participating in a public tender.

The highly regulated market and the pricing policies of the various participants in light of the constant effort to reduce costs in the health sector make it even more important for patentees to pursue their rights against infringers for whom there are various incentives to enter the market. It is certainly recommended to raise the awareness of the authorities in this regard so that infringement can be avoided at a very early stage.

2. *Defendant*

For defendants the greatest risk is to be confronted with a preliminary injunction which would enable the other side to immediately enforce the injunction. In order to avoid at least a decision ex parte it is common to file a so-called protective brief with the relevant courts. This is a brief which allows the defendants to proactively present their position and their arguments as to why the injunction should not be granted. The main purpose of this brief is to convince the court that a hearing should at least be held before the court decides on the motion for a preliminary injunction.

The situation may be unclear with regard to the EPC 2000 claims which have not yet been the considerable subject of case law in Germany. In particular, it remains to be seen if the courts will accept a broader scope of protection compared to conventional Swiss-type claims.

Possible reactions from the potential defendants will have to address the issue of the manifest preparation. Carving out the patented medical indications may be one way but will in most cases not provide sufficient certainty that the courts deny infringement. Another way may be to expressly state that the product should not be used for the specific (patented) indication. At least this makes it arguable whether a manufacturer could be held liable for indirect infringement of a patent when the main act of prescribing or administering the medicament by others is done against the express will of the manufacturer.

Switzerland

Dr. Thierry Calame[1]

A. AVAILABILITY OF PROTECTION

I. Legal framework

1. National statutory laws

1.1 Pharmaceuticals

The Swiss Patents Act sets out the national basis for patent law in Switzerland.

Following the ratification of the European Patent Convention ("EPC"), Switzerland conformed its Patents Act to the provisions of the EPC 1973.

Article 2(b) Patents Act (as amended) excluded methods of surgery, therapy or diagnosis practised on the human or animal body from patent protection. Unlike Article 52(4) EPC 1973, methods of treatment and diagnosis were not considered to lack "industrial application". Rather, the legislator made clear that physicians should be protected from claims for patent infringement for public policy reasons.

At the same time, the legislator recognised the need for the protection of pharmaceuticals. In accordance with Article 54(5) EPC 1973, Article 7c Patents Act provided that any substance or composition that forms part of the state of the art as such, but not in relation to its use in a surgical, therapeutic or diagnostic method, is deemed to be new, provided it is intended solely for such use. Article 7c Patents Act thus established that first medical use inventions would still be deemed novel even if the compound that is used for the first medical use was *per se* already known in the state of the art.

Like the EPC 1973, the Patents Act at the time did not specifically acknowledge the novelty of a claim directed to a second (or further) medical use of a known

1. The author wishes to thank Lara Dorigo for reviewing this chapter and for making helpful suggestions.

pharmaceutical compound/medicament. However, as early as 1984, the Swiss Federal Intellectual Property Office considered it legitimate to allow claims directed to the use of a substance or composition for the manufacture of a medicament for a specified new and inventive therapeutic application. The Office adopted the following wording for claims in the second (or further) medical use format:[2] "the use of substance/compound X for the manufacture of a medicament to treat disease Y".

This claim format was subsequently endorsed by the Enlarged Board of Appeal of the European Patent Office ("EPO") in three parallel decisions (G 1/83, G 5/83, G 6/83) and is now commonly referred to as "Swiss-type" claim format.

The Patents Act was again amended to implement the EPC as revised in 2000, which amendments took effect in Switzerland on 1 July 2008. The exclusion of methods of treatment and diagnosis was transferred to Article 2(2)(a) and the wording of Article 7c was amended to reflect the reference to new Article 2(2)(a) (rather than former Article 2(b)). Importantly, in accordance with Article 54(5) EPC 2000, a new Article 7d acknowledging the novelty of second (or further) medical use claims was introduced into the Patents Act. The relevant provisions in the Patents Act read as follows:

> "**IV. New use of known substances**
>
> *a. First medical use*
>
> Article 7c
> Any substance or composition that forms part of the state of the art as such, but not in relation to its use in a surgical, therapeutic or diagnostic method specified in Article 2 paragraph 2 letter a is deemed to be new provided it is intended solely for such use.
>
> *b. Further medical uses*
>
> Article 7d
> Any substance or composition that forms part of the state of the art as such, but not in relation to a specific use in a surgical, therapeutic or diagnostic method specified in Article 2 paragraph 2 letter a that is distinct from the first medical use specified in Article 7c is deemed to be new provided it is intended for use in the manufacture of a means to a surgical, therapeutic or diagnostic end."

The changes of the Patents Act introduced as a result of the EPC 2000 have not led to any substantive change in what is and is not patentable under Swiss law. However, Article 7d has codified the Swiss-type claim format for Swiss national patents in the Patents Act. This has resulted in different allowable claim formats for Swiss national patents and European patents designating Switzerland ("EP (CH) patents"). While the Swiss-type claim format of Article 7d Patents Act is a process claim, Article 54(5) EPC 2000 now provides for a new claim category, i.e., a purpose-limited product claim. For EP applications having a filing date of 29 January 2011 or later this new claim format is now mandatory, i.e., the Swiss-type claim format is no longer admissible.[3]

---

2. *See* legal advice of Swiss Federal Intellectual Property Office (Bundesamt für Geistiges Eigentum, BAGE) dated 30 May 1984.
3. For EP applications granted after 13 December 2007 (entry into force of EPC 2000) and filed on or before 28 January 2011, applicants are entitled to both formats of second medical

Why does the Swiss Patents Act provide for a different second medical use claim format than the EPC 2000? It appears that the Swiss legislator thought that the protection offered by Article 54(5) EPC 2000 is equivalent to that offered by a Swiss-type claim.[4] This is, however, not the case. As more fully explained below (see section C.), the scope of protection afforded by claims pursuant to Article 54(5) EPC 2000 is broader than that afforded by Swiss-type claims. This has been recognised by the Enlarged Board of Appeal in G 2/08 (reason 6.5) as well as by the Swiss Federal Supreme Court in BGE 137 III 170 (alendronate). The latter decision even prompted the Swiss legislator to introduce new exceptions from patent protection for medical doctors and pharmacists into the Patents Act (see section C. below).

In summary, the legal framework in Switzerland for the grant of medical use claims is as a general matter no different to that of the EPC, i.e., the patenting of first, second or even further medical uses of pharmaceuticals is admissible under Swiss law. However, the format and scope of protection of EPC 2000 second (or further) medical use claims is different to that of the Swiss-type claims allowable under Article 7d Patents Act (see section C. below).

1.2 Biologics

Switzerland is not a member of the European Union. Nevertheless, the Patents Act is to a large extent compliant with harmonised EU law. On 1 July 2008 the Patents Act was amended so as to implement the provisions of Articles 1 to 11 of the European Directive 98/44/EC on the legal protection of biotechnological inventions ("the Biotech Directive"). These provisions confirm that inventions concerning biological material, including gene sequences and proteins, are patentable provided that they comply with the requirements of the Patents Act.

2. *International treaties*

The EPC 2000 was implemented in the Patents Act, as discussed above. Switzerland is also party to the 1883 Paris Convention for the Protection of Intellectual Property, the 1970 Patent Cooperation Treaty (PCT) and the 1994 TRIPS Agreement.

3. *Availability through case law*

The availability of patent protection in Switzerland is governed by the Patents Act, as interpreted by Swiss courts, namely the Federal Patent Court and the Federal Supreme Court. The decisions of the Technical Boards of Appeal of the EPO are also taken into account by the Swiss courts, but they are not binding. The same applies in principle to decisions of the courts of other EPC member states.

Currently, the only decision of the Federal Supreme Court dealing with the availability of patent protection for second medical use claims is BGE 137 III 170 (alendronate).

---

use claims (see Chapter I, "EPO" and section B. I. below).

4. *See* explanatory notes of Swiss delegation, quoted in G 2/08 reason 5.10.4.

4. *Patent term extension/SPCs*

The Patents Act was amended on 1 May 1999 to implement the provisions of the Regulation (EC) No. 469/2009 (the "SPC Regulation"). SPCs are granted in Switzerland under Articles 140a et seqq. Patents Act. The Patents Act will also soon be amended to implement the Regulation (EC) No. 1901/2006 on medicinal products for paediatric use to provide for a six-month extension of the exclusivity if a paediatric investigation plan exists.[5]

Swiss courts have not yet considered the question of whether an SPC is available if the active ingredient in question had been authorised in any earlier marketing authorisation. When adjudicating this issue, Swiss Courts will take into consideration the case law of the European Court of Justice.[6] In Case C-130/11 *Neurim Pharmaceuticals*, the ECJ made it clear that new indications for an already approved drug may be the subject of an SPC. The ruling in *Neurim* is equally supported in Swiss scholarly writing.[7]

II. Policy considerations

1. *Health and social issues*

In Switzerland, access to healthcare is provided through medical doctors and pharmacies, which dispense medicaments (including those prescribed by doctors). Doctors are in principle free in prescribing medicaments. Prescribing by reference to a drug's international non-proprietary name ("INN") is referred to as generic prescribing. Doctors do not tend to write the indication for which the patient is being treated on the prescription. Where pharmacists are presented with a prescription written generically, they are free to dispense either the branded version of the drug or the equivalent generic. However, there is a reimbursement process in place, which encourages pharmacists to prescribe generic versions of the drug. If a drug is prescribed by brand, the pharmacist must dispense the branded product. If the prescribing doctor writes a prescription generically, and generic versions of the drug are available, the doctor will not know whether the branded product or a generic version will ultimately be dispensed by the pharmacist.

---

5. The Swiss parliament has already adopted the respective amendments of the Patents Act in the context of the revision of the Therapeutic Products Act, but the amendments have not yet entered into force. They will likely enter into force in the course of 2017. Under the new law, the right holder can either apply for a specific Pediatric SPC, which will be valid for six months after expiry of the basic patent, or, if the right holder already has an SPC, they can apply for a six-month extension of such SPC (Pediatric SPC Extension).
6. According to the decision B-3064/2008 of 13 September 2010 of the Federal Administrative Tribunal, the provisions of the Patents Act relating to SPCs have to be interpreted in light of the precedents of the European Court of Justice (*see* reason 3).
7. *See* Kilian Schärli, *Das ergänzende Schutzzertifikat für Arzneimittel*, Zurich 2013, pp. 54 et seqq.

2. *Legal issues*

As more fully discussed below (see section C.), specific difficulties arise as a result of the prescribing and dispensing practice in Switzerland (as outlined above). In particular, where a drug is prescribed generically, without safeguards in place it cannot be ensured that it will not be used for the patented indication. Pharmacists may not know what illness a patient is being treated for. Accordingly, in circumstances where for different indications the pharmaceutical form or dosage is similar, if not the same, it may be difficult for the pharmacist to identify whether the drug is being prescribed for a new therapy which is patent protected or for an earlier indication which is no longer patent protected. Furthermore, neither the doctor nor the pharmacist may be aware of the issues of patent protection affecting the drug generally or the new therapy specifically.

B. VALIDITY

I. Allowable claim wording

Prior to the entering in to force of the EPC 2000 on 13 December 2007, second medical use claims (both in EP (CH) patents and Swiss national patents) were only allowed using the Swiss-type process or method claim in the form of "*the use of substance/compound X for the manufacture of a medicament to treat disease Y*".[8]

For Swiss national patents, the new Article 7d Patents Act (implementing the EPC 2000) still prescribes the Swiss-type claim format for second medical uses (see above section A.). In addition, "old" EP (CH) patents with Swiss-type claims are still in force in Switzerland. Furthermore, for EP applications granted after 13 December 2007 (entry into force of EPC 2000) and filed on or before 28 January 2011, the application may provide for both claim formats. For EP (CH) patents having a filing date of 29 January 2011 or later the new purpose-limited claim format of "substance X for use in the treatment of disease Y" is now mandatory. This rather confusing situation may be summarised as follows:

	Granted before or on 13 December 2007 (entry into force of EPC 2000)	*Granted after 13 December 2007 and filed on or before 28 January 2011*	*Filed after 28 January 2011*
EP (CH) patents	Swiss-type claim	Co-existence of Swiss-type claim and purpose-limited product claim	Purpose-limited product claim
CH patents	Swiss-type claim	Swiss-type claim	Swiss-type claim

Therefore, the validity and infringement of Swiss-type claims remain relevant in Switzerland.

8. G 5/83 *Eisai/Second Medical Indication*, approved by the Federal Supreme Court in BGE 137 III 170 (alendronate); see also section A.1.1 above.

No product and method claims are permissible in Switzerland for second medical use patents, since the product is not novel and methods of treatment of the human body by therapy are not themselves patentable (see above section A).

Medical system claims are not permissible (see Chapter I, "EPO").

The Federal Supreme Court has confirmed that second medical use claims for dosage regimes are permissible, as long as the dosage regimes are novel and inventive.[9]

Swiss Courts have not yet considered the patentability of specific second medical use patents for the use of a known compound for the treatment of a known condition in special patient groups. However, the Federal Supreme Court seems to acknowledge that such claims may be patentable, as long as the usual requirements for novelty and inventive step are met.[10] In considering this issue, the Swiss Courts will also take into consideration the case law of the EPO (as to which see Chapter I, "EPO").

II. Novelty

1. General definition of novelty and prior art

While Article 54 EPC (as to which see Chapter I, "EPO") applies to EP (CH) patents, the Patents Act applies to Swiss national patents. However, in applying the Patents Act, Swiss courts will have regard to the case law of the EPO.

Article 1 Patents Act states that one of the requirements for a patentable invention is that it is new. Article 7 states that an invention is new if it does not form part of the state of the art at the relevant priority date of the patent. The state of the art comprises everything made available to the public by means of a written or oral description, by use, or in any other way, before the priority date of the patent.

For the purpose of assessing novelty (but not inventive step), the state of the art also includes information in certain patent applications which have an earlier priority date, but which were not published until after the priority date of the relevant patent (*see* Article 7(3) Patents Act).

It is not permissible, for the purpose of considering novelty, to combine information in multiple prior art documents; an exception may apply where the reader is specifically cross-referred by the first document to the second. Furthermore, it is usually not permissible to combine different features within a prior art document, unless the combination is itself disclosed by the document.[11]

In order for a disclosure to render a patent invalid for lack of novelty, it must be clear, unambiguous and enabling. It is not sufficient that the prior art merely discloses the claimed invention, it must provide sufficient information to allow the skilled person to perform it at the priority date. Nevertheless, the skilled person reads the prior art in the context of their common general knowledge. This means

9. BGE 137 III 170 (alendronate).
10. BGE 137 III 170 (alendronate).
11. *See* Peter Heinrich, *PatG/EPÜ*, 2nd ed., PatG 7 N 23; Robert Briner, in: *SIWR IV*, Basel 2006, pp. 117 et seq.

that not all features of the claimed invention need to be explicitly disclosed in the prior art document if the skilled person would find them to be implicitly disclosed.[12]

2. *Definition of skilled person*

The skilled person is a hypothetical person who is presumed to be aware of all the pertinent prior art. The skilled person is defined based on the closest prior art.[13] Where the skilled person is deemed to be a team, the relevant common general knowledge will be the knowledge held collectively by the team.[14]

3. *Scope of disclosure*

3.1 *General rules*

While Article 83 EPC (as to which see Chapter I, "EPO") applies to EP (CH) patents, Article 50 Patents Act applies to Swiss national patents. Here again, in applying the Patents Act, Swiss courts will have regard to the case law of the EPO.

Article 50 Patents Act provides that the specification of a patent should disclose the invention in sufficiently clear fashion so that the skilled person can perform it. The specification of the patent should contain sufficient information to allow the skilled person to work the invention across the scope of the entire claim in light of the specification read in the light of the skilled person's common general knowledge.[15]

3.2 *First medical use*

As explained above (see section A.), the identification of a first medical use of a known compound may confer novelty and form the basis of a patentable invention. To comply with the requirement of sufficiency of disclosure, the patent specification must disclose the suitability of the compound recited in the claims for the claimed medical use (see Chapter I, "EPO").

3.3 *New subject matter*

The patent specification must disclose the novel subject matter, i.e. the use of the claimed substance for the new therapeutic purpose. The new therapeutic purpose may consist solely in a new dosage regime or a new patient group.[16]

12. *See* Peter Heinrich, *PatG/EPÜ*, 2nd ed., PatG 7 N 19; Robert Briner, in: *SIWR IV*, Basel 2006, pp. 118 et seq.
13. Federal Patent Court of 4 May 2016, O2014_009 (reason 4.9.2).
14. *See* BGE 120 II 71 (reason 2).
15. *See* Robert Briner, in: *SIWR IV*, Basel 2006, pp. 164 et seq.
16. *See* BGE 137 III 170 (alendronate) and section B.I. above.

3.4 *New data*

The information in the patent specification must make it plausible or credible that the claimed substance will be effective with respect to the claimed therapeutic use. New data and post-published evidence may be taken into account to support the initial disclosure (see Chapter I, "EPO").

4. *Requirements for second medical use*

To comply with the requirement of sufficiency of disclosure, the patent specification must contain a plausible or credible teaching as to why the claimed second medical use is workable and it must disclose the suitability of the compound recited in the claims for the claimed second medical use (see Chapter I, "EPO").

4.1 *Distinction from first medical use*

The claims of the second medical use patent must be limited to novel uses, including novel medical conditions, or novel combination therapies, or novel dosage regimes[17] or novel classes of patients who would not have been treated within the scope of the first medical use.

4.2 *Sub-species of second medical use*

Examples of second medical use patents include novel medical conditions, novel combination therapies, novel routes of administration or novel classes of patients. The Federal Supreme Court has specifically approved of second medical use patents where the use is for a novel dosage regime.[18]

4.3 *Dosage regimes*

The Federal Supreme Court has confirmed that second medical use claims for dosage regimes are permissible, as long as the dosage regimes are novel and inventive.[19]

4.4 *Special patient groups*

Swiss Courts have not yet considered the patentability of specific second medical use patents for the use of a known compound for the treatment of a known condition in special patient groups. However, the Federal Supreme Court seems to acknowledge that such claims may be patentable, as long as the usual requirements for novelty and inventive step are met.[20] In adjudicating this issue, the Swiss Courts will also take into consideration the case law of the EPO (as to which see Chapter I, "EPO").

---

17. See BGE 137 III 170 (alendronate).
18. BGE 137 III 170 (alendronate).
19. BGE 137 III 170 (alendronate).
20. BGE 137 III 170 (alendronate).

5. *Timing issues*

5.1 *Relevant time of development of second medical use*

Second medical uses are often identified after a drug has been developed and tested. Therefore, experimental data such as preclinical data from animal models or even data from clinical trials may already be available. Generally speaking, a patent need not contain any experimental data as long as the claims are credible or plausible in light of the information in the specification and the common general knowledge. However, a second medical use patent will usually contain experimental data to make it plausible that the medicament will indeed treat the new claimed indication (see Chapter I, "EPO").

5.2 *Role of new data*

The information in the patent specification must make it plausible or credible that the claimed substance will indeed treat the new claimed indication. New data and post-published evidence may be taken into account to support the plausibility of the initial disclosure (see Chapter I, "EPO").

5.3 *Use of old data*

To comply with the requirement of sufficiency of disclosure, the application as filed must make it plausible or credible that the claimed substance will indeed treat the new claimed indication. Such therapeutic effect may also be derivable from the prior art or other old data (see Chapter I, "EPO"). However, if the therapeutic effect is derivable from the prior art, the second medical use claim may well lack inventive step.

III. Inventive step/non-obviousness

1. *Definition of inventive step/non-obviousness*

While Article 56 EPC (as to which see Chapter I, "EPO") applies to EP (CH) patents, the Patents Act applies to Swiss national patents. However, in applying the Patents Act, the Swiss courts will have regard to the case law of the EPO.

Article 1(2) Patents Act states that anything that is obvious having regard to the state of the art is not patentable as an invention. The state of the art comprises everything made available to the public by means of a written or oral description, by use, or in any other way, before the priority date of the patent.

The Federal Patent Court generally applies the problem-solution approach adopted by the European Patent Office. This approach consists essentially of (i) determining the "closest prior art", (ii) establishing the "objective technical problem" to be solved, and (iii) considering whether or not the claimed invention, starting from the closest prior art and the objective technical problem, would have been obvious to the skilled person.

The closest prior art for assessing inventive step is normally a prior art document, disclosing the combination of features which constitutes the most promising starting point for a development leading to the claimed invention. If there are several promising starting points for assessing inventive step, it is necessary to apply the problem-solution approach to each of these starting points because an invention needs to be inventive vis-à-vis any closest prior art.[21] According to recent case law of the Federal Patent Court, the skilled person must be newly defined for each closest prior art.[22]

2. *Same scope of disclosure as for novelty?*

The patent specification must establish that a technical problem has been solved by the features recited in the claims. A clear, plausible and credible teaching in the patent specification is, therefore, important. If the patent does not solve any technical problem, the claims will be held obvious.

3. *Assessment of inventive step/non-obviousness*

For second medical use patents, the active ingredient will form part of the state of the art. Therefore, the assessment of non-obviousness will often turn upon whether it would have been obvious to the skilled person that a particular use of the product would have a reasonable chance of success in treating the new medical indication or patient group.

IV. Amendment of claims after grant

1. *Admissibility of post-grant amendments in general*

Post-grant amendments are admissible. Patents can be voluntarily amended post-grant via a number of routes. EP (CH) patents can be amended post-grant in opposition proceedings or central limitation proceedings before the EPO (as to which see Chapter I, "EPO"). EP (CH) patents and Swiss national patents can be amended post-grant in limitation proceedings before the Federal Institute of Intellectual Property (FIIP). Alternatively, if the EP (CH) patent or the Swiss national patent is the subject of court proceedings in which validity is put in issue, then the proprietor can amend the patent during the course of such court proceedings before the Court.[23]

In considering whether to allow the amendment, the examiner of the FIIP or the Court, as the case may be, shall have regard to Article 24 of the Patents Act. According to this provision, the proprietor can limit the patent in three ways: (i) by

21. BGE 138 III 111 (reason 2.2); Federal Patent Court of 27 May 2015, O2013_011 (reason 5.6).
22. Federal Patent Court of 4 May 2016, O2014_009 (reason 4.9.2).
23. It is not settled whether an amendment application to the Court is possible in the event the alleged infringer does not file a nullity counter-claim, but only raises nullity as a defence, especially where the proprietor seeks to amend the claims by incorporating features from the specification.

revoking a patent claim, (ii) by combining an independent claim with one or more patent claims that are dependent on it, and (iii) by incorporating features from the specification into an independent claim; in such cases, the limited claim must refer to the same invention and define an embodiment that is included in *the specification of the published patent* and in the version of the patent application that determined the date of filing.

Amendments proposed to distinguish the invention from the new prior art must be such that the claimed invention is novel and inventive. Furthermore, the amendments must not add matter or extend the protection conferred. However, under Swiss law, the amendments must also have a basis in the specification of the published patent. According to the Federal Patent Court, this additional requirement – not foreseen in the EPC – equally applies to EP (CH) patents.[24] As a matter of Swiss law, only the claims can be amended, not the specification.[25]

A proprietor may not amend the patent *after* the Court gives a decision invalidating the patent.[26] The reason is that there is an underlying public interest in finality of litigation. Therefore, if a proprietor considers the claims of the patent are vulnerable, it has to propose auxiliary requests as a fall-back position in the course of the court proceedings rather than awaiting the outcome.

2. *Procedural issues*

2.1 Independent limitation proceedings

EP (CH) patents can be amended post-grant in central limitation proceedings before the EPO (as to which see Chapter I, "EPO").

EP (CH) patents and Swiss national patents can be amended post-grant in limitation proceedings before the Federal Institute of Intellectual Property ("FIIP").

2.2 Opposition proceedings

EP (CH) patents can be amended post-grant in opposition proceedings before the EPO (as to which see Chapter I, "EPO"). If a European patent is upheld in opposition proceedings before the EPO in amended form, those amendments automatically apply to the EP (CH) patent, subject to any appeal.

Swiss national patents are subject to opposition proceedings before the FIIP. The grounds of opposition are, however, limited to certain exclusions of subject matter from patentability, notably the human body and its parts, naturally occurring gene sequences, inventions whose exploitation is contrary to public policy or morality, methods of medical treatment and diagnosis, as well as plant varieties and animal varieties. The proprietor may amend the claims in opposition proceedings before the FIIP to overcome these exclusions from patentability.

24. *See* Federal Patent Court of 17 September 2013, O2012_030 (reason 17); affirmed in BGE 4A_541/2013 of 2 June 2014.
25. *See* Federal Patent Court of 17 September 2013, O2012_030 (reason 18).
26. *See* BGE 4A_541/2013 of 2 June 2014 (reason 2.4).

2.3 *Nullity actions*

If the EP (CH) patent or the Swiss national patent is the subject of court proceedings in which validity is put at issue, including nullity and infringement proceedings, then the proprietor can amend the patent during the course of such court proceedings before the Court. See above section B. IV.1 and section C. below.

3. *Added matter*

Under Swiss practice, a strict assessment takes place as to whether the amendments proposed to distinguish the invention from the new prior art add matter. A post-grant amendment to replace a Swiss-type claim with the new product-limited form of a second medical use claim (according to the EPC 2000) would not be allowable, particularly as the Federal Supreme Court confirmed in BGE 137 III 170 (alendronate) that the new form of EPC 2000 claim has a broader scope than Swiss-type claims. See also TBA T 1673/11 of 20 October 2015 and further below.

4. *Sufficiency*

Second medical use claims must be supported by evidence that the substance or composition recited in the claims is plausibly effective for the specified use.

5. *Multiple indications*

See Chapter I, "EPO".

V. Change of patent category

As discussed above, it is permissible to amend granted claims in the course of Swiss proceedings, provided that the requirements of Article 24 Patents Act 1954 are fulfilled.

Changing a process claim to a product claim is not admissible as a matter of Article 24 Patents Act because it extends the protection conferred.

Similarly, changing a Swiss-type claim to the new product-limited form of a second medical use claim (EPC 2000) would not be allowable, particularly as the Federal Supreme Court confirmed in BGE 137 III 170 (alendronate) that the new form of EPC 2000 claim has a broader scope than Swiss-type claims (see above B. IV. 3. and further below).

Amending a product claim to a use claim does not broaden the scope of protection and is thus allowable as a general matter.[27] However, changing a product claim to a method of treatment claim would not be admissible because method of treatment claims are not allowable pursuant to Article 2(2)(a) Patents Act/Article 53(c) EPC.

27. *See* G2/88 *Mobil/Friction Reducing Additive.*

C. INFRINGEMENT AND LITIGATION

I. Legal framework

1. National statutory laws

As mentioned above, the Patents Act sets out the national basis for patent law in Switzerland.

2. Case law

The scope of patent protection in Switzerland is governed by the Patents Act, as interpreted by the Swiss courts, namely the Federal Patent Court and the Federal Supreme Court. The decisions of the Technical Boards of Appeal of the EPO are also taken into account by Swiss courts, where relevant, but they are not binding. The same applies to decisions of the courts of other EPC member states. Swiss Courts will routinely look to judgments of the German and UK courts as well as other courts of EPC member states.

Infringement of second medical use claims has so far not been the subject of any published court decisions in Switzerland.

II. Claim construction

1. General rules

The extent of the protection conferred by a patent is determined by the claims, which are interpreted according to the description and drawings. This is in line with Article 69 EPC and the Protocol on the Interpretation of Article 69, which are not only applicable to EP (CH) patents, but (indirectly) also to Swiss national patents. The overall aim is to achieve a reasonable balance between the interest of the applicant in obtaining adequate protection for the invention and the interest of third parties and the public in legal certainty.

It is a fundamental principle under Swiss law and procedure that the construction of the claim is the same whether validity or infringement is at issue.

2. Specific issues for use claims

It is well established that the term "for" in patent claims usually means "suitable for". In other words, a claim to a product or method "for" a specific purpose is a claim to such a product or method whatever its intended purpose. Therefore, the indication of the intended purpose of the product or the method in the claim does usually not confer novelty.[28] Conversely, it is, as a general matter, irrelevant to the question of

28. *See* decision of Federal Patent Court of 24 August 2012, S2012_004, p. 6, para. 8. However, novelty is exceptionally established if the product or method disclosed in the prior art is obviously unsuitable for the purpose indicated in the claim.

infringement of a patent claim relating to a method for a particular purpose whether the method is carried out for the purpose recited in the claim.[29]

In a second medical use claim, however, such a construction would not make any sense as it would deprive the claim of novelty (as the product itself was "suitable for" the new use before the discovery of such application). A second medical use claim is characterised in that it protects the use of such product for a specific purpose, i.e., as a medicament. Therefore, a second medical use claim provides a purpose-limited protection only. This means that third parties are only prevented from using the compound or substance recited in the claims for preparation of a medicament for the same indication.

III. Scope of protection

1. *Scope of the use*

1.1 *General definition of the term "use"*

There is no general definition of the term "use". The Swiss Patents Act uses the term "use" in different contexts.

According to Article 8 Patents Act, the patent confers on its proprietor the right to prohibit others from using the invention commercially. The term "use" in this context describes the proprietor's right of exclusivity. The "uses" exclusively reserved to the proprietor include, in particular, manufacturing, storage, offering, placing on the market, importing, exporting and carrying in transit, as well as possession for any of these purposes (see Article 8(2) Patents Act).

The term "medical use" as in Articles 7c and 7d Patents Act is different from the term "use". In this context it refers to the use of a substance or composition in a method for treatment or a diagnostic method.

1.2 *Manufacture of the pharmaceutical*

Manufacturing is among the "uses" which are exclusively reserved to the proprietor, according to Article 8 of the Patents Act. In the absence of the proprietor's consent, manufacturing therefore constitutes an act of infringement.

The manufacture of the medicament comprises the acts necessary to obtain the final and complete product (i.e., the medicament). The preparation of parts of the medicament only (for instance, only some of the raw materials) will usually not be sufficient to constitute an act of manufacturing. However, the person making parts of the medicament may be liable for indirect infringement (Article 66(d) Patents Act).

In the context of second medical use claims, manufacturing will only constitute an act of infringement if it is clear that the manufactured product will be used for the specific (protected) indication (see further below).

---

29. *See* Tobias Bremi, "Wie wirken sich Zweckangaben in Patentansprüchen auf den Schutzbereich aus", in: *Immaterialgüterrecht in kommentierten Leitentscheiden*, Zurich 2015, p. 432.

1.3 *Sale of the product*

Sale of the product is equivalent to putting the product on the market, which is among the "uses" exclusively reserved to the proprietor, according to Article 8 of the Patents Act. In the absence of the proprietor's consent, sale of the product therefore constitutes an act of infringement.

In the context of second medical use claims, sale of the product will only constitute an act of infringement if it is clear that such product will be used for the specific (protected) indication (see further below).

1.4 *Offer for sale*

Offer for sale is among the "uses" exclusively reserved to the proprietor, according to Article 8 of the Patents Act. In the absence of the proprietor's consent, an offer for sale of the product therefore constitutes an act of infringement.

A person makes an offer within the meaning of Article 8 Patents Act if they are prepared to manufacture and/or supply the product to third parties. Offers are usually made through advertising, letters, leaflets, brochures, trade fairs and the like. Offers on the internet are relevant to the extent the website is (also) directed at Swiss customers. Making pre-patent expiry offers to supply the product after patent term expiry also constitutes an act of infringement.[30]

In the context of second medical use claims, offer for sale of the product will again only constitute an act of infringement if it is clear that such product will be used for the specific (protected) indication (see further below).

1.5 *Application to the patient*

The application of a medicament to the patient may also be considered use of the invention. Currently, there is no general exception for the physician from patent infringement. In other words, the doctor who treats a patient may in theory be held liable for patent infringement. However, as a reaction to the Federal Supreme Court decision BGE 137 III 170 (alendronate),[31] the Swiss parliament has recently enacted a general exception from infringement for physicians and pharmacists, which has not yet entered into force.[32]

A patient cannot infringe a patent by using the drug for treatment because private acts are exempt from infringement.

---

30. *See* decision of Federal Patent Court of 27 February 2014, S2014_002; decision of Federal Patent Court of 31 March 2014, S2014_003.
31. In BGE 137 III 170 (alendronate), the Federal Supreme Court specifically alerted the legislator to the fact that due to the broader scope of protection of the new purpose-limited product claim category for second medical uses, medical doctors and pharmacists would risk to be exposed to patent infringement claims (see further below).
32. *See* Articles 9(1)(g) and 9(1)(h) Patents Acts. The amendments will likely enter into force in the course of 2017.

1.6 Combination products

Where a patent claim protects a combination product, i.e., two or more substances to be administered to the patient in combination, the claim will only be infringed if all components, which form part of the combination, are offered or put on the market. The protection does not extend to the offer of one of the components alone. However, the person offering one of the components may be liable for indirect infringement (Article 66(d) Patents Act).

2. Absolute product protection

Under Swiss law, it is well settled that a product claim enjoys absolute protection, i.e., its scope of protection generally encompasses any such product, which has the same properties as the claimed product. In other words, the scope of protection of a product claim encompasses any and all functions, effects and purposes of such claimed product.[33] By contrast, a process claim does not convey absolute protection. A product is only covered by the scope of protection as far as it has been directly obtained by the patented process (see Article 8a Patents Act).

2.1 Limitation through the term "use"

The necessary limitation through the term "use" means that a patentee to a second medical use patent cannot prevent the use of the product *per se*. But the patentee can prevent the use of the substance recited in the claims for the production of a medicament for the same indication. The precise scope of protection depends on the specific claim format. While Swiss-type claims are held to be process claims, the new claim category of Article 54(5) EPC 2000 provides a purpose-limited product protection. This new claim category conveys a protection which comes close to the generally known absolute product protection. Any third party is prevented from using the substance or composition for the production of a medicament for the same indication.

2.2 Off-label use

Off-label use means that an authorised drug is used for an indication, age group, dosage or mode of administration that has not been approved for such drug and is thus not disclosed in the product information. By relying on a marketing authorisation for one indication, clinicians may use their clinical judgment, at their own risk, to prescribe authorised medicaments for unauthorised indications. As long as off-label use is covered by the patented indication, it will be seen as "use" in the meaning of the patent claim and constitute infringement.

Sometimes the term "off-label use" is used, although there is in fact a "cross-label use". The two terms do not mean one and the same thing. Cross-label use generally refers to the use of a drug for a previously approved and patented indication, age

33. *See* BGE 122 III 85.

group, dosage or mode of administration that is not mentioned in the marketing authorisation or packaging information for the particular product in question.

Cross-label use occurs in the context of so-called "skinny labelling". Article 14 of the Therapeutic Products Act provides an abridged procedure for the authorisation of generic products.[34] Swissmedic allows generic suppliers to "carve out" indications which are protected by a second medical use from the summary of product characteristics (and hence the market authorisation) and packaging information.[35]

As with off-label use, doctors are generally free to prescribe a medicament for a cross-label use.

3. *Dosage regimes*

If a specific dosage regime forms an element of a second medical use claim, the scope of protection is limited to the specific dosage. In such circumstances, the patentee is entitled to prevent only the use for such specific dosage regime.

4. *Patient groups*

If a second medical use claim is directed to a new or selected patient population, the scope of protection will again be limited to use for that specific group and will not extend to any use outside that group. In such circumstances, the patentee is again entitled to prevent the use only in such patient groups.

5. *Extension under the doctrine of equivalents*

The doctrine of equivalents also applies in Switzerland. The Federal Patent Court has recently refined the criteria for extending the scope of protection to equivalent embodiments as follows: when an allegedly infringing method or product does not literally fulfil one or more features of the claim but comprises replacing features instead, the following three questions need to be answered in the affirmative in order to conclude that the allegedly infringing method or product is within the scope of the claim:[36]

- Do the replacing features objectively fulfil the same function?
- If so, are the replaced features and their objectively same function rendered obvious to the skilled person by the teaching of the patent?

34. This corresponds to Article 10 of Directive 2001/83/EC relating to medicinal products for human use.
35. See Paragraph 7.13 of Swissmedic Anleitung Zulassung von Humanarzneimitteln mit bekannten Wirkstoffen. This corresponds to Article 11 of Directive 2001/83/EC which provides that: "those parts of the summary of product characteristics of the reference medicinal product referring to indications or dosage forms which were still covered by patent law at the time when a generic medicine was marketed need not be included".
36. *See* decision of Federal Patent Court of 22 March 2013, S2013_001; decision of Federal Patent Court of 25 January 2016, O2014_002.

- If so, with due consideration of the claim wording in view of the description, would the person skilled in the art have taken the replacing features into account as being an equivalent solution?

Generally speaking, the doctrine of equivalents also applies to second medical use claims. It may well be that the alleged infringer uses a derivative of the compound recited in the claims for manufacturing a medicament to treat the same medical condition. This would be a typical situation where the doctrine of equivalents may come into play. On the other hand, it seems rather unlikely that a patentee could prevent the use of the same compound as the one recited in the patent claims for the treatment of a different medical indication on the basis of the doctrine of equivalents. It seems unlikely that one medical indication can merely be substituted by another indication to fulfil the same function. Equally, it would probably be difficult to argue that it would be obvious for the skilled person to replace the indication or that the skilled person would have taken the other indication as being an equivalent solution.

IV. Infringing acts

The possible infringing acts mirror the exclusive rights of the patentee set out above. Here again, the limitation of the claim to the specific purpose has to be taken into consideration. The second medical use claims cover all acts that are linked to the specific use of the substance or the compound recited in the claims. The scope of protection is not limited to the actual use of the substance or medicament (by doctors and patients), but equally covers all acts preceding the concrete use of the substance or medicament if and to the extent these acts are linked to the specific medical use.

With respect to Swiss-type claims, it has been suggested in Swiss scholarly writing this notion be captured by relying on the German doctrine of "manifest preparation" (in German: "*sinnfällige Herrichtung*").[37] Under this doctrine, the substance recited in the claims needs to be manifestly prepared for the specific treatment to constitute an infringement of a Swiss-type claim (see Chapter II, "Germany"). It appears that this approach is also stipulated by the Technical Board of Appeal.[38] While there is no pertinent Swiss case law on this issue so far, one should expect that the Federal Patent Court would also follow the notion that only the manifest preparation of the substance recited in the claims for the specific treatment constitutes an infringement of a Swiss-type claim.[39]

With regard to purpose-limited product claims (i.e., EP 2000 claims), every use of the substance recited in the claims for the specific therapeutic indication infringes the patent regardless of whether the claimed indication is revealed on the product packaging or in the label instructions. However, in order to find direct infringement

37. *See* Thierry Calame, in: *SIWR IV*, Basel 2006, pp. 452 et seq.; Thierry Calame, in: Jan Busche/Michael Trimborn/Bernd Fabry, *Patent Infringement Worldwide – Claim Interpretation – Infringement – Damages*, Cologne 2010, CH 24.
38. See T 1673/11, reason 9.1.
39. Andri Hess-Blumer, Richard Stäuber, "Wann wird ein Swiss-type claim direkt verletzt?", *sic!* 2015, 622, criticise this approach as being overly narrow.

by a manufacturer of such medicaments, it will still be necessary to show that such medicaments have been manifestly manufactured for the patented use.

1. *Infringing person or entity*

Save for a few exceptions (for example private use), any person or entity carrying out, in Switzerland, any of the acts amounting to direct or indirect infringement under Articles 8 and 66 Patents Act is liable for patent infringement. However, the Swiss parliament has recently enacted a general exception from infringement for physicians and pharmacists, which has not yet entered into force.[40]

2. *Direct infringement*

2.1 *Manufacture of the pharmaceutical*

See section C.III.4, above. As explained, manufacturing will only infringe a second medical use claim if it is clear that the manufactured product will be used for the specific (protected) indication. Where the product is manufactured without any indications for the intended use and where it may be used also for other purposes than the patented ones, manufacturing will not constitute infringement.

It needs to be determined in each individual case whether there is manifest preparation or at least manifest use. The patentee will generally rely on the patient information leaflet or product leaflet. However, where label instructions describing the patented use are not available, manifest preparation and use may also be evidenced by other means. For instance, the preparation of the substance itself, the formulation, the dosage, the packaging, documents from regulatory authorities, invoices, or shipping documents may equally reveal the intended purpose. It must be clear from these documents that the intended use of the medicament is for the patented indication. Even advertising, to the extent it relates specifically to the patented use, is sufficient for the purpose of establishing manifest preparation.[41]

It is still unsettled as to whether a manifest preparation could also result from the manufacturing circumstances, such as the quantity of product manufactured. Where the patented indication applies to many more patients than the non-patented indication, the manufactured quantity could manifest the intention to use the product for the patented indication.

---

40. *See* Articles 9(1)(g) and 9(1)(h) Patents Acts. The amendments will likely enter into force in the course of 2017. *See further* below.
41. Andri Hess-Blumer, Richard Stäuber, "Wann wird ein Swiss-type claim direkt verletzt?", *sic!* 2015, 623, rightly criticise the notion that advertising is not sufficient for establishing manifest preparation or use. AIPPI Resolution Q238, para. 9a) states as follows: "The fact that a pharmaceutical does not contain label instructions specifying the patented second medical use should not per se exclude the finding of infringement of a patent for the second medical use. In particular: a) Offering, selling, or promoting a pharmaceutical for a patented second medical use, but without label instructions for such use, as well as placing such pharmaceutical on the market with concomitant references to such second medical use by means other than the label instructions, should constitute infringement."

As mentioned above, there is currently no case law in this area in Switzerland. It may be assumed, however, that where manifest preparation of a pharmaceutical product for use in the treatment of the patented indication can be shown, either by way of label instructions describing the patented use or otherwise, such product will be within the scope of a Swiss-type claim. In contrast, where such manifest preparation cannot be shown, the mere manufacture of such a product should not be encompassed by a Swiss-type claim. As set out above, demonstrating manifest use will be sufficient for an EPC 2000 claim. As explained below, disposing of a skinny label product with the requisite knowledge of its intended use may amount to indirect infringement, according to Article 66(d) Patents Act.

2.2 Offer for sale

2.3 Sale

See sections C.III.3 and 4, above. As explained, the sale or offer for sale of a pharmaceutical product will only infringe a second medical use claim if it is clear that the product will be used for the specific (protected) indication. This is only the case if there is "manifest preparation" or at least "manifest use" in case of EPC 2000 claims, as more fully explained above.

As with manufacturing, there is no case law in this area in Switzerland. It may be assumed, however, that if manifest preparation or use, respectively, can be shown, either by way of label instructions describing the patented use or otherwise, the sale or offer for sale of such a pharmaceutical product may amount to direct infringement of a Swiss-type claim and an EPC 2000 claim, respectively. If a "skinny label" is used, such supply may amount to indirect infringement according to Article 66(d) Patents Act.

2.4 Export

2.5 Import

Export and import are among the "uses" exclusively reserved to the proprietor, according to Article 8(2) of the Patents Act. The individual factual circumstances and claim format are important in connection with export and import.

With regard to Swiss-type claims, if the compound recited in the claims is exported for use in manufacturing abroad, there may well not be any (direct or indirect) infringement within Switzerland. However, if the substance recited in the claims is manufactured in Switzerland and its intended use is manifest, export may very well constitute infringement within Switzerland (regardless of the claim format).

Where the manufacture of a product covered by a patentee's Swiss-type claim takes place outside of Switzerland, it will be an infringement (regardless of the claim format) to import the product into Switzerland, if manifest preparation for a use in Switzerland can be shown. If manifest preparation cannot be shown, e.g., in case of "skinny label" products, the focus will be more on the circumstances of its disposal to third parties, leading to potential liability for indirect infringement.

2.6 *Combination products*

As mentioned above, where a patent claim protects a combination product, the claim will only be infringed if all components, which form part of the combination, are offered or put on the market. This does not necessarily require that all components are offered in one package together. It may well be that the patient prepares the combination.

Another scenario could be that the defendant supplies one of the components which is used further down the chain for the preparation or dispensing by a pharmacist of a combination covered by the patent. The person supplying one of the components may then be liable for indirect infringement (Article 66(d) Patents Act).

3. *Indirect infringement*

Indirect infringement (also known as contributory infringement) is set out in Article 66(d) Patents Act. Indirect infringement is broadly defined: any person who abets any unlawful use of the patented invention, participates in such acts, or aids or facilitates the performance of any of these acts, is liable for indirect infringement.

Swiss law requires that the alleged indirect infringer contributes to an act that qualifies as unlawful direct infringement. If the alleged direct infringement is not unlawful because it is exempted or because the main party can rely on a licence or a prior user right, the party contributing to such lawful act will not be liable for indirect infringement even if its own conduct may be improper. This is a reflection of the principle of accessoriness which governs indirect infringement under Swiss law.

3.1 *Objective acts*

Article 66(d) Patents Act covers the abetting of any unlawful use of the patented invention, the participation in such acts, or the aiding or facilitating of the performance of any of these acts. In practice, the most important example of indirect infringement is the supply and offer to supply any means relating to an essential element of the invention.

3.2 *Subjective conditions*

The Federal Supreme Court requires that the supplier *knows* or that it was obvious that the means are suitable and *intended* (by some ultimate users) for putting the invention into effect.[42]

These subjective conditions are undoubtedly fulfilled if the means are specifically offered to supply or specifically supplied to be used by the recipient for the patented purpose. Equally, if the means are only suitable for the patented purpose and cannot be used for any other purpose than the patented one, the subjective conditions are clearly met.

42. BGE 129 III 588.

Where the means can be used both in an infringing and in a non-infringing manner, one has to establish that the supplier knew or that it was obvious in the circumstances at the time of their offer to supply or when the supply occurred that (i) the means are suitable for putting the invention into effect and (ii) the recipient would intend to use the means so as to infringe. To this effect, the individual factual circumstances will play a major role. For instance, where the medicament is manifestly prepared for the patented use, the supplier should know or at least it should be obvious that the recipient would use the medicament accordingly and thus infringe the patent. In other words, it would be very difficult for the supplier to argue that it had no knowledge of the recipient's intention despite the manifest preparation.

3.3 *Export*

Exporting usually does not amount to indirect infringement.[43] As explained above, Swiss law requires that the alleged indirect infringer contributes to an act that qualifies as unlawful direct infringement. Since the alleged direct infringement does not take place within Switzerland, there is no unlawful act within Switzerland, which the supplier can contribute to. This is again a reflection of the principle of accessoriness.

However, where a party exports a product and the exported product is then re-imported into Switzerland, such party will nevertheless be liable for indirect infringement, if it knew about the re-import from the beginning or it was obvious that this would happen.

3.4 *Import*

Importing product for the purpose of putting it on the Swiss market may well amount to indirect infringement. Here again, it will be relevant whether there is a manifest preparation for the patented use or not.

The transit of goods is among the "uses" exclusively reserved to the proprietor. However, transit of goods may only be prohibited if the proprietor of the patent is permitted to prohibit importation into the country of destination, according to Article 8(3) Patents Act.

3.5 *Combination products*

As mentioned above, where a patent claim protects a combination product, scenarios of indirect infringement may well play a role. One scenario could be that the defendant supplies one of the components which is used further down the chain for the preparation or dispensing by a pharmacist of a combination covered by the patent. The person supplying one of the components may then be liable for indirect infringement (Article 66(d) Patents Act).

43. BGE 122 III 81.

4. *Off-label use*

4.1 General admissibility of off-label use

As set out above, from a regulatory perspective, off-label use is generally permitted in Switzerland, provided that the clinician assumes responsibility for doing so. Cross-label use is also generally permissible.

In principle, the patentee of a second medical use patent should be entitled to prevent off-label use covered by the claims. However, as more fully explained above, the prescribing and dispensing framework in Switzerland presents difficulties. Furthermore, it would be unattractive for a patentee to bring a claim for infringement in respect of an unauthorised use.

With regard to cross-label use, the general principles (in particular in relation to the adoption of "skinny labelling") should apply.

4.2 Liable persons

A patient cannot infringe a patent by using the drug for treatment because private acts are exempt from infringement.

In BGE 133 III 170 (alendronate) the Federal Supreme Court held that clinicians could be found liable for infringement of EPC 2000 claims. Equally, pharmacists could be found liable for dispensing the generic medicament for the patented use. The Court also found that doctors and physicians would unlikely be liable for infringement of the Swiss-type claim format. It is against this background that the Federal Supreme Court, in BGE 133 III 170, specifically alerted the legislator to the broader scope of protection of the new purpose-limited product claim category for second medical uses, which would potentially expose medical doctors and pharmacists to patent infringement claims.

However, for reputational and business reasons it may be unwise for a patentee to sue clinicians and pharmacists. Indeed, there are no reported cases of patentees suing clinicians or pharmacists. Nevertheless, as a reaction to the Federal Supreme Court decision BGE 137 III 170 (alendronate), the Swiss parliament recently enacted a general exception from infringement for physicians and pharmacists, which has not yet entered into force.[44]

If a generic manufacturer markets a drug using "skinny labelling", there will not be any direct infringement (regardless of the claim format). Due to the principle of accessoriness, there is no direct infringement of the Swiss-type claim either. As explained above, Swiss law requires that the alleged indirect infringer contributes to an act that qualifies as unlawful direct infringement. Since the acts of the clinicians and/or pharmacists do not constitute direct infringement, there is no unlawful act that the supplier can contribute to.

In the case of EPC 2000 second medical use claims, the legal situation is currently different. Given that the acts of the clinicians and/or pharmacists currently constitute

44. *See* Articles 9(1)(g) and 9(1)(h) Patents Acts. The amendments will likely enter into force in the course of 2017.

direct infringement of the EPC 2000 claims, there is an unlawful act that the supplier can contribute to. The generic manufacturer will be liable for indirect infringement if the subjective conditions are fulfilled. However, since the Swiss parliament recently enacted a general exception from infringement for physicians and pharmacists, the acts of the clinicians and/or pharmacists will no longer constitute direct infringement once the exception enters into force. This in turn means that there is no longer an unlawful act that the supplier can contribute to.

The liability of the various parties involved in the supply chain can be summarised as follows:

Liable persons	*Swiss-type claim: "use of compound X in the manufacture of medicament for treatment of disease Y"*	*EPC 2000 claim (purpose limited): "compound X for use in treatment of disease Y"*
Patient	No (private use exempted)	No (private use exempted)
Physician prescribing/ pharmacist dispensing drug for patented use	No (obiter dicta in BGE 137 III 170)	Current law: Yes (direct infringement) New law: No (exempted)
Party manufacturing and/ or marketing drug with label instructions which describe patented use (on-label use)	Yes (direct infringement)	Yes (direct infringement)
Party manufacturing and/ or marketing drug with label instructions which do not describe patented use (skinny label), if drug is then dispensed for patented use (cross-label use)	No direct infringement and no contributory infringement (because there is no direct infringement by physician/physicist)	Current law: No direct infringement, but contributory infringement if subjective conditions are fulfilled New law: No direct infringement and no contributory infringement (because there is no direct infringement by physician/physicist)

Swiss law of indirect infringement and specifically the principle of accessoriness therefore indirectly benefit manufacturers and suppliers of skinny-labelled generics. It is not clear why the legislator overlooked this issue.[45] It could have been easily avoided if a defence against enforcement (similar to 35 USC § 287(c)(1)) had been adopted rather than new exemptions from infringement.[46]

45. The legislative process is described in Felix Addor, Christine Vetter, "Der Schutz der medizinischen Behandlungsfreiheit vor patentrechtlichen Verletzungsklagen", *sic!* 2014, 245.
46. *See* Andri Hess, "Der Schutz der zweiten und weiteren medizinischen Indikation – endlich alles klar?", *sic!* 2014, p. 345.

V. Remedies

1. *Injunctions*

Injunctions are not a discretionary remedy in Switzerland. They are automatically issued following a finding of infringement of a second medical use patent.

In some instances an injunction may not always be appropriate. For instance, if the product in question is indicated for multiple medical conditions, only a proportion of the marketed generic drug that is being sold will be infringing (i.e. that which is being used for the patented second medical use). It is not clear how the Federal Patent Court will deal with this issue. It may well be that the Federal Patent Court will refuse injunctive relief on the basis that a claimant's motion is excessive and overreaching.

2. *Damages*

Under Swiss law, damages are intended to be compensatory. Damages are assessed on the basis that the claimant must be placed in the position it would have been in if no infringement had occurred. Awarding damages in respect of infringement of a second medical use patent is likely to be complicated and so far the Swiss courts have not had to deal with this issue.

For example, what level of compensation will be appropriate for a patentee that has been forced to lower the price of its product because of the presence of a generic alternative which was legitimately on the market for the non-patented indications? Will a claimant have to establish the split in the market between patented and non-patented indications to attempt to distinguish non-infringing sales from infringing sales?

Under Swiss law, a reasonable royalty rate is generally not accepted as a method for determining damages. A reasonable royalty rate has to be requested on the basis of unjust enrichment law.

3. *Information*

3.1 *Names of manufacturer, distributors, etc.*

The Federal Patent Court will, in some circumstances, order parties to identify the source of infringing goods or, less commonly, the customer receiving those goods.

As part of this process, an infringing party may be ordered to disclose the levels of sales it has achieved and further information to help a patentee determine whether it will be more beneficial to seek damages or an account of profits.

3.2 *Names of customers*

As a general matter, the provision of the identity of customers will only be appropriate where those customers are trade customers (i.e. wholesalers) rather than consumers. Even if the purpose of the request is the establishment of the intended use (see section 3.3 below), it is unlikely that a court would agree to the disclosure of patients' names, but the disclosed information would at most be limited to the number of customers suffering from a particular indication, if this information is available from the defendant.

3.3 Information about infringing sales

In a case of second medical use infringement, the level of sales to a particular customer may be relevant in establishing the extent to which a generic manufacturer's product is being supplied for the patented use. However, it should not be assumed that the market is static as the availability of cheaper generic drugs for unpatented indications may encourage wider prescribing, and so the attribution of sales to the patented indication may not be straightforward.

3.4 Account of profits

Further to an award of damages, a patentee may opt for the defendant to pay compensation based on the profits the generic has made. Given that the Swiss courts adhere to stringent substantiation requirements and damage claims are difficult to substantiate, this route will often be preferred over damages, even though the patentee will usually have a higher profit margin as compared to the generic.

4. Recall of products and destruction

In Switzerland, following a finding of infringement, the court may order the delivery up or destruction of infringing articles. Whether this would be ordered in the event of a finding of infringement of a second medical use claim remains to be seen since, in theory, some of the infringing product could be put to non-infringing use (at least in a skinny label case).

5. Recovery of legal costs

In Switzerland, the general rule is that costs follow the event such that the overall winning party is entitled to recover its legal costs – although determined according to a statutory tariff depending on the value of litigation – from the losing party. Depending on the value of litigation, the party in whose favour a costs order is made would normally expect to recover just about 30-50% of its actual costs.

VI. Exceptions from patent protection

1. Exhaustion of rights

Switzerland applies a one-sided regional exhaustion doctrine with regard to the European Economic Area ("EEA"). A patent right does not extend to acts in relation to an article that has already been put on the market in a country within the EEA by a patentee or with its consent. Therefore, parallel importation from within the EEA is generally permissible. By contrast, if a patented product has been placed on the market outside the EEA that does not exhaust the patent rights when the product enters Switzerland. Patent products with regulated prices such as pharmaceuticals are not subject to this regime. Switzerland applies a national exhaustion doctrine for pharmaceuticals. Therefore, even parallel importation of pharmaceuticals from within the EEA is not permissible.

2. *Patient welfare*

Patients are protected under Article 9(1)(a) Patents Act, which provides a defence where an otherwise infringing act is done in private and for non-commercial purposes.

In circumstances where a patented drug is not being made available to patients in Switzerland, then the Federal Council (Federal government) may expropriate part or all of the patent, according to Article 32 Patents Act. Alternatively, the Court may grant compulsory licences where, for example, the demand for a patented product is not being met on commercially reasonable terms or where an important technical advance relating to the field of the patent is being hindered. In practice, no applications for compulsory licences have ever been filed. This is likely due to the requirement for the applicant to have first sought to obtain a licence, on reasonable terms, directly from the patentee, followed by the potentially ensuing legal proceedings (with consequent cost and delay).

3. *Exception from infringement for medical doctors and pharmacists*

As mentioned above, the Swiss parliament recently enacted a general exception from infringement for physicians and pharmacists. Article 9(1)(g) Patents Act will exempt from infringement any act performed in the context of medical practice involving an individual human or animal and a medicament. Article 9(1)(h) Patents Act will exempt from infringement the individual preparation of medicaments in pharmacies on the basis of a medical prescription as well as any act related to a medicament prepared in this manner. Mass production and sales of the medicament, however, will not be exempted. It is expected that the new law will enter into force in the course of 2017.

VII. Procedural issues

1. *Preliminary injunction cases*

The Court may award a preliminary injunction, if the following requirements are met: (i) there is a prima facie case of infringement and validity (the burden of proof regarding invalidity lies on defendant); and (ii) the applicant will suffer irreparable harm if the preliminary injunction is not granted. Urgency is not a condition for the grant of interim relief. However, if the applicant has waited for a substantial period of time (i.e., several months) before requesting interim relief, such relief will no longer be available.

The traditional view is that generic entry can cause significant and irreparable harm to the innovator's market where products are typically marketed on an exclusive basis and at a significant price premium.

In the event that a preliminary injunction is awarded, an undertaking in damages may be required from the claimant to compensate the defendant for any loss caused by ordering the preliminary injunction if it later turns out that it was wrongly imposed (for example, if the patent is revoked or it turns out there is no finding of infringement).

1.1 *Availability for second medical use claims*

There have not been any cases in Switzerland where the Federal Patent Court has addressed whether a preliminary injunction should be granted in relation to a second medical use patent. However, it is to be expected that, as with other patents, the Court will issue preliminary injunctive relief if the conditions as set out above are met.

2. *Cases on the merits*

There are no specific procedural requirements that apply in proceedings concerning second medical use patents beyond those which apply in the usual course of proceedings on the merits before the Federal Patent Court.

After the parties have exchanged the first round of pleadings, a preliminary hearing is convened at which a delegation of the court (including the President of the Court and at least one technical judge) will give a preliminary opinion on the merits of the case and try to mediate a court settlement. If the case is not settled, the parties will exchange a second round of pleadings. The technical judge in charge of the file will then issue an expert opinion, which the parties can comment on. At the end of the proceedings a main hearing (trial) is convened at which the parties will make final pleadings. If the court considers that evidence will have to be taken (including hearing of witnesses, appointment of external court expert, or inspections), the proceedings will be continued accordingly. Otherwise the Court will close the proceedings, proceed to the deliberations and then hand down a judgment.

To the extent that infringement and validity issues are both in play, these will be dealt with in the same proceedings, which reflects usual practice in Swiss patent proceedings.

3. *Enforcement of judgments*

Judgments in Switzerland are enforced by order of the court. Failure to comply with an order of the court may be treated as contempt of court.

VIII. Tactical considerations

1. *Plaintiff*

As discussed above, preliminary injunctions are in principle available to prevent generic launch of a product for use for treating a patented indication. The patentee must be alert for grants of marketing authorisation to generic manufacturers and to engage the generic manufacturer in correspondence as to their intentions at an early stage if a marketing authorisation is granted on a product the marketing of which may infringe the patent. It may be that a generic will agree not to launch the product prior to expiry of the patents. If this is not possible, it is essential to take action promptly upon launch of the generic as delay will reduce the chances of success of a preliminary injunction application. Also, to establish that irreparable harm will be suffered by the patentee, the patentee should be in a position to promptly prepare evidence of the commercial impact of a generic launch.

Where there is a substantial non-patent market, it may in practice be difficult or impossible to ask for a conventional injunction as it may prevent legitimate supply for unpatented indications. Careful thought therefore needs to be given as to what relief may be sought that protects, as much as possible, the patented market without disrupting the lawful market. In practice this may be difficult to achieve given the prescribing and dispensing system in Switzerland (as set out above). However, at least it may be possible to require that the generic manufacturer puts prescribers and pharmacists on notice of the patent. Moreover, an injunction should be available to prevent the launch of a product specifically labelled or formulated for the infringing use. This is of course not only an issue for interim relief but also for permanent relief if the patentee is successful in main proceedings.

2. *Defendant*

There is an obvious risk of infringement if a generic manufacturer specifically labels its product for the infringing use. For this reason, it is common for generics to carve out the patented indication from their marketing authorisations and seek to launch "skinny label" products directed only to the unpatented indications, as discussed above. However, given the current, unsettled state of the law on infringement of second medical use claims, it would be unwise for a generic company to rely solely on a skinny label to defeat an allegation of infringement. There is a real risk that the court will infer an intention to supply the patented market from all the circumstances of the launch. For example, if the generic is supplying quantities of product that far exceed the known demand for the unpatented indication, then an intention to infringe may be inferred. The same is of course true in the unlikely event that the generic company takes active steps in alerting doctors and pharmacists that their generic product can be used to treat additional indications.

In conclusion, there is a common interest of responsible patentees and generic manufacturers to cooperate in finding ways to persuade the market to respect second medical use patents while leaving the unpatented market open for generic competition. This is challenging given the prescribing and dispensing practices in Switzerland, which are beyond the control of either party.

France

Isabelle Romet, Dora Talvard

A. AVAILABILITY OF PROTECTION

I. Legal framework

1. National statutory laws

Evolution of the French legislation with respect to patents on drugs

The first French patent act passed on 5 July 1844 excluded drugs from patent protection.

In 1959, a special system was created according to which inventions relating to drugs could be protected only by so-called "*special patents for drugs*" ("*brevets spéciaux de médicaments*", "BSM").

An indication of the pharmacological properties and at least one therapeutic indication of the drug, as well as at least one detailed example for each application described, must be stated in the specification.

Under this system, only a composition for a first medical use can be patented, not a further medical use.

The 2 January 1968 Act suppressed the special patents for drugs, but maintained certain special provisions for patents relating to a drug.

Article 30 specified that, in the case in which a product patent did not describe the therapeutic indication of a product, the rights conferred by the patent did not extend to the use of this product for the manufacturing of drugs and to the importation of drugs, which constituted a significant derogation from the general principles of patent law.

The requirements relating to the content of the specification of pharmaceutical patents were maintained.

Also, Article 10 of this Act maintained the impossibility of protecting a product for a second medical use.

Act No. 78-742 of 13 July 1978 and its implementing decree of 19 September 1979, which aligned French law with the European Patent Convention (EPC) of 1973, removed all specific provisions concerning pharmaceutical patents.

Under the new Act, the patentability of a first medical use resulted from a combination of Article 6 § 4, codified as Article L. 611-16 of the French Intellectual Property Code ("IPC"), and of Article 8 § 4, codified as Article L. 611-11 IPC.

Article 6 § 4, corresponding to Article 52(4) EPC 1973, excluded treatment methods from patentability on the grounds that they were not susceptible of industrial application, but specified that the non-patentability of treatment methods did not preclude obtaining a patent on a drug implementing such a method.

Article 8 § 4, corresponding to Article 54(4) EPC 1973, provided that a therapeutic indication of an already known substance or composition, in a method referred to in Article 6 § 4, could be patented, on the condition that such indication was not disclosed in the prior art, thus allowing patents on a known substance for its first therapeutic use as a drug.

Article 8 § 4 was construed unanimously by the legal authorities as excluding the patentability of a product for a second medical use.

However, as presented in section A.I.3, French case law ultimately admitted Swiss-type claims to protect a second therapeutic use.

Articles 6 and 8 of the 1978 Act were amended by Act No. 2008-776 of 4 August 2008 currently in force.

Legal provisions currently in force

Protection of inventions on drugs is now governed by Articles 132-II and 132-III of Act No. 2008-776 of 4 August 2008, codified under Articles L. 611-11, § 4 and Article L. 611-16 IPC respectively.

Article L. 611-16 IPC, corresponding to Article 53(c) EPC 2000, establishes the principle that methods for treatment of the human body are excluded from patentability; the legal fiction of lack of industrial application was abandoned in favour of a clear statement that methods for treatment shall be excluded from patentability.

Article L. 611-11 IPC on novelty, corresponding to Article 54 EPC 2000, recognises, in § 4, the patentability of a substance or composition comprised in the state of the art for a first therapeutic indication, and § 5 expressly authorises patents on such a substance or composition for a further therapeutic indication.

As explained in section B.1, a second medical use can be protected only through product claims that are, drafted as purpose-limited claims.

1.1 Pharmaceuticals

Articles L. 611-11, § 4, and L. 611-16 IPC apply to all pharmaceuticals as the words "*substance or composition*" in these provisions are very general and cover any product.

1.2 Biologics

Articles L. 611-11, § 4, and L. 611-16 IPC also apply to biologics.

Some specific provisions on biologic products deriving from the human body are worth mentioning.

According to Article L. 611-18 § 2 IPC, deriving from Act No. 2004-800 of 6 August 2004, which implemented Directive 98/44/CE of 6 July 1998 into French law, an element of the human body, such as a gene, cannot be patented as such; it is only the technical application of a function of an element of the human body that can be patented.

Article L. 613-2-1 § 2 IPC sets a derogation from general patent law by limiting the scope of a patent concerning a gene sequence to the function disclosed in the specification, so that it cannot be asserted against a later claim relating to another application of the same sequence.

2. *International treaties*

2.1 TRIPS

The TRIPS Agreement was ratified by France in 1994; French law was amended accordingly in 1996.

Article 27 of the TRIPS Agreement entitled "Patentable Subject Matter" provides for the patentability of "any inventions" "in all fields of technology", but gives Member States the possibility of excluding some inventions from patentability, such as diagnostic, therapeutic and surgical methods for the treatment of humans or animals.

As indicated in section A., French legislation already excluded diagnostic, therapeutic and surgical methods from patentability, but authorised the patentability of compositions and substances used in such methods.

With Act No. 2008-776 of 4 August 2008, Article L. 611-10 § 1 IPC was amended to specify that patents are available for inventions meeting the applicable criteria "in all fields of technology".

2.2 FTAs

No free trade agreement binding on France has consequences on the issue of second medical use.

3. *Availability through case law*

In France, national patents granted by the *Institut national de la propriété intellectuelle* (INPI), the French patent office, and European patents designating France granted by the European Patent Office ("EPO"), coexist.

Ultimately, the French courts having jurisdiction to decide on patent matters, i.e. the *tribunal de grande instance de Paris* ("TGI Paris"), the *cour d'appel de Paris* ("CA Paris") and the *Cour de cassation*, decide on the validity of patents subject to litigation.

3.1 *Second therapeutic use*

In order to place the case law presented below in context, it should be recalled that the Enlarged Board of Appeal of the EPO accepted the patentability of second therapeutic uses, through Swiss-type claims, in Decision G 06/83 of 5 December 1984.

The first French decision examining the validity of a Swiss-type claim was handed down on 25 March 1998[1] in an infringement action brought by Wellcome against Apotex on the basis of European patent No. 0 291 633 on the use of azidothymidine (AZT) for the treatment of AIDS; in this case, Apotex requested revocation of the patent claims, arguing that claim 1 of the patent on the use of AZT was not patentable under Articles 52 § 4 and 54 § 5 EPC 1973 because it pertained to a treatment method of the human body using a product the therapeutic use of which was already known, and that claim 12, drafted in Swiss-type form, was not patentable either but aimed to circumvent the prohibition of patenting such a therapeutic method.

The tribunal examined whether the claimed use corresponded to a first therapeutic use or to a second one and held that no therapeutic use of AZT was known in the prior art; thus, it concluded that claim 1 was valid as it did not relate to a therapeutic method but to a product for implementing such method and for which no previous therapeutic use was known; it considered claim 12 valid for the same reason; thus this decision did not need to decide upon the patentability of a second therapeutic use.[2]

Since then, French courts never denied the patentability of a second therapeutic use protected by a Swiss-type claim; however, these patents were ultimately found invalid for insufficiency, lack of novelty or lack of inventive step in the vast majority of cases.

There are a few famous decisions:

- in a decision dated 22 September 2006, the CA Paris, 4th chamber, section B, in *Laboratoire de contactologie appliquée v Alcon*, concerning Alcon's European patent No. 0 705 095 on combinations of viscoelastics for use during surgery, held that, assuming that the invention concerned a second surgical application – following Alcon's construction that claim 1 was a Swiss-type claim drafted in conformity with Decision G 06/83 of the EPO – claim 1 would be invalid for lack of novelty;[3]
- in a case opposing Teva and Sepracor concerning Sepracor's European patent No. 0 663 828 relating to the use of an enantiomer for the manufacture of a medicament for the treatment of allergic rhinitis and asthma using levocetirizine, the TGI Paris, 3rd chamber, 1st section, in its decision of 6

1. TGI Paris, chamber 3, section 1, 25 March 1998, *The Wellcome Foundation Limited v Apotex France*, docket No. 94/6951.
2. CA Paris, chamber 4, section B, 15 September 2000, *Apotex France v The Wellcome Foundation Limited*, docket No. 1998/16047.
3. CA Paris, chamber 4, section B, 22 September 2006, *Laboratoire de contactologie appliquée v Alcon*, docket No. 04/19659:

   "Yet considering that should this invention concern a second surgical application, the said application lacks novelty"

October 2009, did not examine Teva's nullity ground of non-patentability, but held that the patent was invalid for insufficiency;[4]

- in an order of 12 January 2010 in preliminary injunction proceedings brought by Sepracor and Aventis against Teva concerning European patent No. 0 701 443 on the use of terfenadine metabolites and their optically pure isomers for the preparation of a medicament for treating allergic disorders (fexofenadine), the judge recognised the possibility of claiming a second therapeutic use through a Swiss-type claim,[5] but considered the validity of the patent seriously disputable for insufficiency and lack of novelty, and dismissed the preliminary injunction request;
- in a judgment dated 9 November 2010, in *Teva v Merck Sharp & Dohme*, concerning European patent No. 0 724 444 on the use of a compound for the preparation of a medicament with a specific dosage for treating androgenic alopecia with 5-Alpha reductase inhibitors (finasteride), the TGI Paris, 3rd chamber, 1st section also recognised the availability of Swiss-type claims to patent a known product for a second therapeutic use;[6] but the patent was considered invalid for insufficiency, a finding affirmed on appeal;[7]
- the possibility of protecting a second therapeutic use under EPC 1973 was clearly acknowledged in a decision dated 20 March 2012 by the TGI Paris, 3rd chamber, 1st section, in the case *Teva v Eli Lilly*, concerning Lilly's European patent No. 0 584 952 on the use of benzotiophenes for the preparation of a medicament for treating osteoporosis[8] in a post-menopausal

4. TGI Paris, chamber 3, section 1, 6 October 2009, *Teva v Sepracor*, docket No. 07/16446, English translation available on www.frenchpatentcaselaw.info/.

   There is no appeal decision in this case.
5. TGI Paris, order in preliminary injunction proceedings, 12 January 2010, *Aventis, Sepracor v Teva*, docket No. 09/56031:

   "Therefore, this is about a Swiss-type claim that enables a second therapeutic application to be claimed for a molecule already known."

   There is no appeal decision in this case.
6. TGI Paris, chamber 3, section 1, 9 November 2010, *Teva v Merck Sharp & Dohme*, docket No. 09/12713, English translation available on www.frenchpatentcaselaw.info/:

   "This is the reason why claim 1 of the patent was drafted in the Swiss-type format which, before Decision G2/08 of the EPO Enlarged Board of Appeal, allowed an already known substance to be patented for a second therapeutic use."
7. CA Paris, division 5, chamber 2, 30 January 2015, *Merck Sharp & Dohme v Teva*, docket No. 10/23603.
8. TGI Paris, chamber 3, section 1, 20 March 2012, *Teva Santé and Teva Pharmaceutical Industries v Eli Lilly*, docket No. 09/12706, English translation available on www.french patentcaselaw.info/:

   "It should be noted that part of French case law prior to the implementation of EPC 2000 did not admit the principle of the patentability of a new therapeutic application of a product already known, not on the grounds that a text explicitely excluded it but on the principle that since the molecule is known, the second application was necessarily known.

   Therefore, even under EPC 1973, it was possible to recognise the validity of a second therapeutic application on condition that it was possible to establish that this application was new or inventive and not already included in the prior art".

woman, affirmed on appeal;[9] the patent was ultimately found invalid for lack of inventive step;

- in a recent decision of 3 November 2015,[10] in a case between Ethypharm and Alkermes concerning European patent No. 0 644 755 entitled "surface modified NSAID nanoparticles", the CA Paris recalled again that a new medical use of a known substance can form the subject matter of a patent on condition that the claim be drafted in the Swiss form; however the subject matter of claim 9 of the patent in dispute was found not patent eligible, on the grounds that this claim only taught an accelerated way of therapeutic treatment which could be applied to almost any drug product, to treat any affection and intended for any patient, regardless of the administration mode of the drug and its dosage, so that it was a non-patentable therapeutic method.[11]

---

9. CA Paris, *division 5, chambre 1*, 12 March 2014, *Teva Santé* and *Teva Pharmaceutical Industries v Eli Lilly*, docket No. 12/07203:

   "Considering, as set out, that it is well established that raloxifene was already known for other therapeutic applications (infertility agents, breast cancer etc.), it appears that under the legal provisions applicable on the filing date of the patent, a European patent could be granted on the basis of claims having for object the application of a substance to obtain a medicinal product intended for a new therapeutic use as in this instance."

10. CA Paris, division 5, chamber 1, 3 November 2015, *Ethypharm v Alkermes*, docket No. 12/23743:

    "Considering that under this text, a European patent can be granted for any determined subsequent medical indication of a known substance or composition, provided that the claim be written in the "Swiss-type" format, of the application of a product in view of obtaining a medicinal product used for a new therapeutic application;

    Therefore, it is necessary that a determined specific substance should find a new therapeutic use distinct from the state of the art, it being recalled that a mere process claim relating to a therapeutic treatment is not patentable;

    In this particular instance, claim 9 of the patent at issue relates to any medicinal substance, with the exclusion of naproxene and indomethacine already taught in the state of the art, with the sole purpose of hastening the onset of its action after administration to a mammal;

    Upon reading it appears that this claim refers to no determined known substance or composition in view of obtaining a medicinal product intended to a new determined therapeutic use;

    The claimed hastened onset of the action of the medicinal product is merely a mode of action of a medicinal product, moreover undefined, and cannot be considered as therapeutic use of this medicinal product;

    It follows that claim 9 teaches only a hastened mode of therapeutic treatment applying to any medical substance (with the exclusion of naproxene and indomethacine) to treat any illness and applying to any patient, regardless of the administration of the medicinal product and its dosage;

    Consequently, this claim will held invalid under Articles 53(c) and 138(1) of the Munich Convention and Article L. 614-12 of the French Intellectual Property Code, the appealed judgment being reversed in that it dismissed SA Ethypharm's requests for revocation of this claim;"

11. The CA Paris referred to Article 53 c) EPC 2000 concerning exclusions from patentability as, although the patent was filed on 1 June 1993 well before the entry into force EPC 2000 on 13 December 2007, this provision was applicable according to the transitory provisions

There has been no French case law to date concerning patent claims drafted as purpose-limited product claims.

3.2 Dosage regimes

French case law is reluctant to admit the patentability of claims relating to a dosage regime, notwithstanding the Decision G 02/08 of 19 February 2010 of the EPO Enlarged Board of Appeal expressly recognising this possibility.

A majority of decisions presented below, dated between 2010 and 2014, rejected the patentability of a new dosage form of a known product for the treatment of the same disease as in the prior art, based on the consideration that the choice of a dosage for a drug is the exclusive work of physicians, in consideration of the specificities of their patients, so that dosage claims of a known substance for the same disease would amount to seeking protection for a therapeutic method; they admitted only the possibility of claiming a new dosage of a known substance for the treatment of a new disease:

- in a decision of 28 September 2010, in a case between Actavis and Merck concerning Merck's European patent No. 0 724 444 on the use of a compound for the preparation of a medicament with a particular dosage for treating androgenic alopecia with 5-Alpha reductase inhibitors (finasteride), the TGI Paris, 3rd chamber, 1st section, affirmed the patentability of second therapeutic uses in France, but excluded the possibility of patenting a dosage;[12] in this case, as the tribunal considered that only the dosage taught in the patent was new, it held the patent invalid for lack of patentability;

---

of EPC 2000; but it referred to Article 54 § 5 EPC 1973 concerning novelty as the patent was already granted on the date of the entry into force EPC 2000.

12. TGI Paris, chamber 3, section 1, 28 September 2010, *Actavis v Merck Sharp & Dohme*, docket No. 07/16296, English translation available on www.frenchpatentcaselaw.info/:

    "A specific dosage for the treatment of an illness constitutes neither a first nor a second therapeutic application but simply an indication of the range within which this substance is efficacious so as to treat such or such an illness in light of the tests and research completed and explained in the patent.

    The therapeutic application is therefore limited to the use of a substance to treat a specific illness and not to the choice of such or such a dosage within a range of efficacious dosages.

    The practitioner then has the task of determining in his therapeutic approach and in light of the other many factors to be taken into account (age, weight and gender of the patient, history and other illnesses, other treatments followed) which dosage is adapted to the treatment of the illness treated by this substance.

    The ideal dosage as the only indication belongs to the virtual world and the doctor alone has the right to determine the dosage adapted to the patient by confronting his theoretical knowledge in the field of illnesses and medicaments with the particular case of his patient as he knows it, with all the interactions which the latter is subject to.

    Also, it matters little that the medicament thus protected is marketed by the company which owns the patent or its licensees with a leaflet recommending a certain dosage since such information is merely an indication and only the doctor, in a therapeutic approach, has the right to prescribe the dosage adapted to each patient.

- the non-patentability of a dosage form was also briefly mentioned by the TGI Paris, 3rd chamber, 1st section, in its decision dated 20 March 2012, in *Teva v Eli Lilly,*[13] concerning claims 9 to 12 of Lilly's European patent No. 0 584 952 relating to a dosage form of the drug raloxifene, finding confirmed on appeal in a decision of 12 March 2014;
- the non-patent eligibility of a new dosage for the same disease was reiterated by a decision of the TGI Paris, 3rd chamber, 3rd section, handed down on 5 December 2014 in the infringement proceedings between Akzo Nobel, MSD *and* Teva,[14] concerning MSD's SPC based on European patent No. 0 491 443

In addition, the leaflet which is required for marketing any medicament with an MA, contains the warning in France that these dosages are merely indicative and that a doctor should be consulted.

In the same way, all the cases where the medicament must not be taken and all the warnings relating to the counter-indications due to other illnesses and other treatments or other prohibitions are listed.

In any case, the marketing of the medicament is not a relevant criterion for assessing its patentability.

Consequently, it is possible to patent a medicament for the treatment of a first and then a second illness but not a dosage adapted to the treatment of those illnesses as by doing so, one attempts to patent a therapeutic method, which is excluded in order to belong to the field of care and to depend only on the concomitant freedom and responsibility of each doctor."

13. TGI Paris, chamber 3, section 1, 20 March 2012, *Eli Lilly v Teva*, docket No. 09/12706, English translation available on www.frenchpatentcaselaw.info/:

"Claims 9 to 12 of the limited patent concern particular dosage regimes of administration of raloxifene.

Besides the fact that the dosage is excluded from patentability, since the physicians must assess the doses required by their patients and that the number of times the patient must take the medicinal product must here again be determined by the physician, claims 9 to 12, which protect particular dosages and covering very large dosage ranges from 0.1 to 1,000 mg, from 50 to 400 mg, from 50 to 200 mg, without explaining how these dosages would be relevant and what particular problem they would solve, are invalid for lack of inventive step."

14. TGI Paris, chamber 3, section 3, 5 December 2014, *Akzo Nobel, MSD, v Teva Santé, Ratiopharm, Merckle and Cemelog-BRS*, docket No. 12/13507, English translation available on www.frenchpatentcaselaw.info/.

The decision explains that progestogen-only contraceptives were already known in the prior art and that the patent purported to a specific dosage form of desogestrel or 3-ketodesogestrel presented in the specification as inhibiting ovulation more effectively, while still avoiding some secondary effects; it construes claim 1 as covering a second therapeutic application of a known molecule for the treatment of the same disease in the same administration form, the specific dosage form being the only new element.

The tribunal recognised the possibility of protecting new therapeutic indications of a known substance and also admitted the possibility of claiming a new dosage of a known substance for the treatment of a new disease, but considered that a new dosage form of a known substance for the treatment of the same illness should not be patentable:

"Consequently, it is possible to patent a substance by indicating an efficient dosage scale to solve the posed problem that is the treatment of a first disease and then to patent the

> relating to a contraceptive preparation containing progestogen only, *in a specific daily dosage.*

A decision dated 30 January 2015 of the CA Paris, in the case between *MSD* and *Actavis* about finasteride, seemed to put an end to this line of case law as it recognised the patentability of a new dosage form of a known product for the same therapeutic use as in the prior art, provided this new dosage reflects a different technical teaching; the CA Paris referred to Decision G 02/08 of the EPO Enlarged Board of Appeal, while specifying that it concerned Article 54(5) EPC 2000 which was not applicable to the patent in dispute;[15] in this case, the requirement of a new technical teaching was considered not to be met and the patent was found invalid for lack of novelty.[16]

Notwithstanding this decision of the CA Paris, the TGI Paris of 19 June 2015 in a case opposing Mylan to Richter Gedeon concerning European patent No. 1 448 207 entitled "dosage regime and pharmaceutical composition for emergency contraception" (levonorgestrel), reverted to the previous position according to which a new dosage form of a known product for the same use is not patentable.

---

same substance by indicating a different efficient dosage scale but to solve the posed problem that is a second illness.

(...) however, it is impossible to treat the sole posology adapted for the treatment of the same disease as by doing so, one attempts to patent a therapeutic method, which is excluded in order to belong to the field of care and to depend only on the concomitant freedom and responsibility of each doctor."

15. The CA Paris referred to Article 53(c) EPC 2000 concerning exclusions from patentability, as although the patent was filed on 1 June 1993, well before the entry into force of the EPC 2000 on 13 December 2007, this provision was applicable according to the transitory provisions of the EPC 2000, as did the *tribunal* in first instance; however, according to the transitory provisions, Article 54 EPC 1973 was applicable as the patent was already granted when the EPC 2000 came into force.
16. CA Paris, division 5, chamber 2, 30 January 2015, *Merck Sharp & Dohme v Actavis*, docket No. 10/23603:

"It emerges from all these elements that although the patentability of a claim of a second therapeutic indication based only on the characteristic of a dosage regime may be accepted even for a patent under EPC 1973 interpreted in the light of a subsequent amendment of the convention and resulting case law, it must fulfil the requirement of the existence of a different technical teaching, and to do so to take also account, as contended by Merck, of the characteristics related to the dosage. [...]

Yet Merck's patent, which in no way specifies the technical teaching resulting of the administration of the lower dosage regime, relates to:

- the use of Finasteride for the preparation of a medicinal product taken orally,
- useful for the treatment of adrogenic alopecia,
- the dose of the active ingredient finasteride varying from 0.05 to 1 mg.

With this Stoner document, the overall teachings of the Merck patent are already disclosed while this patent does not contain a technical, specific teaching different from that of the prior art document EP 0 285 382, so that claim 1 of patent EP 0 724 444 is devoid of novelty."

4. *Patent term extension/SPCs*

With Act No. 90-150 of 25 June 1990 creating a French supplementary protection certificate ("SPC"), France was the first country in Europe to introduce a patent term extension regime for patents on drugs to compensate, at least partly, the patent owner for the time period during which he could not exploit its invention before the grant of a marketing authorisation.

This regime was replaced by Regulation 1768/92 (EC) of 18 June 1992, then Regulation 469/2009 (EC) of 6 May 2009.

Although governed by an EU regulation, SPCs are national rights granted by the national patent offices of each Member State, in France the INPI.

Validity and infringement are dealt with by the French courts having jurisdiction for patent matters.

An SPC can be granted on the basis of a patent concerning a first or a second therapeutic indication, as specified in Article 1 c) of Regulation 469/2009, provided that the conditions of Article 3 a) to d) of Regulation 469/2009 are met:

- the product must be "*protected*" by a basic patent in force (Article 3 a));
- a valid authorisation to place the product on the market in the territory for which the certificate is applied must have been granted (Article 3 b));
- the SPC applied for must be the first certificate for the product (Article 3 c));
- the marketing authorisation upon which the application for an SPC is based must be the first authorisation for this product, as a medicinal product (Article 3 d)).

The CJEU issued a decision on 19 July 2012 concerning Article 3 d), under which the marketing authorisation for the product should be the first authorisation to place the product on the market as a medicinal product in *Neurim* (C-130/11), authorising the grant of an SPC on the basis of a second marketing authorisation for a product (in this case melatonin), while a first marketing authorisation had already been granted for the same product, on the grounds that the therapeutic indication was different (the second marketing authorisation concerned the treatment of insomnia in humans while the first one related to the regulation of the reproductive activity of sheep);[17] in this case, the basic patent related to the therapeutic use of a formulation of melatonin.

The CA Paris applied the *Neurim* case law in a decision of 15 February 2013, in *Merck v French patent office*,[18] and held that Merck could obtain an SPC based on a marketing authorisation for the virus varicella zoster as a vaccine for the prevention of

17. CJEU, 19 July 2012, *Neurim* (C-130/11):

    "Articles 3 and 4 [...] must be interpreted as meaning that, in a case such as that in the main proceedings, the mere existence of an earlier marketing authorisation obtained for a veterinary medicinal product does not preclude the grant of a supplementary protection certificate for a different application of the same product for which a marketing authorisation has been granted, provided that the application is within the limits of the protection conferred by the basic patent relied upon for the purposes of the application for the supplementary protection certificate."

18. CA Paris, division 5, chamber 2, 15 February 2013, division 5, chamber 2, *Merck v French patent office*, PIBD 2013, No. 982-III-1131.

zoster, despite the existence of a previous marketing authorisation for the same product for a different application (prevention of varicella); in this case, the patent concerned the use of varicella zoster virus for the manufacture of a vaccine against zoster.

After the *Neurim* decision, the question was raised by legal authors and practitioners as to whether or not it could be construed as authorising the grant of a second SPC for the same product for a new indication, despite the condition set in Article 3 c) that the SPC applied for must be the first certificate for the product.

In Portugal, in a case opposing Boehringer and the Portuguese patent office concerning Boehringer's drug *Pradaxa*, the court held that a second SPC protecting the new indication of a product already protected by an SPC can be granted;[19] in the same case, the French patent office refused to grant a second SPC for a new indication of a product already the subject-matter of an SPC.

The scope of an SPC granted on the basis of a first or second therapeutic application patent will have a scope limited to the said indication, as Articles 4 and 5 of Regulation 469/2009 (EC) limit the protection and the effects of an SPC to that of the basic patent.

The scope of an SPC, obtained on the basis of a patent protecting a therapeutic application of a known active ingredient, limited to the new use of that active ingredient, was confirmed by the *Neurim*[20] decision.

There is no French case law on this issue.

It should be noted that the SPCs granted by the INPI do not specify the indication covered by the SPC.

II. Policy considerations

1. *Health and social issues*

To justify the non-patentability of a second therapeutic use under the 1978 Act, various explanations were put forward by the legislator and the legal authors such as:

- it would be in the interest of public health to encourage researchers to look for new molecules rather than new applications of new molecules;
- the inventor who finds a second therapeutic indication would bear less investment costs than the first one;
- a second therapeutic indication would amount to a treatment method excluded from patentability;

19. "IP Court grants SPC for second medical use", 23 February 2015, Baptista, Monteverde & Associados, http://www.internationallawoffice.com.
20. CJEU, 19 July 2012, *Neurim Pharmaceuticals v Comptroller General of Patents*, C-130/11, § 25:
"Therefore, if a patent protects a therapeutic application of a known active ingredient which has already been marketed as a medicinal product, for veterinary or human use, for other therapeutic indications, whether or not protected by an earlier patent, the placement on the market of a new medicinal product commercially exploiting the new therapeutic application of the same active ingredient, as protected by the new patent, may enable its proprietor to obtain an SPC, the scope of which, in any event, could cover, not the active ingredient, but only the new use of that product."

- if the patentability of several therapeutic indications were allowed, it would not be possible to find out for which application a drug was prescribed without breaching medical secrecy.[21]

These considerations, some of which are highly disputable, show the difficulty to justify the non-patentability of a second therapeutic indication in the past.

Considerations of general policy also seem to have influenced the case law of the TGI Paris, presented in section A.I.3.2, considering that a dosage form should not be patentable, on the grounds that it would impinge the physicians' freedom of prescription.

They also may have influenced the decisions finding Swiss-type claims invalid for insufficiency,[22] presented in section A.I.3: these decisions applied requirements

---

21. Paul Mathély, *Le nouveau droit français des brevets d'invention*, 1991, page 142.
22. Decisions finding patents invalid for insufficiency on the grounds that they are "*speculative*":

TGI Paris, chamber 3, section 1, 6 October 2009, *Teva v Sepracor*, PIBD 2010, No. 914III161, English translation available on www.frenchpatentcaselaw.info/:

> "In the pharmaceutical field, the sufficiency of disclosure of a drug invention entails the specification of pharmacologic properties and of one or several therapeutic uses.
>
> [...]
>
> Accordingly, Sepracor contented itself with speculating on the pharmaceutical usefulness of one of the two enantiomers.
>
> When legal texts require sufficient disclosure, they oblige the inventor, in pharmacology matters, not to prove the result, but to mention that this result was sought and exists.
>
> The absence of any mention of research and result proves the speculative nature of the patent application and, as a consequence, conceals the lack of inventive step."

TGI Paris, chamber 3, section 1, 9 November 2010, *Teva v Merck, Sharp & Dohme*, docket No. 09/12713, English translation available on www.frenchpatentcaselaw.info/:

> "In the field of pharmacology, the sufficiency of disclosure of the invention of a drug requires that the pharmacological properties and one or several therapeutic applications be indicated.
>
> Therefore, although in this field the inventor does not have to demonstrate the results, he must nevertheless state that this result has been sought and exists, that he carried out tests and experiments to demonstrate the alleged therapeutic effect. "

CA Paris, division 5, chamber 2, *Teva v Merck, Sharp & Dohme*, docket No. 10/23603, confirming TGI Paris, chamber 3, section 1, 9 November 2010, docket No. 09/12713, English translation available on www.frenchpatentcaselaw.info/:

> "It falls on the inventor to indicate that the result was sought and that it exists, using for that any information whether experimental or not, explaining and establishing the claimed pharmaceutical effect, as of the date of filing."

Decisions applying the same criteria but finding the requirement met:

CA Paris, division 5, chamber 1, 12 March 2014, *Eli Lilly v Teva*, docket No. 12/07203 (affirming TGI Paris, chamber 3, section 1, 20 March 2012, docket No. 09/12706):

> "Considering that the law provides no particular requirement as to the therapeutic inventions for which there is no need to request a description that would enable the person skilled in the art to deduce the pharmacological properties of the invention and its real possibilities of use;
>
> Considering that the indication of the pharmacological properties constitutes a sufficient description of the invention, if it is demonstrated that this result was sought and that it

diverging from those generally applicable when assessing sufficiency, notably by requiring that the specification of a drug invention mentions the pharmacological properties and one or several therapeutic uses, as well as technical information in support, such as experimental data or plausible explanations, and demonstrate that a result was searched for and exists; in the absence of these mentions, the patents were considered speculative and thus invalid.

2. Legal issues

Drugs are highly regulated products.

In French law, most provisions concerning health products can be found in the *Code de la santé publique*, the Public Health Code ("PHC"), and the *Code de la sécurité sociale*, the Social Security Code ("SSC").

These provisions can be of importance concerning infringement (see section C.).

B. VALIDITY

A change of patent category does not call for specific comments.

I. Allowable claim wording

1. Product claims

Concerning first therapeutic use of a known product, the guidelines of the INPI governing the grant of French patents provide, by reference to Article L.611-11 IPC, that a first therapeutic indication is patentable, and that it should be drafted as follows:

> "Substance or composition X, followed by the indication of the use, for example, '... for the use as a medicinal product' or '... for use as an antibacterian' or '... for the treatment of condition Y'."

It should be noted that a first medical use claim can protect the product for any use of the product as a drug.

Concerning second therapeutic use, before the entry into force of the 2008 Act, the INPI accepted Swiss-type claims for second therapeutic indications.

Since the entry into force of the 2008 Act, the INPI guidelines provide that a second therapeutic indication is patentable and give the following drafting example:

> "An example of claim drafting acceptable for the second therapeutic use could be formulated as follows: 'Substance or composition containing compound X for its use in the treatment of condition Y'."[23]

---

exists; in this particular case, the contemplated pharmacological results and therapeutic application were the object of research the examples of which are disclosed on pages 16 to 21 of the description;"

23. Guidelines of the French patent office, title I, section C, chapter VII, point 4.2.f:

The INPI no longer accepts Swiss-type claims.

The new drafting will be referred to as "purpose-limited product claim", following the terminology used by the EPO.

Accordingly, a second therapeutic application can be claimed only with reference to a specific therapeutic use.

2. *Method claims*

Claims referring to a "method of use" or "treatment method" were never accepted by the INPI, due to the non-patentability of treatment methods.

3. *Use claims*

Claims referring to the "use of a substance X for the treatment of Y" were never accepted in France either, as they would be considered as covering a treatment method.

4. *System claims*

A system claim will be dealt with either as a product claim or a use claim depending on the meaning of the word "system" in a given context.

"f) *Therapeutic use*

The Code does not exclude the patentability of a substance or composition comprised in the state of the art on condition that its therapeutic use is not comprised in the state of the art.

The code neither excludes the patentability of a substance or composition referred to above for any specific use, on condition that this use is not comprised in the state of the art.

First therapeutic use

A claim concerning a known substance or composition that would be used for the first time in therapy should be formulated as follows: 'Substance or composition X', followed by the indication of the use, for example, '... for the use as a medicinal product ' or '... for use as an antibacterian ' or '... for the treatment of condition Y'.

These types of claims will be interpreted as being limited to the substance or the composition such as presented in view of the use. These are claims relating to a first therapeutic use of the substance or the composition.

Second (and subsequent) therapeutic use

When a substance or composition is already known for a therapeutic use, a claim relating to a different use, which is not described in the state of the art, will not be rejected for lack of novelty. It is a claim relating to a second therapeutic use or a subsequent therapeutic use.

The use not comprised in the state of the art will be considered new, regardless of the fact that other uses in therapy were already known.

An example of claim drafting acceptable for the second therapeutic use could be formulated as follows: 'Substance or composition containing compound X for its use in the treatment of condition Y'".

5. *Dosage regimes*

To date, the INPI has not accepted claims purporting to a dosage regime.[24]

The INPI's guidelines refer in this respect to the decision by the TGI Paris dated 28 September 2010, in *Actavis v Merck*, concerning a patent claiming a dosage of finasteride,[25] presented in section A.I.3.1.

6. *Patient groups*

Several French decisions admitted the possibility of claims limited to a specific patient group:

- the order by the TGI Paris dated 12 January 2010, in *Sepracor and Aventis v Teva*,[26] concerning European patent No. 0 701 443 on fexofenadine, where the claimed use was limited to a "a human patient whose hepatic function is not impaired"; this claim did not raise particular objections from the court which however specified that such limitation should be based on tests to demonstrate inventive step;
- the decision by the TGI Paris dated 20 March 2012, in *Teva v Eli Lilly*, concerning Lilly's European patent No. 0 584 952, where claim 1 had been limited to a group of patients corresponding to post-menopausal women, admitted the patentability of such a claim,[27] confirmed on appeal;[28]
- the decision by the CA Paris dated 15 February 2013, in *Merck v French patent office*,[29] holding that Merck could obtain an SPC based on a marketing authorisation for the virus varicella zoster as a vaccine for the prevention of zoster, despite the existence of a previous marketing authorisation for a different application, while claim 1 of the basic patent purported to a

24. Guidelines of the INPI, title 1, section C, chapter VII, 2.1.1 b:

    "Are thus likely to be rejected [...] a claim concerning the dosage regime of a medicinal product [...], TGI Paris, 28/09/2010, *Actavis Group v Merck Sharp & Dohme*
25. TGI Paris, chamber 3, section 1, 28 September 2010, *Actavis v Merck Sharp & Dohme*, docket No. 07/16296, English translation available on www.frenchpatentcaselaw.info/.
26. TGI Paris, order in preliminary injunction proceedings, 12 January 2010, *Aventis, Sepracor v Teva*, docket No. 09/56031.

    There is no appeal decision in this case.
27. TGI Paris, chamber 3, section 1, 20 March 2012, *Teva Santé and Teva Pharmaceutical Industries v Eli Lilly*, docket No. 09/12706, English translation available on www.french-patentcaselaw.info/.
28. CA Paris, division 5, chamber 1, 12 March 2014, *Teva Santé* and *Teva Pharmaceutical Industries v Eli Lilly*, docket No. 12/07203:

    "Considering furthermore that the first-instance judges rightly noted that Eli Lilly had limited the scope of its claim to post-menauposal women for protecting a medicinal product suitable for a particular section of the population which alone suffers from this condition owing to gender and the fact that the effect of oestrogens has ceased because of their disappearance caused by the menopause, whether is it natural or surgical."
29. CA Paris, division 5, chamber 2, 15 February 2013, *Merck v French patent office*, PIBD No. *982-III-1131*.

specific patient group corresponding to "a person older than fifty who has had varicella or who has had a live varicella vaccine".

II. Novelty

1. General definition of novelty and prior art

The novelty requirement in French law, defined by Article L. 611-11 IPC, is the same as that provided by Article 54 EPC.

2. Definition of the skilled person

The skilled person is the one possessing the ordinary knowledge and skills of the relevant field; it may also be a team when the invention requires combined skills in several fields.[30]

3. Scope of disclosure

3.1 General rules

To be comprised in the state of the art and deprived of novelty, the invention must be disclosed entirely in a single prior art reference, with the same elements composing it in the same form, the same arrangement, and the same function to achieve the same result.[31]

3.2 First medical use

For a first medical use, the general rules for assessment of novelty of a use of known means apply, i.e. that said use shall not have been disclosed before the priority date.

3.3 New subject-matter

There are no specific issues with respect to new subject-matter.

3.4 New data

New data would not be sufficient to confer novelty on a known therapeutic use.

30. TGI Paris, chamber 3, section 3, 14 January 2009, *Abbott v Evysio*, PIBD No. 2009, 901-III-1267.
TGI Paris, 3rd ch., 3rd s, 25 March 2009, *Novartis v Johnson & Johnson*, docket No. 07/13504.
TGI Paris, 3rd ch., 23 May 2013, *The General Hospital v Clinipro*, docket n° 11/18480, English translation available on www.frenchpatentcaselaw.info/.
31. Cass. Com., 6 June 2001, *Galverpor v Technel and Hervé Dartois*, PIBD 2001, No. 726-III-427.

4. *Requirements for second medical use*

To assess the novelty of a second therapeutic use, the criterion should be whether this second use of the known means was disclosed in the prior art.

As an example, the CA Paris, 4th chamber, section B, in the decision of 22 September 2006, *Laboratoire de contactologie appliquée v Alcon*, concerning Alcon's European patent No. 0 705 095 on combinations of viscoelastics for use during surgery held that claim 1 would be invalid for lack of novelty, on the grounds that the two viscoelastic agents were claimed for their respective known use, without a new use being mentioned.[32]

4.1 *Distinction from first medical use*

French case law suggests that a second medical use is more difficult to establish when the disease is the same and when the difference between the first and the second use relates to aspects such as side effects.

4.2 *Sub-species of first medical use*

The comments above apply *mutatis mutandis*.

4.3 *Dosage regimes*

A dosage regime will be new if such dosage and its technical effect were not disclosed in the prior art.

The CA Paris, in its decision dated 30 January 2015 about finasteride, admitting the principle of patentability of a new dosage form of a known product for the same therapeutic use as in the prior art, provided this new dosage reflects a different technical teaching, considered that MSD's patent was invalid for lack of novelty as the claimed use of 0.05 to 1 mg of finasteride for the treatment of androgenic alopecia was disclosed in the prior art and the patent did not specify a technical teaching different from the prior art.[33]

4.4 *Special patient groups*

A claim to a limited specific patient group will be new if the use of the drug for the said patient group was not disclosed in the prior art.

In the 12 January 2010 order in preliminary injunction proceedings, in *Sepracor and Aventis v Teva* concerning European patent No. 0 701 443 on fexofenadine, the judge considered that the claimed use limited to "a human patient whose hepatic function is not impaired" by way of a disclaimer had serious chances to be found invalid for lack of novelty in the proceedings on the merits, as the prior art disclosed

32. CA Paris, chamber 4, section B, 22 September 2006, *Laboratoire de contactologie appliquée v Alcon*, docket No. 04/19659.
33. CA Paris, division 5, chamber 2, 30 January 2015, *Merck Sharp & Dohme v Actavis*, docket No. 10/23603.

the use of fexofenadine as an antihistaminic drug for any patient without limitation, thus necessarily including those with hepatic problems, and considering that the validity of disclaimers was subject to debate.[34]

In *Teva v Eli Lilly*,[35] concerning Lilly's European patent No. 0 584 952 on the use of benzotiophenes in osteoporosis, claim 1 of the patent in dispute had been limited to a group of patients corresponding to post-menopausal women; it was held both in first instance and on appeal that the prior art documents did not disclose the use of raloxifene for the treatment of osteoporosis in post-menopausal women; the patent was, however, revoked for lack of inventive step.

5. *Timing issues*

French case law does not provide specific teachings about timing issues.

III. Inventive step/non-obviousness

1. *Definition of inventive step/non-obviousness*

The definition of inventive step is presented in Article L. 611-14 IPC, which has the same wording as Article 56 EPC.

The definition of the skilled person is the same as for novelty.

To determine whether an invention is obvious, French courts increasingly rely on an approach similar to the problem–solution approach of the EPO; the wording of French decisions on inventive step, however, is less formal.

2. *Same scope of disclosure as for novelty?*

The French rules for French patents are identical to the rules of the EPC.

3. *Assessment of inventive step/non-obviousness*

As an illustration of assessment of inventive step, two decisions are summarised:

- the decision by the TGI Paris, 3rd chamber, 3rd section, dated 5 December 2014, in the infringement proceedings between Akzo Nobel and Teva concerning MSD's SPC based on European patent No. 0 491 443 relating to a contraceptive preparation containing progestogen in a specific daily dosage from 70 to 80 micrograms: according to the patent, the invention consisted in increasing the known daily dosage of 50 micrograms to obtain a complete inhibition of ovulation while avoiding secondary effects; the court considered that the patent was deprived of inventive step over the prior art which disclosed a

34. TGI Paris, order in preliminary injunction proceedings, 12 January 2010, *Aventis, Sepracor v Teva*, docket No. 09/56031.
35. CA Paris, division 5, chambre 1, 12 March 2014, *Teva Santé* and *Teva Pharmaceutical Industries v Eli Lilly*.

complete inhibition with a dosage of 60 micrograms, as nothing prevented the skilled person from checking with routine operations whether a slightly higher dosage would increase efficacy while avoiding secondary effects;

- in the decision by the CA Paris, dated 12 March 2014, in *Teva v Eli Lilly*, Lilly's patent relating to the use of raloxifene against osteoporosis of post-menopausal women was found deprived of inventive step on the grounds that the skilled person knew from the prior art that raloxifene had positive effects for the prevention of osteoporosis in rats, which could be transposed to humans, and that the first anti-estrogen, tamoxifen, which raloxifene followed, was efficient in treating osteoporosis in post-menopausal women; the judges considered that no obstacle to overcome would have discouraged the skilled person from using raloxifene to treat osteoporosis in a post-menopausal woman, the only document considering that raloxifene would not have such effect being an isolated opinion not followed, and even criticised, by the scientific community, whereas the bioavailability of raloxifene would amount to a mere routine work on the dosage for the drug.

IV. Amendment of claims after grant

Added matter, sufficiency and multiple indications do not call for specific comments with respect of second medical use and are thus not considered in this section.

1. Admissibility of post-grant amendments in general

The 4 August 2008 Act introduced the post-grant amendment of a patent into French law.

Article L. 613-24 IPC governs the amendment procedure of a French patent before the INPI.

Articles L. 613-25 and L. 614-12 IPC concern the amendment of a French patent and a European patent in revocation proceedings respectively.

2. Procedural issues

2.1 Independent limitation proceedings

Under Article L. 613-24 IPC, a patentee can request the limitation of a French patent before the INPI; he can also request the INPI to limit the French designation of a European patent.[36]

Central limitation of a European patent before the EPO is also an option.

2.2 Opposition proceedings

The limitation of the claims of the French designation of a European patent remains possible even if the patent is the subject matter of an opposition pending before

36. CA Paris, division 5, chamber 2, 1 July 2011, *Teva v Eli Lilly*, PIBD No. 948-III-598.

the EPO, as held in a decision by the CA Paris, dated 26 June 2015, in *Honeywell v Arkema.*[37]

2.3 Nullity actions

Limitation can be done in revocation or infringement proceedings, at any stage.

In *Lilly v Teva,*[38] claim 1 of Lilly's patent was amended during the proceedings to limit it to a group of patients corresponding to post-menopausal women; Teva challenged the validity of the patent notably on the grounds that it would constitute an extension over the patent application as filed, but this argument was dismissed as the court considered that the patent specification referred to any menopausal women and was not restricted to elderly women, contrary to what Teva had argued.

Similarly, in *Mylan v Gedeon Richter,*[39] the patent claims originally granted were amended before litigation, to specify the dosage of 1.5 mg of levonorgestrel to be taken in a single dose; the limitation did not raise specific attacks from Mylan.

C. INFRINGEMENT AND LITIGATION

I. Legal framework

1. National statutory laws

The provisions on patent infringement are contained in the IPC; national law was harmonised with the European Union directives and regulations, notably Directive 2004/48/EC of 25 April 2004 on the enforcement of intellectual property rights.

Article L. 613-3 IPC governs direct infringement and Article L. 613-4 IPC indirect infringement, while Article L. 613-5 IPC sets out a list of exempted acts.

2. Case law

French courts are known for having a broad concept of infringement.

Case law distinguishes three main forms of infringement:

- literal infringement ("*contrefaçon à l'identique*"), i.e. the reproduction of each and every feature of the claim, taken in its structure, function and result;
- infringement by reproduction of the essential means ("*contrefaçon par reproduction des moyens essentiels*"), i.e. the reproduction of the new and inventive means which are necessary to perform the function of the invention, despite minor differences;
- and infringement under the doctrine of equivalents ("*contrefaçon par équivalence*"), i.e. means which differ from the patented means by their

37. CA Paris, division 5, Chamber 2, 26 June 2015, *Honeywell v Arkema*, TG No. 14/23888, English translation available on www.frenchpatentcaselaw.info/.
38. CA Paris, division 5, chambre 1, 12 March 2014, *Teva Santé* and *Teva Pharmaceutical Industries v Eli Lilly*, docket No. 12/07203.
39. TGI Paris, chamber 3, section 3, 19 June 2015, *Mylan v Richter Gedeon*, docket No. 13/08566.

structure but perform the same function for the same result (see section C.III.5).

II. Claim construction

1. General rules

Patent construction is governed by Article 69 EPC for the French designation of European patents and by Article L. 613-2 IPC for national patents, which provide that "the extent of the protection conferred by a patent shall be determined by the terms of the claims" but that "nevertheless, the description and the drawing shall be used to interpret the claims".

Construction of the specification and of the claims is usually discussed first.

French judges' approach is purposive in that they aim to give full meaning to the claim and to define the substance of the claimed invention by understanding, with the eyes of the skilled person, the technical problem solved by the patent, the means taught to solve the said problem and their function.[40]

The scope given to the claims is the same for validity and infringement.

2. Specific issues for use claims

Use claims are dealt with as process claims. Swiss-type claims belong to use claims. But claims protecting a compound for a second therapeutic use correspond to product claims. In both cases, it is necessary to prove the infringing use of the accused product.

III. Scope of protection

This section deals with the scope of the claim only; liability for infringement will be considered in section C.IV.

---

40. The French approach was notably defined by the decision issued by the court of appeal of Paris on 11 October 1990 in the first case involving a European patent, in 1990 (*Dolle v Emsens*):

> "Article 69, as completed by its protocol, has chosen a middle way between a literal construction of the claim, in which the description and the drawings should be used only to dissipate ambiguities, and a broad construction in which the claim would be used just as a guideline and in which the protection would extend to what, according to the skilled person, the patentee has intended to protect.
>
> This compromise must ensure a fair protection for the patentee against the skill of the infringer to disguise infringement and enable third parties to know with certainty what is protected.
>
> In view of Article 69, the judge must construe the claims by reference to the description and to the drawings.
>
> He must give to the claim its full meaning, so that this condensed text is understood.
>
> The construction leads to define the substance of the claimed invention, without adding any element which the claim did not include and did not suggest."

1. *Scope of the use*

1.1 *General definition of the term "use"*

The provisions of the IPC on patents distinguish between product claims and process claims but do not refer to use claims; a use claim is considered as a process claim, and thus is governed by the same rules concerning scope of protection and infringement.

A distinction should be drawn between:

- a second medical use claim drafted in Swiss-type form, comprising a reference to the manufacturing step: "use of a substance or composition X for the manufacture of a medicament for therapeutic application Z";
- and a purpose-limited claim following the new authorised drafting which covers a product: "product X for use in the treatment of Z".

1.2 *Manufacture of the pharmaceutical*

The mere manufacture of the product infringes both a Swiss-type claim and a purpose-limited product claim if the manufacturer is aware that the product is intended for the patented use (see section C.IV on infringing acts).

1.3 *Sale of the product*

Article L. 613-3 a) IPC on direct infringement refers to the "putting on the market" of the product, which is broader than the term "sale", as it covers any act of making a product available, either free of charge or against payment, and either temporarily or definitively.

The putting on the market of a product would be within the scope of a Swiss-type claim or a purpose-limited product claim if it is done with reference to the claimed use (see section C.IV.).

1.4 *Offer for sale*

The term "offer" corresponds to a proposition, announcement or preparation to put a product on the market.

The notion of offer for sale, or more broadly putting on the market, is construed broadly by case law as encompassing acts putting a product in contact with the public, even when the product is not available in France, unless it is explicitly indicated that the product is not available to the public in France or in any other country covered by a patent.[41]

41. TGI Paris, chamber 3, 19 September 1997, *Aktiebolaget Hassle and Laboratoires Astra France v Chong Kun Dang*, PIBD 1998, No. 645III4: this decision construed broadly the terms "*putting into the market*" of Article L. 6133 IPC as encompassing the circulation of any document putting a product into contact with the market.

CA Paris, 19 November 1997, *Aktiebolaget Hassle and Laboratoires Astra France v Lek DD Ljubljana*, PIBD 1998, No. 647III69 and Cass. Com., 30 January 2001, *Lek DD Ljubljana v*

As for the act of sale or putting on the market, the offer would fall within the scope of a Swiss-type claim or purpose-limited product claim only if performed with reference to the patented use (see section C.IV).

1.5 Application to the patient

Prescription and administration of the drug do not correspond to any of the infringement acts triggering liability (see section C.IV).

1.6 Combination products

A combination product (for example A + B) would infringe a claim referring to A or B. Conversely, product A would not infringe a claim referring to A + B.

2. Absolute product protection

2.1 Limitation through the term "use"

A product claim grants the patentee a monopoly on the product as such, for any use of the product, regardless of its manufacturing process and its intended or effective use; the patentee can prevent non-authorised third parties from manufacturing, offering, putting on the market, using, importing, exporting, transshiping, or holding for the above-mentioned purposes, a product that is the subject of the patent (see section C.IV.2. on direct infringement).

The exclusive right conferred by a Swiss-type claim or a purpose-limited product claim is much narrower as the claim includes a feature in relation to a specific use.

As indicated in section B.I.3, for a first medical use of a known product, it is possible to claim the medical use of the product in general, without limiting it to a specific use; on the contrary, for second medical uses, it is required to identify the specific medical use, so that the scope of such claims is much narrower.

It should be noted that for inventions on the use of a product, issues of dependency with respect to previous patents on the product or a first use thereof may arise:

- when the product for which a new use is claimed is protected as such by a previous patent in force, the patent on the new use will be dependent on the first one;

Aktiebolaget Hassle and Laboratoires Astra France, PIBD 2001, No. 723III329: the court held that Lek was liable for infringement because it presented documents concerning a drug at an exhibition and thus, although Lek did not offer the product for sale at the exhibition, the drug was presented to potential clients who could engage in business with Lek.

TGI Paris, 22 December 2006, *Evysio v Abbott and Guidant,* PIBD 2007, No. *848*III201: this decision held that Article L. 6133 IPC "encompasses any act intended to put a product in contact with a relevant public and it covers any presentation of the product even if the marketing is not immediately effective".

- when a first medical use patent covers any use of the product as a drug, the second patent claiming a second specific therapeutic use will be dependent on the first one.

2.2 Off-label use

Off-label use of a drug refers to a use of a drug which was not authorised by the regulatory agencies and is thus not on the package leaflet of the drug.

Skinny labelling, or carving out, means that an indication, although authorised for the reference drug, is not included in the summary of product characteristics for the generic drug because it is covered by a patent.

An off-label use of a drug will be covered by the first or second medical use patent claiming such use; the fact that the actual use of the product is authorised by the regulatory authorities or is off-label is irrelevant.

The difficulty will be to evidence the off-label use of a product to demonstrate infringement (see section C.IV).

3. Dosage regimes

A claim on a dosage regime confers narrower protection than a product claim as its scope is limited to the use of the product following said dosage regime.

4. Patient groups

Similarly, a claim limited to a patient group will have a narrow scope as compared to a product claim as it covers only the use of the product in relation to the specific patient group mentioned in the claim.

5. Extension under the doctrine of equivalents

The doctrine of equivalents applies to all categories of inventions, including first and second therapeutic use patents; it may also be relevant concerning biologic and biosimilar drugs.

Under the doctrine of equivalents, means which differ from the patented means by their structure are infringing if they perform the same function with the same result:

- the "function" designates the primary technical effect (which can be defined as the effect directly and immediately produced by the implementation of the patented means) and should be distinguished from the advantages of the invention;[42]
- the "result" is defined as the advantages provided by the means; it should be pointed out that two means are considered as having the same result when

42. Cass. Com., 26 January 1993, *Hovione, Sarget and Plantier v Pfizer*, PIBD 1993, No. 542III256.

they have a result of the same nature, so that two means will be considered as having the same result despite a difference in quality or degree.[43]

It happens that French judges also take into account the way in which the patented means perform their function.

The doctrine of equivalents can apply only if the claimed means perform a novel function:

- if the claimed means differ from the prior art only by their structure, then the scope of the claim is limited to the claimed structure (or variants reproducing its essential features): the doctrine of equivalents cannot apply;[44]
- if the claimed means differ from the prior art not only by their structure, but also by their function, the scope of the claims extends to any other structure performing the same function for the same result: in this case, the claim is said to cover "general means" ("*moyen général*") and the doctrine of equivalents can apply.

French judges do not take into account whether or not the accused variant was obvious to the skilled person.

Furthermore, in general, French judges do not take into account whether or not the patentee intended to cover the accused variant; nevertheless, the doctrine of equivalents does not apply when the patent explicitly and unambiguously excludes the variant from its scope, or when the variant goes directly and unambiguously against the teaching of the patent.

IV. Infringing acts

1. *Infringing person or entity*

Under French law, the acts of infringement of Articles L. 613-3 and L. 613-4 IPC and the exceptions to infringement of Article L. 613-5 IPC are defined objectively, with reference to specific acts, and not to persons or entities.

---

43. Until recently, French case law considered that the result obtained by the means at issue had to be similar, without necessarily being identical: as a consequence, the result could be of a different quality (less perfect, or higher or poorer) or of a different degree than the result obtained by the patented means.

    However, a few recent decisions considered that the result shall be of "the same nature and of identical quality and efficacy" (TGI Paris, chamber 3, section 1, 3 April 2014, *Société d'équipement pour l'environnement v Rabaud*, PIBD 2014, No. 1010III597 and TGI Paris, chamber 3, section 3, 22 November 2013, *Manitou v Haulotte*, docket No. 10/10117).

44. Cass. Com., 16 April 2013, *Cycles Lapierre and Lesage v Decathlon and Promiles*, PIBD 2013, No. 986III1243.

    CA Paris, division 5, chamber 1, 26 September 2012, *Beaba v Seb France and Tefal*, PIBD 2012, No. 972III735.

    CA Paris, division 5, chamber 2, 17 June 2011, *Salomon v Merrell and Wolverine Worldwide*, docket No. 09/09418.

Thus, in theory, any person or entity can be held liable, as long as the material element of infringement (i.e. the act of infringement), in some cases the moral element (*i.e.* knowledge of the facts), and the legal element are established.

The persons and entities involved in the manufacturing and sale of a drug correspond to the manufacturer of the active ingredient, the manufacturer of the drug, the importer, the distributor, the pharmacist; their liability will be examined in sections C.IV.2 on direct infringement and C.IV.3 on indirect infringement.

Although no specific exceptions apply to physicians, who could in theory be liable for infringement, the acts performed by physicians, the prescription of the drug, or its administration to the patient, do not constitute one of the infringement acts presented in sections C.IV.2 and C.IV.3 below.

All the persons performing infringing acts can be held liable independently of each other.

In the case of a pharmaceutical group, the liability of each of the companies involved has to be demonstrated separately.

2. *Direct infringement*

Acts of direct infringement of a patent covering a product are exhaustively listed in Article L. 613-3 IPC; they consist in:

a) for a patented product, manufacturing, offering, putting on the market, using, importing, exporting, transshiping, or holding for the above-mentioned purposes of the product;
b) for a patented process, the utilisation of the process or, when the third party knows or when the circumstances make it clear that the use of the process is prohibited without the consent of the owner of the patent, the offer of its use on French territory;
c) for the product directly obtained from a patented process, the offer, the putting on the market, use, import, export, transshipment or holding for the above-mentioned purpose of the product.

A Swiss-type claim corresponds to a process claim, so that only § b) and c) of Article L. 613-3 IPC concerning a patented process and a product obtained through this process apply, whereas a purpose-limited claim is a product claim.

As far as liability is concerned, a distinction has to be made between primary and secondary infringers:

- acts of manufacture and importation of an infringing product trigger the liability of the infringer, irrespective of its good faith;
- acts of offering for sale, putting on the market, using, holding with a view to use or putting on the market an infringing product, committed by a person other than the manufacturer or the importer, require the demonstration that they have acted with the knowledge of the alleged infringement .[45]

45. Article L. 615-1 IPC.

Concerning a patented process, its use triggers liability irrespective of the good faith of its user; however, the offer for use of a patented process can be held infringing only upon the demonstration that the third party offering it knew or should have known that its use was prohibited.

2.1 *Manufacture of the pharmaceutical*

The manufacture of a pharmaceutical for a patented use would infringe a purpose-limited product claim under Article L. 613-3 § a) IPC.

According to Article L. 613-3 § b) IPC, the use of the process constitutes an infringement; thus, the manufacturer could be liable of infringement of a Swiss-type claim if it manufactures the drug for the patented use.

In *Warner Lambert v Sandoz*, concerning pregabalin ("the pregabalin case"), in the presence of a Swiss-type claim, the judge held that Article L. 613-3 § b), concerning the use and offer for use of a patented process, could be asserted only against the manufacturer, not the distributor.[46]

2.2 *Offer for sale*

The offer for sale of the drug for a patented use would infringe a purpose-limited product claim, under Article L. 613-3 a) IPC.

Following Article L. 613-3 c) IPC, the offer for sale of a product directly obtained by a patented process is prohibited, so that infringement of a Swiss-type claim would also be constituted; in the pregabalin case, the judge considered that Article L. 613-3 c) could be asserted against the distributor of the drug; it considered that in this case the offer for sale of the drug for the patented use, which was carved out, was not demonstrated.[47]

When it is done by a person other than the manufacturer or the importer, an offer for sale can be considered infringing only if it is demonstrated that this person acted with the knowledge of the alleged infringement .

The entity whose liability would be at stake in an infringement action corresponds, in the first place, to the pharmaceutical company offering for sale the infringing drugs to the pharmacists.

---

46. TGI Paris, order in PI proceedings, 26 October 2015, *Warner Lambert, Pfizer v Sandoz*, docket No. 15/58725, page 16, English translation available on www.frenchpatentcaselaw.info/:

    "It is established that the conditions in subparagraphs a and b of Article L. 613-3 of the French Intellectual Property Code are not applicable to the present case since subparagraph a) relates to a product claim and since subparagraph b) relating to a process invention can only be asserted against the manufacturer.

    In the case of (c), it should be established whether the offer for sale by Sandoz France of the product obtained using the process and manufactured outside France, and the import of that product by Sandoz GmbH, are in breach of the conditions of (b)."

47. TGI Paris, order in PI proceedings, 26 October 2015, *Warner Lambert, Pfizer v Sandoz*, docket No. 15/58725, English translation available on www.frenchpatentcaselaw.info/.

When the indication corresponding to the patented use is that appearing in the marketing authorisation, evidence of infringement is much easier to provide than in case of off-label use or skinny labelling (see section C.IV.4).

Infringement can be evidenced by any means, such as commercial documents, advertisements, letters to pharmacists, or press releases.

A *saisie-contrefaçon*, performed on the premises of the pharmaceutical company or the *Agence nationale de sécurité du medicament et des produits de santé* ("ANSM"), the French Health Agency, can be used to obtain evidence of infringement.[48]

To fulfil the requirement of knowledge of the alleged infringement, the sending of a warning letter or the service of summons may be necessary.

In the second place, the pharmacists offering for sale the drug to the patient could also be held liable if their knowledge of the use of the drug for the patented use was demonstrated; however, in France, the indication of the treatment is not indicated on the prescription so that generally pharmacists are not aware of the use of the drugs they sell.

2.3 Sale

The explanations concerning the offer for sale also apply to the sale of a drug for the patented use.

2.4 Export

Under Article L. 613-3 a) IPC, exporting would constitute infringement of a purpose-limited product claim.

It results from Article L. 613-3 c) IPC that the act of exporting of the product directly obtained by a patented process can constitute infringement of a Swiss-type claim.

The exporter is liable for infringement only if its knowledge of the alleged infringement is demonstrated, as it is the case for a mere distributor (and in contrast with the situation of the manufacturer and the importer).

2.5 Import

The above explanations concerning export also apply to import.

2.6 Use

A purpose-limited product claim would be infringed by the use of a product covered by the claim under Article L. 613-3 a) IPC.

---

48. *Saisie-contrefaçon*, governed by Article L. 615-5 IPC, is a probative measure allowing a patentee to have a bailiff conduct investigations on the premises of the seized party in order to gather evidence of the alleged infringement; it is a preliminary step in almost all patent cases.
In several cases, saisies were performed in the premises of the ANSM.

Under Article L. 613-3 c) IPC, the unauthorised use would also amount to infringement of a Swiss-type claim.

Use by a person other than the manufacturer or the importer can be considered infringing only if it is demonstrated that it acted with knowledge of the alleged infringement .

The term "use" is very broad and encompasses any kind of use, it being recalled that "acts done privately and for non-commercial purposes" constitute one of the exceptions to infringement listed in Article L. 613-5 IPC and that exhaustion of rights may apply in some circumstances (see section C.VI below).

Use by the patient would fall within the exception of the acts done privately and for non-commercial purposes of Article L. 613-5 IPC.

2.7 Holding

Holding, for example stockpiling, for the purpose of offering, putting on the market, exporting, importing, using, a patented product or a product directly obtained through an unauthorised process is an act of infringement under Article L. 613-3 a) and c) IPC respectively.

When it is done by a person other than the manufacturer or the importer, it can be considered infringing only if it is demonstrated that they have acted with the knowledge of the alleged infringement .

2.8 Combination products

For a combination product, liability for direct infringement will follow the same rules as for any product.

3. ***Indirect infringement***

Acts of indirect infringement, or contributory infringement, are defined by Article L. 613-4 IPC prohibiting the "supply or offer to supply, on the French territory, to a person other than a person entitled to exploit the patented invention, the means of implementing, on that territory, the invention with respect to an essential element thereof where the third party knows, or it is obvious from the circumstances, that such means are suitable for putting and are intended to put the invention into effect."

Article L. 613-4 § 2 specifies that the supply of staple commercial products amounts to contributory infringement when the supplier induces the person supplied to commit infringement acts prohibited by Article L. 613-3 IPC.

3.1 Objective acts

The objective acts of contributory infringement consist in the supply or offer to supply of the means for implementing the invention with respect to an essential element thereof, to a person not entitled to exploit the patented invention; the means must be supplied in France and implemented in France.

In the case of a Swiss-type claim, the means, consisting in the active ingredient, or one of them in the case of a combination product, have to be supplied in France in view of the manufacturing in France of the product, so that only the supply to the manufacturer can be considered infringing.

In the pregabalin case,[49] the judge held that under Article L. 613-4 § 1 IPC, only the supply of the means to implement the patented process would be infringing, so that in this case where the liability of the distributor was at stake, it was considered that, under Article L. 613-4 § 2 IPC, only the supply of staple commercial products would constitute infringement; the judge held that a drug available on the market corresponds to a staple commercial product but that, in this case, inducement of physicians to prescribe the product, and of pharmacists to sell the product for the patented use, was not demonstrated.

In the case of a purpose-limited product claim, infringement could be constituted if the means are supplied for any infringing act, such as the sale of the drug.

3.2 *Subjective conditions*

Under Article L. 613-4 § 1 IPC, contributory infringement is constituted only when the third party knows, or it is obvious from the circumstances, that such means are suitable for putting, and are intended to put, the invention into effect.

The manufacturer of the active ingredient could be held liable if it can be demonstrated that it knows that the drug will be used for the patented used.

Article L. 613-4 § 2 IPC, concerning the supply of staple products, requires the demonstration of inducement.

3.3 *Export*

A double territorial requirement applies: the means must be supplied on the French territory, for use within that territory.

Thus, exportation of the active ingredient for manufacturing abroad cannot constitute contributory infringement.

---

49. TGI Paris, order in PI proceedings, 26 October 2015, *Warner Lambert, Pfizer v Sandoz*, docket No. 15/58725, English translation available on www.frenchpatentcaselaw.info/:

> "In this case, although Pfizer does not specify which subpararaph of Article L. 613-4 it is relying upon, it is clear, first, from reading its pleading and from oral presentations, and, second, from the "Swiss form" claims involved in this application, that the provisions of subpararaph (1) do not apply because Sandoz does not supply any third party in France with the means to exploit the protected process in France.
>
> Only subparagraph (2) might apply because the drugs in question are products that are readily commercially available.
>
> Thus, it has to be proven that Sandoz induced third parties, in this case doctors and pharmacists, to dispense the product manufactured pursuant to the process the provisions of Article L. 613-3 (c) of the Intellectual Property Code."

3.4 Import

There is no decision, at least for the time being, holding that the double territorial requirement of Article L. 613-4 § 1 IPC would be met when the infringing means are supplied abroad and the supplier is aware, or should be aware, that the final product is intended to come back to France.

3.5 Combination products

The supply of part of the means of a combination product could trigger liability for contributory infringement if all the conditions of Article L. 613-4 IPC, presented above, are met.

4. *Off-label use*

The French carve-out mechanism results from the implementation into French law of Directive 2001/83 as modified in 2004.

Article L. 5121-10 PHC provides that a marketing authorisation for a generic drug can be granted before the expiry of the intellectual property rights on the reference drug; the marketing authorisation holder has to inform the ANSM of the indication, pharmaceutical forms and dosage forms for which the intellectual property rights have not expired; the same provision exists for biosimilars.

Under Article R. 5121-29-2 PHC, when the ANSM is informed that certain indications are covered by the patent, it suppresses from the summary of product characteristics the parts referring to those indications, forms or dosages.

However, it should be noted that the mechanism of automatic substitution of generic drugs to reference drugs in France limits to some extent the efficacy of this provision:

- when a marketing authorisation is granted for a generic drug, within 60 days, the said generic drug is registered on the list of generic groups, or for a biosimilar the list of biosimilar groups; these lists do not refer to the authorised indications of the generics or biosimilars;
- the physician has the obligation to prescribe the drugs which are registered on the list of generic drugs with reference to their international non-proprietary names (INN), in accordance with Article L. 5125-23 PHC, notwithstanding the use for which they are prescribed;
- it results from the same provision that the pharmacist shall dispense a generic drug, when it is available, for any drug referred to in the prescription by its INN, unless the physician excluded this option on the prescription; in this respect, a decision of the *Conseil d'Etat* ("CE"), the highest administrative law court, held that pharmacists are authorised to substitute a generic drug to a reference drug, even when the marketing authorisations for the two drugs do not refer to the same therapeutic indications;[50] in any case, as the prescription does not mention the indication of the drug, the pharmacist

50. CE, 23 July 2003, case No. 246716, *Lilly*.

does not know it and will automatically substitute a generic drug for the reference one without considering the therapeutic indication.

The pregabalin case[51] concerns a scenario where the patented indication, i.e. the treatment of pain, had been carved out from the summary of product characteristics of Sandoz' generic.

The claimants, Warner-Lambert and Pfizer, contended that Sandoz' generic pregabalin was sold for the patented indication despite the skinny labelling on the marketing authorisation, and relied in particular on an advertisement by Sandoz, indicating the size of the potential market for its generic, as well as on data about the actual market share gained by Sandoz which, according to the claimants, exceeded the potential generic market for the non-patented indications of the drug.

The judge agreed that Sandoz' market share exceeded that of the authorised indications and concluded that physicians had prescribed and pharmacists had sold the drug for the non-authorised indications, but found that no infringement act, i.e. offer for sale, sale or importation, for the patented indication, was established, and that Sandoz complied with its obligations by carving out the indication covered by the patent from its generic's label and informing physicians and pharmacists that the generic should not be prescribed or dispensed for the treatment of pain, so that it could not be held liable for either direct or contributory infringement and dismissed the measures requested.

4.1 General admissibility of off-label use

As indicated in section C.III.1.4, the off-label use of a drug can constitute infringement of a first or second medical use claim; the fact that the actual use is not authorised from a regulatory point of view has in principle no consequence on liability for infringement.

In the pregabalin case, the judge considered that the sales of Sandoz' generic that should be taken into account to assess whether Sandoz' sales exceeded the market share of the generic for the non-patented indications, would be those relating to the treatment of pain in general, as the patent covered the use of pregabalin for the preparation of a pharmaceutical composition for treating pain, and not, contrary to Sandoz' position, only the sales specifically relating to neuropathic pain, corresponding to the indication of the reference drug; the judge confirmed that off-label use is not a relevant factor to an infringement claim, but a public health matter .[52]

---

51. TGI Paris, order in PI proceedings, 26 October 2015, *Warner Lambert, Pfizer v Sandoz*, docket No. 15/58725, English translation available on www.frenchpatentcaselaw.info/.
52. TGI Paris, order in PI proceedings, 26 October 2015, *Warner Lambert, Pfizer v Sandoz*, docket No. 15/58725, English translation available on www.frenchpatentcaselaw.info/:

    "However, although Pfizer only has a MA for the treatment of neuropathic pain, this action is based on Patent EP061, particularly claims 1 and 3, relating to the use of pregabalin in the preparation of a pharmaceutical composition for the treatment of pain and, more particularly for the treatment of neuropathic pain.

    Consequently, Pfizer's Patent EP061 covers pain treatment in the broad sense even if only one MA was issued for the treatment of neuropathic pain, so that Prégabaline Sandoz GmbH cannot be marketed for pain treatment in general.

The difficulty will be to evidence the actual use of the drug in the absence of the mention of its use on the leaflet and knowledge of the said use by the entity whose liability is at stake.

4.2 *Liable persons*

The liability regimes presented in section C.IV concerning direct and indirect infringement apply the same way in case of off-label use and skinny labelling, with the difficulty of demonstrating knowledge that the drug is aimed for an off-label use.

The entity of the pharmaceutical group which deals with the marketing authorisation necessarily knows the use of the product presented in the dossier.

However, the entity holding the marketing authorisation and the one offering the drug for sale may be distinct, and knowledge of the latter should specifically be demonstrated.

4.3 *Objective requirements for infringement*

The objective requirements for direct and indirect infringement presented above apply.

The proof of the material element of infringement can be difficult to obtain, in the absence of mention of the actual use of the drug on the leaflet.

4.4 *Subjective requirements for infringement*

The subjective requirements presented in section C.IV concerning direct and indirect infringement apply.

5. ***Dosage regimes***

The same general conditions apply for infringement of a claim on a dosage regime.

6. ***Patient groups***

The same general conditions apply, with the difficulty to demonstrate that the drug is intended for the patient groups referred to in the patent.

Although Lyrica may have been used by practitioners for a much broader range of pain, therefore outside the MA, this is not a relevant factor to an infringement claim (it is a public health matter).

Accordingly, the reference market to take into account with regard to the asserted claims is the global pain treatment market, i.e. 86 % of the pregabalin market, although, at this stage, Sandoz's objection that the patent cannot offer valid protection for all pain treatments should not be overlooked."

V. Remedies

1. *Injunctions*

In France, permanent injunctions are a remedy as of right in the case of a finding of infringement.

In the situation of a first or second medical use claim, the scope of the injunction has to be precisely drawn in order not to impinge on the non-patented use of the known product.

As an example, in the pregabalin case,[53] the claimants requested the limitation of the sales of the generics to a percentage reflecting the market share of the drug for the non-patented indications.

2. *Damages*

The award of damages aims to compensate the loss actually suffered due to infringement, corresponding to lost profits, in case the patent was exploited, or a reasonable royalty.

Article L. 615 7 IPC concerning damages also refers to the profits made by the infringer:

> "To set the amount of damages, the court distinctly takes into account: the negative economic consequences of the infringement, including the loss of earnings and any loss suffered by the injured party, the moral prejudice caused to the latter and the profits made by the infringer, including the savings in intellectual, material and promotional investments that it achieved from the infringement."

Thus, some decisions considered that the claimant can be granted the infringer's profits.[54]

Concerning first and second medical use claims, it is necessary to determine the sales and profits linked to the patented use and those made lawfully in respect of the non-patented use.

3. *Information*

To obtain information about the extent of infringement and the financial damage, two main tools are available: saisiecontrefaçon (Article L. 615-5 IPC) and right of information (Article L. 615-5-2 IPC).

---

53. TGI Paris, order in PI proceedings, 26 October 2015, *Warner Lambert, Pfizer v Sandoz*, docket No. 15/58725, English translation available on www.frenchpatentcaselaw.info/.
54. CA Paris, division 5, chamber 1, 23 January 2013, *TYC Europe v Valeo*, docket No. 10/13867.
TGI Paris, chamber 3, section 4, 24 January 2013, *Hydr Am v Gimaex and Weber Hydraulik*, docket No. 10/14541.
TGI Paris, chamber 3, section 1, 14 November 2013, *Time Sport International v JCR*, docket No. 11/16713.

3.1 *Names of manufacturers, distributors etc.*

Information about the names of manufacturers and distributors can be obtained in the context of a *saisie* and of the exercise of the right of information.

3.2 *Names of customers*

The names of customers will generally not be disclosed as they constitute very sensitive information.

3.3 *Information about infringing sales*

Concerning a second medical use patent, only the sales relating to the patented indication will be relevant, which requires in determining which sales were made for that specific use.

3.4 *Account of profits*

Similarly, only the profits linked to the patented use will be relevant.

4. *Recall of products and destruction*

Article L. 615-7-1 IPC makes it possible for the claimant to request the recall of infringing products from the channels of commerce as well as their confiscation and destruction; it can be requested both in preliminary injunction proceedings or proceedings on the merits, but is not frequently ordered since it has severe consequences both on the infringer and its distributors.

The recall and destruction of products, as a result of a finding of infringement of a second medical use claim, could be authorised only for the products pertaining to the patent use.

As an illustration, in the pregabalin case,[55] the claimants had requested the recall of the products exceeding a percentage of units deemed acceptable in consideration of the market share for the non-patented indications of the generic.

5. *Recovery of legal costs*

The successful party can recover part of its attorneys' fees, the amount being up to the discretion of the judge.

55. TGI Paris, order in PI proceedings, 26 October 2015, *Warner Lambert, Pfizer v Sandoz*, docket No. 15/58725, English translation available on www.frenchpatentcaselaw.info/.

VI. Exceptions from patent protection

1. Exhaustion of rights

According to Article L. 613-6 IPC, the introduction of the patented product within the European economic area by the patentee or with the patentee's consent exhausts the patentee's rights.

French case law requires that there be express consent of the patentee.

2. Patient welfare

Patient welfare or public health considerations do not constitute exceptions to the exclusive right of the patentee and do not prevent, in principle, an injunction.

They could also be taken into account when assessing the balance of interests in preliminary injunction proceedings.

3. Others specific to second medical use claims

Article L. 613-5 IPC sets out a list of exempted acts.

Under § a) of this Article, acts done privately and for noncommercial purpose, such as the use of a drug by a patient, are exempted; it should be stressed that the requirements of a private and non-commercial use are cumulative.

Article L. 613-5 d) corresponds to the French "Bolar exemption" resulting from the introduction into French law of the exception provided for in Article 10 § 6 of Directive No. 2001/83/EC of 6 November 2001 .[56]

The French Bolar exemption is not limited to marketing authorisations for generic and biosimilar drugs, but also applies for innovator drugs, and applies not only to the acts performed to obtain a marketing authorisation for France or countries within the European Union, but also for other countries.[57]

VII. Procedural issues

1. Preliminary injunction cases

Preliminary injunction proceedings, governed by Article L. 615-3 IPC, can be started to prevent imminent infringement or prohibit the defendant from continuing the infringement.

Preliminary injunctions can be ordered "only if evidence, reasonably accessible to the claimant, make it likely that its rights are infringed or that such infringement is about to be committed"; thus, the judge takes into consideration the arguments of the parties as to the alleged infringement and also as to the validity of the asserted patent.

56. Directive No. 2001/83/EC of 6 November 2001 establishing a Community code for medicinal products for human use as amended by Directive 2004/27/EC of 31 March 2004.
57. TGI Paris, presiding judge, 15 December 2014, *SanofiAventis Deutschland v Lilly France*, docket No. 14/58023, English translation available on www.frenchpatentcaselaw.info/.

Also, the balance of interests between the parties is more often taken into account by judges than in the past to decide whether or not to order a preliminary injunction.[58]

Concerning imminent infringement, according to case law, the obtention of a marketing authorisation is not sufficient to prove the imminent launch of the accused product.

Further administrative acts preceding the launch are not sufficient either:[59] nor the submission of a file to the *Commission de la transparence*, in charge of assessing the medical service and the improvement of the medical service given by the drug, nor does the request for a price or the request for the registration on the list of refundable drugs suffice.

It is only the letter sent by a generic company to the *Comité économique des produits de santé*[60] ("CEPS"), in charge of the registration of the drug on the list of refundable drugs, confirming the request for registration of the generic drug on the list of refundable drugs more than six months before the expiry of the intellectual property rights, despite the patent rights declared to the CEPS by the right holder,[61] that is considered by current case law as sufficient to characterise imminent infringement.

---

58. This approach started with the decision TGI Paris, presiding judge, 12 February 2010, *EI Du Pont de Nemours and Merck Sharp & Dohmechibret v Mylan and Qualimed,* docket No. 10/51453, English translation available on www.frenchpatentcaselaw.info/, granting a preliminary injunction, affirmed by CA Paris, 15 March 2011, PIBD 2011, No. 943III451, English translation available on www.frenchpatentcaselaw.info/, relating to Losartan, where the judge ruled as follows:

    "The Judge in preliminary proceedings should, when confronted with a serious dispute, weigh opposing interests so as to ensure that a balance between the rights of the parties is maintained, that is, between the seriousness of an imminent damage and its potential compensation and the seriousness of the prohibition measure sought."

    See also TGI Paris, presiding judge, 28 January 2011, *Novartis v Actavis,* docket No. 11/5 0892, English translation available on www.frenchpatentcaselaw.info/, reversed by CA Paris, 16 September 2011, PIBD 2011, No. 951III692, English translation available on www.frenchpatentcaselaw.info/, quashed by Cass. Com. 15 January 2013, *Novartis v Actavis,* PIBD 2013, No. 979III1005, English translation available on www.frenchpatentcaselaw.info/.

    TGI Paris, chamber 3, section 1, 17 January 2013, *Uretek v Sols et Fondations*, docket No. 12/11634, recalling the principle (decision granting a preliminary injunction).

    TGI Paris, presiding judge, 23 June 2014, *Gedeon Richter v Mylan,* docket No. 14/54903, recalling the principle (decision refusing the preliminary injunction).
59. Several decisions of the French courts, handed down in preliminary injunction proceedings, considered that the setting of a price and the listing on the list of refundable drugs are not sufficient to characterise imminent infringement, for example:

    CA Paris, division 1, chamber 3, 15 March 2011, *Mylan Qualimed/EI DuPont de Nemours,* English translation available on www.frenchpatentcaselaw.info/,

    CA Paris, division 1, chamber 2, 21 March 2012, *Novartis/Mylan, Qualimed,* English translation available on www.frenchpatentcaselaw.info/.
60. In English *"Economic committee of health products"*.
61. Article 3 of the framework agreement between the CEPS and the LEEM provides that:

    "For information purpose, companies exploiting pharmaceutical products to which they hold one or more patents or SCPs declare these titles and their expiry dates to

1.1 *Availability for second medical use claims*

With respect to a second medical use claim, the scope of the injunction will have to be limited to the claimed use.

In the pregabalin case,[62] the claimants requested a limitation of the sales to a percentage corresponding to the sale of the drug for the non-patented indications; the recall of the products when the sales would exceed the said percentage; the prohibition for Sandoz from participating in tenders for pregabalin unless specifically limited to the non-patented indications; the sending of letters to physicians, pharmacists and hospitals stating that the generic cannot be prescribed and sold for the patented indication; the prohibition to use advertisement material not limited to the non-patented indications.

1.2 *Specific requirements*

No specific requirements apply to second medical use claims.

However, as indicated in section A.I.3, French judges are very strict when examining the validity of second medical use claims.

2. *Cases on the merits*

There are no specific issues with respect to proceedings on the merits.

3. *Enforcement of judgments*

Enforcement relating to a second medical use patent may be more complex than for a product patent, as it shall be limited to the specific patented use.

---

the Committee in Annex 4 of the convention mentioned in article 5 of the framework agreement for the next three years following the initial signature and for each update. The Committee shall make such declarations accessible to any pharmaceutical company that requests access to them.

No registration of any generic pharmaceutical product in the national health insurance reimbursable medicines lists and where applicable in the public hospital approved medicines list shall be published more than six months before the declared expiry date of the intellectual property rights concerned, where the committee has been notified of such date.

However, any pharmaceutical company which believes that it is able to sell the generic products in question without infringing the declared rights may apply for their product to be registered in the appropriate lists. In this event, the pharmaceutical company must inform the Committee, which in turn shall promptly inform the company selling the referenced drug as mentioned in the first paragraph hereabove and shall then begin the registration procedure."

62. TGI Paris, order in PI proceedings, 26 October 2015, *Warner Lambert, Pfizer v Sandoz*, docket No. 15/58725, English translation available on www.frenchpatentcaselaw.info/.

VIII. Validity

1. Relevance for infringement cases

Validity of the patent is challenged in the majority of patent infringement proceedings; infringement will be considered in the decision of the court only if the patent is held valid.

2. Specifics for second medical use claims

As indicated in section A.I.3.1, second medical use patents were often found invalid for insufficiency, lack of novelty or lack of inventive step by the French courts.

The Netherlands

Gertjan Kuipers

A. AVAILABILITY OF PROTECTION

I. Legal framework

1. National statutory laws

One should distinguish between European patents granted by the European Patent Office ("EPO") designating the Netherlands and that thus have to be validated in the Netherlands, and Dutch Patents granted by the Dutch Patent Office. The requirements for validation of a European patent are listed in the Dutch Patents Act 1995 ("DPA") (Rijksoctrooiwet 1995). According to Article 52(1) DPA, validation requires submission of a translation of the patent claims into Dutch to the Dutch Patent Office, and a payment of a fee within three months after granting of the European patent. Additionally, if the patent is not granted in English, a Dutch or English translation of the entire document should be submitted to the Dutch Patent Office. If these requirements are not met, the patent is considered to have never had legal effect in the Netherlands (Article 52(4) DPA).

The Dutch system for granting patents on the other hand is a registration system. This means that a patent will always be granted after application if the information listed in Articles 24 and 25 DPA is submitted and the applicant requests the grant of a patent. Although a search will be carried out, there is no examination as to patentability prior to grant.

With the planned United Patent System, a new patent form will be introduced in the Netherlands – the unitary patent.

The general requirements for patentability under the DPA are set forth in Article 2 DPA:[1]

1. All translations of the Dutch Patents Act in this article are derived from a non-official translation by The Netherlands Enterprise Agency: http://english.rvo.nl/sites/default/files/2013/12/ROW95_ENG_niet_officiele_vertaling_0.pdf.

> "Inventions that are new, that involve an inventive step and that are susceptible of industrial application shall be patentable."

Art. 3(1)(f) DPA explicitly excludes the patentability of methods of treatment, including surgical and therapeutic treatments and diagnostic methods applied "in vivo":

> "No patent shall be issued for methods of treating the human or animal body by means of surgery or medical treatment and diagnostic methods that are applied to the human or animal body, with the exception of products, in particular substances or compositions, for the application of such methods."

Pursuant to Article 4(5) and 4(6) DPA, patents are granted for first and further medical uses by giving an exception to the requirement of novelty in Article 4(1) DPA:

> "(1) An invention shall be considered new if it does not form part of the state of the art.
>
> (2) The state of the art shall comprise everything made available to the public by means of a written or oral description, by use or in any other way before the date of filing of the application.
>
> [...]
>
> (5) Notwithstanding the provisions contained in paragraphs (1) to (4) above, *substances or compositions* included in the state of the art *may be patented* insofar as they are intended *for use in one of the methods referred to in Article 3(f)*, provided that their use for any method referred to in that paragraph *is not included in the state of the art.*
>
> (6) Without prejudice to the provisions contained in paragraphs (1) to (4), the substances or compositions as referred to in paragraph (5) *may be patented for a specific application in a method as referred to in Article 3(f)* provided that such application is not included in the state of the art." [Emphasis added]

"First medical uses"

Following the European Patent Act (Article 54(5) EPC1973), the patentability of first medical uses was implemented in the Dutch Patent Act 1995 in Article 4(5) (see above). The formulation of a first medical use claim could be:

> "Substance X, for use as a medicament/in a therapy/in vivo diagnostics/in surgery" (Guidelines for Examinations, Part G, II 4.2).[2]

For a more detailed explanation on the patenting of first medical uses reference is made to A.I.1.a) of Chapter I, "EPO".

2. Guidelines for Examination in the European Patent Office, Edition November 2015: http://documents.epo.org/projects/babylon/eponet.nsf/0/A62ECC3718E570B3C1257EF100351F38/$File/guidelines_for_examination_2015_en.pdf.

"Second medical uses"

It took Dutch courts until 1998 to accept the patentability of second medical use claims. First, no acceptable form of the claims was found because of the problem with novelty and non-patentability of treatment methods. Novelty had to be derived from the manifestation of new acts or measures in the subject matter, while second medical uses constituted the exact same acts or measures (Octrooiraad AvB 19 June 1990, BIE 1991, p. 97). Even reasons of harmonization with European law could not persuade the appeal division of the Dutch Patent Office.[3] Eventually, following the EPO, and after implementing Article 54(5) EPC1973 in Article 4(5) DPA, the Dutch Supreme Court accepted the patentability of second medical use claims in 1998,[4] albeit in this case the patent was held invalid for lack of novelty. Because of the origination in Swiss case law, the second medical use claims were called "Swiss-type" claims. The formulation of a Swiss-type claim is:

> "Use of substance X in the manufacture of a medicament for the therapeutic application or disease Y." (Guidelines for Examination, Part G, VI 7.1).

With the amendment of the European Patent Convention (EPC 2000), "EPC 2000" claims were introduced (Article 54(4) EPC) (see A.I.1 Chapter I, "EPO"). This article is implemented in the DPA in Article 4(6). Since 29 January 2011, Swiss-type claims are no longer allowed in new patent applications.[5] Instead, the wording of EPC 2000 claims is mandatory for second medical use claims. This EPC 2000 claim wording reads:

> "Compound X for use in the treatment of disease Y characterized in that [other features; e.g. the dosage regime]" (Article 4(6) DPA and Guidelines for Examination, Part G, VI 7.1.2).

The major difference between the two types of second medical use claims is that a Swiss-type claim is a *purpose-limited process* claim, and an EPC 2000 claim is a *purpose-limited product* claim.[6]

For a more detailed explanation on the patenting of second medical uses reference is made to A.I.1.b) of Chapter I, "EPO".

1.1 Pharmaceuticals

The DPA is likewise applicable to patents relating to pharmaceuticals. Patenting first, second or further medical uses of chemical substances is allowable pursuant to the DPA. With regard to the novelty of patents relating to chemical pharmaceuticals, Dutch courts tend to follow the Technical Boards of Appeal (TBA) and the Enlarged Board of Appeal (EBA) of the EPO. Therefore, reference is made to A.I.1.1.1 of Chapter I, "EPO", where certain issues regarding novelty are discussed.

3. Octrooiraad (Afdeling van Beroep) 30 September 1987, ECLI:NL:XX:1987:AM1191, BIE 1988/8.
4. Court of Appeal The Hague 25 June 1998, ECLI:NL:GHSGR:1998:AM2688 (*Taxol*).
5. OJ EPO 2010, 514.
6. T1780/12 Technical Board of Appeal EPO; District Court The Hague 25 November 2015, ECLI:NL:RBDHA:2015:14337 (*Sun/Novartis*), at. 4.51.

1.2 Biologics

The DPA is likewise applicable to patents relating to biotherapeutics. In, for example, Articles 2a and 53a DPA specific rules regarding biological inventions are set forth, implementing the EU biotech directive 98/44/EC. Patenting first, second or further medical uses of biological substances is allowable pursuant to the DPA. With regard to the novelty of patents relating to biotherapeutics Dutch courts tend to follow the TBAs and the EBA of the EPO. Therefore, reference is made to A.I.1.1.2 of Chapter I, "EPO", where certain issues regarding novelty are discussed.

2. International treaties

The Netherlands is a member of the European Patent Convention. See A.I.2 of Chapter I, "EPO" about the interpretation of the provisions of the EPC.

2.1 TRIPS

The Netherlands is party to the TRIPS Agreement. TRIPS is implemented in the DPA (Stb. 1995, 668, entry in force on 29 December 1995).

2.2 FTAs

In the Netherlands, TRIPS is the only fair trade agreement regarding intellectual property rights.

3. Availability through case law

There is much case law on medical patents. However, case law on first and second medical uses is limited in the Netherlands, especially with regard to infringement. In first instance, the District Court of The Hague has sole jurisdiction in patent cases (Article 80 DPA). The European case law of the Technical Boards of Appeal and the Enlarged Board of Appeal of the EPO is often considered by the Dutch courts and in general the legal principles decided therein are followed.

4. Patent term extension/SPCs

Pursuant to Article 36(6) DPA, the patent term in the Netherlands is 20 years starting from the application date. Articles 90-97 DPA provide for an additional protection of a maximum of five years for medicines by granting Supplementary Protection Certificates (SPCs). These Articles are the implementation of Council Regulation (EEC) No 1768/92 of 18 June 1992. The Court of Justice of the European Union (CJEU) clarified in July 2012 that an SPC could also be granted for further medical uses.[7]

7. C-130/11, Neurim Pharmaceuticals.

II. Policy considerations

1. Health and social issues

It is likely that allowing patent protection of second and further medical uses encourages the research and development of new indications of known medical substances.[8] This is a positive consequence, since the side effects and (optimal) dosage regime of the substance are already known. The need for less research into the side effects and (optimal) dosage regime for second and further medical uses decreases the costs and risks of the medicine.[9] However, granting further medical use protection enhances the monopoly of pharmaceutical companies. This is controversial, especially when pharmaceutical companies purposely extend the lifetime of patent protection for inventions with minor, insignificant improvements to the original invention.

2. Legal issues

The adverse effects of patenting second medical uses may be decreased by the general requirements for patentability. Minor, insignificant improvements are likely to not be inventive, and thus the patent will be held invalid.

Considering the importance of harmonization of patent law within the European Union, it was desirable to allow second medical use claims in the Netherlands.[10]

B. VALIDITY

I. Allowable claim wording

1. Product claims

Art. 53(1)(a) DPA provides for protection for product claims. The simplest allowable formulation is:

> "Substance X, consisting of ..."

However, there is no mandatory formulation. For first medical uses, the formulation of a claim is for example:

> "Substance X, for use as a medicament/in a therapy/in vivo diagnostics/in surgery." (Guidelines for Examinations, Part G, II 4.2).

2. Method claims

Method of treatment claims are not allowed pursuant to Article 3(1)(f) DPA. However, with the new Article 4(5) and 4(6) DPA, it is possible to patent treatments by

---

8. Q238 AIPPI second medical use or indication claims (The Netherlands), p. 11.
9. AIPPI Question 238 Working Guidelines, p. 3.
10. Q238 AIPPI second medical use or indication claims (The Netherlands), p. 11.

patenting the new and inventive use of a known compound for the treatment of an illness. This use may also be a new method of administration, a new patient group, or a new dosage regime.[11]

3. *Use claims*

To patent medical inventions, it is established practice to patent novel and inventive medical uses. Until 2011, Swiss-type claims could be used for this purpose. Swiss-type claims circumvent the prohibition of patenting treatment methods, because a use for the *manufacture* of a medicine for the medical use was patented. Novelty is found by applying Article 4(5) DPA by analogy in the case of second medical uses.[12] As stated in I.1 above, for first medical uses, an exception is made in Article 4(5) DPA with regard to novelty. Although the substance is not new, it is possible to patent the known substance for use in a first medical indication.

The (mandatory) formulation of a Swiss-type claim is:

> "Use of substance X in the manufacture of a medicament for the therapeutic application or disease Y." (Guidelines for Examination, Part G, VI 7.1).

With the amendment of the European Patent Convention (EPC 2000), EPC 2000 claims were introduced (section 54(4) EPC). Since 29 January 2011, Swiss type claims are not allowed anymore in new patent applications.[13] Instead, EPC 2000 claims are mandatory for second medical use claims. The novelty of a second medical use claim may be based on a new therapeutic purpose, a different dosage regime, a different administration regime, a new patient group, etc. The basic formulation of an EPC 2000 claim is:

> "Compound X for use in the treatment of disease Y, characterized in that [other features; e.g. the dosage regime]." (Art. 4(6) DPA). (See Guidelines for Examination, Part G, VI 7.1.2 for variations on this formulation).

The major difference between the claims is that a Swiss-type claim is a *purpose-limited process* claim, and an EPC 2000 claim is a *purpose-limited product* claim.[14]

4. *System claims*

In the European patent regime, system claims are construed in the same way as product claims (Guidelines for Examination, Part F, IV 3.8). The Dutch regime follows this approach.[15] Thus far, there is no Dutch case law concerning second medical use patents for medical devices and systems. Reference is made to B.I.4. Chapter I,

11. Court of Appeal The Hague 14 July 2015, ECLI:NL:GHDHA:2015:1899 (*Schering/Teva*); Court of Appeal The Hague 25 June 1998, ECLI:NL:GHSGR:1998:AM2688 (*Taxol*); Q238 AIPPI second medical use or indication claims (The Netherlands), p. 2.
12. G5/83 'Eisai'.
13. OJ EPO 2010, 514.
14. T1780/12 Technical Board of Appeal EPO.
15. Court of First Instance 29 November 2000, ECLI:NL:RBSGR:2000:AM2847.

"EPO", where it is discussed that it is not likely that medical devices and medical systems are covered by Article 54(4) and 54(5) EPC.

5. *Dosage regimes*

Second medical use claims with regard to dosage regimes are valid claims in the Netherlands.[16] The claims are construed in the same way as other types of second medical use claims. A possible formulation could be:

> "Substance X for use in the treatment of disease Y, whereby X is administered by the dosage regime Z." (Guidelines for Examination, Part G, VI 7.1.2).

6. *Patient groups*

Second medical use claims with regard to patient groups are valid claims in the Netherlands.[17] The claims are construed in the same way as other types of second medical use claims. A possible formulation could be:

> "Substance X for use in the treatment of disease Y in a subgroup of patients carrying genotype Z".

II. Novelty

1. *General definition of novelty and prior art*

A valid patent requires absolute novelty (Articles 2(1) and 4 DPA). This means that an invention shall be considered new if it does not form part of the prior art (Article 4(1) DPA). The prior art comprises everything that has been made available to the public by whatever means prior to the application date. This includes prior applications that are published in the patent register after the application date of the subsequent application (Article 4(3) and 4(4) DPA). Available to the public means that at least one person is able to gain access to the information. In order to hold a patent invalid for the lack of novelty, the skilled person should be able to derive all claimed technical features directly and unambiguously from *one* publication in the prior art without undue burden.

2. *Definition of skilled person*

The skilled person is an average person skilled in the relevant art with average knowledge on the field of the invention. Traditionally not much emphasis was placed on defining the skilled person in a particular case in Dutch decisions. More recently, this aspect is getting more attention, probably as a result of decisions from the UK.

---

16. Court of Appeal The Hague 25 June 1998, ECLI:NL:GHSGR:1998:AM2688 (*Taxol*); Q238 AIPPI second medical use or indication claims (The Netherlands), p. 2.
17. Court of Appeal The Hague 14 July 2015, ECLI:NL:GHDHA:2015:1899 (*Schering/Teva*).

3. *Scope of disclosure*

3.1 General rules

The publication should be sufficiently clear and complete to enable the skilled person to carry out the whole range claimed in the invention without undue burden (Article 25 DPA). Since the Dutch system for granting patents is a registration system, as mentioned above in A.I.1, and the number of Dutch patents tested in litigation is small, in particular in the area of pharmaceuticals. For this part of the chapter we will mainly rely on B.II.3 of Chapter I, "EPO".

3.2 First medical use

Pursuant to Article 4(5) DPA, a first medical use of a known substance is patentable, although the substance is already known. The application should disclose how the product is suitable for the claimed medical use (see B.II.3.2 Chapter I, "EPO")

3.2 New subject matter

A first, second or further medical use should disclose the new subject matter (see B.II.3.3 Chapter I, "EPO").

3.4 New data

In the Netherlands it is possible to add post-filed data to the patent application after the patent is granted. Post-published evidence that the patent solves the problem as claimed, is admissible, but may not be the only evidence.[18] (See B.II.3.3 Chapter I, "EPO".)

4. *Requirements for second medical use*

4.1 Distinction from first medical use

A patent for a first medical use protects all medical uses of the substance (Article 4(5) DPA). A patent for a second medical use only protects the specified second medical use (Article 4(6) DPA). Therefore, the application should specify the specific medical use that is claimed.

18. Q217 AIPPI The patentability criterion of inventive step /non-obviousness (The Netherlands), p. 8.

4.2 *Sub-species of second medical use*

In the Netherlands all known sub-species of second medical use patents are allowable. For example a new therapeutic purpose,[19] a new patient group,[20] a new dosage regime, a new administration regime, a new technical effect, or the avoidance of an undesired side effect.[21]

4.3 *Dosage regimes*

The second medical use may be the invention of a new dosage regime.[22] No additional novelty requirements apply as compared to normal patents (see B.II.4.3 Chapter I, "EPO").

4.4 *Special patient groups*

The second medical use can be the use of the medicine for a completely new patient group. This can be a completely different patient group; for example heart patients instead of patients suffering from a headache. It is also possible that the special patient group is a subgroup of the group for which the substance already was prescribed.[23] No additional novelty requirements apply as compared to patents for other subject matter (see B.II.4.4 Chapter I, "EPO").

4.5 *Special technical effect or mechanism leading to a truly novel clinical/ medical situation*

The second medical use may be the invention of a new technical effect or mechanism leading to a truly novel clinical/medical situation.[24] No additional novelty requirements apply as compared to patents for other subject matter (see B.II.4.5 Chapter I, "EPO").

5. ***Timing issues***

5.1 *Relevant time of development of second use*

Second medical uses of known drugs will most likely be found after development of the drug. This will enhance the availability of experimental laboratory data, which will support the application.

19. District Court The Hague 25 November 2015, ECLI:NL:RBDHA:2015:14337 (*Sun/Novartis*).
20. Court of Appeal The Hague 14 July 2015, ECLI:NL:GHDHA:2015:1899 (*Schering/Teva*).
21. Q238 AIPPI second medical use or indication claims (The Netherlands), p. 2
22. Court of Appeal The Hague 25 June 1998, ECLI:NL:GHSGR:1998:AM2688 (*Taxol*).
23. Court of Appeal The Hague 14 July 2015, ECLI:NL:GHDHA:2015:1899 (*Schering/Teva*).
24. Court of Appeal The Hague 25 June 1998, ECLI:NL:GHSGR:1998:AM2688 (*Taxol*).

5.2 *Role of new data*

New data has to be collected in order to research whether a known substance can be used in a new indication. When invalidity of a patent is claimed, data supporting the claimed effect of the invention is very important.

5.3 *Use of old data*

Old data on medicines for prior medical uses can be used to prove the validity of the second or further medical use patent. After all, the substance or composition of the medicines is identical. Moreover, it is cost- and timesaving not having to conduct detailed research into the side effects, since it is likely that these will be the same.[25]

III. Inventive step/non-obviousness

1. *Definition of inventive step/non-obviousness*

Pursuant to Article 6 DPA, "An invention shall be deemed to be the result of inventive activity if, for a person skilled in the art, it does not manifestly ensue from the state of the art." Whether the invention involves an inventive step depends on the state of the art at the application date. Having regard to the state of the art, the inventive step should not be evident for the person skilled in the art or already suggested in the prior art. As for novelty, the prior art constitutes everything that has been made public verbally or in writing prior to the application date. Contrary to the scope of disclosure for novelty, prior applications that are published in the patent register after the application date of the subsequent application are not included.

2. *Same scope of disclosure as for novelty?*

The skilled person should be able to derive from the patent that a certain problem is solved by the inventive step claimed in the patent.

3. *Assessment of inventive step/non-obviousness*

The assessment of the inventive step is somewhat more subjective than the assessment of novelty. To assess the inventive step, the problem-solution approach is most used in the Netherlands. However, judges are not obliged to use this approach.[26] Reference is made to B.III.1.3 of Chapter I, "EPO" and to Q217 AIPPI.[27]

25. Q238 AIPPI second medical use or indication claims (Summary Report), p. 18.
26. HR 7 June 2013, ECLI:HR:2013:BZ4115, *Lundbeck/Tiefenbacher.*
27. Q217 AIPPI The patentability criterion of inventive step /non-obviousness (The Netherlands), p. 8.

IV. Amendment of claims after grant

1. Admissibility of post-grant amendments in general

Post-grant amendments are in general accepted under Dutch practice. Such amendments should however not extend the scope of protection or add subject matter.

2. Procedural issues

2.1 Independent limitation proceedings

A patent holder may surrender its patent in whole or in part through filing an appropriate deed with the Dutch Patent Office (Article 63 DPA). This deed will not be examined. It will have retroactive effect. For European patents the patentee may moreover use the central limitation procedure. Reference is made to Chapter I, "EPO" B.IV.2.1

2.2 Opposition proceedings

Opposition proceedings are only possible with regard to European patents granted for the Netherlands (Article 51(2) DPA and Article 99 ff. EPC). During the opposition proceedings the patent holder can limit the scope of protection (Article 138(3) EPC). Reference is made to Chapter I, "EPO" B.IV.2.2.

2.3 Nullity actions

In a nullity action, the judge can partially invalidate a patent. This is provided for in Article 75(1) and 75(3) DPA. Typically, unless the patentee has submitted specific requests for maintenance of the patent in a particular limited form during the course of the proceedings, the patent will only be limited based on the dependent claims granted.

3. Added matter

The patent application may not be amended in such a way that it extends beyond the subject of the invention (Article 75(1)(c) DPA). The amendment of the application should directly and unambiguously follow from the original application. Otherwise the patent will be held (partially) invalid.

In addition, pursuant to Article 75(1)(d) DPA, a patent may be invalidated for reasons of extension of scope after granting of the patent. This is the case when the scope of protection is impermissibly broadened, for example because the elements of the claims are left out in opposition proceedings, nullity actions or because of a request to surrender. Recent case law on this matter is for example Court of Appeal The Hague 16 February 2016, ECLI:NL:GHDHA:2016:339 (*Shionogi c.s./Resolution*); Court of Appeal The Hague 18 November 2014, ECLI:NL:GHDHA:2014:3611 (*Novartis/Alvogen c.s.*).

4. *Sufficiency*

After partial surrender or invalidation of the patent pursuant to Articles 63 and 75 DPA, the patent should still specify sufficiently clearly how the invention can be carried out by a person skilled in the art (Article 25 DPA). Otherwise the patent may be invalidated (Article 75(b) DPA).

5. *Multiple indications*

Multiple therapeutic indications may be claimed in the patent application (see IV.5 Chapter I, "EPO"). However, after granting of the patent, new indications may not be introduced. Pursuant to Article 63 and 75 DPA, one claimed therapeutic indication may be surrendered or held invalid.

V. Change of patent category

1. *General admissibility*

As long as the changes comply with the requirements, in particular those relating to added subject matter and extension of scope, changes in patent category may be allowable. Reference is made is made to B.V.1 of Chapter I, "EPO".

2. *Use claim as a category*

There is no Dutch case law about this specific amendment of the patent application.

3. *From product to method claim*

Method of treatment claims are not allowed pursuant to Article 3(1)(f) DPA.

4. *From method to product claim*

There is no Dutch case law about this specific amendment of the patent application.

5. *System claims*

Probably, second medical use claims of medical systems or devices are not allowable in the Netherlands, according to the EPO (see B.I.4 above).

6. *Use claims*

There is no Dutch case law about this specific amendment of the patent application.

C. INFRINGEMENT AND LITIGATION

I. Legal framework

1. National statutory laws

The DPA applies to all patents granted for the Netherlands. In addition, the Code of Civil Procedure (Wetboek van Burgerlijke Rechtsvordering) gives some rules on the enforcement of intellectual property rights in general.

2. Case law

- *Schering/Teva*: Court of Appeal The Hague 14 July 2015, ECLI:NL:GHDHA:2015:1899 & District Court The Hague 10 November 2010.
- *Sun/Novartis*: District Court The Hague 25 November 2015, ECLI:NL:RBDHA:2015:14337 & Court of Appeal The Hague in preliminary relief proceedings 27 January 2015, ECLI:NL:GHDHA:2015:1769 & District Court The Hague in preliminary relief proceedings 12 May 2014.
- *Warner-Lambert/College ter Beoordeling van Geneesmiddelen (CBG)*: Court of first instance 15 January 2016, ECLI:NL:RBDHA:2016:334.

II. Claim construction

1. General rules

See B.I for the allowable claim wording. In construing the claims, the way of assessing the scope of protection should be taken into account. Until 1995, the scope of protection of the patent was assessed by establishing the essence ("*het wezen*") of the patent. In 1995, the Supreme Court accepted the criterion as used in section 69 EPC and the Protocol on the interpretation of section 69 EPC,[28] although the essence of the invention continued to play some role. The scope of protection will be determined by the claims, and the description and drawings should be used to interpret the claims.[29]

Using the prosecution history to interpret the claims is allowed. However, using the prosecution history for the benefit of the patent holder is only allowed to a limited extent.[30]

28. HR 13 January 1995, ECLI:NL:HR:1995:ZC1609 (*Ciba Geigy/Oté Optics*).
29. HR 25 May 2012, ECLI:NL:HR:2012:BV3680 (*AGA/Occlutech*); HR 4 April 2014, HR:NL:HR:2014:816 (*Medinol/Abbott*).
30. HR 13 January 1995, ECLI:NL:HR:1995:ZC1609 (*Ciba Geigy/Oté Optics*); HR 22 December 2006, (*Dijkstra/Saier*).

2. *Specific issues for use claims*

The general rules for claim construction, as mentioned above in C.II.1, apply to use claims.

III. Scope of protection

1. *Scope of the use*

1.1 *General definition of the term "use"*

In case infringement is found, Dutch courts will impose a prohibition on direct and indirect infringement. Often, in this prohibition it is not specified what "use" constitutes the infringement. However, all prohibited types of use are listed in Article 53(1) DPA:

> "(1) Subject to the provisions contained in articles 54 to 60, a patent shall confer on its owner the exclusive right:
>
> (a) to make, use, put on the market or resell, hire out or deliver the *patented product*, or otherwise deal in it in or for his business, or to offer, import or stock it for any of those purposes;
>
> (b) to use the patented process in or for his business or to use, put on the market, or resell, hire out or deliver the product obtained directly as a result of the use of the *patented process*, or otherwise deal in it in or for his business, or to offer, import or stock it for any of those purposes." (Emphasis added).

For product claims, the prohibited types of use are to manufacture, use, put on the market, resell, hire out or deliver the product for the patented use, or deal in it otherwise, as well as to offer, import or stock the product for the patented use for any of those purposes.[31] For process claims these same acts constitute use of the patent when performed in connection with the product directly obtained through the patented process. In addition, for process claims the use of the patented process is a prohibited act.

In any case, the use should be in the context of an occupation or business activity.

1.2 *Manufacture of the pharmaceutical*

See 1.1.

1.3 *Sale of the product*

See 1.1.

31. Q238 AIPPI second medical use or indication claims (The Netherlands), p. 13.

1.4 *Offer for sale*

See 1.1.

1.5 *Application to the patient*

Application to the patient constitutes "use" of the product. Both a doctor and a patient apply the medicine to the patient. The patient is not acting in the context of an occupation or business activity, therefore, this is not a protected use. In G2/08, the Enlarged Board of Appeal decided that a doctor should be free in treating the patient and should not be limited by patents.[32] This decision is likely to be followed by the Dutch courts.[33]

1.6 *Combination products*

It is possible to patent a product in which two active substances are combined. When patenting a combination product, the normal requirements for patentability apply. In Court of Appeal The Hague 1 November 2011, ECLI:NL:GHSGR:2011:BU6588 (Sanofi/Ratiopharm) the patent for the combination of clopidogrel and aspirin was held to be invalid, since it lacked an inventive step. Clopidogrel and aspirin were combined in a Swiss-type claim. In District Court The Hague in preliminary relief proceedings 14 September 2012 (Sanofi/Pharmachemie & Teva) it is clarified that supplementary product protection for a combination product is allowed as well.

2. *Absolute product protection*

2.1 *Limitation through the term "use"*

Second medical use claims do not enjoy absolute product protection. In Swiss-type claims, only the use of the product for the preparation of a medicine for the treatment of the patented indication is protected. Using the product for something other than preparing that medicine, or using the medicine for a different indication, is not protected. In EPC 2000 claims, only the product for use in the treatment of the patented indication is protected. The product for use in another treatment is not protected.

2.2 *Off-label use*

The patented indication should be carved out from the SmPC (Summary of Product Characteristics) and the PIL (Patient Information Leaflet) of the (generic) medicine used for the non-patented indication. When the patented indication is carved out, this is called a skinny label.[34] Cross-label use means that the medicine is used for an indication not indicated in the specific (skinny) SmPC or PIL. Off-label use means

---

32. G2/08 '*Dosage regime/ABBOTT RESPIRATORY*'.
33. Q238 AIPPI second medical use or indication claims (The Netherlands), p. 5.
34. Court of Appeal The Hague 14 July 2015, ECLI:NL:GHDHA:2015:1899 (*Schering/Teva*).

that the medicine is used for an unapproved indication (not indicated in the SmPC or PIL). However, please note that cross-label use is often (wrongly) referred to as "off-label use". Both cross-label use and off-label use are not allowed.[35]

3. *Dosage regimes*

A new dosage regime can be a new patentable indication.[36]

4. *Patient groups*

A new patient group can be a new patentable indication.[37]

5. *Extension under the doctrine of equivalents*

In assessing the scope of protection due account should be taken of equivalent elements (Article 2 of the Protocol on the interpretation of Article 69 EPC). Equivalent use will not constitute infringement when looking to the exact wording of the claims of the patent. However, an equivalent leads to an equivalent result, and under some circumstances this can lead to infringement. Under Dutch law, an equivalent does not infringe a patent if it is obvious for the person skilled in the art that the patent holder made a deliberate choice in using the substance as described in the claims, instead of the substance used in the equivalent.[38]

There is no reason not to assume that the doctrine of equivalents can be applied to second medical use patents in the same way as to other patents. As far as we know, there is however no case law in this respect with regard to second medical use claims.

IV. Infringing acts

1. *Infringing person or entity*

All parties engaging in directly or indirectly infringing activities and all parties taking undue advantage of these infringing activities may be liable for infringement of a second medical use claim either under the DPA or under civil tort law.[39]

In *Schering/Teva* and *Sun/Novartis*, Teva and Sun were held liable, both as manufacturer as well as supplier. Except for the preliminary proceedings in *Schering/Teva*, in all decisions in both proceedings infringement was not established. However, they being manufacturer and supplier did not rule out the possibility of infringement under Dutch law.

35. Q238 AIPPI second medical use or indication claims (Working Guidelines), p. 8.
36. Court of Appeal The Hague 25 June 1998, ECLI:NL:GHSGR:1998:AM2688 (*Taxol*); Q238 AIPPI second medical use or indication claims (The Netherlands), p. 2.
37. Court of Appeal The Hague 14 July 2015, ECLI:NL:GHDHA:2015:1899 (*Schering/Teva*).
38. Supreme Court 5 February 2016, ECLI:NL:HR:2016:196 (*Bayer/Sandoz*); Supreme Court 4 April 2014, ECLI:NL:HR:2014:816 (*Medinol/Abbott*).
39. Q238 AIPPI second medical use or indication claims (The Netherlands), p. 13.

Furthermore, the Dutch Medicines Evaluation Board (CBG) was held liable in *Warner-Lambert/CBG*. Although CBG did not infringe the patent as it was providing information, but not supplying or offering to supply the product or a means relating to an essential element of the invention, it was held liable under civil tort law. The court ruled that CBG committed a wrongful act by not carving out the patented indication in the SmPCs on its website.

In Dutch case law, no other types of persons or entities were held liable for infringement of a second medical use claim. A physician may probably not be held liable following the Enlarged Board of Appeal of the EPO in G2/08; a physician should not be subject to limitations in treating a patient. This decision is likely to be followed by the Dutch courts.[40] Patients may not be held liable because the use is not in or for their business (Article 53(1) DPA). There is no Dutch law preventing the liability of pharmacists.

2. *Direct infringement*

2.1 *Manufacture of the pharmaceutical*

Schering/Teva is the only relevant Dutch case where a patent holder claimed direct infringement. In *Sun/Novartis* direct infringement was not claimed until the pleadings in the proceedings on the merits. Because neither party fully prepared this claim, the court decided to postpone the proceedings. According to the court, the possibility of direct infringement could not be excluded, also not in cases where the new use is not specifically mentioned, but better preparation was required in order to proceed. A decision on this matter is not yet available. In *Warner-Lambert/CBG* no finding of direct infringement was made, because, according to the court, CBG did not sell, offer, put on the market or deliver the product, or otherwise dealt in it.

In *Schering/Teva*, Schering had a patent for the use of ribavirin for a method for manufacturing a medicine for hepatitis C. This (second medical use) patent expired, which meant that Teva could enter the market with the same medicine. However, Schering had a further medical use patent for the use of ribavirin for a method for manufacturing a medicine for hepatitis C subtype 1 (Swiss-type claim). The further medical use is a use for a new patient group, while the new patient group is a subcategory of the old patient group. Thus, both groups overlap. According to Schering, Teva's generic product is also prescribed for hepatitis C subtype 1, and thus infringing Schering's patent. For these particular circumstances in establishing direct infringement of a Swiss-type claim, the Court of Appeal made a distinction between a *new subgroup* and a *new indication*. For direct infringement of a patent for a new indication, the Court of Appeal referred to the decision in *Sun/Novartis*, suggesting that the scope on direct infringement could extend to include the trade in the compound, even if it is not accompanied by a specific statement that it is intended for the new indication. For direct infringement of a patent for a new subgroup however it is, according to the Court of Appeal, necessary that a person skilled in the art considers that the medicine is intended specifically for the new patient

40. Q238 AIPPI second medical use or indication claims (The Netherlands), p. 5.

group. This can be proven when the patented use is specifically mentioned in the SmPC or PIL. The Court of Appeal considered that the medicine was already being prescribed to patients within the subgroup before it was found that the medicine works well especially for such patients. According to the Court of Appeal, the generic manufacturer can thus only benefit from its acts when the use for the subgroup is specifically mentioned. The decision of the Court of Appeal is presently under appeal to the Supreme Court.

Thus far, there is no Dutch case law with regard to the (indirect) infringement of EPC 2000 claims. However, EPC 2000 claims are expected to have a broader scope of protection, since they are product claims.[41] For infringement of an EPC 2000 claim fewer components are to be fulfilled than for a Swiss-type claim, which should make it easier to prove infringement.

2.2 *Offer for sale*

See 2.1.

2.3 *Sale*

See 2.1.

2.4 *Export*

Export as such is not an infringing act. For infringement by exporting products, evidence should be provided that one of the infringing activities as stated in Article 53(1) DPA (e.g. manufacturing the product or delivering the product) was conducted in the Netherlands before the product was exported.

2.5 *Import*

It is prohibited to import a patented product in the Netherlands in order to undertake any of the infringing activities as stated in Article 53(1) DPA (e.g. delivering the product, or deal in it otherwise) in the Netherlands.

2.6 *Combination products*

No specific requirement would apply here.

41. T 1780/12; District Court The Hague 25 November 2015, ECLI:NL:RBDHA:2015:14337 (*Sun/Novartis*), at. 4.51.

3. *Indirect infringement*

3.1 Objective acts

Indirect infringement is provided for in Article 73 DPA. A crucial element in the context of indirect infringement is that it should concern means relating to an essential element of the invention. In HR 31 October 2003, ECLI:NL:PHR:2003:AI0346 (Sara Lee/Integro), the Supreme Court gave some guidance on the meaning of these words in holding that such means should be part of what sets the invention apart from the prior art.

In *Schering/Teva*, Schering had a patent for the use of ribavirin for a method for manufacturing a medicine for hepatitis C. This (second medical use) patent expired, which meant that Teva could enter the market with the same medicine. However, Schering had a further medical use patent for the use of ribavirin for a method for manufacturing a medicine for hepatitis C subtype 1 (Swiss-type claim). The further medical use is a use for a new patient group, while the new patient group is a subcategory of the old patient group. Thus, both groups overlap. According to Schering, Teva's generic product is also prescribed for hepatitis C subtype 1, and thus infringing Schering's patent. According to the Court of Appeal, the invention would be in the subgroup. Compound X, in this case ribavirin, would according to the Court of Appeal not be a means relating to an essential element of the invention, as it (i) is not essential to the concept of the invention, (ii) does not point towards the use in the subgroup, and (iii) does not form what sets the patent apart from the prior art. As a result, Teva's sale of ribavirin would not constitute indirect infringement. The decision of the Court of Appeal on this point is under appeal to the Supreme Court.

A few months later in *Sun/Novartis* in the proceedings on the merits, the District Court had a different view for dismissing the claim for indirect infringement. Novartis has a Swiss-type claim for the use of zoledronic acid for a method for manufacturing a medicine for osteoporosis, while zoledronic acid is free to be used in treating Paget's disease. Sun manufactures zoledronic acid and participated in a tender from a health insurance company without mentioning the disallowed patented use. In addition, although Sun carved out the patented use in the hardcopy of the SmPC, such carve out was not present online (see Pfizer-CBG matter). Examination of the market share clarifies that 97.3% of zoledronic acid is prescribed for osteoporosis, while 2.7% is prescribed for Paget's disease. In view thereof, Sun manufactures way too much zoledronic acid for it to be solely used for Paget's disease. For this reason Novartis claimed that Sun indirectly infringed the second medical use patent. According to Novartis, Sun delivered zoledronic acid *for application* in the invention, since in the chain of purchasers the patented destination is given to the product several times.

In assessing indirect infringement, the court would not even investigate whether zoledronic acid is a means relating to an essential element of the invention, because even when assuming that zoledronic acid would be such means, the possibility of indirect infringement of Swiss-type claims would be dismissed on other grounds. According to the court, giving a destination to the product is not the same as application of the invention protected by a Swiss-type claim. Only manufacturing the product would be an application of such an invention. As nowhere in the downstream chain of purchasers of zoledronic acid would the product be manufactured, the delivery of zoledronic acid by Sun can for that reason not amount to indirect infringement.

In *Warner-Lambert/CBG*, CBG committed a wrongful act by not carving out the patented indication in the SmPC on its website. With regard to indirect infringement, the court considered that means relating to an essential element has to be something physical. It cannot be the knowledge that compound X, in this case pregabalin, can be used for a specific indication.

The assessment of indirect infringement is probably different for purpose-limited product claims, as is explicitly mentioned in *Sun/Novartis* in the proceedings on the merits. EPC 2000 claims do not have the element "for a method for manufacturing". This means that for application of the patent downstream it is probably not necessary that the infringer actually manufactures the patent. However, it is still required that the component delivered for application of the invention is a means relating to an essential element of the invention.

3.2 Subjective conditions

Interestingly, the Court of Appeal in preliminary relief proceedings in *Sun/Novartis* came to the conclusion that Sun's acts constitute indirect infringement of Novartis' patent. In the preliminary relief proceedings, zoledronic acid being an essential element is not disputed by Sun. The application of zoledronic acid by giving the product a destination is not explicitly mentioned in the decision. Instead, the court determined the subjective conditions for indirect infringement. For indirect infringement, the alleged infringer should know about the use of the invention, or it should have been evident given the circumstances. Examination of the use of zoledronic acid clarifies that 97.3 % of zoledronic acid is prescribed for osteoporosis, while 2.7 % is prescribed for Paget's disease, so Sun manufactures too much zoledronic acid for it to be solely used for Paget's disease. In these circumstances, it is evident for Sun that its zoledronic acid will be used for the patented indication. Therefore, Sun should have done everything to prevent the use of zoledronic acid for the patented indication. According to the Court of Appeal Sun did not do so. On the contrary, Sun did not even mention the not-allowed patented use when taking part in the tender for the health insurance company. Please note that this decision on indirect infringement has been overruled in the proceedings on the merits, as according to the District Court in the proceedings on the merits no application of the invention takes place downstream of Sun.

3.3 Export

Export as such is not an infringing act. For infringement by exporting products, evidence should be provided that one of the infringing activities as stated in Article 53(1) DPA (e.g. manufacturing the product or delivering the product) was conducted in the Netherlands before the product was exported.

3.4 *Import*

It is prohibited to import a patented product in the Netherlands in order to undertake any of the infringing activities as stated in Article 53(1) DPA (e.g. delivering the product, or deal in it otherwise) in the Netherlands.

3.5 *Combination products*

No specific requirement would apply here.

4. ***Off-label use***

4.1 *General admissibility of off-label use*

For off-label use, as well as cross-label use, see III.2.2.2.

4.2 *Liable persons*

In *Schering/Teva* it was established that the manufacturer would be liable for direct infringement if the patented use was specifically mentioned in the SmPC or PIL. This concerned a second medical use based on a subgroup. For direct infringement of a patent for a new indication, the Court of Appeal referred to the interim decision in *Sun/Novartis*, for suggesting that the scope on direct infringement could extend to include the trade in the compound, even if it is not accompanied by a specific statement that it is intended for the new indication. A further decision in *Sun/Novartis*, explicitly considering this point, is however not yet available.

In *Sun/Novartis* in the preliminary relief proceedings the manufacturer who had not explicitly asked for a carve out in a tender for a health insurance company was held liable for indirect infringement. The decision on indirect infringement was however overruled in the main proceedings in which the District Court held that there was no use of the invention downstream of Sun. In *Warner-Lambert/CBG*, CBG committed a wrongful act by not carving out the patented indication in the SmPC on its website. Probably the same persons and entities can be liable as with other infringing activities, see IV.1.

4.3 *Objective requirements for infringement*

For direct infringement, see C.IV.2.1. For indirect infringement the acts should related to a means relating to an essential element of the invention. See C.IV.3 for a broader explanation of infringement of a second medical use claim.

4.4 *Subjective requirements for infringement*

According to the DPA there are no subjective requirements for direct infringement. See further C.IV.2.1 and C.IV.3

5. *Dosage regimes*

As far as we know, there is no Dutch case law on infringement of a second medical use claim for a dosage regime. There is no reason not to assume that the requirements for infringement can be applied to second medical use claims for dosage regimes in the same way as to other second medical use claims.

6. *Patient groups*

In *Schering/Teva*, Schering had a second medical use claim for a subgroup. In IV.2.2.1 and IV.3.3.1 both direct and indirect infringement of a second medical use claim for a subgroup and a new patient group are explained.

V. Remedies

1. *Injunctions*

The patent holder can claim an injunction, as was done by Schering in *Schering/Teva* and by Sun in *Sun/Novartis* (Article 70(1) DPA). The court may impose a penalty payment in connection with the injunction (Article 611a ff. Code of Civil Procedure). In Dutch case law, only in *Sun/Novartis* in the preliminary proceedings was infringement of a second medical use claim established. The Court of Appeal imposed a general injunction of non-infringement subject to a penalty payment. In addition, Novartis claimed a specific injunction that Sun would not be allowed to take part in tenders for the supply of the generic product for the patented use in the Netherlands. According to the Court of Appeal, this injunction was already covered by the general injunction of non-infringement. However, the Court of Appeal did order that, when taking part in a tender, Sun has to clarify that the product cannot be used for the patented use.

Apart from an injunction, the patent holder may claim a declaratory decision that the infringer does infringe the patent (Article 3:302 of the Dutch Civil Code). In addition, the infringer may be ordered to send a rectification to all customers or to put a rectifying statement on its website (Article 70(12) DPA).

2. *Damages*

Damages can only be claimed if the infringer knew or should reasonably have known of the infringement (Article 70(4) DPA; Article 45 TRIPS). Profits may be claimed as well (Article 70(5) DPA). It is not possible for the court to allocate both the profits and the damages. Only an amount equal to the highest amount of either profits or damages may be allocated.[42]

42. Supreme Court 14 April 2000, ECLI:NL:HR:2000:AA5519 (*HBS/Danestyle*).

3. *Information*

3.1 *Names of manufacturer, distributors etc.*

The infringer may be ordered to supply the names of manufacturers, distributors, etc. (Article 70(10) DPA).

3.2 *Names of customers*

The infringer may be ordered to supply the names of customers (Article 70(10) DPA).

3.3 *Information about infringing sales*

The infringer may be ordered to supply information about infringing sales (Article 70(5) DPA).

3.4 *Account of profits*

The infringer may be ordered to supply information about the account of profits (Article 70(5) DPA).

4. *Recall of products and destruction*

The patent holder has the right to recall the infringing products, as well as the materials and instruments that are used to manufacture the products. Destruction of the infringing products and infringing advertisement may be granted for relief as well.[43] The infringer may be ordered to send a letter to all customers for recall of the infringing products (Article 70(7) DPA).

5. *Recovery of legal costs*

Under Dutch law, Article 1019h of the Code of Civil Procedure provides for the recovery of legal costs in intellectual property cases. The unsuccessful party shall be ordered to pay both its own legal costs and the legal costs of the other party in full, unless this is not in accordance with the requirements of reasonableness and fairness. In any case, the costs should be reasonable and proportionate.

---

43. Q238 AIPPI second medical use or indication claims, p. 9.

VI. Exceptions from patent protection

1. *Exhaustion of rights*

When a product has been put on the market lawfully in the Netherlands, the patent holder can no longer exercise its intellectual property rights (Article 53(5) DPA). The rights are exhausted.

2. *Patient welfare*

In G2/08 it is stated by the Enlarged Board of Appeal of the EPO that physicians should be free to take all actions necessary to cure or prevent a disease, and that they should not be limited by patents. This decision is likely to be followed by the Dutch courts.[44] Furthermore, obtaining a patent for the treatment of a patient is not possible (Article 3(1)(f) DPA).

3. *Others specific to second medical use claims*

Under Dutch law no specific exceptions from patent protection are made for second medical use claims.

VII. Procedural issues

1. *Preliminary injunction cases*

1.1 Availability for second medical use claims

Preliminary injunction cases can be brought to court in relation to all patent claims, including second medical use claims (*Warner-Lambert/CBG*; *Sun/Novartis*). In first instance, only the District Court in The Hague has jurisdiction in patent cases (Article 80 DPA).

1.2 Specific requirements

A preliminary injunction can only be given when there is sufficient evidence of interest in obtaining urgent relief.

2. *Cases on the merits*

Apart from bringing a normal action on the merits, a party can request the accelerated regime in patent cases (Versneld Regime Octrooi). If the requesting party submits all documents necessary for the request, the court will allow the case in the accelerated regime.[45] The accelerated regime facilitates both the increasing complexity of patent

44. Q238 AIPPI second medical use or indication claims (The Netherlands), p. 5.
45. VRO Regulations.

cases and the need for a fast decision. In first instance, only the District Court in The Hague has jurisdiction in patent cases (Article 80 DPA).

3. *Enforcement of judgments*

The enforcement of judgments in second medical use cases may be difficult. First of all it is difficult to enforce a general injunction of infringement, since the generic product may still be used for the non-patented indication. More specifically, it is difficult to hold pharmacists liable. Under Dutch law physicians are not obliged to specify the medical indication on the prescription. For that reason, it is hard to prove the requisite knowledge of a pharmacist.[46]

VIII. Validity

1. *Relevance for infringement cases*

If the patent is held invalid, the court cannot establish infringement. Thus, when the counterparty claims infringement of its patent, it is important to claim invalidity of the patent. However, the court can hold the patent partially invalid, in which case a part of the patent may still be infringed (Article 75(1) DPA).

2. *Specifics for second medical use claims*

There are no specific comments about validity in infringement cases of second medical use claims.

IX. Tactical considerations

1. *Plaintiff*

If possible, always claim both indirect and direct infringement. In *Sun/Novartis*, direct infringement was not claimed until the pleadings in the proceedings on the merits. Because neither party fully prepared this claim, the court decided to postpone the proceedings. According to the court the possibility of direct infringement could not be excluded, but a better preparation was required in order to proceed. As was established in *Warner-Lambert/CBG*, apart from liability for indirect or direct infringement, an alleged infringer can be held liable for civil tort.

2. *Defendant*

Defendants should always avoid using the still patented indication in the SmPC, PIL and any other communications. Furthermore, defendants should be able to demonstrate that they took adequate measures to avoid use for the patented indication.

46. Q238 AIPPI second medical use or indication claims (The Netherlands), p. 12.

Italy

Lamberto Liuzzo, Bianca M. Gutierrez

A. AVAILABILITY OF PROTECTION

I. Legal framework

1. National statutory laws

1.1 Pharmaceuticals

The Italian Industrial Property Code ("IPC", Legislative Decree No. 30 of 10 February 2005, as implemented, among other laws, by Legislative Decree No. 140 of 16 March 2006, by Law No. 99 of 23 July 2009, and by Legislative Decree No. 131 of 13 August 2010), provides that, where a substance or a composition of substances is already known to be used in a *first medical use,* it may still be patentable for any second or further new utilization (i.e. *second medical use*).

The basis for patent protection is provided for in Article 46 IPC.

Article 46(1) states that an invention shall be considered novel if it is not anticipated in the prior art.

Article 46(4) contemplates an exception from the general principle that patents can only be obtained for novel products. Article 46(4) allows the patentability of new uses of a substance or a composition of substances, by admitting claims to products already included in the prior art, "provided that they are for the purpose of a new utilization", without any limitation of the technical field (medical or other).

In this case, a known substance or composition of substances can be patented if the second or further use claims fulfil all other requirements of patentability, especially that of inventive step. The new use is inventive if for a person "who is an expert in the field, it is not evident from the prior art" (Article 48 IPC).

Article 45(5) IPC makes it clear that the provisions of Article 45(4), which excludes patentability of methods for surgical or therapeutic treatment of human or animal bodies and diagnostic methods applied to human or animal bodies, does not apply to products (substances and compositions) for the use of one such method.

According to the IPC, any type of second medical use is patentable if novel and inventive (Articles 46 and 48 IPC).

The IPC does not provide any further indication about the possible object of second medical use claims.

The Italian Patent Office also provides no guidelines in relation to second medical use claims.

1.2 Biologics

The IPC was amended in order to implement EC Directive 1998/44, first by Law No. 78 of 22 February 2006, and secondly by Legislative Decree No. 131 providing for the patentability of biotechnological inventions (Articles 81-bis et seq.).

2. International treaties

The 1994 TRIPs Agreement was implemented with the creation of the IPC by Legislative Decree No. 30, amended by Legislative Decree No. 131.

3. Availability through case law

The availability and scope of patent protection in Italy is governed by the IPC, as applied by the Italian courts.

4. Patent term extension/SPCs

SPCs are granted in Italy under Regulation EC No. 469/2009 and the IPC, in particular Articles 61, 68(1-bis) and 81 et seq.

II. Policy considerations

Public policy requires that second medical uses be patentable and no arguments exist to the contrary.

Research activities by pharmaceutical companies in the medical field are clearly desirable and they must be supported and fostered by giving an appropriate patent reward.

In terms of the interests involved, secondary research, i.e. research study into uses of known compounds, deserves to be given the same rewards as the search for new compounds with respect to patent protection.

Italian law ensures the right balance between the interests of the relevant stakeholders.

B. VALIDITY

See section A.I.1.1.

Italian courts have decided on cases regarding the validity of European patents issued for Italy having as an object second medical use claims.

To quote a few court decisions:

- The Court of Milan declared the nullity in Italy of a European patent concerning the second medical use of repaglinide as an antidiabetic for lack of inventive activity according to Article 48 IPC (Court of Milan, 7 July 2011, No. 10997/2011, in Darts).
- The Court of Milan declared the partial nullity for lack of novelty of a European patent concerning the synergic combination of an essential fatty acid and a biocompatible disulphide claimed for use in the treatment of a wide range of disorders including diabetic, inflammatory, neurodegenerative and cardiovascular conditions (Court of Milan, 23 September 2010, No. 14437/2010, in www.eplawpatentblog.com).
- The Court of Turin declared the nullity in Italy of a European patent claiming the use of levobupivacaine or a salt thereof for the manufacture of a medicament for use as an anesthetic in obstetrics for lack of inventive activity according to Article 48 IPC (Court of Turin, 18 September 2015, No. 5972/2015, in Darts).
- In a proceeding concerning the nullity of a European patent, the Court of Appeal of Turin declared that the claim setting out the use of transferosomes to convey pharmacologically active principles inside the human body was not contrary to Article 45(4) because its object cannot be considered a therapeutic treatment according to Article 52(4) EPC (Court of Appeal of Turin, July 2009, in Giur. Ann. Dir. Ind., 2010, No. 5507).

I. Allowable claim wording

See above, section B.

II. Novelty

See section A.I.1.1.

1. General definition of novelty and prior art

Article 46(1) IPC states that an invention shall be considered novel if it is not anticipated in the prior art. Prior art consists of all that has been made available to the public in the territory of the country or abroad prior to the date of filing of the patent application, through a written or verbal description or any other means.

2. Definition of skilled person

The definition of a skilled person depends on the facts and on what is the object of the invention. According to Article 48 IPC, the skilled person is "an expert in the field".

3. *Scope of disclosure*

3.1 *General rules*

Article 51 IPC states that the invention must be described in a sufficiently clear and complete manner so that any person who is an expert in the field (*homme du mètier*) can implement it.

3.2 *First medical use*

See Chapter I, "EPO".

3.3 *New subject matter*

See Chapter I, "EPO"

3.4 *New data*

See Chapter I, "EPO"

4. *Requirements for second medical use*

See Chapter I, "EPO"

5. *Timing issues*

See Chapter I, "EPO"

III. Inventive step/non-obviousness

1. *Definition of inventive step/non-obviousness*

According to Article 48 IPC, an invention is considered as involving inventive activity if for a person "who is an expert in the field, it is not evident from the prior art".

See above, section A.

2. *Same scope of disclosure as for novelty?*

See Chapter I, "EPO".

3. *Assessment of inventive step/non-obviousness*

See Chapter I, "EPO".

IV. Amendment of claims

1. *Admissibility of amendments in general*

According to Articles 172(2), 79 and 76(1)(c) IPC, an application for a patent or a granted patent may be amended on request of the owner. The request must be accompanied by the modified description and drawings.

The requirements for assessing amendments made to description, figures and/or claims depend on the timing:

- the assessment of amendments made before the patent is granted is ruled by Articles 172(2) and 76(1)(c) and in principle any kind of amendment is allowed (even adding examples to the description) on condition that it concerns non-substantial aspects of the invention; whereas,
- amendments made to a granted patent, i.e. post grant amendments, are based on Article 79 and can only limit the scope of protection.

Amendments that extend the subject matter beyond the content of the application as filed will lead to nullity of a granted patent.

In proceedings concerning nullity of a patent, the owner may submit to the court, at any stage or instance of judgement, amended claims (Article 79(3) IPC). The modified claims must remain within the limits of the content of the patent application as originally filed and must not extend the protection conferred by the granted patent.

According to some Italian judges, amendments of claims during proceedings concerning nullity are permitted only if a declaration signed by the owner of the patent or by their specifically authorized representative is filed with the court. The declaration must include the text of the amended claims (Court of Milan, May 21, 2015, No. 10512/2015 in Darts; Court of Milan, 1 December 2014).

Italian courts will admit amendments of second medical use claims submitted to the court during the proceedings, if the modified claims remain within the limits of the content of the patent application and do not extend the protection conferred by the granted patent according to Article 79(3) IPC (Court of Milan, 21 May 2015, No. 10512/2015, in Darts; Court of Appeal of Milan, 10 July 2014, No. 3642/2014: "the only condition is that the object of the patent does not extend beyond the content of the patent application as initially filed").

> "Italian and European laws allow amendments to the claims of a patent first of all during the examination procedure. After the filing of the application and before the office has granted the patent ... the applicant may [supplement it with new examples or limit the description, claims and drawings originally filed] (Article 172.2 IPC), on condition that these amendments do not extend the patent beyond the content of the initial application (Article 76. 1, as implemented by D. Lgs. 131/10; Articles 102.3, 123.2 EPC; Article 172.2 IPC) ... Amendments to a granted patent are possible too, limitations of its object on request of the owner are allowed (Article 79) also in proceedings concerning nullity of the patent in case of declaration of a partial nullity (Article 76.2). An application for conversion to a different patent is allowed, if the original patent contains the requirements of validity of the new one and this protection would have been desired by the

requesting party if he had known of the nullity (Article 76.3)."(Court of Milan, 23 September 2010, No. 14437/2010, in www.eplawpatentblog.com).

2. *Procedural issues*

2.1 Independent limitation proceedings

See above, section B.IV.1.

2.2 Opposition proceedings

See above, section B.IV.1.

2.3 Nullity actions

See above section B.IV.1.

3. *Added matter*

See above section B.IV.1.

4. *Sufficiency*

See above section B.IV.1.

V. Change of patent category

See Chapter I, "EPO".

C. INFRINGEMENT AND LITIGATION

I. Legal framework

1. *National statutory laws*

According to Article 66 IPC ("Patent right") the owner of a patent has the exclusive rights to implement the invention and profit from it in the territory of Italy. In particular, the patent grants the owner the rights: i) if the object of the patent is a product, to prohibit third parties from producing, using, putting on the market, selling or importing the product in question, ii) if the object of the patent is a process, to prohibit third parties from applying the process and to put on the market, sell or import a product directly obtained from the patented process pursuant to Article 67.

Although the IPC does not contain any specific provision regarding infringement of use (in particular, second medical use) claims, the right attached to such claims can be derived from the above mentioned provisions of Article 66 IPC.

The exclusive rights conferred by a patent extend within the limits and the conditions established by the IPC (Article 68 "Limitations on patent rights").

Whatever the object of the invention may be, the exclusive rights of a patented invention do not extend to: a) actions carried out in the private sphere and for non-commercial purposes; b) studies and trials aimed at obtaining a marketing authorization for a drug, including in foreign countries, and the resulting practical requirements including the preparation and utilization of the pharmacologically active raw materials strictly necessary for the same; c) the occasional preparation of unit doses of drugs in pharmacies on prescription (so called galenic preparations) and the drugs thus prepared, provided that no industrially produced active principles are utilized.

The *ratio* is that the exempted actions must be justified by reason of the overriding public health interest.

The principles contemplated by Articles 66, 67 and 68 IPC fully apply to second medical use claims.

A party marketing a drug with label instructions which describe a patented use may be considered liable to infringement of second medical use claims.

On the contrary, a physician prescribing a drug for a patented second medical use may not in principle be liable to infringement. The activity of physicians can be considered to fall within the exception of Article 68(1)(a) IPC: "Physicians should be free to take all actions they considered suitable to prevent or to cure a disease, and in this exercise they should remain uninhibited by patents" (Enlarged Board of Appeal of EPO, 19 February 2010 - Case No. G 0002/08).

The patient taking the drug is not responsible for infringement according to Article 68(1)(a) IPC because "actions carried out in the private sphere and for non-commercial purposes" are not covered by the exclusive rights attributed by a patent.

Under Italian law, second medical use claims may be enforced both on the basis of direct and indirect infringement, depending on the circumstances.

According to Article 53(2), (3) and (4) IPC, the enforcement may also occur before the granting of the patent, after the date on which the application with the description, claims and designs is made available to the public as per Article 132(1).

Manufacturing, importing, marketing, offering for sale, distributing and selling of a drug protected by a second medical use claim are considered forms of direct infringement, particularly: (a) where the drug is immediately connected to the patented second medical use (e.g. the packaging refers to the patented use), or (b) even if not declared on packaging, the drug is unequivocally destined for the second medical use.

A pharmacist who sells a drug for the patented use on medical prescription for use other than that for which said drug has been officially approved (off-label sales) is liable for direct infringement. In these cases, it is not relevant whether or not the pharmacist is aware of the infringing use.

The manufacture, sale and supply of a generic version of a medicament for any use constitutes an infringement if the said medicament is approved for more than one indication and some fall within the second medical use claims. In this case, liability can be excluded if the sale of the generic version is accompanied by clear information that it cannot be used for the patented use.

Accordingly, in the case of a medicament which is legally on the market for a use not covered by a second medical use claim, a manufacturer omitting any and all reference (on the packaging or in advertising) to a protected second medical use, could be liable – in specific circumstances – for indirect infringement. Particularly, the responsibility of the manufacturer is ascertained if the medicament is sold for a condition other than that for which the medicament has been officially approved (i.e. off-label).

More specifically, under the relevant case law, a claim for indirect infringement requires either (a) the supply of means that are unequivocally intended to be used for the infringing use, or (b) where the means can also be for purposes other than the infringing uses (as in the case of a medicament which is legally on the market for a non-patented use), the knowledge (or wilful ignorance) of the supplier that the supplied means will however be used for the infringing purposes.

In the case of an infringement of second medical use claims, the owner of the patent may act before the Italian courts:

(a) with a preliminary procedure, to obtain one or more of the preliminary, interim and precautionary measures contemplated by the IPC, such as preliminary injunctions, preliminary seizures and description (Articles 129, 131 and 132 IPC); or
(b) with a procedure on the merits to obtain final relief (Articles 124-126 IPC).

The exclusive licensee can also act before an Italian court to obtain the above mentioned measures in its own interest.

2. *Case law*

Italian courts determine direct or indirect infringement of a second medical use claim based on: i) labels, packaging and any form of instruction and technical information given to physicians, hospitals, pharmacies and patients; ii) scientific articles and studies, medical conferences showing the use of the product, including its listing in the Transparency List of Italian Medicine Agency.

> "On the packaging of the product 'Cereal-YO' there are no indications about a hypothetical use in the medical field, nor that the consumption of the biscuit is indicated for functional bowel disorders. There is no evidence at all that Cereal-YO is sold with the indication of use in the treatment of bowel disorder syndrome ... The exclusive rights attributed by the patent are the ones related to the use of lactic bacteria for the preparation of bakery, according to claims 1 and 4, for the prevention and treatment of functional bowel disorders. On the contrary, the product Kraft-Mondelez named Cereal-YO, being sold without any medical-therapeutic use and indications for the treatment of functional bowel disorders, does not infringe the EP'372 patent" (Court of Milan, 21 May 2015, No. 10512/2015, in Darts).

> "The therapeutic indication that Meda Pharma assumes to be infringed is diabetic neuropathy. The evidence of the counterfeiting should have to be given by the defendant [the owner of the patent], who should have demonstrated that Alanerv was and is actually indicated for diabetic neuropathy or diabetic

> polyneuropathy" (Court of Appeal of Milan, 10 July 2014, No. 3642/2014; Court of Milan, 23 September 2010, No. 14437, in www.eplawpatentblog.com).
>
> "The second medical use has been deemed patentable; the second medical use regards the treatment of diabetic disorders. Thus the infringement must be judged considering this particular use ... Considering the chemical composition there are no differences between Alanerv and the patented products ... However the infringement has not been sufficiently proved, considering that no package or brochure showing the medical use object of the patent have been filed with the Court" (Court of Milan, 23 September 2010, No. 14437/2010, in www.eplawpatentblog.com).

For a case of description issued according to Article 129 IPC against the supplier and the hospital using a drug covered by three EP patents, the Court of Turin (June 13, 2012, in Darts) excluded the exemption provided for in Article 68 IPC because of the hospital's entrepreneurial dimension. The patents concerned: i) the use of botulinum toxin to treat urinary incontinence (EP 1475099) and recalcitrant voiding dysfunction (EP 1658858); ii) the use of neurotoxin therapy for treatment of urologic and related disorders (EP 2145629).

II. Claim construction

1. General rules

See above, section C.I.

2. Specific issues for use claims

See above, section C.I.

III. Scope of protection

1. Scope of the use

1.1 General definition of the term "use"

The IPC does not contain any specific provision regarding infringement of use (in particular, second medical use) claims. The right attached to such claims can be derived from Article 66 IPC. See above, section C.I.1.

1.2 Manufacture of the pharmaceutical

See above, section C.I.1.

1.3 Sale of the product

See above, section C.I.1.

1.4. Offer for sale

See above, section C.I.1.

1.5 Application to the patient

See above, section C.I.1.

1.6 Combination products

See Chapter I, "EPO".

2. Absolute product protection

2.1 Limitation through the term "use"

See above, section C.I.

2.2 Off-label use

See above, section C.I.

3. Dosage regimes

See above, section C.I.

4. Extension under the doctrine of equivalents

The IPC was amended by Legislative Decree No. 131 to bring Italian law in line with EPC 2000, by adding Article 52(3-bis). According to this Article: "To determine the scope of the protection granted by the patent, every element that is equivalent to an element indicated in the claims must be considered".

In any case, before this change, the Italian courts already recognized the theory of equivalents.

IV. Infringing acts

See the examples in section C.I.2.

1. Infringing person or entity

See above, sections C.I.1 and C.IV.

2. *Direct infringement*

2.1 Manufacture of the pharmaceutical

See above, sections C.I.1 and C.IV.

2.2 Offer for sale

See above, sections C.I.1 and C.IV.

2.3 Sale

See above, sections C.I.1 and C.IV.

2.4 Export

See Chapter I, "EPO".

2.5 Import

See Chapter I, "EPO".

2.6 Combination products

See Chapter I, "EPO".

3. *Indirect infringement*

3.1 Objective acts

See above, section C.I.1 and C.IV.

3.2 Subjective conditions

See above, section C.I.1.

3.3 Export

See Chapter I, "EPO".

3.4 Import

See Chapter I, "EPO".

4. *Off-label use*

4.1 *General admissibility of off-label use*

See above, sections C.I and C.IV.

4.2 *Liable persons*

See above, sections C.I.1 and C.IV.

V. Remedies

1. *Injunctions*

The requirements to obtain a preliminary measure (injunction, seizure, etc.) are *fumus boni iuris* and *periculum in mora* in accordance with the provisions of the Italian Code of Civil Procedure concerning proceedings for interim relief (Articles 669-bis et seq.).

Statements provided on the product packaging may justify the granting of a preliminary injunction as well as advertising or other activities showing implementation of the second medical use.

To obtain a final injunction (Article 124 IPC) the owner of the patent must file full and clear evidence of the infringing acts with the court.

2. *Damages*

According to Article 125 IPC, the owner of the infringed patent may seek compensation for damages and restitution of profits from the infringer. The compensation due to the damaged party shall be set according to Articles 1223, 1226 and 1227 of the Italian Civil Code.

3. *Information*

Article 121-bis IPC states that in both proceedings, for interim relief and for the merits, the court may order that information (regarding the origin, the distribution networks of goods or the provision of services) be provided by the infringing party. The right to information contemplated by Article 121-bis is granted in case of commercial violation. In the other cases in which there is no commercial violation, Article 121 IPC provides that under certain conditions the court can order the infringing party to file elements of information with the court for “the identification of the persons involved in the production and distribution of the goods or services that constitute an infringement of the industrial property rights”.

It must be pointed out that Articles 121 et seq. IPC have been implemented by Legislative Decree No. 140, which harmonized Italian law with Directive 2004/48/EC.

3.1 *Names of manufacturer, distributors etc.*

See above, section C.V.3.

3.2 *Names of customers*

See above, section C.V.3.

3.3 *Information about infringing sales*

See above, section C.V.3.

3.4 *Account of profits*

See above, section C.V.3.

4. ***Recall of products and destruction***

As per Article 131 IPC, the owner of the patent rights may obtain an order from the court for the delivery up or destruction of the infringing articles.

5. ***Recovery of legal costs***

The winning party generally obtains recovery of the costs of proceedings from the other party. The award of the costs depends on: the value of the lawsuit; the kind of assistance, also considering the number of the briefs filed with the court; the kind of trial (hearing of witnesses, technical expert consultancy, etc.).

VI. Exceptions from patent protection

1. ***Exhaustion of rights***

According to Article 5 IPC, patented products brought to the market by the patentee or with their consent in Italy or within the EU or EEA, are not covered by patent protection.

2. ***Patient welfare***

The exclusive right to a patented invention does not extend to actions carried out in the private sphere or for non-commercial purposes (Article 68(1) IPC). See above, section C.I.1.

3. ***Other issues specific to second medical use claims***

Other than the points set out above, there are no specific issues relevant to second medical use claims.

VII. Procedural issues

1. Preliminary injunction cases

According to Articles 129 and 131 IPC, the patent owner may request of the Judge preliminary measures, such as injunction and seizure, against the manufacture, sale and use of the items constituting an infringement of the right. See above, section C.I.1.

1.1 Availability for second medical use claims

Preliminary measures can be also requested by the owner of a second medical use patent.

1.2 Specific requirements

See above, section C.I.1.

2. Cases on the merits

See above, section C.I.2. See also section B.

3. Enforcement of judgments

According to Article 124, from the judgement that determines the infringement of an industrial property right, an injunction may be ordered against the manufacture, sale and use of the items constituting an infringement of the right and an order to definitively withdraw those items from the market. In issuing the injunction, the court may set a sum due for any infringement or instance of non-compliance subsequently determined, and for any delay in carrying out the order.

VIII. Validity

Italian courts have decided on cases regarding the validity of European patents issued for Italy having as an object second medical use claims. To quote a few decisions: Court of Milan, 7 July 2011, No. 10997/2011, in Darts; Court of Milan, 23 September 2010, No. 14437/2010, in www.eplawpatentblog.com; Court of Turin, 18 September 2015, No. 5972/2015, in Darts; Court of Appeal of Turin July 2009, in Giur. Ann. Dir. Ind., 2010, No. 5507 – see above, section B.

IX. Tactical considerations

1. Plaintiff

To prevent generic launch of a product that constitutes an infringement of a patented second medical use, the patent owner may ask for preliminary measures such as injunction and seizure against the producer and those making use of the infringing product on the market. See above section C.I.1.

2. *Defendant*

A party marketing a drug with label instructions which do not describe the patented use may not be considered responsible for counterfeiting. Special attention must be given to the label and other indications accompanying the product.

Sweden

Jonas Westerberg

A. AVAILABILITY OF PROTECTION

I. Legal framework

1. National statutory laws

1.1 Pharmaceuticals

The central legislation in the field of patents is the Patents Act (Swe. *Patentlagen* – SFS 1967:837). Sweden became a member of the European Patent Convention ("EPC") in 1978, and the Act was then and has since been amended to conform to the EPC (including the latest revisions in connection with the EPC 2000).

Both the Supreme Administrative Court – for administrative proceedings – and the Supreme Court – for proceedings in the general courts – have established that the Patents Act shall be interpreted in line with the material provisions of the EPC and the case law of the European Patent Office ("EPO") provided that such practice is not in conflict with Swedish legislation (RÅ 1990 ref 84 and NJA 2000 p. 49, respectively).

The Patents Act allows patents covering any aspect of new uses of known pharmaceutical compounds (hereafter referred to as "second medical use claims") provided that the ordinary patentability criteria, as applied to second medical use patents, are met. The Swedish Patent and Registration Office's assessment of patentability is generally harmonised with the practice of the EPO.

Section 1d of the Patents Act corresponds to Article 53(c) of the EPC 2000 and thus prohibits the grant of patents for methods directed to surgical or therapeutic treatments and to diagnostic methods practiced on humans or animals, while it acknowledges the patentability of products, including compounds and mixtures of compounds for use in such methods.

It was added to the Patents Act after the entry into force of EPC 2000.

1.2 Biologics

The Biotech Directive (98/44//EC) has been implemented in the Patents Act.

2. International treaties

2.1 TRIPS

The Patents Act reflects the changes made in the EPC 2000, intended to harmonise EPC with the 1994 TRIPS Agreement.

3. Availability through case law

Availability of protection for second medical use inventions are governed by statute as interpreted by case law. As noted above case law of the EPO is of direct relevance for the Swedish context.

4. Patent term extension/SPCs

SPCs and six-month paediatric extensions thereof are available pursuant to Regulation (EC) No. 469/2009 and No. 1901/2006. The European Court of Justice decision in case C-130/11 (*Neurim*) meant that also a new and patented indication for a known drug that had already been the subject of an earlier marketing authorisation may give right to an SPC.

II. Policy considerations

1. Health and social issues

The current Swedish benefit system for prescription drugs involves that patients which has been prescribed an original medicine are normally dispensed a cheaper generic equivalent instead, if generic medicinal products exist in the market. This generic substitution is mandatory (unless the patient is willing to pay the difference in price themself). The aim is to reduce government costs and to increase competition after the expiry of the patent for the originator product.

While the patents for second or further medical uses still are in force it is possible for generic manufacturers to obtain a generic marketing authorisation ("MA") for the first medical use in an easy and inexpensive way. To avoid patent infringement of the patent protecting the second medical use, the generic applies for a "skinny label" MA, which only covers the indications that no longer have patent protection. But because the medicinal products are identical in terms of active ingredient, the generic medicinal product can despite this also be used for the still-patented areas.

The assessment of whether products are medically substitutable for the purpose of generic substitution is made by the Swedish Medical Products Agency ("MPA") on its own initiative. This means that the company which has obtained a generic MA with a skinny label does not need to apply for such an assessment and cannot avoid that such decision is taken. When deciding on the substitutability according to the regulations the MPA does not take into account the existence of patents. Neither is the decision on substitutability limited to the patent-free areas of use for which the generic medicinal product is formally approved. A decision on substitutability therefore means that the exchange at the pharmacy will take place even if the patient is being treated for a condition which the generic medicinal product is not formally approved for and which is still patent protected.

Since the Swedish reimbursement system is product-based (as opposed to indication based), there is no system for controlling the indication for which a medicinal product has been prescribed in the individual case and a generic medicinal product will also be reimbursed, even when its actual use as substituted is for an unapproved and still patent protected indication.

2. *Legal issues*

The Swedish regulatory system for generic substitution involves that patients will receive the generic product which is the cheapest at the time of dispensation, regardless of the condition which the patient has received the product for, and even if the use of the medicinal product for the patient's condition is still patented. There is no system for monitoring for which indications a medicinal product is dispensed at the pharmacy. This creates an uncertainty for all parties, both generic manufacturers and originators: What measures could constitute patent infringement of a second medical use patent? What steps need to be taken in order to be able to market a generic product for non-patented uses without risk of running foul of patent law? What liability do the other actors in the system (the MPA, physicians, county councils and pharmacies) have when they play their part in the system? These issues have not yet been tried by Swedish courts.

There is a clear need for some kind of a coordination between the regulatory systems and the patent system in order to both give effective protection to patents claiming a second medical use and allow third parties to exploit off-patent medical uses without – involuntarily – running foul of patent protection.

For a third party who desires to exploit a first use of an active ingredient that has become off patent, but at the same time respect the patented second medical use, the available course of action is to obtain a marketing approval for the generic product that covers the first medical use only (a so-called carve out or skinny labelling).

However, even so there are three aspects that complicate the situation both for the patentee of the second medical use and the third party wanting to exploit the patent free medical use:

The free prescription right of physicians, which means that cross-label and off-label prescription is possible. Notably a prescription does not have to state the indication for which the medication is prescribed (and normally does not). This means that the generic product approved only for the first medical use may be prescribed also for the patented second medical use without real possibilities to monitor such use.

The mandatory substitution of generic medicines at the pharmacy level which means that a generic product approved only for off-patent use is provided by the pharmacy for the patented second medical use even if the prescription states the original product sold by the patentee (or their licensees).

The fact that the benefit system for pharmaceuticals is product based and thus not limited to the use of a pharmaceutical product in an approved indication. This means that also cross-label and off-label use benefits from such subsidies.

Hence, there is room for improving the regulatory provisions to improve the practical protection of the second medical use patentee and minimise the risks for unintended infringement of such patents.

B. VALIDITY

I. Allowable claim wording

The Swedish practice of what constitutes impermissible subject matter follows the practices of the EPO.

For applications filed before 29 January 2011, Swedish practice allowed second medical use claims in the "Swiss-type" form in accordance with the set practice of the EPO (i.e."Use of [active ingredient X] for the manufacture of a medicament to treat [disease Y]").

Applications for second medical use patents filed after 29 January 2011 must be drafted as EPC 2000 purpose-limited product claims (i.e. "[Active ingredient X"] for use in the treatment of [disease Y]".

This amendment to Swedish practice was performed in line with the publication in the Official Journal of decision G2/08 of the EPO EBoA on 20 September 2010. Together with this publication, it was confirmed that for European applications filed from 29 January 2011, the EPO does not allow Swiss-type claims. The decision had no retroactive effect.

According to Section 15 of the Swedish Patent Rules (issued by the Swedish Patent and Registration Office), the claims of a second medical use invention must contain a precise definition of the intended medical application.

The guidelines for the examiners at the Swedish Patent and Registration Office define a new second medical use as the "provision of a new medical effect of a known substance". This medical effect needs to be "specifically provided" in the application. No more details regarding the concept of a medical effect are given. However, it is the Swedish Patent and Registration Office's standard practice to follow the EPO in this respect. The Guidelines for Examination in the EPO (GL) and case law of the EPO Boards of Appeal ("BoA") and Enlarged Board of Appeal ("EBoA") provide additional, although not extensive, information on this subject.

II. Novelty

Section 2 of the Patents Act, sets out the novelty criteria. This paragraph comprises a provision corresponding to Article 54(5) EPC 2000, providing that the novelty requirement does not prevent the grant of a patent for a known substance or a known mixture of substances for specific use in a method referred to in Section 1d (surgical or therapeutic treatment), if such use is not known.

1. *General definition of novelty and prior art*

According to Section 2 of the Patents Act, a patent may only be granted for an invention which is new in relation to what was known prior to the date of the patent application and shall differ significantly therefrom (i.e. have inventive step). What was "known" includes everything which was publicly available by means of writing, lectures, exploitation, or otherwise. Furthermore, the content of a patent application submitted for Sweden prior to such date shall be considered known for purpose of assessing novelty (only), where such application was later available to the public in accordance with Section 22 (publication).

Prior art does not need to exist physically or be commercially available. It is sufficient that someone earlier has described, presented or produced something that contains the use of a certain technology. An existing product is the most obvious form of prior art. Nevertheless, many inventions never become products, yet there may be evidence of them somewhere. That evidence – whatever form it may take – will be prior art.

Swedish law does not expressly set out any criterion for how the state of art should be interpreted, but it is generally understood that the state of the art should be interpreted as it would by a person skilled in the art.

2. *Definition of skilled person*

There is no statutory definition of the skilled person but what is set out in Section C, IV, 9.6 of the EPO Guidelines would generally apply in the Swedish context.

The person skilled in the art should be presumed to be an ordinary practitioner aware of what was common general knowledge in the art at the relevant date. They should also be presumed to have had access to everything in the "state of the art", in particular the documents cited in the search report, and to have had at their disposal the normal means and capacity for routine work and experimentation. There may be instances where it is more appropriate to think in terms of a group of persons, e.g. a research or production team, than a single person. This may apply, for example, in certain advanced technologies such as computers or telephone systems and in highly specialised processes such as the commercial production of integrated circuits or of complex chemical substances.

3. *Scope of disclosure*

3.1 *General rules*

The specification of a patent should disclose the invention clearly enough for it to be performed by the skilled person. Furthermore, the specification of the patent should contain sufficient information to allow the skilled person to make a reasonable prediction that the invention will work with substantially everything falling within the scope of the claim, i.e. the claim must be plausible or credible across its scope in light of the data in the specification read in the light of the skilled person's common general knowledge.

3.2 First medical use

When for the first time someone finds a way to use a substance or a mixture of substances for medical purposes, it is called the first medical use. In other words, the substances are already known, when for the first time they are shown to be effective as drugs. The possibility to obtain a patent for the first medical use is found in Section 2 of the Patents Act, which corresponds with Article 54(4) EPC. The patentability for first medical uses is an exception from the novelty requirement. However, it requires that the use of the substance was not previously known in a method for surgical or therapeutic treatment, or other method for diagnosis which is intended for use on humans or animals.

4. Requirements for second medical use

See section B.I, above.

5. Timing issues

5.1 Relevant time of development of second use

It is not necessary for a patent to contain experimental data from clinical trials or otherwise, as long as the claims are credible or plausible in light of the information in the specification and the common general knowledge of the skilled person. The applicant may thus rely on pre-clinical data from animal models or similar if this is sufficient to make it plausible that the medicament will treat the newly claimed indication.

5.2 Role of new data

Post-published data may be relied upon to support the plausibility of the disclosure in the application as filed.

5.3 Use of old data

Old data may be used in order to establish that the claims are credible or plausible.

III. Inventive step/non-obviousness

1. Definition of inventive step/non-obviousness

An invention is considered as involving an inventive step if, having regard to the state of the art, it is not obvious to a person skilled in the art.

Thus the question to consider, in relation to any claim defining the invention, is whether before the filing or priority date valid for that claim, having regard to the art known at the time, it would have been obvious to the person skilled in the art to arrive at something falling within the terms of the claim. If so, the claim lacks inventive step. The term "obvious" means that which does not go beyond the normal progress of technology but merely follows plainly or logically from the prior art, i.e. something which does not involve the exercise of any skill or ability beyond that to be expected of the person skilled in the art.

2. *Same scope of disclosure as for novelty?*

In considering inventive step, as distinct from novelty, it is fair to construe any published document in the light of knowledge up to and including the day before the filing or priority date valid for the claimed invention and to have regard to all the knowledge generally available to the person skilled in the art up to and including that day.

3. *Assessment of inventive step/non-obviousness*

The Swedish Patent Office and courts generally apply the problem-solution approach adopted by the EPO.

IV. Amendment of claims after grant

1. *Admissibility of post-grant amendments in general*

Post-grant amendments of patent claims are admissible provided certain criteria are met. Under Swedish law the term used for this measure is a "patent limitation" as it is not possible to extend the patent claims. Other requirements are that the proposed amended claims are sufficiently clear to enable a person skilled in the art to utilise the invention and that the proposed amended claims do not cover subject matter which did not appear in the patent application as filed.

A patent may be amended by the Swedish Patent Office, only if there is no pending opposition proceedings before the EPO and/or court action for invalidation. When an action for revocation of a patent has been filed with a court it is not possible to amend the patent claims administratively any more. As long as the court case is pending only the court is competent to decide a matter regarding amendment (Section 40 a of the Patents Act).

2. *Procedural issues*

2.1 *Independent limitation proceedings*

The holder of a patent may at any time during the patent term, except in a few particular situations, request an amendment to the patent claims at the Swedish Patent and Registration Office. If there are pending opposition proceedings before the Swedish Patent and Registration Office or the EPO or nullification proceedings in respect of the patent, a request for amendment should be denied. If the patent holder has requested at the EPO that a European patent validated for Sweden is amended or revoked, any request for an amendment at the Swedish Patent and Registration

Office should be stayed. Also, if the patent is subject to seizure, charged with a lien, claimed through attachment or if a dispute concerning the transfer of the patent is pending before a court, a request for an amendment is only allowable subject to concerned stakeholders' consent.

The patent holder does not have to provide any reason for its request for an amendment. The new wording of the claims must be filed together with the request. Also, an amended specification should be submitted if the changes to the claims make it necessary. If new characteristics are introduced to the proposed wording of the amended claims the patent holder must state where the corresponding information can be found in the original application as filed.

2.2 Opposition proceedings

Amending national Swedish patent claims in opposition proceedings is admissible under Swedish law. In opposition proceedings the patent holder will be provided with the opposition together with the documents submitted by the opponent and given an opportunity to submit a reply to the opposition. In the response the patent holder may choose to request an amendment to the claims as one way to defend the patent against the opposition. The judgment by the Patent and Registration Office on the opposition will include a decision on the requested amendment of claims if it is found that the patent claims in its original wording are invalid.

2.3 Nullity actions

Patent claims may be amended in nullity actions upon request by the patent holder. The patent claims will be amended if the court finds the patent claims as granted to be invalid and the proposed amended claims valid (i.e. the basic requirements of novelty, inventive step and industrial applicability are met) and subject to the general criteria for amendments.

3. Added matter

Patent claims may not be amended after grant so that the patent covers subject matter which did not appear in the application as filed.

4. Sufficiency

The patent specification must be sufficiently clear to enable a person skilled in the art to utilise the invention, also when the patent claims have been amended after grant.

5. Multiple indications

See Chapter I, "EPO".

V. Change of patent category

1. *General admissibility*

If a patent is amended so that a claim to a product is replaced by a claim to a method for producing the product, this change of category is allowable, provided that the method now claimed only results in the product previously claimed. As it is a fundamental principle of European patent law that the protection conferred by a product claim covers all methods for production of the product, the limitation to one of these methods cannot extend the protection conferred originally (see T 5/90 and T 54/90).

2. *From method to product claim*

If a patent is so amended that a claim to a method of operating a device is replaced by a claim directed to the device itself, this change of category is allowable, provided that the original claim contains the claimed features of the device exhaustively, whether in structural or functional terms (see T 378/86 and T 426/89).

If, however, the device as now claimed is for its features no longer dependent on the circumstances of its operation whereas it depended on them under the terms of the prior method claim, then such a change of category should not be allowed (see T 82/93).

A change in claim category from a method in which an apparatus is used to the apparatus itself is not allowable (see T 86/90).

C. INFRINGEMENT AND LITIGATION

I. Legal framework

1. *National statutory laws*

The Patents Act provides the general framework for assessing infringement.

2. *Case law*

Case law of relevance for the proper understanding of the Patents Act comes from both the administrative courts and the general courts but infringement is exclusively handled by the general courts. As noted above the interpretation of the (harmonised) provisions of the Patents Act is also influenced by EPO case law.

Case law on infringement of second medical use is however scarce and none of the issues arising in relation to so-called skinny labelling or off-label use have been decided.

II. Claim construction

1. *General rules*

Section 39 of the Swedish Patents Act states that the scope of protection of a patent is determined by the patent claims but the description may serve as a guide when the patent claims are construed.

This provision corresponds to Article 69 of the EPC. Thus, the Protocol on the Interpretation of Article 69 is used in Swedish courts as a tool in the evaluation of the scope of the patent protection also in infringement cases.

When determining the scope of protection the objective meaning of the wording should be considered. Also, if a particular meaning to a word has been given in the patent, this meaning should be used when interpreting the claims.

Unclear expressions in the claims cannot be used to extend the scope of protection but this does not mean that the wording of the claims is construed restrictively. The interpretation of the claims is based on the person skilled in the art, considering the description, drawings and the state of the art. If there is a real uncertainty as to the meaning of a claim, which cannot be resolved, the narrower meaning should be applied.

It is permissible to interpret a claim as including a limiting characteristic not covered by the wording, if this characteristic is essential for the invention and it is obvious for the person skilled in the art who reads the description that the claim must be interpreted as including the limiting characteristic.

2. *Specific issues for use claims*

Use claims are subject to the same general principles for claim interpretation as other claims. However, in the context of second medical use claims there are specific issues in respect of the scope of protection afforded by Swiss-type claims in themselves and also in relation to EPC 2000 claims. There is still uncertainty regarding the possible difference in scope of protection provided by claims drafted in applications filed before and after the entry into force of the EPC 2000 and the issuance of G2/08 of the EPO EBoA (Swiss-type claims versus purpose-limited product claims). However, as noted above the Swedish courts are likely to follow the EPO case law in this respect meaning that Swiss-type claims could be given a more limited scope of protection as process claims than purpose-limited product claims according to EPC 2000.

III. Scope of protection

1. *Scope of the use*

1.1 *General definition of the term "use"*

The term "use" appears in several contexts; in the claim defining the invention as such, in the statutory provisions defining the exclusivity afforded by the patent and as part of the question of when an invention has been used and by who.

In the context of the exclusivity afforded by a patent Section 3 of the Patents Act provides that no one without the consent of the patentee may use the patented invention in certain ways. In respect of *direct infringement* these uses include:

a) Manufacture, offer for sale, put on the market or use of a patented *product* or import or possess such product for any of these purposes.
b) Use a patented process or, if it is known or obvious under the circumstances that the process may not be used without the consent of the patentee, offer such process for use in Sweden.
c) Offer for sale, put on the market or use a *product which has been manufactured according to a patented process* or import or possess such product for any of these purposes (so-called indirect product protection).

The Patents Act also affords protection against *indirect (or contributory) infringement* of a patented invention. Thus, no one may without the consent of the patentee use the invention by offering or supplying third parties essential means for using the invention in Sweden if the party providing such means knows or it is obvious under the circumstances that it is suitable and intended to be used in exercising the invention. In case the means offered or provided consist of staple goods ("goods which are common in the trade"), liability for indirect infringement requires that the party providing the means seeks to influence the recipient to use it for exercising the invention.

As noted above there is not yet any Swedish case law dealing with the precise limits of the protection afforded by Swiss-type and EPC 2000 claims concerning second medical use. The following comments can therefore only be taken as a general analysis of the likely protection.

1.2 *Manufacture of the pharmaceutical*

A second medical use claim of the Swiss-type would typically cover the manufacture of a pharmaceutical since it specifically concerns "use of [active ingredient X] for the manufacture of" etc. That is of course as long as it can be established that the manufactured pharmaceutical is intended for the second medical use. With this proviso an EPC 2000 claim (purpose-limited product claim) should also cover the manufacture of the patented product.

An issue of special interest for the second medical use claims is what actually constitutes "manufacture" of a pharmaceutical intended for the second medical use in question. It could at least be argued that such manufacture occurs not only when someone undertakes all the technical steps of synthesising the active substance, formulating tablets/injections etc. but also when someone decides to use (or label) an already existing pharmaceutical with the relevant active ingredient for the patented indication (i.e. the "manufacture" of the pharmaceutical for the second medical use would not have to involve all the technical steps of "real" manufacture).

1.3 *Sale of the product*

As appears from the general account for the exclusivity afforded by patents, putting the product on the market is defined as an infringing act in respect of patented products and products obtained by a patented process (indirect product protection). The expression "put on the market" is meant to encompass any manner for putting the products into circulation, for example the acts of selling, lending, renting and giving away the product in question.

1.4 Offer for sale

The offer for sale is already an infringing act. In the context of pharmaceuticals and the regulatory steps involved in a launch it has been established in case law that neither the application for an MA or obtaining a price decision for inclusion in the governmental subsidy of prescription drugs involve an offer for sale. However, under the right circumstances, where the intention of a subsequent infringing launch can be established, these steps can be considered to be preparatory acts of infringement which entitles the patentee to injunctive relief (also as a preliminary measure).

1.5 Application to the patient

The patient's own use of a pharmaceutical falls under the exemption for private use. A pharmacists' preparation of patented pharmaceutical products in accordance with individual prescriptions (*ex tempore*) is also exempted from patent protection. Physicians are otherwise not exempt from liability for patent infringement and the prescription or physical administration of a patented product could be considered a use of such product also on behalf of the physician or at least their employer (as part of the operation of the hospital and providing health care services). However, there are as far as we are aware no instances where such liability has been claimed in court.

1.6 Combination products

The aforesaid in principle applies also to combination products but direct infringement would require the manufacture, use, etc., of the claimed combination. Indirect infringement could occur when only one of several products to be used in combination is provided to a third party.

2. *Absolute product protection*

2.1 Limitation through the term "use"

The fact that the claimed invention is limited to a specific second medical use means that pharmaceutical product as such (without the addition of an intended or actual use for the patented purpose) is not protected.

2.2 Off-label use

Physicians have traditionally had great freedom to use their professional judgment based on science and clinical experience, in prescribing drugs also for unapproved indications, so-called off-label use. Similar to off-label use is so-called cross-label use

(use of a pharmaceutical approved for one indication for another approved indication), which is of special interest since it occurs in connection with generic substitution at pharmacy level and therefore is of great interest for the protection and value of second medical use patents (cf. section A.II above regarding generic substitution).

As soon as the actual use of a pharmaceutical concerns a patented second medical use it should in principle be covered by the patent protection for a purpose-limited product claim (EPC 2000 type of claim). In respect of Swiss-type claims the question is whether the intention to use a pharmaceutical for the patented indication must have existed at the time of manufacturing in order for subsequent dealings with the product to be covered by the patent protection (in the form of indirect product protection).

3. *Dosage regimes*

Use claims covering dosage regimens prevents the use of a pharmaceutical in such regimen and also the offering for sale or putting on the market of a pharmaceutical with instructions to use in the patented dosage regimen.

4. *Patient groups*

In case the claim only covers use for certain patient groups its scope of protection is limited to use for the specified group.

5. *Extension under the doctrine of equivalents*

The doctrine of equivalents has been developed in case law and can extend the scope of protection beyond literal infringement in cases where one feature of the claimed invention is missing in the alleged infringing product/process but has been substituted with what can be considered an equivalent feature.

The finding of equivalence requires that the missing feature is not vital for the patentability of the invention and that the substitute feature has the same purpose and gives the same functional result as the missing feature of the patent. It has been thought that a further requirement for equivalence is that the substitute feature is considered to be an obvious alternative by the skilled person. However, the fact that the equivalent solution had been found to be patentable over the invention of the infringed patent by the EPO did not prevent the courts from applying the doctrine of equivalence and finding infringement in a court of appeal case (*DeLaval International AB and Lely Industries N.V. v Lely Sverige AB*, Svea Court of Appeal, 10 March 2008, leave to appeal not granted by the Supreme Court).

IV. Infringing acts

1. *Infringing person or entity*

The primary liability for infringing acts lies with the individuals involved in performing the acts defined as being within the exclusivity afforded by the patent (see above). Legal entities are then made liable for the acts of such individuals based on statutory provisions and legal principles concerning the liability for acts done by employees and acts done by legal representatives.

In respect of liability there might arguably be some difference depending on whether the second/further medical use claim has been drafted as a Swiss-type claim or according to the EPC 2000 regime. The fact that the latter type of claims do not refer to the "use of [active ingredient X] for the manufacture of" etc. may involve an increased risk that, for example, a physician could be held directly liable for infringement in case of off-label use of a *per se* non-infringing pharmaceutical for the patented second medical use indication.

As noted above patients are exempt from liability due to the exemption for private use and pharmacists has a limited exemption for *ex tempore* preparations of pharmaceuticals for individual patients.

2. *Direct infringement*

In respect of the general definition and prerequisites for direct infringement, reference is made to section III above.

2.1 *Manufacture of the pharmaceutical*

As noted above the manufacture of a pharmaceutical with the manifest intent to use it for the patented second medical use would no doubt involve an infringement of a Swiss-type claim and probably also an EPC 2000 claim.

For direct infringement, an intention to use the product for the patented indication must be demonstrated to exist at the time of the manufacture of the product. Such intention is usually evidenced by the approved indications in the MA and the content of the SmPC and/or PIL.

2.2 *Offer for sale*

See section C.III, above.

2.3 *Sale*

See section C.III, above.

2.4 *Export*

Export is not explicitly mentioned as an act covered by the exclusivity afforded by a patent. However, in case law it has been found that it is sufficient that an offer/sale of an infringing product has been made in (from) Sweden in order for a Swedish patent to be infringed (in said case the products were manufactured and delivered abroad). This means that exports based on offers/sales made from Sweden would normally involve infringement in Sweden.

2.5 *Import*

Import is explicitly defined as an infringing act in Section 3 of the Patents Act, see section C.III, above.

2.6 *Combination products*

See section C.III, above.

3. ***Indirect infringement***

3.1 *Objective acts*

The objective acts required for indirect infringement are offering or actual supply of an essential means for exercising the invention. The essential means does not have to be part of what makes the invention patentable but must relate to what is defined as the invention (i.e. cannot be a generic utility). For staple goods the infringer must also have tried to induce the recipient to use the means supplied for purpose of exercising the invention.

3.2 *Subjective conditions*

It is required that the party offering or supplying the essential means is aware or ought to have been aware that it is suitable and intended for use in exercising the invention.

3.3 *Export*

Indirect infringement requires that both the offering/supply and the subsequent use of the essential means for exercising the invention takes place in Sweden (the so-called double territoriality requirement).

3.4 *Import*

In case the party offering or supplying the essential means does so in Sweden, liability for indirect infringement occurs also when the means is supplied from abroad.

3.5 *Combination products*

The essential means supplied can typically be one of several substances in a combination product.

4. *Off-label use*

4.1 *General admissibility of off-label use*

As noted above physicians are generally allowed to prescribe and use pharmaceuticals off-label, provided that such use is based on science and clinical experience.

Cross-label use occurs as a matter of course as the result of the Swedish system for generic substitution where the MPA decides on substitution without regard to the indications for which the (skinny labelled) generic medicine has been approved. Pharmacies then dispense the cheapest generic for all prescriptions without regard to which indication the medicine has been prescribed for. As a matter of fact the pharmacies do not even know the relevant indication since that is not in the prescription.

4.2 *Liable persons*

In theory physicians can as noted above be liable for off-label use which involves a patented second medical indication at least in respect of EPC 2000 claims, and with a broad definition of the term "manufacture" also in respect of Swiss-type claims. However, off-label use is difficult to detect and prove in the individual case (the indication is not stated in the prescription) and there is no tradition in pursuing patent issues with physicians.

In respect of cross-label use in the context of generic substitution the issue of liability is very complex since the regulatory system itself causes infringing cross-label use. There is as yet no case law on who should eventually be liable for this effect of the system. However, once the different parties playing roles in the system (the generic company, the MPA, the physicians and the pharmacies) have been made aware of the occurrence of infringement for an individual product they can in theory all be liable either as the direct or indirect infringer or as one of several joint infringers.

V. Remedies

There is no relief available which is specific to infringement of second medical use claims, but the general provisions in the Patents Act apply.

1. *Injunctions*

The court may at the request of a patentee or a licensee, prohibit an infringer from continuing the infringement, subject to the penalty of a fine. It is sufficient that there has been an objective infringement and the plaintiff does thus not have to show that the infringement was made by negligence or with intent.

In case law concerning permanent injunctions on the basis of community trademarks, the Supreme Court has established that a permanent injunction does not require an ongoing infringement. Since the provisions on permanent injunctions on the basis of patents correspond with the provisions concerning community trademarks, it is suggested in the legal commentaries that the same should apply to patents.

Even if the legal requirements for an injunction are met, there is still some room for the court to apply a form of judicial discretion before granting the injunction. This follows from the wording that the court "may" grant an injunction. The extent of the courts' discretion is not however settled in case law and there is no case where the court despite a finding of infringement has refused to grant a permanent injunction.

2. *Damages*

The successful plaintiff is entitled to damages in the form of reasonable compensation for use of the invention regardless of whether or not the plaintiff has suffered any actual damage because of the infringement, if the infringement was made intentionally or by negligence. Someone who has infringed a patent in good faith should only pay compensation for use of the invention where, and to the extent, reasonable. However, it is very rare that courts find an infringer to be in good faith, considering that patent rights are registered rights and as such in principle 'known to all'.

Reasonable compensation for use is normally calculated as a reasonable licence fee for the use of the invention. With a "reasonable licence fee" is meant the fee which the infringer would have had to pay the patentee if he had entered into a licence agreement in an arm length's transaction regarding the use. An assessment is often established as a royalty rate (a percentage), which varies depending on the nature and value of the invention and the industry sector in question, and the value of the net sales of infringing products. However, in case law other factors have also been the basis for the calculations.

Reasonable compensation may also be awarded for infringements of a published patent application which eventually is granted, for the period between the publication and the grant (provided that a claim is made within certain specified time limits).

If the infringement was made by negligence or intent, the plaintiff is also entitled to damages for any further loss it has incurred as a result of the infringement. In most cases, this will be compensation for lost profits on sales that have been taken by the infringer. Some case law suggests that if further damages are claimed for actual loss of sales, reasonable compensation for use should be deducted from the damages awarded for these further losses. Exceptions to this view can also be found in case law.

Damages can also be awarded for example if the infringer has damaged the goodwill of the patentee or, in connection with the infringement, has acted in a manner which has otherwise damaged the patentee's reputation or share of the market.

The plaintiff has full burden of proof for the loss it has incurred. In many instances it may be difficult to prove damages as it is based on a hypothetical course of events as if the infringement had never occurred. In practice, plaintiffs often rely on a provision of the Code of Judicial Procedure whereby the court may estimate the damages to a reasonable amount. However, case law has established that a plaintiff must produce all evidence that possibly can be obtained.

3. *Information*

3.1 *Names of manufacturer, distributors, customers, sales etc.*

The Patents Act provides the patentee with a right to an order for information about the origin and distribution network for infringing products or services against anyone who has participated in the infringement or taken possession or used the products or services concerned by the infringement. The information may in particular include the names and addresses of the manufacturers, distributors, suppliers, intended wholesalers and retailers as well as information on how many products that have been manufactured, delivered, received or ordered, and the price obtained for the goods or services.

Notably the obligation to provide information according to an order is limited by a self-incrimination exception – information that shows that the addressee of the order or someone closely related have committed a criminal act does not have to be provided. Since grossly negligent and intentional patent infringement is penalised in Sweden this exception may significantly reduce the possibility to obtain information.

An information order may be issued outside or within the framework of main proceedings on infringement and in order to obtain such order the patentee must show probable cause for infringement. A proportionality test applies – an information order may be issued only if the reasons in favour of granting the measure outweigh the inconvenience or other harm that the measure would cause to the party against which it is directed or any other opposing interest.

If it can reasonably be assumed that someone has committed an infringement, contributed thereto or attempted or prepared an infringement, Swedish courts may also, in order to preserve evidence relating to the infringement, order that an investigation shall be undertaken with respect to the alleged infringer in order to search for objects or documents which can be assumed to be of importance for the investigation of the infringement.

An infringement investigation as part of evidence protection measures may be granted before or after infringement proceedings have been initiated, but only if the reasons in favour of the measures outweigh the disadvantages or other harm caused to the person against whom it is directed or to any other opposing interest. If the applicant and the defendant are competitors, one obvious risk is that trade secrets of the defendant are disclosed through the infringement investigation.

The main rule is that the defendant shall be given the opportunity to respond before the decision is taken. However, if there is a risk of sabotage – in other words if a delay (or communication of the application or decision to the opposing party) would entail a risk that objects or documents would be removed, destroyed or distorted, a court may issue an order *ex parte* without communicating the application with the alleged infringer.

In addition to the above specific measures the Code of Judicial Procedure also includes provisions allowing parties to obtain orders for production of documents or objects which have evidentiary value. It is also possible to hear witnesses in order to establish the existence of documents or objects which may be subject to an order for production. However, these provisions do not provide a general right to "discovery" and can only (with very limited exceptions) be used once proceedings on the merits have been initiated.

3.2 Account of profits

Account of an infringer's profits is not available as a sanction in itself but the court is allowed and shall, if invoked by the patentee, consider the profit of the infringer as one of several relevant circumstances when establishing the damage caused to the patentee by the infringement.

4. Recall of products and destruction

It is possible for the plaintiff to request that any infringing goods should be recalled from the market, seized and destroyed or placed in custody for the remainder of the patent term. Also in this respect, an assessment of proportionality is made by the court before issuing the order of such corrective measures.

5. Recovery of legal costs

In general court proceedings, the winning party should be fully compensated for reasonable legal costs, provided that a claim for compensation for costs has been submitted. This includes legal fees, costs related to evidence and the party's own work made necessary because of the proceedings. If a party is only partially successful, the costs should be divided between the parties in relation to what each party has won. Consequently, it is important to submit realistic claims for damages; if only part of the claimed amount of damages is granted this may result in the plaintiff losing the right to compensation for a proportionate part of its litigation costs.

VI. Exceptions from patent protection

1. Exhaustion of rights

Sweden applies national exhaustion of patent rights except for that regional exhaustion applies to the European Economic Area (EEA). The patent right to a product is thus exhausted when the product is put on the market within the EEA by the patentee or with the patentee's consent.

2. Patient welfare

The Patents Act contains certain provisions on the right to compulsory licences in case an invention is not exploited in Sweden within three years of patent grant or if such licence is motivated by a public interest of special importance. However, these provisions have been of very limited practical importance.

3. *Others specific to second medical use claims*

There are no exceptions that apply specifically to second medical use claims but the so-called "Bolar exception" that was introduced in the Patents Act in 2006 based on EU directives may be of special interest in the context of second and further medical use patents. It is now clearly set out in the Act that studies, tests, investigations and practical measures attributable to a reference pharmaceutical necessary to obtain marketing approval in accordance with national Swedish or EU pharmaceutical legislation is exempted from the protection conferred by patent protection.

What is referred to as scientific research with the aim to develop the pharmaceutical as such falls under the research exemption.

VII. Procedural issues

1. *Preliminary injunction cases*

The patentee may claim for an interlocutory injunction as part of the proceedings on the merits. As a main rule, the defendant shall be given an opportunity to respond and the court normally thoroughly examines the question of infringement and validity (if raised as a defence) before deciding on a request for an interlocutory injunction. However, if a delay could cause irreparable harm, the court may issue an injunction *ex parte* without giving the defendant an opportunity to respond. In practice, the court rarely finds that there are sufficient reasons to issue an injunction *ex parte*.

To succeed with a claim for an interlocutory injunction, the patentee must show probable cause that the patent is being infringed. Furthermore, it must be established that there is reason to believe that the defendant, by continuing the infringement, will depreciate the value of the exclusive right provided by the patent. The plaintiff must also, prior to a decision on the grant of a preliminary injunction, present a sufficient security (normally a bank guarantee), covering the damage that the defendant may suffer as a result of the injunction. According to general principles of law, the court must balance the opposing interests of the parties in each individual case. However, in cases where the court finds infringement of valid patent to be at hand it normally issues a preliminary injunction.

The courts are required to ensure – within the framework of the plaintiff's claim – that the scope of a preliminary and/or final injunction is clear and specific and not wider than necessary. The court can thus rephrase the scope of the injunction in order to make it clearer, specific and more limited in scope than has been requested by the plaintiff.

The injunction issued will prohibit the defendant from continuing specific infringing activities under the penalty of a fine (payable to the state) for example importing, offering for sale and putting on the market of a specific pharmaceutical for a use covered by a second medical use claim.

If the defendant violates the injunction, a separate action must be brought in order for the penalty to be awarded.

1.1 *Availability for second medical use claims*

Preliminary injunctions are also available for second medical use claims and in the clear cases where the marketing authorisation, SmPC and/or PIL show a clear intention to use the relevant pharmaceutical for the patented use, the scope of the injunction should not be problematic. However, in respect of cross-label use occurring as a result of generic substitution of skinny labelled generics the problem with drafting an appropriate injunction is inherent. As noted before this issue has yet to be addressed in case law.

1.2 *Specific requirements*

There are no specific requirements applicable to preliminary injunctions concerning second medical use patents.

2. ***Cases on the merits***

As noted above preliminary injunctions are decided as part of the main proceedings. Once the issue of the grant of preliminary relief has been decided, the case handling continues with possible further exchange of briefs, preliminary hearing (case conference) to prepare the case for the main hearing and finally a main hearing. The total time from initiation of an action until judgment is currently about 24 months in average.

3. ***Enforcement of judgments***

If the defendant violates an injunction (preliminary or final) a separate action must be brought in order for the penalty to be awarded. In connection with such an action the court may set a new penalty for any further breach of the injunction.

Monetary judgments and judgments concerning other specific performance are ultimately enforced by the Enforcement Authority, which may, inter alia, levy execution on assets and order the obligated party to comply with a judgment involving specific performance subject to a penalty of a fine.

VIII. Validity

1. ***Relevance for infringement cases***

A granted and valid patent is a basic prerequisite for a finding of infringement. In case the defendant wishes to rely on an invalidity defence in the infringement action, a separate action for revocation of the patent must be initiated. The two actions are then normally heard together.

As noted above the court will also consider the validity of the patent in connection with a decision on the grant of a preliminary injunction, if the validity is questioned by the defendant.

2. *Specifics for second medical use claims*

Actions concerning second medical use claims do not differ from other cases in respect of the handling of the issue of validity in relation to infringement.

IX. Tactical considerations

1. *Plaintiff*

A patentee wishing to successfully enforce its patents against launch of a product which may be used for treating the patented indication should be active and well-prepared. However, there is no requirement of taking action within a certain period of time in order to obtain a preliminary injunction, but swift action will of course minimise the harm caused by the infringement and will support arguments made for the urgency of the grant of preliminary relief.

Preparations should start early and would typically include gathering of relevant arguments on infringement and contacts with potential experts. As Swedish patent infringement proceedings are brought on the merits along with a claim for a preliminary injunction, it is advisable to start preparing a summons application early on. Since it is necessary to lodge a sufficient security with the court to obtain a preliminary injunction calculations should be made so that it can be showed to the court that the amount covers all potential loss of the alleged infringer, in particular if seeking an *ex parte* or otherwise swiftly granted injunction with minimum exchange of briefs.

Monitoring of grants of relevant marketing authorisations should be in place to quickly initiate contacts with the relevant company after such grant to exchange information about relevant patent rights and to try and ascertain intentions in respect of launch.

If a generic product is labelled for infringing use the matter of enforcement should be straightforward. Assuming that the generic company has used a so-called skinny label, which excludes the patented indications from the marketing authorisation the patentee must try and collect sufficient evidence on actual or expected use of the generic product for the patented indication. In this regard, it is relevant to consider the market volumes in respect of the patented and non-patented indications. Supply and sales of the generic product which are clearly over what is required to satisfy the market for off-patent use would be a strong indication that the generic product is in fact intended and used for the patented second medical use. Proving infringement would thus likely be easier where the off-patent use represents a very small market compared to the patented use, but will be more troublesome where there is a real and substantial market for the non-patented indications.

Different considerations may apply between Swiss-type claims ("use of [active ingredient X] for the manufacture of a medicament for treating [disease Y]") and EPC 2000 type claims ("product X for treating indication Y"). Swiss-type claims, being aimed at the time of preparation of the product in question, would require additional convincing arguments in order to prove an intention to infringe or knowledge of infringing use sufficient to establish indirect infringement. Absent Swedish case law, arguments made and judgments handed down in foreign jurisdictions could be considered relevant also in Sweden.

Tactical considerations may differ depending on if the product in question is – mainly – a hospital drug or a prescription drug.

Prescriptions are usually made by brand name but as noted there is mandatory substitution to the cheapest available substitutable generic at pharmacy level meaning that physicians will not be able to control which product is ultimately provided to the patient. Further, pharmacies are under an obligation to dispense the cheapest generic product available (set forth in the "product of the period" list of substitutable products issued by the Dental and Pharmaceutical Benefits Agency) regardless of the indication intended by the prescription. Since the indication for which a pharmaceutical is prescribed is normally not set forth in the prescription there is no way for the pharmacies to know for which indication the substitutable generic product is dispensed. The aforesaid regulatory structure thus operates in a way which causes skinny labelled generics to be used for patented second medical use and does not provide tools for either physicians or pharmacies to avoid this. Generic companies could potentially avoid substitution at pharmacies by contacting the Dental and Pharmaceutical Benefits Agency and refuse to supply the product in question during the period of listing. Such refusal would mean that the generic in question would be excluded from the list which forms the basis for substitution at pharmacies but it would however also mean that it is excluded from substitution for non-patented indications.

In respect of medical products which are only or mainly used in hospitals there are more opportunities to take action against infringing use. Such products are publicly procured, and County Councils which purchase the products can be put on notice of the patented indications and the possibility of infringement in case of cross-label use of (skinny labelled) generic medicines. The patentee can furthermore require of County Councils that procurements be made separately for medicinal products for the different indications in order to avoid infringement. Likewise, the patentee can require of generic companies not to participate in tenders which include use for the patented indication.

The main problem for the enforcement of second medical use patents in Sweden arises out of the conflict between patent law and the current regulatory legislation in the context of generic substitution, which ultimately requires political action to be resolved adequately.

Such changes could probably be facilitated by case law that clarified the liability for the respective actors in the system (mainly the generic companies, pharmacies and the MPA deciding on substitution without regard to approved indications and existence of second medical use patents).

2. *Defendant*

Generic manufacturers wishing to avoid infringement should obviously follow what has become the industry standard of so-called "skinny labelling", where the patented indications are left out of the marketing authorisation, creating a narrower scope of indicated treatment for the generic product.

As discussed in relation to plaintiff tactics, mere skinny labelling is, however, unlikely to suffice, in particular unless the generic company takes positive action to avoid infringing use.

For prescription products the defendant scenario and the limited possibilities to avoid what could amount to infringement in connection with generic substitution is described in section 1 above.

For hospital products the (potential) defendant could initiate a dialogue with County Councils to ensure that they understand the limitations imposed by patent legislation. That way, public procurements can be tailored to differentiate between patented and non-patented indications, allowing for the generic manufacturer to participate in a tender without running afoul of patent law.

To further avoid claims of infringement, generic manufacturers may take action to inform health care providers of the approved indication of the generic product and those covered by relevant patents, to ensure that the generic product is only used for non-patented indications. Such actions may also be communicated to the plaintiff/patentee, along with clear statements that the generic company has no intention of having its product used for the patented indication.

However, to avoid the current uncertainties in relation to second medical use patents, generic companies may also consider engaging in seeking to bring about changes in the current regulatory legislation.

Denmark

Nicolai Lindgreen, Nicolaj Bording

A. AVAILABILITY OF PROTECTION

I. Legal framework

1. National statutory laws

1.1 Pharmaceuticals

Section 2, subsection 5, of the Danish Patents Act expressly permits the grant of patents for a known product for use in medicine or for a specific first or further medical use.

Section 2, subsection 5, reads:

> "The requirement under subsection 1 that inventions be new shall also not prevent the grant of patents for the substance or compositions referred to in subsection 4 for use in accordance with the methods referred to in Section 1(3), provided that the use is a specific use of the substance or composition and that specific use is not known for any of those methods."

The provision was implemented in the Danish Patents Act in 2007 in order to harmonise the Danish Patents Act with the revised European Patent Convention EPC 2000.

In addition to second medical use claims as statutorily defined in Section 2, subsection 5, of the Danish Patents Act, Danish law also acknowledges so-called "Swiss-type claims" (i.e. patents for use of a known compound to manufacture a drug for use for the treatment of a specific medical indication). These types of second medical use claims were accepted prior to the revision of the Danish Patents Act introducing Section 2, subsection 5, and continue to be accepted by the Danish PTO for new applications.

Danish courts will generally take into account corresponding provisions of the EPC when interpreting provisions in the Danish Patents Act in order to ensure a uniform interpretation and application of the law.

By and large the legal framework in Denmark for the grant of medical use claims is no different to that of the EPO, apart from the continued accept of Swiss-type claims.

1.2 Biologics

The Danish Patents Act was amended in 2000 in order to implement European Directive 98/44/EC on the legal protection of biotechnological inventions.

2. International treaties

The Danish Patents Act was amended in 1995 in order to implement the 1994 TRIPS Agreement.

3. Availability through case law

The availability and scope of patent protection in Denmark is governed by statute, as interpreted by the Danish courts.

4. Patent term extension/SPCs

SPCs are granted in Denmark under Regulation (EC) No. 469/2009 and related Danish regulations, i.e. Section 91 of the Danish Patents Act and Sections 69-85 of the Danish Executive Order No. 25 of 18 January 2013 ("Patentbekendtgørelsen").

II. Policy considerations

1. Health and social issues

In Denmark, primary healthcare is provided through general practitioners, whereas secondary healthcare is provided in hospitals.

The fundamental principle of prescription practice in Denmark is the clinician's clinical freedom to prescribe the drug that is deemed relevant for treating the patient. The prescription shall include the trade name for the drug, if a marketing authorisation is issued for the drug, the dosage form of the drug, the concentration, if several concentrations are available, and information regarding indication and dose, cf. Sections 7 and 8 in the Danish Executive Order No. 1671 of 12 December 2013 on prescriptions ("Receptbekendtgørelsen").

In Denmark, there is free price formation for medicine. Medicine prices are fixed by pharmaceutical companies and medicinal products are sold at the same price by all pharmacies. The medicine prices are fixed for 14-day periods, and pharmaceutical companies report their prices every fortnight to the Danish Medicines Agency.

When a clinician has prescribed a medicine product defined by its trade name, pharmacies must dispense another and cheaper medicine, which contains the same active substance, in the same quantity, and which is used in the same way (generic medicines). This is due to the Danish rules on substitution of medicine, which are primarily regulated in the Receptbekendtgørelsen.

The rules on substitution are complex and have been changed several times. However, the main rule is that pharmacies must always dispense the cheapest medicine in a substitution group, unless the patient demands a specific product in the group, or unless the clinician has designated "*ej S*" ("not S[ubstitution]"). In the latter case, the pharmacy must dispense the medicine specifically designated in the prescription. If the price difference between the cheapest medicine and the one specifically prescribed is only marginal (DKK 5 to DKK 20 depending on the specific medicine price), pharmacies are not obliged to dispense the cheapest medicine, but can choose to dispense the medicine specifically prescribed.

Whether a given medicine falls within a given substitution group is exclusively determined by the Danish Medicines Agency.

If a medicine is prescribed for the treatment of a patent-protected indication, the pharmacy must dispense the medicine with the originator product and cannot substitute a cheaper product within the same substitution group. However, if the same medicine is prescribed for treatment of another indication, which is not patent protected, the pharmacy must substitute to a cheaper product within the same substitution group, cf. Section 38a of the Receptbekendtgørelsen.

2. Legal issues

In order to protect doctors from claims for patent infringement, a patent cannot be granted for a method of treatment of the human (or animal) body using the drug in question, cf. Section 1, subsection 3, of the Danish Patents Act.

A fundamental issue previously arose due to the Danish rules on generic substitution as outlined above, in particular when a drug was prescribed for a specific indication and pharmacies, because of the Danish rules on generic substitution, were obliged to hand out the cheapest drug in the substitution group, and therefore in some cases would hand out a generic drug for the patented indication.

The issue was recently tested in a preliminary injunction case (2015) concerning pregabaline where the holder of a patent containing a Swiss-type claim was successful in obtaining a preliminary injunction against a number of pharmacies prohibiting them from handing out a generic drug for the patented indication, although the Danish rules on generic substitution obliged the pharmacies to do so.

Apparently as a consequence of this decision, the Danish rules on generic substation were subsequently amended, so that pharmacies, in case a prescription specifies the patented indication, must hand out the originator drug, whereas the Danish Health and Medicines Authority was obliged to notify pharmacies when a drug has a patented indication, cf. Section 38a in the Receptbekendtgørelsen, as explained above.

B. VALIDITY

It is a prerequisite in order for an invention to be patentable with a use-specific product claim, that the later-established specific use of the drug (i.e. the second indication) fulfils the fundamental requirements of novelty and inventive step in relation to the drug's previously known therapeutic use.

The Danish PTO and Danish courts will to a large extent attempt to harmonise their decisions with the case law of the EPO. Accordingly, in relation to validity of second medical use claims, we generally refer to the Chapter I "EPO", part B. However, as already indicated, the Danish PTO still accepts so-called Swiss-type claims, provided that the use of the drug for that indication is novel and involves an inventive step.

I. Allowable claim wording

Prior to the entering into force of the EPC 2000 on 13 December 2007, second medical use claims were only allowed using the Swiss-type process or method claim in the form of "the use of substance X for the manufacture of a medicament to treat disease Y". Since patents of this form are still in force and the Danish PTO still accepts patents in this form, provided that the specific use of the drug in question is novel and implies an inventive step, the validity and infringement of Swiss-type claims remains relevant in Denmark.

No product, use or system claims are permissible in Denmark for second medical use patents, since the product is not novel and methods of treatment of the human body by therapy are not themselves patentable. However, dosage claims relating to either the form of the medicament, or the particular dosing regimen, are permitted, provided that they are novel and imply an inventive step. Second medical use claims may also relate to the use of a known compound for a different patient group, so long as the new patient group is entirely distinct from the previously claimed patient group.

II. Novelty

1. General definition of novelty and prior art

Section 2 of the Danish Patents Act states that one of the requirements for an invention to be patentable is that it is new. Section 2 states that an invention is new if it does not form part of the "state of the art" at the relevant priority date of the patent. The "state of the art" is defined as all matter (i.e. information) which was available to the public before the relevant priority date. The requirement of novelty is objective and global.

The "state of the art" comprises everything made available to the public by means of a written or oral description, by use, or in any other way, before the priority date of the patent.

Novelty is assessed on the basis of each specific piece of prior art and the invention as defined in the patent claims.

For the purpose of assessing novelty (but not inventive step), the "state of the art" also includes information in certain patent applications which have an earlier priority date, but which were not published until after the priority date of the relevant patent, cf. Section 2, subsection 2, 2nd sentence, of the Danish Patents Act.

We also refer to Chapter I, "EPO".

The validity of a Danish Swiss-type patent claim was tested in a case concerning pathological treatment of fish for infestation in the form of sea lice by use of pyrethroids and was found to be invalid for lack of novelty, cf. the decision by the Maritime and Commercial Court reported in U 2012.1330S. The patent claimed use of pyrethroids to treat sea lice in immature phases, but the treatment of fish for infestation in the form of sea lice by use of pyrethroids as such was already known, and although it had previously been assumed that the efficacy of the treatment with pyrethroids was associated with its effect on the sea lice in their mature phases, the new realisation that pyrethroids were also effective against sea lice in their immature phases, did not confer novelty to the claimed invention, as it did not concern a new medical indication or a different patient group.

2. *Definition of skilled person*

The skilled person is legal fiction used to determine a certain knowledge profile to be applied when comparing the state of the art with the invention. The definition of the skilled person has to be determined on the particular facts of the case and depends on the characteristics of the invention. For complicated inventions, the skilled person will often possess skills that equal the skills of a whole team of individuals. The skilled person has extensive knowledge covering all prior art and common general knowledge, but on the other hand has no inventive skills.

3. *Scope of disclosure*

3.1 *General rules*

Section 8, subsection 2, of the Danish Patents Act provides that the specification of a patent should disclose the invention sufficiently clearly for it to be performed by the skilled person. Furthermore, the specification of the patent should contain sufficient information to allow the skilled person to work the invention across its scope in light of the data in the specification read in the light of the skilled person's common general knowledge.

3.2 *First medical use*

It is clear from the EPC both as originally enacted and as amended by the EPC 2000 that the identification of a first medical use of a known compound may confer novelty and form the basis of a patentable invention.

3.3 *New subject matter*

The patent specification must provide clear and unambiguous support for the novel subject matter, i.e. the use of the claimed substance for the new therapeutic purpose. The new therapeutic purpose may consist solely in a new dosage regime or in a novel class of patients treatable by the claimed substance.

3.4 *New data*

See Chapter I, "EPO".

4. *Requirements for second medical use*

It is a requirement that the specification contains sufficient documentation to support that the product in question (the compound or mixture of compounds) is useful in the treatment of a specific therapeutic indication. If the patent application relates to several different indications and it does not follow from the patent application that there is a relation between these indications, then the application will have to be divided into several independent applications concerning each specific indication.

Reference is also made to Chapter I, "EPO".

4.1 *Distinction from first medical use*

See Chapter I, "EPO".

4.2 *Sub-species of first medical use*

See Chapter I, "EPO".

4.3 *Dosage regimes*

See Chapter I, "EPO".

4.4 *Special patient groups*

See Chapter I, "EPO".

5. *Timing issues*

5.1 *Relevant time of development of second use*

See Chapter I, "EPO".

5.2 *Role of new data*

See Chapter I, "EPO".

5.3 *Use of old data*

See Chapter I, "EPO".

III. Inventive step/non-obviousness

1. Definition of inventive step/non-obviousness

According to Section 2 of the Danish Patents Act, it is a requirement that the invention at the priority date involves an inventive step over the prior art. The Danish PTO and Danish courts generally follow the problem-solution approach adopted by the EPO.

2. Same scope of disclosure as for novelty?

See Chapter I, “EPO”.

3. Assessment of inventive step/non-obviousness

See Chapter I, “EPO”.

IV. Amendment of claims after grant

1. Admissibility of post-grant amendments in general

Generally speaking, post-grant amendments to patent claims in force in Denmark may occur in the following five scenarios:

1) Opposition proceedings before the Danish PTO concerning a Danish patent, cf. Section 21 of the Danish Patents Act. It is a requirement that the amended patent claims still fulfil the patentability conditions, including novelty, inventive step and the prohibition against added matter.
2) Opposition proceedings at the EPO.
3) A voluntary administrative re-examination of a Danish patent (the option is also available for third parties), cf. Section 53b of the Danish Patents Act, although not as long as any court proceedings concerning the patent are pending. It is a requirement that the amended patent claims still fulfil the patentability conditions, including novelty, inventive step and the prohibition against added matter.
4) A voluntary administrative re-examination of the Danish part of a European patent, cf. Section 53b of the Danish Patents Act, although not as long as any court proceedings concerning the patent are pending. It is a requirement that the amended patent claims still fulfil the patentability conditions, including novelty, inventive step and the prohibition against added matter.
5) A voluntary limitation of a European patent, cf. Article 105(a) EPC.

Reference is also made to Chapter I, “EPO”.

2. *Procedural issues*

2.1 Independent limitation proceedings

See Chapter I, "EPO".

2.2 Opposition proceedings

See Chapter I, "EPO".

If a European patent which designates Denmark is upheld in opposition proceedings before the EPO in amended form, those amendments automatically apply to the Danish part of the European patent, subject to any appeal.

2.3 Nullity actions

See section C., below.

3. *Added matter*

See Chapter I, "EPO".

4. *Sufficiency*

See Chapter I, "EPO".

5. *Multiple indications*

See Chapter I, "EPO".

V. Change of patent category

1. *General admissibility: product to use claims and vice versa*

See Chapter I, "EPO".

C. INFRINGEMENT AND LITIGATION

I. Legal framework

1. *National statutory laws*

As set out above, the Danish Patents Act sets out the national basis for patent law in Denmark.

2. *Case law*

Case law interprets the provisions of statutory law and determines its application. The courts are likely to take into consideration the case law of the EPO and other European Patent Convention jurisdictions where relevant, but will not consider such case law as binding, neither in regard to decisions in individual cases nor on a general level.

II. Claim construction

1. *General rules*

Danish courts attempt to follow the approach set out in Article 69 EPC and its Protocol, both in relation to Danish national patents and (Danish parts of) European patents. Danish courts do not adhere to a strict literal reading of the claims of a patent but will determine the extent of the protection conferred by a patent by reference to the claims, read in light of the description and drawings, cf. Article 69 EPC and Section 39 of the Danish Patents Act. The starting point is the skilled person's "natural" reading of the claim language, within the relevant technical area and in the relevant context, including the purpose of the invention. The prosecution history may be relevant where this leads to a more restrictive reading of the claims. The prosecution history cannot be used to expand the scope of the claims beyond the natural reading of the claims.

The construction of the claim should be the same whether validity or infringement is considered.

Danish courts do not always clearly distinguish between situations where a claim is construed and where a doctrine of equivalents (see below) is used; courts strive to extend protection to the characteristic or essential features of the invention, see the Supreme Court decision from 2009 reported in U 2009.1523H. The aim is to render a realistic protection that reflects the inventor's contribution to the art, while at the same time taking into account the need for legal certainty and predictability for third parties.

2. *Specific issues for use claims*

The term "for" in patent claims means "suitable for". In other words, a claim to an article "suitable for" a specific purpose is a claim to such an article whatever its intended purpose. This became clear in a recent preliminary injunction case (2016) holding a (mechanical) patent invalid for lack of novelty over a prior art object intended for another use, but nevertheless suitable for the claimed use. In the case of second medical use claims, a similar claim construction would appear to deprive claims of novelty. In infringement terms, something more than suitability of a product for the claimed purpose must be required. Case law has not yet determined what it takes, although some indications have emerged (see below).

The few (preliminary injunction) decisions that have been issued require that the defendant product is "directed to" the protected use, either via the indications defined in the SmPC and MA, or otherwise via direct or indirect statements, the text of the SmPC, MA, product inserts, etc. This has led courts to focus preliminary injunction grant on marketing, sales, etc., of products combined with the use of specific language in SmPCs, product inserts, etc., indicating, directly or indirectly, the protected use.

III. Scope of protection

1. Scope of the use

1.1 General definition of the term "use"

There is no general definition of the term "use" in Danish patent law.

1.2 Manufacture of the pharmaceutical

Section 3(1)(1) of the Danish Patents Act provides that, where the invention is a product, a person infringes the patent for the invention where, amongst other things, that person makes the product. Section 3(1)(2) of the Danish Patents Act provides that, where the invention is a process, a person infringes the patent for the invention where, amongst other things, that person uses the process or offers it for use.

1.3 Sale of the product

Section 3(1)(1) of the Danish Patents Act provides that, where the invention is a product, a person infringes the patent for the invention where, amongst other things, that person disposes of the product. Section 3(1)(3) of the Danish Patents Act further provides that, where the invention is a process, a person infringes the patent for the invention where that person, amongst other things, disposes of any product obtained directly by means of that process or keeps any such product for that purpose.

1.4 Offer for sale

Section 3(1)(1) of the Danish Patents Act provides that, where the invention is a product, a person infringes a patent for the invention where, amongst other things, he offers to dispose of the product. Section 3(1)(3) of the Danish Patents Act further provides that, where the invention is a process, a person infringes the patent for the invention where that person, amongst other things, offers to dispose of any product obtained directly by means of that process or keeps any such product for that purpose.

1.5 Application to the patient

Not applicable.

1.6 Combination products

As set out above, a combination product for a new or non-obvious combination treatment can be patentable.

2. *Absolute product protection*

2.1 Limitation through the term "use"

The necessary limitation through the term "use" means that a patentee to a second medical use patent cannot prohibit the product *per se*.

2.2 Off-label use

Off-label use (i.e. the use of a drug for an unapproved indication, age group, dosage or mode of administration) is relatively common in some therapeutic areas. By relying on a marketing authorisation for one indication, clinicians may use their clinical judgment, to prescribe authorised medicaments for unauthorised indications (the so-called "free prescription right" of clinicians).

Cross-label use generally refers to the use of a drug for a previously approved and patented indication, age group, dosage or mode of administration that is not mentioned in the marketing authorisation or packaging information for the particular product in question. This arises in the context of so-called "skinny labelling". Article 10 of Directive 2001/83/EC relating to medicinal products for human use provides an abridged procedure for the authorisation of generic products. Article 11 of Directive 2001/83/EC provides that: "those parts of the summary of product characteristics of the reference medicinal product referring to indications or dosage forms which were still covered by patent law at the time when a generic medicine was marketed need not be included". Thus, European law allows generic suppliers to "carve out" indications which are protected by a second medical use patent from SmPC, MA and packaging information. This came into play in the Danish pregabaline preliminary injunction decision (see below).

3. *Dosage regimes*

As set out above, novel dosage regimes can be patentable as a second medical use. In such circumstances, the patentee is entitled to prevent the sale, etc., of products directed to use for such dosage regimes.

4. *Patient groups*

As set out above, a claim directed to a new or selected patient population may also be patentable. Again, in such circumstances the patentee is entitled to prevent the sale, etc., of products directed to use for such patient groups. This was the case in the Danish fexofenadine preliminary injunction case in 2008, where the patent concerned use of this substance for humans who were "not hepatically impaired". A preliminary injunction was granted against manufacture, sale and use of medicinal products containing the compound, where the specific text of the SmPC and/or product insert indicated, directly or indirectly, that the product was directed to use for humans who were not hepatically impaired.

5. *Extension under the doctrine of equivalents*

Section 39 of the Danish Patents Act does not expressly mention the possibility of extending protection beyond what can be brought within a construction of the claim language. However, it is well established in case law from the Danish Supreme Court that protection is also available by way of equivalence.

The doctrine can be summarised as implying that the decisive question is whether the central or most important characteristics of the invention are recognised in the allegedly infringing object, such that deviations occur only on less important points. If the deviations are, moreover, obvious alternatives in the eyes of the skilled person, an infringement by equivalence will normally be found. What the central characteristics of the invention are must be determined on the basis of the claims. The object held to be equivalent with what is defined in the claims must not belong to the prior art.

The doctrine of equivalents will also be applicable, in principle, to second medical use claims. It remains to be seen whether such an expansive protection will apply both in terms of uses (therapeutic indications) that do not fall within a normal construction of the claim as such, and in terms of derivatives of the active substance defined in the claim.

IV. Infringing acts

1. *Infringing person or entity*

Save for a few exceptions (for example, private, non-commercial use), any person or entity carrying out, in Danish territory, any of the acts amounting to direct or indirect infringement under Section 3(1) and/or Section 3(2) of the Danish Patents Act, is liable for patent infringement.

2. *Direct infringement*

2.1 *Manufacture of the pharmaceutical*

See section C.III, above.

A Swiss-type claim, as a process claim, may be infringed under Section 3(1)(2) or Section 3(1)(3) of the Danish Patents Act. In the common scenario that the manufacture of the product takes place outside Denmark, Section 3(1)(2) does not apply.

2.2 *Offer for sale*

See section C.III, above.

As set out above, a Swiss-type claim, being a process claim, may be infringed under Section 3(1)(3), which entitles the patentee to prevent the sale or offer for sale of a product obtained directly by means of that process.

As with manufacturing, there is no case law in this area in relation to EPC 2000 claims.

2.3 *Sale*

See 2.2 "Offer for sale", above.

2.4 *Export*

There is no specific prohibition on "export" in the Danish Patents Act, and it is doubtful whether this can be seen as a special case of disposal of the product. Keeping the product is not a delict, unless the keeping is for a prohibited purpose, such as offering or disposing of the product (presumably limited to disposal in Denmark).

2.5 *Import*

Section 3(1)(1) of the Danish Patents Act provides that, where the invention is a product, a person infringes the patent for the invention where, amongst other things, he imports the product with the purpose of disposing of, using, etc., the product in Danish territory. Section 3(1)(3) of the Danish Patents Act further provides that, where the invention is a process, a person infringes the patent for the invention where that person, amongst other things, imports any product obtained "directly" by means of that process or keeps any such product, with the purpose of disposing of, using, etc., the product in Danish territory.

2.6 *Combination products*

In terms of infringement, combination products covered by second medical use claims should, in principle, be treated in the same way as non-combination products. There is no specific case law in a second medical use context.

3. *Indirect infringement*

3.1 *Objective acts*

The provisions regarding indirect (contributory) infringement are set out in Section 3(2) of the Danish Patents Act, which covers the acts of supplying and offering to supply any means relating to an essential element for putting the invention into effect. A double territoriality requirement applies, requiring the offering/supply to take place in Denmark, as well as requiring the use of the invention by another being intended to take place in Denmark. Both conditions must be fulfilled.

3.2 *Subjective conditions*

Section 3(2) of the Danish Patents Act requires that the supplier *knows* (or that it ought to be obvious to the supplier) that the "means essential" are suitable and *intended* (by the ultimate users) for putting the invention into effect in Danish territory. It is not enough that the means are suitable for putting the intention into effect. Based on UK and German case law, a preliminary injunction decision from

2011 outside the pharmaceutical area held that it was sufficient that the supplier/offeror of the "means essential" recommended or referred to the prohibited use in his marketing, in order for a court to hold that such use was also the use intended by (some) ultimate users.

3.3 Export

Exporting is not an act amounting to contributory infringement, due to the double territoriality requirement (see above).

3.4 Import

Importing is not an act amounting to contributory infringement.

4. *Off-label use*

4.1 General admissibility of off-label use

As set out above, off-label use is generally permitted in Denmark.

4.2 Liable persons

For EPC 2000 claims, where there is a "skinny label", a pharmacist dispensing the generic medicament for the second medical use (i.e. cross-label) is arguably liable for infringement.

As to Swiss-type claims, neither clinicians nor pharmacists manufacture medicaments. However, at least pharmacists may be liable for disposing of a product of the patented process. In theory, a clinician may also be alleged to "procure" the infringement by writing a generic prescription.

In the Danish pregabaline preliminary injunction decision (2015), pharmacies were held to infringe Pfizer's Swiss-type claim by handing out Krka's generic pregabaline in cases where the protected indication (pain relief) was specified on a sticker on the product, which is normal and required procedure for prescribed medicines in Denmark (the clinician sets out the indication for which he prescribes the drug, see above). Krka only marketed its product for two off-patent indications. Pfizer had sued practically all Danish pharmacies, who defended themselves by saying that under the (then) current Danish health regulations, they were *obliged* to hand the cheapest substitutable drug, no matter whether it was prescribed for a patent-infringing use or not. The court held that the health-law obligations of pharmacies did not override patent law, so the pharmacies infringed by carrying out their obligation under health law to hand out the cheapest product when doing this for a patented indication. Meanwhile, health regulations were amended so that pharmacies must now hand out the originator product for patent-protected indications.

V. Remedies

1. *Injunctions*

Injunctions are generally available in cases involving a finding of patent infringement. However, the availability and scope of injunctions on the basis of a finding of infringement of a second medical use patent are unsettled. Assuming the product in question is indicated for multiple medical conditions, only part of the marketed generic drug that is being sold will be infringing, so presumably there would be no basis for injuncting the product as such.

In the Danish fexofenadine preliminary injunction case (2008, above), Sanofi-Aventis had not even tried to obtain a preliminary injunction against the sale of Merck Generics' products as such. Moreover, the Court refused a general injunction formulated as an injunction against manufacture, sales, etc., of the product where this was "directed against" the protected indications (listed in the injunction request).

An injunction could only be entertained to the extent that it injuncted the manufacture, sales, etc., of the product in combination with the use of *specified* statements in the SmPC and/or product insert that indicated that the product was directed to the infringing use.

2. *Damages*

Under Danish patent law, damages are available to compensate the patentee's actual loss (of gross profits).

As an alternative, the patentee may seek compensation in the form of a reasonable royalty, thereby avoiding the necessity of showing an actual loss.

There is no basis for requiring an account of defendant's profits, although available information in respect of defendant's profits can be a factor in assessing the patentee's loss.

3. *Information*

3.1 *Names of manufacturer, distributors etc.*

Danish courts may order parties to identify the source of infringing goods or distributors receiving those goods. Information orders are only available once infringement has been determined by the court or accepted by the defendant.

3.2 *Names of customers*

The provision of the identity of customers will only generally be appropriate where those customers are trade customers (i.e. wholesalers) rather than consumers. As mentioned, information orders are only available once infringement has been determined by the court (or accepted by the defendant).

3.3 *Information about infringing sales*

An infringing party may be ordered to disclose the levels of sales it has achieved and further information to help a patentee determine whether it will be more beneficial to seek damages or a reasonable royalty. Again, information orders are only available once infringement has been determined by the court (or accepted by the defendant).

3.4 *Account of profits*

There is no basis for requiring an account of defendant's profits, although available information in regard of defendant's profits can be a factor in assessing the patentee's loss.

4. *Recall of products and destruction*

In Denmark, following a finding of infringement, the court may order the delivery up or destruction of infringing articles. Whether this would be ordered in the event of a finding of infringement of a second medical use claim remains to be seen since some of the infringing product could be put to non-infringing use (at least in a skinny label case).

5. *Recovery of legal costs*

The winning party is generally entitled to recovery of "reasonable costs" from the other party. The award of costs is in the court's discretion and is not clearly predictable. However, if a party is only partly successful, it will only be eligible for cost recovery in proportion to the parts of the case it has won. In a recent case, the defendant had defended itself by arguing invalidity and non-infringement; as invalidity can only be argued if a counterclaim for revocation is brought, it had done so. The patent was upheld as valid, but not infringed. Since the defendant had lost its revocation counterclaim, it was only awarded cost recovery in respect of the infringement issue.

Even where a party wins a case completely, it is unlikely to recover its full costs, and often far from it.

VI. Exceptions from patent protection

1. *Exhaustion of rights*

According to Section 3(3)(2), acts pertaining to products that have been brought on the market by the patentee or with his consent, in Denmark or within the EU or EEA, are not covered by patent protection. In respect of such goods, patent protection has been exhausted.

2. *Patient welfare*

Section 3(3)(1) of the Danish Patents Act provides a defence where an otherwise infringing act is done for non-commercial purposes. This would cover a patient's use and keeping of a patented product.

Sections 45 *et seq.* of the Danish Patents Act provide for compulsory licences in various scenarios. Although some of these would, in principle, be relevant for medicinal products, they are never used in practice.

3. *Other issues specific to second medical use claims*

Other than the points set out above, there are no specific issues relevant to second medical use claims that are of interest in the present context.

VII. Procedural issues

1. *Preliminary injunction cases*

A competent court may award a preliminary injunction to restrain the defendant from infringement of a valid patent right.

The conditions are that the claimant shows that there is a likelihood that defendant infringes a valid patent, or is going to do so in the near future ("within a short timeframe"). The claimant has to render it likely that infringing acts currently take place or will take place "within a short timeframe". This test was established in a fairly recent case where it was held to be insufficient in itself that the defendant had obtained a marketing authorisation. It was also not sufficient that defendant had refused to undertake not to market for as long as claimant's patent was in force, nor was it sufficient that defendant had refused to undertake to give the claimant 28 days' notice before launch, in order that the claimant could seek injunctive relief before the defendant's actual launch. The defendant had declared that it had no current plans regarding marketing of the allegedly infringing product in Denmark, and the Supreme Court held that there was no concrete basis for doubting the sincerity of that declaration.

It follows that any statement from the defendant indicating that it is intending to launch within a short timeframe would suffice. Refusal to respond to a query as to whether defendant is planning to market the infringing product in Denmark is also likely to suffice, depending on the circumstances. Submitting a price to the official pricelist ("Taksten") would imply that the defendant is currently prepared to supply and would amount to actual infringement in the form of offering, so this would also clearly suffice.

There is no balance of convenience test or similar in Danish procedural law relating to preliminary injunctions.

1.1 Availability for second medical use claims

Preliminary injunctions are also available in cases involving second medical use claims, although special care has to be taken in relation to the requests for injunction, so as not to seek injunction against a defendant's lawful acts.

1.2 Specific requirements

The assessment of whether a preliminary injunction should be granted is based upon the usual requirements set out in the Administration of Justice Act.

As mentioned above, the limited case law from Danish courts indicates that an injunction must relate to specific marketing statements (or product characteristics) which indicate that the defendant's product is directed to the infringing use, for example by statements in the SmPC, MA or product insert referring, directly or implicitly, to the infringing use.

2. Cases on the merits

There are no specific procedural requirements that apply in proceedings concerning second medical use patents.

There is no procedure for disclosure or discovery under Danish law.

In Danish patent cases on the merits, it is not possible for the parties to present evidence by their individual experts. Instead, evidence is usually provided in the form of one or more reports from court-appointed experts, which respond to – often quite detailed – questions prepared by the parties. Cases are heard by a panel comprising both legally and technically qualified judges.

Infringement and validity issues will be dealt with at the same trial. Fact witnesses and experts are examined by the parties at trial, both in examination-in-chief and in cross-examination.

3. Enforcement of judgments

Judgments, if not respected by defendants, are enforced by the enforcements courts. Failure to comply with a preliminary or permanent injunction may lead to criminal charges (fines).

VIII. Tactical considerations

1. Plaintiff

As discussed above, preliminary injunctions are in principle available to prevent generic launch of a product for use for treating a patented indication. The patentee must be alert for grants of marketing authorisations to generic manufacturers and to engage generic manufacturers in correspondence as to their intentions at an early stage if a marketing authorisation is granted on a product the marketing of which may infringe the patent.

It is not possible to obtain injunctive relief against offering or sale of the product as such, as this will prevent legitimate supply for unpatented indications. Careful thought therefore needs to be given as to what relief may be sought that protects, as much as possible, the patented market without disrupting the lawful market. However, an injunction should be available to counter the launch of a product specifically labelled or formulated for the infringing use. This is of course not only an issue for interim relief but also for final relief if the patentee is successful at full trail.

2. *Defendant*

There is an obvious risk of infringement if a generic manufacturer specifically labels its product for the infringing use or mentions the protected indications in its SmPC or in product inserts. For this reason, it is common for generics to carve out the patented indication from their marketing authorisations and seek to launch "skinny label" products directed only to the unpatented indications, as discussed above.

Poland

Justyna Rasiewicz, Marta Sznajder

A. AVAILABILITY OF PROTECTION

I. Legal framework

Poland is a member of the European Patent Organisation since 1 March 2004. Poland is bound by most international treaties and agreements concerning the protection of intellectual property, in particular the Agreement of Trade-Related Aspects of Intellectual Property Rights (TRIPS) as well as Paris Convention for the Protection of Industrial Property.

In principle, Polish statutory provisions either entirely reflect the provisions of international agreements and conventions or, in case of discrepancies, should be interpreted in such manner so as to provide priority to respective international law provisions (Article 91(2) of the Constitution[1]).

Poland is a participant in enhanced cooperation concerning the European patent with unitary effect. Nevertheless, the Polish government has not signed the Agreement on the Unified Patent Court.

Polish patent provisions are based on a bifurcated system. The Patent Office has exclusive competence to recognize patent revocation cases, whereas infringement cases are within the jurisdiction of the common courts which recognize suits concerning the infringement of patents.

Patent applications are recognized by the Polish Patent Office which conducts their examination and grants patents. The Polish Patent Office has developed its own version of official Guidelines for Examination entitled 'Inventors' Manual'. This publication does not constitute binding law, but it provides the most extensive information concerning the practice applied by the Office.

1. The Constitution of the Republic of Poland of 2 April 1997 as published in Official Journal No. 78, item 483.

1. *National statutory laws*

Statutory provisions on second medical use are stipulated in the Act of 30 June 2000 – Industrial Property Law (O.J. 2001 No. 49 item 508, hereinafter referred to as "IPL"). Article 25 of this Act stipulates the statutory notion of the novelty requirement, including the following:

(1) definition of novelty (an invention shall be considered to be new if it does not form a part of the state of the art),
(2) definition of the state of the art (it shall be held to comprise everything available to the public by means of a written or oral description, by use, displaying or disclosure in any other way, before the date according to which priority to obtain a patent is determined), and
(3) provision on contents of patent or utility model applications (the content of any patent applications or utility model applications which enjoy the earlier priority, not made available to the public, shall also be considered included in the state of the art, provided that they were published in the manner as specified in this Act).

Moreover, in Article 25(4) of this Act it has been provided that the provisions of paragraphs (1) to (3) shall not prevent a patent from being granted for an invention concerning a new use of a substance or mixtures of substances included in the state of the art for use or use in strictly specified manner in therapy or diagnostics methods, provided for in Article 29(1) point 3,[2] if such use does not form a part of the state of the art.

The cited wording of Article 25(4) is valid from 1 December 2015. According to its previous version, the provisions of paragraphs (1) to (3) shall not prevent a patent from being granted for an invention concerning a new use of a substance included in the state of the art or the use of such substance for the purpose of obtaining a product for a new use.[3]

In the light of the above, the new wording explicitly provides that new use of a substance may concern not only a substance, but also mixtures of substances.[4] In addition to that, now the protected use may include use in a strictly specified manner

2. Article 29 IPL stipulates which inventions are excluded from patent protection. Paragraph 1 point 3 relates to methods for treatment of the human or animal body by surgery or therapy or diagnostic methods applied on human or animal bodies; this provision shall not apply to products, and in particular to substances or compositions applied in diagnostics or treatment.
3. Previous wording of Article 25(4) IPL was not consistent with EPC's provision before 12 December 2007. In fact, the Polish law has already anticipated the amendments introduced in EPC 2000.
4. The introduction of 'mixtures of substances' in the analysed provision eliminated a prior inconsistency in relation to relevant EPC provisions. Before the introduction of this amendment, the purposive interpretation has been proposed for resolution of this inconsistency. Such an interpretation has been often supported by EPO's decision T-0009/81 *Cytostatic Combination*.

in therapy or diagnostic methods.[5] Finally, the current version of this provision does not explicitly refer to Swiss-type claims as in previous wording ('the use of such substance for the purpose of obtaining a product for a new use').

According to the official grounds for this amendment, the reason for its introduction involved the necessity to depart from imposing on an applicant a specific method of formulating patent claims for further applications of known substances or composition, so called Swiss-type method.

This is important information as to the general approach to second medical use patents which should be adopted by the Polish Patent Office – and subsequently, also common courts recognizing infringement cases – in regard to the wording of claims and their further interpretation.

Rules for examination and interpretation of second medical use patents and patent applications developed by European Patent Office have been vastly absorbed by the Polish Patent Office by means of incorporating extensive parts of EPO's Guidelines for Examination in the Polish Inventors' Manual.

1.1 Pharmaceuticals

Polish Pharmaceutical Law[6] contains several provisions relating to medical applications.

Article 11 of the Act may be related to second medical use patents. It provides requirements for the content of the Summary of Medical Product Characteristics (hereinafter referred to as "SmPC"), stipulating that SmPC shall include the following information:

- pharmaceutical form of a medicinal product,
- clinical data comprising indications as to application, dosage regime and manner of administration to adults and children and, if applicable, contraindications.

In Article 11(3) it is further provided that until lapse of the patent rights on the territory of Republic of Poland for medical indications or pharmaceutical forms, a Marketing Authorization ("MA") holder applying for marketing authorization for a generic of reference medicinal product or a generic of reference medicinal veterinary product, is not obliged to present in the SmPC this part of the SmPC which refers to the medical indications or forms being covered by the patent protection on the territory of the Republic of Poland on the date of introduction on the market of the generic of reference medicinal product or the generic of reference medicinal veterinary product.

5. Previous wording allowed for patenting products the manufacturing of which involved a use of known substance, having new properties (i.e. not directed to product-by-use claims). No limitation has been provided as to the field of this use, so unlike EPC, this use did not have to relate to medicinal or veterinary products. Thus, potentially second use patents could be granted not only for medical inventions.
6. The Pharmaceutical Law Act of 6 September 2001, published in Polish Journal of Laws/ Dz. U. of 2008 No. 45, item 27, as amended.

In the situation discussed above, MA holder is obliged to file a declaration confirming that data not have been included in the SmPC, relating to medical indications or pharmaceutical forms, are covered by a patent protection.

1.2 Biologics

Pursuant to IPL's provisions implementing the EU Biotechnology Patent Directive, inventions capable of industrial application - even when they concern a product made of or containing a biological material or a procedure for producing, processing, or using biological material - are patentable. As has been approved in legal literature, such inventions may also relate to use of a particular product (i.e. known protein) for manufacture of a medicinal product for treatment of a particular disease.[7] The function of the nucleic acid or protein is required, and claiming a use based upon a predicted (but not proven) function fails to meet the requirement of industrial applicability.

2. International treaties

2.1 TRIPS

Poland is a signatory to the TRIPS Agreement.

2.2 FTAs

Poland is bound by free-trade agreements with the European Free Trade Association (EFTA), other Central European Free Trade Agreement (CEFTA) parties as well as bilaterally with the Baltic States, Turkey and Israel.

3. Availability through case law

The Polish legal system is based on statutory law which is interpreted and applied by the courts and relevant authorities. Case law does not bind courts or administrative bodies to recognize cases based on similar factual and legal grounds[8] but it constitutes an important and persuasive source of legal argumentation.

Under the laws of the previous Act on Inventive Activitiy dated 1972, the Polish Patent Office had not approved the patentability of inventions whose essence lay in the new application of a known medical substance. However, some decisions of the Office's Appeal Committee, rendered under the laws of the previous Act, had accepted the patentability of second medical use inventions.[9] Claims accepted by virtue of those decisions have not been formulated as Swiss-type claims, but rather product-by-use claims: a substance for treatment of disease X, characterized in that

7. Judgment of the Administrative Court in Warsaw, ref. II SA 1722/03.
8. Exceptions to this rule relate, for instance, to judgments which are given a value of legal principle by the Supreme Court.
9. Decisions of the Appeal Committee of the Patent Office, ref. Odw. 1407/97, Odw. 1002/98 and Odw. 1691/98.

it contains substance X as an active substance. This situation constitutes an example of availability of protection rendered through case law.

4. *Patent term extension/SPCs*

A supplementary protection certificate was introduced into Polish patent law on the date of Poland's accession to the European Union. As the provisions governing the SPC system have been provided for in Community Regulation No. 469/2009 of 6 May 2009 on supplementary protection certificates for medicinal products, the general rules are the same as in other European countries.[10] This applies also to the application of ECJ judgments on decisions of the Polish Patent Office as well as Polish common courts. In particular, Polish practice follows ECJ judgments rendered in cases C-31/03 *Pharmacia Italia SpA* and C-202/05 *Yissum*. Thus, in case a basic patent covers a different use of a product and such product has been already introduced on the market, while application for an SPC relates to the very same product but with different indication provided for in another marketing authorization, an SPC cannot be granted due to the failure to meet the requirements of Article 3d of the Regulation.

According to the practice of the Polish Patent Office, for a patent which protects a new use which is explicitly provided in the patent claims, the first marketing authorization is the one which exhausts this new use. In relation to second medical use SPC applications, the Polish Patent Office seems to be particularly devoted to ECJ judgment rendered in case C-431/04 MIT while it disregards C-130/11 Neurim judgment. This practice is being questioned by the administrative courts, which may finally lead to its abandonment.

II. Policy considerations

1. *Health and social issues*

As far as health issues are concerned, patenting second medical use inventions is justified by a need to provide pharmaceutical companies with protection for achievements in the field of new applications of known substances. Rapid development of biotechnological, pharmaceutical and medical technologies has led to an increased tendency to conduct research aimed at examination of whether known substances may be applied in the treatment of new diseases. In many cases, new and non-obvious applications have been established. This has resulted in increased demand for patent protection of second medical use inventions. Due to that, their admissibility may be considered as an incentive for pharmaceutical industry to invest in research which will solve health issues relating to new diseases, including civilization diseases.

On the other hand, providing cheaper generic drugs constitutes an existing objective of national health authorities resulting in accepting such drugs on the list of

10. The Polish Patent Office applies also the Explanatory Memorandum of European Commission (COM(90) 101 published on 11 April 1990), in which Article 1c of Regulation 1768/92 was interpreted by indication that not only a new product, but also a new method of manufacture or new application of a product may be protected by a supplementary protection certificate (item 12).

reimbursed medicinal products. The reimbursement limit is established on the basis of the price of the least expensive product within the group with the same medical indication. As a result, if a generic drug is included on the list, the limit is set on the basis of its price, which very often leads to substantial discrepancies between the prices of generic and innovative drugs to be paid by a patient.

2. *Legal issues*

Polish law and practice allows generic drugs to be granted marketing authorization and to be included on the reimbursement list irrespective of the fact that the innovative drug is still protected by a valid second medical use patent. Thus, it is positively incentivised by a drug reimbursement policy to use a generic substitute rather than the originator brand.

However, Polish medical practitioners prescribe medicinal products by reference to their brand name, not the INN. Patients are more willing to buy a product that has been chosen by a physician and explicitly indicated on the prescription, rather than a cheaper generic drug. Nevertheless, generic drugs having same active substance are often proposed for substitution by pharmacists.

B. VALIDITY

Patent applications are examined by the Polish Patent Office. The general prerequisites of patentability are provided in Article 24 IPL which stipulates that patents shall be granted – regardless of the field of technology – for any inventions which are new, which involve an inventive step and which are susceptible of industrial application.

For examination of second medical use patent applications the Polish Patent Office adopts the guidelines of the European Patent Office. In principle, second medical use inventions have to fulfil the general prerequisites of patentability for the grant of a valid patent.

The Inventors' Manual provides the following additional requirements for patent applications and assessment of their patentability. The specification of the problem in the state of the art should present its technical features, which, compared to the features describing the subject matter of the application presented in the specification, would allow for identification of the essence of an invention. It needs to be proved which specific technical problem is solved by the invention and how it will be exploited (applied) in the industrial activity.[11]

I. Allowable claim wording

Independent patent claims should describe an invention with technical means appropriate for each category of invention and these means should lead to achieving a desirable result. Thus, solutions featured in these claims should be complete to solve a technical problem with sufficiently disclosed technical means.[12]

---

11. Judgment of the Administrative Court in Warsaw, ref. VI SA/Wa 1474/04.
12. Judgment of the Administrative Court in Warsaw, ref. VI SA/Wa 112/08.

In principle, claims should be worded in a two-part form. The pre-characterizing part should contain an indication of the designation of the subject matter of the invention, i.e. the technical class of a given device or method, as well as prior art features defining the claimed subject matter. The characterizing part of the claim should indicate the features which constitute the contribution added to the prior art by the invention. Both parts of the claim combined constitute the scope of the protection sought.

In practice, a two-part form of independent patent claim is not applied for inventions relating to new chemical compounds or groups of chemical compounds, inventions relating to biological material, or inventions relating to use in a field of medicine. Examination of a patent claim of a one-part form should consider it entirely as the characterizing part of a patent claim in two-part form. In case a patent application relates to a chemical compound, it is sufficient to present its chemical structure in a claim.

In order to meet the criterion of unity of an invention, it is possible in particular to include in the application apart from an independent claim relating to a product also one independent claim relating to a method specifically adopted for the manufacture of this product, as well as one independent claim relating to a use of this product.

1. Product claims

An invention relating to a product should be characterized by the technical features relevant for a given chemical compound or a mixture of chemical compounds, in particular its chemical structure.[13] If the field of use of a chemical compound or a mixture, or a method of manufacture of a chemical compound, constitutes an essential feature of a subject matter of an invention, then this field should also be classified in accordance with a use or a method.

In principle, in the examination of claims in a product category, a use of this product is not considered to be a feature to distinguish it from the state of the art. If the contribution to the state of the art lies in a previously unknown property of a known substance, leading to achieving new technical result, then these newly discovered properties will not render the known substance novel. Thus, a product claim formulated in a manner presented above would not meet the critetion of novelty. Exceptions to this general rule relate to first and second medical use claims.

A product claim form is used for first medical use inventions, where a known chemical not previously used as a pharmaceutical is found to have a therapeutic effect.

Product-by-use claims are recommended for second medical use inventions since the revision of the EPC in 2000 and decision G 2/08 of the Enlarged Board of Appeal.[14] Nevertheless, Swiss-type claims are preferred by the Polish Patent Office and their indication is provided in the Inventors' Manual.

13. Judgment of the Supreme Administrative Court, ref. II GSK 109/05.
14. OJ EPO 2010, 514.

2. *Method claims*

An invention relating to a method should be characterized by a set of actions, operations or technological processes ordered according to a pre-determined priority, as well as technical means for performing such method and potential conditions to be applied.

Inventions relating to a new therapeutical application of a known substance cannot be put in method claims as they would be considered to be a therapeutic method excluded by EPC and Polish law provisions (Article 29(1) item 3 IPL).

A patent claim formulated as a use, for instance, a use of substance X as a biocidal preparation, should be treated as equivalent to a claim in the method category formulated as a method of exterminating insects with the use of substance X.

3. *Use claims*

Novelty of inventions involving new applications of known substances rests in the new technical effect resulting from the indicated therapeutical application. There are no grounds for treating inventions relating to second medical use differently. New, documented therapeutical applications should be significantly different from the known ones to be considered as a positive prerequisite of patentability.[15]

In case of compositions of active substances having known therapeutic effect it should be proved that the overall therapeutic effect is greater than a sum of the effects of the single substances (synergy). In order to prove inventive step it is advisable to present the relevant comparative data in the patent specification. An invention in a field of a compound (means, pharmaceutical set) needs to contain experimental material documenting discovered properties related to an expected use.[16] It is essential that disclosure of a medical invention provides information necessary not only to apply the invention, but also that this application of disclosed technical solution is safe for its recipients.[17]

4. *System claims*

Polish patent law and practice do not recognize a category of system claims.

5. *Dosage regimes*

Polish patent law provisions do not explicitly provide for granting patents for second medical use inventions formulated by new dosage regime. Admissibility of such a form of second medical use invention is, however, noted in the legal literature – a new dosage regime understood as a new administration of known medicine should be allowed patent protection, provided that it leads to achievement of non-obvious effects due to such administration. Administration as such has to meet the criteria of novelty and inventive step.

15. Decision of the Appeal Commission of the Polish Patent Office, ref. Odw. 1036/97.
16. Decision of the Appeal Commission of the Polish Patent Office, ref. Odw. 1985/97.
17. Judgment of the Administrative Court in Warsaw, ref. VI SA/Wa 112/08.

In light of the above, potential innovations in a dosage regime could involve the following solutions:

- new routes of delivery: for instance, to simplify ease of administration, effectiveness and access,
- improved efficacy: for instance, by addition of an additive or a second active ingredient and combining them in order to ensure dosage compliance,
- increased compliance: for instance, decreased frequency of administration could lead to a more stable drug level and decreased side effects,
- improved storage characteristics: for instance, improved heat stability enabling access in resource-poor settings.

6. *Patient groups*

Polish patent law provisions do not explicitly provide for granting patents for second medical use inventions formulated by their application to new patient groups. Again, admissibility of such a form of second medical use invention is stipulated in legal literature: use of known drug by a new, non-obvious group of patients, which is distinguishable in its physiological or pathological condition and simultaneously does not have any common part with a patient group which has been treated by a given therapy in the past, should be allowed as a second medical use invention. Examples are use of a substance by geriatric and pediatric patient groups or use for seropositive animals while previously it has been used for seronegative animals.

Polish legal literature has also emphasized that, according to EPO decision T 1399/04, inventions involving use of a known substance by a new group of patients should not be assessed as regards its novelty within the framework established by guidelines concerning selection inventions.

These findings would be likely applied by the Polish Patent Office in its examination of second medical use invention involving use by a new patient group.

II. Novelty

1. *General definition of novelty and prior art*

An invention shall be considered to be new if it does not form part of the state of the art.

The state of the art shall be held to comprise everything made available to the public by means of a written or oral description, by use, displaying or disclosure in any other way, before the date according to which priority to obtain a patent is determined. The content of any patent applications or utility model applications which enjoy earlier priority and not made available to the public, shall also be considered as included in the state of the art, provided that they were published in the manner as specified in the IPL. It is worth noting that in the state of the art relevant for assessment of novelty utility model applications are also included.[18]

18. A utility model is any new and useful solution of a technical nature affecting shape, construction or durable assembly of an object (Article 94(1) IPL).

An invention is considered to be a part of the state of the art if information disclosed to a person skilled in the art before the priority date is sufficient for the practical application of the technical teaching which is the subject matter of such a disclosure, including common knowledge in the field related to the invention available in that date.[19]

An invention does not meet the criterion of novelty if it is possible to indicate evidence which proves that all features of the solution or a variant of the solution included in an application, considered together, form a part of the state of the art. In the assessment of novelty, a prior document should be read as it would be read by a person skilled in the art on the date of its publication as regards previously published documents, or on the date of application (or priority, if relevant) in the case of a document considered in light of Article 25(3) IPL.

Assessment of novelty shall not be conducted on the basis of several combined documents. Neither is it possible to combine separate teachings of various embodiments described in one document, unless such combination is suggested therein.

It is permissible to use dictionaries or similar publications for interpretation of special terms used in the documents.

2. *Definition of skilled person*

While the Polish patent law refers to a skilled person as an 'expert' according to the literal wording of IPL, it should be understood as a common concept of a person skilled in the art or having ordinary skill in the art.

Polish patent law and practice generally follows the guidelines developed by the EPO, although explicit identification of the relevant skilled person is rarely provided for in Polish case law. For instance, it is accepted that in certain cases a person skilled in the art may be in fact a group or a team of persons, rather than just one person. Patients having very serious diseases may be examined by entire teams of medics who analyse various aspects of the disease. Finally, such identification of a person skilled in the art' affects the interpretation of the inventive step requirement.

3. *Scope of disclosure*

Pursuant to Article 25 (3) IPL, the content of any patent application or utility model application which enjoy earlier priority and not made available to the public, shall also be considered the state of the art, provided that it was published in the manner as specified in the IPL. Such an application represents the state of the art subject to its publication in Polish Patent Office's Bulletin – even if the date of such publication is later than the date of priority for the analysed invention. Thus, information contained in a patent or utility model application enjoying earlier priority, after its publication in accordance with statutory provisions, is included in the state of the art relevant for examination of novelty – irrespective of how proceedings regarding these earlier applications would have ended. Therefore, Article 25 (3) provides that abandoning

19. Judgment of the Supreme Administrative Court, ref. II GSK 271/12.

an earlier patent application before it is published results in a situation in which the earlier application does not lead to the loss of novelty of subsequent applications for very same invention.

In the assessment of novelty a general disclosure does not typically lead to an obstacle to lack of novelty for a particular embodiment of such a solution lying within the scope of such a disclosure. Nevertheless, a particular solution being part of the state of the art, covered by the broad scope of the subject matter of an application, would be destructive for the novelty of such an application.

3.1 General rules

Patents may be granted for new solutions involving products (substances or compositions) for use in therapeutic, surgery or diagnostic methods.

The Polish Patent Office applies the findings provided for in EPO decision G 5/83 – in order to fully characterize new medical indication of a known medical substance it is necessary to indicate not only a disease to be treated by the given substance, but also provide information on this substance and target patient group. A change in any of these element may justify patentability of second or further medical use invention.

3.2 First medical use

Pursuant to the general rules, it is permissible only within a field of medical inventions that a product dedicated for therapeutical use known from another field may be patented in a form of a first medical use, if the therapeutical use of known product has been revealed for the first time.

Patent claims relating to a known product used for a first medical use require particular wording. Such a claim should include the name of a compound (composition of compounds) followed by the indication of its use, for example "substance/ composition X" followed by "for use as a medicine", "for use as an antibacterial preparation", "used for treatment of disease Y", etc. The claimed invention in the category of a first medical use should meet not only this particularly understood criterion of novelty, but also other requirements for patentable inventions, including the prerequisite of inventive step.

3.3 New subject matter

The subject matter of a first medical use invention relates to new therapeutical properties of a given product. The product does not have to be novel itself. First medical use inventions may relate also to known products which have not been previously known for any medical use.

3.4 New data

New use should be supported in the patent specification by providing detailed results of biochemical research which prove this therapeutical application, and in particular, confirmed by acknowledged international tests, including statistical data and a profit risk analysis.[20]

Providing exhaustive evidence constitutes an essential requirement in Polish practice. In many cases patent applications have been rejected due to lack of sufficient documentation confirming that the claimed solutions (i.e. new medical uses of known product) actually achieve the claimed result.

4. *Requirements for second medical use*

Guidelines applied by the Polish Patent Office explicitly provide that second medical use patents are allowed, following the model applied by other patent offices (EPO decision G 5/83 is referred to as a basis of such admissibility). Thus, general rules developed by the EPO would be applicable to second medical use applications filed with the Polish Patent Office.

The wording of second medical use patent claims should indicate both the treated disease and particular active substance. For instance, claiming an invention as "use of substance or composition X for treatment of disease Y" would be considered as a method of treatment. Thus, such a form is not admissible since methods of treatment are excluded from patenting, pursuant to Article 29(1) point 3 IPL.

It is permissible to formulate the claim as "use of substance or composition X for manufacture of a medicinal product for new use Y" or as "product X for use in treatment of particular disease Y".

A therapy or therapeutical use includes treatment of particular diseases or by particular substances or compositions in group of either humans or animals. Essential features of second medical use inventions consist of a disease, a medicinal substance or treated group of patients. Other features of such treatment cannot be considered as relating to therapeutical use.

Novelty of a second medical use invention is derived from its novel feature understood as a new pharmaceutical application. Nevertheless, such an invention actually also covers within its scope development of a new opportunity for therapeutical use of a known medicament. Such an invention has been described in a Polish Patent Office decision as inventing a medicinal product for treatment of a particular disease including indications as to its application.[21]

The Inventors' Manual lists the following solutions as examples of inventions that may be granted a second medical use patent, provided that the general criteria of patentability are fulfilled:

- a new medical indication;
- use of a known medicament by a new, non-obvious group of patients, distinguishable in its physiological or pathological condition and simultaneously devoid of common part with a group which has been previously treated with the same therapy before;
- a new dosage regime understood as a route of administration for a known medicament, provided that non-obvious results are achieved due to such

20. Judgment of the Supreme Administrative Court, ref. II GSK 271/12.
21. Decision of the Polish Patent Office's Appeal Committee, ref. Odw. 1691/98.

administration i.e. improvement of therapeutic efficacy or elimination of side effects.[22]

Rules governing second medical use are applicable also to further medical uses. Should a patent application disclose more than one further therapeutic use, claims of such a type are allowable in one application only if they clearly constitute one inventive idea (Article 34 IPL).

Claimed use needs to be supported on the date of application by results of research (biological examination) confirming the claimed result. An invention in the category of a compound (means, pharmaceutical set) needs to present experimental material documenting discovered properties relating to the expected application.

4.1 *Distinction from first medical use*

The most important difference is that second medical use invention relates to the use of a substance which is already known in medicine as having known therapeutical properties. First medical use, on the other hand, relates to a use of substance which does not have any recognized therapeutical application. Thus, the scope of a first medical use patent is broader.

Furthermore, an indication of therapeutical application in a second medical use has to describe it in a very specific manner, while first medical use may be formulated as a general therapeutical application of a product.

4.2 *Sub-species of first medical use*

In Polish patent literature the following exemplatory sub-species of first medical use inventions have been listed:

- treatment of a disease by use of a previously unknown substance or treatment of other causes of same disease (provided that it may be used in different clinical situation),
- treatment of a new group or population of animals,
- treatment of a new group of patients,
- new route of administration of a medicinal product,
- new combination of known medicinal products,
- new detailed instructions as to administration of a medicinal product relating to particular doses or concentration (dosage regime).

Such sub-species could be related to fields of application of these inventions, i.e. therapeutic method invention, surgical method invention or diagnostic invention.

4.3 *Dosage regimes*

A new dosage regime may form a basis for grant of a second medical use patent if the general requirements of patentability are met.

22. Judgment of the Supreme Administrative Court, ref. II GSK 52/10.

In the practice of the Patent Office it has been noted that for a declaration that the essence of the invention lies in a new dosage regime, claims should be formulated for example in the following manner: "composition for treatment of diabetes type 2 consisting of administering a medicament once a week". If indication of the dosage regime is added only on the date of an SPC application, it should be considered an extension of protection, since a new dosage regime which fulfils the inventive step criterion may lead to a grant of the patent, but it does not necessarily constitute a new product within the meaning of the SPC Regulation.[23]

4.4 Special patient groups

The inventiveness of a second medical use invention involving a use for a new group of patients requires proof in the patent specification that new, unexpected results have been achieved by use of a given medicament on a new group of patients. In particular, it needs to be clear that such an unexpected effect is detected only in one, new group. Should it also be present for the previously known group, the invention cannot be considered patentable.[24]

5. Timing issues

5.1 Relevant time of development of second use

As patent applications relating to second medical use inventions are examined on the basis of the same criteria of patentability as other inventions, development of a second use would have to remain non-obvious in the light of the prior art, in particular in relation to the first use of the same substance or mixture of substances. A prerequisite of an inventive step requires that the development of second use is made preferably at least some time after the first medical use, so that it may be argued that making such a development required long-term efforts.

Polish practice does not provide any particular findings as regards the relevant time for the second use.

5.2 Role of new data

An indication of new data in the second medical use patent application plays an important role in the prosecution proceedings. As discussed above, a new use should be supported in the patent specification by providing data concerning the biochemical research which proved the validity of a new therapeutical application. New data may also include acknowledged international tests, including statistical data and a profit risk analysis.

23. Judgment of the Administrative Court in Warsaw, ref. VI SA/Wa 2130/14.
24. Judgment of the Administrative Court in Warsaw, ref. VI SA/Wa 1997/09.

5.3 *Use of old data*

Use of old data – understood as previous biochemical research, known statistical data or clinical studies – would be considered by the Polish Patent Office as an argument for lack of patentability of an invention presented by such a use. Second medical use needs to be clearly distinguishable from known applications. In order to provide such a distinction, new data should be used in the patent application.

III. Inventive step/non-obviousness

1. *Definition of inventive step/non-obviousness*

An invention shall be considered as involving an inventive step if, having regard to the state of the art, it is not obvious to a person skilled in the art.

In Poland, just like in other EPC countries, inventive step is considered as a criterion which is separate and independent from novelty. However, the question whether a given solution involves inventive step, is analysed only if the subject matter of the invention is considered to be novel.

In the present Industrial Property Law the term 'inventive step' (replacing the previous 'non-obviousness') has been introduced as an adaptation to European standards. It has been also followed by a general definition. This replacement does not involve an essential difference in a manner of assessment of patentability and thus previous case law and legal literature remain generally applicable.

The solution is obvious if it could have been achieved by a person having ordinary skill in the art in a certain field on the basis of the relevant state of the art before the date of the priority. It means that for a person skilled in the art such a solution does not extend beyond typical technical development, but still it clearly and logically follows the state of the art – it does not involve a use of extraordinary skills or knowledge, as compared to those ascribed to a person skilled in the art.

The subject matter of the invention does not need to involve only milestone achievements which would revolutionize the state of the art. It is sufficient for the invention to be something more than the routine knowledge of an engineer. It needs to be evaluated whether a person skilled in the art, knowing the closest prior art, while considering the technical problem could achieve the claimed solution using regular reasonable thinking and routine professional skills, i.e. without any inventive activities.[25]

Unlike analysis of novelty, analysis of inventive step requires published documents to be interpreted in the light of the knowledge available for the person skilled in the art as well as referring this knowledge to that known on the date of priority. The claimed invention has to be considered as a whole. If a claim includes combination of features, it is not correct to argue that each of features of this combination separately is known or obvious and hence whole claimed solution results from the state of the art in the obvious manner. If a claim includes a combination of elements or components, such combination may obviously follow the state of

25. Judgment of the Administrative Court in Warsaw, ref. VI SA/Wa 2183/04.

the art, but if the interaction of combined features leads to achievement of an effect which is different from expected, for example it is greater than a sum of effects of separate features (synergy effect), then such a solution may be considered to involve inventive step. Case law uniformly provides that an obstacle of obviousness should be laid against the solution in its entirery, and not its individual element. Even a combination of known devices or methods may require an inventive contribution.[26]

2. *Same scope of disclosure as for novelty?*

As provided in Article 26(2) IPL, in deciding whether there has been an inventive step, the content of patent applications or utility model applications which enjoy an earlier priority and not made available to the public, shall not be taken into consideration. This provision reflects the wording of second sentence of Article 56 EPC and provides for a difference between the scope of disclosure for inventive step in comparison with the relevant scope for novelty.

3. *Assessment of inventive step/non-obviousness*

Provisions of the Polish Industrial Property Law do not stipulate any particular method for the assessment of an inventive step. While questioning the inventive step, the Patent Office is obliged only to indicate evidence of the state of the art which would support a conclusion that the invention results directly from the state of the art, taking into account an average knowledge possessed by a person skilled in the art.

Polish case law accepts the EPO's 'problem-solution' approach. Assessment of an inventive step should include the following three steps:

(1) finding the nearest prior art,
(2) defining the problem to be solved,
(3) consideration of whether a person having the relevant knowledge of the state of the art, while considering a given technical problem laying behind a given invention, would have an opportunity to reach claimed solution during routine professional activities without employing inventiveness.[27]

Inventive step is considered in the light of one or more prior documents combined. A relevant point of reference is based on the state of the art known on the date of priority of the examined application, as opposed to the state of the art which existed on the date of disclosure of the opposed solutions. The closest state of the art is deemed to consist of a document which discloses a combination of technical means having most features in common with analysed invention, which – in the light of its technical effect, goal or manner of application – is most similar to the analysed invention.

A further step involves the determination of the objective technical problem to be solved by the examined invention. Therefore, it is necessary to analyse the application and the closest state of the art and compare them feature by feature.

26. Judgment of the Administrative Court in Warsaw, ref. VI SA/Wa 307/06.
27. Judgment of the Administrative Court in Warsaw, ref. VI SA/Wa 89/08.

Those which are not essential should not be taken into account. Technical problems may relate to improvement of some effect.

If a solution of a technical problem is unexpected within the closest state of the art or may be related only to a remote state of the art, then it may be assumed that the invention involves an inventive step. Furthermore, if it is not possible to indicate the state of the art relating to the technical problem solved by given invention, i.e. if the state of the art does not present a technical effect resulting from the invention, there are usually no factors that could lead a person skilled in the art to the analysed solution and then the invention may be considered to involve inventive step.

It does not mean, however, that an invention is deemed to be patentable should such new effect be detected, even if the invention relates to a product which has been known as such. In such a case it is necessary to determine other state of the art relating to this new use. The use is then in the right category to grant patent protection.

If the relevant state of the art exists for a given invention, it is important to assess whether one may be lead to the analysed invention on the basis of conclusions drawn from the state of the art.

The Polish Patent Office tends to be reluctant to admit the evidence of an expert opinion for assessment of inventive step, although Polish administrative courts (which examine the validity of the Patent Office's decisions) very often used to remand the cases assessed without such evidence. Recent change in IPL (Article 253[1]) has confirmed the Patent Office's approach that the evidence of the expert opinion is not admitted for verification of whether the statutory prerequisites for the grant of the patent are fulfilled, unless the Patent Office considers such evidence necessary.

In the examination of whether a selection of two or more distinctive features makes an invention non-obvious, it is in particular considered:

- whether the disclosure is of such a kind that when a person skilled in the art faces a given technical problem to be solved, it may combine those features; if, for instance, two analysed disclosures from the state of the art may not practically be easily combined since they describe opposing features, then such combination is usually considered to be non-obvious;
- whether disclosures originate from similar or a distant field of the art,
- whether combination of two or more parts of the same document could be obvious if it were suggested as a reasonable course of action to the person skilled in the art; what may be obvious is connection of a document from the state in the art with common general knowledge derived from textbooks or combination of two or more documents from the state of the art if they include clear mutual reference information,
- whether an invention may be considered as a replacement of, among other things, a component of a preparation with an equivalent component known from the state of the art as appropriate for this purpose; in such case, the solution is deemed to be obvious.

If an independent claim is novel and nonobvious, there is no need to examine whether claims dependent on such independent claim are novel and nonobvious too. In a similar manner, if a product is new (does not form a part of the state of the art) and involves inventive step, there is no need to examine novelty and inventive step of a method of manufacture of such a product or its use (provided that all categories fulfil the condition of unity of invention).

However, it needs to be considered that if a product, method and use have different dates of application, then it may be necessary to conduct a separate examination relating to their novelty and inventive step.

IV. Amendment of claims after grant

In principle, an applicant may amend or supplement patent specification, patent claims and drawings only until a final decision is rendered in the prosecution proceedings (that is, also during the proceedings concerning re-examination of the case). These amendments and supplementations cannot extend beyond the scope disclosed as subject matter of a solution in the application, including the specification, claims, drawings, except for the abstract and the priority document.

Polish patent literature (supported with some case law) provides the following possibilities for amending or supplementing the patent specification:

- limitation of the range of parameters,
- introduction of a change in a feature by replacing its general description with more detailed one (provided that this detailed description may be found somewhere in the application),
- introducing features disclosed in dependent claims into independent claims,
- adding auxiliary features disclosed in the specification or drawings,
- moving features of the characterizing part to pre-characterizing portion of patent claim.[28]

1. Admissibility of post-grant amendments in general

Polish patent law provisions admit post-grant amendments in very limited situations.

In principle, post-grant amendments may be considered only in the following situations:

(1) in relation to national patents – as a result of revocation proceedings,
(2) in relation to European patents – if an amendment is required to adapt the translation of the European patent to amended original wording or in case of filing of a correction of the translation.

As to the first situation, it has been discussed in the case law that the patent holder is not allowed to amend the patent post-grant upon its own initiative. There are no statutory post-grant amendment proceedings as such. It may be considered whether a patent holder's post-grant amendment could be based on revocation in which a patent holder would request on its own to amend or limit a patent. As for now, such an opportunity has been explicitly ruled out by case law. The main reason for that is it is required to have legitimate interest in revoking one's patent. A legitimate interest is interpreted, in general, as a serious need for revoking a patent due to a fact that this patent already constituted an actual basis for claims against a prepared

28. Decision of the Appeal Committee of the Polish Patent Office, ref. Odw 1901/98.

or manufactured solution that is considered as infringing the patent.[29] It is claimed that this interest needs to be real and imminent. In this context, it had been discussed that patent holder would never have an interest in revoking its own patent. Thus, the patent holder would also not be allowed to amend its own patent after its grant.

In the second option, if the scope of a European patent as defined in the translation is narrower than its scope as defined in the language of proceedings before European Patent Office, the translation is deemed to constitute an authentic text of European patent, except from European patent revocation proceedings.

A patent holder may submit a corrected translation at any time with a legal effect after it is published by the Polish Patent Office.

2. *Procedural issues*

2.1 *Independent limitation proceedings*

No independent limitation proceedings are available under Polish patent law.

2.2 *Opposition proceedings*

Polish patent law does not distinguish between opposition proceedings and nullity actions in terms of substantive prerequisites. Proceedings aimed at nullifying one's patent are called revocation proceedings.

Potential post-grant amendments resulting from the revocation proceedings should be dependent on the outcome of the assessment concerning re-examined patentability of a given patent. A patent holder's proposals for amendment of patent claims (potentially including also relevant changes in patent specification) are not binding on the Patent Office.

The Patent Office is not bound by the extent of the revocation request by the applicant. In other words, even if the applicant requests that the patent is revoked in its entirety, and such request is not entirely supported in the course of the proceedings, the Patent Office should not merely follow such a request but rather revoke the patent in part, introducing necessary changes into wording of its claims (and potentially also in patent specification).

It is unclear whether the amendments of the patent in the revocation proceedings should be confirmed with the patent holder. One may assume that the amendments should be introduced in a manner which is practised during prosecution proceedings, i.e. by introducing a more specific description of claimed features, introducing dependent claims into independent claims, etc.

2.3 *Nullity actions*

The remarks presented in point 2.2. are applicable here.

29. For instance, an applicant in the revocation proceedings has been served with a cease-and-desist demand or with a court action relating to an infringement of the patent in question.

3. *Added matter*

If the patent adds matter to the content of the patent application or priority patent application, this fact may constitute a basis for revocation (Article 89(1) item 3 IPL).

In such a situation, the patent holder may consider limiting the scope of the patent by returning to the originally filed application.

4. *Sufficiency*

Lack of sufficiency of disclosure is interpreted as a lack of relevant technical information which would prove that the realization of the intended purpose of the invention is present within the entire scope of the claims.[30]

For instance, pharmacological properties should be confirmed for various types of chemical compounds. The applicant should disclose the information in such an extent so as to allow a person skilled in the art to apply the invention after analysis of the whole content of the application, without the necessity to conduct an additional examination in order to supplement the technical information.[31]

5. *Multiple indications*

Multiple indications provided in one patent may be accepted by the Patent Office if they form a single inventive concept. Otherwise, such a situation may lead to a lack of unity obstacle against the grant of the patent.

The Polish patent law does not stipulate, however, that lack of unity of the patent may form a basis for the revocation proceedings (Article 89 IPL).

V. Change of patent category

1. *General admissibility*

As explained in the preceding section, post-grant changes may be considered only in relation to potential limitations introduced as a result of revocation proceedings.

Polish practice has developed guidelines relating to amendments of a patent's category only in the pre-grant proceedings. As it has been not ruled out that these guidelines could be applied also to post-grant revocation amendments, they will be briefly discussed below.

A change of category is permissible if it does not lead to an extension of the scope of protection.

More specifically, permissibility of change in a patent category is dependent on whether a new category could be derived from the content of the application (in particular its title) and relevant prerequisites may be found in the specification.[32]

30. Judgment of the Administrative Court in Warsaw, ref. II Wa/SA 2896/03.
31. Decision of the Appeal Committee of the Polish Patent Office, ref. Odw. 1841/97.
32. Decision of the Appeal Committee of the Polish Patent Office, ref. Odw. 1901/98.

It is permissible to change a claim relating to a compound, or composition containing a compound, for a claim relating to a use of a compound in a composition for a particular purpose. A use claim confers narrower protection than a product claim as such. For instance, a claim "use of transistor in amplifying device" should not be interpreted as directed to "amplifying device" in which a transistor is applied. Thus, it is not permissible to change a use claim to product claim.

Introduction of a new category is allowable only if it does not extend the scope of the protection of the invention as a whole and it may be derived from the content of the application.

2. *Use claim as a category*

Use claim is accepted as a separate category of an invention. It is required that the subject matter of the patent should be defined by technical features which are appropriate for the claimed category, clear from a technical point of view and capable of distinguishing the subject matter of an invention from solutions known in the state of the art.

3. *From product to method claim*

If a claim relating to a product has been changed into claim relating to a method of manufacture of this product, such a change of category is permissible if the method now claimed leads to manufacture only of a product previously claimed. It is also possible to claim "a method of application of a product".

4. *From method to product claim*

Protection resulting from a product claim embraces this product manufactured by any method. A change from the manufacture method (including protection of products directly obtained in a claimed process) into a product (obtained by any process) is not permissible.

5. *System claims*

Polish patent law and practice do not recognize a category of system claims.

6. *Use claims*

Information concerning use claims is provided in point V. 2. above.

C. INFRINGEMENT AND LITIGATION

I. Legal framework

1. National statutory laws

Patent protection in general and by specific provisions concerning the protection of patents for second medical use is regulated by the IPL. A comprehensive approach to the infringement may require in addition the application of provisions of the Code on Civil Proceedings, Pharmaceutical Law, Public Procurement Law and Unfair Competition Law.

2. Case law

Unlike prosecution and validity, infringement of second medical use patents is very rarely assessed in Poland. Most cases are settled and the majority of final decisions which are available were rendered in preliminary injunction proceedings. There is no Supreme Court judgment referring specifically to the principles of construing second medical use patent claims and forms of infringements.

II. Claim construction

1. General rules

Polish law provides explicitly for three categories of patents: product patents, process patents (including product-by-process protection) and use patents (including product-by-use protection).

According to Article 65 of the IPL, a patent which protects the invention concerning the use of a substance belonging to the prior art to obtain a product having a novel application also covers products prepared specifically in accordance with the invention for such an application.

Therefore, Polish patent law provides for protection of said inventions in a broader scope than it has been provided in the EPC, resulting in protection similar to the UK approach. Furthermore, the concept of “specific preparation” resembles the German construction of “specific manufacture”, unknown in Polish law.

The extent of protection conferred by a national patent is determined by the terms of the claims. Polish courts tend to apply a strict meaning to the patent claims. One of the major differences between the EPC and Polish law is that the latter does not require that the description and the drawings are used to construe the claims. The description and the drawings may be used to interpret the claims when necessary. In accordance with the *clara non sunt interpretanda* principle, Polish courts, especially in the preliminary injunction proceedings, often do not refer to the description or the drawings if the claims are *prima facie* clear and unambiguous.

In the main action, claims are almost always construed with the assistance of a court-appointed expert. As a first step, the meaning of the words contained in the claim is determined on the basis of the patent description (the patent is its own dictionary). Then, based on the court-appointed expert's opinion, the court ascribes the usual meaning of such terms in the relevant area of technology. The claim construction should not lead to a broadening of the extent of the protection which follows from the terms of the claim.

The prosecution files are not used for construing the claims although there is no such explicit prohibition.

2. *Specific issues for use claims*

2.1 Non-medical use claims

Non-medical use claims are subject to a narrowing construction. In particular a claim format: "use of substance X as a biocidal" should be construed as the method of insect extermination with the application of substance X and not as a product-by-use claim.

2.2 First medical use

First medical use claims should include a name of a compound (composition of compounds) followed by the indication of its use, i.a. "substance/composition X" followed by "for use as a medicine", "for use as an antibacterial preparation", "used for treatment of disease Y" etc. (see point B. II. 3.2).

2.3 Second medical use

Polish courts have so far assessed only infringements of Swiss-type claims which usually do not raise doubts as to the product-by-process protection and the claim construction was made within the simplified frame of the preliminary injunction proceedings. Preliminary injunctions have been refused in cases where the information leaflet (SmPC) did not specifically cover the patented use.

III. Scope of protection

1. *Scope of the use*

1.1 General definition of the term "use"

A patent can only be infringed when the invention is used in a professional or commercial manner.

The major factor which determines the scope of protection and the exclusive use is the format of the claims. A product claim is infringed by manufacturing, using, offering, putting on the market or importing for those purposes of the product. A process claim is infringed by using the claimed method or by using, offering, putting on the market or importing for those purposes of a product obtained directly by means of the claimed process.

The term "use" represents a separate form of the product and process claims infringement. It applies to products only but is understood broadly as comprising reprocessing, mixing, or even destroying.

1.2 Manufacture of the pharmaceutical

The manufacture of the pharmaceutical may be prohibited insofar as it is limited by the purpose, i.e. the product is solely destined for the patented use. The manufacture should not be prohibited if the product in question is destined for both non-patented and patented use. The relevant case law requires that the judicial decision contains such a limitation, for example that the manufacture is prohibited for the application of medicine X used for the treatment of disease Y. For that reason, we may expect that the difficulty of proving the actual infringement which plaintiffs face in the litigation will expand to cover the enforcement proceedings as well.

1.3 Sale of the product

The IPL uses the term "putting on the market" instead of the term "sale". This term is understood as having a broad meaning consisting of all legal and actual actions allowing third parties the use of the claimed products. According to the Court of Appeal in Gdansk (case I ACa 320/12) "putting on the market" should be understood broadly as any activity leading to a transfer of the control over the patent-protected product regardless of the form and the legal title of such act. The decisive factor is that the third person during the term of the patent protection puts the infringing product on the market for commercial purpose.

1.4 Offer for sale

The term "offering" is understood as having a broader meaning than the offer according to the general provisions of the civil law. It concerns any preparatory action which is made with the intent of putting the product on the market. As for the broader meaning of the term "offering", the Court of Appeal in Gdansk (case I ACa 320/12) held that it should contain information about the possibility of purchasing a particular product, even without specifying the price and commercial terms, or solicitation to conclude a transaction. Such an interpretation, in court's view, is supported by the purpose of patent protection, which is absolute and exclusive. Therefore providing information about the availability of a particular substance, the possibility of purchasing it and contact details of the seller may be deemed legally relevant acts of patent infringement. This view has been accepted by the Supreme Court (case IV CSK 92/13).

1.5 Application to the patient

Although the application to the patient is a form of use which in the majority of cases takes place within the professional or commercial activity of the doctor/hospital, the practical significance of this finding is very low because patent holders do not take actions against this category of potential infringers.

1.6 *Combination products*

There is no relevant case law with respect to combination products protected under second medical use patents.

2. ***Absolute product protection***

2.1 *Limitation through the term "use"*

The Swiss-type claims which represent the only type of claims of second medical use patents that have been brought the Polish courts' attention so far extend to product-by-process protection. On the basis of such claims courts have granted preliminary injunctions prohibiting from all forms of infringement as long as the plaintiff: (i) properly evidenced that the infringing actions were taken with the purpose of use within the claimed second medical use and (ii) properly formulated its demands by restricting the scope of requested judicial protection to the said purpose. The courts required on-label infringement proof. In practice, skinny labelling would be sufficient to comply with the preliminary injunction.

2.2 *Off-label use*

Off-label use theoretically would be recognized as patent infringement. The complexity of such cases rests in gathering evidence of such use and the intention to infringe. Although most remedies for patent infringement do not require proof of anintention to infringe, many off-label use cases cannot be directly attributed to manufacturers or wholesalers of generic drugs. The infringement is attributable rather to those who administer drugs for off-label application or doctors who prescribe them and pharmacists who dispense them (although we tend to believe that doctors' and pharmacists' liability should be perceived as indirect infringement of accessories). In one recent off-label preliminary injunction case, the application was dismissed despite the fact that the SmPC contained special warnings, precautions for use and pharmacokinetics specific for the claimed second medical use. The court found that even such data would not be sufficient to corroborate the infringement.

3. ***Dosage regimes***

There is no case law pertaining to infringement of the second medical use for dosage regimes in Poland. Theoretically, the major difficulty with pursuing such claims would rest in determining the person or entity liable for infringement. With the lack of evidence of promoting such dosage regimes in the SmPC, leaflets or other materials provided by the generic company, the infringement can only be attributed to the doctor prescribing the patented dosage regime.

4. *Patient groups*

There is no case law pertaining to infringement of second medical use for patient groups in Poland. Again, as discussed above, the major difficulty rests in establishing who is liable for the infringement.

5. *Extension under the doctrine of equivalents*

There is no case law pertaining to infringement of second medical use under the doctrine of equivalents in Poland. Understanding of the specific test for infringement by equivalents has increased in recent years in other patent cases, though. Polish courts accept that in certain instances patent protection may extend beyond the literal meaning of the claims.

Infringement under the doctrine of equivalents may be considered only if it is obvious for a person skilled in the art that a given measure may be applied in the invention instead of its protected feature in order to achieve the same objective, meet the same technical function and achieve the same result. A similar view has been expressed in the judgment of the Court of Appeal in Lodz (case I ACa 612/12) where the admissibility of applying the doctrine of equivalents as such was confirmed and the criterion of "obviousness" of the equivalent for a person skilled in the art was emphasized.

Furthermore, in a recent judgment of the Supreme Court (case V CSK 149/15), it was confirmed that the patent infringement needs to be evaluated also in the context of the doctrine of equivalents involving particular consideration as to whether essential features of the invention have been used in the contested solution.

IV. Infringing acts

Note: the subsequent considerations apply to Swiss-type claims only.

1. *Infringing person or entity*

An act of infringement may be committed by an individual as well as a legal entity provided that such a person or entity acts within commercial or professional terms. Directors, shareholders or members of companies' bodies cannot be sued for infringements committed by the company. The possibility to sue third parties who have not directly participated in the infringing acts but have induced, facilitated or benefited from the infringement will be discussed within the section "Indirect infringement". Although Polish law does not expressly provide for indirect patent infringement, the existing case law allows this type of civil liability to be construed.

2. Direct infringement

2.1 Manufacture of the pharmaceutical

Manufacture of the pharmaceutical would infringe the Swiss-type claims as long as the manufacturing process of the infringing products takes place in the territory of Poland and such products are destined exclusively for the patented use, e.g. when the SmPC contains the patented indication as the sole product indication (purpose-limited claims). When a product was manufactured both for a non-patented and patented use, the courts granted preliminary injunctions prohibiting the manufacture for the patented purpose only; in such cases, however, in the enforcement proceedings the plaintiff would be required to evidence that a specific batch was manufactured for the patented use. When the product's SmPC contains only non-patented indication but the product is prescribed for the patented use, the manufacture would not establish infringement unless extraordinary circumstances are proved (e.g. the intention to manufacture the product for the patented indication follows from evidence other than the SmPC).

2.2 Offer for sale

Any offer indicating the patented use would encroach upon the patent protection regardless of whether for sale or any other commercial or professional use. If the patented indication is contained in the SmPC, products leaflet or other materials disseminated by or on behalf of the MA holder it amounts to direct infringement. Although OTC products may potentially be offered (or – more often – advertised) for patented use, the essential application of this form of infringement in Poland concerns drugs administered in hospitals which in a vast majority of cases represent reimbursed medicines for which public tenders play a particularly important role. Based on the wide interpretation of the term "offering" by the Court of Appeal in Gdansk (case I ACa 320/12) and the Supreme Court (case IV CSK 92/13) it may be argued that the application for reimbursement for the patented indication infringes the patent directly. Such an application may establish an offer, within a broad understanding, especially that the reimbursed medicine must be permanently supplied onto the market, which the applicant shall declare in writing. Although there have been controversies in case-law as to whether the application for reimbursement represents an infringement, more recent decisions issued in preliminary injunction proceedings confirm that at least participation in the reimbursement list represents a form of offer.

The same principle applies to participation in public tenders organized by hospitals as long as the tender specifications include reference to the desired patented indication. In such a case, even if the participating generic does not include this indication in the SmPC, an argument can still be made that such an offer is assumed. A preliminary injunction prohibiting the offer of the claimed product may be used to intervene in public tenders and, in certain scenarios, may lead to rejection of the infringing offer or give a basis to object to the result of the tender. Another option is intervening in the course of public tender proceedings in order to ensure that the tender specification requires that the medicine is authorized for the patented indication. This usually decreases the risk of infringement and such a narrowing of the specification is permitted in justified instances (case KIO/UZP 2588/10).

2.3 Sale

As mentioned above, IPL uses the term "putting on the market" instead of the term "sale". This term is understood as having a broad meaning consisting of all legal and actual actions allowing third parties the use of the claimed products.

2.4 Export

Export is not explicitly listed as a form of direct patent infringement in the IPL. Therefore, export from the country in which the product is not protected to a country covered by the patent protection should not be considered, in principle, as a patent infringement by the exporter in the country from which the export is made as long as the exporter does not exercise any activities in the country of destination. The patent holder may only prohibit those activities that occur within the territory where the patent is protected, in this case, the importer's actions (see below). In certain circumstances the exporter may be liable for the indirect infringement.

2.5 Import

Import is explicitly listed as a form of direct patent infringement in the IPL but is limited by its purpose. Import represents the patent infringement insofar as it is undertaken for the purpose of offering, putting on the market of use of the product within the scope of the patent protection. In case of second medical use patents, it is therefore double-limited, first – it has to be shown that the import was exercised for the purpose of using the product in Poland and second – that such use remains within the patented use.

2.6 Combination products

There is no relevant case law with respect to combination products protected under second medical use patents.

3. Indirect infringement

3.1 Objective acts

Polish law does not contain provisions which would expressly address the issue of indirect infringement. Therefore, this concept under Polish law can only be inferred from general principles of civil law and intellectual property law. A provision of the law, which is commonly taken into account in similar cases, is Article 422 of the Polish Civil Code (CC) pertaining to tortuous liability. Article 422 CC regulates the liability of three categories of persons: accessories, instigators and persons who knowingly take advantage of the damage caused to the injured entity. An accessory is a person who assists in the commission of an infringement by supporting the principal infringer either psychologically or materially (e.g. by providing the principal infringer with the devices necessary for the commission of the infringement).

The possibility of employing Article 422 CC outside the realm of classic civil law, as a legal basis of indirect infringement of intellectual property rights, is, however, subject to differing views, but was supported by the Supreme Court in case II CR 161/74.

Moreover, there are differing views as to the scope of claims available against the indirect infringer as Article 422 CC expressly only provides for the claim for damages. The majority of views as well as the Supreme Court in the ruling in case II CR 161/74 accept a broad interpretation of the application of this provision in patent infringement cases and allow all claims available against the direct infringer also against the perpetrator of the indirect infringement. Yet, a cautious approach is recommended.

Polish legal literature almost uniformly supports the view that an actual direct patent infringement must occur, in order to consider an indirect patent infringement. The above issue is relevant to second medical use. Whereas the fact of manufacturing and putting on the market of drugs intended for the patented use can be ascertained, the actual use of these products for the protected purpose often depends on the patient's actions (for drugs which are not administered in hospitals). One can merely assume with a very high likelihood that such use will take place, since the purchase of the medicine serves this purpose. Yet, if the SmPC contains indications for both patented and non-patented use, it is almost impossible to prove which use actually took place. Another issue is that the patented use in case of drugs not administered in hospitals is undertaken beyond the scope of commercial exploitation of the invention, i.e. beyond the scope of patent exclusivity and thus does not constitute direct infringement.

3.2 Subjective conditions

In the absence of established case-law, we refer to legal writing where it is fairly well accepted that the liability of an accessory is not purely objective and is dependent on culpable conduct. Different views are expressed as to whether the negligence of an accessory in not realizing that they are contributing to patent infringement is sufficient or whether intent on the part of the accessory is required.

The liability of an instigator and a person, who knowingly took advantage of the damage caused to the injured entity is, of essence, depended upon culpable conduct, which also encompasses gross negligence.

3.3 Export

There is no case law regarding export as a form of indirect infringement but some authors tend to adopt the position that the exporter may be considered liable for indirect infringement (as an accessory to the importer's infringement) provided that the exporter is aware of the patent protection in the country of destination (in particular when both the exporter and importer belong to the same capital group).

Moreover, according to some views expressed in the literature, the assessment of whether a given activity should be considered as exporting or putting the product on the market strongly depends on the place where the act takes place. For example, if the agreement relating to the export of the product is concluded in the territory of Poland, it is assumed that the products were put on the market in Poland (i.e. the export is deemed equal to putting on the market). If the purchaser is seated in Poland the contract must also contain an explicit provision that the products will be put on the market outside of Poland.

3.4 Import

Import for the purpose of using, offering or putting on the market is explicitly listed as a form of direct patent infringement in the IPL, i.e. there is no need to evaluate actions of the importer in view of the indirect infringement because all forms of indirect infringement require culpable conduct or at least gross negligence.

3.5 Combination products

There is no case law pertaining to indirect infringement of second medical use patent by supplying medicines which can be used together within the scope of the patent. Theoretically offering one of several active substances can pertain to indirect infringement provided that the intended, protected use can be proved.

4. ***Off-label use case***

4.1 General admissibility of off-label use

Off-label use is neither defined nor explicitly allowed in the Polish Pharmaceutical Law. It is construed on the basis of Article 4 of the Act on Doctor and Dentist Professions which provides that doctors are obliged to exercise their profession in accordance with the current medical knowledge available to them and with due diligence. Off-label use is explicitly regulated only with regard to reimbursed drugs in the Reimbursement Act which provides for the following criteria: such use is necessary for saving patients' lives or health and no other possible applicable clinical procedures exist which are financed from public funds. Off-label use of reimbursed medicines may apply to all types of drugs. The reimbursement is granted by the Minister of Health in an administrative decision which is appealable to administrative courts.

The criteria provided for in the Reimbursement Act, although strict, have often been applied in a very flexible manner by the reimbursing authority.

The reimbursement rate must be indicated in the prescription and both doctors and pharmacists can be fined for prescribing and dispensing medicine for non-reimbursable off-label use as the reimbursed drug.

A majority of Polish prescriptions refer to the brand name rather that the INN which in practice narrows off-label substitution for pharmacists. Another very complex issue which has not been resolved, except for drugs reimbursed within patented use (see above) is that there is no system allowing tracing of the actual indication for which the drug was prescribed in a given case.

If the tender specification requires the medicine containing the active substance and certain clinical indications, medicine of the same active substance but narrower indications do not meet these requirements. In case KIO/UZP 2588/10 the National Appeal Chamber found that the use of a drug beyond the official indications is of course acceptable, but it may raise the risk of refusal to reimburse treatment by the National Health Fund, because there are no clear and transparent rules for funding in this area.

4.2 *Liable persons*

The vast majority of liable persons are those who, within their commercial or professional activity, administer drugs off-label for patented use (doctors, hospitals). Any person who manufactures, offers and puts on the market a product with the intention of off-label use should also be liable for infringement but it causes significant difficulties in proving such intent on the manufacturer's or wholesaler's part. In one of the preliminary injunction cases, the Regional Court in Warsaw dismissed a request against the MA holder and manufacturer of a drug whose SmPC did not contain explicitly the patented indication but amongst special warnings referred to the indication covered by the second medical use patent. The court also held that even though the MA holder and manufacturer offered the drug to wholesalers who then took part in a public tender covering the patented use – this was not sufficient to establish liability of the MA holder and the manufacturer.

Finally, those who knowingly prescribe, dispense or substitute drugs for the purpose of off-label use (doctors and pharmacists) may be liable but rather under the principles of indirect infringement.

4.3 *Objective requirements for infringement*

Objective requirements for infringement of second medical use patents through off-label use are the same as infringement indicated in point 2 above.

4.4 *Subjective requirements for infringement*

Due to the purpose-limited claims protecting second medical use, liability for off-label use will require proving intention to use the product off-label. If the decision to use off-label is made by the patient on the basis of his own research, no infringement would occur. The liability is not dependent upon the culpable conduct of the infringer.

5. *Dosage regimes*

There is no case law which would specifically address off-label infringement of dosage regime patents.

6. *Patient groups*

There is no case law which would specifically address off-label infringement of patient group patents.

V. Remedies

1. *Injunctions*

This remedy is applicable irrespective of whether the infringer acted intentionally or even negligently. Article 287(3) of the IPL stipulates that in case the act of infringement is committed unintentionally, the court may order that the person infringing the patent pays the patent holder an adequate amount of money, if an injunction would be excessively severe for the infringing person and the payment of an adequate sum of money properly satisfies the interests of the patent holder.

2. *Damages*

Damages are available in case of an intentional or negligent infringement. Damages may be pursued and awarded twofold: either as compensation for actual damage and hypothetical but highly probable profits or in the form of an adequate licence fee or other type of remuneration which would be due from the patent holder's consent to exploit the invention as of the date of pursuing this remedy. In practice, damages are rarely pursued in patent litigation in Poland but this situation is most likely going to change in view of several pending cases. Neither punitive damages nor other types of civil penalties are available in patent cases, except for certain enforcement measures.

3. *Information*

Requests for information can be filed either prior to institution of the full action or during the patent litigation. Only information enumerated in the IPL may be requested.

3.1 *Names of manufacturer, distributors etc.*

The applicant may request names and addresses of manufacturers, distributors, suppliers and other prior holders of infringing products, intended wholesalers and retailers, including those who render patented services. It is unclear whether this category also encompasses hospitals where drugs are administered.

3.2 *Names of customers*

Only the names and addresses of intended wholesalers and retailers can be requested. Names and addresses of other customers, in particular patients, cannot be disclosed.

3.3 *Information about infringing sales*

The request for information can only encompass volumes of manufactured, sold, received and ordered infringing products and prices paid for such products.

3.4 Account of profits

Although the IPL does not specify the account of profits as a type of information available to the patent holder, in several patent cases such data was allowed by the courts in the course of the main action on the basis of general rules of civil proceedings.

4. Recall of products and destruction

There is no case-law concerning these remedies for second medical use patents. The recall of products is controversial although has been recently accepted in an unfair competition case by the Court of Appeal in Bialystok. The destruction of infringing products is generally available, although the Court of Appeal in Warsaw dismissed such request in relation to goods which were put on the market during the term of the patent, but the remedy was sought after the patent expiry (case I ACa 1100/14).

5. Recovery of legal costs

Legal costs can be recovered only within the statutory limits which are very tight. Recovery of expenses necessary to litigate can also be requested.

VI. Exceptions from patent protection

1. Exhaustion of rights

Patent exhaustion extends to products which were previously put on the market in the territory of Poland or another EEA country with the patent holder's consent. The following actions are mentioned in the legal writing as actions which do not amount to "putting on the market": manufacturing, transit, and storing with the intent of putting on the market. The term is construed narrowly in comparison with the identical term that refers to the form of infringement and it is accepted that it does not encompass lending, rent or lease. The contractual provisions between the patent holder and the first purchaser of the patented product which prohibit putting products on the market in other countries are not effective on subsequent purchasers and do not eliminate the exhaustion.

Poland is bound by the rules of a so-called "specific mechanism" provided for in point 2 of Annex 4 to the Accession Treaty. Pharmaceutical products, which are protected by patents in the EU and which were marketed in Poland prior to the Polish revision which allowed patenting of pharmaceutical products (i.e. prior to 16 April 1993) may be prevented from the import into the EU until the expiry date of the patents concerned or until the expiry of the relevant SPC as long as the first market authorization was obtained prior to the date of accession (1 May 2004).

There is no specific case law which would relate to the exhaustion of second medical use patents.

2. *Patient welfare*

There are no specific provisions of law for patient welfare. Patient welfare may be taken into account on the basis of the abuse of patent defence. Although Polish law does not require that the patentee exploits its invention, in cases where the protected product is not available in sufficient volumes or is available at excessive prices the patent holder's legal action may qualify as abuse of patent rights and be dismissed. The abuse of the patent may also consist in posing excessive requirements for potential licensees. It is commonly accepted that healthcare and patient welfare is the most likely scenario of the application of the abuse of patent defence.

3. *Others specific to second medical use claims*

In a decision dated 23 October 2013 (IV CSK 92/13), the Polish Supreme Court held that the Bolar exemption does not cover activities by third-party manufacturers, i.e. supplying active ingredients for studies and trials to be conducted by third-party generic manufacturers. One may assume that the Bolar exemption has to be interpreted narrowly because it is an exception to patent protection.

VII. Procedural issues

1. *Preliminary injunction cases*

1.1 *Availability for second medical use claims*

A preliminary injunction is available in second medical use cases. Unlike in the majority of European jurisdictions, the preliminary injunction shall in principle be granted *ex parte* based on facts and evidence offered only by the applicant. Subsequently it is served on the defendant who automatically becomes bound by the injunction. Additional temporary measures available to the patent owner include the seizure of infringing products. However, seizure is generally perceived as posing an excessive burden on the defendant, therefore it is rarely upheld by the Court of Appeal (see: e.g. decision of the Court of Appeal in Warsaw, case VI ACz 6163/14).

1.2 *Specific requirements*

There are no requirements specific for second medical use patents. The general requirements apply, i.e. corroboration of claims (which is understood as showing that the claim is more likely to be well-grounded than not) and legitimate interest. The latter is assumed in IP cases without the necessity to furnish specific evidence.

2. *Cases on the merits*

The major difficulty in second medical use cases pertains to providing evidence of infringement (specifically in off-label use cases). Polish law does not provide for a *saisie-contrefacon* type of proceedings although collecting evidence is allowed in the manner of requesting the opponent to supply specific documents or samples to the court. In off-label use cases the reimbursement decision for off-label application may be the main evidence of infringement.

3. *Enforcement of judgments*

As a majority of patent cases in general are settled, there is almost no case law on the enforcement of judgments available. One may, however, assume that due to the nature of enforcement proceedings in Poland, the plaintiff will face similar difficulties in these proceedings as in litigation, namely – proving the breach of the injunctive measure.

Since 2013, Polish law has introduced a new enforcement measure which is similar to the civil penalty and has quickly become a basic tool in IP cases. Namely, in case of non-compliance with the injunctive relief, the plaintiff may apply for a monetary award the amount of which has not been specified other than by referring to its adequacy to the breach and accuracy to force the defendant to comply with the judgment. In addition, a fine to the State Treasury (in no event exceeding 1,000,000 PLN) can be awarded.

The enforcement of injunctive relief is handled fully by common courts.

VIII. Validity

1. *Relevance for infringement cases*

There is a purely bifurcated system of assessment of validity (the Patent Office and administrative courts of two instances) and infringement (common courts). According to prevailing case law, common courts are bound by the decision on the grant of the patent and shall presume its validity.

Doubts as to the validity of the patent are not sufficient to influence preliminary injunction proceedings unless they are very significant (straightforward lack of novelty). Participation of the alleged infringer in invalidation proceedings before the Polish Patent Office or EPO is not decisive for the refusal of the preliminary injunction in the first instance or its reversal in the appeal.

In general, appeal proceedings are focused only on the corroboration of the infringement. A very clear-cut invalidity argument (lack of novelty rather than lack of inventive step) may be used to rebut the preliminary injunction but it very rarely succeeds as the sole argument against the preliminary injunction.

Until recently, a pending invalidity proceeding was not sufficient to stay the infringement case. The situation is likely to evolve when the written grounds to the Supreme Court's judgment dated 18 February 2016, case II CSK 282/15 are published. The bench, in the oral presentation of the basic motives of this decision held that the Supreme Court will divert from the established view and recommend to stay infringement proceedings pending an invalidity case. It should be mentioned though that the discussed case concerned an industrial design and it cannot be predicted whether and to what extent it will influence patent litigation.

2. *Specifics for second medical use claims*

There are no considerations specific to second medical use patents.

IX. Tactical considerations

1. *Plaintiff*

The plaintiff can gain a strong position with the preliminary injunction in place. It is relatively easy in the first instances taking into account the *ex parte* nature of the preliminary injunction proceedings. Arguments of the parties are weighed usually only in the appeal. As damages awarded for IPR infringement are very low, not to mention the costly and lengthy proceedings with court appointed expert opinions and judgments of the courts of appeal being often reversed by the Supreme Court, it is safe to advise all patent holders to apply for the preliminary injunction as a first step in any patent litigation.

Another consideration is connected with a highly formalistic approach taken by Polish courts which requires plaintiffs in second medical use cases to thoroughly analyse the scope of claims which they can reasonably prove and pursue. A good example of this consideration is a recent case where despite the preliminary injunction being granted and upheld in the appeal, the Regional Court in Warsaw dismissed the action entirely during the first hearing based on the fact that the plaintiff failed to prove that the defendant - the MA holder - actually exploited the invention and infringed the patent. The sole proof that the product with the questioned application was available in Poland and that the defendant held the marketing authorization for the disputed product were found insufficient to prove the infringement (judgment of the Regional Court in Warsaw dated 29 January 2015, XX GC 311/14).

2. *Defendant*

For the defendant it is crucial to prepare for the preliminary injunction proceedings in advance. In most cases, defendants learn about the preliminary injunction on the date when it is served and becomes binding on them. Then they have a very tight deadline of seven days to appeal against the preliminary injunction.

Finally, the formalist approach of the Polish courts may well be explored by the defendants because a lot of patent cases are dismissed on formal grounds or due to insufficient evidence rather than upon an in-depth analysis of the merits and sophisticated patent law based argumentation.

United Kingdom

Tim Powell, Dr. Penny Gilbert[1]

A. AVAILABILITY OF PROTECTION

I. Legal framework

1. National statutory laws

1.1 Pharmaceuticals

As a signatory to the Convention for the European Patent for the Common Market, the United Kingdom resolved to conform its laws in respect of patents to those set out in the European Patent Convention ("EPC"), leading to the Patents Act 1977 which contained the following provisions as originally enacted:

> Section 2:
> (6) In the case of an invention consisting of a substance or composition for use in a method of treatment of the human or animal body by surgery or therapy or of diagnosis practised on the human or animal body, the fact that the substance or composition forms part of the state of the art shall not prevent the invention from being taken to be new if the use of the substance or composition in any such method does not form part of the state of the art.
>
> Section 4:
> (2) An invention of a method of treatment of the human or animal body by surgery or therapy or of diagnosis practised on the human or animal body shall not be taken to be capable of industrial application.

1. The authors wish to acknowledge the contributions of Dr. Bethan Hopewell, Sidd Kusumakar, Dr. David Lancaster and Dr. Joel Coles in the preparation of this chapter.

> (3) Subsection (2) above shall not prevent a product consisting of a substance or composition being treated as capable of industrial application merely because it is invented for use in any such method.

The Patents Act 1977 was subsequently amended, by the Patents Act 2004, to implement the EPC as revised in 2000, which took effect on 13 December 2007. This led to the repeal of Sections 4(2) and 2(6), introducing a new Section 4A to the 1977 Act which expressly permits the grant of a patents for a known product for use in medicine or for a specific first or further medical use.

> 4A. (1) A patent shall not be granted for the invention of
> (a) a method of treatment of the human or animal body by surgery or therapy, or
> (b) a method of diagnosis practised on the human or animal body.
>
> (2) Subsection (1) above does not apply to an invention consisting of a substance or composition for use in any such method.
>
> (3) In the case of an invention consisting of a substance or composition for use in any such method, the fact that the substance or composition forms part of the state of the art shall not prevent the invention from being taken to be new if the use of the substance or composition in any such method does not form part of the state of the art.
>
> (4) In the case of an invention consisting of a substance or composition for a specific use in any such method, the fact that the substance or composition forms part of the state of the art shall not prevent the invention from being taken to be new if that specific use does not form part of the state of the art.

The changes introduced by Patents Act 2004 have not in fact led to any substantive change in what is and is not patentable under UK law although the scope of protection afforded by EPC 2000 claims may be different to the Swiss-type claims allowable prior to EPC 2000 coming into effect (as to which, see section B below).

In interpreting the Patents Act 1977, the courts will have regard to the wording of the corresponding provisions of the EPC in order to resolve any ambiguity arising from any difference in wording. Additionally, whilst not bound by decisions of the European Patent Office ("EPO"), the courts have confirmed that decisions of the Technical Boards of Appeal ("TBA") and the Enlarged Board of the EPO should be highly persuasive to avoid differing constructions of the EPC.[2]

---

2. See Lord Hoffmann in *Merrell Dow Pharmaceuticals v Norton* [1996] RPC 76 at paragraph 82:

   "... the United Kingdom Courts ... must have regard to the decisions of the European Patent Office ("EPO") on the construction of the EPC. These decisions are not strictly binding upon courts in the United Kingdom but they are of great persuasive authority; first, because they are decisions of expert courts (the Boards of Appeal and Enlarged Board of Appeal of the EPO) involved daily in the administration of the EPC and secondly, because it would be highly undesirable for the provisions of the EPC to be construed differently in the EPO from the way they are interpreted in the national courts of a Contracting State."

Accordingly the legal framework in the United Kingdom for the grant of medical use claims is, in theory, no different to that of the EPO.

1.2 Biologics

The Patents Act 1977 was amended, by the Patents Regulations 2000 (SI 2000/2037), so as to implement the provisions of Articles 1 to 11 of the European Directive 98/44/EC on the legal protection of biotechnological inventions ("the Biotech Directive"). These provisions confirmed that inventions concerning biological material, including gene sequences and proteins, are patentable provided that they comply with the requirements of Patents Act 1977.

2. International treaties

The EPC 2000, which brings the EPC in line with the 1994 TRIPS Agreement and deals with enforcement issues, was implemented by the Patents Act 2004, as discussed above.

3. Availability through case law

The availability and scope of patent protection in the United Kingdom is governed by statute, as interpreted by precedential case law of the UK courts. Settled case law of the Technical Boards of Appeal of the EPO is also influential but not decisive, as emphasised by Lord Neuberger in *Human Genome Sciences v Eli Lilly*:[3]

> "87. ... while national courts should normally follow the established jurisprudence of the EPO, that does not mean that we should regard the reasoning in each decision of the Board as effectively binding on us. There will no doubt sometimes be a Board decision which a national court considers may take the law in an inappropriate direction, misapplies previous EPO jurisprudence, or fails to take a relevant argument into account. In such cases, the national court may well think it right not to apply the reasoning in the particular decision. While consistency of approach is important, there has to be room for dialogue between a national court and the EPO (as well as between national courts themselves). Nonetheless, where the Board has adopted a consistent approach to an issue in a number of decisions, it would require very unusual facts to justify a national court not following that approach."

4. Patent term extension/SPCs

SPCs are granted in the UK under Regulation (EC) No. 469/2009 (the "SPC Regulation") and related UK legislation, i.e. Section 128B and Schedule 4A of the UK Patents Act 1977 (as amended), which makes clear that references in the Act to patents apply equally to supplementary protection certificates. Regulation (EC) No.

3. [2011] UKSC 51.

1901/2006 on medicinal products for paediatric use amended the pharmaceutical products Regulation to provide for a six-month extension of an SPC.

Article 1(c) of the SPC Regulation makes clear that a patent which protects the use of a medicinal product can be a "basic patent" for the purpose of Article 3(c). Nevertheless, prior to the decision of the European Court of Justice in Case C-130/*11 Neurim Pharmaceuticals*, on a referral from the UK Intellectual Property Office, it was thought that an SPC was precluded (or its duration was truncated) if the active ingredient in question had been authorised in any earlier marketing authorisation within the EU, even if the earlier authorisation related to a different use in a different species. The ruling in *Neurim* made it clear that new indications for an already approved drug may be the subject of an SPC:

> 25 Therefore, if a patent protects a therapeutic application of a known active ingredient which has already been marketed as a medicinal product, for veterinary or human use, for other therapeutic indications, whether or not protected by an earlier patent, the placement on the market of a new medicinal product commercially exploiting the new therapeutic application of the same active ingredient, as protected by the new patent, may enable its proprietor to obtain an SPC, the scope of which, in any event, could cover, not the active ingredient, but only the new use of that product.
>
> 26 In such a situation, only the MA of the first medicinal product, comprising the product and authorised for a therapeutic use corresponding to that protected by the patent relied upon for the purposes of the application for the SPC, may be considered to be the first MA of 'that product' as a medicinal product exploiting that new use within the meaning of Article 3(d) of the SPC Regulation...

II. Policy considerations

1. Health and social issues

In the United Kingdom, the vast majority of medicaments are prescribed publicly through the National Health Service (the "NHS"). Primary healthcare is provided through general practitioners ("GPs"), who provide access to healthcare through clinics, and pharmacies, which dispense medicaments (including those prescribed by GPs). Secondary healthcare is generally provided in hospitals by specialist consultants and their teams.

The public body NHS England is responsible for providing guidance to Clinical Commissioning Groups (statutory bodies responsible for commissioning medical services within their geographic area of England). Healthcare has been devolved in Scotland, Wales and Northern Ireland. As a result, there are differing arrangements for the provision of healthcare in those countries, with guidance provided on a more local basis.

The starting point of any consideration of prescribing practice is the fundamental principle of the clinician's clinical freedom. Nevertheless, generic prescribing (i.e. prescribing by reference to a drug's international non-proprietary name ("INN")) is encouraged at all levels of the healthcare system, for both clinical and financial reasons. Clinical software used by most GPs also promotes generic prescribing. The vast majority of prescriptions are thus written generically. Furthermore, GPs do not tend to write the indication for which the patient is being treated on the prescription.

Where pharmacists are presented with a prescription written generically, they are free to dispense either the branded version of the drug or the equivalent generic. There is a complicated reimbursement process in place which, amongst other things, encourages pharmacists to hold a wide stock to enable them to provide for the majority of prescriptions whilst obtaining the best possible reimbursement, averaged across all medicaments. However, if a drug is prescribed by brand, the pharmacist must dispense the branded product. In general, if the prescribing doctor writes a prescription generically, and generic versions of the drug are available, the doctor will not know whether the branded product or a generic version will ultimately be dispensed by the pharmacist.

2. *Legal issues*

Whilst the courts of the United Kingdom recognise that valuable, sometimes life-saving, inventions are made through the discovery of the new use of a known drug, they also acknowledge that their protection in patent law is problematic. First, as the drug molecule itself is not novel, there is no question of awarding the inventor of the new use absolute protection for the substance itself. Secondly, for reasons connected with protecting doctors from claims for patent infringement, a patent cannot be granted for a method of treatment of the human body using the drug in question.

Further difficulties arise as a result of the prescribing and dispensing practice in the United Kingdom (as outlined above). In particular, where a drug is prescribed generically, without safeguards in place it cannot be ensured that it will not be used for the patented indication. Pharmacists may not know what illness a patient is being treated for (and, that information may not be available from the patient since prescriptions may be brought to the pharmacist by someone other than the patient, on their behalf). Consequently in circumstances where the pharmaceutical form or dosage is similar, if not the same, for different indications it may be difficult for the pharmacist to identify whether the drug is being prescribed for a new therapy which is patent protected or for an earlier, off patent, indication. Furthermore, neither doctor nor pharmacist may be aware of the issues of patent protection affecting the drug generally or the new therapy specifically.

Recent case law has wrestled with this conundrum and attempted to move toward a solution that seeks to balance the protection to be afforded to those developing new medicaments, to encourage such development, with the desire to minimise public spending on expensive drugs when cheaper alternatives may be available, as well as to allow generic manufacturers access to the legitimate, non-patented, market. This is discussed in more detail below, in particular at section V in relation to the availability of remedies for patent infringement.

B. VALIDITY

I. Allowable claim wording

Prior to the entering in to force of the EPC 2000 on 13 December 2007, second medical use claims were only allowed using the Swiss-type process or method claim in the form of "the use of substance X for the manufacture of a medicament to treat disease Y".[4] Since patents of this form are still in force, the validity and infringement of Swiss-type claims remains relevant in the United Kingdom.

Since 13 December 2007, the simpler purpose-limited product claim form of "substance X for use in the treatment of disease Y" is now permitted. This simpler form coexisted with Swiss-type claims until the Enlarged Board of Appeal decision in G2/08 *Abbott Respiratory/Dosage regime*. Following that decision, the United Kingdom Intellectual Property Office issued a practice note, dated 26 May 2010, rendering Swiss-type claims impermissible for lack of clarity with immediate effect. After that date, all pending or new patent applications before the Intellectual Property Office had to use the simpler, EPC 2000 format. Although it took slightly longer for this change to take effect at the EPO, all EP (UK) patents must now adopt the simpler form of claim in order to be granted.

There has so far been no binding case law in the United Kingdom in respect of infringement or validity of the EPC 2000 form of second medical use patents. It remains to be seen whether they will be found to have the broader scope hinted at by the TBA in *University of Texas Board of Regents/Cancer treatment* (T 1780/12), whereby a claim to a physical activity (the Swiss-type claim) is narrower than a claim to a physical entity (EPC 2000 claim), or if they will be found to have the same scope of protection, as suggested by the preparatory documents for the EPC 2000. However, given the consistent jurisprudence of the EPO (see below) it is probable that the UK courts will consider EPC 2000 claims to have a broader scope than Swiss-type claims.

No product, use or system claims are permissible in the United Kingdom for second medical use patents, since the product is not novel and methods of treatment of the human body by therapy are not themselves patentable. However, dosage claims relating to either the form of the medicament, or the particular dosing regimen are permitted provided that they are novel. Second medical use claims may also be framed in relation to the use of a known compound in a different patient group, so long as the new patient group is entirely distinct from the previously claimed patient group.

The validity and scope of second medical use claims will be discussed further below.

4. G5 /83 *Eisai/Second Medical Indication*, approved by the UK Court of Appeal in *Actavis UK Ltd v Merck & Co Inc* [2008] EWCA Civ 444.

II. Novelty

1. General definition of novelty and prior art

Section 1 of the Patents Act 1977 states that one of the requirements for a patentable invention is that it is new. Section 2 states that an invention is new if it does not form part of the "state of the art" at the relevant priority date of the patent. The "state of the art" is defined as all matter (i.e. information) which was available to the public before the relevant priority date.

The "state of the art" comprises everything made available to the public by means of a written or oral description, by use, or in any other way, before the priority date of the patent. It is not usually permissible, for the purpose of considering novelty, to combine information in multiple prior art documents, unless the reader is cross-referred by the first document to the second.[5] Furthermore, it is not usually permissible to combine different features within a prior art document, unless the combination is itself disclosed by the document.

Information will have been made available to the public if it has been made available to at least one person who is free in law and equity to use it.[6] It is not, however, necessary for any member of the public to have actually received the information, it is sufficient that the information was made publicly available[7].

For the purpose of assessing novelty (but not inventive step), the "state of the art" also includes information in certain patent applications which have an earlier priority date, but which were not published until after the priority date of the relevant patent.

In order for a disclosure to render a patent invalid for lack of novelty, it must be: (i) clear and unambiguous;[8] and (ii) enabling. Whilst any ambiguity may prevent a finding of anticipation (although the prior art may still render the claimed invention obvious), the skilled person reads the prior art in the context of his common general knowledge. This means that not all features of the claimed invention need to be explicitly disclosed in the prior art document if they would be held to be implicitly disclosed.[9] Furthermore, it is not sufficient that the prior art merely discloses the claimed invention, it must provide sufficient information to allow the skilled person to perform it at the priority date.[10]

2. Definition of skilled person

The skilled person is the notional individual (or notional team of individuals) to whom the patent is addressed, and who has a practical interest in the subject matter of the invention. Where the skilled person is deemed to be a team, the relevant common

5. *Sharpe & Dohme Inc v Boots Pure Drug Co Ltd* (1927) 44 R.P.C. 367.
6. *Bristol Myers Co's Appn* [1969] R.P.C. 146.
7. *Lux Traffic Controls Ltd v Pike Signals* [1993] R.P.C. 107.
8. *General Tire v Firestone* [1972] RPC 457.
9. *Hoechst Celanese v BP Chemicals* [1998] F.S.R. 586.
10. *Synthon BV v SmithKline Beecham Plc (Paroxetine)* [2006] R.P.C. 10.

general knowledge will be the knowledge held collectively by the team and not only the knowledge that was common to all.

The skilled person has been described by the English judges as being "very boring – a nerd".[11] They are well-acquainted with standard techniques and have carefully read the relevant literature, however, they are incapable of a scintilla of invention.[12]

3. *Scope of disclosure*

3.1 General rules

Section 72(1)(c) Patents Act 1977 provides that the specification of a patent should disclose the invention clearly enough for it to be performed by the skilled person. Furthermore, the specification of the patent should contain sufficient information to allow the skilled person to make a reasonable prediction that the invention will work with substantially everything falling within the scope of the claim, i.e. the claim must be plausible or credible across its scope in light of the data in the specification read in the light of the skilled person's common general knowledge.[13]

3.2 First medical use

It is clear from the EPC both as originally enacted and as amended by the EPC 2000 that the identification of a first medical use of a known compound may confer novelty and form the basis of a patentable invention.

3.3 New subject matter

The patent specification must provide clear and unambiguous support for the novel subject matter, i.e. the use of the claimed substance for the new therapeutic purpose. The new therapeutic purpose may consist solely in a new dosage regime[14] or in a novel class of patients treatable by the claimed substance.

3.4 New data

The information in the patent specification must make it plausible or credible that the claimed substance will be effective with respect to substantially all the claimed therapeutic uses.[15] However, in a recent decision from the English Patents Court it was held that there is no requirement that a patent should contain data or experimental

11. *Technip France SA's Patent* [2004] R.P.C. 46.
12. *Technograph v Mills & Rockley* [1972] R.P.C. 346.
13. *Regeneron Pharmaceuticals Inc v Genentech Inc* [2013] EWCA Civ 93.
14. *Actavis v Merck* [2008] R.P.C. 26.
15. *Regeneron Pharmaceuticals* (*supra*).

proof to support its claims, so long as the claims are plausible or credible in light of the specification and the common general knowledge.[16]

4. *Requirements for second medical use*

There are no special requirements under English law in relation to the sufficiency of disclosure with regard to claims to a second medical use. As for other types of invention, the claims must be plausible or credible in the light of the specification and the common general knowledge, and must be workable across their scope.

4.1 Distinction from first medical use

The claims of the second medical use patent must be limited to novel uses, including novel medical conditions, or novel combination therapies, or novel dosage regimes or classes of patients who would not have been treated within the scope of the first medical use.

4.2 Sub-species of first medical use

The English courts have approved of second medical use patents where the use is for: (i) a novel medical condition; (ii) a novel combination therapy;[17] and (iii) a novel dosage regime.[18] A claim to the use in a selected patient population may be patentable if it can be established that the combination therapy or the use in the selected patient population is novel. It may be necessary to establish that there is no overlap between the selected patient population and the patient populations in which the substance was previously used.

4.3 Dosage regimes

The English courts have confirmed that second medical use claims for dosage regimes are permissible, so long as the dosage regimes are novel and inventive.[19]

4.4 Special patient groups

The English courts have not yet considered the patentability of second medical use patents for the use of a known compound for the treatment of a known condition in special patient groups. Such claims may be held to be patentable, so long as the usual requirements for novelty and inventive step are met. In considering this issue, the English courts are likely to have regard to the case law of the EPO and other European jurisdictions.

---

16. *Actavis v Eli Lilly* [2015] EWHC 3294 (Pat).
17. *Plough v Norbrook* [2005] EWHC 2532 (Ch).
18. *Actavis v Merck* [2008] EWCA Civ 444.
19. *Actavis v Merck* [2008] EWCA Civ 444.

5. *Timing issues*

5.1 *Relevant time of development of second use*

It is not necessary for a patent to contain data from clinical trials, but may instead contain pre-clinical data from animal models[20] provided that they make it plausible that the medicament will treat the new claimed indication. Furthermore, a patent need not contain any experimental data, so long as the claims are credible or plausible in light of the information in the specification and the common general knowledge.[21]

5.2 *Role of new data*

New data are necessary insofar as the claims would not be credible or plausible without them. Post-published data may be relied upon to support[22] the plausibility of the disclosure in the application as filed and to determine, therefore, whether or not any particular technical advance had actually been achieved.[23]

5.3 *Use of old data*

Old data may be used in order to establish that the claims are credible or plausible.

III. Inventive step/non-obviousness

1. *Definition of inventive step/non-obviousness*

Section 3 of the Patents Act 1977 states that an invention shall be taken to involve an inventive step if it is not obvious to the skilled person at the priority date in light of the prior art. Instead of the problem/solution approach adopted by the European Patent Office, the English courts generally apply the *Windsurfing/Pozzoli* test for obviousness.

The *Windsurfing/Pozzoli* test involves the following four steps:

- Identify the skilled person and his common general knowledge.
- Identify the inventive concept of the claim in question or if that cannot readily be done, construe it.
- Identify what, if any, differences exist between the matter cited as forming part of the "state of the art" and the inventive concept of the claim or the claim as construed.
- Viewed without any knowledge of the alleged invention as claimed, ask whether the differences constitute steps which would have been obvious to the person skilled in the art or do they require any degree of invention?

20. *Generics (UK) t/a Mylan & Ors v Warner-Lambert* [2015] EWHC 2548 (Pat).
21. *Actavis v Eli Lilly (supra).*
22. *Human Genome Sciences v Eli Lilly* [2011] UKSC 51.
23. *Generics (Mylan) v Yeda & Teva* [2013] EWCA CIV 925.

It is not, however, sufficient for it to be obvious to try the substance for the claimed second medical use. For the claim to be obvious, the skilled person must also have a fair expectation that the substance will be effective for the claimed use.

2. Same scope of disclosure as for novelty?

If the patent makes no technical contribution to the state of the art, the claims will be held to be obvious.[24] Therefore, the patent specification must establish that the invention makes a technical contribution to the art.

3. Assessment of inventive step/non-obviousness

For second medical use patents, the active ingredient(s) will generally form part of the state of the art. The question of inventiveness will therefore often turn upon whether it would have been obvious to the skilled person that a particular use of the product would have a reasonable chance of success in treating the new indication.

IV. Amendment of claims after grant

1. Admissibility of post-grant amendments in general

Patent specifications can be voluntarily amended post-grant via a number of routes. If the patent is not the subject of proceedings in which validity may be put in issue,[25] either before the UK Intellectual Property Office (UK IPO) or the Court, then the proprietor can apply in writing to the UK IPO giving details of the proposed amendment and reasons for the application.[26] In particular, if the amendments are intended to distinguish the claimed invention from any published prior art which might invalidate the patent, this should be disclosed and the prior art identified. In considering whether to allow the amendment, the examiner shall have regard to the relevant principles under the EPC. An application to amend a patent specification is advertised by a preliminary notice in the *Patents Journal* prior to examination, but without specifying the proposed amendments. Amendment applications are recorded in the UK IPO register and can be inspected by the public.

Amendments proposed to distinguish the invention from specified prior art must be such that the claimed invention is novel and involves an inventive step. The amendments must not add matter, extend the protection conferred or introduce any other objection into the specification. For example, the description and claims must continue to be clear.

If the examiner considers that the amendment is not allowable and agreement cannot be reached with the applicant, then an oral hearing is convened. Where proposed amendments appear to be allowable, a notice is published in the *Patents Journal* declaring that the amendments are open to opposition for a period of four

24. *Idenix v Gilead* [2014] EWHC 3916 (Pat).
25. Such proceedings are listed in s.74(1) Patents Act 1977.
26. s.27 Patents Act 1977.

weeks. Assuming no opposition is filed, the proprietor will be required to file, within a specified time, a copy of the amended specification,[27] which will carry a "C" rather than a "B" designation. Amendments are deemed to have had effect from the grant of the patent.[28]

The above principles apply to both UK patents and European patents (UK). Where an EP (UK) is sought to be amended and the specification is not in English, the applicant must also supply a translation of proposed amended specification and a translation of the proposed amendment.[29]

Patent specifications may also be amended during the course of proceedings before either the UK IPO or the Court.[30] The Court formally retains a discretion as to whether to exercise its power to amend a patent specification, although the scope of that discretion has become limited and considerations of delay, covetous claiming and the proprietor's conduct generally are no longer to be considered relevant.

It is important to note, however, that the Court still retains the power to refuse amendments if they amount to an abuse of the Court's process. This can arise where a proprietor applies to amend the patent *after* the Court gives a decision invalidating the patent in such a way that may necessitate a new trial. The general principle is that there is an underlying public interest in finality in litigation and ensuring proceedings are conducted efficiently. In assessing whether conduct is abusive, the Court adopts a broad, merits-based judgment, taking account of the public and private interests involved and ultimately focuses on the question of whether, in all the circumstances of the case, a party is misusing or abusing the process of the Court by seeking to raise before it an issue which could have been raised before. A particularly relevant factor in patent cases is that a proprietor ought to know what its invention is. Therefore, if a proprietor considers the claims of the patent are vulnerable, it should propose a fall-back position in good time, with supporting evidence, rather than awaiting the outcome of the trial before making an amendment application.[31]

Amendment applications to the Court must be by way of an application notice, giving particulars of the proposed amendment and the grounds upon which it is sought. The applicant must also state whether it contends that the claims prior to amendment are valid. This application notice must be served on all parties to the proceedings and at the UK IPO within seven days of being filed at Court. Unless the Court orders otherwise, the UK IPO will advertise the amendment in the *Patents Journal*. Any oppositions by third parties must be filed and served on all parties (and the UK IPO) within 14 days of the advertisement. If the Court allows an amendment after a decision of partial invalidity and all likely opponents are already before the Court, the Court may order that the requirement to advertise the proposed amendment be dispensed with. It is also usual practice for the proprietor to serve on the UK IPO a copy of the order allowing the amendment together with an amended patent specification.

---

27. r.35(6), Patents Rules 2007.
28. s.27(3) Patents Act 1977.
29. r.35(4) Patents Rules 2007.
30. s.75 Patents Act 1977.
31. For a summary of the relevant law, see *Warner-Lambert v Actavis* [2015] EWHC 3370 (Pat) at paragraphs 7-14.

In addition, European patents may be amended through the EPO opposition or limitation procedures. Such amendments will automatically apply to any EP (UK), subject to any appeal.

2. *Procedural issues*

2.1 *Independent limitation proceedings*

See Chapter I, "EPO".

2.2 *Opposition proceedings*

See Chapter I, "EPO".

If a European patent which designates the UK is upheld in opposition proceedings before the EPO in amended form, those amendments automatically apply to the EP (UK), subject to any appeal. In addition, it is important to note that, where an EP (UK) is under opposition at the EPO and the patentee seeks amendments in those proceedings, an action for infringement cannot be pursued unless the desired amendments are also sought in parallel.

2.3 *Nullity actions*

See Infringement and litigation below.

3. *Added matter*

Under UK practice, a request to make a post-grant amendment to replace Swiss-type claims with the new form of second medical use claim (EPC 2000) is unlikely to succeed, particularly as the Enlarged Board in G 02/08 suggested that the new form of claim may have a broader scope than Swiss-type claims. See further below.

4. *Sufficiency*

Second medical use claims to the further medical use of a substance or composition must be supported by evidence that the substance or composition is (or at least is plausibly) effective for the specified use.

5. *Multiple indications*

See Chapter I, "EPO".

V. Change of patent category

1. *General admissibility: product to use claims and vice versa*

As discussed above, amendment of granted claims in the course of UK proceedings may be permitted provided that there is no extension in scope of protection (Patents Act 1977 Section 76(3)(b), equivalent to EPC Article 123(3)).

The Patents Court has recently confirmed that Swiss-type claims are process claims (see *Warner Lambert v Actavis*[32]) and are directed to the manufacturer of a medicament.[33] By contrast, the new EPC 2000 form of second medical use claims are "purpose-limited" product claims. In G2/88 *Mobil/Friction Reducing Additive*, the EPO Enlarged Board confirmed that amending a product claim to a use claim does not broaden the scope of protection under Article 123(3). However, a request to make a post-grant amendment to replace Swiss-type claims with the new form of second medical use claim is unlikely to succeed since the latter may have a broader scope.[34]

In T 250/05 *Use of Nitric Oxide for Systemic Treatment/The Brigham and Women's Hospital*, the TBA held that a post-grant amendment from a Swiss-type claim to the new form of second medical use claim would extend the scope of protection and so would not be allowable under Article 123(3) EPC (equivalent to Patents Act 1977 Section 76(3)(b)).

The same conclusion was reached more recently in T 1673/11 *Treatment of Pompe's disease/Genzyme*. In the course of opposition proceedings the patentee had applied to amend a granted Swiss-type claim into EPC 2000 format. The argument advanced by the patentee was that a product directly obtained by the process of a Swiss-type claim was protected as such (by virtue of Article 64(2) EPC) and therefore the scope of protection was the same as that of the proposed EPC 2000 claim. The TBA decided that even if this 'product directly obtained' analysis was the correct approach to assessing extension of protection under Article 123(3), there was in any event extension of protection. The TBA took the view that because the Swiss-type claim was for the manufacture of a medicament then the direct product would be the active ingredient in a form which is packaged and/or provided with instructions for use in the treatment of the patented indication (in that case infantile Pompe's disease). Conversely the EPC 2000 claim covered the active ingredient whenever it is being used for the patented treatment.

This difference in scope was also highlighted in T 1780/12 *Cancer treatment/Board of Regents, University of Texas* and T 879/12 *Genentech* where it was held that where a divisional application included the new claim form and the granted parent claimed the same medical use in the Swiss type, this did not constitute "double-patenting".

---

32. [2015] EWHC 2548 (Pat).
33. [2015] EWCA Civ 556.
34. In G 02/08 *Kos Life Science*, the EPO Enlarged Board of Appeal suggested that the new form of claim may have a broader scope than Swiss-type claims.

C. INFRINGEMENT AND LITIGATION

I. Legal framework

1. National statutory laws

As set out above, the Patents Act 1977 sets out the national basis for patent law in the United Kingdom. It is to be interpreted as having, as nearly as practicable, the same effect as the relevant articles of the EPC.

2. Case law

The United Kingdom is a common law jurisdiction and, as such, the application of statutory law is set out in the decisions of the courts. The courts of the United Kingdom will also consider the case law of the EPO and other Convention jurisdictions where relevant.

II. Claim construction

1. General rules

The accepted approach to claim analysis is "purposive construction", which embraces Article 69 of the EPC (*Kirin-Amgen Inc and others v Hoechst Marion Roussel Limited and others* [2004] UKHL 46). The extent of the protection conferred by a patent is determined by the claims, which are interpreted according to the description and drawings. It is, of course, a fundamental principle, under UK law and procedure, that the construction of the claim is the same whether validity or infringement is to be considered.

2. Specific issues for use claims

It is well-established that the term "for" in patent claims means "suitable for". In other words, a claim to an article "for" a specific purpose is a claim to such an article whatever its intended purpose. In second medical use claims, however, such a construction would deprive the claim of novelty (as the product itself was "suitable for" the new use before the discovery of such application). The word "for" in second medical use claims is therefore understood to mean "suitable and *intended* for" (*Hospira UK Ltd v Genentech Inc* [2014] EWHC 1094 (Pat)). The questions remain (and are yet to be finally answered): what is meant by "intended", and whose intention is relevant?

In recent and evolving case law on the question of the patentability and infringement of Swiss-type claims, the Court of Appeal rejected tests based on subjective intention (i.e. where the generic manufacturer actually intends the product to be used for the patented indication) and foreseeability (i.e. where it is merely foreseeable to the generic manufacturer that some of its product may be used for the patented indication). Instead, the Court of Appeal proposed that the word "for" in a second medical use claim requires that the alleged infringer knows (or can reasonably foresee) the ultimate intentional use for the patented indication (not that they had that specific intention or desire themself) (*Warner-Lambert Company, LLC v Actavis Group Ptc EHF & Others* [2015] EWCA Civ 556). Thus, the Court of Appeal in *Actavis* proposed a test for infringement of Swiss-type claims having two elements: (i) foreseeability on the part of the manufacturer that (ii) somewhere further down the chain there will be intentional use for the patented indication. At the time of writing, the Court of Appeal is being asked to revisit this interpretation (in the context of the ongoing dispute between Warner-Lambert and Actavis in relation to the compound pregabalin).

III. Scope of protection

1. Scope of the use

1.1 General definition of the term "use"

There is no general definition of the term "use".

Since Swiss-type claims are purpose-limited process claims, direct infringement is concerned with the manufacture of the medicament (including questions about what it is manufactured "for") along with the handling of the resultant product. This is governed under Sections 60(1)(b) (use etc. of the process) and 60(1)(c) (disposal etc. of a product obtained directly by means of the process) of the Patents Act 1977. Whilst there is yet to be any case law on the issue, the infringement of EPC 2000 claims, being purpose-limited product claims, would concern the product itself (rather than the process) and be governed by Section 60(1)(a) (making, disposing etc. a product) of the Patents Act 1977.

The Court of Appeal stated in *Warner Lambert v Actavis* that the skilled person would understand that the technical features of a Swiss-type claim extend beyond making the product, yet fall short of including the step of actually using the product for treating the patented indication. Instead, it includes a feature concerned with the ultimate purpose of the product manufactured, namely the intentional treatment of the patented indication. The subject matter of the claim, therefore, was making the product for patients to whom it will be intentionally administered for treating the patented indication. Making the product for patients to whom it is to be administered for the non-patented indications is not within the technical subject matter of the claim. Only the former category of manufacture makes use of the technical contribution of the patentee.

1.2 Manufacture of the pharmaceutical

Section 60(1)(a) of the Patents Act 1977 provides that, where the invention is a product, a person infringes the patent for the invention where, amongst other things, they make the product. Section 60(1)(b) of the Patents Act 1977 provides that, where the invention is a process, a person infringes the patent for the invention where, amongst other things, they use the process or offer it for use.

1.3 *Sale of the product*

Section 60(1)(a) of the Patents Act 1977 provides that, where the invention is a product, a person infringes the patent for the invention where, amongst other things, they dispose of the product. Section 60(1)(c) of the Patents Act 1977 further provides that, where the invention is a process, a person infringes the patent for the invention where they, amongst other things, dispose of any product obtained directly by means of that process or keep any such product.

1.4 *Offer for sale*

Section 60(1)(a) of the Patents Act 1977 provides that, where the invention is a product, a person infringes the patent for the invention where, amongst other things, they offer to dispose of the product. Section 60(1)(c) of the Patents Act 1977 further provides that, where the invention is a process, a person infringes the patent for the invention where they, amongst other things, offer to dispose of any product obtained directly by means of that process or keep any such product.

1.5 *Application to the patient*

Pursuant to Section 60(1)(a) of the Patents Act 1977, the patentee is entitled to prevent the keeping of any and all product deemed infringing, whether by the patient or by someone else. While a patient (or anyone else) cannot infringe a patent by using the drug for treatment, according to the Court of Appeal's proposed test for infringement in *Actavis* the patient's intention may nevertheless be relevant in assessing infringement by the manufacturer.

1.6 *Combination products*

As set out above, a combination product for a new or non-obvious combination treatment can be patentable.

2. **Absolute product protection**

2.1 *Limitation through the term "use"*

The necessary limitation through the term "use" means that a patentee to a second medical use patent cannot prevent the use of the product *per se*.

2.2 *Off-label use*

Off-label prescribing (i.e. the use of a drug for an unapproved indication, age group, dosage or mode of administration) is relatively common in some therapeutic areas. By relying on a marketing authorisation for one indication, clinicians may use their clinical judgment, at their own risk, to prescribe authorised medicaments for unauthorised indications. This is not however as relevant in a typical second medical use case as "cross-label use".

Cross-label use generally refers to the use of a drug for a previously approved and patented indication, age group, dosage or mode of administration that is not mentioned in the marketing authorisation or packaging information for the particular product in question. This arises in the context of so-called "skinny labelling". Article 10 of Directive 2001/83/EC relating to medicinal products for human use provides an abridged procedure for the authorisation of generic products. Article 11 of Directive 2001/83/EC provides that: "those parts of the summary of product characteristics of the reference medicinal product referring to indications or dosage forms which were still covered by patent law at the time when a generic medicine was marketed need not be included". Thus, European law allows generic suppliers to "carve out" indications which are protected by a second medical use from summary of product characteristics (and hence marketing authorisation) and packaging information. This was the case in *Warner-Lambert v Actavis*. As with off-label use, GPs are generally permitted to prescribe for cross-label use if they see fit.

3. *Dosage regimes*

As set out above, novel dosage regimes can be patentable as a second medical use. In such circumstances, the patentee is entitled to prevent the use for such dosage regime.

4. *Patient groups*

As set out above, a claim to a new or selected patient population may also be patentable. Again, in such circumstances the patentee is entitled to prevent the use in such patient groups.

5. *Extension under the doctrine of equivalents*

The United Kingdom does not employ a doctrine of equivalents approach. As set out above, the courts follow the Protocol on the Interpretation of Article 69 of the EPC.

IV. Infringing acts

1. *Infringing person or entity*

Save for a few exceptions (for example, private, non-commercial use), any person or entity carrying out, in the United Kingdom, any of the acts amounting to direct or indirect infringement under Section 60(1) and/or Section 60(2) of the Patents Act 1977 is liable for patent infringement.

2. *Direct infringement*

2.1 *Manufacture of the pharmaceutical*

See "Scope of protection", above.

A Swiss-type claim, as a process claim, may be infringed under Section 60(1)(b) or Section 60(1)(c). In the common scenario that the manufacture of the product takes place outside of the United Kingdom, Section 60(1)(b) does not apply. This was the case in *Actavis*. If the interpretation of the Court of Appeal in *Actavis* is established and followed, then a Swiss-type claim will be infringed where, at the time of manufacture (no matter where manufacture takes place), the manufacturer can foresee the ultimate intentional use for the patented indication (in the United Kingdom). A consequence of such a construction is that that all products deemed to infringe at the time of manufacture, whether or not ultimately used for the patented indication, will thus be "infringing" products.

There is no case law in this area in relation to EPC 2000 claims. It may be assumed, however, that a pharmaceutical product manufactured and packaged in a form suitable for use in the treatment of the patented indication (i.e. a "full label" product) will be within the scope of an EPC 2000 claim. In contrast, where a "skinny label" is used, the mere manufacture of such a product should not be encompassed by an EPC 2000 claim. As explained below, however, disposing of such a product with the requisite knowledge of its intended use may amount to indirect infringement of an EPC 2000 claim.

2.2 *Offer for sale*

See "Scope of protection", above.

As set out above, a Swiss-type claim, as a process claim, may be infringed under Section 60(1)(c), which entitles the patentee to prevent the sale or offer for sale of a product obtained directly by means of that process.

As with manufacturing, there is no case law in this area in relation to EPC 2000 claims. It may be assumed, however, that the sale or offer for sale of a pharmaceutical product may amount to direct infringement of an EPC 2000 claim unless a "skinny label" is used. Furthermore, such supply may amount to indirect infringement of an EPC 2000 claim whether or not a "skinny label" is used.

2.3 *Sale*

See "Offer for sale", above.

2.4 *Export*

There is no specific prohibition on "export" covered by the Patents Act 1977. Where the export is in relation to an infringing product, however, the person exporting is likely to be carrying out at least the act of "keeping", contrary to Section 60(1)(a) of the Patents Act 1977.

2.5 *Import*

Section 60(1)(a) of the Patents Act 1977 provides that, where the invention is a product, a person infringes the patent for the invention where, amongst other things, they import the product. Section 60(1)(c) of the Patents Act 1977 further provides that, where the invention is a process, a person infringes the patent for the invention where they, amongst other things, import any product obtained directly by means of that process or keep any such product.

Where the manufacture of a product covered by a patentee's Swiss-type claim takes place outside of the jurisdiction, it will be an infringement to import the product where manufacture amounted to an infringement of the Swiss-type claim.

With regard to EPC 2000 claims, the importation of a product with a "full label" may amount to infringement. For "skinny label" products the focus will be more on the circumstances of its disposal to third parties, leading to potential liability for indirect infringement.

2.6 *Combination products*

Subject to their patentability, combination products covered by second medical use claims should, in principle, be treated in the same way as non-combination products. There is no specific case law in a second medical use context, but two general scenarios can be envisaged: (i) cross-label-type cases, where the generic manufacturer wishes to supply a product (combination or otherwise) into the non-patented market, the active ingredients of which overlap with the patented combination product; and (ii) where the generic product may be used further down the chain for the preparation or dispensing by a pharmacist of a combination covered by the patent. In the former case, infringement is likely to arise unless the generic manufacturer adopts a "skinny label". In the latter case, the usual principles as to indirect infringement should apply (see below).

3. *Indirect infringement*

3.1 *Objective acts*

Indirect infringement (also known as contributory infringement) is set out in Section 60(2) of the Patents Act 1977, which covers the acts of supplying and offering to supply any means relating to an essential element for putting the invention into effect.

3.2 *Subjective conditions*

Section 60(2) of the Patents Act 1977 requires that the supplier *knows* (or it ought to be obvious to them) that the "means essential" are suitable and *intended* (by some ultimate users) for putting the invention into effect. This is to be proved on the usual standard of balance of probabilities. It is not enough that the means are suitable for putting the intention into effect, but it is likely to be the case where the supplier knew (or it was obvious in the circumstances) at the time of their offer to supply or supply that some (disregarding freak use) ultimate users would intend to use, adapt or alter the "means essential" so as to infringe (*Grimme Landmaschinenfabrik GmbH & Co. KG v Derek Scott (t/a Scotts Potato Machinery)* [2010] EWCA Civ 1110, 15 October 2010 and *KCI Licensing Inc and others v Smith and Nephew plc and others* [2010] EWCA Civ 1260).

3.3 *Export*

Exporting is not an act specifically covered by the Section 60(2) provisions in relation to indirect infringement.

3.4 *Import*

Importing is not an act specifically covered by the Section 60(2) provisions in relation to indirect infringement. However, any subsequent supply or offer to supply may amount to indirect infringement if the conditions set out above are met.

4. ***Off-label use***

4.1 *General admissibility of off-label use*

As set out above, off-label use is generally permitted in the United Kingdom, provided that the clinician assumes responsibility for doing so. Cross-label use is also generally permissible.

In principle, the patentee to a second medical use patent should be entitled to prevent off-label use covered by the claims. However, for the same reasons explained in the Policy section above regarding the prescribing and dispensing framework in the United Kingdom, the policing of such use and enforcement of such protection presents difficulties. Furthermore, it would be difficult and unattractive for a patentee to bring a claim for infringement in respect of an unlicensed use.

With regard to cross-label use, the general principles discussed above (in particular in relation to the adoption of "skinny labelling") should apply.

4.2 *Liable persons*

For EPC 2000 claims, where there is a "skinny label", it might be argued that clinicians could be found liable for infringement for cross-label prescribing (such cross-label use amounting to the therapy covered by the second medical use patent). Since prescriptions are generally written by INN rather than by brand, however, the GP will not know whether the pharmacist is going to use the generic or the branded product. It may be argued, that, given the cost-saving approach of the NHS, GPs should know that a pharmacist receiving a prescription written by INN is likely to dispense the generic rather than the branded product. Likewise, a pharmacist dispensing the generic medicament for the second medical use (i.e. cross-label) would not generally know that the patient was being treated for such (for the policy framework reasons set out above).

Whilst there is no case law in this area, it is arguable that the GP or patient will not in either case have the necessary intention or foresight required to satisfy the use element of an EPC 2000 claim.

As to Swiss-type claims, neither GPs nor pharmacists manufacture medicaments (subject to the argument that the acts of GPs or pharmacists are within a broad definition of "manufacture" in Swiss-type claims). However, at least pharmacists may be liable for disposing of a product of the patented process of manufacturer. In theory, a clinician may be alleged to "procure" the infringement by writing a generic prescription, although it may be unwise for a patentee to sue clinicians and there may be issues surrounding the exclusion of methods of treatment.

V. Remedies

1. *Injunctions*

Injunctions are a discretionary remedy that are generally available in cases involving a finding of patent infringement. However, it is arguable that where there is a finding of infringement of a second medical use patent, an injunction may not be appropriate. Assuming the product in question is indicated for multiple medical conditions, only a proportion of the marketed generic drug that is being sold will be infringing (i.e. that which is being used for the patented second medical use).

The Court of Appeal in *Warner-Lambert Company LLC v Actavis Group PTC EHF & Ors*[35] stated that a general injunction prohibiting sale of the product of a second medical use claim is plainly not justifiable, and that it may be unjust and inconvenient to grant an injunction at all since this will prevent the manufacturer from selling the product for legitimate, unpatented purposes. The Court of Appeal also questioned whether any form of injunction would be justifiable given the difficulty of defining what will and will not be infringing. This is in part a consequence of the current test for infringement (i.e. foreseeability that the drug will intentionally be used for the patented indication), since if infringement is found, all of a manufacturer's product will be infringing as it will be impossible to differentiate between batches where the foreseeability does not apply and batches where it does, unless some other part of the factual matrix is altered.

Whilst a general prohibitory injunction is not appropriate, the High Court in *Warner-Lambert Company, LLC v Actavis Group PTC EHF & Others*[36] issued a mandatory injunction requiring NHS England to issue guidance to Clinical Commissioning Groups about the prescription of medicaments for either patented or unpatented indications. In requiring that such guidance be issued, the court also ordered that the manufacturer give an undertaking in damages to certain interested parties, namely generic manufacturers, entitling them to whatever relief the court might order in the event that the guidance caused loss to those interested parties.

35. [2015] EWCA Civ 556.
36. [2015] EWHC 485 (Pat).

2. *Damages*

Under UK law, damages are intended to be compensatory. The measure of damages is, as far as possible, a sum that will put claimants in the same position that they would have been in if they had not sustained the wrong. Awarding damages in respect of infringement of a second medical use patent is likely to be complicated and so far it is not a matter that the UK court has had to grapple with in the context of a damages inquiry.

For example, in the face of a finding of patent infringement, what level of compensation will be appropriate for a patentee that has been forced to lower the price of its product because of the presence of a generic alternative which was legitimately on the market for the non-patented indications? Establishing the split in the market between patented and non-patented indications to attempt to distinguish legitimate, non-infringing sales from infringing sales is likely to be relevant, but the court may also need to find a creative way of arriving at an outcome which provides adequate compensation for patentees without unduly penalising generic competitors from accessing a legitimate, non-patented market.

3. *Information*

3.1 *Names of manufacturer, distributors etc.*

The United Kingdom courts will, in some circumstances, order parties to identify the source of infringing goods or, less commonly, the customer receiving those goods.

3.2 *Names of customers*

The provision of the identity of customers will only generally be appropriate where those customers are trade customers (i.e. wholesalers) rather than consumers. As part of this process, an infringing party may be ordered to disclose the levels of sales it has achieved and further information to help a patentee determine whether it will be more beneficial to seek damages or an account of profits.

3.3 *Information about infringing sales*

In a case of second medical use infringement, the level of sales to a particular customer may be relevant in establishing the extent to which a generic manufacturer's product is being supplied for the patented use. However, it should not be assumed that the market is static as the availability of cheaper generic drugs for unpatented indications may encourage wider prescribing, and so the attribution of sales to the patented indication may not be straightforward.

3.4 *Account of profits*

Further to a finding of infringement, a patentee may opt for the defendant to pay compensation based on the profits the generic has made. However, as it is likely that the patentee will have a higher profit margin overall, it is doubtful that this route will be chosen in most cases.

4. *Recall of products and destruction*

In the United Kingdom, following a finding of infringement, the court may order the delivery up or destruction of infringing articles. Whether this would be ordered in the event of a finding of infringement of a second medical use claim remains to be seen since, in theory, some of the infringing product could be put to non-infringing use (at least in a "skinny label" case).

5. *Recovery of legal costs*

In the United Kingdom, the general rule is that costs follow the event such that the overall winning party is entitled to recover its legal costs from the losing party. In patent cases, the Court adopts an issue-based approach to costs, which means that in practice a discount is applied to the costs of the winning party to reflect the issues upon which it lost. Once the relevant deduction has been taken into account, the party in whose favour a costs order is made would normally expect to recover 65-75% of their costs. If the costs budgeting provisions have been followed (which require the parties to submit costs budgets to the Court, for the Court to endorse), the winning party is likely to recovery a higher percentage of their costs (e.g. 80 - 95%).

VI. Exceptions from patent protection

1. *Exhaustion of rights*

The United Kingdom applies a regional exhaustion doctrine based upon its membership of the European Economic Area ("EEA") and Articles 34 and 36 of the Treaty on the Functioning of the European Union (the "EU Treaty"). Thus, a patent right does not extend to acts in relation to an article that has already been put on the market in a country within the EEA by a patentee or with their consent. Therefore, parallel importation from within the EEA is generally permissible, subject to trademark issues on repackaging. By contrast, if a patented product has been placed on the market outside the EEA, that does not exhaust the patent rights when the product enters the United Kingdom.

The United Kingdom also has a principle of implied licence, which functions as an exhaustion doctrine. This was established in 1871 in *Betts v Willmott*[37] where it was held that, on selling a patented product, the patentee transfers with the goods a licence for the purchaser to sell or use the article. That principle applies regardless of whether the first sale is made in the UK or elsewhere.

37. (1871) LR 6 Ch App 239.

2. *Patient welfare*

Section 60(5) of the Patents Act 1977 sets out a list of statutory defences to patent infringement. Patients are protected under Section 60(5)(a), which provides a defence where an otherwise infringing act is done in private and for non-commercial purposes.

In circumstances where a patented drug is not being made available to patients in the UK then Section 48 of the Patents Act 1977 provides a potential solution. The UK Intellectual Property Office may grant compulsory licences where, for example, the demand for a patented product is not being met on commercially reasonable terms or where an important technical advance relating to the field of the patent is being hindered. In practice, the UK Intellectual Property Office receives very few applications for compulsory licences (estimated to be less than one per year on average since the Patents Act 1977 came into force) and even fewer of these are granted. The requirement for the applicant to have first sought to obtain a licence, on reasonable terms, directly from the patentee, followed by the potentially ensuing legal proceedings (with consequent cost and delay) could explain the reluctance to apply.

Alternatively, Section 55 provides for any government department, or person authorised by that department in writing, to carry out acts for the services of the Crown that would otherwise amount to patent infringement. This "Crown use" provision is limited to patents relevant to foreign defence purposes or drugs and medicines. The permission of the patentee is not required and Crown use effectively provides a compulsory licence in the national interest. *Pfizer Corp v Ministry of Health*,[38] a decision of the Court of Appeal under the Patents Act 1949, confirmed that the use of drugs in the treatment of NHS patients amounts to use for services of the Crown.

The patent proprietor, or exclusive licensee, is entitled to receive compensation from the Crown where such rights are exercised. Section 57A of the Patents Act 1977 provides that the measure of compensation will include the loss of profit from not being awarded a contract to supply the patented medicine.

There are no recent examples of Crown use being ordered. In reality, the Crown use provision is intended to deal with emergencies where a particular patented product is not available in the UK at all, rather than to enable a cheaper version of a drug to be produced. The fact that the patentee is entitled to compensation for its lost profits suggests that, in any event, the route of Crown use would not provide an economic means of obtaining an alternative supply of a drug that is already available.

3. *Other issues specific to second medical use claims*

Other than the points set out above, there are no exceptions specific to second medical use claims that are material to consideration of their scope of protection.

38. [1965] AC 512, [1965] 1 All ER 450.

VII. Procedural issues

1. *Preliminary injunction cases*

Where it is considered just or convenient, the Court may award a preliminary injunction, which may be prohibitory or mandatory in character, to restrain the defendant from infringement pending judgment in an action on the merits. The standard applied by the UK Court in assessing whether a preliminary injunction should be awarded is set out in the *American Cyanamid* case and requires that: (i) there is a serious question in issue; (ii) damages are not an adequate remedy for the patentee; and (iii) taking all the circumstances into account, the balance of convenience lies in favour of granting an interim injunction.

In pharmaceutical cases, there is clear judicial guidance that the onus is on the alleged infringer to "clear the way" of any relevant blocking patents if they intend to launch a generic product. If the alleged infringer has failed to do this, that fact can be taken into account when deciding whether or not to grant an interim injunction (*SmithKline Beecham v Apotex Europe Ltd*[39]). The traditional view is that generic entry can cause significant and irreparable damage to the innovator's market where products are typically marketed on an exclusive basis and at a significant price premium. In order to avoid a preliminary injunction, a generic entrant should allow time for first instance and appeal proceedings to be decided before product launch (*Novartis AG v Hospira UK Limited*[40]).

In the event that a preliminary injunction is awarded, a cross-undertaking in damages is required from the claimant to compensate the defendant for any loss caused by ordering the injunction if it later turns out that it should not have been made (for example, if the patent is revoked or it turns out there is no finding of infringement).

1.1 Availability for second medical use claims

There have been two cases in the United Kingdom where the court has addressed whether preliminary relief should be granted in relation to a second medical use patent which included claims of the "Swiss type". Both actions were commenced by Warner-Lambert and concerned the supply of generic pregablin.

In *Warner Lamber LLC v Actavis Group PTC ehf & Ors*,[41] Warner-Lambert sought mandatory relief requiring Actavis to put in place a number of measures in relation to its generic "skinny label" pregabalin product to try to ensure that generic pregabalin was neither prescribed nor dispensed for neuropathic pain, which was subject to patent protection[42]. By the time of the hearing Warner-Lambert itself had taken a number of steps to prevent supply into the pain market, such as writing to

39. [2003] EWCA Civ 137.
40. [2013] EWHC 1285 (Pat).
41. [2015] EWHC 72 (Pat).
42. Pregabalin was also indicated for the non-patented indications, epilepsy and generalised anxiety disorder (GAD).

Clinical Commissioning Groups[43] and entering into a dialogue with the NHS and other organisations. As well as launching under a so-called "skinny label", Actavis had agreed to write to Superintendent Pharmacists and Clinical Commissioning Groups on grant of their "skinny label" marketing authorisation. The Court had to consider whether Actavis should also be required to put a notice on its packaging warning that the generic product should not be dispensed for pain and impose contractual terms on its customers requiring *inter alia* the use of reasonable endeavours not to suppy or dispense generic pregabalin for pain.

In applying the the *American Cyanamid* test, the Judge found there was no serious issue to be tried on the basis that there was no evidence that the generic manufacturer intended the drug to be used for the patented use, and therefore no infringement. Even if there had been a serious issue to be tried, it was held that the balance of the risk of injustice would favour refusal of the relief sought by Warner-Lambert. In applying the principles for granting preliminary relief, the Court considered it particularly important that the relief being sought was intended to affect the conduct of third parties as well the defendant, which required the established legal principles to be applied with particular care.

In assessing the balance of convenience and whether preserving the status quo favoured relief, the court took into consideration the fact that there was a non-patented market which the defendant was entitled to enter, the fact that:

- other generic competitors were likely to enter the market;
- Warner-Lambert had already had some success in trying to change the behaviour of others; and
- Warner-Lambert was seeking that the defendant be compelled to take additional measures that aimed to further change such behaviour.

The court considered that the best solution to the problem was to try to ensure that prescribing doctors prescribe pregabalin for the treatment of pain by reference to the brand name (Lyrica) rather than by reference to the generic name pregabalin. The court considered this would be best achieved by the NHS issuing appropriate guidance.

In *Warner-Lambert Co LLC v Sandoz GmbH & Ors*,[44] Warner-Lambert sought interim injunctions restraining Sandoz from infringing its patent by dealing in a "full label" generic pregabalin product and to prevent Lloyds (a pharmacy chain) from dispensing quantities of that product in its possession.

In this case, the court granted the injunction. According to the usual principles, the judge acknowledged that when a generic supplier intended to market a product covered by a patent, it was appropriate for it to "clear the path" for the launch of its product sufficiently far in advance of the launch to enable the patent's validity or non-infringement to be determined before the launch date. On this basis, Sandoz should have cleared the path for their launch of full-label generic pregabalin by seeking a declaration of non-infringement, which they had not done. The judge found that granting a prelimilary injunction would create a lower risk of irremediable harm than if it were refused and that it would preserve the status quo, this being the absence in the market of full-label generic pregabalin products. In contrast, if no injunction

43. CCGs are organisations that deal with the deliver of NHS services in England.
44. [2015] EWHC 3153 (Pat).

was granted, the arrival of full-label generic pregabalin on the market would make it significantly more difficult for the court to ensure appropriate compensation of those parties who ultimately merited it.

1.2 *Specific requirements*

The assessment of whether a preliminary injunction should be granted is based upon the usual principles laid out in *American Cyanamid*. In determining an application for interim relief, the court adopts whichever course seems likely to cause the least irremediable prejudice to one party or the other. This amounts to an assessment based upon the particular facts of each case. In a second medical use case, as well as considering whether the defendant has taken steps to "clear the way", other steps that the defendant has taken to prevent the generic product being used for the patented indication(s) are also of relevance. How the outcome of the assessment may differ is exemplied by the Warner-Lambert cases against Actavis and Sandoz.

2. *Cases on the merits*

There are no specific procedural requirements that apply in proceedings concerning second medical use patents beyond those which apply in the usual course of proceedings on the merits.

After the parties have exchanged pleadings, a case management hearing is convened at which the court orders directions to trial to the extent they cannot be agreed between the parties. Unless disclosure is dispensed with, the each party is obliged to disclose information which adversely affects its case or supports the other party's case. This may be ordered by way of standard disclosure, or by reference to specific categories of documents that are relevant to the issues in the case. In relation to infringement of second medical use patents, relevant documents may include, for example, those that concern: (i) the intention or foresight of the alleged infringer regarding use of the relevant pharmaceutical product for the patented indication; (ii) measures that have been taken by the parties to prevent the relevant pharmaceutical product being used for the patented indication; and (iii) plans concerning the marketing and launch of the relevant pharmaceutical product.

To the extent that infringement and validity issues are both in play, these will be dealt with at the same trial, which reflects usual practice in UK patent proceedings. The parties can rely upon evidence of expert witnesses (who are normally used in relation to technical validity issues) and witnesses of fact. For the purpose of infringement, fact witnesses may be able to address issues concerning, for example, levels of market supply and the intentional administration for the patented indication. Witnesses are cross examined at trial, which is heard by a specialist patents judge.

3. *Enforcement of judgments*

Judgments in the United Kingdom are enforced by order of the court. Failure to comply with an order of the court may be treated as contempt of court.

VIII. Tactical considerations

1. *Plaintiff*

As discussed above, preliminary injunctions are in principle available to prevent generic launch of a product for use for treating a patented indication. The patentee must be alert to grants of marketing authorisation to generic manufacturers and to engage the generic manufacturer in correspondence as to their intentions at an early stage if a marketing authorisation is granted on a product the marketing of which may infringe the patent. It may be that a generic manufacturer will agree not to launch pending a full infringement trial if appropriate cross undertakings are given by the patentee. If this is not possible, it is essential to take action promptly upon launch of the generic as delay will be fatal to an interim injunction application. Also, since the focus of the court will be on whether irreparable harm will be suffered by the patentee during the period before a full trial on the merits, the patentee should be in a position promptly to prepare evidence of the commercial impact of a generic launch.

Where there is a substantial non-patent market, it may in practice be difficult or impossible to ask for relief in the conventional form as a generally drawn injunction may prevent legitimate supply for unpatented indications. Careful thought therefore needs to be given as to what relief may be sought that protects, as much as possible, the patented market without disrupting the lawful market. In practice this may be difficult to achieve given the prescribing and dispensing system in the UK. However, at least it may be possible to require that the generic manufacturer puts prescribers and pharmacists on notice of the patent and of course, an injunction should be available to prevent the launch of a product specifically labelled or formulated for the infringing use. This is of course not only an issue for interim relief but also for final relief if the patentee is successful at full trial.

As mentioned above, in the recent *Warner Lambert v Actavis* case an injunction was obtained requiring the NHS to issue guidance to prescribers that when prescribing for the patented indication the prescription should be written by reference to the patentee's brand. Both the patentee and the generic company agreed that this would be the most effective way to preserve the patented market pending full trial as prescribers were more likely to comply with NHS issued guidance that with communications issued by the parties themselves.

One further point is that the patentee should enter a dialogue with the health authorities as soon as possible after becoming aware of the risk of generic entry. This maximises the chance of the health authorities putting appropriate guidance in place to facilitate educating prescribers and dispensers as to the patent position before generic launch. Consideration may be given to the launch of an "authorised generic" labelled for the unpatented indications coincident with an education campaign during the period of market exclusivity to condition the market ahead of third party generic launch.

2. *Defendant*

There is an obvious risk of infringement if a generic manufacturer specifically labels its product for the infringing use. For this reason, it is common for generic manufacturers to carve out the patented indication from their marketing authorisations and seek to launch "skinny label" products directed only to the unpatented indications, as discussed above. However, given the current, unsettled state of the law on infringement of second medical use claims, it would be unwise for a generic company to rely solely on a "skinny label" to defeat an allegation of infringement. There is a real risk that the court will infer an intention to supply the patented market from all the circumstances of the launch. For example, if the generic is supplying quantities of product that far exceed the known demand for the unpatented indication, then an intention to infringe may be inferred. Also, given the availability of disclosure in UK litigation, a generic company risks having to disclose documents relating to its launch plans and market projections as these may be relevant to its real intention.

The more steps a generic company can take to notify prescribers and pharmacists of the patent position, the more likely it will be that it will be able to argue a lack of intention to infringe. This in itself may not defeat an infringement claim if it is still foreseeable that the generic manufacturer's product may be intentionally dispensed for the infringing use, following the approach of the Court of Appeal in *Warner Lambert v Actavis*. However, it is bound to help if it can be shown that the market is well educated and ready to comply with guidance and notifications of this nature. Supporting steps taken to secure central guidance, as happened in that case, will also reduce the risk of foreseeable use for the patented indication.

In conclusion, there is a common interest of responsible patentees and generic manufacturers to cooperate in finding ways to persuade the market to respect second medical use patents while leaving the unpatented market open for generic competition. This is challenging given the prescribing and dispensing practices in the UK, which are beyond the control of either party. However, it is encouraging that the health authorities are now alert to the particular issues posed by second medical use patents and are open to exploring ways in which patents can be respected while maintaining legitimate competition.

Israel

Tal Band, Yair Ziv

A. AVAILABILITY OF PROTECTION

I. Legal framework

1. National statutory laws

The Israeli law with respect to patents is governed by statute, the Patents Law, 1967 ("the Patents Law"). There is also secondary legislation in the form of the Patents (Office Practice, Rules of Procedure, Documents and Fees) Regulations, 1968.

According to Section 3 of the Patents Law, to qualify for a patent, an invention must be a product or process in any technological field which is new, non-obvious and susceptible to industrial use; and satisfy the utility requirement.

The Manual of Patent Examining Procedure, published by the Israeli Patent Office ("the Israeli MPEP"), provides working guidelines for patent examiners. In a nutshell, the Israeli MPEP provides guidance with respect to the examination and prosecution process of patent applications and the implementation of pertinent legislation and case law in relation thereto. From a normative point of view, the Israeli MPEP is considered as administrative guideline.

1.1 Pharmaceuticals

In general, patent protection is available both for products and for processes in the pharmaceutical field. Patent term extensions are also available under certain conditions, as described herein below. However, according to Section 7 of the Patents Law, methods of therapeutic treatment of the human body (which are considered processes) may not be patentable subject matter.

1.2 Biologics

According to Section 7 of the Patents Law, patent protection is unavailable for new varieties of plants or animals, except for microbiological organisms that did not derive from nature. It should be noted that plant breeders' rights are protected separately under a specific law, in view of the fact that Israel is a member of the UPOV Convention.[1]

The Patents Law contains no provisions specifically referring to stem cells; nor does it exclude them from patentability. Natural substances are excluded from patentability, but a process for isolating natural substances (e.g., stem cells) or any other inventive modification may be patented.

It should be noted that the Patents Law provides that where the invention is a biological material, or a process for the production of a biological material, or involves the use of a biological material, and where the biological material has been deposited in an international depositary authority according to Article 7 of the Budapest Treaty on the International Recognition of the Deposit of Microorganisms for the Purposes of Patent Procedure, then part of the description of the invention or of the manner of performance thereof may consist of referral to such deposit.

2. International treaties

Israel is a member of the World Trade Organization ("WTO"), WIPO and the OECD and party to several international patent treaties including, *inter alia*: the Paris Convention, the Patent Cooperation Treaty ("PCT") and the Trade-Related Intellectual Property Rights ("TRIPS") Agreement. The latter is reviewed below.[2]

2.1 TRIPS

Israel became party to the TRIPS Agreement within the framework of becoming a member of the WTO. On 1 January 2000, the Intellectual Property Amendment Law (according to the TRIPS Agreement), came into force, the purpose of which was to harmonize the Israeli legislation concerning intellectual property with the TRIPS Agreement. Thus, while the provisions of the TRIPS Agreement are not self-implemented directly in Israel, Israeli domestic legislation is TRIPS-compliant.

1. Plant Breeders Rights Law, 1973.
2. Israel is a party to the following multinational conventions relating to patents: Convention Establishing the World Intellectual Property Organization ("WIPO"); Paris Convention (Stockholm text); Patent Cooperation Treaty ("PCT") 1994; Budapest Treaty; Strasbourg Agreement; Trade Related Intellectual Property Rights ("TRIPS") 1994. The Conventions are not self-executory, and rights are granted only on the basis of domestic legislation, which may be enacted to implement Israel's undertakings under the said Conventions.

   In addition, the Israeli Patent Office signed several bilateral PPH and PCT-PPH agreements with different national offices, which enables it, under certain circumstances, to use work products which were created by such offices. The Israeli Patent Office has also joined a Global Patent Prosecution Highway ("GPPH") pilot arrangement.

2.2 FTAs

Israel is party to several Free Trade Agreements ("FTAs") with major global players, including the US and the EU.

Article 14 of the FTA between Israel and the US states that:

> "The Parties reaffirm their obligations under bilateral and multilateral agreements relating to intellectual property rights, including industrial property rights, in effect between the Parties. Accordingly, nationals and companies of each Party shall continue to be accorded national and most favored nation treatment with respect to obtaining, maintaining and enforcing patents of invention, with respect to obtaining and enforcing copyrights, and with respect to rights in trademarks, service marks, trade names, trade labels, and industrial property of all kinds."

Article 39 of the FTA between Israel and the EU states that:

> "Pursuant to the provisions of this Article and of Annex VII, the Parties shall grant and ensure adequate and effective protection of intellectual, industrial and commercial property rights in accordance with the highest international standards, including effective means of enforcing such rights."

3. *Availability through case law*

Israeli law is independent of any foreign law or legal system. However, the courts in Israel develop the patent case law, *inter alia*, by carefully considering comparative law from the US and the EU, where appropriate. Cases from the UK are also often cited. For example, the courts in Israel "imported" and applied the doctrine of contributory infringement, even though such doctrine did not (and still does not) form part of the Patents Law.

4. *Patent term extension/SPCs*

Generally, patents are granted for 20 years from the date of filing.[3] Patent term extension ("PTE"), also known as "Supplementary Protection Certificate" ("SPC"), is available in Israel, in certain circumstances, for a pharmaceutical product protected by a basic patent. The patentee can select the basic patent to be extended. In general, a basic patent is a patent protecting an active pharmaceutical ingredient ("API"), a process for manufacturing an API, its use or a pharmaceutical product containing an API, or medical equipment for which regulatory approval is required in Israel. PTE is available only for the first regulatory approval allowing the use of an active ingredient in a pharmaceutical product in Israel. In other words, PTE is unavailable for second medical use. Similarly, PTE is not available for new formulations of a previously approved compound.

In general, the Patents Law provides that subject to the following, an extension order shall remain valid for a period equal to the shortest extension afforded to the

3. Notably, patents of addition are granted for the period remaining in the main patent and do not require the addition of inventive step beyond that included in the main patent.

reference patent in a "Recognized Country" (which term is defined to mean Italy, the UK, Germany, Spain, France and the United States).

Nonetheless, the term of an extension order cannot exceed five years beyond the 20-year patent term referred to above. In addition, the overall period of the basic patent and the extension order therefor shall terminate no later than 14 years from the date marketing approval was first received in a Recognized Country. Moreover, the extension order shall expire no later than the first date of expiry of the extension period granted to the reference patent in a Recognized Country, in which marketing approval has been obtained, or the revocation of any reference patent.

II. Policy considerations

1. *Health and social issues*

In *Merck & Co. Inc v Teva Pharmaceutical Industries Ltd.*,[4] the Supreme Court presented the competing interests concerning pharmaceuticals: on the one hand, the protection of intellectual property encourages the development of new drugs, while on the other hand, the freedom of occupation and the public interest in open and free competition work together to encourage the generic industry. The Supreme Court emphasized that decisions concerning the point of balance between those competing interests are especially delicate in the pharmaceutical sector, where any decision may well be a matter of life and death.

2. *Legal issues*

From a legal perspective, second medical use claims relate to a product or a process which are not considered to be novel, and whose novelty resides in the new use itself. Hence, the claims of a patent protecting second medical use must be carefully phrased, using either of the following options: (1) the claims may be phrased as "Swiss-type" claims (see section B.I.3 below); or (2) the claims may be phrased as purpose-limited product claims (see section B.I.1 below), which make it clear that the novelty resides in the second use itself, rather than in the product.

It should be noted that new chemical entities ("NCE") registered in Israel are entitled, under certain circumstances, to a period of market exclusivity, during which the Ministry of Health will not issue a marketing authorization for a new medicinal product containing said NCE. However, no regulatory exclusivity period is granted for a new indication.

4. LCA 6025/05 *Merck & Co. Inc. v Teva Pharmaceutical Industries Ltd.* (19.5.2011).

B. VALIDITY

I. Allowable claim wording

It should be noted that according to Section 7 of the Patents Law, methods of therapeutic treatment of the human body are not allowed as such.[5] However, according to the Israeli MPEP (Appendix C, section 4), claims which are not intended to treat a disease, may be allowed. Specifically, according to the Israeli MPEP, a method for preventing pregnancy, a method for cosmetic treatment, diagnostic methods or claims referring to a medical device for the treatment of the human body – may be allowed.

1. Product claims

According to Section 3 of the Patents Law, and in so far as the relevant subject matter is concerned, an invention which is a product may be patentable. According to Circular M.N. 30 published by the Registrar of Patents[6] on 17 August 2004 ("Circular M.N.30"), purpose-limited product claims (e.g., "Product X for use in Y", "Compound X for use as a medicament") are allowed, provided that they meet all other requirements of patentability under the Patents Law. Product claims may also be allowed in order to claim a dosage regimen (see below).

2. Method claims

Method claims may be allowed if they are viewed as process claims.

3. Use claims

According to Section 3 of the Patents Law, only an invention that is either a product or a process may be granted a patent. Thus, in order to protect a use, it must refer to a product, or a process, or both. This would also be the case where *second* use – including, but not limited to, second *medical use* – is concerned. In general, in order to protect a new use (e.g., second use) of a known product (or process), one cannot claim protection over the new use itself. Three conditions must be met in order to procure the desired patent protection: (1) the use should be incorporated into a product or process claim, as required under the Patents Law; (2) the new use must demonstrate inventive step over the previous use (or uses) of the same product or process (analogous use will be insufficient to satisfy this condition); and (3) the inventive step may refer to the idea concerning the new use itself, its method of implementation, or both.[7]

---

5. The word "animal" includes human beings. Thus, claims referring to processes or methods of treating animals, which specifically exclude human beings, may be allowed (see the Israeli MPEP, Appendix C, section 3).
6. The Registrar of Patents regulates the examination procedures, *inter alia*, through the publication of "Circulars". From a normative point of view, a Circular is an administrative guideline.
7. CA 804/89 *Lanplast (1971) Ltd. v Berkman*, PD 46(2) 295 (1992).

According to Circular M.N.30, use claims *per se* (for example, "use of X as a paint", "use of X in the treatment of disease Y") are not allowed. However, in the context of second medical use, use claims may be allowed if they are formulated as Swiss-type claims, *viz.*: "use of X in the manufacture/preparation of Y".[8]

It is clarified in Circular M.N.30 that Swiss-type use claims must still satisfy all other requirements of patentability according to the Patents Law.

Section 4.9 of Appendix K to the Israeli MPEP provides that a "medical use claim" is considered to be, *inter alia*, any of the following: a claim referring to, *inter alia*, prevention, diagnosis, treatment or improvement of a medical condition (such as disease, syndrome or functional disorder), symptoms thereof or side effects of such medical condition or treatment.

The definition of a medical use in a claim will be considered clear, if the specific diseases which are included in the claimed scope are mentioned therein.

Where the claim to a medical use is defined as a means or step to perform a certain act (e.g., activity of a protein or biological mechanism), the detailed description must contain an inclusive list of all the diseases that fall within the scope of such definition. Moreover, in some cases, if there is another claim in a set of claims which relate to the same diseases, such other claim may be considered redundant.

Where a claim relates to second medical use of a known compound, the second medical use must be clear and well distinct from the known (first) use.

Where the claimed use refers directly to a biological function (rather than to the diseases that relate to that function), such biological function must be distinct from the medical use outlined above. Thus, the scope of use defined by such claim will be considered "clear" when the claim only refers to the specific use defined therein (e.g., "The compound of claim 1 for use as tyrosine kinase inhibitor").

To sum up: second medical use may only be allowed as either a product or process claim, and provided that such claim will not cover a method of therapeutic treatment of the human body and will not limit the discretion of physicians.

4. *System claims*

System claims may be allowed if they are viewed as product claims.

5. *Dosage regimes*

According to the Israeli MPEP (Appendix C, section 5), a dosage regimen may be presented as a technical feature in a product claim. Such claim will not be classified as a "method for treating the human body", since it is considered as guidance for the manufacturer that is not intended to limit the discretion of treating physicians. Like any other invention, a dosage regimen must satisfy the requirements for subject matter eligibility, otherwise the patent will not be granted.[9]

---

8. Swiss-type claims contain the word "use", but actually describe a process and are thus considered as process claims.
9. Decision of the Registrar of Patents re Opposition to Patent Application No. 153109 *Teva Pharmaceutical Industries Ltd. v Merck & Co. Inc.* (5.8.2010); LCA 6837/12 *Merck Sharp & Dohme Corp. v Unipharm Ltd.* (28.4.2013).

It should be noted that in order to overcome arguments of prior art being raised concerning use of the same compound for the identical indication or disease, the applicant must convince the examiner that the claimed dosage regimen led to unexpected results.

6. *Patient groups*

The patentability of claims relating to new "patient groups" has not yet been discussed in Israeli case law.

II. Novelty

1. *General definition of novelty and prior art*

According to Section 4 of the Patents Law, an invention is considered "new", if not "published" before the application date, either in Israel or abroad. "Publishing" is considered as providing a description which enables a person of ordinary skill in the art to perform the invention. The relevant publication may comprise a written document, but it may also be done orally, visually, or in any other way. Exploiting the invention or displaying it (e.g., during an exhibition), may also constitute publication.

2. *Definition of skilled person*

A "skilled person" is considered a person who is familiar with the entire prior art in the relevant field, but is not expected to have any inventive capabilities. In some cases, especially when the subject matter is rather complicated, a "skilled person" can be a group of persons trained in different technological disciplines.

3. *Scope of disclosure*

The scope of disclosure in the description must be sufficient to enable a "skilled person" to perform the invention. Thus, the patent application must satisfy the requirement concerning sufficiency of description.

3.1 *General rules*

Any claim must be reasonably supported in the detailed description of the patent application. The scope of the claims should represent a reasonable generalization of the detailed parts in the description.[10]

Not every aspect of the invention must be described with the same level of detail. For example, there is no need to provide specific examples of a kit containing a new compound, if sufficient details are given concerning the new compound itself.

10. CA 407/89 *Zuk Or Ltd. v Car Security Ltd.*, PD 48(5) 661 (1994) ("*Zuk Or*").

3.2 *First medical use*

The scope of disclosure concerning first medical use is the same as the requirement generally applicable for disclosure of any invention.

3.3 *New subject matter*

The applicant may, at any time before the application is allowed, amend the specification in their application; however, where amendments of a substantive nature have been introduced to the specification, they will be post-dated, i.e., the effective date of the amendments will be the date of the submission thereof. Substantial amendments made in the description during the prosecution of a patent application may shift the date attributed to the patent application in its entirety.

3.4 *New data*

Generally, the disclosure in the specification must enable a skilled person to perform the invention without undue experimentation. In addition, according to the Supreme Court in *Sanofi*,[11] the utility requirement may be met by providing a reasonable "promise" to achieve the purpose of the invention, but there is no need to provide, in the patent application, evidence of fulfilment of the promise. Thus, for example, it was held that an applicant or patentee in the pharmaceutical field bears no burden for providing experimental data concerning human beings (since some experimental data concerning animals may be sufficient in this regard). However, where the utility is challenged, the patentee bears the burden to provide "some proof" (the level of which will largely depend on the field of the invention) during the opposition proceedings. Although Israeli case law is not completely clear on these issues, it seems that the proof for both sufficiency of disclosure and the utility requirement may include the presentment of new data (i.e., data which was not submitted in the original patent application).[12] It should be noted, however, that with respect to inventive step, it was held that additional effects or advantages discovered after the date of the patent application cannot be considered in the obviousness analysis.[13]

4. **Requirements for second medical use**

Second medical use can be viewed as a private case, in the medical context, of the more general case – new use of a known product or compound. However, within the medical context, an additional factor needs to be taken into consideration, namely, the unpatentability of methods of therapeutic treatment of the human body, as provided in Section 7 of the Patents Law.

---

11. C.A. 665/84 *Sanofi Ltd. v Unipharm Ltd.*, PD 41(4) 729 (1987) ("*Sanofi*").
12. Decision of the Registrar of Patents re Opposition to Patent Application No. 142809 *Teva Pharmaceutical Industries Ltd. v Pharmacia AB* (26.2.2015).
13. Decision of the Registrar of Patents re Opposition to Patent Application No. 136294 *Teva Pharmaceutical Industries Ltd. v Pharmacia & Upjohn AB* (30.9.2014).

A rather old case in this context is *Plantex*,[14] in which the Supreme Court expressed different views of the various Justices (albeit, *in obiter*, as the case before it was decided under the previous statute). While Justice Vitkon held a view widely in favour of the patentability of second medical use, Justice Kahan was more hesitant and restrictive.[15] He expressed the view that, in general, second medical use of a substance already known as a medically active substance should not be granted a patent. However, on the facts of the case before him, Justice Kahan came to the conclusion that the substance had not been used previously as a medicament for human beings, hence it was patentable. Since the result would have been identical in any event, the third Justice in the panel was reluctant to choose which view to endorse on the issue. It should be noted, however, that, as mentioned above, the *Plantex* case was not decided according to the Patents Law, since the previous statute, the Patent Ordinance, still applied to the patent that was being adjudicated in that case.

As explained in section B.I above, Circular M.N.30 outlines the permissible claim wording.

4.1 *Distinction from first medical use*

In general, sometimes a fine line is drawn between first and second use. In certain cases, apparent second use might eventually be classified as "analogous" to the first use, thus rendering the second use unpatentable. Second use must include inventive step over the first use, in order to be recognized as distinctive.[16]

4.2 *Sub-species of first medical use*

First medical uses may include uses of pharmaceutical compounds, dosage regimens and modes or routes of administration.

4.3 *Dosage regimes*

See section B.I.5 above.

4.4 *Special patient groups*

The patentability of claims relating to new "patient groups" has not yet been discussed in Israeli case law (see section B.I.6 above).

14. C.A. 244/72 *Plantex Ltd. v The Wellcome Foundation Ltd.*, PD 27(2) 29 (1973) ("*Plantex*").
15. *Ibid.*, p. 59.
16. C.A. 314/77 *Lipski v Manor*, PD 32(1) 205 (1977).

5. *Timing issues*

5.1 Relevant time of development of second use

Since second medical use claims are aimed to overcome lack of novelty in the product itself and any known use thereof, the relevant time for the development of second medical use is usually after the product and its first use are published. Thus, in so far as previous medical use does not anticipate the claimed (second) use, the second use may be considered novel.

5.2 Role of new data

See section B.II.3.4 above.

5.3 Use of old data

As detailed in section B.II.3.4 above, the disclosure in the specification must enable a skilled person to perform the invention without undue experimentation. In addition, there is no need to provide, in the patent application, evidence of fulfilment of the promise to achieve the purpose of the invention. The proof for both sufficiency of disclosure and the utility requirement may include the use of old data (i.e., data referencing first use), similar to any other publication or common general knowledge.

III. Inventive step/non-obviousness

As outlined in section B.I.3 above, the new use must demonstrate inventive step over the previous use (or uses) of the same product or process (analogous use will be insufficient to satisfy this condition).

1. *Definition of inventive step/non-obviousness*

The term "inventive step" is defined in the Patents Law as a step which does not appear obvious to a skilled person, in the light of information published prior to the application date in a way that enables a skilled person to perform the invention according to the particulars of the description so published.

2. *Same scope of disclosure as for novelty?*

A patent application must include the disclosure of inventive step. An applicant must, therefore, provide a description that is sufficiently detailed to evaluate the inventive step of the invention over the prior art. Since the assessment of novelty is considered to be a more technical issue, the assessment of novelty would generally require less detail.

3. *Assessment of inventive step/non-obviousness*

The requirement for inventive step is broader than that for novelty. In determining obviousness (i.e., evaluating inventive step), it is possible to combine several prior art references to arrive at a complete picture, provided that the applied combination was obvious to a skilled person at the relevant time. However, according to the Israeli MPEP, when more than three documents are used (not including common general knowledge documents), there will be a *prima facie* finding of non-obviousness. With respect to use claims, see also section B.I.3 above.

IV. Amendment of claims after grant

Israel employs a pre-grant opposition system. Therefore, the amendment of claims following acceptance (including before grant), is subject to certain restrictions, which do not apply to amendments before acceptance, as detailed below.

1. *Admissibility of post-grant amendments in general*

Pre-acceptance amendments are quite liberally allowed, while post-acceptance amendments are allowed only for one or more of the following purposes: (a) clarification (b) elimination of a mistake or error in the specification; or (c) a narrowing of the claims. It was held that Section 65 of the Patents Law (stipulating the circumstances under which a patentee may request to amend his patent) and Section 66 of the same law (stipulating the conditions for allowing such amendment) specify cumulative, rather than alternative, requirements with which the requested amendment must comply.[17]

2. *Procedural issues*

2.1 *Independent limitation proceedings*

Independent limitation proceedings are allowed by the patentee.

2.2 *Opposition proceedings*

Any person can oppose the permission granted to amend the claims. The opposition must be filed within three months from the date of publication of the permission granted to amend the claims.

2.3 *Nullity actions*

The Patents Law allows both the patentee as well as any person other than the patentee to initiate a nullity or revocation action.

17. Opposition to Patent Application No. 149567, *Schwartz Pharma AG v Teva Pharmaceutical Industries Ltd.* (16.11.2010).

3. *Added matter*

According to Section 66 of the Patents Law, added matter is not allowed.[18]

4. *Sufficiency*

A patentee seeking to amend the description and/or claims, must, in similar fashion to an applicant seeking to amend the description and/or claims in a patent application, fulfil all the requirements stipulated in the Patents Law. Among other things, the amended description must contain sufficient disclosure supporting the amended version.

5. *Multiple indications*

There is no case law suggesting that an amendment of claims relating to medical use will not be treated in the same manner as any other claim.

V. Change of patent category

The Patents Law does not refer to or contain definitions of patent categories.

1. *General admissibility*

Not applicable.

2. *Use claim as a category*

Not applicable.

3. *From product to method claim*

Not applicable.

4. *From method to product claim*

Not applicable.

5. *System claims*

Not applicable.

18. *Ibid.*

6. Use claims

Not applicable.

C. INFRINGEMENT AND LITIGATION

I. Legal framework

1. National statutory laws

The substantial provisions with respect to patent infringement are found in the Patents Law. Issues of procedure and evidence are governed by the Civil Procedure Regulations, 1984 and the Evidence Ordinance [New Version], 1971. The procedural aspects of litigation before the Registrar of Patents are governed by the Patents Regulations (Authority Procedures, Documents, Procedure, and Fees), 1968.

2. Case law

Case law concerning patent infringement was laid down by the Supreme Court in the matter of *Hughes Aircraft Company v State of Israel*,[19] in which it was clarified that the reference for demonstrating infringement is first and foremost the patent claims. Subject to the doctrines of equivalents and variants (see section C.III.5 below), any subject matter which is not explicitly mentioned in the claims – even if included in the description of the patent application – would not afford protection. In other words, the scope of monopoly defined by the patent is that covered by the claims.

In general, commercial exploitation of an invention may be considered infringing, subject to the "Bolar" exemption. Experiments conducted in order to improve an invention or to develop other inventions are considered as non-infringing.

Subject to the aforegoing and having regard to the scope of any specific claim, the commercial manufacture, supply or use, directed to a patented indication, may be considered infringing. With respect to Swiss-type claims, and depending on the particular circumstances of the case and the interpretation of the specific patent in question, manufacturing a generic version of a drug may be deemed infringing, if such manufacturing includes at least the packaging of the drug with instructions for use in the treatment of the patented indication.

Where a claim for second medical use is found enforceable on the basis of indirect infringement, such enforcement is subject to the conditions detailed in section C.IV.3 below.

19. CA 345/87 *Hughes Aircraft Company v State of Israel*, PD 44(4) 45 (1990) ("*Hughes*").

II. Claim construction

1. *General rules*

As decided in *Hughes* and as further discussed in *Zuk Or v Car Security Ltd.*,[20] the interpretation of a patent is no different from that of any other document, hence, the basic rules of interpretation would apply. However, since a patent defines a monopoly, any such interpretation must be made with caution.

As a basic rule, it was held that the patent must be read as a whole document. Thus, the claims cannot be read out of context of the detailed description or the drawings, which, in any event, serve as an aid during the claim construction.

It was also held in *Zuk Or* that the criterion that is used for evaluating the scope of both the monopoly and the invention, is that of the skilled person and not of the layman.

Referring to claim construction, the Supreme Court emphasized in *Zuk Or* that a "technical bypass" of the literal wording should not be allowed. Thus, the process of claim construction also includes determining the essential features, or 'pith and marrow', of the claim. It was also noted that the scope of protection granted by a patent is decided by its inventive step and the extent of contribution of that invention to the relevant technological field.

Regarding the scope of the invention, it was held in *Zuk Or* that in the context of a legal dispute which concerns the monopoly or its scope, the starting point would always be the patent claims, with the detailed description only serving as a tool to assist in the interpretation of unclear terms that may be found in the claims. The detailed description cannot be used to broaden the scope of the monopoly, which is exclusively defined by the patent claims. However, where the legal dispute concerns the actual meaning of the invention, the claims will not prevail over the detailed description.

In essence, the principles for patent construction can be summarized as follows:[21]

(1) The invention, subject matter of the patent, is defined by its claims and specification, including any diagrams, all of which must be read together as a whole.
(2) The invention, subject matter of the patent, and the monopoly claimed by the patent, are distinct from one another. The scope of the monopoly is delineated by the claims.
(3) Obscure terms or expressions in claims are to be interpreted within the context of the specification.
(4) A patent is to be read and construed through the eyes of a person skilled in the art, at the relevant time, i.e., the interpretative question is how a skilled person would understand the invention and the scope of the monopoly, when reading the patent claims and specification, at the pertinent time.

20. See *Zuk Or, supra*, note 10.
21. See *Zuk Or, supra*, note 10; *Hughes*, *supra*, note 19.

(5) There is no distinction between literal and non-literal infringement. A variant in an invention, as literally described and claimed in the patent, infringes the patent, if a skilled person understands the scope of the monopoly as encompassing the variant.
(6) Designing around the literal scope of the patent monopoly, by replacing an element of the invention with an equivalent or by omitting a nonessential element, does not cure the infringement. If the accused product or process performs substantially the same function, in essentially the same way, to obtain the identical result as the patented invention, it constitutes an infringement of the patent.
(7) The scope of protection afforded to a patent is affected by the extent of its inventive step over the prior art.

2. Specific issues for use claims

There are no specific issues for use claims. As explained above, use claims as such are not eligible for patent protection.

III. Scope of protection

1. Scope of the use

1.1 General definition of the term "use"

The scope of protection of a patent is determined in Section 49 of the Patents Law which provides, *inter alia*, that a patentee may exclude others from unlawfully exploiting the invention, subject matter of the patent. The term "use" is included within the framework of the definition "exploitation of an invention", which expression is defined in the Patents Law as follows:

> "(1) In respect of an invention that is a product - any act that comprises one of the following: manufacture, use, offer for sale, sale or import for purposes of one of the enumerated acts;
>
> (2) In respect of an invention that is a process - use of the process, and in respect of a product directly derived from the process - any act that is one of the following: manufacture, use, offer for sale, sale, or import for purposes of one of the enumerated acts;
>
> but excluding any of the following:
> (1) any act which is not on a commercial scale and does not have a commercial character;
> (2) any experimental act in connection with the invention, the objective of which is to improve the invention or to develop another invention;
> (3) any act performed under the provisions of Section 54A."[22]

22. Section 54A provides as follows (please note in this regard that all quotes from the applicable Israeli law throughout this chapter are unofficial translations from the original Hebrew):

1.2 Manufacture of the pharmaceutical

Manufacture of the pharmaceutical is a separate alternative included in the definition of "exploitation of an invention" (see section C.III.1.1 above).

1.3 Sale of the product

Commercial sale of the product is a separate alternative included in the definition of "exploitation of an invention" (see section C.III.1.1 above).

1.4 Offer for sale

Offer for sale is a separate alternative included in the definition of "exploitation of an invention" (see section C.III.1.1 above).

1.5 Application to the patient

Application to the patient is normally considered private non-commercial use and, therefore, non-infringing.

1.6 Combination products

See section C.IV.3.5 below.

2. Absolute product protection

The doctrine of absolute product protection has not been followed nor discussed in Israeli law jurisprudence. However, a product claim may cover the product regardless of the process used for obtaining the product.

2.1 Limitation through the term "use"

Certain acts are excluded from the definition of "exploitation of an invention" (see section C.III.1.1 above).

"An experimental act, which is part of a process to obtain a licence to market the product (marketing approval) after the patent has lapsed, does not constitute 'exploitation of an invention', if the following two conditions are met:

(1) the process to obtain a licence is made in order to obtain a licence in Israel or in a country, in which an experimental act on a patent protected invention for the purpose of obtaining a licence is permitted before the patent lapses;

(2) any product manufactured under the terms of this section is not used – both while the patent is in effect or thereafter – for any purpose other than obtaining a licence as aforesaid;

For the purposes of this section, 'licence' means certification, permit or any other document required under law in order to market the product."

2.2 *Off-label use*

See section C.IV.4 below.

3. ***Dosage regimes***

See section B.I.5 above. Where a dosage regimen is presented as a technical feature in a product claim, the use of the product, as claimed, falls within the scope of the claim.

4. ***Patient groups***

The patentability of claims relating to new "patient groups" has not yet been discussed in Israeli case law (see section B.I.6 above).

5. ***Extension under the doctrine of equivalents***

The doctrines of equivalents and variants have both been adopted by the Supreme Court and are generally applicable.[23] There is no specific case law applying the doctrine of equivalents or variants with respect to second medical use claims.

IV. Infringing acts

1. ***Infringing person or entity***

Subject to the wording of the claims, an infringing person or entity may be the party manufacturing or marketing the drug with label instructions which describe the patented use; the physician prescribing the drug for such use; or the pharmacist dispensing a drug for such purpose.

2. ***Direct infringement***

2.1 *Manufacture of the pharmaceutical*

Manufacture of the pharmaceutical may constitute direct infringement.

2.2 *Offer for sale*

Offer for sale may constitute direct infringement.

2.3 *Sale*

Sale may constitute direct infringement.

23. *Ibid.*

2.4 Export

The definition of "exploitation of an invention" (see section C.III.1.1 above) does not include the act of export. However, in one case,[24] the district court in Jerusalem expressed the opinion that commercial activity resulting in export may constitute exploitation of the invention, provided that such activity is of a commercial scale or nature.

2.5 Import

Import may constitute direct infringement.

2.6 Combination products

See section C.IV.3.5 below.

3. *Indirect infringement*

Second medical use claims may be enforceable on the basis of indirect infringement. The question with respect to indirect infringement of second medical indication patents has not yet been addressed by the Israeli courts. Nevertheless, the issue of indirect infringement was generally discussed in connection with a mechanical patent for a combination (see section C.IV.3.5 below).

3.1 Objective acts

See section C.IV.3.5 below.

3.2 Subjective conditions

See section C.IV.3.5 below.

3.3 Export

Commercial activity resulting in export may constitute part of indirect infringement. However, it is unclear whether the requirement that there has been direct infringement of the patent in the territory (to the extent such requirement exists, see section C.IV.3.5 below) can be fulfilled where a non-infringing product is exported.

24. CA (J-M) 7076/05 *Orbotech Ltd. v Camtech Ltd.* (1.5.2005).

3.4 *Import*

Since "import" is included in the definition of "exploitation of an invention" (see section C.III.1.1 above), such act may constitute indirect infringement where the appropriate conditions are met (see section C.IV.3.5 below).

3.5 *Combination products*

In general, in order for the court to impose liability with respect to contributory infringement, the following conditions must be fulfilled:[25]

(1) the components sold by the defendant form a substantial part of the protected invention;
(2) the defendant knew, or should have known, under the circumstances, that the article sold was especially made or especially adapted for use in infringement of the relevant patent;
(3) the components sold by the defendant are not a "staple product" or commodity suitable for substantial non-infringing use;
(4) it is still unclear whether the plaintiff must show that there has been direct infringement of the patent in the territory.

4. ***Off-label use***

4.1 *General admissibility of off-label use*

According to the Pharmacists Regulations (Medical Products) 1986, a drug approved for a certain indication may still be administered by a physician for off-label use. An administrative guideline published by the Director General of the Israeli Ministry of Health[26] provides that a physician may, within the scope of their responsibility, prescribe the off-label administration of a drug.

4.2 *Liable persons*

See section C.IV.1 above.

4.3 *Objective requirements for infringement*

The requirements concerning patent infringement are classified as objective, save in the case of indirect infringement (see section C.IV.4.4 below).

25. CA 1636/98 *Rav Bariah Ltd. v Beit Mishar Leavizaray Rehev Havshush* (1987) Ltd., PD 55(5) 337 (2001).
26. Circular 19/07 published by the Director General of the Ministry of Health on 16 October 2007.

4.4 *Subjective requirements for infringement*

In general, direct patent infringement does not involve subjective requirements. However, one of the conditions for demonstrating indirect infringement involves a subjective requirement: whether or not the defendant knew, or should have known, under the circumstances, that the article sold was especially made or especially adapted for use in infringement of a patent (see section C.IV.3.5 above).

5. *Dosage regimes*

See section B.I.5 above. Where a dosage regimen is presented as a technical feature in a product claim, the use of the product, as claimed, falls within the scope of the claim.

6. *Patient groups*

The patentability of claims relating to new "patient groups" has not yet been discussed in Israeli case law (see section B.I.6 above)

V. Remedies

Under Israeli law, the typical remedies granted to a successful plaintiff include the following:

1. *Injunctions*

If a plaintiff is successful, the court will usually grant a permanent injunction or restraining order. As a rule, permanent injunctions remain in effect until the patent expires. The US judgment in *eBay, Inc v MercExchange* (547 US 388 (2006)) ("*eBay*") has not been adopted in Israeli case law as such. Nevertheless, in recent years the Israeli courts have been more willing to entertain general considerations (e.g., those concerning the public) when hearing applications for preliminary injunctions.[27] This tendency may result in the grant of permanent injunctions becoming less frequent.

2. *Damages*

The basic rule in this context is that damages are aimed at putting the injured party, namely the patentee, in the position they would have been had the infringement not occurred.

In awarding damages, the court shall have regard to the act constituting the infringement and to the position of the plaintiff in consequence of that act and it may take into account, *inter alia*:

(1) the direct damage caused to the plaintiff;
(2) the extent of the infringement;

27. CA 10717/05 *Florist de Kwakel B.V v Hajaj* (3.9.2013).

(3) the profits derived by the infringer from the act constituting the infringement; and
(4) reasonable royalties which the infringer would have had to pay if they had been granted a licence to exploit the patent to the extent so infringed by them.

Until amendment of the Patents Law in 2012 ("the 2012 Amendment"), the Patents Law provided that patent applications and the accompanying Patent Office files relating thereto would be made public only upon publication of the notice of acceptance (i.e., after completion of the examination and prosecution process). According to the 2012 Amendment, patent applications, including the respective Patent Office files, would be made public on the internet "as soon as possible after the Determining Date". The term "Determining Date" has been defined to mean 18 months following the filing date of the application or, if a claim for priority has been made for the application, 18 months following the earliest priority date. Notices for patent applications filed under the PCT Treaty will be published within 45 days from the date of compliance by the applicant with the requirements for entering the national phase in Israel.

The 2012 Amendment also provides that, under certain circumstances, a patentee will be retroactively entitled – upon issuance of the patent – to damages in the form of reasonable royalties for the unauthorized exploitation of the invention during the period between the date of publication and the date of acceptance. As was the case prior to the entry into effect of the 2012 Amendment, the patentee will still be retroactively entitled to full damages for any unauthorized exploitation of the invention done following the date of acceptance and throughout the life of the patent. Legal proceedings for patent infringement (including for any unauthorized exploitation of the invention prior to the grant of the patent) may only be initiated after the patent is granted.

3. *Information*

3.1 Names of manufacturer, distributors, etc.

It is within the discretion of the court to order that the defendant will provide such details.

3.2 Names of customers

It is within the discretion of the court to order that the defendant will provide such details.[28]

28. LCA 1536/95 *On Track Innovations Inc. v Electo Galil Inc.* (6.12.1995).

3.3 Information about infringing sales

Where damages have been claimed, the court may order the defendant to render information about infringing sales in the framework of accounts of profits (see section 3.4 below).

3.4 Account of profits

Where damages have been claimed, the court may order the defendant to render an account showing the extent of the infringement; however, in setting the amount of damages, the court shall not be bound by the account but may set the amount taking into account all the circumstances of the case. The account usually comprises a report, detailing all sales made of the infringing items, the consideration received, the expenses incurred in manufacturing and marketing such items and the like. It is also accepted practice that the report be certified by a chartered public accountant.

4. Recall of products and destruction

Delivery up of infringing material - although the Patents Law does not specifically provide for delivery up, in one case the District Court found that this remedy falls within its inherent jurisdiction. However, the Court emphasized that delivery up will be granted only in exceptional circumstances (i.e., where enforcement of the injunction is ineffective or impossible).

5. Recovery of legal costs

As in other commercial and civil litigation in Israel, in principle, the successful party can obtain costs from the losing party. The successful party is entitled to real costs - in particular, the costs that it incurred or undertook to incur. However, the courts will also consider whether real costs are reasonable, proportionate and necessary for conducting the case in the circumstances. In practice, the level of costs determined by the courts is lower (and in most cases, significantly lower) than the costs actually incurred.

Other remedies - in general, courts adjudicating civil matters are competent to grant declaratory judgments, prohibitive orders, orders for specific performance and any other relief, as they see fit.

VI. Exceptions from patent protection

1. Exhaustion of rights

In an *obiter dictum* the Supreme Court indicated that it tends to adopt the "international exhaustion" doctrine and held that parallel import does not constitute patent infringement.

2. *Patient welfare*

As mentioned in section C.V.1 above, although the US judgment in *eBay* has not been adopted into Israeli case law as such, in recent years the Israeli courts have been more willing to consider general considerations (e.g., those concerning the public) when hearing motions for interlocutory injunctions. As aforesaid, according to Section 7 of the Patents Law, methods of therapeutic treatment of the human body may not be patentable subject matter. Nonetheless, the question of whether patient welfare, in and of itself, would be considered an exception to patent protection has not yet been discussed in Israeli case law.

3. *Others specific to second medical use claims*

Not applicable.

VII. Procedural issues

1. *Preliminary injunction cases*

The considerations of the court in granting interim relief in a patent infringing case are no different than any other case.[29]

1.1 *Availability for second medical use claims*

Although this issue has not yet been discussed in Israeli case law, we do not expect second medical use claims to differ from other claims.

1.2 *Specific requirements*

The criteria for granting interim relief include: (1) the apparent existence of a cause of action, based on proper *prima facie* evidence; (2) the balance of convenience (or hardship) that the injury likely to be suffered by the applicant if the injunction is denied will be greater than that likely to be suffered by the respondent if the injunction is granted; (3) equity considerations, including good faith and whether the grant of injunctive relief is justified and appropriate under the circumstances and not unduly harmful. The court will deny a motion for injunctive relief on a preliminary basis if the motion was filed following a considerable delay (i.e., laches), particularly where the subject matter concerns proprietary rights, since any delay in the filing of such motion would contradict the contention that the relief is urgent and must be granted prior to consideration of the claim on the merits. The question of laches might also affect the balance of convenience. The court may also take into consideration the public interest.

29. CA 700/78 Issesco, *The International Co. for Solar Energy Systems Ltd. v Banit*, PD 34(1) 757.

2. *Cases on the merits*

Cases are decided on the merits according to the evidence. In general, the evidence on infringement and validity will often include expert opinions (as well as the giving of testimony by factual witnesses). The witnesses are cross-examined and the parties submit their summations (usually, in writing). The Israeli court system does not employ a jury.

3. *Enforcement of judgments*

Enforcement of judgments and Execution Office proceedings are available in similar fashion as in any civil case.

VIII. Validity

1. *Relevance for infringement cases*

The issue of validity is relevant for infringement cases since a common defence is based on the argument that the patent should not have been granted in the first place, hence, it should be revoked as invalid.

2. *Specifics for second medical use claims*

Not applicable.

IX. Tactical considerations

1. *Plaintiff*

In opposition proceedings, the applicant may prolong the proceedings by applying to amend the patent specification and/or claims. Divisional applications may also be filed in certain circumstances. The applicant, therefore, gains *de facto* monopoly, since competitors will often be deterred from entering the market knowing that a patent application which is relevant to them is pending and may eventually be allowed and also serve as basis for claiming retroactive damages.

In patent infringement actions, the plaintiff may estimate the value of the claim in a way that would allow them to "choose" the appropriate forum (either a District Court or a magistrates' court). Similarly, the specific district in which the suit is filed may be chosen according to the location in which the infringing action took place. Applying to amend the specification and/or the claims during infringement suits is also allowed in certain circumstances.

2. *Defendant*

Since Israel employs a pre-grant opposition system, some opponents may, in certain cases, be interested in filing and then delaying the opposition proceedings for as long as possible.

Where a defendant in a patent infringement action argues that an invention is not new or is obvious, its statement of defence must include full particulars of any prior publication or use. In addition, defendants may submit an application for revocation of the patent, even after filing an infringement suit. If a revocation suit is filed while an infringement action or other revocation suit is pending in court, the Registrar of Patents will entertain it only with the express permission of the court. If an infringement suit is filed with the court after an application for revocation has been filed with the Registrar of Patents, the Registrar of Patents will entertain the application, unless otherwise ordered by the court. Therefore, a person receiving a cease and desist letter with respect to a patent should consider filing an application for revocation of the patent.

United States of America

Dan Altman

A. AVAILABILITY OF PROTECTION

I. Legal framework

The basis for all subject matter eligible for patent protection in the United States of America can be found in 35 U.S.C. § 101, which states:

> "Whoever invents or discovers any new and useful process, machine, manufacture, or composition of matter, or any new and useful improvement thereof, may obtain a patent therefor, subject to the conditions and requirements of this title."

This statute is written in extremely broad terms, and the United States Supreme Court has held that it covers "anything under the sun made by man."[1] Consistent with this decision, at least three judicially created exceptions have been established by the courts, which represent concepts not "made by man": (1) natural laws, (2) natural products, and (3) abstract ideas. Nevertheless, the Supreme Court has recently significantly cut back on this broad interpretation in its decisions concerning each of these three judicial exceptions.[2] In these decisions, a claim that recites any of the three judicial exceptions must also recite something "significantly more" than the judicial exception in order to be eligible for patent.

1. National statutory laws

These recent decisions may occasionally impact the availability of patent claims for second medical uses, where the claims recite a natural product or if the second

1. *Diamond v Chakrabarty*, 447 U.S. 303 (1980).
2. *Mayo Collaborative Services v Prometheus Laboratories Inc.* for natural laws, *Association for Molecular Pathology v Myriad Genetics, Inc* for natural phenomena, and *Alice Corporation Pty. Ltd. v CLS Bank International* for abstract ideas.

medical use includes a diagnostic assay. However, in general, the recitation of a therapeutic method recited in the claim should constitute "significantly more" than the corresponding judicial exception. The Supreme Court specifically recognized this in *Mayo Collaborative Services v Prometheus Laboratories Inc.*, when it stated that:

> "Unlike, say, a typical patent on a new drug or a new way of using an existing drug, the patent claims do not confine their reach to particular applications of those laws."

Thus, the Supreme Court specifically characterized a new way of using an existing drug as a particular application of a law of nature, which should be considered sufficient to render it eligible for patent protection.

Nothing in the statute or case law prohibits a patent claim directed to a method of carrying out a medical treatment. Accordingly, under U.S. law, patent protection is available for new uses of previously known pharmaceutical compounds. Instead of being available in a "second medical use" format, proper U.S. format relates to "methods of treatment" of the new use.

In addition to 35 U.S.C. § 101, further basis for the patent-eligibility of a method of carrying out a new use of an old compound can be found in 35 U.S.C. § 100(b), which states that the "term 'process' means process, art, or method, and includes a new use of a known process, machine, manufacture, composition of matter, or material."

Under U.S. law, second medical use patent protection should be available for all of "classic" second medical use (later research shows an old drug is useful for a new purpose), for a new use of a known compound that was not previously successful for its initial purpose, and for new uses of known compounds previously discovered for non-medical uses.

A new dosage regime of a known drug to treat a known illness may be patentable under U.S. law, depending on what sort of unexpected results may be available to support an assertion of non-obviousness over that which was previously known.

No specific types of second medical use are impermissible subject matter under U.S. law, although as noted below claims in the format of a "use" are generally considered impermissible as indefinite. The only issues are whether such second medical use would be novel and non-obvious in view of the teachings in the art.

As mentioned above, second medical use claims in the U.S. take a "method of treatment" format. Such claims would be directed to a method of treating a patient suffering from new disease Y by administering an effective amount of old compound X to the patient. No other format is available to protect second medical uses in the U.S. For example, use claims, Swiss-type claims, pharmaceutical formulation for use claims, and claims to the compound when used to treat a specific disease are all not permissible under U.S. law.

> "Use claims are generally regarded (1) as indefinite because such claims merely recite a use without any active positive steps delimiting how this use is actually practiced and/or (2) as not falling into any of the statutory categories of subject

> matter eligible for patent protection because the claimed recitation of a use, without setting forth any steps involved in the process. *See* MPEP 2173.05(q)"[3]
>
> "The discovery of a new use for an old structure based on unknown properties of the structure might be patentable to the discoverer as a process of using. *In re Hack*, 114 USPQ 161, 163 (CCPA 1957). However then the claim recites using an old composition or structure and the "use" is directed to a result or property of that composition of structure, then the claim is anticipated. *In re May*, 197 USPQ 601, 607 (CCPA 1978), *See* MPEP 2112.02"[4].

Medical method claims are much more straightforward in their meaning than other claim formats. The meaning of specific treatment steps recited in such claims should be no different than what is recited in the claim.

Based on prior court decisions, the USPTO requires that patent-eligible method of medical treatment must include specific treatment steps. As set forth in M.P.E.P. 2173.05(q). attempts to claim a process without setting forth any steps involved in the process generally raises an issue of indefiniteness under 35 U.S.C. 112(b) or pre-AIA 35 U.S.C. 112, second paragraph.[5] For example, a claim which read: "[a] process for using monoclonal antibodies of claim 4 to isolate and purify human fibroblast interferon" was held to be indefinite because it merely recites a use without any active, positive steps delimiting how this use is actually practiced.[6]

Other decisions suggest that a more appropriate basis for this type of rejection is 35 U.S.C. 101. In *Ex parte Dunki*, 153 USPQ 678 (Bd. App. 1967), the Board held the following claim to be an improper definition of a process: "The use of a high carbon austenitic iron alloy having a proportion of free carbon as a vehicle brake part subject to stress by sliding friction." In *Clinical Products Ltd. v Brenner*, 255 F. Supp. 131, 149 USPQ 475 (D.D.C. 1966), the district court held the following claim was definite, but that it was not a proper process claim under 35 U.S.C. 101: "The use of a sustained release therapeutic agent in the body of ephedrine absorbed upon polystyrene sulfonic acid."

1.1 Pharmaceuticals

The general statutory framework discussed above was primarily designed in the context of pharmaceuticals. Thus, the general principles described in the section above are readily adapted to the field of pharmaceuticals.

---

3. Catalogue of Remaining Differences 2012 Update of the Catalogue of Differing Practices 2011, page 28 obtained from http://www.trilateral.net/catalogue.html.
4. Catalogue of Remaining Differences 2012 Update of the Catalogue of Differing Practices 2011, page 87 obtained from http://www.trilateral.net/catalogue.html.
5. Under the recent "America Invents Act" (AIA) certain of the pre-AIA statutes in the U.S. are applicable to applications having an effective filing date prior to the March 16, 2013 implementation date of the AIA. With respect to under 35 U.S.C. 112(b) or pre-AIA 35 U.S.C. 112, second paragraph, the statutes are identical.
6. Ex parte Erlich, 3 U.S.P.Q.2d 1011 (Bd. Pat. App. & Inter. 1986).

1.2 Biologics

In the pharmaceutical industry, the term "biologic," another term for biological, encompasses pharmaceutical drug products which are extracted from, synthesized from, or manufactured in biological sources. Biologics includes natural products, such as vaccines, anti-venoms, blood components, and engineered products, such as monoclonal antibodies, gene therapies, genetically altered cells, altered hormones, fusion proteins and transgenic animals.

In addition to its general meaning used in the pharmaceutical industry, the term "biologic" has a specific legal meaning. Under the Biologics Price Competition and Innovation Act, "biologic" means "virus, therapeutic serum, toxin, antitoxin, vaccine, blood, blood component or derivative, allergenic product, protein (except any chemically synthesized polypeptide), or analogous product, or arsphenamine or derivative of arsphenamine (or any other trivalent organic arsenic compound), applicable to the prevention, treatment, or cure of a disease or condition of human beings." 42 U.S.C. § 262(i)(1) (2010).

Biologics may be claimed in terms of the structure and/or function of the product. For example, a monoclonal antibody may be claimed by

(i) structure: its primary amino acid sequence,
(ii) function: by epitope to which it binds;
(iii) source: the hybridoma from which it was produced;
(iv) process by which is was made: antigen which was used for immunizing the mouse

Biologics may also be claimed in terms of their methods of preparing the products or methods of using the products. Methods of use may encompass both diagnostic methods, methods of treatments and methods of both diagnosing and then treating.

In view of recent decisions, the USPTO has updated its guidelines with respect to subject matter eligibility of biologics and their accompanying methods claims. [7] Though this guidance is not legally binding, it serves as a useful indicator of what subject matter may be deemed patent eligible.

Example 29 provides claims directed to methods of diagnosing and/or treating a hypothetical autoimmune disease with a nature-based product (anti-TNF antibody) , some of which meet and others which do not meet the patent subject matter eligibility requirements according to the USPTO.[8] In particular, claim 1 of the example reads:

"1. A method of detecting JUL-1 in a patient, said method comprising:
a) Obtaining a plasma sample from a human patient; and
b) Detecting whether JUL-1 is present in the plasma sample by contacting the plasma sample with an anti-JUL-1 antibody and detecting binding between JUL-1 and the antibody."

---

7. See Subject Matter Eligibility Examples: Life Sciences, published by the USPTO on May 1, 2016, available at www.uspto.gov/sites/default/files/documents/ieg-may-2016-ex.pdf.
8. See pages 10-16 of the Subject Matter Eligibility Examples.

Regarding this claim, the USPTO first concludes that the claim does not recite a judicially recognized exception.[9] The USPTO then states that that performing the markedly different characteristics analysis is unnecessary as the claim is focused on a process of detecting whether JUL-1 is present in a plasma sample – not on the products per se.[10]

Example 31, directed to methods of Screening for Gene Alterations, also contains claims which meet or do not meet the patent subject matter eligibility requirements. (See pages 23-28 of the Subject Matter Eligibility Examples.) Claim 1 reads:

> "1. A method of screening germline of a human subject for an alteration of a BRCA1 gene which comprises comparing germline sequence of a BRCA1 gene or BRCA1 RNA from a tissue sample from said subject or a sequence of BRCA1 cDNA made from mRNA from said sample with germline sequences of wild-type BRCA1 gene, wild-type BRCA1 RNA or wild-type BRCA1 cDNA, wherein a difference in the sequence of the BRCA1 gene, BRCA1 RNA or BRCA1 cDNA of the subject from wild-type indicates an alteration in the BRCA1 gene in said subject."

Again, the USPTO concludes that there is no need to perform the markedly different characteristics analysis. The USPTO explains that this is because analysis as a whole indicates that this claim is focused on a process of comparing information about the products rather than focused on the products per se. This is notwithstanding the claims recitation o fnature-based product limitations (*e.g.*, genes).

Finally, note that companies seeking to market biologics to the public must first obtain approval from the FDA through a biologics license application.[11]

2. *International treaties*

The United States is a contracting party to The Agreement on Trade-Related Aspects of Intellectual Property Rights (TRIPS), the Patent Law Treaty, and the Patent Cooperation Treaty ("PCT"). Neither the Patent Law Treaty nor the PCT has had any direct impact on the availability of patent protection for pharmaceutical products or methods of use in the United States. In fact, very few court decisions even *mention* the implementing legislation of the Patent Law Treaty – the Patent Law Treaty Implementation Act of 2012 – and, when they do, generally do so in passing.[12] Accordingly, the discussion that follows covers only the impact TRIPS has had in this respect. However, it is worth noting that between 2003 and 2007, roughly four out of every five pharmaceutical patents granted through PCT filings were to only 13 developed countries.[13] Additionally, research and development investments in the

9. *Id.* at 11.
10. *Id.*
11. In re Genzyme Corp. Securities Litigation, 754 F.3d 31, 34 (Fed. Cir. 2014).
12. *See, e.g.*, *Glycobiosciences, Inc. v Innocutis Holdings, LLC*, Civil Action No. 12-1901, 2015 WL 3609343 (D. D.C. June 10, 2015).
13. Pharmaceutical Companies and Global Lack of Access to Medicines: Strengthening Accountability under the Right to Health, 40 J.L., Med. & Ethics 234, 238 (2012).

United States have steadily increased over the last decade and a half.[14] Indeed, the National Institutes of Health's expenditures more than doubled in 2014.[15]

2.1 TRIPS

TRIPS sets minimum safeguards for intellectual property in all member states, including patented pharmaceuticals.[16]

Due to the increasing globalization of the medicine, TRIPS plays a vital role in protecting U.S. patent holders in the pharmaceutical industry. This was made clear earlier this year by the United States Court of Appeals for the Federal Circuit ("Federal Circuit").[17] The Federal Circuit had previously held in *Jazz Photo* that merely selling or authorizing the sale of a U.S.-patented article abroad does not authorize the buyer to import the article and sell and use it in the United States.[18] In its recent *Lexmark* decision, the Federal Circuit was faced with the decision of whether to overturn *Jazz Photo*. The court noted that overruling *Jazz Photo* might cause significant disruption in the pharmaceutical industry, given the phenomenon of U.S.-patented medicines being sold outside the United States at much lower prices than those charged domestically. A 2003 World Trade Organization ("WTO") decision served as powerful evidence of this phenomenon, in the court's view. In that agreement, the WTO "waived certain TRIPS patent-recognition provisions in order to allow certain countries to import generic versions of needed medicines." However, the WTO conditioned the waiver on the importing countries' agreement "to control re-exportation of drugs they import in this fashion." Ultimately, the Federal Circuit declined to overturn *Jazz Photo*.

2.2 FTAs

The violation of intellectual property rights, including infringement of pharmaceutical patents, is a global problem.[19] A decade ago, the World Health Organization ("WHO") reported that counterfeiting of medicines costs the pharmaceutical industry over $ 45 billion annually. And in 2009, WHO reported that "20 million pills, bottles and sachets of counterfeit and illegal medicines were seized in a five-month operation coordinated by [Interpol] across China and seven of its south-east Asian [neighbors]."[20] Free Trade

14. http://www.ifpma.org/wp-content/uploads/2016/02/IFPMA_-_Facts_And_Figures_2015_web.pdf.
15. *Id.*
16. Agreement on Trade-Related Aspects of Intellectual Property Rights, Apr. 15, 1994, Marrakesh Agreement Establishing the World Trade Organization, Annex IC, The Legal Texts: The Results of the Uruguay Round of Multilateral Trade Negotiations 319, 33 I.L.M. 1125, 1197 (1994).
17. *Lexmark Intern., Inc. v Impression Products, Inc.*, 816 F.3d 721 (Fed. Cir. 2016).
18. *Jazz Photo Corp. v Int'l Trade Comm'n*, 264 F.3d 1094 (Fed. Cir. 2001).
19. Cortney M. Arnold, *Protecting Intellectual Property in the Developing World: Next Stop – Thailand*, 2006 Duke L. & Tech. Rev. 10, 1 (2006).
20. http://www.who.int/bulletin/volumes/88/4/10-020410/en/.

Agreements, or FTAs, serve as one tool for strengthening relations between the United States and other countries while improving protections of intellectual property rights.

The most recent U.S. FTAs have included patent term restoration provisions to compensate for unreasonable delays in the issuance of patents for pharmaceutical products. For example, the FTA between the United States and Colombia and effective May 15, 2012 provides:

> "Each *may* provide the means to and may, at the request of the patent owner, compensate for *unreasonable delays* in the issuance of a patent for a pharmaceutical product by restoring patent term or patent rights. ... For purposes of this subparagraph, an unreasonable delay shall at least include a delay in the issuance of the patent of more than five years from the date of filing of the application in the territory of the Party, or three years after a request for examination of the application has been made, whichever is later, provided that periods attributable to actions of the patent applicant need not be included in the determination of such delays."

United States-Colombia Trade Promotion Agreement ("TPA"), Art. 16.9, paragraph 6.

However, unlike the TPA which permitted the contracting parties to provide means for restoring patent terms, the U.S.-Korea Free Trade Agreement requires the parties to do so. The relevant provisions of the agreement read as follows:

> "With respect to patents covering a *new pharmaceutical product* that is approved for marketing in the territory of the Party and methods of making or using a new pharmaceutical product that is approved for marketing in the territory of the Party, each Party, at the request of the patent owner, shall make available an adjustment of the patent term or the term of the patent rights of a patent covering a *new pharmaceutical products*, its approved method of use, or a method of making the product to compensate the patent owner for unreasonable curtailment of the effective patent term as a result of the marketing approval process related to the first commercial use of that pharmaceutical product in the territory of that Party."[21]

Notably, a footnote to this FTA clarifies that "new pharmaceutical product" means "a product that at least contains a new chemical entity that has not been previously approved as a pharmaceutical product in the territory of the Party.[22]

The United States was recently in negotiations in Thailand but suspended them in 2006 following the dissolution of the Thai Parliament and military-led coup.[23] However, if and when negotiations resume and result in an FTA between the two countries, the FTA will probably include patent term extension provisions for pharmaceutical patents for at least the two following reasons: (1) such provisions have been included in the most recent U.S. FTAs); and (2) the Thai pharmaceutical industry has a strong interest in extending the terms of its pharmaceutical patents due to the Thai drug regulatory office's frequent delays in approving drugs.[24]

21. U.S.-Korea Free Trade Agreement, Art. 18.8, paragraph 6 (emphasis added).
22. *Id.* at note 21.
23. https://ustr.gov/countries-regions/southeast-asia-pacific/thailand.
24. Arnold, supra note []. at 19.

3. *Availability through case law*

In the United States, patent law, like other bodies of law, is developed through a common law system. After statutes are enacted, such as the Patent Act of 1952 and the Leahy-Smith America Invents Act of 2011, the availability of patent protection in specific cases is litigated. In resolving these disputes, U.S. courts clarify the meaning of these statutes and, therefore, the availability of patent protection. This common law development of the law, of course, extends to patents on pharmaceutical products and methods of use. Indeed, though this is relatively rare, courts sometimes devise judicially-created doctrine that stems from, but is not expressly supported by, the statutory provisions at issue. (For example, in its construction of 35 U.S.C. § 101, the Supreme Court of the United States has ruled that "laws of nature, natural phenomena, and abstract ideas" are not patent eligible subject matter.[25] Section 101 states that "[w]hoever invents or discovers any new and useful process, machine, manufacture, or composition of matter, or any new and useful improvement thereof, may obtain a patent therefor, subject to the conditions and requirements of this title." Nowhere in this provision are laws of nature, natural phenomena, or abstract ideas mentioned.)

Due to the common law system of the United States, case law is conceptually intertwined with the statutes that govern patenting of pharmaceuticals. Accordingly, the availability of patent protection *as developed through case law* on such products and methods of use is discussed throughout each section of this chapter as appropriate.

4. *Patent term extension/SPCs*

In general, patents that issued from applications filed on or after June 8, 1995, expire twenty years from the U.S filing date of the application.[26] This "twenty-year term" default rule was put into place by § 532(a)(1) of the Uruguay Round Agreements Act (Public Law 103-465, 108 Stat. 4809 (1994)), which amended 35 U.S.C. 154.[27] If the issue of an original patent is delayed due to certain failures of the Patent and Trademark Office (*e.g.*, failure to send a timely response), the patent's term may be extended.[28] This general patent term extension provision applies to all technologies - not just pharmaceuticals.[29]

However, the patent term for pharmaceutical products or methods subject to Federal and Drug Administration ("FDA") regulation may be further extended to compensate for delay caused by the FDA's regulatory review.[30] The Drug Price Competition and Patent Term Restoration Act ("the Hatch Waxman Act") provides that patent owners generally have sixty (60) days from the time of FDA approval to apply for such patent term extensions.[31] If the request for an extension is approved, the exact length of the extension depends on the regulatory review periods following

25. See, e.g., *Diamond v Diehr*, 450 U.S. 175, 185 (1981).
26. Manual of Patent Examining Procedure ("MPEP") § 2701.
27. *Id.*
28. 35 U.S.C. § 154(b).
29. *Id.*
30. 35 U.S.C. § 156.
31. 35 U.S.C. § 156(d)(1).

the issuance of the patent.[32] The regulatory review periods, in turn, consist of a testing phase and a regulatory approval phase. *Id.* The testing phase is the period that begin "on the date an exemption under subsection (i) of section 505 or subsection (d) of section 507 becom[es] effective for the approved product" and ends "on the date an application was initially submitted for such drug product under section 351, 505, or 507."[33] Simply put, this is the period that begins on the date an Investigational New Drug ("IND") Application is filed and ends on the date a New Drug Application ("NDA") is filed.[34] The regulatory review period begins and ends with the NDA's filing and the FDA's approval.[35]

The extension of the patent term is determined by first taking the time period corresponding to the length of the regulatory review period that occurred after the issuance of the patent.[36] Then, that time period is reduced by any period during the regulatory review period during which the applicant did not act with due diligence. *Id.* The resulting time period is added to one-half of the time of the testing phase. *Id.* This sum is the total period eligible for a patent term extension under the Hatch Waxman Act restoration provisions. *Id.*

The United States Court of Appeals for the Federal Circuit ("Federal Circuit") has clarified the meaning of some of the terms of the Hatch Waxman Act. Specifically, the term "product" appears repeatedly in the statute. Whether something constitutes a "product" within the meaning of the statute affects the availability of a patent term extension under the Act's restoration provisions. In *PhotoCure ASA v Kappos*, the Federal Circuit clarified that the term "product" should be construed according to a plain meaning statutory construction. As a result, what a "product" is under the statute is determined by looking at the active ingredient of the drug in question rather than the biologically active species of the active ingredient of the drug. Thus, according to the Federal Circuit's relatively broad construction, more prodrugs may qualify as new chemical entities ("NCEs") eligible for the five-year period of exclusivity.[37]

II. Policy Considerations

1. Health and social issues

U.S. Courts are just beginning to interpret key provisions of the Biologics Price Competition and Innovation Act ("BPCIA"). The BPCIA was enacted in 2010 as part of the Patient Protection and Affordable Care Act to reduce the costs passed on to consumers

32. 35 U.S.C. § 156(g).
33. *Id.*
34. http://www.fda.gov/drugs/developmentapprovalprocess/howdrugsaredevelopedandapproved/approvalapplications/investigationalnewdrugindapplication/default.htm.
35. 35 U.S.C. § 156(g).
36. 35 U.S.C. § 156(c).
37. *Actavis Elizabeth LLC v U.S. Food and Drug Administration*, 625 F.3d 760, 764 (D.C. Cir. 2010).

by introducing competition from generic manufacturers.[38] The idea behind the new law is that generics can avoid steep research and development costs and, as a result, afford to provide biologic medicine at much lower costs to consumers.[39] In *Amgen v Sandoz*, the Federal Circuit found that notice of commercial marketing - which is required to start the 180 day countdown to market entry - can be given only after licensure by the FDA.[40] According to the Federal Circuit's interpretation, a biosimilar must wait at least 180 days after it has been approved.[41] As a result, consumers have decreased access to important biologic medicines and are charged more.

2. Legal issues

Although the United States has a federal system with power shared between the federal government and the states, patent law is covered exclusively under federal law. Moreover, unlike most trial court decisions, which are reviewed on appeal by regional appellate courts, the Federal Circuit has exclusive jurisdiction over all appeals of trial court decisions relating to patent law, regardless of the region of the United States where the trial occurred. Thus, patent law is remarkably consistent throughout the United States. This has permitted legal issues relating to second medical uses to be enforced throughout the United States without regard to the significant differences in culture and laws in the different regions of the country.

B. VALIDITY

I. Allowable claim wording

The subsections below review courts' treatment of different possible claim language and terms that are likely to be found in claims directed to pharmaceutical products or methods of use. In addition, some general claim language is not specific to pharmaceuticals but may nonetheless affect the validity of pharmaceutical patents. For example, claim language that makes optional certain steps or features but does not require them may or may not state a condition that is material to patentability. In particular, the Federal Circuit has held that whether "adapted to" clauses, "wherein" clauses, and "whereby" clauses are to be construed as claim limitations "depends on the specific facts of the case.[42]

It should be noted that specific claim terms are generally found to be valid or invalid per se. Rather, courts construe claims terms as necessary and determine whether the claim in question meets all statutory requirements. If not, then the claim is invalid. Thus, the adept U.S. patent practitioner must understand how a court is

38. Julie D. Polovina, *Mutant Biologics: The 2010 Health-Reform Legislation's Potential Impact on Reducing Biologic Research and Development Costs*, 100 Geo. L.J. 2291, 2295 (August 2012).
39. *Id.*
40. *Sandoz, Inc. v Amgen*, Inc., 794 F.3d 1347 (Fed. Cir. 2015).
41. Jenny M. Alsup, *You Can Dance if You Want to? Initial Interpretations of the BPCIA's Patent Dance with Sandoz and Amgen*, 8 Hastings Sci. & Tech. L.J. 137, 151 (Summer 2016).
42. *See, e.g., Griffin v Bertina*, 283 F.3d 1029, 1034, 62 USPQ2d 1431 (Fed. Cir. 2002).

likely to construe any given claim term in light of the applicable case law, guidance, and, most importantly, the intrinsic record.

1. Product claims

The Manual of Patent Examining Procedure (MPEP) provides valuable, though not legally binding, guidance on claim drafting.[43] Courts often look to provisions in the MPEP as persuasive authority on granular issues of patent law. Indeed, the Federal Circuit has even held that "§ 2163.04(I)(B) as written [in 2007] is a *lawful formulation of the prima facie standard* for a lack of written description rejection."[44] Patents on pharmaceuticals often include claims directed to chemical formulas. Section 2173.05(t) makes clear that such claims are not invalid as indefinite merely because a structure is not presented or is only partially presented.[45]

Another common term used in method claims is "pharmaceutically effective amount." This term is generally accepted claim language. However, its exact meaning has frequently been litigated and depends, as do the meaning of all claim terms, on the intrinsic record (*i.e.*, specification, prosecution history, claims). For example, in *Key Pharmaceuticals*, Hercon argued that the term should be construed by looking to FDA-approved dosages and that, therefore, the lower limit of the term "pharmaceutically effective amount" was 2.0 mg/day.[46] Even though the FDA considered transdermal patches to be bioequivalent to an FDA-approved patch, the Federal Circuit concluded that a person skilled in the art would not necessarily have so construed the term "pharmaceutically effective amount" based on the evidence in the record.[47]

2. Method claims

In one case, the Federal Circuit reviewed three claims directed to a "method of producing antidepressant activity which comprises internally administering" certain compounds.[48] These three claims stood before the court as rejected as failing to define and particularly point out the invention under 35 U.S.C. § 112. In particular, the Examiner argued indefiniteness on the basis that there was no "host." The court, however found that the lack of a host did not render the claim indefinite but merely broad. Similarly, the court found that the term "effective amount" was broad – not indefinite.[49]

43. *Molins PLC v Textron*, Inc. 48 F.3d 1172, 1180 n. 10 (Fed. Cir. 1995).
44. *Hyatt v Dudas*, 492 F.3d 1365, 1370 (Fed. Cir. 2007) (emphasis added).
45. *See also* In re Fisher, 427 F.2d 833, 166 USPQ 18 (CCPA 1970).
46. *Key Pharmaceuticals v Hercon Laboratories Corp.*, 161 F.3d 709, 718 (Fed. Cir. 1998).
47. *Id.*
48. Application of Gardner, 427 F.2d 786, 786 (CCPA 1970).
49. *Id.* at 787-88.

3. *Use claims*

4. *System claims*

5. *Dosage claims*

In U.S. patent law, the term "dosage claim" does not refer to a legally distinct type of claim. Rather, the term is sometimes used as a useful descriptor of a claim that requires a certain dosage – often within a specific range.

6. *Patient groups*

U.S. patent law does not treat claims directed to "patient groups" as a legally distinct type of claim. Such claims are considered a type of method claim. A representative example of a method claim directed to a patient group is as follows:

> "1. A method of treating an individual suffering from rheumatoid arthritis whose active disease. ..."[50]

The Federal Circuit, indeed, described the above claim language – referring to the patient group consisting of individuals with active disease – as a patient group. However, in doing so, the court did not attribute any legal significance per se to the claim language but merely found "patient group" to be a useful descriptor.

II. Novelty

1. *General definition of novelty and prior art*

2. *Definition of skilled person*

The validity of a patent in the United States depends, in part, on what would have been obvious to a person skilled in the art at the time the application from the patent issued was filed. Accordingly, identifying the hypothetical person skilled in the art is crucial to assessing the validity of a patent. Neither the Federal Circuit nor the Supreme Court has laid down a rule delineating the exact meaning of "person skilled in the art" for all future cases. However, the Federal Circuit has held that determining the level of ordinary skill in the art may include looking to: "(1) the educational level of the inventor; (2) type of problems encountered in the art; (3) prior art solutions to those problems; (4) rapidity with which innovations are made; (5) sophistication of the technology; and (6) educational level of active workers in the field."[51]

More nuanced, but case-specific definitions of "person skilled in the art" are available at the federal district court level. District courts frequently must pin down

50. *Abbvie Inc. v Mathilda and Terence Kennedy Institute of Rheumatology Trust*, 764 F.3d 1366, 1370 (Fed. Cir. 2014).
51. *Envtl. Designs, Ltd. v Union Oil Co.*, 713 F.2d 693, 696 (Fed. Cir. 1983).

with great precision what this term means in order to hold one way or the other on the issue of validity. For example, one district court found:

> [T]he ordinary person skilled in the art pertaining to the '741 patent would have a medical degree, experience treating patients with ear infections, and knowledge of the pharmacology and use of antibiotics. This person would be ... a pediatrician or general practitioner – those doctors who are often the first line of defense in treating ear infections and who, by virtue of their medical training, possess basic pharmacological knowledge.[52]

Sometimes courts are able to sidestep the determination of the ordinary level of skill in the art. For example, one district court addressed this determination in a footnote but deemed it unnecessary. Specifically, the court reasoned, following the Federal Circuit in *Ultradent Prods., Inc. v Life-Like Cosmetics, Inc.*, 127 F.3d 1065, 1069 (Fed. Cir. 1997), that "one patent could incorporate another patent by reference." Thus, the court concluded that "each and every limitation of the four asserted claims" were disclosed in a single prior art reference.[53]

The validity of U.S. patents can be challenged in a number of different manners. Patents having claims to second medical uses are not treated differently than other patents in this regard. Patents directed to second medical uses can be challenged at the USPTO through either two *inter partes* proceedings. The first of these is Post Grant Review ("PGR"), which is available within nine months of grant of a patent application granted under the first-to-file statutes of the AIA.[54] In a PGR proceeding, virtually any challenge to the validity of a patent can be made by a third party. The second *inter partes* proceeding is Inter Partes Review ("IPR"), which is available for any granted patent at any time. Grounds for challenge in an IPR are generally limited to novelty and non-obviousness over the prior art.

There have been very few PGR proceedings because the first patents eligible for them have only recently been granted. However, a substantial number of IPR proceedings have been conducted and decided. A very high percentage of proceedings where IPR has been instituted have resulted in a final decision in which at least one claim was canceled. In fact, as of December 2015, 84.2% of final decisions resulted in cancellation of at least one claim. The rate of cancellation is about the same in pharmaceutical patents as in other patents.[55]

One of the reasons for the high rate of cancellation is that the USPTO generally uses a "broadest reasonable interpretation" standard in interpreting the validity of the claims. The USPTO uses this standard because, in theory, it is possible for the patentee to amend the claims during the proceeding. However, in practice, only a negligible percentage of motions to amend claims is granted. Thus, claims will almost always stand or fall as they are granted.

---

52. *Daiichi Sankyo Co., Ltd. v Apotex, Inc.*, 501 F.3d 1254, 1256 (Fed. Cir. 2007) (reviewing the district court's determination regarding the level of skill in the art).
53. *Semcon Tech, LLC v Micron Technology*, Inc., Civil Action No. 12-532, 2015 WL 4910467 (D. Del. Aug. 17, 2015).
54. *See, Id.*
55. *IPR 360*, "3 Years of IPR: A Look at the States," available at http://www.law360.com/articles/699867/3-years-of-ipr-a-look-at-the-stats (downloaded May 14, 2016).

A third route of challenging patents at the USPTO is "*ex parte* reexamination". Such proceedings can be brought by a challenger on the basis of a substantially new issue that was not considered during the original prosecution of the patent. If the USPTO agrees that such a new issue is present, the USPTO will conduct an *ex parte* proceeding with the patentee in a manner similar to the original prosecution of the application. Amendments are far more easily granted in *ex parte* reexamination than in IPR. In addition, because once *ex parte* reexamination is instituted, the challenger has no further input in the proceeding, this type of proceeding has a much lower rate of invalidating patents.

The validity of patents can also be challenged in the courts in conjunction with infringement proceedings. Claims cannot be amended during suit. A majority of proceedings outside of the USPTO for second medical use patents occur in infringement actions under the Hatch-Waxman Act.[56] Under paragraph IV of the Act, a generic drug manufacturer applying for approval to market a generic copy of an approved pharmaceutical product must provide notice to the holder of the approval to market that product and provide a detailed statement of its basis for believing that the listed patents are either invalid or not infringed. If the holder of the approval disagrees with the basis, it must sue the applicant desiring to sell the generic product, in which the act of infringement is the submission of the application to market the generic product. The issue of validity of the patent will then be litigated along with all other issues in the case.

Validity can also be raised in the courts as a defense to an ordinary lawsuit for infringement or in connection with a Declaratory Judgment Action in which a party with a reasonable apprehension of suit can sue the patentee for a judgment that the patent is either invalid or not infringed.

III. Allowable claim wording: patent eligible under 101

> "The 2014 Interim Guidance on Patent Subject Matter Eligibility (2014 IEG) is for USPTO personnel to use when determining subject matter eligibility under 35 U.S.C. 101 in view of recent decisions by the U.S. Supreme Court, including Alice Corp., Myriad, and Mayo."[57]

Note the following examples and analysis is taken from USPTO's recent Subject Matter Eligible Examples in the Life Sciences areas.[58]

1. Product claims

> 1. Claim A vaccine comprising live attenuated Pigeon flu virus.
>
> Subject Matter Eligible. "The recited live attenuated virus is a nature-based product that must be compared to its naturally occurring counterpart to

---

56. Formally known as the Drug Price Competition and Patent Term Restoration Act of 1984.
57. http://www.uspto.gov/patent/laws-and-regulations/examination-policy/2014-interim-guidance-subject-matter-eligibility-0.
58. See Subject Matter Eligibility Examples: Life Sciences, published by the USPTO on May 1, 2016, available at www.uspto.gov/sites/default/files/documents/ieg-may-2016-ex.pdf.

determine if it has markedly different characteristics than the counterpart." In Example28, "the live attenuated virus has a different structural characteristic (the nucleotide sequence of its polymerase gene was changed due to the mutation), which has resulted in the live attenuated virus having a different functional characteristic (reduced virulence). No mutations of this gene are known to occur in nature. Thus, under the holding in Myriad, this structural difference is a markedly different characteristic, because it causes the claimed virus to have a nucleotide sequence that is different from anything found in nature. *Association for Molecular Pathology v Myriad Genetics*, Inc., 133 S. Ct. 2107, 2119 (2013)"[59].

Claim 3. A vaccine comprising Peptide F and a pharmaceutically acceptable carrier.

Subject Matter Ineligible. Although Peptide F and water do not naturally coexist in nature, both Peptide F and water "are naturally occurring, so neither would be eligible as claimed on their own. While the mixture of these two naturally occurring components is novel and does not occur in nature, there is no indication that mixing these components changes the structure, function, or other properties of the peptide or water."[60]

Example 28 goes on to explain that "the claimed mixture is like the novel bacterial mixture of Funk Brothers, which was held ineligible because each species of bacteria in the mixture (like each component in the peptide-carrier mixture) continued to have "the same effect it always had", *i.e.*, it lacked markedly different characteristics. *Funk Brothers Seed Co. v Kalo Inoculant Co.*, 333 U.S. 127, 131 (1948), discussed in Myriad Genetics, 133 S. Ct. at 2117 (explaining that the bacterial mixture of Funk Brothers "was not patent eligible because the patent holder did not alter the bacteria in any way")."[61]

2. *Method claims*

From Example 29

Claim 1. A method of detecting JUL-1 in a patient, said method comprising:
  a. obtaining a plasma sample from a human patient; and
  b. detecting whether JUL-1 is present in the plasma sample by contacting the plasma sample with an anti-JUL-1 antibody and detecting binding between JUL-1 and the antibody.

Subject Matter Eligible

"The claim recites a series of steps or acts, including detecting the presence of JUL-1 in a plasma sample. Thus, the claim is directed to a process, which is one of the statutory categories of invention… These steps do not recite or describe any recognized exception. See, e.g., *Mayo Collaborative Svcs. v Prometheus Labs.*, 566 U.S. __, 132 S. Ct. 1289, 1297 (2012) (recited steps of administering a drug to a patient and determining the resultant level of 6-thioguanine in the

59. See Subject Matter Eligibility Examples, page 3.
60. See Subject Matter Eligibility Examples, pages 4-5.
61. See Subject Matter Eligibility Examples page 5.

patient "are not themselves natural laws"). Accordingly, the claim is not directed to an exception"[62]

2. A method of diagnosing julitis in a patient, said method comprising:
   a. obtaining a plasma sample from a human patient;
   b. detecting whether JUL-1 is present in the plasma sample by contacting the plasma sample with an anti-JUL-1 antibody and detecting binding between JUL-1 and the antibody; and
   c. diagnosing the patient with julitis when the presence of JUL-1 in the plasma sample is detected.

Subject Matter Ineligible:

Step c requires a correlation that "is a consequence of natural processes, similar to the naturally occurring correlation found to be a law of nature by the Supreme Court in Mayo. Additionally, step c could be performed by a human using mental steps or basic critical thinking, which are types of activities that have been found by the courts to represent abstract ideas (e.g., the mental comparison in Ambry Genetics, or the diagnosing an abnormal condition by performing clinical tests and thinking about the results in Grams)...."Further, it is well established that the mere physical or tangible nature of additional elements such as the obtaining and detecting steps does not automatically confer eligibility on a claim directed to an abstract idea (see, e.g., *Alice Corp. v CLS Bank Int'l*, 134 S.Ct. 2347, 2358-59 (2014))."[63]

3. *Use claims*

As noted above, use claims are not permissible under U.S. practice.

4. *System claims*

A system claim is permissible under U.S. law. However, if a system claim does not recite the interaction between the elements of that system, there is a risk that the claim will be viewed as indefinite.[64]

5. *Dosage regimes*

Dosage regime claims may be patent eligible under U.S. law unless the dose regime patent claims are simply "statements of the correlations to allow the processes they describe" then those claims do not "add enough ... to qualify as patent eligible processes that apply to natural laws."[65] For example, consider a claimed process that describes "'[a] method of optimizing therapeutic efficacy for treatment of [a disease], comprising: (a) administering a drug ... to a subject; and (b) determining the level

62. See Subject Matter Eligibility Examples, page 11.
63. See Subject Matter Eligibility Examples page 12.
64. See M.P.E.P. 2173.02(II).
65. *Mayo Collaborative Servs. v Prometheus Labs., Inc.*, 566 U.S. __, 132 S. Ct. 1289, 1297 (2012).

of [said drug] in said subject, wherein the level [of the drug]" at a particular blood concentration indicates the drug amount needs to be either increased or decreased.[66] "The 'administering' step simply refers to the relevant doctors, ... the 'determining' step tells the doctor to determine the level of relevant metabolites in the blood ... [and] the 'wherein' clause[] simply tell[s] a doctor about the relevant natural laws, at most adding a suggestion that he should take those laws into account when treating his patient."[67] Finally, considering, "the three steps as an ordered combination adds nothing to the laws of nature that is not already present when the steps are considered separately."[68] Thus, these steps do not sufficiently "transform unpatentable natural correlations into patentable applications."[69]

6. *Patient groups*

From Example 29

Subject Matter Eligible:

Claim 6. A method of diagnosing and treating julitis in a patient, said method comprising:

a. obtaining a plasma sample from a human patient;
b. detecting whether JUL-1 is present in the plasma sample;
c. diagnosing the patient with julitis when the presence of JUL-1 in the plasma sample is detected; and
d. and administering an effective amount of anti-tumor necrosis factor (TNF) antibodies to the diagnosed patient.

Even though steps in claim 6 are within the framework of a law of nature or abstract idea, it is still eligible subject matter because it recites "specific and unconventional reagents and/or treatments that amount to significantly more than" a law of nature or abstract idea.[70]

C. INFRINGEMENT AND LITIGATION

I. Legal framework

The two sections that follow provide a brief overview of the legal framework regarding infringement of pharmaceutical patents in the United States. The first section covers the applicable national statutory laws. The second covers the applicable case law. As a result of the U.S. common law system, the material in these two sections cannot easily be separated. The case law discusses and interprets the statutes. And the statutory provisions, discussed in the first section below, cannot be fully understood absent a discussion of the relevant case law. But the authors have made an earnest effort to separate the two to the extent possible.

---

66. *Mayo*, 566 U.S. __ at 1295.
67. *Mayo*, at 1297-98.
68. *Id.* at 1298.
69. *Id.*
70. See Subject Matter Eligibility Examples, pg. 9.

1. *National statutory laws*

35 U.S.C. § 271(a) provides that "whoever without authority makes, uses, offers to sell, or sells any patented invention, within the United States, or imports into the United States any patented invention during the term of the patent therefor, infringes the patent." Furthermore, anyone who "actively induces infringement of a patent shall [also] be liable as an infringer."[71] Thus, under the plain interpretation of these statutes, any of a number of parties, for example, the physician prescribing the drug for the claimed method, the pharmacist dispensing the drug for the claimed method, the party marketing the drug with label instructions that describe the patented use, and the patient using the drug for the claimed method, may be liable for infringement of any second medical use claims.

None of the above listed parties are exempt from infringement or liability for infringement of a claim directed to a method of using a pharmaceutical product to treat a patient. 35 U.S.C. § 287(c)(2) provides that "medical practitioners" are exempt for liability for "performance of a medical activity" that constitutes an infringement under 35 U.S.C. § 271(a) or (b).[72] However, the term "medical activity" is limited to "the performance of a medical or surgical procedure on a body," and specifically does not include (i) "the use of a patented machine, manufacture, or composition of matter in violation of such patent;" (ii) "the practice of a patented use of a composition of matter in violation of such patent;" or (iii) "the practice of a process in violation of a biotechnology patent."[73] Thus, under the plain meaning of the language of the statute, medical practitioners are not exempt for liability for the use of a patented drug or the practice of a patented use of a drug. Furthermore, the legislative history indicates that the statute was meant to protect medical practitioners from liability for infringement of medical treatment method patents, but specifically not to include an exemption from liability for the use of drugs.[74] Notwithstanding the foregoing, patients and physicians are rarely the targets of a lawsuit.

Second medical use claims could be enforceable on the basis of either direct or indirect infringement. Whether second medical use claims could be enforceable on the basis of direct or indirect infringement depends entirely upon the circumstances of the case. For example, a party marketing the drug with label instructions that describe the patented use may be liable for inducing either the direct infringement of the doctor administering the drug according to the patented use, or the direct infringement of a patient using the drug. A doctor may be liable for directly infringing a patented method of use of a drug in the course of treatment, or for inducing the direct infringement of a patient who takes the drug at the physician's direction. Likewise, a pharmacist may be liable for either direct or indirect infringement depending on the facts of a specific case.

The most common target of a lawsuit for infringement of a medical method claim is the medical manufacturer, and infringement is determined based on proving indirect infringement. One theory of indirect infringement, as set forth in 35 U.S.C. §

71. 35 U.S.C. § 271(b).
72. 35 U.S.C. § 287(c)(1).
73. 35 U.S.C. § 287(c)(2)(A).
74. *See generally*, § 616 of the Conference Report to accompany H.R. 3610, 104th Cong. (1996).

271(c), is contributory infringement. This type of infringement requires that the drug not be a "commodity of commerce suitable for substantial noninfringing use." Since a claim directed to a second medical use presupposes the existence of substantial noninfringing uses, contributory infringement would generally not be applicable. However, where the first medical use is not approved for any purpose in the United States, it may be possible to prove contributory infringement.

Contributory infringement under 35 U.S.C. § 271(c) requires proof of knowledge of the patent. In the context of a medical method claim, the defendant must know that the material or apparatus they are providing is especially made or especially adapted for use in an infringement of a patent. The U.S. courts have interpreted this to require actual knowledge of the patent.

Proving infringement is a question of fact that is decided by a trier of fact. The plaintiff must prove the infringement by a preponderance of the evidence. Thus, if a plaintiff is seeking to prove that a manufacturer actively induces (or will induce) patent infringement of a patented method, the plaintiff must prove that direct infringement occurred by a preponderance of the evidence, and that the defendant actively induced the infringement by a preponderance of the evidence.

2. *Case law*

In cases where a theory of contributory infringement is not available, infringement would need to be proven under a theory of induced infringement. Induced infringement under 35 U.S.C. § 271(b) might be found if the party sells the drug by advertising or instructions to carry out the infringing use. Case law also establishes that the party must know of the existence of the patent, and also know that their activities would lead to infringement of the patent. Thus, there is a requirement that the accused infringer intend that the direct infringement should occur. Nevertheless, circumstantial proof that the person accused of inducing infringement knew of the patent, and knew that their activities would lead to infringement of the patent is generally sufficient to establish the requisite intent.[75]

Liability for both active inducement of infringement and contributory infringement is still dependent upon the existence of direct infringement. The patent holder in a patent litigation lawsuit must still prove that all of the steps of the patented method are performed, e.g., by the medical device practitioner or the patient himself. Recent case law in the United States has further held that "all the steps of a claimed method must be performed in order to find induced infringement."[76]

Beyond proving direct infringement, a patent holder alleging inducement of infringement must prove not just that the defendant intended to cause the acts that produced direct infringement, but that the defendant had an affirmative intent to cause direct infringement.[77] Typically this will require actual knowledge of the patent,

75. See *DSU Med. Corp. v JMS Co., Ltd.*, 471 F.3d 1293 (Fed. Cir. 2006).
76. *Move, Inc. v Real Estate Alliance Ltd.*, 709 F.3d 1117, 1123 (Fed. Cir. 2013).
77. *DSU Medical Corp. v JMS Co.*, 471 F.3d 1293, (Fed. Cir. 2006).

though the U.S. Supreme Court in *Global-Tech Appliances, Inc. v SEB S.A.* held that willful blindness to a known patent will also satisfy the intent requirement.[78]

The general rule is that an act of direct infringement is required to find liability under induced infringement. Thus, any acts found to be infringing would need to be done in connection with the infringing use. The "single entity rule," requiring that to find indirect infringement, direct infringement by a single entity must be found first, has been reestablished by the Supreme Court in *Limelight Networks, Inc. v Akamai Technologies, Inc.* Thus, if a claim requires multiple actors who have no agency to each other, it may be very difficult to prove infringement.

If a drug is approved for more than one indication, one or more of which (but not all) falls within the claims of a patent, it is still possible to prove an infringement if a party makes, supplies or uses a generic version of the drug. Such acts would be an infringement. If a party has a patent covering a method of using a drug for a second medical use, then infringement would generally be proven under a theory of induced infringement and/or contributory infringement.

Each of the acts of making, supplying and using may constitute a form of infringement. In such a case, the infringing acts would generally be the inducement of others to infringe. Thus, merely making, supplying, and using would not be infringement by the party offering the generic drug. While the use of the drug by the patient or the physician prescribing it may be considered acts of infringement, as mentioned above, they are rarely the targets of a lawsuit. Nevertheless, the acts of direct infringement by these parties are considered a necessary component of the induced infringement by the party making and supplying the drug.

Statements used in product packaging may be used as evidence that a medical manufacturer actively induced the infringement of a patent. However, proof of direct infringement and proof of intent to cause the infringement would still be required.

The writing of a prescription may be used as evidence to prove direct infringement, e.g., to prove that a patient actually took a particular medication as covered by a patented method. To successfully prove induced infringement by a medical manufacturer, additional evidence may be needed to prove that the physician was instructed by the manufacturer to prescribe the medication for a particular patented purpose. This may be difficult if the prescription does not indicate for what purpose a drug is being prescribed.

Because of the foregoing difficulties, in the large majority of cases involving second medical uses, infringement is proved based on the proposed label applied to a product used for the second medical use. Thus, through a process colloquially termed "skinny labeling," the United States Food and Drug Administration ("FDA") may permit "carve out" of infringing uses from a copyist's drug product labeling. This may reduce the chance of infringement liability under 35 USC 287(b).[79]

---

78. *563 U.S.* ___; 131 S. Ct. 2060 (2011) "[A] willfully blind defendant is one who takes deliberate actions to avoid confirming a high probability of wrongdoing and who can almost be said to have actually known the critical facts." *Global-Tech*, slip opin. at 14.
79. *See*, 21 U.S.C. § 355(j)(2)(A)(viii).

II. Claim construction

1. General rules

In U.S. law, there is a distinction drawn between questions of fact and those of law. Questions of fact are presented to the factfinder, which may be a jury or a judge in a bench trial. Questions of law, on the other hand, are submitted to the judge.

Issues of infringement are usually questions of fact.[80] But courts have traditionally treated issues of claim construction, which arise in infringement suits, as questions of law.[81]

In construing claims, U.S. courts cannot consider any and every document or other piece of evidence. Instead, claims "must be read in view of the specification, of which they are a part." In fact, the specification is usually dispositive of issues of claim construction.[82] However, the claims themselves, as well as the prosecution history, are also key parts of the intrinsic record that courts review when construing claims. Courts may also consider extrinsic evidence – evidence other than the claims, specification and prosecution history – if needed in order to construe the claims.[83]

2. Specific rules for use claims

Restated from Section A.I.1. of this chapter, second medical use claims in the U.S. take a "method of treatment" format. Such claims would be directed to a method of treating a patient suffering from new disease Y by administering an effective amount of old compound X to the patient. No other format is available to protect second medical uses in the U.S. For example, use claims, Swiss-type claims, pharmaceutical formulation for use claims, and claims to the compound when used to treat a specific disease are all notpermissible under U.S. law.

III. Scope of protection

> 35. S.C. § 154(a)(1) states a patent holder has the "right to exclude others from making, using, offering for sale, or selling the invention throughout the United States or importing the invention into the United States, and, if the invention is a process, of the right to exclude others from using, offering for sale or selling throughout the United States, products made by that process, referring to the specification for the particulars thereof." Additionally, § 154(d) provides the right of a patent holder to "obtain a reasonable royalty from any person who, during the period beginning on the date of publication of the application for such patent ... and ending on the date the patent is issued –
>
> (A)
>
> (i) makes uses, offers for sale, or sells in the United States the invention as claimed in the published patent application or imports such an invention

80. *See* 5A-18 Chisum on Patents § 18.06 (2015).
81. *Id.*
82. *Phillips v AWH Corp.*, 415 F.3d 1303, 1315 (Fed. Cir. 2005).
83. *See* 5A-18 Chisum on Patents § 18.06[2] (2015).

into the United States; or

(ii) if the invention as claimed in the published patent application is a process, uses, offers for sale, or sells in the United States or imports into the United States products made by that process as claimed in the published patent application ..."

In other words, a patent grants a patent holder's right "to exclude others from making, using, and selling the invention" and not the "affirmative right to make, use or sell."[84] Therefore, if a court determines that a party participated in any of these exclusive rights either directly or indirectly without the patent holder's authorization, it can determine that party is liable for patent infringement under 35 U.S.C. § 271.

1. *Scope of the use*

1.1 General definition of the term "use"

The Federal Food, Drug and Cosmetic Act (FFDCA) provides an abbreviated way to enable a generic drug to get to market more quickly and with less expense than the traditional approval route for a new or "pioneer" pharmaceutical.[85]

"An ANDA may be filed for a generic drug that is the same as a so-called 'pioneer drug' previously approved, see 21 U.S.C. § 355(j)(2)(A), or that differs from the pioneer drug in specified ways, see 21 U.S.C. § 355(j)(2)(C). The ANDA applicant can substitute bioequivalence date for the extensive animal and human studies of safety and effectiveness that must accompany a full new drug application. Compare 21 U.S.C. § 355(j)(2)(A)(iv), with § 355(b)(1). "[86] An ANDA application contains a "statement regarding the patent status of the approved product, including, potentially, a 'Paragraph IV' certification that a patent listed with the FDA as covering a drug product is invalid or is not infringed by the proposed generic equivalent."[87] In response to an ANDA filing related to a patented drug, the patent holder can file a § 271(e)(2) patent infringement suit, which elicits a "30-month stay" of FDA approval of the ANDA while the patent holder and the ANDA-filer undergo patent infringement litigation.[88] Particularly, a timely § 271(e)(2)(A) suit filing "results in an automatic stay of FDA approval for up to 30 months," however, the court can shorten or extend this stay if the patent holder or the accused infringer, respectively, fails to cooperate. *Id.* The court "can grant (1) an order that the effective date of any FFDCA approval should be the date of expiration of the patent; (2) injunctive relief against commercial manufacture, use or sale; (3) damages for any such commercial activity; and (4) attorney's fees under 35 U.S.C. Section 285.[89]

However, 35 U.S.C. § 271(e)(1) provides a "reasonably related uses" exception to patent infringement for ANDA applicants if "the act [is] 'solely for uses reasonably

84. 5-16 Chisum on Patents §16.02.
85. *Eli Lilly & Co. v Medtronic, Inc.*, 496 U.S. 661, 676 (1990).
86. *Eli Lilly*, 496 U.S. at 676.
87. 5-16 Chisum on Patents § 16.03.
88. *Id.*
89. *Id.*

related to the development and submission of information [to the FDA].' ... The infringing acts must be 'solely' for the exempt use, but to be exempt, a use need be only 'reasonably related' to the [above] stated objective."[90]

1.2 Manufacture of the pharmaceutical

See "2. Direct Infringement"

1.3 Sale of the product

See "2. Direct Infringement"

1.4 Offer for sale

See "2. Direct Infringement"

1.5 Application to the patient

Not applicable in U.S. law.

1.6 Combination products

Not applicable in U.S. law.

2. Absolute product protection

Not applicable in U.S. law.

2.1 Limitation through the term "use"

Not applicable in U.S. law.

2.2 Off-label use

See "1.1 General definitions of the term 'use'"

3. Dosage regimes

Not applicable in U.S. law.

90. *Id.*

4. *Patient groups*

Not applicable in U.S. law.

5. *Extension under the doctrine of equivalents*

Alternative to showing that an alleged infringer literally infringes on a patent holder's patent. The patent holder can assert that an infringer infringes under the doctrine of equivalents. Under the doctrine, the patent holder would claim that either the product or process "performs substantially the same function in substantially the same way to obtain the same result as the claimed subject matter."[91] Just as in determining literal infringement, a court will define the asserted claims using claim construction.

IV. Infringing acts

1. *Infringing person or entity*

Both individuals and entities can be held liable for patent infringement.

2. *Direct infringement*

The statutory provisions governing direct infringement are located in 35 U.S.C. § 271(a) which reads:

> "Except as otherwise provided in this title, whoever without authority makes, uses, offers to sell, or sells any patented invention, within the United States or imports into the United States any patented invention during the term of the patent therefor, infringes the patent."

2.1 *Manufacture of the pharmaceutical*

Whether a party's manufacture of a pharmaceutical constitutes an infringing act of direct infringement depends on how the claim is written. If the claim is written as a method, then merely manufacturing the pharmaceutical by *any* method is not an infringing act. Manufacturing the pharmaceutical would infringe a method claim only if done *according to one of the particular methods covered by the claim*. For example, one federal district court known for handling a large number of infringement suits concluded in one case that "[d]efendants themselves will not directly infringe because even if they manufactured and marketed generic ribavirin, they would not be "treating," "modulating," or "inhibiting." The court went on to recognize that the defendant pharmaceutical companies, in fact, do not treat diseases at all, but rather sell drugs to wholesalers and pharmacists, who sell the drugs to patients. Other forms of liability, such as induced infringement, may attach, but not direct

---

91. 5B-18 Chisum on Patents § 18.04.

infringement. Thus, in that case, which is paradigmatic of U.S. infringement suits, the pharmaceutical companies were not liable for direct infringement.[92]

2.2 *Offer for sale*

While an "offer for sale" may constitute an infringing act under 35 U.S.C. § 271(a), whether there was such an offer is often not disputed. Courts can determine whether such an offer occurred by applying traditional principles of contract law. However, in infringement suits, issues may arise as to *what* was offered for sale. For example, "the Supreme Court recently recognized that a patented method may not be sold in the same way as an article or device."[93] Indeed, the Federal Circuit has declined to decide whether selling a process may give rise to liability under § 271(a) – that is, direct infringement.[94] But the Federal Circuit has, more narrowly, held "that a party that ... offers to sell software containing instructions to perform a patented method" is not liable for direct infringement under § 271(a).[95]

2.3 *Sale*

Similarly, courts apply traditional principles of contract law to determine whether there was an actual sale. Typically, more nuanced issues relating to sales arise when courts are determining whether the alleged infringer is liable under some other theory. An alleged infringer may be liable under a theory of induced infringement if there is a showing of intent to induce infringement.[96] Whether a sale "evince[s] an intent to induce infringement" is fact-specific and may merely evidence "an intent to sell at the highest price."[97]

Whether a sale has occurred is also a highly litigated issue in determining whether a claim is valid. For instance, whether there was a sale and when it occurred affect whether the on-sale bar – under the post-America Invents Act 35 U.S.C. § 102(b) – applies. The Federal Circuit has held, for example, "that a contract manufacturer's sale to the inventor of manufacturing services where neither title to the embodiments nor the right to market the same passes to the supplier does not constitute an invalidating sale under § 102(b)."[98] Courts, however, have not drawn a distinction between what constitutes a sale for validity purposes under § 102(b) – or the pre-AIA provisions – and what constitutes a sale for direct infringement purposes. Accordingly, U.S. patent lawyers may study cases turning on whether there was an on-sale bar to better predict whether there may be liability for a sale under § 271(a).

92. *ICN Pharmaceuticals, Inc. v Geneva Pharmaceuticals Technology Corp.*, 272 F.Supp.2d 1028, 1046 (C.D. Cal. July 14, 2003).
93. *Quanta Computer, Inc. v LG Elecs., Inc.*, 553 U.S. 617, 128 S. Ct. 2109, 2117 (2008).
94. *Ricoh Co., Ltd. v Quanta Computer Inc.*, 550 F.3d 1325, 1336 (Fed. Cir. 2008).
95. *Id.*
96. 5-17 Chisum on Patents § 17.04.
97. *Moba, B.V. v Diamond Automation, Inc.*, 325 F.3d 1306, 1318 (Fed. Cir. 2003).
98. *Medicines Company v Hospira, Inc.*, Nos. 2014-1269, 2014-1504, 2016 WL 3670000, *14 (July 11, 2016).

It is worth emphasizing that under 35 U.S.C. § 271(a), an offer for sale and a sale are distinct infringing acts. In order for there to be direct infringement liability for a sale, there must be an actual sale before the expiration of the patent.[99] But there need not be an actual sale for liability to attach for *offering* to sell. The purpose of enacting § 271(a), in fact, "was to permit a patentee to act against threatened infringing sale[s] by establishing a cause of action before [an] actual sale occurred."[100] A patentee may try to mitigate economic loss resulting from infringement by suing *before* an actual sale has occurred and seeking relief in the form of a prohibitory injunction preventing the competitor from actually selling the covered product.

2.4 *Export*

In the United States, there is no liability per se under the theory of direct infringement for exporting a patented product or method. Indeed a plain reading of 35 U.S.C. § 271(a), reveals that the term "export" does not appear once. Indeed, as the title of this section suggests, this material covers only liability under the theory of direct infringement.

However, the reader should be aware that there may be liability for exporting patented goods under 35 U.S.C. § 271(f). In fact, the Federal Circuit recently found in one case that the exportation of a single component sufficed for liability to attach.[101] The court rejected the contention that § 271(f)(1) requires *two* components to be exported in order to create liability, emphasizing that that statutory provision "assigns infringement to anyone who supplies or causes to be supplied 'all or a substantial portion of the components of a patented invention.'"[102] If, on the other hand, a single component does not constitute a "substantial portion" of the patented system, the mere exportation of that single component is unlikely to expose the exporter to liability under § 271(f)(1).

2.5 *Import*

In contrast with exporting, importing a patented invention plainly constitutes an act of direct infringement under § 271(a), which reads, in pertinent part: "[W]hoever without authority ... imports into the United States any patented invention during the term of the patent therefor, infringes the patent." Section 271(g) also creates liability for the unauthorized importation of patented goods and reads, in pertinent part: "Whoever without authority imports into the United States or offers to sell, sells, or uses within the United States a product which is made by a process patented in the United States shall be liable as an infringer, if the importation, offer to sell, sale, or use of the product occurs during the term of such process patent."

---

99. 12B Chisum on Patents 5111.60.
100. Thomas L. Irving and Stacy D. Lewis, Proving a Date of Invention and Infringement After GATT/TRIPS, 22 AIPLA Q.J. 309, 351–52 (Summer/Fall 1994).
101. *Promega Corp. v Life Technologies Corp.*, 773 F.3d 1338 (Fed. Cir. 2014).
102. *Id.* at 1353.

2.6 *Combination products*

Under the liability theory of direct infringement, "combination products" are not treated as legally distinct per se. However, as explained under the subsection above titled "Exports", whether selling or exporting a single component patented as part of a combination product can give rise to liability will depend heavily on the circumstances of the case. Due to the complicated nature of combination products, infringing acts are more likely to give rise to liability under other theories – such as induced infringement and contributory infringement. [35 U.S.C. § 271(b),(c)].

3. *Indirect infringement*

In U.S. law, there are types of indirect infringement: induced infringement and contributory infringement. Accordingly, the subsections that follow are divided along those lines as appropriate. 35 U.S.C. § 271(b) assigns liability under an *inducement theory* to "[w]hoever actively induces infringement of a patent." Section 271(c) assigns liability under a *contributory theory* to:

"Whoever offers to sell or sells within the United States or imports into the United States a component of a patented machine, manufacture, combination or composition, or a material or apparatus for use in practicing a patented process, constituting a material part of the invention, knowing the same to be especially made or especially adapted for use in an infringement of such patent, and not a staple article or commodity of commerce suitable for substantial noninfringing use, shall be liable as a contributory infringer."

3.1 *Objective acts*

The objective acts that constitute infringing acts or induce or contribute to infringement are generally the same as those acts discussed in the context of direct infringement. Indeed, for there to be induced infringement, which is a form of secondary liability, there must also be direct infringement – primary liability.

3.2 *Subjective conditions*

The Supreme Court has held that both induced infringement and contributory infringement require knowledge that the induced acts constitute acts of patent infringement.[103] More recently, the Supreme Court clarified the knowledge requirement, explaining that Global-Tech requires not only knowledge of the patent, but also knowledge of infringement. Thus, the defendant is liable only "if the defendant knew of the patent *and* knew as we that the induced acts constitute patent infringement.[104]

103. *Global-Tech Appliances, Inc. v SEB S.A.*, 131 S. Ct. 2060 (2011).
104. 5-17 Chisum on Patents § 17.04.

3.2 *Export*

The term "export" is not recited as an infringing act in either of the above provisions. However, exportation of a patented good may constitute an infringing act under the inducement theory of liability.

3.4 *Import*

While the above statutory language plainly recites "imports" as an element, whether an alleged infringer has imported within the meaning of this provision is not an issue specific to indirect infringement. Accordingly, the reader is referred to discussion of this possibly infringing act above.

3.5 *Combination products*

As in direct infringement, whether the patented invention is a combination or product or not does not make a difference per se in indirect infringement suits. (Note that, as shown above, § 271(c) does create contributory infringement liability for unauthorized selling, offering to sell, or importing of components of combination products. But the statute merely clarifies that combination products are protected under this type of liability. That there may be various component parts, that may or may not have separate uses apart from the patented system, is a relevant consideration in determining whether the alleged infringer possessed the requisite level of scienter.

4. *Off-label use*

Off-label uses have not generated much patent litigation in the United States. As the Federal Circuit stated in *Warner-Lambert* and subsequently reaffirmed, generic drug companies may not seek Abbreviated New Drug Application approval for an unapproved or off-label use of a drug under 21 U.S.C. § 355(j)(2)(A)(i).[105] Accordingly, where a brand-name drug company owns a patent covering only an off-label use for a drug, that company cannot invoke 35 U.S.C. § 271(e)(2)(A) – the Hatch-Waxman Act provision making the submission of an ANDA an act of infringement. Furthermore, in U.S. patent law, as opposed to FDA regulations, there is no legal distinction drawn between off- and on-label uses of drugs. Whether a use is "off-label" is purely related to whether it is eligible for approval from the FDA. There is no necessary relationship between whether a patented drug's is "off-label" and liability for infringement.

4.1 *General admissibility of off-label use*

Not applicable in U.S. law.

105. *Bayer Schering Pharma AG v Lupin, Ltd.*, 676 F.3d 1316, 1319 (Fed. Cir. 2012).

4.2 *Liable persons*

Not applicable in U.S. law.

4.3 *Objective requirements for infringement*

Not applicable in U.S. law.

4.4 *Subjective requirements for infringement*

Not applicable in U.S. law.

5. *Dosage regimes*

Not applicable in U.S. law.

6. *Patient groups*

Not applicable in U.S. law.

V. Remedies

A plaintiff who successfully proves infringement of a medical method of use claim may be entitled to injunctive relief (35 U.S.C. § 283). and/or damages (35 U.S.C. § 284, 285). Injunctive relief is often the only relief available when a generic drug manufacturer is sued based on its challenge to a patent in the Orange Book.[106] Nevertheless, in cases of an "at risk" launch by a generic drug manufacturer, damages could also be awarded.

1. *Injunctions*

A preliminary injunction is available if the patentee can prove that it is (1) likely to succeed on the merits; (2) likely to suffer irreparable harm in the absence of preliminary relief; (3) the balance of equities tips in its favor; and (4) an injunction is in the public interest.[107] A preliminary injunction may properly be denied where a movant fails to establish any one of these four factors.[108]

Permanent injunctions in U.S. patent cases are not automatic. After a plaintiff proves direct infringement and indirect infringement, if alleged, to obtain a permanent injunction, the plaintiff will usually also need to prove by a preponderance of the evidence:

---

106. The Drug, Price and Competition Act (Hatch-Waxman Act) requires the FDA to publish a list of Approved Drug Products with Therapeutic Equivalence Evaluations, commonly known as the Orange Book.
107. *Apple, Inc. v Samsung Elecs. Co.*, 678 F.3d 1314, 1323 (Fed. Cir. 2012).
108. *See Apple*, 678 F.3d at 133.

(1) that it has suffered an irreparable injury;
(2) that remedies available at law are inadequate to compensate for that injury;
(3) that considering the balance of hardships between the plaintiff and defendant, a remedy in equity is warranted; and
(4) that the public interest would not be disserved by a permanent injunction.[109]

A temporary restraining order ("TRO") may also be sought by the patent holder. The legal standard for obtaining a TRO is the same as a preliminary injunction. The main differences are that a preliminary injunction requires the adverse party to have adequate notice (unlike a TRO which may be entered without notice), and a preliminary injunction is of indefinite duration while a TRO is of a short, limited duration (e.g., 14 days).

Quite distinct from injunctive relief, and in some ways more powerful because of the heightened certainty is the 30-month stay available to a party who timely files an infringement action in a federal district court on an Orange Book listed patent claiming an approved drug against a filer of a generic application seeking approval to market that drug, The FDA is prohibited from approving the generic application for a period of 30 months from the filing of the infringement action. Without an approval, the generic filer cannot market the drug. Second medical use patents can and have been used to obtain such 30-month stays.

2. *Damages*

Injunctive relief is most commonly sought as most relevant cases occur before the launch of a product into the market. However, damages can be awarded under circumstances in an amount "adequate to compensate for the infringement, but in no event less than a reasonable royalty for the use made of the invention by the infringer, together with interest and costs as fixed by the court."[110] Enhanced damages of up to three times the amount found or assessed may also be awarded to the plaintiff if the plaintiff can prove that the defendant willfully infringed the patented method.[111]

3. *Information*

While parties in patent litigation do not seek information as a remedy, information regarding names of customers and manufacturers is nonetheless important as a means to obtaining money damages or an injunction. For example, a plaintiff may try to obtain these names in order to know which third parties to join as defendants. Remedies in trade secret law may require one party to refrain from distributing customer lists, e.g., but trade secret law is outside the scope of this chapter. Furthermore, there is no subfield of trade secret law that deals exclusively with and is specific to trade secrets in the pharmaceutical industry.

109. *eBay, Inc. v MercExchange, LLC*, 547 U.S. 388 (2006).
110. 35 U.S.C. § 284.
111. 35 U.S.C. § 285.

3.1 Names of manufacturer, distributors etc.

Not applicable in U.S. law.

3.2 Names of customers

Not applicable in U.S. law.

3.3 Information about infringing sales

Not applicable in U.S. law.

3.4 Account of profits

See "2. Damages"

4. Recall of products and destruction

Not applicable in U.S. law.

5. Recovery of legal costs

See "2. Damages"

VI. Exceptions from patent protection

1. Exhaustion of rights

The term "exhaustion of rights" in U.S. law is typically used to refer to the "exhaustion of rights doctrine" under copyright law.[112] The "exhaustion of rights" doctrine refers to the Copyright Act's definition of when a copyright owner's exclusivity rights expire. This topic is outside the scope of this chapter.

However, the Supreme Court of the United States has recognized an exhaustion of patent rights doctrine commonly referred to as the "patent exhaustion doctrine."[113] Under the patent exhaustion doctrine, the initial authorized sale of a patented article terminates all patent rights to that article.[114] Any conduct *after* the patent rights have been exhausted does not constitute infringement.[115] In addition to applying to an

112. Javier M Leija, *The Patent Exhaustion Doctrine: Patent Holders' Rights versus The Public's Interest in Using the Invention*, 2 Phoenix L. Rev. 163, 171 (Spring 2009).
113. *Quanta Computer, Inc. v LG Electronics, Inc.*, 128 S. Ct. 2109 (2008).
114. *Id.* at 2115.
115. *LifeScan Scotland, Ltd. v Shasta Technologies, LLC*, Case No. 11-cv-04494-WHO, 2014 WL 2159331, *1 (N.D. Cal. May 23, 2014).

"outright sale," the doctrine also applies to "the disposition of a product under a license."[116]

The patent exhaustion doctrine plays an important role in the U.S. pharmaceutical industry.[117] Pharmaceutical companies frequently charge much higher prices in the United States than they do in other countries.[118] Retailers of pharmaceutical products are able to maintain this price differential by prohibiting the resale of such products in the United States. Under present U.S. patent law, importers of such products may be liable for infringement.[119] Importers sued for infringement under these circumstances may counter with a patent exhaustion doctrine defense.

But in *Lexmark*, a recent landmark Federal Circuit decision, the court reaffirmed the rule that, where the sale of a patented article occurs abroad, the patent exhaustion doctrine is not available as a defense to infringement. Thus, in U.S. patent law, there is *domestic* patent exhaustion but no *foreign* patent exhaustion. Furthermore, sales within the United States do not result in per se exhaustion of patent rights. The Federal Circuit in *Lexmark* ruled that sales under a single-use license – *i.e.*, sales subject to contractually binding use restrictions – do not exhaust patent rights per se.[120] Recognizing that private parties are free to contract around the terms and conditions of a sale, the court stated:

> "[A] patentee's own sale of its patented article subject to a clearly communicated restriction does not confer authority to sell or use the article in violation of that restriction, *i.e.*, does not exhaust the patentee's § 271 rights against such conduct involving that article."[121]

Note that this doctrine applies to all technologies in patent law and is not specific to pharmaceuticals.

2. *Patient welfare*

Not applicable in U.S. law.

3. *Others specific to second medical use claims*

Not applicable in U.S. law.

116. *Forest Laboratories, Inc. v Abbott Laboratories*, No. 96-CV-159-A, 1999 WL 33299123, *23 (W.D.N.Y. June 23, 1999).
117. Daniel J. Hemel et al., *Trade and Tradeoffs: The Case of International Patent Exhaustion*, 116 Colum. L. Rev. Sidebar 17, 17 (April 2016).
118. *Id.*
119. *Id.*
120. *Lexmark Intern., Inc. v Impression Products, Inc.*, 816 F.3d 721 (Fed. Cir. 2016).
121. *Id.* at 737.

VII. Procedural issues

1. *Preliminary injunction cases*

Because a preliminary injunction is an equitable remedy, courts evaluate and balance all four "factors and the circumstances surrounding each."[122] Additionally, courts "weigh and measure each of the four factors against the other factors and against the magnitude of the relief requested."[123] A patent holder will not be granted a preliminary injunction unless he "establishes both ... [a] likelihood of success on the merits and irreparable harm."[124]

1.1 *Availability for second medical use claims*

A patent holder can file a preliminary injunction against a copyist drug manufacturer to prohibit that manufacturer from distributing its generic version of the patent holder's drug.[125] As articulated in Section C.2. of this chapter, the patent holder may be able to assert that allowing the copyist drug manufacturer to distribute its drug would directly, indirectly and/or induce infringement of his patent(s) resulting in the patent holder suffering irreparable harm.

1.2 *Specific requirements*

Success on the merits

"A patent holder must show a likelihood of success on the merits both with respect to validity of its patent and with respect to infringement of its patent."[126] Thus, under the same standard of proof that the patent holder is held to at trial, the patent holder must show that the copyist drug product manufacturer infringes on his patents and that the patent will likely withstand an invalidity claim.[127] Because a patent is presumed valid, when a patent holder moves for a preliminary injunction, he does not have to establish validity beyond question but must "present a clear case supporting the validity of the patent in suit."[128] The patent holder must also show by a preponderance of the evidence that the copyist infringed on his patent.

Irreparable harm

"Irreparable harm is presumed when a clear showing of patent validity and infringement has been made."[129] In the circumstance that a patent holder did not make a

122. *Ill. Tool Works, Inc., v Grip-Pak, Inc.*, 906 F.2d 679, 680 (Fed. Cir. 1990).
123. *Chrysler Motors Corp. v Auto Body Panels of Ohio, Inc.*, 908 F.2d 951, 954 (Fed. Cir. 1990) citing *Hybridtech Inc. v Abbott Labs.*, 849 F. 2d 1446, 1451 n. 12, (Fed. Cir. 1988).
124. *Amazon.com, Inc. v Barnesandnoble.com, Inc.*, 239 F.3d 1343, 1350 (Fed. Cir. 2001).
125. *AstraZeneca LP v Apotex, Inc.*, 633 F.3d 1042 (Fed. Cir. 2010).
126. *Hybridtech Inc. v Abbott Labs.*, 849 F. 2d 1446, 1451 (Fed. Cir. 1988).
127. *Amazon.com*, 239 F.3d 1343, 1350.
128. *Id*, at 1359.
129. *Id*, at 1350.

clear showing then the presumption does not apply.[130] The patent holder must then show how he will suffer harm that is not quantifiable or compensable with money damages.[131]

Balance of hardships

The balancing of hardships is a fact-specific inquiry. Based on the evidence offered by both parties, a court will evaluate the likely harm that the patent holder will suffer if the preliminary injunction is not issued and the generic drug goes to market versus the harm the alleged infringer will suffer if the preliminary injunction does issue and the drug is prohibited from going to market (at least until after the trial).

Public interest

Determining what is the best outcome regarding the public interest is also a fact-specific inquiry. Again, based on the evidence offered by both parties, the court will weigh the impact on the public if the preliminary injunction is not granted and the generic drug is allowed to go to market versus the effect on the public if the generic is withheld from the market at least until after trial.

2. *Cases on the merits*

In *AstraZeneca LP v Apotex, Inc.*[132] the Federal Circuit affirmed the district court's ruling to grant AstraZeneca a preliminary injunction prohibiting Apotex from marketing its generic version of AstraZeneca's asthma medication until after trial.[133] AstraZeneca held two patents related to its asthma medication and both patents contained method claims instructing users how to administer the medication.[134] Per FDA drug label dose instruction requirements, AstraZeneca's drug label included directions to "titrate to the lowest effective dose once asthma stability is achieved" using once daily dosing.[135] These titration instructions were also articulated in AstraZeneca's method claims.[136] Apotex was granted its ANDA application for its generic version of the asthma medication.[137] The proposed label included instructions to titrate the drug dose to the lowest effective dose but did not explicitly describe once-daily dosing.[138] The day after Apotex was granted its application, AstraZeneca moved for a preliminary injunction.[139] The district court granted AstraZeneca its preliminary injunction barring Apotex from distributing its drug until after trial.[140]

130. *AstraZeneca, LP v Apotex, Inc.*, 623 F.Supp. 2d 579, 608 (D. N.J. 2009).
131. *AstraZeneca*, 623 F.Supp. 2d at 608.
132. *AstraZeneca LP v Apotex, Inc.*, 633 F.3d 1042 (Fed. Cir. 2010).
133. *AstraZeneca* at 1045.
134. *Id.* at 1047.
135. *Id.*
136. *Id.*
137. *Id.*
138. *Id.* at 1048.
139. *Id.*at 1047.
140. *Id.* at 1048.

Apotex appealed the preliminary injunction to the Federal Circuit and the Federal Circuit reviewed the district court's ruling for abuse of discretion.[141]

The Court affirmed the district court's ruling that AstraZeneca's method claims would likely withstand a validity challenge at trial.[142] Specifically, the Court rejected Apotex's arguments that AstraZeneca's method claims were invalid because (1) those claims were anticipated by prior art and therefore not novel and (2) the prior art also rendered those claims obvious.[143] Apotex also argued that its proposed label was not evidence of induced infringement because the FDA required such language in its label and the FDA advised Apotex that no "carve out" was needed in their label because it did not expressly describe once daily dosing.[144] The Court was unpersuaded and affirmed that AstraZeneca would likely be able to prove that Apotex induced medication users to infringe on AstraZeneca's method claims because its proposed titrating dose instructions effectively directed users to use once-daily dosing.[145] Moreover, FDA-required labeling was not a defense against induced infringement because the FDA "is not the arbiter of patent infringement issues."[146]

The Court also agreed with the district court that distribution of Apotex's drug would cause AstraZeneca irreparable harm.[147] First, AstraZeneca had an exclusive licensing deal with Teva to distribute a generic version of AstraZeneca's asthma medication.[148] It would not be possible to accurately calculate the economic harm to both AstraZeneca and Teva that would result if Apotex's drug went on the market.[149] Second, there would also be unquantifiable damage to its reputation and goodwill if Apotex's drug were put on the market and then subsequently removed.[150] This is because there would likely be consumer confusion and harm to AstraZeneca's good will if Apotex's drug went to market and was then subsequently pulled from the market because at trial it was determined that Apotex's drug did infringe on AstraZeneca's patents.[151] Third, premature entry of a generic version of AstraZeneca's drug would force AstraZeneca to lay off personnel and those damages would also be large and unquantifiable.[152] Therefore, the Federal Circuit affirmed the preliminary injunction because the Court found there was no abuse of discretion by the district court in its analysis of whether AstraZeneca would likely succeed on the merits and suffer irreparable harm.[153]

In contrast, the Federal Circuit in *Takeda Pharms* affirmed the district court's denial of Takeda's motion for a preliminary injunction against defendants West-Ward Pharmaceutical Corporation, Hikma Americas Inc. and Hikma Pharmaceuticals PLC

141. *Id.* at 1049.
142. *Id.* at 1053-54.
143. *Id.* at 1050-56.
144. *Id.* at 1058-59.
145. *Id.* at 1061.
146. *Id.*
147. *Id.* at 1063.
148. *Id.* at 1061.
149. *Id.* at 1062.
150. *Id.*
151. *Id.*
152. *Id.* at 1063.
153. *Id.* at 1065.

(collectively "Hikma").[154] Colchicine itself, which has known medicinal use, is not covered by Takeda's patents.[155] Takeda owned patents directed at using colchicine to treat acute gout flare ups.[156] Takeda also owned "drug-drug-interaction" patents which articulated methods for using "colchicine for prophylaxis of gout in patents who [were] concomitantly taking certain drug inhibitors."[157] Takeda had FDA approval via the New Drug Application (NDA) process to market colchline under the brand name Colcrys for gout flare ups.[158] Hikma also filed an NDA and received FDA approval to market colchicine for prophylaxis of gout flares under the name Mitigare.[159] Takeda sued Hikma asserting both direct and induced infringement claims against Hikma based on its Mitigare label.[160] Hikma did not include a "Paragraph IV" filing in its FDA approval application certifying that Mitigare did not infringe on Takeda's patents or that Takeda's patents were invalid because Hikma did not seek FDA approval for use covered by Takeda's patents.[161] Hikma also relied on older FDA findings that colchicine was safe and efficacious.[162] According to Hikma's label, Hikma planned on marketing Mitigare for prophylaxis of gout and not acute gout flare ups.[163] "The label also said that '[i]f you have a gout flare while taking [Mitigare], tell your healthcare provider.'"[164] The district court denied Takeda's preliminary injunction motion on the grounds that "Takeda did not meet its burden of showing a likelihood of success on the merits for its direct or induced infringement claims or irreparable injury."[165]

Takeda appealed to the Federal Circuit and argued Hikma's label induced physicians to infringe on its method claims.[166] Particularly, in case of a flare up, a physician would tell patients to use Mitigare, which would infringe on Takeda's claims that articulate to use colchicine for gout flare ups.[167] Takeda asserted that the present case was like the situation in *AstraZeneca LP v Apotex, Inc.*[168] and Hikma's label was evidence of induced infringement.[169] The Federal Circuit disagreed and stated that in *AstraZeneca*, while the label did not expressly direct drug users to infringe because it did not say to use the drug "once a day" which would constitute infringement, the label did say to use the lowest possible dose, which would result in once daily dosing.[170] The Court determined that present circumstance was different because unlike the drug label in *AstraZeneca,*[171] Hikma's label instruction was not enough to

154. *Takeda Pharms, U.S.A., Inc v West-Ward Pharm. Corp.*, 785 F.3d 625, 627 (Fed. Cir. 2015).
155. *Takeda* Pharms, 785 F.3d at 627.
156. *Id.*
157. *Id.*
158. *Id.* at 628.
159. *Id.*
160. *Id.*
161. *Id.* at 629.
162. *Id.*
163. *Id.* at 630.
164. *Id.*
165. *Id.* at 628.
166. *Id.* at 630.
167. *Id.*
168. *AstraZeneca*, 633 F.3d 1042.
169. *Id.* at 634.
170. *Id.*
171. *AstraZeneca*, at 1059.

"'necessarily lead' to infringement" and "evidence of knowledge of infringing uses is not sufficient to prove induced infringement."[172] Takeda also argued that Hikma's label was also evidence of direct infringement of its drug-drug interaction method claims because the "label warn[ed] patients that co-administration of colchicine and certain inhibitors 'have been reported to lead to colchicine toxicity,' that drug interactions must thus 'be considered prior to and during therapy,' and that concomitant use 'should be avoided if possible.'"[173] The Court rejected Takeda's argument because the label indicated that concomitant use of colchicine with other drugs should be avoided instead of prescribed.[174] Therefore, the Court affirmed the district court's preliminary injunction denial because Takeda had not shown it would likely succeed in trial at showing that Hikma had directly or induced others to infringe on its patents.[175]

3. *Enforcement of judgments*

If a patent holder is granted an injunction (preliminary or permanent) or damages by a court and the adverse party (in this case, the copyist) does not comply with the court's ruling, the court has the authority to enforce its judgment.[176] In the case of injunctions, the court can find the copyist in contempt of court.[177]

VIII. Validity

1. *Relevance for infringement cases*

In U.S. law, infringement and validity of the patent are two separate issues. Indeed, the Supreme Court has explained that when infringement is the issue, the validity of the patent is not the question to be confronted. [178] In fact, the two issues are treated in separate parts of the Patent Act.[179]

2. *Specifics for second medical use claims*

The general rules of patent validity are also true for second medical use claims.

D. SUMMARY

Under United States law, patent protection for medical treatments is broadly available, covering both new uses of previously known pharmaceutical compounds and previously known medical devices. The proper format for such claims is a "method

172. *Takeda Pharms*, at 634.
173. *Id.*
174. *Id.* at 635.
175. *Id.* at 635.
176. Fed. R. Civ. P. 70.
177. Fed. R. Civ.P. 70(e).
178. *Commil USA, LLC v Cisco Systems, Inc.*, 135 S. Ct. 1920 (2015).
179. *Id.* at 1928.

of treatment" reciting the active steps of the new use. Claims reciting a product limited only by an intended use or that do not recite an active step are currently impermissible. United States law provides that medical practitioners are exempt from liability for performance of a medical activity that constitutes an infringement. However, under current law, medical practitioners are not exempt for liability for the use of a patented drug or the practice of a patented use of a drug. Method of medical treatment claims can be enforced on the basis of either direct or indirect infringement. In order to prove indirect infringement, it generally must be shown that at least one party is a direct infringer. Thus, proof that a manufacturer of a medical product is indirectly infringing a claim directed to a method of medical treatment will often require proof that a medical practitioner is carrying out the steps of that claim, even if the medical practitioner is exempt from liability.

United States practitioners broadly agree that harmonization is desirable in this area. Many believe that "method of treatment" claims represent the most desirable format, provided that a broad exemption from liability of medical practitioners is adopted. Other practitioners believe that such method claims may be perceived as inflammatory even with a broad exemption for medical practitioners.

Canada

Steven Garland, Dan Davies, Dr. Lei Liu

A. AVAILABILITY OF PROTECTION

I. Legal framework

1. National statutory laws

The Canadian patent system is governed by the Federal Patent Act.

Section 2 of the Canadian Patent Act defines the term "invention" as "any new and useful art, process, machine, manufacture or composition of matter." Therefore, subject matter must fall within one of the categories to be patentable. The Supreme Court of Canada has held that these categories of patentable subject matter are exhaustive.[1] Additionally, the Patent Act specifically bars "any mere scientific principle or abstract theorem" from being patented.[2] There are no other restrictions in the current Patent Act on the types of subject matter that can be patented, though some further prohibitions arise pursuant to the jurisprudence.

The Patented Medicines (Notice of Compliance) Regulations ("NOC Regulations") serve to link Canada's patent and pharmaceutical regulatory regimes. Under the NOC Regulations, a subsequent entry manufacturer ("SEM") seeking regulatory approval of a generic drug or subsequent entry biologic ("SEB") must address patents that are listed on the Patent Register against an innovator's drug or biologic for which the innovator has obtained approval (receipt of an NOC[3]) and to which the generic drug or SEB is directly or indirectly compared. An SEM in addressing such listed patents must either indicate that it will not seek an NOC in advance of

1. *Harvard College v Canada (Commissioner of Patents)*, 2002 SCC 76 ("*Harvard*").
2. Patent Act, s. 27(8).
3. A Notice of Compliance is a notification, issued pursuant to paragraph C.08.004(1)(a) of the Food and Drug Regulations, indicating that a manufacturer has complied with sections C.08.002 or C.08.003 and C.08.005.1 of the Food and Drug Regulations. An NOC is required in order to sell a drug product in Canada.

the patents expiring, or otherwise allege in a Notice of Allegation that the patents are invalid and/or not infringed.

1.1 *Pharmaceuticals*

A patent containing claims directed to second medical uses of pharmaceuticals may be eligible for listing in the Patent Register, and thus can trigger the NOC Regulations when an SEM attempts market entry. If an SEM serves a Notice of Allegation alleging that a listed patent is invalid or not infringed, the innovator may in response to the Notice of Allegation bring an Application to prohibit the Minister of Health from granting an NOC to the generic. In the application, the innovator must establish that the generic manufacturer's invalidity and/or non-infringement allegations are not justified. Upon commencement of an NOC proceeding by the innovator, Health Canada is prohibited from issuing an NOC to the SEM for up to 24 months, or until the proceeding is decided, whichever is earlier.

Another form of protection for pharmaceuticals is data protection, a form of exclusivity under the Food and Drug Regulations ("FDR") that protects the data filed in support of a regulatory submission for an "innovative drug"[4] for which an NOC issued on or after June 10, 2006.[5] Subsequent regulatory approvals for second medical uses will not extend data protection afforded by the first NOC.

1.2 *Biologics*

Biologics are governed by the same NOC Regulations. The data protection provisions also apply equally to pharmaceuticals and biologics.

2. *International treaties*

2.1 *TRIPS*

Canada is a member of the World Trade Organization ("WTO") and is thus required to ensure its pharmaceutical patent laws are harmonized with the criteria as set out in the Agreement on Trade-Related Aspects of Intellectual Property Rights ("TRIPS"). Canada's harmonization of its patent law in line with the TRIPS Agreement is

4. An "innovative drug" is defined in Food and Drug Regulations, CRC, c 870 as amended (FDR) at s. C.08.004.1(1) as "a drug that contains a medicinal ingredient not previously approved in a drug by the Minister and that is not a variation of previously approved medicinal ingredient such as a salt, ester, enantiomer, solvate or polymorph."
5. An SEM may not file a submission making a direct or indirect comparison to an innovative drug until six years after issuance of the innovator's first NOC for the innovative drug. There is a further two years of market exclusivity, which prohibits the Minister from issuing an SEM NOC. Additional six months of protection can be obtained if information regarding pediatric use is provided and there is no requirement for obtaining a pediatric indication. Thus, the total period of protection is eight years (or eight and a half years if the pediatric extension applies) from the innovator's first NOC.

expressed in Bill S-17, An Act to Amend the Patent Act, which became law on June 14, 2001.

2.2 *FTAs*

Canada is also a member of a number of free trade agreements, including: Canada-Korea Free Trade Agreement, Canada-Honduras Free Trade Agreement, Canada-Panama Trade Agreement, Canada-Jordan Free Trade Agreement, Canada-Columbia Free Trade Agreement, Canada-Peru Free Trade Agreement, Canada-European Free Trade Association, Canada-Costa Rica Free Trade Agreement, Canada-Chile Free Trade Agreement, Canada-Israel Free Trade Agreement, and the North American Free Trade Agreement ("NAFTA") between Canada, the United States and Mexico.

3. *Availability through case law*

In Canada, claims that recite or are directed to methods of medical treatment are considered to be unpatentable. The seminal Supreme Court of Canada decision in *Tennessee Eastman Co. v Canada (Commissioner of Patents)*[6] ('*Tennessee Eastman*') is the leading authority concerning the prohibition against patent claims for methods of medical treatment. In *Tennessee Eastman*, the applicant had discovered that a known adhesive was able to bond human tissue and could therefore be used to close wounds in surgical procedures, and claimed a "method for surgical bonding of body tissues which comprises applying to at least one of the tissue surfaces to be bonded an adhesive composition comprising a monomeric ester of a-cyanoacrylic acid of" a specifically defined chemical formula.

In holding that the claims at issue were not patentable as a method of medical treatment, the Supreme Court reasoned that if a method of medical or surgical treatment fell within the definition of "invention" (as a "process"), "then the inventor, by making such a process claim, would have an easy way out of the restriction in s. 41(1)."[7]

Section 41(1) of the Patent Act referred to in *Tennessee Eastman*, as it stood at the time, served to restrict the scope of patents "relating to substances prepared or produced by chemical processes and intended for food or medicine" such that medicines could be claimed only in product-by-process form.[8]

While section 41(1) is no longer in the Patent Act, the prohibition against patent claims for methods of medical treatments remains.[9]

Despite the jurisprudence-based prohibition against the patentability of methods of medical treatment in Canada, it is possible to obtain protection for inventions

6. *Tennessee Eastman Co. v Canada (Commissioner of Patents)*, [1974] S.C.R. 111.
7. *Ibid.* at para. 14.
8. Patent Act, R.S.C. 1952, c. 203.
9. The Supreme Court of Canada, in an *obiter* statement in *Shell Oil Co. v Commissioner of Patents*, [1982] 2 S.C.R. 536, further explained the decision in *Tennessee Eastman* as follows: "[i]n effect, [the invention in *Tennessee Eastman*] was not patentable because it was essentially non-economic and unrelated to trade, industry or commerce. It was related rather to the area of profession skills."

relating to the use of compounds to treat medical conditions by presenting method claims as use claims. Indeed, drafting second medical use claims had been a widely used practice in response to the method of medical treatment prohibition decision of *Tennessee Eastman*. However, it was not until *Apotex Inc. v Wellcome Foundation Ltd.* ('*Wellcome Foundation*'),[10] almost 30 years after *Tennessee Eastman*, that the validity of one specific form of use claim was upheld by the Supreme Court of Canada.

In *Wellcome Foundation*, the Supreme Court of Canada held claims directed to formulations comprising a known compound (AZT) for use in the treatment of HIV/AIDS as well as claims directed to the containerized product (a "kit" claim) to be patentable, including the following:

> "21. A pharmaceutical formulation for use in the treatment or prophylaxis of human retrovirus infections comprising an effective amount of 3'-azido-3'-deoxythymidine [AZT] in association with a pharmaceutically acceptable carrier.
>
> 24. A containerized pharmaceutical product comprising a container containing a formulation comprising 3'-azido-3'-deoxythymidine [AZT] and a pharmaceutically acceptable carrier thereof, and instructions associated with said container directing use of the formulation in the treatment or prophylaxis of AIDS."

In *Wellcome Foundation*, the Supreme Court distinguished composition-for-use-type claims from methods of medical treatment, commenting:

> "*Tennessee Eastman* was concerned with the patentability of a surgical method for joining incisions or wounds by applying certain compounds. The decision was based on the former s. 41 of the Patent Act, now repealed. The Court concluded that the method (apart from the compounds) was not patentable. The policy rationale, as explained by Wilson J. in *Shell Oil, supra*, at p. 554, was that the unpatentable claim was
>
> > ... essentially non-economic and unrelated to trade, industry, or commerce. It was related rather to the area of professional skills.
>
> The AZT patent does not seek to "fence in" an area of medical treatment. It seeks the exclusive right to provide AZT as a commercial offering. How and when, if at all, AZT is employed is left to the professional skill and judgment of the medical profession."[11]

It is important to note that the claims upheld in *Wellcome Foundation* are not directed to use *per se*, and that the Supreme Court drew a distinction between a claim directed to a matter of "professional skill and judgment" and a claim directed to a "commercial offering."

Not long after the Supreme Court of Canada upheld the validity of "composition for use" claims in *Wellcome Foundation*, there were a series of decisions whereby lower courts considered the patentability of claims relating to various dosage regimes (e.g., dosage range and schedule).

---

10. *Apotex Inc. v Wellcome Foundation Ltd.*, 2002 SCC 77 ("*Wellcome Foundation*").
11. *Ibid.* at paras. 49-50.

Representative claims for dosage regimes that were held to be patentable by the courts include:

- use claims, pharmaceutical composition for use claims and compound for use claims relating to alendronate used in the treatment of osteoporosis, reciting a specific dosage of alendronate ("about 70 mg") and a fixed dosing schedule ("once weekly");[12]
- a use claim relating to azithromycin used in the treatment of an antimicrobial infection, specifying the use of the compound in patients who have eaten;[13]
- a use claim relating to finasteride used in the treatment of male pattern baldness, reciting a specific dosage ("about 1.0 mg");[14]
- a use claim relating to Bayer's medicine YAZ (drospirenone and ethinylestradiol) used for birth control, reciting a single dosage of each of two compounds;[15]
- use claims relating to HUMIRA (an anti-TNF alpha antibody) used in the treatment of an arthritic disease or an inflammatory bowel disease, reciting a specified fixed amount (40 mg) and fixed interval (bi-weekly).[16]

Representative claims for dosage regimes that were held to be non-patentable by the courts as being methods of medical treatment (in encompassing the skill and judgment of the physician) include:

- a composition for use claim relating to Urso® (ursodeoxyscholic acid) used in the treatment of primary biliary cirrhosis, reciting "a dose of 13 to 15 mg/kg/day"; [17]
- a use claim relating to the medicine galantamine used in the treatment of Alzheimer's disease, reciting "from a first dosage of about 8 mg/day to a final dosage of about 16 mg/day to 24 mg/day" and "said first dosage is for use for a period from about two weeks to about ten weeks";[18]
- use claims relating to Novartis' ACLASTA (zoledronic acid) used in the treatment of a condition of abnormally increased bone turnover, reciting "intermittent administration, with a period of about one year between a first administration and each subsequent administration in the intermittent administration."[19]

The current jurisprudence appears to suggest that when second medical use claims recite a dosage regimen, the patentability of such claims could be challenged as methods of medical treatment claims even if they are not written as method claims. Under the current law, if an invention resides in providing a choice of a treatment, be it a dosage or a treatment interval, the claims (no matter in which form they

12. *Merck & Co. v Apotex Inc.* 2005 FC 755.
13. *Pfizer Canada Inc. v Apotex Inc.* 2005 FC 1421.
14. *Merck & Co. v Pharmascience Inc.* 2010 FC 510.
15. *Bayer Inc. v Cobalt Pharmaceuticals Co.* 2013 FC 1061.
16. *Abbvie Biotechnology Ltd. v Canada (Attorney General)* 2014 FC 1251.
17. *Axcan Pharma Inc. v Pharmascience Inc.* 2006 FC 527.
18. *Janssen Inc. v Mylan Pharmaceuticals ULC* 2010 FC 1123, appeal dismissed for mootness 2011 FCA 16.
19. *Novartis Pharmaceuticals Canada Inc.v. Cobalt Pharmaceuticals* 2013 FC 985 ("*Novartis*").

are written) are likely to be considered unpatentable as being methods of medical treatment.

4. *Patent term extension*

Currently, the Patent Act does not provide for any measures to restore patent term for loss of effective term caused by the time required for regulatory approval. This may soon change in view of the consolidated text of the Comprehensive Economic and Trade Agreement (CETA) which was released to the public in September of 2014.[20] CETA is a free trade agreement between Canada and the European Union that has been in negotiations since 2009.

Chapter 22 of the consolidated CETA text addresses intellectual property and contains two provisions that relate to patent protection for drugs in Canada, namely (1) the availability of patent term restoration (PTR), which effectively extends the patent term to account for marketing delays resulting from the time required to obtain regulatory approval,[21] and (2) the implementation of "equivalent and effective right of appeal" for all litigants that engage in a "linkage" mechanism where the granting of market authorization for pharmaceuticals is linked with patent protection (this is a reference to proceedings under the NOC Regulations, discussed above).[22]

Regarding the patent term restoration provision, Article 9.2, entitled "*Sui Generis* Protection for Pharmaceuticals," outlines the parties' obligations regarding PTR as follows:

- The protection will apply to a product defined as "the active ingredient or combination of active ingredients of a pharmaceutical product" that is protected by a basic patent defined as "a patent which protects a product as such, a process to obtain a product or an application of a product in force."
- The protection will be granted upon request by the "holder of the patent or his successor in title" provided:
  a. marketing approval for the product has been granted;
  b. the product has not already been the subject of protection; and
  c. the marketing approval is the first such approval as a pharmaceutical product.
- There may be only one term of protection per product, and if the product is protected by more than one patent, the single applicable patent will be selected as follows:
  a. where all the patents are owned by the same person, selected by the person requesting the protection; and

20. Government of Canada, "Canada-European Union: Comprehensive Economic and Trade Agreement (CETA) Consolidated Text," online: Foreign Affairs, Trade and Development Canada <http://www.international.gc.ca/trade-agreements-accords-commerciaux/agr-acc/ceta-aecg/text-texte/toc-tdm.aspx?lang=eng> (CETA text).
21. *Ibid.* at Chapter 22 Article 9.2.
22. *Ibid.* at Chapter 22 Article 9 bis.

b. where the patents are not owned by the same person and this gives rise to conflicting requests, selected by agreement between the "patent holders."

- The period of protection will commence at the end of the lawful term of the relevant patent. The term will be for "a period equal to the period which elapsed between the date on which the application for a patent was filed and the date of the first authorization to place the product on the market of that Party as a pharmaceutical product reduced by a period of five years," which "may not exceed a period of two to five years, to be established by each Party."[23]
- The protection will extend only to the pharmaceutical product covered by the marketing approval and any use of that product as a pharmaceutical product approved before the expiry of the protection. The protection will confer the same rights as conferred by the patent and will be subject to the same limitations and obligations.
- The protection may be revoked if the patent is invalidated, the claims of the patent no longer cover the product, marketing approval is withdrawn, or if the protection had been granted contrary to the requirements set forth in Article 9.2.

II. Policy considerations

1. Health and social issues

There is no applicable Canadian content.

2. Legal issues

Similar to the patent law in many other countries, the requirement that an invention have utility is one of the key conditions for patentability. Section 2 of the Canadian Patent Act defines an "invention" as "... any new and *useful* art, process, machine, manufacture or composition of matter ..." (emphasis added) or improvement thereof.

An aspect of Canadian law of utility is the concept of a "promise" of a patent. Briefly stated, to satisfy the requirement for utility, no particular level of utility is required, and a "mere scintilla" of utility will suffice, unless the patent promises some elevated level of utility.[24]

The courts have concluded that a "promise" of utility in the patent should be "clear and unambiguous" and constitute an "explicit promise of a specific result," and that not every patent will necessarily contain a promise of utility.[25] However, for a second medical use invention, the claimed new use of a known compound

23. The Canadian government has publicly suggested that it intends to set the maximum time available at two years.
24. *Eli Lilly Canada Inc. et al. v Novopharm Limited* 2010 FCA 197 at para. 76; *Sanofi-Aventis v Apotex Inc.* 2013 FCA 186 (clopidogrel) at paras. 49 and 54.
25. *Sanofi-Aventis* (clopidogrel), *ibid.* at para. 66.; *Pfizer Canada Inc. v Apotex Inc.* 2014 FCA 250 at paras. 65-67.

presumably promises that the compound is useful for the claimed purpose. In other words, second medical use inventions would at least "promise" the claimed uses (see section B.II.2 below for a further discussion on this point).

Once the applicable level of utility is established ("mere scintilla" or a "promise" of a specific utility), the patentee must be able to show that, as of the Canadian application *filing date* (which, for a national phase entry case, is the PCT international filing date), the utility of the invention either had been demonstrated or could be "soundly predicted."[26]

With respect to demonstrated utility, the patentee is permitted to rely on data obtained *before* the filing date that is not disclosed in the patent.[27] However, it may be necessary that the patent at least make reference to a study from which the data demonstrating utility was obtained.[28] The threshold for demonstrated utility can be high depending on the "promise," if any, of the patent, particularly in pharmaceutical cases, in which pre-filing clinical studies have been found in some cases to be insufficient to constitute demonstrated utility, for example, on the basis that the study was not of sufficient scale or duration.[29]

For a "sound prediction" of utility, there must be:

(1) a factual basis for the prediction;
(2) an articulable and sound line of reasoning from which the desired result can be inferred from the factual basis; and
(3) proper disclosure.[30]

A number of Federal Court and Federal Court of Appeal decisions have held that based on the earlier decision of the Supreme Court of Canada in *Wellcome Foundation*, the factual basis and line of reasoning for a sound prediction must be disclosed in the patent (sometimes referred to as an enhanced or elevated disclosure requirement) or be within the common general knowledge of the person of ordinary skill in the art.[31] However, the law is currently unsettled as to what, if anything, must be disclosed in the patent in order to support a sound prediction in view of recent *obiter* comments of the Supreme Court of Canada in *Teva Canada Ltd. v Pfizer Canada Inc.*,[32] wherein the Supreme Court of Canada noted that its earlier *Wellcome Foundation* decision does not stand for the proposition that there is any enhanced disclosure requirement for

26. *Sanofi-Aventis* (clopidogrel), *ibid.*, at para. 46.
27. *Teva Canada Ltd. v Pfizer Canada Inc.* 2012 SCC 60 (sildenafil) at para. 42. The patent referenced but did not disclose the results of a pre-filing clinical trial demonstrating the use of sildenafil citrate to treat erectile dysfunction.
28. See e.g. *Laboratoires Servier and Servier Canada Inc. v Canada (Health)*, 2015 FC 108 at paras. 213-216, citing *Apotex Inc. v Pfizer Canada Inc.*, 2011 FCA 236 at para. 30. However, the issue is unsettled. More recently courts have found that there is no requirement to make reference in the patent to the study demonstrating utility: see e.g. *Eli Lilly Canada Inc. v Apotex Inc.*, 2015 FC 1016 at para. 142.
29. See e.g. *Eli Lilly & Co. v Teva Canada Limited* 2011 FCA 220 at paras. 31-43.
30. *Wellcome Foundation*, *supra* note 10, at para. 70.
31. *Eli Lilly Canada Inc. v Apotex Inc.* 2009 FCA 97 at para. 15; *Eli Lilly and Company v Teva Canada Limited* 2011 FCA 220 at para. 57; *Bell Helicopter Textron Canada Limitée v Eurocopter 2013 FCA 219* at para. 155.
32. *Teva* (Slidenafil), *supra* note 27, at paras. 37 and 40.

the purposes of sound prediction and the issue of utility. Subsequently, some lower courts have also questioned whether there is any such disclosure requirement based on utility, and suggested that at best it may be limited to new use patents.[33] The issue of whether the utility requirement creates an enhanced disclosure requirement in the patent is expected to be considered by the Supreme Court of Canada in *AstraZeneca Canada Inc., et al. v Apotex Inc., et al.*,[34] the hearing for which is expected to be heard in November 2016.

B. VALIDITY

I. Allowable claim wording

1. Product claims

Product claims are generally acceptable in Canada. However, product claims for "higher life forms," such as transgenic animals or plants, are not patentable subject matter.[35] A cell of a higher life form, methods of making highlife forms, and use of a higher life form, on the other hand, may constitute patentable subject matter.[36]

2. Method claims

As stated above in section A.I.3, methods of medical treatment claims are not permissible in Canada. With regard to business methods, the Court has stated in *Canada (Attorney General) v Amazon.com, Inc.*,[37] that "no Canadian jurisprudence determines conclusively that a business method cannot be patentable subject matter" and the Patent Office should have a mind open to the possibility that a novel business method may be patentable.

3. Use claims

In *Shell Oil Co. v Canada (Commissioner of Patents)*,[38] the Supreme Court of Canada was asked to determine whether new uses for known compounds were patentable. The Court allowed the claims, holding that a new use (i.e., as plant growth regulators) for previously known chemical compounds constitutes a patentable "new and useful art." In addition, as discussed in section A.I.3 above, claims directed to formulations

33. *AstraZeneca Canada Inc. v Apotex Inc.*, 2014 FC 638. Justice Rennie (as he then was), distinguished *Wellcome Foundation* by limiting Justice Binnie's remarks concerning disclosure to new use patents. However, in *Eli Lilly Canada Inc.v. The Minister of Health et al.*, 2016 FC 47, Justice Barnes disagreed with Justice Rennie and held that there remains a requirement to disclose the factual basis and sound line of reasoning in the specification for patents not relating to new uses.
34. SCC Case Information: 36654.
35. *Harvard, supra* note 1.
36. *Monsanto Canada Inc. v Schmeiser*, 2004 SCC 34.
37. *Canada (Attorney General) v Amazon.com, Inc.* 2011 FCA 328 ("*Amazon.com*").
38. *Shell Oil Co. v Canada (Commissioner of Patents)*, [1982] 67 C.P.R. (2d) 1 (S.C.C.).

comprising a known compound (AZT) for use in the treatment of HIV/AIDS were held to be patentable by the Supreme Court in *Wellcome Foundation*.[39]

4. *System claims*

It is possible to protect computer implemented inventions in the form of system claims. In *Amazon.com*,[40] both system claims and method claims were held by the Court of Appeal to be patentable.

5. *Dosage regimes*

See section A.I.3. above.

6. *Patient groups*

No court decision has dealt with the patentability of second medical use claims where the invention resides in identification of a novel patient group (e.g., a patient group identified by a biomarker). Based on its interpretation of jurisprudence, the Patent Office considers such claims to be patentable but suggests that such claims may nonetheless lack novelty.[41]

II. Novelty

1. *General definition of novelty and prior art*

Section 28.2(1)(a) and (b) of the Canadian Patent Act, governing novelty in Canada, state that the claimed invention in a Canadian patent application must not have been disclosed:

(a) more than one year before the filing date by the applicant, or by a person who obtained knowledge, directly or indirectly, from the applicant, in such a manner that the subject-matter became available to the public in Canada or elsewhere; or
(b) before the claim date by a person not mentioned in paragraph (a) in such a manner that the subject-matter became available to the public in Canada or elsewhere.

Section 28.3 of the Canadian Patent Act, governing obviousness, has a similar provision in respect of what constitutes relevant prior art. Thus, the statute provides a one-year grace period for disclosures made by the applicant. This one-year grace period runs from the filing date in Canada, *not* the priority date. In the case of a PCT national phase entry, the Canadian filing date is deemed to be the PCT international filing date.

39. *Wellcome Foundation.*, *supra* note 7.
40. *Amazon.com*, *supra* note 37.
41. Patent Notice: Revised Examination Practice Respecting Medical Uses – PN 2015-01.

In order for a claim to be anticipated, the Supreme Court of Canada in *Sanofi*[42] has indicated that two requirements must be met: first, there must be a disclosure of the invention as claimed; secondly, that disclosure must be enabling.

The disclosure requirement is set out in *Beloit Canada Ltd. v Valmet OY*,[43] cited with approval by the Supreme Court of Canada in *Free World Trust v* Électro *Santé Inc.*[44] and *Sanofi*. Anticipation requires that a single prior disclosure contain sufficient information such that the skilled person will be led inevitably to the claimed invention:

> "One must, in effect, be able to look at a prior, single publication and find in it all the information which, for practical purposes, is needed to produce the claimed invention without the exercise of any inventive skill. The prior publication must contain so clear a direction that a skilled person reading and following it would in every case and without possibility of error be led to the claimed invention."

The Supreme Court of Canada in *Sanofi* further buttresses *Beloit*'s requirement of "without possibility of error" by citing the following excerpt from the English Court of Appeal in *General Tire & Rubber Co. v Firestone Tyre & Rubber Co.*, [1972] R.P.C. 457, at p. 486:

> "If, on the other hand, the prior publication contains a direction which is capable of being carried out in a manner which would infringe the patentee's claim, but would be at least as likely to be carried out in a way which would not do so, the patentee's claim will not have been anticipated, although it may fail on the ground of obviousness. To anticipate the patentee's claim the prior publication must contain clear and unmistakable directions to do what the patentee claims to have invented ..."

In terms of the enablement requirement, according to *Sanofi*, a skilled person is permitted to engage in trial and error experiments to make the disclosure work:

> "[27] Once the subject matter of the invention is disclosed by the prior patent, the person skilled in the art is assumed to be willing to make trial and error experiments to get it to work. *While trial and error experimentation is permitted at the enablement stage, it is not at the disclosure stage.* For purposes of enablement, the question is no longer what the skilled person would think the disclosure of the prior patent meant, but whether he or she would be able to work the invention." [Emphasis added]

2. Definition of skilled person

In *Beloit*, a person skilled in the art is described as:

> "the technician skilled in the art but having no scintilla of inventiveness or imagination; a paragon of deduction and dexterity, wholly devoid of intuition; a triumph of the left hemisphere over the right. The question to be asked is whether this mythical creature (the man in the Clapham omnibus of patent law)

42. *Apotex Inc. v Sanofi-Synthelabo Canada*, 2008 SCC 61. (*Sanofi*)
43. *Beloit Canada Ltd. v Valmet OY* (1986), 8 C.P.R. (3d) 289 (F.C.A.) at p. 297 ("|*Beloit*").
44. *Free World Trust v* Électro *Santé Inc.*, 2000 SCC 66.

would, in the light of the state of the art and of common general knowledge as at the claimed date of invention, have come directly and without difficulty to the solution taught by the patent."[45]

3. *Scope of disclosure*

3.1 General rules

See section B.II.1.

3.2 First medical use

The Canadian Patent Office may allow first medical use claims (e.g., use of a compound X as a medicament) if the compound is a novel chemical entity. To the authors' best knowledge, the validity of such claims has not been considered by courts.

3.3 New subject matter

There is no applicable Canadian content.

3.4 New data

There is no applicable Canadian content.

4. *Requirements for second medical use*

4.1 Distinction from first medical use

Permitted second medical use claims typically relate to new uses in respect of specific diseases and/or conditions, and may optionally contain features defining patient populations and/or dosage regimes.

4.2 Sub-species of first medical use

There is no applicable Canadian content.

4.3 Dosage regimes

In *Merck & Co. v Apotex Inc.*,[46] the Court found that none of the prior art references anticipated various forms of use claims reciting a specific dosage of alendronate ("about 70 mg") and a fixed dosing schedule ("once weekly") because "[t]he articles

45. *Beloit, supra* note 43.
46. *Supra* note 12.

indicate that they are positing hypotheses and that these ideas require further testing."[47]

In *Pfizer Canada Inc. v Apotex Inc.*,[48] the Court found that the claim at issue relating to azithromycin in a pharmaceutical dosage form which does not exhibit an adverse food effect used in the treatment of an antimicrobial infection, specifying that the patient receiving the treatment has eaten, was not anticipated by any of the prior art references. It was known that the oral bioavailability of azithromycin in the capsule form was adversely affected by the presence of food in the patient's system. Although Apotex argued that the prior art references did not restrict the use of azithromycin with or without food, the Court recognized that none of them discussed or mentioned an adverse food effect and stated that "to conclude that the tablets disclosed in that patent do not exhibit a food effect, one has to have reference to the test results obtained for the dosage forms disclosed in [Pfizer's patent at issue]."[49]

In *Merck & Co. v Pharmascience Inc.*,[50] the Court found that the claim at issue relating to finasteride used in the treatment of male pattern baldness, reciting a specific dosage ("about 1.0 mg"), is not novel. The prior art references only disclosed a range of dosages from 5 mg/day to 2000 mg/day. However, in reaching the conclusion of lack of novelty, the Court stated that "the selection of a dosage range was within the skill of an ordinary person skilled in the art" and that "[n]o new technical feature has been disclosed or claimed" respecting the dosage of 1 mg/day.[51] Notably, the Court appeared to have accepted the "new technical effect" test set forth in a decision of the Enlarged Board of Appeal of the European Patent Office relied on by Pharmascience.[52]

In *Axcan Pharma Inc. v Pharmascience Inc.*,[53] the Court found that the claim at issue to be novel over prior art for reciting a dosage range of Urso® (i.e., 13 to 15 mg/kg/day) outside the teachings of the prior art. The prior art included prior knowledge of Urso® (which was known as a liver medication since 1957) and the prior publication of a dosage of 10 mg/kg/day of the drug for treating chronic liver diseases.

5. *Timing issues*

There is no applicable Canadian content.

47. *Ibid.* at para [119].
48. *Supra* note 13.
49. *Ibid.* at para. [97].
50. *Supra* note 14.
51. *Ibid.* at para. [176].
52. Pharmascience argued that "all that [Merck's patent at issue] does is to use adjectives such as "unexpected" or "surprising" and offers no solid foundation for distinguishing itself from the prior art, nor distancing itself from any previous prejudices" and relied on *Kos Life Sciences*, Case No. G 0002/08 decided by the Enlarged Board of Appeal of the European Patent Office February 19, 2010. According to Pharmascience, *Kos Life Sciences* requires that "a subsequent invention that comes within broader disclosures in the prior art must distinguish itself so as to provide "a particular technical effect as compared with the known state of the art" and, in considering dosage selected from a prior broader disclosure a "new technical effect" must be considered." *Ibid.* at para. [175].
53. *Supra* note 17.

III. Inventive step/non-obviousness

1. *Definition of inventive step/non-obviousness*

See section B.III.3. below.

2. *Same scope of disclosure as for novelty*

There is no applicable Canadian content.

3. *Assessment of inventive step/non-obviousness*

The Supreme Court of Canada in *Sanofi* also sets out the Canadian approach to obviousness, with the Court adopting the approach taken in the United Kingdom:

> "[67] It will be useful in an obviousness inquiry to follow the four-step approach first outlined by Oliver L.J. in *Windsurfing International Inc. v Tabur Marine (Great Britain) Ltd.*, [1985] R.P.C. 59 (C.A.). This approach should bring better structure to the obviousness inquiry and more objectivity and clarity to the analysis. The Windsurfing approach was recently updated by Jacob L.J. in *Pozzoli SPA v BDMO SA*, [2007] F.S.R. 37 (p. 872), [2007] EWCA Civ 588, at para. 23:
>
> 'In the result I would *restate* the *Windsurfing* questions thus:
> (1) (a) Identify the notional "person skilled in the art";
> (b) Identify the relevant common general knowledge of that person;
> (2) Identify the inventive concept of the claim in question or if that cannot readily be done, construe it;
> (3) Identify what, if any, differences exist between the matter cited as forming part of the "state of the art" and the inventive concept of the claim or the claim as construed;
> (4) Viewed without any knowledge of the alleged invention as claimed, do those differences constitute steps which would have been obvious to the person skilled in the art or do they require any degree of invention?' [Emphasis added.]
>
> It will be at the fourth step of the *Windsurfing/Pozzoli* approach to obviousness that the issue of 'obvious to try' will arise."

This decision of the Supreme Court also supports the application of an "obvious to try" analysis, in appropriate circumstances and with the following limitations:

> "[69] If an 'obvious to try' test is warranted, the following factors should be taken into consideration at the fourth step of the obviousness inquiry. As with anticipation, this list is not exhaustive. The factors will apply in accordance with the evidence in each case.
> 1. Is it more or less self-evident that what is being tried ought to work? Are there a finite number of identified predictable solutions known to persons skilled in the art?
> 2. What is the extent, nature and amount of effort required to achieve the invention? Are routine trials carried out or is the experimentation prolonged and arduous, such that the trials would not be considered routine?

3. Is there a motive provided in the prior art to find the solution the patent addresses?

[70] Another important factor may arise from considering the actual course of conduct which culminated in the making of the invention. It is true that obviousness is largely concerned with how a skilled worker would have acted in the light of the prior art. But this is no reason to exclude evidence of the history of the invention, particularly where the knowledge of those involved in finding the invention is no lower than what would be expected of the skilled person."

IV. Amendment of claims after grant

1. *Admissibility of post-grant amendments in general*

It may be possible to amend an issued patent in Canada via one or more of the following approaches:

- disclaimer under Section 48 of the Patent Act;
- re-examination under Section 48.1 of the Patent Act;
- reissue under Section 47 of the Patent Act.

2. *Procedural issues*

2.1 Independent limitation proceedings

Section 48 of the Patent Act relates to disclaimers and dictates that a patentee may disclaim parts of the invention where a patent specification is too broad and claims more than what was invented, and that the defect must have resulted from "mistake, accident or inadvertence, and without any willful intent to defraud or mislead the public." The purpose of the disclaimer is to reduce the scope of a patent claim and not to broaden it or change the point of the invention.[54] In a disclaimer, one cannot add inventive elements which have the effect of broadening the scope, but only essential elements which narrow the scope of the patent claim.[55] If a disclaimer is challenged in litigation, the burden is on the patentee to establish that the disclaimer was prompted by "mistake, accident, or inadvertence" as required by Section 48.[56] An invalid disclaimer may result in invalidation of the original claims since a disclaimer is viewed as an act of renunciation of subject matter that serves as an admission by the patentee that the original claims were invalid.[57]

Section 48.1 of the Patent Act relates to re-examination and dictates that re-examination may be requested by any person, including the patent owner, on the basis that there is a substantial new question affecting patentability of a claim with

54. *Hershkovitz v Tyco Safety Products Canada Ltd.* 2010 FCA 190 affirming 2009 FC 256 at para. [25].
55. *Ibid.* at para. [35].
56. *Ibid.* at para. [36].
57. *Ibid.* at para. [24].

respect to novelty or obviousness over prior art. Re-examination permits the claims to be narrowed but not broadened. A request for re-examination may be made at any time after a patent has issued, until the expiration date of the patent.

Section 47 of the Patent Act relates to reissue and dictates that reissue is possible whenever any patent is deemed defective or inoperative by reason of insufficient description and specification, or by reason of the patentee's claiming more or less than he had a right to claim as new, but at the same time it appears that the error arose from inadvertence, accident or mistake, without any fraudulent or deceptive intention. Reissue is only available within the first four years of the grant of the patent. Claim amendments are possible, including broadening amendments. The patentee must explain the nature of the error and how it came to be realized that one had occurred. In addition, there must be a showing that there was an intent to protect in the original patent that which is claimed in the reissue.

2.2 Opposition proceedings

Re-examination is the only post grant procedure available in the Canadian Patent Office that allows a third party to challenge the validity of a Canadian patent.[58] Re-examination is a summary procedure and is limited to the issues of anticipation and/or obviousness based on prior patents, published applications or other publicly available documents. Other types of prior disclosures, such as offers for sale or prior uses, etc., cannot form the basis for a re-examination procedure. It is commenced by the requesting party filing written submissions and the relevant prior art. There are no hearings, no cross-examinations and no opportunities for discovery in a re-examination. As noted above, re-examinations can only raise issues of anticipation or obviousness, and other validity attacks such as lack of patentable subject matter, non-disclosure, lack of best mode, etc., cannot be relied upon. Upon the Patent Office determining that there is a substantial new question affecting patentability, a re-examination board is convened to consider the matter further, but only the patentee may participate (if re-examination is commenced by a third party, that party's role is limited to the initial filing of the prior art and supporting written submissions). A re-examination decision of the Patent Office may be appealed to the Federal Court, but only by the patentee.

In Canada, there is no formal method for opposing a pending patent application. A third party is permitted to file prior art against a pending application, along with an explanation of its relevance.[59] However, other than an acknowledgment of receipt of its submissions, there is no further notification to the third party of any action taken by an Examiner as a consequence of the submitted materials, nor is there an apparent requirement to cite the prior art against the application or to otherwise consider it.

58. Validity can also be challenged by way of impeachment pursuant to Section 60 of the Patent Act but that is via an action brought in the Federal Court of Canada.
59. Patent Act, s. 34.1 and Patent Rules, s. 10.

2.3 Nullity actions

Validity of an issued patent can be challenged in court proceedings. Proceedings for impeachment may be brought against any issued patent before the Federal Court and may be instituted by any interested person. "Interested person" has been interpreted broadly by the Court, and can include, for example, a party which may expect to have the patent asserted against it (e.g. in view of the manufacture or sale of a product in Canada which may arguably fall within the scope of the patent).[60] An impeachment proceeding can raise any ground of invalidity, including obviousness and novelty attacks based on prior art, lack of utility, non-patentable subject matter, and other grounds pertaining to certain intrinsic defects in the patent itself.[61]

3. *Added matter*

There is no applicable Canadian content.

4. *Sufficiency*

There is no applicable Canadian content.

5. *Multiple indications*

There is no applicable Canadian content.

V. Change of patent category

1. *General admissibility*

There is no explicit prohibition against changing the category of claims of a patent application, but claim amendments that introduce new subject matter are not permissible. Amendments to specifications and drawings are governed by section 38.2 of the Patent Act, which permits any amendment to a specification that is reasonably inferable from the original specification and drawings, or that adds matter that is admitted to form part of the prior art.

2. *Use claim as a category*

See section B.I.3. above.

3. *From product to method claim*

There is no applicable Canadian content.

---

60. *Purcell Systems Inc. v Argus Technologies Ltd.*, 2008 FC 1210.
61. Patent Act, s. 60.

4. *From method to product claim*

There is no applicable Canadian content.

5. *System claims*

There is no applicable Canadian content.

6. *Use claims*

The Canadian Patent Office generally does not object to use claims converted from method claims even if the specification as originally filed does not disclose uses *per se*.

C. INFRINGEMENT AND LITIGATION

I. Legal framework

1. *National statutory laws*

Although Canada does not have a specific statutory definition of infringement, Section 42 of the Patent Act defines the monopoly given to a patentee upon being granted a patent, namely "the exclusive right, privilege and liberty of making, constructing and using the invention and selling it to others to be used, subject to adjudication." This Section gives rise to a patentee's right to enforce the patent against others who infringe upon those exclusive rights by way of an infringement action.

The Federal Court and the provincial courts have concurrent jurisdiction over patent infringement actions. Thus a patentee bringing an infringement action has a choice of forum between the Federal Court or the appropriate provincial court, although almost all patent infringement proceedings in Canada are brought in the Federal Court due to the national reach of the Federal Court's judgments, and its experience in handling patent matters.

The Patent Act also provides a right of action for interested third parties to seek to expunge a patent from the register (see section B.IV.2.3 above), or to seek a declaration as to non-infringement of a patent. The Federal Court has exclusive jurisdiction over these types of proceedings.[62]

For pharmaceutical patents only, there is also the additional procedure under the NOC Regulations available to address potential patent infringement in the context of the drug approval process overseen by Health Canada and pursuant to which an innovative or generic drug company obtains an NOC. See section A.I.1. above.

Since proceedings under the NOC Regulations do not give rise to final decisions on the infringement or the validity of the patent, they can be brought concurrently or sequentially with infringement or impeachment actions relating to the same patent. For instance, an innovator that is unsuccessful under the NOC Regulations can nevertheless bring a subsequent infringement action based on the same patent.

62. Patent Act, s. 60.

Similarly, an SEM that is unsuccessful under the NOC Regulations can subsequently bring an action to impeach the same patent.

2. *Case law*

The leading case defining what constitutes an infringement under the Patent Act is the Supreme Court of Canada decision in *Monsanto Canada Inc. v Schmeiser.*[63] In this decision, the Supreme Court defined the general test for infringement: whether the inventor has been deprived, in whole or in part, directly or indirectly, of the full enjoyment of the monopoly conferred by the patent pursuant to section 42 of the Patent Act (see above).

II. Claim construction

1. *General rules*

The leading cases on claim construction are the Supreme Court of Canada decisions in *Whirlpool Corp. v Camco Inc.*[64] and *Free World Trust v* Électro *Santé Inc.*[65] These decisions were released concurrently. Together, they provide the foundation of the current "purposive construction" approach to claim analysis in Canada.

According to the *Whirlpool* and *Free World Trust* decisions, claim construction is a matter of law to be determined by the court, and is an exercise that is to be undertaken in advance of any validity or infringement analysis.

Under "purposive construction," a patent is to be construed from the perspective of a person of ordinary skill in the art or science that is the subject of the patent ("skilled person") taking into account the common general knowledge that such a person would have. The skilled person is uninventive, but is considered to be reasonably diligent in keeping up with advances in the field of technology to which the patent relates. The "common general knowledge" of the skilled person undergoes continuous evolution and growth, and must be such that it is common among skilled workers and is well known and available to those with a practical interest in the subject matter of the invention.

In construing a patent purposively, the patent is to be read with a mind willing to understand, not by a mind desiring of misunderstanding. It must be given an interpretation that best ensures the attainment of the patent's objects. Reference to extrinsic materials (including the file history) to construe a claim is not permitted in Canada.

According to *Whirlpool*:

> "[45] The key to purposive construction is therefore the identification by the court, with the assistance of the skilled reader, of the particular words or phrases in the claims that describe what the inventor considered to be the "essential" elements of his invention..."

---

63. *Monsanto Canada Inc. v Schmeiser* (2004), 31 C.P.R. (4th) 161 (S.C.C.); 2004 SCC 34.
64. *Whirlpool Corp. v Camco Inc.*, 2000 SCC 67.
65. *Supra* note 44.

In *Free World Trust*, the Supreme Court outlined the following approach for determining "essential elements" of an invention:

> "[31] ... The claims language will, on a purposive construction, show that some elements of the claimed invention are essential while others are non-essential. The identification of elements as essential or non-essential is made:
> (i) on the basis of the common knowledge of the worker skilled in the art to which the patent relates;
> (ii) as of the date the patent is published;
> (iii) having regard to whether or not it was obvious to the skilled reader at the time the patent was published that a variant of a particular element would not make a difference to the way in which the invention works; or
> (iv) according to the intent of the inventor, expressed or inferred from the claims, that a particular element is essential irrespective of its practical effect;
> (v) without, however, resort to extrinsic evidence of the inventor's intention."

2. *Specific issues for use claims*

In the case of a claim directed to a "use," the general rules of claim construction as set out above still apply.

However, it should be noted that where a claim references a "use," that use will generally be construed as a promised utility of the invention. The Supreme Court of Canada has held that "[w]here the new use is the *gravamen* of the invention, the utility required for patentability (s. 2) must, as of the [relevant] date, either be demonstrated or be a sound prediction based on the information and expertise then available."[66]

The Federal Court of Appeal has similarly noted that "when a result or advantage is asserted in a patent's claims, it will general be seen as a promise of utility" and that "statements going to utility are particular vulnerable to being read as promises when they are expressed in a patent's claim."[67]

For a further discussion on the utility requirements under Canadian patent law, and the role of a "promise" in the patent, in relation to second medical use claims, see section A.II.2. above.

66. *Apotex Inc. v Wellcome Foundation Ltd.*, [2002] 4 S.C.R. 153, 2002 SCC 77 [*AZT*] at para 56. Note that later jurisprudence has held that the relevant date for establishing utility is the Canadian filing date of the patent, rather than the "priority date" as referenced in this passage.
67. *Apotex Inc. v Pfizer Canada Inc.*, 2014 FCA 250 at para. 71.

III. Scope of protection

1. *Scope of the use*

1.1 *General definition of the term "use"*

According the Manual of Patent Office Practice,[68] a patent claim directed to a "use" is distinct from a claim directed to a method. A *use* is defined only in terms of the means to be applied, the circumstances in which the means are applied, and the result to be achieved, leaving the "how" to the skilled person:

> "A *use* is distinguished from a *method* in that the latter involves directing the person skilled in the art to take a step or series of steps to arrive at the desired result. In contrast, a use must not require any specific step or steps to be followed. Rather, a *use* is defined only in terms of the means to be applied, the circumstances of this application, and the result to be achieved. The "how" of implementing a *use* must be left to the common general knowledge of the person skilled in the art. A claim that purports to be a *use* claim (e.g. a claim that begins "the use of") but that defines specific steps to be followed is, in effect, a method and must be examined as such."[69]

The Supreme Court of Canada in *Wellcome Foundation* distinguished the pharmaceutical "use" claims at issue in that case from a method of medical treatment (for which patenting is prohibited in Canada) by observing that such use claims did not seek to "fence in" an area of medical treatment, but rather only sought the exclusive right to provide a product as a commercial offering, while leaving the method of its employment to the professional skill and judgment of the medical profession.[70]

1.2 *Manufacture of the pharmaceutical*

As discussed above, in Canada it is considered an infringement to interfere with a patentee's "exclusive right, privilege and liberty of making, constructing and using the invention and selling it to others to be used." Thus, manufacturing (i.e. making) an infringing product in Canada is an infringement.

However, where a particular use of a product is an essential element of the claim, manufacture of the product alone is insufficient to give rise to infringement. In order to be liable, the manufacturer must be found to have induced or procured the actual users (such as doctors, patients or pharmacists) to directly infringe the patent by using the product for the claimed use.

In order to be held liable for inducing infringement, three criteria must be met:

> "First, the act of infringement must have been completed by the direct infringer. Second, the completion of the acts of infringement must be influenced by

68. Note that the Manual is a set of guidelines reflecting the Canadian Intellectual Property Office's interpretation of the law, but is not itself legislation or an authoritative legal source.
69. At chapter 12.06.08.
70. *Wellcome Foundation, supra* note 10, at para 50.

> the acts of the alleged inducer to the point that, without the influence, direct infringement would not take place. Third, the influence must knowingly be exercised by the inducer, that is, the inducer knows that this influence will result in the completion of the act of infringement..."[71]

Canadian courts have generally been hesitant to find inducement in relation to second medical use patents, especially in the context of NOC proceedings, for fear of extending the monopolies of patent holders over compounds *per se*.[72]

Additionally, Canadian courts have held that it is not an infringement to manufacture and/or sell a product which in itself does not infringe, even if the product will inevitably be used to infringe, and even if the seller knows that it will be used to infringe, as long as the seller does not engage in active conduct to influence the infringement.[73] The exception to this is where the product has no significant commercial use other than the infringing one, in which case the seller will likely be found to be liable for inducing infringement.[74]

Cases dealing with allegations of inducing infringement in the context of second medical use claims often revolve around the content of the generic manufacturer's product monograph. Inducement can take place "through inferences reasonably drawn" from a product monograph,[75] although inducement generally cannot be inferred from a mere reference to the new use in the product monograph in the course of explaining contraindications or drug interactions, or as part of a list of scientific references.[76]

1.3 Sale of the product

As noted above in section 1.2, selling a patented product to others is an infringement. However, also as discussed in section 1.2, sale alone is insufficient to give rise to infringement if the claim is to a particular use of the product (by a purchaser, physician, patient, etc.). The seller would only be liable if it induced or procured others to use the product for the claimed use as discussed above.

1.4 Offer for sale

In general, offering to sell or promoting a patented product in Canada will constitute an infringement.[77]

71. *Weatherford Canada Ltd v Corlac Inc*, 2011 FCA 228 at para 162.
72. *AB Hassle v Canada (Minister of National Health and Welfare)*, 2002 FCA 421 at para 57.
73. *Lundbeck Canada Inc. v Ratiopharm Inc.*, 2009 FC 1102 at para 370.
74. *Abbvie Corp. v Janssen Inc.*, 2014 FC 55 at para 106.
75. *Bayer Inc. v Pharmaceutical Partners of Canada Inc.*, 2015 FC 797 at para 51. Also see *AB Hassle v Genpharm Inc.*, 2003 FC 1443.
76. *Novopharm Limited v Sanofi-Aventis Canada Inc*, 2007 FCA 167 at para 11.
77. See generally *Monsanto Canada Inc. v Schmeiser* (2004), 31 C.P.R. (4th) 161 (S.C.C.).

1.5 *Application to the patent*

In cases where manufacturers have been alleged to be inducing infringement, Canadian courts have accepted that using a pharmaceutical compound for a claimed use by administering the same to a patient would constitute a "direct infringement" (which is the first step of the test for inducing infringement).[78] For further details on inducing infringement see section 1.2 above.

1.6 *Combination products*

Where a patent is directed to the use of a combination, the manufacture or sale of only one component of that combination is not, by itself, an infringement. The seller of a component of the combination is only liable if they induce or procure the use of the combination. For example, in Canada there is no cause of action that corresponds with the U.S. "contributory infringement" cause of action. Inducing or procuring infringement is further discussed in section 1.2 above.

In Canadian jurisprudence, the following has been held *not* to constitute inducing or procuring infringement in relation to a combination:

- Where the product monograph does not refer to the use of the drug, the absence of a disclaimer not to use the drug as part of the patented combination does not in itself give rise to inducing or procuring infringement.[79]
- A reference in a drug's product monograph to its "compatibility" with other elements that, if used, would result in infringement, has been held not to constitute an inducement.[80]

2. ***Absolute product protection***

2.1 *Limitation through the term "use"*

Reference to a particular use in a patent claim is limiting insofar as the use is construed to be an essential element of the claim. See section II above as to how essential elements are determined in Canada.

If a use is deemed to be an essential element of the claim, as discussed in section 1.2 above, there will only be liability for infringement on the part of an manufacture or seller that does not itself use the product if:

(a) the seller induces or procures infringement; or
(b) the patented use is the only significant commercial use of the product.

---

78. See, for example, *AB Hassle v Canada (Minister of National Health and Welfare)*, 2002 FCA 421.
79. *Lundbeck Canada Inc. v Ratiopharm Inc.*, 2009 FC 1102 at paras. 386-387.
80. *Bayer Inc. v Pharmaceutical Partners of Canada Inc.*, 2015 FC 797.

2.2 Off-label use

See section C.IV.4. below for a discussion of off-label use in Canada.

3. Dosage regimes

See section C.IV.5. below for a discussion of dosage regimes in Canada.

4. Patient groups

See section C.IV.6. below for a discussion of patient groups in Canada.

5. Extension under the doctrine of equivalents

Canada does not have a doctrine of equivalents. See section II above for a discussion of the law of claim construction in Canada.

IV. Infringing acts

1. Infringing person or entity

See section C.III. above for a full discussion of infringement in the context of second medical use patents.

2. Direct infringement

See section C.III. above for a full discussion of infringement in the context of second medical use patents.

2.1 Manufacture of the pharmaceutical

See section C.III. above for a full discussion of infringement in the context of second medical use patents.

2.2 Offer for sale

See section C.III. above for a full discussion of infringement in the context of second medical use patents.

2.3 Sale

See section C.III. above for a full discussion of infringement in the context of second medical use patents.

2.4 Export

See section C.III. above for a full discussion of infringement in the context of second medical use patents.

2.5 Import

See section C.III. above for a full discussion of infringement in the context of second medical use patents.

2.6 Combination products

See section C.III. above for a full discussion of infringement in the context of second medical use patents.

3. Indirect infringement

See section C.III. above for a full discussion of infringement in the context of second medical use patents.

3.1 Objective acts

See section C.III. above for a full discussion of infringement in the context of second medical use patents.

3.2 Subjective conditions

See section C.III. above for a full discussion of infringement in the context of second medical use patents.

3.3 Export

See section C.III. above for a full discussion of infringement in the context of second medical use patents.

3.4 Import

See section C.III. above for a full discussion of infringement in the context of second medical use patents.

3.5 Combination products

See section C.III. above for a full discussion of infringement in the context of second medical use patents.

4. *Off-label use*

4.1 General admissibility of off-label use

In Canada, generic drugs are often used off-label, due in part to the way in which drugs are prescribed and dispensed. Off-label prescription, the practice of physicians prescribing pharmaceuticals for uses not set out in the product monograph, often occurs in Canada. Additionally, generally speaking, prescriptions do not indicate the condition for which a drug has been prescribed and pharmacists will generally dispense lower cost generic drugs where available, without considering patent issues. Additionally, even if a drug is prescribed using an innovator's brand name, pharmacists may substitute a generic version unless the prescription specifically indicates that no substitutions should be made. As such, even if generic manufacturers do not label their products for patented second medical uses (for example, in order to avoid liability for inducing or procuring infringement), their products can nevertheless be prescribed, dispensed or consumed for such uses.

4.2 Liable persons

As discussed in section C.III.1.2. above, use of a generic drug for a patented second medical use may constitute direct infringement by the patient, doctor or pharmacist administering the drug. This includes off-label use. However, as previously discussed, this may not create liability on the part of the generic drug manufacturer.

Canadian courts have specifically held that the fact that infringing off-label use will inevitably occur does not to give rise to liability on the part of the generic manufacturers in the absence of additional activities by the manufacturer to promote (i.e. induce) such off-label use:

> "It strikes me as clear that [the generic]'s recognition that 'off-label' prescription by doctors, dispensation by pharmacists, and subsequent consumption by patients does not meet the 'something more' requirement established by Sexton J.A. in *AB Hassle, supra.* Whether the 'something more' consists of inducement, procurement, marketing or some other nexus will depend upon the facts of each particular case. However, there must be a nexus. Mere passive recognition that 'off-label' prescription and/or consumption will occur does not amount to 'something more'."[81]

See section C.III.1.2. above for a further discussion on manufacturer liability for inducing or procuring infringement.

4.3 Objective requirements for infringement

See section C.III. above for a full discussion of infringement in the context of second medical use patents.

81. *Aventis Pharma Inc. v Apotex Inc.*, 2005 FC 1461, at para. 32.

4.4 *Subjective requirements for infringement*

See section C.III. above for a full discussion of infringement in the context of second medical use patents.

5. *Dosage regimes*

To the extent patentable, a dosage regime may be infringed where the manufacturer induces or procures infringement, as discussed in section III.1.2 above. Moreover, selling a drug in a dosage form or "kit" that facilitates compliance with a patented dosage regime has been held to constitute direct infringement of claims directed to such dosage form or "kit."[82]

6. *Patient groups*

In Canada, there has been no distinction made between claims directed to second medical uses for particular patient groups and other types of second medical use claims.

V. Remedies

1. *Injunctions*

In Canada, a successful patentee is typically awarded a permanent injunction restraining the defendant (and persons under its control) from further infringing the patent.[83] However, it is an "equitable remedy" and therefore subject to the Court's discretion. Additionally, a defendant who breaches an injunction can be found to be in contempt of court.[84]

2. *Damages*

Any person who infringes a patent is liable for all damages sustained by the patentee (e.g. lost profits from lost sales or loss of a reasonably royalty) after the grant of the patent by reason of the infringement. Alternatively, at the Court's discretion, a successful plaintiff may be permitted to elect between recovery of the plaintiff's damages or an accounting (i.e. disgorgement) of the defendant's profits made as a result of the infringing activity.[85] The remedy of an accounting of the defendant's profits is different from the remedy of damages in that, in an accounting of profits,

82. See, for example, *Merck & Co. v Apotex Inc.*, 2005 FC 755; *Procter & Gamble Pharmaceuticals Canada Inc. v Canada (Minister of Health)*, 2004 FC 204.
83. *Merck & Co. v Apotex Inc.* (2000), 5 C.P.R. (4th) 2 at 22 (F.C.T.D.); Patent Act, s. 57.
84. *Merck & Co. v Apotex Inc.* (2003), 25 C.P.R. (4th) 289 at 312-322 (F.C.A.).
85. Patent Act, ss 55, 57.

compensation is measured by the profits made by the infringer, whereas for damages, compensation is measured by the loss suffered by the patentee.[86]

In addition to the remedies of damages or an accounting of profits for infringing acts that occurred after the patent had issued, a defendant is also liable to pay 'reasonable compensation' for any infringing activity that takes place after the patent application became open to the inspection of the public and before the grant of the patent.[87]

3. *Information*

3.1 Names of manufacturer, distributors etc.

There is no stand-alone remedy in Canada that entitles a successful party in a patent infringement suit to obtain names of other possible infringing parties. However, if relevant to the action, information of this kind may be able to be obtained in the course of the discovery process. However, information obtained from the discovery process is subject to an "implied undertaking" by the recipient not to disclose or use the information for purposes other than the litigation. Breach of the "implied undertaking" is considered a contempt of court.

Where the identity of an infringer cannot be ascertained, but it can be established that it is known to a third party, it is also possible to seek an order permitting discovery of the third party prior to commencement of an action against an infringer (otherwise known as a "Norwich Order") where:

1) there is a *bona fide* case against the unknown alleged wrongdoer;
2) the person from whom discovery is sought must be in some way involved in the matter under dispute; they must be more than an innocent bystander;
3) the person from whom discovery is sought must be the only practical source of information available to the applicants;
4) the person from whom discovery is sought is reasonably compensated for their expenses arising out of compliance with the discovery order in addition to their legal costs; and
5) the public interests in favour of disclosure outweighs the legitimate privacy concerns.[88]

Additionally, in the context of an action, it is possible to seek discovery of a third party where:

1) the third party may have information on an issue in the action;
2) the requesting party has been unable to obtain the information informally from the person or from another source by any other reasonable means;
3) it would be unfair not to allow the requesting party an opportunity to question the person before trial; and

86. *Monsanto Canada Inc. v Schmeiser* (2004), 31 C.P.R. (4th) 161 at 189 (S.C.C.)
87. *Patent Act*, ss. 55 (1), (2).
88. *BMG Canada Inc. v John Doe*, 2005 FCA 193 at paras. 15 and 32.

4) the questioning will not cause undue delay, inconvenience or expense to the person or to the parties.[89]

3.2 *Names of customers*

See section C.V.3.1. above.

3.3 *Information about infringing sales*

Information regarding infringing sales, to the extent it is relevant, is typically obtained through the discovery process.

3.4 *Account of profits*

See section C.V.2 above.

4. *Recall of products and destruction*

In Canada, a successful plaintiff in a patent case may be entitled to obtain a "delivery up or destruction order" whereby any infringing product in the possession of the defendant (manufacturer, distributor, customer, etc.) is ordered to be delivered to the plaintiff or destroyed.

5. *Recovery of legal costs*

In Canada, a successful litigant (be it the plaintiff or the defendant) is typically awarded its 'costs' which consists of full reimbursement for all reasonable disbursements (such as reasonable fees for experts) and a portion of its attorney's fees (usually based on a tariff or schedule of allowable fees contained in the applicable court rules). In exceptional circumstances, full or substantial indemnity for actual legal costs incurred for the litigation may be awarded.

VI. Exceptions from patent protection

1. *Exhaustion of rights*

The sale of a patented article to a purchaser is presumed to give the purchaser an implied licence to use, sell or deal with the patented article as they please, unless restrictive conditions are put in place at the time of purchase. Any limitation intended to affect the rights of subsequent purchasers must also be expressed clearly and unambiguously to the subsequent purchasers when the patented article is acquired in order for the subsequent purchaser to be bound by such limitations.[90]

89. *Apotex Inc. v H. Lundbeck A/S*, 2011 FC 88.
90. *Eli Lilly and Co. v Novopharm Ltd.* (1998), 80 C.P.R. (3d) 321 at 363-364 (S.C.C.).

2. *Patient welfare*

There is no specific law in Canada that provides an exception to patent infringement for patient welfare. However, pursuant to Section 32 of the Competition Act, a patentee may be prevented from using the exclusive rights under a patent to "prevent, limit or lessen, unduly, the manufacture or production of any such article or commodity or unreasonably enhance the price thereof." Although there is no law on this point, this Section could conceivably apply where a patent was being used to prevent patients from obtaining necessary medical treatment. Further, Subsection 65(1) of the Patent Act provides: "The Attorney General of Canada or any person interested may, at any time after the expiration of three years from the date of the grant of a patent, apply to the Commissioner alleging in the case of that patent that there has been an abuse of the exclusive rights thereunder and asking for relief under this Act." One of the grounds for seeking relief is "if the demand for the patented article in Canada is not being met to an adequate extent and on reasonable terms." The Government of Canada may also apply to use patented inventions based on Section 19 of the Patent Act.

3. *Others specific to second medical use claims*

There are no exceptions from patent protection in Canada that relate specifically to second medical use claims. Other exceptions to infringement under Canadian patent law include the following:

(a) It is not an infringement to use a patent solely for non-commercial experimental purposes.[91]
(b) Pursuant to Section 55.2(1) of the Patent Act, it is not an infringement to make, construct, use or sell a patented invention solely for uses reasonably related to the development and submission of information required under any law of Canada or any other country that regulates the manufacture, construction, use or sale of the product. This would include activity related to obtaining an NOC for the sale of a pharmaceutical product in Canada, or similar government approval elsewhere. See section A.I.1. above.

VI. Procedural issues

1. *Preliminary injunction cases*

In a patent infringement action, a preliminary injunction (referred to as an interim or interlocutory injunction) can be obtained upon satisfying a tripartite test, namely:

(a) Is there a serious question to be tried (on the merits of the case)?
(b) Will the plaintiff suffer irreparable harm if the injunction is refused? and
(c) Does the balance of convenience favour the granting of an injunction?[92]

---

91. *Micro Chem. Ltd. v Smith, Kline & French Inter-American Corp.*, [1972] S.C.R. 506 at 520.
92. *RJR-Macdonald Inc. v Canada (A.G.)*, [1994] 1 S.C.R. 311 at 340-342.

Irreparable harm is harm that cannot be cured simply by way of the payment of money, for example, because one party cannot collect damages from the other.[93]

In practice, preliminary injunctions have proven difficult to obtain, as the Federal Court has set a high standard for establishing "irreparable harm," including a requirement that evidence of irreparable harm must be "clear and non-speculative."[94]

As discussed above in section I, the NOC Regulations provide a mechanism whereby a generic may be prevented from obtaining government approval, and thereby prevented from entering the market, pending expiry of a listed patent.

1.1 Availability for second medical use claims

The same principles discussed in section C.VII.1. above apply to second medical use claims.

1.2 Specific requirements

See section VII.1. above for the requirements to obtain a preliminary injunction.

2. Cases on the merits

In Canada, patent proceedings, including for second medical use claims can brought pursuant to Section 42 of the Patent Act (an infringement action), or under the NOC Regulations (an NOC proceeding), both discussed in section C.I.1. above.

3. Enforcement of judgments

Upon obtaining a judgment, it is generally immediately enforceable. Injunctive relief can be enforced through contempt proceedings. Judgments for monetary relief can be enforced through the typical enforcement mechanisms including writs of execution, garnishment and charging orders.[95]

VIII. Validity

1. Relevance for infringement cases

Validity can be raised as a defence to infringement in any infringement action. A defendant can also bring a counterclaim to have the asserted patent (or claims thereof) declared void.

93. *RJR-Macdonald Inc. v Canada (A.G.)*, [1994] 1 S.C.R. 311 at 340-342.
94. *Centre Ice Ltd. v National Hockey League* (1994), 53 C.P.R. (3d) 34 at 46 (F.C.A.).
95. *Federal Courts Rules* (SOR/98-106), Rules 423-474.

2. *Specifics for second medical use claims*

The same law applies to second medical use claims as set out in section 1 above.

IX. Pre-litigation strategic considerations

1. *Plaintiff*

The main pre-litigation strategic considerations that may be considered by plaintiffs or potential plaintiffs to proceedings based on second medical use patents include:

(a) Ensuring patent claims are drafted so as to provide the best possible coverage as against infringing manufacturers to the extent possible, including ensuring that all requirements are met to permit a patent to be listed, and including possible claims for dosage form products where available.
(b) Listing, if applicable, the patent on the Patent Register to ensure proceedings under the NOC Regulations can be brought in appropriate circumstances.
(c) Obtaining data protection, where applicable, which is independent of patent status and applies to an "innovative drug," granting the innovator a six-year "no-file" period and an eight-year "no-grant" period.
(d) Considering the various procedural options for addressing infringement, including choice of forum (Federal Court versus appropriate provincial court), and choice of procedure (NOC Regulations versus infringement action).

2. *Defendant*

The main tactical considerations that may be considered by defendants or potential defendants to proceedings based on second medical use patent include:

(a) Deciding on the indications (including possible "off label" use considerations) and other content to be included in the product monograph (and any other materials to be distributed) so as to ensure that doctors, pharmacists and patients others are not induced or procured to infringe.
(b) Whether and when to serve a Notice of Allegation under the NOC Regulations, and the grounds of invalidity and non-infringement to advance.
(c) Pre-emptively bringing actions for declarations of non-infringement or invalidity, or commencing a re-examination procedure.

Australia

Sarah Matheson, Matthew Swinn[1]

A. AVAILABILITY OF PROTECTION

I. Legal framework

1. National statutory laws

Australian patents are granted by the Patent Office of IP Australia. The legislation which governs the registration and enforcement of patents in Australia is the Patents Act 1990 (Cth) ("Patents Act").[2] The Australian patent system provides for two types of patents: standard patents and innovation patents.[3] For the sake of brevity, this chapter primarily deals with the requirements for standard patents only.

The Intellectual Property Laws Amendment (Raising the Bar) Act 2012 (Cth) ("RTB Act") introduced sweeping changes to the Patents Act, including measures to raise the standard of disclosure in patent specifications and the standard for inventive step. The *post-RTB Act regime* applies to all patents or patent applications filed on or after 15 April 2013, or for patent applications for which examination is requested after this date. It does not apply to applications for standard patents for which examination was requested before 15 April 2013, or standard patents granted on applications for which examination was requested before 15 April 2013 ("preRTB patents"). The changes introduced by the RTB Act were intended to align Australia's patent laws with those of overseas jurisdictions, principally England.

---

1. The authors gratefully acknowledge the assistance of Lauren Gore, King & Wood Mallesons and Lauren John, Allens, in drafting this Chapter.
2. All references to sections are references to sections of the Patents Act.
3. Innovation patents were introduced to provide a relatively quick and inexpensive way for inventors to obtain patent protection. Innovation patents undergo no substantive examination prior to grant (although must do so prior to enforcement), have a lower threshold of patentability than standard patents, have a term of eight years and the claim set is limited to five claims.

It should be noted that many Australian patents are still governed by the *pre-RTB Act regime*. At present, there is very little case law which has considered the new patentability standards under the post-RTB Act regime, although much of the case law decided under the pre-RTB Act regime (in particular the case law on manner of manufacture, novelty and inventive step) will continue to apply.

For the sake of brevity, this chapter deals with the post-RTB Act regime, unless it is necessary to refer to the pre-RTB Act regime to explain changes to the law.

An invention is a patentable invention for the purposes of a standard patent if the invention, so far as claimed in any claim:

- is a manner of manufacture within the meaning of section 6 of the Statute of Monopolies;
- is novel;
- involves an inventive step;
- is useful; and
- was not secretly used in Australia by or with the authority of the patentee or the patentee's predecessor in title before the priority date.[4]

The Patents Act excludes human beings or the biological processes for their creation from patentability in the case of both standard and innovation patents.[5] The Patents Act also excludes plants and animals, and the biological processes for the generation of plants and animals, other than a microbiological process or a product of such a process, from patentability in the case of innovation patents.[6]

Relevantly, the Patents Act does not prohibit patents for methods or processes of medical treatment of the human body, nor subsequent medical uses of previously known products. Apart from the discrete subject matter exceptions noted above, there is no restriction on the type of second medical use that may be patentable.

2. *Availability through case law*

To qualify as patentable subject matter in Australia, an invention claimed in a standard patent or an innovation patent must be "a manner of manufacture" within the meaning of section 6 of the Statute of Monopolies.[7] The use of section 6 of the Statute of Monopolies to define the meaning of "invention" in patent legislation has a long history.

Since decided by the High Court of Australia ("HCA") in 1959, *National Research Development Corporation v Commissioner of Patents*[8] ("NRDC") has been considered the leading decision in Australia for the test of whether an invention satisfies the manner of manufacture test within the meaning of section 6 of the Statute

4. Subsection 18(1).
5. Subsection 18(2).
6. Subsections 18(3)–(4).
7. The *Statute of Monopolies* was enacted in 1623 and was the first patent statute of England. Although the Statute of Monopolies has been repealed in the United Kingdom, it remains part of Australian law.
8. (1959) 102 CLR 252.

of Monopolies.[9] The HCA considered an invention for a process that used a known chemical for a purpose for which it was not known previously to be useful. The HCA held that the meaning of section 6 requires that the alleged invention satisfy a threshold requirement of inventiveness by being more than a mere new use of an old substance. An invention must belong to the "useful arts" rather than the "fine arts"; it must provide a material advantage; and its value to the country must be in the field of economic endeavour. *NRDC* confirmed that a new use of a known substance is patentable provided the use takes advantage of a previously unknown property.[10]

The HCA in *NRDC* speculated that the exclusion of methods for treating the human body could lie outside the conception of invention because the whole subject is conceived as essentially non-economic.[11] However, any uncertainty was resolved in the HCA case of *Apotex Pty Ltd v Sanofi-Aventis Australia Pty Ltd*[12] ("*Leflunomide*"), which confirmed that processes or methods for medical treatment of humans, having economic utility, are patentable.[13] The majority held that as long as the requirements for patentability are met, a method for medical treatment can be considered a manner of manufacture which is a patentable invention. In light of *NRDC's* recognition that a second, previously unknown use of a chemical as a pesticide was patentable, the HCA in *Leflunomide* held that, provided the new therapeutic use satisfied the other requirements for patentability, there was no basis in economics or ethics to distinguish between a first or subsequent therapeutic use.[14]

2.1 Pharmaceuticals

In Australia, there is no distinction between pharmaceutical products and other products in terms of the availability of patent protection for their second or later uses.

A drug may potentially be the subject of a patent in Australia irrespective of whether:

- it was previously developed for another therapeutic purpose;
- its intended first medical use was not successful; or
- it was previously known for a non-medical use.

---

9. The very recent HCA case of *D'Arcy v Myriad Genetics Inc.* [2015] HCA 35 has cast doubt on *NRDC's* status as a leading decision on patentability. In that case, the HCA cautioned against the formulaic application of the principles articulated in *NRDC* that to be patentable an invention must consist in a mode or manner of achieving an end result which is an artificially created state of affairs of utility in the fields of economics endeavour. The HCA said that whether a new class of invention is patentable should be decided on a case-by-case basis by reference to a wider range of factors, including policy-based considerations.
10. *National Research Development Corporation v Commissioner of Patents* (1959) 102 CLR 252 at [7].
11. *Ibid.* at [22].
12. (2013) 253 CLR 284.
13. Earlier decisions of the Full Federal Court in *Anaesthetic Supplies Pty Ltd v Rescare Ltd* (1994) 50 FCR 1 and *Bristol-Myers Squibb Co. v FH Faulding & Co. Ltd* (2000) 97 FCR 524 had discussed the patentability of methods of medical treatment of the human body, and prior to the HCA's decision in *Leflunomide* it was the Australian Patent Office practice to grant patents for methods of medical treatment.
14. *Apotex Pty Ltd v Sanofi-Aventis Australia* Pty Ltd (2013) 253 CLR 284 at [282].

2.2 Biologics

Like pharmaceutical products, biologic products are patentable in Australia and second medical uses of such products are also patentable.

3. *International treaties*

Australia is a signatory to a number of international treaties.

3.1 TRIPS

Australia is a party to the TRIPS Agreement. Article 27(1) of the TRIPS Agreement states that patents shall be granted to "any inventions, whether products or processes, in all field of technology, provided that they are new, involve an inventive step and are capable of industrial application".

Article 27(2) of the TRIPS Agreement permits members of the World Trade Organization ("WTO") to exclude certain inventions from patentability: see the discrete subject matter exceptions in the Patents Act that are identified in section 1 above.

Article 27(3) of the TRIPS Agreement permits members of the WTO to exclude "diagnostic, therapeutic and surgical methods for the treatment of humans or animals" from patentability. In Australia, unlike in some other jurisdictions, treaties are not self-executing and the provisions of a treaty have to be enacted as part of Australian domestic law to take effect. Amendments to the Patents Act following the TRIPS Agreement did not enact Article 27(3) into Australian domestic law. Further, as discussed above in section A.I.2, under the common law concept of "manner of manufacture", methods of medical treatment are patentable in Australia.

3.2 FTAs

Australia is a member state of various Free Trade Agreements, including the Australia-United States Free Trade Agreement ("AUSFTA") and the Trans-Pacific Partnership Agreement ("TPP"). The TPP has not yet been ratified.

Article 17.9(1) of the AUSFTA states that patents shall be made available "for any invention, whether a product or process, in all fields of technology, provided that the invention is new, involves an inventive step, and is capable of industrial application" and "for any new uses or methods of using a known product". Article 17.9(2)(b) permits the parties to exclude "diagnostic, therapeutic and surgical methods for the treatment of humans or animals" from patentability.

Article 18.37(1) of the TPP mirrors Article 27(1) of TRIPS and Article 17.9(1) of the AUSFTA. Article 18.37(2) of the TPP states that each party confirms that patents are available for inventions claimed as at least one of the following: new uses of a known product, new methods of using a known product, or new processes of using a known product. Article 18.37(3) permits the parties to exclude "diagnostic, therapeutic and surgical methods for the treatment of humans or animals" from patentability.

4. *Patent term extension/SPCs*

The term of a standard patent in Australia is 20 years from the date of filing of the corresponding application.

The Patents Act provides that extensions of the term of a standard patent are available only for patents that disclose and claim a pharmaceutical substance *per se* or a pharmaceutical substance produced by a process that involves the use of recombinant DNA technology.[15] A substance that is mentioned only in the context of a claim for a method or process and not *per se* does not satisfy those requirements.[16] Accordingly, patents which claim new uses of previously known pharmaceutical compounds cannot be extended.

II. Policy considerations

1. *Health and social issues*

In *Leflunomide*, the majority of the court observed that, despite earlier authorities having doubted the patentability of methods of medical treatment of human beings, no clear and consistent rationale had been identified in support of that proposition.[17] The Chief Justice was comfortable to decide that methods of medical treatment should not be excluded from patentability, although he recognised that the decision may have significant consequences for public policy.[18]

2. *Legal issues*

An issue that remains unresolved in Australia is whether the activities or procedures of doctors when physically treating patients are patentable. In *Leflunomide*, two judges questioned whether such activities, to the extent they involve a method or a process, satisfy the *NRDC* test for the patentability of processes because they are not capable of being practically applied in commerce or industry.[19] Whether or not such activities or procedures (and second or further uses of such activities or procedures) are patentable may be the subject of judicial consideration in the future. In the very recent HCA case of *D'Arcy v Myriad Genetics Inc.*,[20] the majority cautioned against simply applying the test articulated in the *NRDC* case as an exhaustive verbal formula when deciding the question of patentable subject matter.[21] The HCA emphasised that when a new class of claim involves a significant new application or extension of the concept of "manner of manufacture", policy, moral or social considerations should

---

15. Section 70.
16. *Prejay Holdings Ltd v Commissioner of Patents* (2003) 57 IPR 424 at [24].
17. *Apotex Pty Ltd v Sanofi-Aventis Australia* Pty Ltd (2013) 253 CLR 284 at [30] and [50] per French CJ, at [281]–[282] per Kiefel and Crennan JJ, and at [314] per Gageler J.
18. *Ibid.* at [50] per French CJ.
19. *Ibid.* at [287] per Kiefel and Crennan JJ.
20. [2015] HCA 35.
21. *Ibid.* at [5], [20] and [74].

not necessarily be disclaimed when addressing the question of patentability.[22] The case represents a shift in the traditional approach taken to determining the issue of patentability in Australia to one that is more policy-driven.

B. VALIDITY

The validity of Australian patents can be challenged on a number of grounds. Patents having claims to second medical uses are not treated differently to other patents in this regard.

I. Allowable claim wording

In Australia, "method of treatment", "compound when used" and "Swiss-type" claims are all permissible and are often used in the same claim set on the basis that they have different scope respectively.

1. Product claims

The monopoly granted in respect of second medical use claims is necessarily limited given that the substance has known prior therapeutic uses. Any novelty and inventive step reposes in, and is confined to, the previously unknown therapeutic use of the compound.[23] As a result, second medical uses cannot be claimed through product claims.

"For use" claims

Article 54(4) of the EPC 2000 allows claims in the form "[Compound X] for use in the treatment of [condition Y]".

EPC 2000-style "compound for use" claims are not permissible in Australia if the compound is known. The words "for", "for use in", "used to", "used for" and the like are considered to place a limitation on what is claimed only to the extent that it must be "suitable for" the specified purpose (as opposed to confined to that specified purpose).[24] As a result, such claims are equivalent to a claim simply to the compound *per se* (i.e., a product claim). Accordingly, where a second medical use is being claimed in this form, the fact that the compound is known means that the claim will be rejected on novelty or inventive step grounds.

22. *Ibid.* at [22]–[28].
23. *Apotex Pty Ltd v Sanofi-Aventis Australia* Pty Ltd (2013) 253 CLR 284 at [289].
24. *Root Quality Pty Ltd v Root Control Technologies Pty Ltd* (2000) 49 IPR 225 at [33]–[34]; *Raleigh Cycle Co. Ltd v Miller & Co. Ltd* (1946) 63 RPC 113.

2. *Method claims*

"Method of treatment" claims

As discussed in section A.I.2 above, method of treatment claims are considered to relate to patentable subject matter. The typical form of a "method of treatment" claim is: "A method of treating [condition Y] comprising administering [compound X]".

A method of treatment claim is given a purpose-limited construction, such that the method of treatment is only realised or expressed through the deliberate administration of "compound X" to prevent or treat "condition Y" – it will not be realised or expressed by its administration with some other object or end in view that happens to achieve the results of preventing or treating "condition Y" accidentally or as an unsought consequence.[25]

"Swiss-type" claims

The constraints on permissible claim drafting in some jurisdictions (namely the prohibition on method of treatment claims) which led to the adoption of the Swiss-type claim format do not apply in Australia. Accordingly, it is not necessary to draft a Swiss-type claim to overcome objections to claim format; nevertheless, the use of such claims is common in Australia. This is largely because claims sets in foreign patent applications are not usually amended to delete Swiss-type claims, although method of treatment claims will be added to cover the field given that Swiss-type claims and method of treatment claims have different scope.

The fundamental question of whether Swiss-type claims are a valid form of claiming has not been considered in Australia. However, a recent decision has rejected the argument that a Swiss-type claim is not a process or method claim. Swiss-type claims are considered to be manufacturing process claims, directed to the use of a substance in the manufacture of a pharmaceutical product (i.e., they are concerned with the purpose for which the medicaments are to be used).[26] Whereas a method of treatment claim is concerned with the use of a compound, a Swiss-type claim does not encompass the administration of the compound. The therapeutic use defined in a Swiss-type claim qualifies, and thus confines, the scope of the monopoly that is claimed.[27] However, the manufacture of the medicament itself does not stand as use of the medicament for the defined purpose.[28]

Whereas the typical form of a Swiss-type claim is: "The use of [substance X] for the manufacture of a medicament for the therapeutic and/or prophylactic treatment of [medical condition Y]" or "The use of [substance X] in the manufacture of a medicament for the therapeutic and/or prophylactic treatment of [medical condition Y]", the Australian Patent Office Manual of Practice and Procedure ("Patent Examiners

25. *Apotex Pty Ltd v Sanofi-Aventis Australia Pty Ltd* (2013) 103 IPR 217 at [177] and [289] per Crennan and Kiefel JJ, French CJ and Gageler J agreeing at [51] and [316]; *Apotex Pty Ltd v Sanofi-Aventis Australia Pty Ltd (No 2)* [2012] FCAFC 102 (2012) at [37], [40], [45] and [122]–[129].
26. *Otsuka Pharmaceutical Co., Ltd v Generic Health Pty Ltd (No 4)* [2015] FCA 634 at [120].
27. *Ibid.* at [169].
28. *Ibid.* at [168].

Manual")[29] states that claims in the form of "[Substance X] in the manufacture of a medicament for the therapeutic and/or prophylactic treatment of [medical condition Y]" or "[Substance X] for use in the treatment of [medical condition Y]" are not Swiss-type claims (and are to be construed according to the usual rules of construction).[30]

3. *Use claims*

"When used" claims

In Australia, a claim in the form of "[compound X] when used in the treatment of [condition Y]" is understood to be a "disguised" process claim and is allowable.[31] The words "when used" or "whenever used" are considered to have the effect of limiting the scope of a claim to a particular application, environment or timing (unlike "for use" claims).[32] Accordingly, where a second medical use is being claimed in this form, the claim will be construed in a similar fashion to a "method of treatment" claim.

4. *System claims*

In Australia, the question of whether an invention relating to a second or further use of a medical device or corresponding medical system (so-called "system claims" in the EPO) can be protected under the second medical use claims format does not appear to have received specific judicial consideration; however, such inventions are likely to be governed by the same principles of construction that apply to second medical uses generally (i.e., the "when used" format should be used).

The Patent Examiners Manual cites, in the context of discussing "when used" claims, a case where a claim to an apparatus "for carrying out" a process was held to be equivalent to a claim to the apparatus *per se*, but an amendment to the claim to add the words "when used" before "carrying out" was sufficient to restrict the claim to the apparatus when used in the particular manner.[33] There is no suggestion that the same principles of construction would not apply to inventions where the apparatus is a medical device.

5. *Dosage regimes*

A second medical use relating to the use of a known compound according to a new treatment/dosage regime is patentable, provided the dosage regime is novel and inventive (and the other requirements for patentability are met).

---

29. The Patent Examiners Manual is not a legislative instrument. The Patent Examiners Manual provides guidance for patent examiners on procedural and legal matters relevant to their deliberations during examination, but it is not binding on any courts.
30. Patent Examiners Manual, section 2.11.2.3.10.
31. *Wellcome Foundation Ltd v Commissioner of Patents* (1980) 145 CLR 520 at 529.
32. Patent Examiners Manual, section 2.11.2.3.3A.
33. Patent Examiners Manual, section 2.11.2.3.3 citing *L'Aire Liquide Societe Anonyme pour L'Etude et L'Exploitation des Precedes George Claude* (1932) 49 RPC 428.

A claim of this type will typically take the following form: "A method of treating a patient suffering from [condition Y] which comprises administering [compound X by dosage regime Z]".

6. *Patient groups*

A second medical use relating to the treatment of a new group or sub-group of patients using a known compound is patentable, provided the treatment of this new group or sub-group of patients is novel and inventive (and the other requirements for patentability are met).

A claim of this type will typically take the following form: "A method of treating [condition Y] comprising administering [compound X] in a [sub-group of patients Z]".

By way of example, a second medical use of a compound can be targeted at:

- a particular patient population, such as paediatrics;
- patients with certain conditions. For example, in *Otsuka Pharmaceutical Co., Ltd v Generic Health Pty Ltd*[34] the patent claimed use of aripiprazole to treat cognitive impairment caused by schizophrenia, where the patient failed to respond adequately to the previous administration of at least two other specified antipsychotic drugs; or
- a particular stage of a particular disease, for example, in *Roche Therapeutics, Inc. v GenRx Pty Ltd*[35] the patent claimed the use of the known compound carvedilol for the manufacture of a medicament for decreasing mortality resulting from congestive heart failure.

II. Novelty

1. *General definition of novelty and prior art*

An invention is taken to be novel when compared with the prior art base unless it is not novel in light of any one of the following kinds of information ("prior art information"), each of which must be considered separately:[36]

- prior art information made publicly available in a single document or through a single act;
- prior art information made publicly available in two or more related documents, or through doing two or more related acts, if the relationship between the documents or acts is such that a person skilled in the relevant art (anywhere in the world)[37] would treat them as a single source of that information; or

34. (2015) 113 IPR 191.
35. [2007] FCA 83.
36. Subsection 7(1).
37. For pre-RTB patents filed before 1 April 2002, the skilled person is a person skilled in the relevant art in Australia.

- prior art information contained in a single specification which has an earlier priority date but which is published after the priority date of the claim(s) under consideration (this is referred to as "whole of contents" novelty, and is akin to, but potentially broader than, the concept of "prior claiming").

The Patents Act defines "prior art information" by reference to the definition of "prior art base", and the prior art base for novelty purposes means:[38]

- information in a document that is publicly available anywhere in the world;
- information made publicly available through doing an act, anywhere in the world; and
- information contained in a published patent specification which has an earlier priority date but which is published after the priority date of the claim(s) under consideration.

The Patents Act only prescribes the kinds of information that can be considered for the purpose of assessing novelty; it does not define novelty. The test applied to determine whether an invention is novel is often referred to as the "reverse infringement" test and asks whether the alleged prior disclosure or publication would, if the patent were valid, constitute an infringement.[39] The Full Federal Court recently clarified the application of the "reverse infringement" test and emphasised that it is not applied by simply asking whether something within the prior art document would, if carried out after the grant of the patent, infringe the invention as claimed - a prior art document must contain a clear description of, or a clear direction, recommendation or suggestion to do or make, something that would infringe the patentee's claim if carried out after the grant of the patentee's patent.[40]

Whether a prior publication anticipates a subsequent claimed invention will depend upon the quality of the disclosure in that prior publication and the context in which that disclosure appears, as assessed through the eyes of the skilled addressee having regard to the state of knowledge at the date of publication of the document.[41] If the skilled person would add missing information to what is disclosed in the prior art as a matter course and without inventive ingenuity or undue experimentation, the invention will lack novelty.[42]

2. *Definition of skilled person*

The "skilled person" is a hypothetical person of ordinary skill in the relevant art possessed of the common general knowledge in the art before the priority date. The characteristics of the skilled person, including their experience, skill and knowledge, will depend on the relevant field of art or science to which the invention relates.

38. Schedule 1.
39. *Meyers Taylor Pty Ltd v Vicarr Industries Ltd* (1977) 137 CLR 228; *Minnesota Mining & Manufacturing Co. v Beiersdorf (Australia) Ltd* (1980) 144 CLR 253; *Ramset Fasteners (Aust) Pty Ltd v Advanced Building Systems Pty Ltd* (1999) 44 IPR 257. These foundational cases are cited in the numerous cases on novelty which follow and are still cited today.
40. *AstraZeneca AB v Apotex Pty Ltd* [2014] FCAFC 99 at [301].
41. *Bristol Myers Squibb Co. v F H Faulding & Co. Ltd* (2000) 97 FCR 524.
42. *Hill v Evans* (1862) 45 ER 1195.

Further, depending on the nature of the invention in a given case, the skilled person may be an individual or it may be a team whose combined skills would normally be employed in the relevant art.

3. *Scope of disclosure*

3.1 *General rules*

The requirements for a complete specification and its claims are that:

- a complete specification must disclose the invention in a manner which is clear enough and complete enough for the invention to be performed by a person skilled in the relevant art (this is referred to as the "sufficiency" requirement);[43]
- a complete specification must disclose the best method known to the applicant of performing the invention;[44] and
- the claim or claims must be clear and succinct and supported by matter disclosed in the specification (this is referred to as the "support" requirement).[45]

A patent may be revoked on the ground that it does not comply with these requirements.[46] A revocation action is akin to a nullity action in Europe.

An enabling disclosure is one that provides sufficient information to enable the skilled person to perform the invention over the full width of the claim or claims without undue burden or the need for further invention. A complete specification may therefore need to describe a number of examples, or describe alternative embodiments or variations, extending over the whole scope of the claims, depending on the nature of the invention and the breadth of its application.

The requirement that the claim or claims be "supported" by matter disclosed in the specification is intended to ensure that there is a basis in the description for each claim and the scope of the claims is not broader than is justified by the extent of the description, drawings and contribution to the art. A contribution to the art is something that is disclosed in the specification that is novel, inventive and enabled by that disclosure.

For pre-RTB patents, the requirements for a complete specification are that:

- the complete specification "describe the invention fully, including the best method known to the applicant of performing the invention", and this simply requires a disclosure that would enable the addressee of the specification to produce *something* (i.e., one embodiment) within each claim without

43. Subsection 40(2)(a). The wording of subsection 40(2)(a) is similar to section 14(3) of the Patents Act 1977 (UK) and to Article 83 of the European Patent Convention.
44. Subsection 40(2)(aa).
45. Subsection 40(3). The wording of subsection 40(3) is similar to section 14(3) of the Patents Act 1977 (UK) and to Article 83 of the European Patent Convention.
46. Subsection 138(3)(f).

new inventions or additions or prolonged study of matters presenting initial difficulty.[47]

- the claim or claims of a patent must be "fairly based on the matter described in the specification", which requires that there be a "real and reasonably clear disclosure" in the complete specification of what is claimed such that the claims are consistent with what the specification as a whole describes as the invention.

Unlike in many other jurisdictions today, it is still a requirement in Australia (under both the pre-RTB Act regime and the post-RTB Act regime) that a complete specification disclose the "best method" known to the applicant of performing the invention.[48] This must be the best method known to the applicant at the filing date of the patent (this probably also applies to enablement and support under the post-RTB Act, although there is no case law on the issue yet).[49] An applicant is not required to identify which, out of a range of methods, is the "best".[50] Further, where the best method of performance does not differ in any way from that which is disclosed in the complete specification for the purposes of disclosing the invention in a clear enough and complete enough manner, then there is no requirement to provide any additional information to satisfy the best method requirement.

3.2 First medical use

A claim to a therapeutic use of a new pharmaceutical compound (i.e., first therapeutic use) will lack support in the absence of evidence of the new therapy working over the whole scope of the use as claimed.[51] Further, a complete specification must disclose a specific, substantial and credible use for the claimed invention.[52] A mere assertion in the specification that a pharmaceutical composition or medicament will treat a medical condition does not provide adequate support for claims to a method of treatment. Accordingly, an objection of lack of support and utility may arise where claims are broad and speculative.

For example, the Patent Examiners Manual cites, in the context of the requirement of "support", a case where the description referred to the medical use and provided some statements indicating that certain compounds had been tested and found to exhibit specific activity, but no data or details of the testing procedures were provided, which meant that the claimed therapeutic activity was not a reality for each disease falling with the scope of the claims.[53] Further, where a patent claims the use of "compound X and its derivatives" for the preparation of a medicament to

47. *Kimberly-Clark Australia Pty Ltd v Arico Trading International Pty Ltd* (2001) 207 CLR 1 at [25].
48. Subsection 40(2)(aa); in the case of pre-RTB patents, subsection 40(2)(a).
49. *Rescare Ltd v Anaesthetic Supplies Pty Ltd* (1992) 25 IPR 1; *Pfizer Overseas Pharmaceuticals v Eli Lilly and Company* [2005] FCAFC 224 at [375].
50. *Eli Lilly and Company v Pfizer Overseas Pharmaceuticals* (2005) 64 IPR 506.
51. Patent Examiners Manual, section 2.11.7.10A.
52. Section 7A.
53. Patent Examiners Manual, section 2.11.7.10A citing *Consultant Suppliers Ltd's Application* [1996] RPC 348.

treat "condition Y", and in the absence of any indication that the treatment was a principle of general application such that the skilled person would have a reasonable expectation that the treatment would work with any derivative of compound X, the specification must contain a disclosure enabling the skilled person to determine which of the many possible derivatives will work (e.g., by identifying those derivatives or providing a testing procedure to identify the derivatives with the relevant activity).

For patents under the pre-RTB Act regime, the claims must be consistent with what the specification as a whole describes as the invention and the specification must provide sufficient information to enable the skilled person to make something within each claim. Further, examiners are not required to consider whether the claimed invention is useful, however they are required to consider the use to which an invention is to be put.[54] For that reason, in the case of *PhotoCure v Queen's University*,[55] the patent claimed a method for the treatment of skin disorders but the examples in the specification were limited to five disorders, with other uses merely "contemplated". The Federal Court held that the reference to the further uses in the specification indicated that the treatment was directed more broadly than the five examples and provided fair basis for the wide range of disorders (even though data or descriptions of tests undertaken with respect to those other contemplated disorders were not included in the specification).[56]

3.3 *New subject matter*

For an invention which is a second or further medical use of a known compound, the novel subject matter (i.e., the new therapeutic effect) must be disclosed in the patent. Further, claims to a second or further medical use will lack support in the absence of any evidence of the idea working for the new use.[57] The Patent Examiners Manual states that the tests that must be disclosed in order to support a claim to a method of treatment depend on the nature of the invention, but that "rudimentary" tests that credibly and plausibly demonstrate that the specified compounds possess an activity that could lead to the treatment of a given disorder will be sufficient.[58]

3.4 *New data*

The Patent Examiners Manual states that in order to comply with the requirement that the claims be "supported", the description in the specification should identify the condition (or conditions) that may be treated and should demonstrate by reference to tests (with rudimentary tests such as *in vivo* tests or *in silico* modelling being sufficient) that the treatment is a reality and not just a possibility against the claimed condition (or each of the claimed conditions).[59]

---

54. Patent Examiners Manual, section 2.9.3.4.
55. (2005) 64 IPR 314.
56. *PhotoCure v Queen's University* (2005) 64 IPR 314 at [137].
57. Patent Examiners Manual, section 2.11.7.10A.
58. *Ibid.*, section 2.11.7.10A.
59. *Ibid.*, section 2.11.7.10A.

Under the post-RTB Act regime, a proposed amendment which adds further embodiments, examples or illustrations to the specification will not be allowable if it adds new matter to the specification that extends beyond what the skilled addressee could directly derive from reading the complete specification as filed, together with other prescribed documents. The Patent Examiners Manual states that if the specification as filed referred to tests having been carried out and the results of those tests, then amendments to add an example to this effect may be allowable.[60] Post-filing date data or evidence may be relied upon to demonstrate the utility of a claimed invention (provided that the specification as filed discloses a specific, substantial and credible use).[61]

Under the pre-RTB Act regime, it is permissible to amend a specification to include data which post-dates the date of filing provided that the addition does not broaden the scope of the claims. The Patent Examiners Manual states that the addition of a further example or a description of further embodiments may change the scope of a generic claim, although if further embodiments, examples or illustrations which fall within the framework of the original disclosure are added to the specification, the inclusion of that further material in a claim will generally be allowable.[62]

4. *Requirements for second medical use*

4.1 Distinction from first medical use

It is also the case in Australia that whereas the claims on first medical uses protect any therapeutic use of a given compound, second and further medical uses are limited in their scope of protection to specific medical settings. For example, treatment of a specific disorder or disease, treatment of a specific patient group and/or treatment in accordance with a specific treatment or dosage regime.

4.2 Sub-species of second medical use

As noted above in section B.I, it is possible for there to be separate patents granted in respect of inventions which are sub-species of second medical uses relating to the same known compound (provided the requirements for patentability are otherwise met). For example, separate inventions might lie in the use of a known compound in the treatment of a novel disease, using a different route of administration, using a novel dosage regime or treating a novel patient group.

4.3 Dosage regimes

As noted above, claims comprising a method of treatment according to a novel dosage regime are permissible, however, such claims may be susceptible to a finding of obviousness or lack of novelty. By way of example, in the recent case of *AstraZeneca*

60. *Ibid.*, section 2.23.8.2A.
61. Section 7A.
62. Patents Examiners Manual, section 2.23.8.2.

AB v Apotex Pty Ltd,[63] the so-called "low dose" patent (a pre-RTB patent filed before 1 April 2002), which claimed a method of treatment involving the single, once-daily oral administration of 5mg to 10mg of rosuvastatin, was found to be obvious. An earlier patent (which disclosed a broad class of compounds with cholesterol lowering activity, including rosuvastatin, and a dosage regimen) and an article, were held to be relevant prior art documents. Further, the evidence established that the skilled person, armed only with the common general knowledge and the information in the earlier patent or the article would have been led as a matter of routine to carry out the methods of treatment claimed in the earlier patent in the expectation that they would work. The HCA upheld this finding on inventive step and also held that it was a routine step to test rosuvastatin in the claimed dosage range in clinical trials which could be conventionally carried out.[64]

4.4 Special patient groups

As noted above, a second medical use relating to the treatment of a new group or sub-group of patients using a known compound is patentable, provided the treatment of this new group or sub-group of patients is novel and inventive (and the other requirements for patentability are met).

5. ***Timing issues***

5.1 Relevant time of development of second use

At present, there is no case law on the application of the post-RTB Act provisions of the Patents Act. According to English case law relating to sufficiency (which is expected to inform the application of the law of sufficiency and support under the post-RTB Act regime), the specification must make it "plausible or credible" that the invention would work across the scope of the claim.[65] Accordingly, the timing of the discovery of a novel therapeutic use of a known compound, and its proximity to the development of the compound itself, will impact on the amount and the nature of data available at the time of filing. Further, the field of art to which the invention relates and the state of common general knowledge in that field will impact the determination of whether the disclosure in a specification provides a plausible or credible disclosure. For example, where the second medical use is discovered during the development and/or testing of the compound in relation to the first medical use, it may be the case that little is known about the compound and its effects by those skilled in the art such that more information will be required to enable the skilled person to make a reasonable prediction the invention will work across the scope of the claim.

63. [2014] FCAFC 99.
64. *AstraZeneca AB v Apotex Pty Ltd* (2015) 114 IPR 445.
65. For example, see *Generics (UK) Limited v Warner-Lambert Company LLC* [2015] EWHC 2548 (Pat) at [341].

5.2 *Role of new data*

As discussed above in section B.II.3.4, the description in the specification should identify the condition(s) that may be treated and should demonstrate by reference to tests that the treatment is a reality and not just a possibility against the claimed condition(s).[66] Further, in relation to assessment of the utility of a claimed invention, it provides that an applicant can establish the existence of a reasonable correlation between an activity and the asserted use by relying on data such as data from *in vitro* or *in vivo* tests that the person skilled would accept as being reasonably predictive of an asserted use or human clinical data.[67] Accordingly, it is necessary to include new data going to the efficacy of the treatment in the specification to satisfy the requirements of sufficiency, support and utility.

5.3 *Use of old data*

In Australia, data relating to the first medical use of the compound may conceivably be used to support a claimed second medical use, however, the use of such data alone may invite objections on the grounds of lack of novelty and inventive step and is unlikely to be adequate to satisfy the requirements of sufficiency, support and utility.

III. Inventive step/non-obviousness

1. *Definition of inventive step/non-obviousness*

Section 7 sets out the requirements for inventive step. It has been the subject of considerable amendment since its introduction. As a result, different tests of inventive step apply depending on the date of filing of a patent application.

Under the post-RTB Act regime, an invention is taken to involve an inventive step when compared with the "prior art base" unless the invention would have been obvious to a person skilled in the relevant art in light of the common general knowledge as it existed anywhere in the world before the priority date of the relevant claim, whether that knowledge is considered separately or together with "section 7(3) information", being either:

- any single piece of prior art information; or
- a combination of any two or more pieces of prior art information that the skilled person could, before the priority date of the relevant claim, be reasonably expected to have combined.

The "prior art information" which comprises the "prior art base" for inventive step purposes is information in a document that is publicly available anywhere in the world and information made publicly available anywhere in the world through doing an act.[68]

---

66. Patent Examiners Manual, section 2.11.7.10A.
67. *Ibid.*, section 2.9.3.4.3A.
68. Schedule 1.

Under the pre-RTB Act regime, two different tests apply:

- for pre-RTB patents filed before 1 April 2002, the common general knowledge is limited to that in Australia. Inventive step may be assessed in light of the common general knowledge alone, or together with certain kinds of information[69], each of which must be considered separately. The prior art information that can be considered together with the common general knowledge must be information that the skilled person could, before the priority date of the relevant claim, "be reasonably expected to have ascertained, understood and regarded as relevant" to work in the relevant art in Australia; or
- for pre-RTB patents filed after 1 April 2002, the common general knowledge is also limited to that in Australia. The information that can be combined with the common general knowledge can be a combination of two or more pieces of prior art information if the skilled person could "be reasonably expected" to have combined them, provided the skilled person had already "ascertained, understood and regarded as relevant" the information combined.[70]

2. *Same scope of disclosure as for novelty?*

The scope of disclosure is the same as for novelty. As discussed above in section B.II.3.1, the claim or claims in a complete specification must be "supported" by matter disclosed in the specification.[71] Accordingly, a specification must disclose enough information to allow an assessment to be made of the technical contribution to a problem which has been solved by the features recited in the claims, and the evaluation of this technical contribution will be closely aligned (if not synonymous) with the identification of the inventive step or concept which lies at the heart of the invention.[72]

3. *Assessment of inventive step/non-obviousness*

The test for obviousness is whether the skilled person (having reference to the relevant prior art and common general knowledge at the time) would have been directly led as a matter of course to try the invention in the expectation that it would have produced a useful result.[73] The reference to "expectation" means a reasonable expectation of achieving the result. Further, the reference to "directly be led as a matter of course to try" does not mean that an invention is obvious if it is "worthwhile" or "obvious to try".[74] Where there is no expectation of success, an inventive step can lie equally in a complex and laborious course of action and in a sudden flash of genius.

69. Subsection 7(3).
70. Subsection 7(3).
71. Subsection 40(3).
72. C. Bodkin, *Patent Law in Australia* (2nd ed, Thomson Reuters, 2014), [5630].
73. *Aktiebolaget Hässle v Alphapharm Pty Ltd* (2002) 212 CLR 411.
74. *Alphapharm Pty Ltd v H Lundbeck A/S* (2008) 76 IPR 618.

IV. Amendment of claims after grant

1. Admissibility of post-grant amendments in general

It is possible to amend patent claims after grant in Australia, either before the Patent Office or before the court, where relevant proceedings are already on foot.

In summary, the types of amendments that are prohibited are:

- any amendment that would add and claim subject matter that extends beyond that disclosed in the complete specification as filed taken together with other prescribed documents (for pre-RTB patents, the prohibition is any amendment that would result in the complete specification claiming matter not in substance disclosed in the complete specification);[75]
- any amendment that would broaden the scope of the patent;[76] or
- any amendment that would result in the complete specification no longer complying with the requirements of sufficiency and support.[77]

2. Procedural issues

2.1 Independent limitation proceedings

In Australia, the procedures which are most closely analogous to independent limitation proceedings in the EPO (i.e., where the patentee voluntarily seeks an amendment) are those provided for post-grant amendments depending on whether the patent is subject to litigation.

- If there is no litigation pending, an applicant or patentee may ask the Commissioner of Patents (the Patent Office) for leave to amend a patent request or complete specification or any other filed document for any purpose, including removing a lawful ground of objection to the request or specification;[78] and
- If court proceedings for infringement or revocation of the patent, or in which the validity of the patent, or of a claim, is in dispute, are on foot, the court may, on the application of the patentee, direct the amendment of a complete specification.[79]

In the latter case, the court has a discretion whether to refuse an amendment even where the amendment is otherwise allowable according to the criteria set out in section B.IV.1 above.[80] An amendment may be refused, for example, on the basis of the patentee's conduct in delaying making an application to amend or for failing to satisfy the obligation for full and frank disclosure (which requires an applicant to

---

75. Subsection 102(1).
76. Subsection 102(2)(a).
77. Subsection 102(2)(b).
78. Section 104.
79. Section 105 and Schedule 1.
80. *Wimmera Industrial Minerals Pty Ltd v RGC Mineral Sands Ltd (No 3)* (1997) AIPC 91-366.

disclose all matters relevant to its reasons for seeking amendment). It is therefore desirable to make any application to amend before any proceedings are commenced, as the Commissioner of Patents does not have any such discretion to refuse an amendment that otherwise satisfies the allowability requirements.

2.2 *Opposition proceedings*

In Australia, the term "opposition proceedings" refers to proceedings in connection with a patent application or a patent in which third parties can attempt to prevent some Patent Office action in relation to the application or patent[81] (unlike in the EPO, where the opposition procedure is a post-grant procedure). In order to challenge a patent, a person may request that the Patent Office re-examine the patent (both before and after grant) or they may apply to the court for an order revoking a patent (which is akin to a nullity action).

The Patent Office is obliged to conduct a re-examination of a granted patent if requested to do so by a third party. A patentee may make an application to amend a patent to remove a lawful ground of objection that is raised during re-examination, and this application may then be opposed by any person.[82]

2.3 *Nullity actions*

In Australia, a "revocation action" is akin to a "nullity action". Any person may apply to a court in Australia for an order revoking a patent on the grounds that the:

- patentee is not entitled to the patent;
- invention is not a patentable invention;
- patent was obtained by fraud, false suggestion or misrepresentation;
- an amendment of the patent request or the complete specification was made or obtained by fraud, false suggestion or misrepresentation; or
- specification does not comply with section 40 (i.e., the requirements of sufficiency and support).[83]

As noted above, if a patentee wishes to apply to amend a patent once revocation proceedings are on foot, the patentee can only apply to the court pursuant to section 105.[84]

3. *Added matter*

The prohibition on amendments which result in the specification disclosing new matter is similar to Article 123 of the European Patent Convention and section 76 of the Patents Act 1977 (UK). The Explanatory Memorandum of the RTB Act explains that the intended effect of the amendments to the allowability requirements is

81. C. Bodkin, *Patent Law in Australia* (2nd ed, Thomson Reuters, 2014), [14020].
82. Subsection 104(4).
83. Subsection 138(1). See also section B.II.3.1.
84. Section 112.

to prevent applicants from amending a specification to add any material that the hypothetical skilled person could not directly derive by reading the information in the specification as filed.

4. *Sufficiency*

As noted above in section B.IV.1, any amendment that would result in the complete specification no longer complying with the requirements of sufficiency and support, is not an allowable amendment.[85]

5. *Multiple indications*

In Australia, the claim or claims of a complete specification must relate to one invention only;[86] however, there is no limitation on the number of independent claims that can be made in each category, such that separate claims directed to different medical uses are allowable provided they relate to the one invention.

V. Change of patent category

1. *General admissibility*

The "change of patent category" concept is of limited relevance in Australia due to the allowability of various claim types that can be employed to protect second medical use inventions.

As discussed above in section B.IV.1, a patentee is entitled to request amendment of claims either before a request for examination is made, during examination or after acceptance or grant.

2. *Use claim as a category*

As discussed above in section B.I.3, for claims to first, second or further medical uses, the only type of "use" claims allowable are "compound when used" claims.

3. *From product to method claim*

As discussed above in section B.I.2, method of treatment claims are allowable in Australia.

4. *From method to product claim*

As discussed above in section B.I.1, second medical uses cannot be claimed through product claims given that any novelty and inventive step reposes in the second

85. Subsection 102(2)(b).
86. Subsection 104(4).

medical use and the monopoly granted in respect of such claims must therefore be limited to that second medical use.

5. System claims

As discussed above in section B.I.4, to be valid a "system claim" should take the form of a "when used" claim so that the claim is construed as being limited to the use of the medical device to the particular second or further use.

6. Use claims

As discussed above in section B.I.3, claims in the form "[compound X] for use in the treatment of [condition Y]" are not allowable as such claims are construed as claims directed to "compound X" *per se*.

C. INFRINGEMENT AND LITIGATION

I. Legal framework

1. National statutory laws

As discussed above in section A.I.1, the Patents Act governs the enforcement of patents by providing the patentee with the power to commence an infringement proceeding against a party who has exercised, without authorisation, the patentee's exclusive rights.

An infringement proceeding can be commenced in a Federal Court or State Supreme Court in respect of a standard patent, where the patent is granted.[87] Only the patentee or an exclusive licensee has standing to bring an infringement proceeding. If the exclusive licensee commences an infringement proceeding, it must join the patentee in the proceeding (unless the proceeding is against the patentee).[88] An infringement proceeding must be commenced before the later of three years from the day on which the patent is granted, or six years from the day on which the infringing act was done.[89]

2. Case law

As discussed above in section A.I.2, the uncertainty concerning the exclusion of methods for treating the human body was resolved by the HCA in *Leflunomide*. Since then, the case law concerning infringement of second medical use claims has continued to develop.[90]

87. Subsections 120(1), (1A).
88. Subsection 120(2).
89. Subsection 120(4).
90. For example, see *Warner-Lambert Company LLC v Apotex Pty Ltd* [2014] FCAFC 59 and *Otsuka Pharmaceutical Co., Ltd v Generic Health Pty Ltd* (2015) 113 IPR 191.

II. Claim construction

1. *General rules*

A second medial use claim is infringed when all of the essential integers of the claim have been taken.[91]

An integer is determined to be essential by taking a purposive approach to construction of the claim.[92] General principles of construction are relevant, including:[93]

- construing the patent from the position of the non-inventive person skilled in the art as at the priority date, with the benefit of the common general knowledge in the relevant field as it then stood;
- reading the patent specification as a whole and construing the terminology in light of the manner in which it is used in the specification;
- terms of art given meaning that the non-inventive person skilled in the art would give them. If no technical meaning exists, terms of art are given their ordinary meaning.

2. *Specific issues "for use" claims*

As discussed above in section B.I.1, claims to second medial uses in the form *"[compound X] for use in the treatment of [condition Y]"* are not allowable.[94]

III. Scope of protection

The patentee's exclusive rights are to "exploit" the invention, and authorise another person to exploit the invention, throughout Australia.[95] The right of exploitation covers the following: [96]

- the doing of certain acts in relation to products;
- the use of a method or process; and

---

91. *PhotoCure ASA v Queen's University at Kingston* [2005] FCA 344 at [200] citing *Root Quality Pty Ltd v Root Control Technologies Pty Ltd* [2000] FCA 980 at [44]–[45].
92. *Ibid.* at [158].
93. *Ibid.* at [169]–[174].
94. Patent Examiners Manual, section 2.11.2.3.3A.
95. Subsections 13(1) 13(3); the exclusive rights of the patentee are within the "patent area" which means Australia, its continental shelf, the waters about the continental shelf and the airspace above Australia and the continental shelf: Schedule 1 definition of "patent area".
96. The acts of exploitation in relation to a "product" include to make, hire, sell or otherwise dispose of the product, offer to make, sell, hire or otherwise dispose of it, use or import it, or keep it for the purpose of doing any of those things. The acts of exploitation in relation to a "method or process" include to use the method or process or to make, hire, sell or otherwise dispose of, offer to make, sell, hire or otherwise dispose of, use or import, keep for the purpose of doing any of those things, in respect of a product resulting from use of the method or process: Schedule 1 definition of "exploit".

- the doing of certain acts in relation to products that result from use of a method or process.

The rights of exploitation attached to second medical use claims are, however, limited to method or process claims (i.e., method of treatment, compound when used or Swiss-type claims), as discussed above in section B.I.

1. Scope of the use

The scope of use is limited by the exclusive rights of exploitation.

1.1 General definition of the term "use"

The patentee's exclusive rights include the right to "use".

Although the exclusive right to use is ordinarily given a broad meaning,[97] this right in respect of a second medical use claim is limited to use of the compound for the second medical use, not the right to use the compound *per se*.[98] To illustrate, in *Leflunomide*, claim 1 of the patent claimed the use of leflunomide for the purpose of treating or curing psoriasis; therefore the exploitation of leflunomide for the treatment of psoriatic arthritis was not within the patentee's exclusive rights.

1.2 Manufacture of the pharmaceutical

A patentee has an exclusive right to "make", and this encompasses the right to manufacture.[99] This right in respect of a second medical use claim is limited to the making or manufacturing of the known compound for the second medical use; not the right to make or manufacture the compound for any use.

1.3 Sale of the product

A patentee has an exclusive right to "sell" or "dispose of" the compound.[100] This right in respect of a second medical use claim is limited to instances of sale or disposal for the second medical use, and not any use.[101]

97. For example, see *Abbott v Williams* (1837) 2 Carp Pat Cas 381 at 383; *Noakes v Meharey* (1915) 32 RPC 307.
98. Schedule 1 definition of "exploit".
99. *Pinefair Pty Ltd & Anor v Bedford Industries Rehabilitation Association Inc.* [1998] FCA 1181.
100. Schedule 1 definition of "exploit".
101. For example, see *Leflunomide* at [294] where the sale of leflunomide for the treatment of psoriatic arthritis would not fall within the patentee's exclusive rights, which were to the use of leflunomide for psoriasis only.

1.4 *Offer for sale*

A patentee has an exclusive right to "offer for sale" the compound. [102] This right in respect of a second medical use claim is limited to the offering for sale of the compound for the second medical use, and not any use.

1.5 *Application to the patient*

A patentee's exclusive right can extend to administration or application of the compound to the patient, if the second medical use claim is construed, with reference to the specification, as requiring administration.[103] In *Leflunomide*, the Full Federal Court said that description showed "that the object or end in view of the claimed method is the prevention or treatment of psoriasis by the administration of leflunomide", which gave Sanofi a resulting exclusive right that included administration.[104]

1.6 *Combination of products*

The compound that is the subject of the method or process in which the patentee has exclusive rights can comprise a combination of two or more compounds, where the combination is to produce a new method or process and where it was not obvious to place those compounds in the interactive combination.[105]

The scope of the patentee's exclusive rights depends on construction of the claim. That is, whether the claim is directed to the physical combination of two or more compounds, which would confer a narrow monopoly, or the use together of two or more compounds, which would confer a wider monopoly.

2. ***Absolute product protection***

2.1 *Limitation through the term "use"*

Second medical use claims place a limit on the patentee's exclusive rights to use the compound in the treatment of the second medical use.

2.2 *Off-label use*

The patentee's exclusive rights include off-label use that is for the second medical use claimed. This is because off-label use would, despite being use contrary to the indication that is approved by the Therapeutic Goods Administration ("TGA"), still constitute use of the method or process as claimed.

---

102. Schedule 1 definition of "exploit".
103. For example, see *Roche Therapeutics, Inc. v GenRx Pty Ltd* [2007] FCA 83 at [52]–[53] where the patent claimed a dosing regime for the administration of carvedilol.
104. *Apotex Pty Ltd v Sanofi-Aventis Australia Pty Ltd (No 2)* [2012] FCAFC 102 at [124]–[125].
105. *Firebelt Pty Ltd v Brambles Australia Ltd* (2002) 54 IPR 449 at [39].

3. *Dosage regimes*

As discussed above in section B.I.5, a dosage regime of a compound for a second medical use based upon known properties and involving no new method of administration is patentable provided the second medical use claimed is novel and inventive. For example, in *Bristol-Myers Squibb Co. v FH Faulding & Co. Ltd*[106] the claims were to methods of treating cancer involving infusion to a cancer patient of a specified amount of taxol over a defined period. The Full Federal Court held that the claims were invalid on the basis that they lacked novelty because there was an abstract, published in Australia before the priority date, which taught the infusion period claimed in the patent.[107]

4. *Patient groups*

As discussed above in section B.I.6, a second medical use of a compound can be targeted at particular patient groups.

5. *Extension under the doctrine of equivalents*

There is no US-style doctrine of equivalents under Australian patent law. Whilst Australian courts do recognise a doctrine of mechanical equivalents, the adoption of the purposive approach to claim construction means that the courts now rarely permit a claim feature to be replaced by a mechanical equivalent.

The purposive construction approach involves the court considering whether a person with practical knowledge in the relevant field would understand that terms or phrases employed in the specification were to be understood as having their purely literal meaning, or whether they could instead embody some variation, and thereby provides for non-literal infringement. Where the courts do apply the doctrine of mechanical equivalents (which is at the courts' discretion), it can only apply to non-essential features of the claimed invention, which significantly distinguishes the Australian position from the US and the European positions.

IV. Infringing acts

1. *Infringing person or entity*

The Patents Act does not expressly identify who can engage in infringing conduct; nonetheless, the reference to "persons" in the Patents Act is construed with reference to the Australian legislative interpretation rules, which define "person" as an individual, corporation or body politic.[108] Accordingly, acts of infringement can be engaged in by individuals or entities, such as corporations.

106. (2000) 97 FCR 524.
107. *Ibid.* at [72].
108. Acts Interpretation Act 1901 (Cth) s 2C(1) which provides "in any Act, expressions used to denote persons generally (such as 'person', 'party', 'someone', 'anyone', 'no-one', 'one',

2. *Direct infringement*

The claims of a patent are directly infringed where a person, without authorisation of the patentee, engages in one or more of acts of exploitation.[109] For second medical use claims, the patentee's rights are limited to circumstances where there has been infringement of a method of treatment, "compound when used" or Swiss-type claim.

2.1 Manufacture of the pharmaceutical

A patentee's rights are not directly infringed by the mere manufacture of the compound for any purpose, because rights in second medical use claims extend only to manufacture of the compound for the second medical use.[110] Infringement can only be found where the process or method has been followed, or where there is the manufacture of a compound for the second medical use.

2.2 Offer for sale

A Swiss-type claim can be directly infringed by the offering for sale of a product containing the known compound, where that offer is accompanied by marketing or advertising of the compound for the second medical use.[111] The form of advertising or marketing includes product information documentation that is required by the TGA to accompany the compound.[112]

Infringement of a patentee's rights in Swiss-type claims can also be found where the claim is directed to the use of the compound as "effective for" or "effective in" the second medical use, irrespective of any marketing or advertising. The question is whether, objectively ascertained, the compound that results from the manufacture of the medicament is one that is nevertheless effective in the treatment of the second medical use.[113] Absent the words "effective for" or "effective in", however, there may be no infringement of a method or process, or Swiss-type claim in the offer for sale of the compound, if there is no marketing or advertising of the product for the second medical use.[114]

'another' and 'whoever'), include a body politic or corporate as well as an individual".

109. Section 13 and Schedule 1 definition of "exploit".
110. *Otsuka Pharmaceutical Co., Ltd v Generic Health Pty Ltd* (2015) 113 IPR 191 at [168] where Yates J held that "the manufacture of the medicament itself does not stand as use of the medicament for the defined purpose".
111. *Ibid.* at [172].
112. *Therapeutic Goods Act 1989* (Cth) s 23(2)(ba).
113. *Otsuka Pharmaceutical Co., Ltd v Generic Health Pty Ltd* (2015) 113 IPR 191 at [172].
114. *Apotex Pty Ltd v Sanofi-Aventis Australia Pty Ltd* (2013) 253 CLR 284 at [302]; we note that the decision in *Otsuka Pharmaceutical Co., Ltd v Generic Health Pty Ltd* (2015) 113 IPR 191 is on appeal which is likely to provide further guidance on this issue.

2.3 *Sale of the product*

A Swiss-type claim can be directly infringed by the sale of the compound, if the sale is accompanied by marketing or advertising for the second medical use.[115] As with the offering for sale of a product, direct infringement can also be found where the claim is directed to the use of the compound as "effective for" or "effective in" the second medical use, irrespective of any marketing or advertising, and absent those words, there may be no infringement by the sale of the compound, without marketing or advertising of the product for the second medical use.[116]

2.4 *Import*

A Swiss-type claim can be directly infringed through the importation of a compound resulting from the use outside of Australia of the claimed method or process, if the scope of the therapeutic use of the product, as listed on the Australian Register of Therapeutic Goods ("ARTG"), includes the second medical use.[117]

2.5 *Export*

The exclusive right to "otherwise dispose of" products resulting from methods or processes is sufficiently broad to encompass the act of exportation,[118] and the act of exportation presupposes the carrying out of the method or process in Australia to produce the product. Therefore, depending on the structure of the claim, a patentee's rights can be directly infringed. For example, a Swiss-type claim is directed to the manufacture of the medicament for the second medical use and a patentee's exclusive rights may be directly infringed by the manufacture of the compound in Australia for the second medical use and the subsequent exportation of the medicament manufactured.

2.6 *Combination products*

A patentee's rights in second medical use claims can be directly infringed through the use of a combination of two or more compounds. The patentee must show the

115. *Otsuka Pharmaceutical Co., Ltd v Generic Health Pty Ltd* (2015) 113 IPR 191 at [172].
116. *Apotex Pty Ltd v Sanofi-Aventis Australia Pty Ltd* (2013) 253 CLR 284 at [302]; we note that the decision in *Otsuka Pharmaceutical Co., Ltd v Generic Health Pty Ltd* (2015) 113 IPR 191 is on appeal which is likely to provide further guidance on this issue.
117. *Otsuka Pharmaceutical Co., Ltd v Generic Health Pty Ltd* (2015) 113 IPR 191 at [170]–[174] where Yates J held "[f]or the purpose of determining infringement of a Swiss type claim, does it matter that the alleged infringer does not actually advertise or promote the medicament specifically for the therapeutic use defined in the claim? I do not think it necessarily does. The question is whether, objectively ascertained, the medicament that results from the claimed method or process is one that has the therapeutic use defined in the claim".
118. *Seafood Innovations Pty Ltd v Richard Bass Pty Ltd* [2010] FCA 723 at [29]–[30].

taking of the combination of the compound; if the alleged infringer omits one of them, the infringer escapes liability.[119]

3. *Indirect infringement*

Indirect infringement of a patent is provided for under the Patents Act and the common law.

A patentee's rights in second medical use claims (in the form of a method of treatment claim) can be indirectly infringed where a supplier has supplied a product containing the compound to another person, and where:[120]

- the compound is not a staple commercial product and the supplier had reason to believe that the person would put the compound to an infringing use;[121] or
- the compound is used in accordance with any instructions for the use of the product, or any inducement to use the compound, which were given to the person by the supplier or contained in an advertisement published by or with the authority of the supplier.[122]

Under the common law, a patentee's rights in second medical use claims can be indirectly infringed:

- where the supplier's supply of the compound aids, induces or procures the infringement of the patent by persons who use the compound according to the patented method or process; or
- where the supplier has authorised the use of the compound by patients who use the compound according to the patented method or process.

Indirect infringement by supply concerns only method or process claims in the form of method of treatment claims; the indirect infringement provisions have no relevant application to Swiss-type claims. This is because the supplier of the compound is highly unlikely to have a reason to believe that the person to whom it supplied the compound will engage in an infringing process of manufacture.[123]

The remainder of this section B.IV.3 focusses on indirect infringement by supply, which is most commonly raised in infringement proceedings concerning second medical use claims.

3.1 *Objective acts*

Whether a supplier has "reason to believe" that the person would put the compound to an infringing use is determined objectively. Australian courts looks at whether

119. *Nicaro Holdings Pty Ltd v Martin Engineering Co.* (1990) 16 IPR 545 citing *Populin v H B Nominees Pty Ltd* (1982) 59 FLR 37 at 41.
120. Subsection 117(1).
121. Subsection 117(2)(b).
122. Subsection 117(2)(c).
123. *Otsuka Pharmaceutical Co., Ltd v Generic Health Pty Ltd* (2015) 113 IPR 191 at [168].

there are factual matters that would lead a reasonable person to believe that the compound would be used in the method or process that is the subject of the claims.[124]

The factual matters that Australian courts have considered include:

- the respective size of the markets for the infringing and non-infringing uses of the compound;[125]
- whether the use of the compound for the non-infringing use would, due to the nature of the therapeutic condition, nevertheless overlap with the infringing use;[126]
- whether the compound is routinely prescribed off-label for the infringing use;[127]
- whether there is any evidence of actual infringing use of the compound;[128]
- whether the product information for the compound specifically disclaims or instructs against the use in a manner that would be infringing;[129]
- whether the product information for the compound carves out use in a manner that would be infringing (known as "skinny-labelling");[130] and
- whether the alleged infringer has taken any steps, by way of marketing or promotional materials, to deter use of the compound in a manner that would be infringing.[131]

3.2 *Subjective conditions*

Subjective conditions, such as the requirement for actual belief or knowledge on the part of the supplier, are not prerequisites for a finding that the supplier had a reason to believe that the person would put the compound to an infringing use.[132]

3.3 *Import*

A patentee's rights in second medical use claims can be indirectly infringed if the supplier had reason to believe that the supply of the imported compound would be put to an infringing use. Matters relevant to a finding of infringement include

124. *Ibid.* at [193]; *Collins v Northern Territory* (2007) 161 FCR 549 at [64]–[66].
125. *Warner-Lambert Company LLC v Apotex Pty Ltd* [2014] FCAFC 59.
126. In *Leflunomide*, the HCA acknowledged that the administration of leflunomide to treat rheumatoid arthritis and psoriatic arthritis would also be likely to relieve the patient's psoriasis, but the claim was construed so as to require a deliberate administration of the compound to prevent or treat psoriasis.
127. *Warner-Lambert Company LLC v Apotex Pty Ltd* [2014] FCAFC 59.
128. *AstraZeneca AB v Apotex Pty Ltd* [2014] FCAFC 99 at [437].
129. *Apotex Pty Ltd v Sanofi-Aventis Australia Pty Ltd* (2013) 253 CLR 284 at [304].
130. *Ibid.* at [304].
131. *Warner-Lambert Company LLC v Apotex Pty Ltd* [2014] FCAFC 59.
132. *Generic Health Pty Ltd v Otsuka Pharmaceutical Co., Ltd* [2013] FCAFC 17 at [106]; *Collins v Northern Territory* (2007) 161 FCR 549 at [64]–[66]; *Otsuka Pharmaceutical Co., Ltd v Generic Health Pty Ltd* (2015) 113 IPR 191 at [66].

whether the scope of the therapeutic use of the compound, as registered on the ARTG, includes the second medical use.[133]

3.4 *Export*

A patentee's rights in second medical use claims cannot be indirectly infringed by exporting the compound. This is because, as discussed above in section C.IV.2.2.5, exportation presupposes the carrying out of the method or process in Australia. If the use of the method or process is not an infringement in Australia, the supply of the product outside of Australia cannot be an infringement.

3.5 *Combination products*

A patentee's rights in second medical use claims can be indirectly infringed where the individual compounds comprising a combination product are supplied to a person who then combines them for second medical use, where the combination is ordinarily sold in an unassembled form.[134] It is unclear, however, whether there is infringement where the combination is not ordinarily sold in an unassembled form.[135]

4. ***Off-label use***

4.1 *General admissibility of off-label use*

Evidence of off-label use of a known compound for a second medical use, for which the compound is not approved by the TGA and registered on the ARTG, is admissible evidence in infringement proceedings.

In *Warner-Lambert Company LLC v Apotex Pty Ltd*,[136] Apotex's pregabalin product was approved by the TGA for the non-infringing use. However Warner-Lambert's evidence from pharmacists was that there was no professional or legal obligation preventing a medical practitioner from prescribing, or a pharmacist dispensing, a medicine for an off-label indication if the medicine was approved by the TGA. This evidence was accepted by the Full Federal Court as relevant to whether there was a *prima facie* case that Apotex had a reason to believe its product would be put to an infringing use.[137]

133. *Alphapharm Pty Ltd v H Lundbeck A/S* (2008) 76 IPR 618 at [693]-[694], cited with approval in *Otsuka Pharmaceutical Co., Ltd v Generic Health Pty Ltd* (2015) 113 IPR 191 at [165].
134. *Windsurfing International Inc. v Petit* [1984] 2 NSWLR 196.
135. *Beadcrete Pty Ltd v Fei Yu trading as Jewels 4 Pools (No. 2)* (2013) 100 IPR 188 at [51]-[53].
136. [2014] FCAFC 59.
137. *Warner-Lambert Company LLC v Apotex Pty Ltd* [2014] FCAFC 59 at [39]-[42], [46]-[47], [86]-[87].

4.2 *Liable persons*

The liable person for infringing off-label use of a compound is, most commonly, the manufacturer or supplier of the product.[138]

Pharmacists and medical practitioners who prescribe off-label are generally not pursued for liability, even though their conduct would constitute direct infringement of the patent's claims. The National Competency Standards Framework for Pharmacists in Australia issued by the Pharmaceutical Society of Australia has been interpreted as stating that if a product is bioequivalent with a prescribed brand, and there are no contraindications, substitution is completely acceptable, without need to have reference to the indications as approved by the TGA.[139]

4.3 *Objective requirements for infringement*

The objective requirements for infringement as a result of off-label use are the same requirements discussed above at section C.IV.3.3.1.

In the context of off-label use, Australian courts have also considered the following matters:

- the size of the market for the off-label use, for instance, if the off-label use market is larger than the approved indicated use, it is more likely that the compound would be used off-label;[140]
- whether the compound would be sold at a discount which would encourage substitution and off-label prescriptions;[141]
- how the compound is prescribed, i.e., whether it is prescribed by drug name or without the indication being specified on the prescription, which would increase the likelihood of off-label use;[142] and
- how the compound is promoted, i.e., whether there are advertising or promotional materials warning against off-label use.[143]

4.4 *Subjective requirements for infringement*

As discussed above in section C.IV.3.3.2, subjective conditions, such as the requirement for actual belief or knowledge, are not prerequisites for the finding of infringement.

5. **Dosage regimes**

A finding of indirect infringement of second medical use claims that include a dosing regime depend on whether, for example, the compound is registered by the

138. For example, see *Warner-Lambert Company LLC v Apotex Pty Ltd* [2014] FCAFC 59.
139. *Ibid.* at [42].
140. *Ibid.* at [79], [83], [90].
141. *Ibid.* at [57].
142. *Ibid.* at [88].
143. *Ibid.*

TGA as bio-equivalent to the patentee's product, such that it will be put to the same use, including the same dosing regimen, as the patentee's product, or whether the product information provides for dosing regimens that are claimed in the patent.[144]

6. *Patient groups*

A finding of indirect infringement of second medical use claims that is targeted at a certain patient group depend on whether the compound is registered by the TGA as bio-equivalent to the patentee's product, such that it could be used for the group that is the subject of the second medical use claim.

V. Remedies

A patentee is entitled to a range of remedies for relief for infringement of the second medical use claim(s).

1. *Injunctions*

A patentee can obtain an injunction as relief for infringement, subject to the terms that the court thinks fit.[145]

2. *Damages*

A patentee can elect to obtain damages,[146] to put the patentee in the position it would have been had the infringement not occurred. The patentee may elect damages or an account of profits.[147]

In addition, the court can award exemplary damages having regard to the following matters:[148]

- the flagrancy of the infringement;
- the need to deter similar infringements of patents;
- the conduct of the party that occurred after the act constituting the infringement or after that party was informed that it had allegedly infringed the patent;
- any benefit shown to have accrued to that party because of the infringement; or
- all other relevant matters.

---

144. For example, see *Roche Therapeutics, Inc. v GenRx Pty Ltd* [2007] FCA 83 at [88]–[89] where in an application for a preliminary injunction the court held that it was at least arguable that GenRx had reason to believe that its products would be used for the patented purpose, including the dosing regimen.
145. Subsection 122(1).
146. *Ibid.*
147. *Colbeam Palmer Ltd v Stock Affiliates Pty Ltd* (1968) 122 CLR 25 at 32.
148. Subsection 122(1A).

There has only been one case in Australia where a court has ordered exemplary damages in addition to compensatory damages.[149]

3. *Information*

3.1 *Account of profits*

A patentee can obtain an account of the infringers profits made as a result of the infringing conduct.[150] As stated above, the patentee may elect damages or an account of profits.[151]

3.2 *Names of manufacturer, distributions etc., names of customers and information about infringing sales*

A patentee is entitled to limited discovery of documents that relate to the supply and sale by the defendant of the infringing product, in order to assist in the election by the patentee of an account of profits or damages. This is because such documents and the information which they contain are in the possession and within the knowledge of the defendant and the patentee otherwise has no means of knowing what sales or what supplies of the infringing product have been made.[152]

4. *Recall of products and destruction*

A patentee can obtain orders for the recall, delivery up, or the destruction of products found to infringe second medical use claims.

5. *Recovery of legal costs*

The successful party is generally entitled to its costs. The successful party in an infringement or revocation proceeding is entitled to the costs for work done and services performed by their legal representative(s), incurred from the commencement of the proceeding. A successful party may be awarded less than its costs, or there may be an order apportioning costs, on the basis of success on different issues raised in a proceeding.

A party will not recover all of its legal costs. The amount of costs that a successful party can obtain from the unsuccessful party are the costs that have been

149. *Pacific Enterprises (Aust) Pty Ltd v Bernen Pty Ltd* [2014] FCA 1372, where the Federal Court ordered $40,000 in exemplary damages in addition to $355,487.16 in compensatory damages against a supplier of window components.
150. Subsection 122(1).
151. *Colbeam Palmer Ltd v Stock Affiliates Pty Ltd* (1968) 122 CLR 25 at 32.
152. *Minnesota Mining & Manufacturing Co. v C Jeffries Pty Ltd t/as Seibulite of Australia* (1992) 37 FCR 294.

fairly and reasonably incurred by the party in the conduct of the proceeding, limited to the amount set out in the scale as determined by Australian courts.[153]

VI. Exceptions from patent protection

1. Exhaustion of rights

There is a presumption that the sale of a patented product is unfettered and that the on-sale exhausts the patentee's rights.[154] For second medical use claims, the claim is to methods or systems of use of the compound, and not the compound *per se*; therefore the exhaustion of rights doctrine has no application. Rather, it is whether the on-sale, or supply, constitutes an indirect infringement by supply, as discussed above in section C.IV.3.

2. Patient welfare

As discussed above in section C.IV.4.4.2, pharmacists and medical practitioners can prescribe a product off-label, for a second medical use, provided the product is bioequivalent with the prescribed brand and there are no contraindications.

VII. Procedural issues

1. Preliminary injunction cases

1.1 Availability for second medical use claims

The application for, and obtaining of, preliminary injunctions (called interlocutory injunctions in Australia) for threatened infringement of a second medical use claim is known as seeking "*quia timet* relief" and is available for, and commonly undertaken by, patentees.

The circumstances prompting a preliminary injunction often involve the following:

- notification by a generic company, either directly to the patentee or to pharmacists, of the launch of a compound for the claimed second medical use, or, the launch by a generic company of a compound for the first medical use;[155] or
- detection that a generic version of the product has been applied to be registered on the ARTG.

153. For example, see *Federal Court Rules 2011* rule 40.01 and Schedule 2.
154. *National Phonograph Co. Australia v Menck* [1980] GCA 96.
155. For example, see *Roche Therapeutics, Inc. v GenRx Pty Ltd* [2007] FCA 83 at [35] where GenRx informed 5,000 pharmacists that it was proposing to sell carvedilol tablets.

1.2 Specific requirements

The specific requirements for a preliminary injunction include the following:[156]

- whether the plaintiff for relief has established a *prima facie* case, i.e., whether there is a sufficient likelihood of success in establishing of direct or indirect infringement to justify, in the circumstances, the preservation of the status quo pending trial; or
- whether the balance of convenience and justice favours the grant of an injunction or the refusal of that relief, which involves a consideration of whether the patentee would suffer irreparable harm for which damages would not be adequate compensation.

The decision in *Warner-Lambert Company LLC v Apotex Pty Ltd*[157] concerned a preliminary injunction in relation to a second medical use claim to the method of use of pregabalin in the treatment of pain, including neuropathic pain. The first medical use for pregabalin was for seizures, for which Apotex sought registration with the TGA. Warner-Lambert sought a preliminary injunction against Apotex to restrain the making, importing or supplying or keeping for the purposes of supply, pregabalin on the basis that Apotex had reason to believe that its pregabalin product would, contrary to its approved use, be used for the patented purpose. The Full Federal Court held the following:

- There was a *prima facie* case of indirect infringement because the evidence showed that off-label substitution of pregabalin would not be unlikely, the market for the non-infringing use was virtually non-existent as compared to the market for the infringing use and the evidence did not show that the marketing materials distributed to doctors and intended to deter off-label substitution would be effective.[158]
- The balance of convenience favoured the grant of a preliminary injunction because the usual undertaking as to damages would have been likely to provide Apotex with an adequate remedy if it prevailed at the final hearing, and in the event it was entitled to a permanent injunction at trial, it would be extremely difficult for Warner-Lambert to raise its prices once it had to meet the discounts proposed by Apotex if the preliminary injunction was not granted.[159]

As a condition on the grant of preliminary injunctive relief in patent infringement proceedings, a patentee or exclusive licensee is ordinarily required to give the "usual undertaking as to damages", i.e., an undertaking to submit to such order (if any) of the court for the payment of compensation to any person (whether or not a party) adversely affected by the operation of the preliminary injunction. If the patentee is ultimately unsuccessful in its infringement claim, the alleged infringer can make a

156. *Samsung Electronics Co. Limited v Apple Inc.* [2011] FCAFC 156; see also *Otsuka Pharmaceutical Co., Ltd v Generic Health Pty Ltd* [2012] FCA 239.
157. [2014] FCAFC 59.
158. *Warner-Lambert Company LLC v Apotex Pty Ltd* [2014] FCAFC 59 at [83].
159. *Ibid.* at [98].

claim on the undertaking for compensation on the basis that it has suffered loss or damage by virtue of the launch of its product having been delayed.

2. *Cases on the merits*

As discussed above at section C.I.2, since *Leflunomide,* a number of cases on the merits have been determined concerning second medical use claims, including *Otsuka Pharmaceutical Co., Ltd v Generic Health Pty Ltd*[160] which concerned the use of a known compound, aripiprazole, for the treatment of certain forms of schizophrenia, and *AstraZeneca AB v Apotex Pty Ltd*[161] which concerned the use of a known compound, rosuvastatin, in low dosage levels to lower cholesterol.

3. *Enforcement of judgments*

Where a party is successful in an infringement proceeding, the judgment takes effect and can be enforced by way of court order.[162]

VIII. Validity

1. *Relevance for infringement cases*

If an infringement proceeding is commenced, the alleged infringer has the option to counter-claim seeking revocation of the patent on the available grounds of invalidity as set out in section B.IV.2.3.[163]

2. *Specifics for second medical use claims*

For second medical use claims, the invalidity grounds that are commonly raised in a counter-claim for revocation include lack of novelty and lack of inventive step, and/or the invention as claimed is not a manner of new manufacture.[164]

IX. Tactical considerations

It is common in patent cases for liability to be heard separately from and before issues as to the quantum of pecuniary relief, which can reduce costs and the length of the trial (although ultimately document discovery and evidence will be required for both parts of the proceeding).

---

160. [2012] FCA 239.
161. (2015) 114 IPR 445.
162. For example, see *Federal Court Rules 2011* rule 39.01.
163. Subsections 121, 138(3).
164. For example, see *Otsuka Pharmaceutical Co., Ltd v Generic Health Pty Ltd* (2015) 113 IPR 191 where Generic Health Pty Ltd counter-claimed for revocation of claims 1 and 7 of the patent on the basis that the invention as claimed was not novel, was not a manner of new manufacture and was obvious.

1. *Plaintiff*

When faced with infringement of second medical use claims, a plaintiff should consider whether a preliminary injunction should be sought early to preserve the status quo before a case on the merits is commenced. Where a defendant proposes to use "skinny-labelling", a plaintiff should ensure that it can adduce sufficient evidence that off-label use will be prevalent or that the market for the skinny-label use is small or insignificant such that the product will be put to an infringing use.[165]

A plaintiff should also appreciate the potential consequences of giving the usual undertaking as to damages as the price for securing a preliminary injunction.

2. *Defendant*

When faced with infringement of a second medical use claims, a defendant should consider bringing an action for revocation of the patent. A revocation action can be brought before a product containing the compound that is the subject of the patent is launched by the defendant, to mitigate the risk of an preliminary injunction being sought by the plaintiff (known as "clearing the way"), or by way of counter-claim in an infringement proceeding.

Where a defendant proposes to use "skinny-labelling", the defendant should ensure that it can adduce sufficient evidence to support its case that the market for the skinny-label use is significant and therefore it will suffer considerable damage by being kept out of that market.[166]

A defendant should also consider seeking from the court a non-infringement declaration after the plaintiff has given a written admission that the doing of the particular act by the defendant does not constitute infringement of the second medical use patent's claims.[167]

165. For example, see *Warner-Lambert Company LLC v Apotex Pty Ltd* [2014] FCAFC 59.
166. *Ibid.*
167. Sections 124–127.

Japan

Dr. Shoichi Okuyama

A. AVAILABILITY OF PROTECTION

I. Legal framework

1. Basics

Article 29(1) of the Japanese Patent Act[1] provides that: "Any person who has made an invention which is industrially applicable may obtain a patent therefor, except in the case of the following inventions," followed by the itemized list of circumstances in which novelty is lacking.

The definition of "invention" is in the Patent Act. According to Article 2(1), "invention" for the Patent Act means a highly advanced creation of a technical idea utilizing a law of nature. Also, an invention is categorized into: "an invention of a product," "an invention of a process," and "an invention of a process for manufacturing a product" (Article 2).

2. JPO Examination Guidelines

The Patent and Utility Model Examination Guidelines[2] published by the Japan Patent Office ("JPO") (Part III, Chapter 1, Section 3.1.1) identify a "method of surgery,

1. English translation of Japanese laws is available at: http://www.japaneselawtranslation.go.jp/?re = 02. The Patent Act is available at: http://www.japaneselawtranslation.go.jp/law/detail_main?vm = &id = 42.
2. In September 2015, the Japan Patent Office published a new set of the "Examination Guidelines for Patent and Utility Model" (herein referred to as "Examination Guidelines") and the "Examination Handbook for Patent and Utility Model" (herein referred to as "Handbook") to replace previous the "Examination Guidelines for Patent and Utility Model." The entire examination manuals have been revised for readability and up-to-date

therapy or diagnosis on humans"[3] as not industrially applicable, and no other inherent exclusion from patentability is stipulated as far as traditional medical inventions are concerned. Therefore, a second medical use may be patented so long as it is not claimed as a "method of surgery, therapy or diagnosis of humans."

Annex B of the Examination Handbook (Chapter 3, entitled "Medicinal Inventions") explicitly states that a medicinal invention based on a second medical use is "an invention of a product." As Case 1 in this Chapter, an invention directed to "a drug for treating Alzheimer's disease containing compound A as an active component" is novel over the known use of compound A as an antibiotic (Annex B, Chapter 3, section 3.1, page 13).

Incidentally, the following instructions are found in another part (Part II, Chapter 2, Section 3 on Clarity Requirement, page 7) of the Examination Guidelines:

> "'Use' or 'utilization' is treated as a term meaning a method of using a thing which belongs to the category of 'method'.
>
> Example 11: 'Use of substance X as an insecticide' is interpreted as 'method for using substance X as an insecticide.'
>
> Example 12: 'Use of substance X for the manufacture of a medicament for treating Y' is interpreted as 'method for using substance X for the manufacture of a medicament for treating Y.'"

Because a second medical use should be framed as a product invention according to the JPO, it is a normal and recommended practice to claim such second medical use as such: for example, "A pharmaceutical composition for treatment of condition X, comprising Y as an active component."

On the other hand, as discussed above, as the JPO accepts claims directed to "use" or "utilization," it may allow a Swiss-type claim or a method of manufacture claim in which a second medical use is identified, provided the other requirements are met. In fact, there exist many Japanese patents involving such types of claims.

In the enforcement phase, however, such Swiss-type claims or method claims tend to give rise to a controversy over the scope of protection and encounter problems with proof of infringement. Thus, it is advisable to claim such an invention as a product in accordance with Japanese practice.

3. *International treaties*

The TRIPS Agreement and numerous FTAs Japan has with many countries do not have any direct impact on the protection of second medical uses in Japan. The TRIPS

examples, but according to the JPO, the new set of Examination Guidelines and Handbook does not represent a significant departure from the examination practice that the JPO has been using last 15 years or so. Aside from some notable court decisions, the statutory provisions and such the Guidelines and Handbook are the source of law and practice in Japan. English translations of the Examination Guidelines and Handbook are available and can be easily found in the JPO website.

3. Methods of treating animals may be patented.

Agreement sets out the basic framework for patent protection. Japan is believed to be fully compliant with the TRIPS Agreement.

4. *Patent term extension*

Patent term extensions of up to five years are available on drugs and agricultural chemicals. Basically the term of a patent as a whole is extended, but the extended patent is effective only for the product that is the subject of a marketing authorization based on which the patent term extension was successfully requested. If the marketing authorization specifies a particular use of the product, the extended patent is effective only on such use.[4] Currently, a patent term extension is available for each marketing authorization of the same active component for a different dosage or efficacy.

5. *Biologics*

Biologics can be isolated from a variety of natural sources – human, animal, or microorganisms. Biologics may be composed of sugars, proteins, or nucleic acids or complex combinations of such substances, or may even be living entities such as cells and tissues. Under Japanese practice, biologics are patentable subject matter. No provisions, rules or case law exist which would exclude biologics from the subject of patent protection. If such biologics are isolated from natural sources for the first time and their efficacies are unknown, we can see a great likelihood of getting a patent on such biologics, provided regular patentability requirements such as inventive step and enablement (see below) are satisfied.

6. *Historical overview*

In 1975, as part of amendments to the Patent Act, Japan introduced a system for patenting substances and abolished provisions stating that pharmaceuticals are not eligible for patent protection. Prior to this, pharmaceuticals could only be protected under the Patent Act for their methods of manufacture. In preparation for this amendment, the Industrial Property Council was organized by the Ministry of International Trade and Industry (which is now the Ministry of Economy, Trade and Industry) to hear opinions from academics, industrial experts and lawyers.

From the viewpoint of public interests, the Council decided that: "pharmaceutical patents will not have adverse effects on people's lives because there are many types of similar pharmaceutical products available in the market these days."

The pharmaceutical industry commented that: "Since the prohibition of chemical and pharmaceutical patents is one of the factors that have brought about

4. Article 68-2 of the Patent Act provides that: "Where the duration of a patent right is extended (including the case where the duration is deemed to have been extended under Article 67-2(5)), such patent right shall not be effective against any act other than the working of the patented invention for the product which was the subject of the disposition designated by Cabinet Order under Article 67(2) which constituted the reason for the registration of extension (where the specific usage of the product is prescribed by the disposition, the product used for that usage).

technical gaps with other countries, we hope that these gaps will be gradually closed after lifting the prohibition."

There was no discussion, in particular, on whether there should be a distinction between first and second medical uses. Prior to the introduction of the substance patent system, use inventions had already been accepted for other than pharmaceutical and food uses, without distinction between first and second uses. Partly because of this situation, it seems that there was no special reason for distinction between first and subsequent medical uses.

Relatively recently pharmaceutical inventions characterized by dosages and/or administrations (including cell/tissue-based medicines) have become explicitly eligible for patent protection. According to a report dated May 29, 2009 by the Advanced Medical Patent Review Committee, a reason behind this change was as follows:

(i) importance of dosage and administration of a drug;
(ii) public need and importance of incentive measures;
(iii) adequacy of a system in which pharmaceutical inventions related to new dosages or administrations are protected as inventions directed to products, as opposed to methods; and
(iv) impact on costs and free access for patients.

After discussions, the Committee reached the following conclusion:

> "It is important to promote R&D of drugs that may dramatically reduce the occurrence of side effects or greatly improve the quality of life of patients, through finding new dosages and/or administrations. To expand the availability of these drugs, it is necessary to provide protection to pharmaceutical inventions of new dosages and/or administrations that achieve greater effects than expected by the experts. This type of invention should be protected as an invention of 'a product,' and to this end, the Examination Guidelines should be revised by taking into consideration the presented specific examples."

II. Policy considerations

With its aging population and national insurance system covering basically 100% of its population, increasing social costs of providing medical services are a big issue in Japan. While the use of generic drugs has been encouraged and a high bar has been set for their use, the use of generic drugs remains at about 56% as of September 2015.

Also, the patent term extension system has been in place in Japan since 1988. Two recent sets of Supreme Court decisions,[5] and several High Court decisions that led to the Supreme Court decisions, had very significant impacts on the practical application and operation of the system. When the system started in 1988, it was understood that a single patent term extension would be available for a particular active component. Now, more than one patent term extension is available if there is more than one marketing authorization for different dosages and/or efficacies of the

5. Supreme Court decisions of April 28, 2011 (Case Nos. 2009(gyo-hi)324-326) and of November 7, 2015 (Case No. 2014(gyo-hi)356).

same active component. Currently, the need for reforming the patent term extension system has been discussed, but so far no clear directions have emerged.

B. VALIDITY

I. Allowable claim wording

1. Product claims

As noted above, second medical uses of different types should invariably be claimed as a product for two reasons. One is that a method of treating a human patient is not patentable in Japan because such method is "not industrially applicable". This stems from the idea that medical doctors should not have to worry about patent infringement when they are trying to give the best treatment to a particular patient. The other reason is that a product claim generally provides the broadest scope of protection under the Japanese law. A patented product claim may be infringed when an unauthorized party makes, sells, uses, offers for sale, imports or exports an infringing product, whereas a patented method claim may be infringed only if the method is used.[6]

A claim directed to use or a Swiss-type claim is considered as a method claim in Japan. While the Swiss-type claim would most likely be considered as directed to a process of manufacturing a drug and that would afford patent protection over products manufactured by such process, the more direct claiming of a product would also avoid any potential problems, such as collection of evidence from the other party in litigation.

According to Annex B of the Examination Handbook, second medical use inventions are broadly classified into two types.

One type is a pharmaceutical invention related to a known compound. A second medical use of a known compound which is intended for a disease different from the one previously associated with the compound may be patentable.

Allowable claim formats include:

(1) A pharmaceutical for treatment of disease Y comprising active compound A;

---

6. Article 2 of the Patent Act defines "working of an invention" in paragraph (3) as "working" of an invention in this Act means the following acts:
   (i) in the case of an invention of a product (including a computer program, etc., the same shall apply hereinafter), producing, using, assigning, etc. (assigning and leasing and, in the case where the product is a computer program, etc., including providing through an electric telecommunication line, the same shall apply hereinafter), exporting or importing, or offering for assignment, etc. (including displaying for the purpose of assignment, etc., the same shall apply hereinafter) thereof;
   (ii) in the case of an invention of a process, the use thereof; and
   (iii) in the case of an invention of a process for producing a product, in addition to the action as provided in the preceding item, acts of using, assigning, etc., exporting or importing, or offering for assignment, etc. the product produced by the process.

(2) A disease Y drug comprising active component B;
(3) A disease Y drug comprising active component A and active component B in combination; and
(4) A treatment kit for disease Y comprising …

A claim directed to "compound X for treatment of disease Y" may not be patentable due to lack of novelty when compound X is already known in general, even if the treatment of disease Y with compound X is new. This is because the claim is considered to be directed to compound X itself.

The other type is a pharmaceutical product that uses the same active component as an existing drug for the same indication, but with a particular dosage and/or administration. If such dosage and/or administration produces a striking effect beyond expectation of one skilled in the art, then this invention may be patentable. Even this type of second medical use should be drafted as a product claim under Japanese practice. For examples of acceptable claim formats, see the section on "Dosage claims" below.

2. *Method claims*

As noted earlier, a method of surgery, treatment or diagnosis on a human patient is not patentable in Japan.

Claims such as the following are *not* permissible:

(1) A method of treating a patient suffering from disease Y, comprising administering an effective amount of compound X to the patient; and
(2) Use of compound X for treatment of disease Y.

As discussed above, a use claim is interpreted as a method claim according to the JPO.

3. *Use claims*

A Swiss-type claim, which is not recommended for Japan, can be patented as a method of manufacture provided that other patentability requirements are satisfied.

As noted above, "use of compound X for treatment of disease Y" is considered as a method of treatment and is not patentable unless it is explicitly designated for animals excluding humans.

4. *System claims*

A claim directed to a system is considered to be a product claim in Japan. It is therefore potentially patentable.

5. *Dosage claims*

A particular dosage and/or administration should also be claimed as a product. Possible claim formats include:

(1) An anti-asthma drug containing compound A, characterized in that 30-40 µg per kg of body weight is administered orally once every three months to a human patient;
(2) An ovarian cancer drug containing compound A as active component, characterized in that 100-120 µg per kg of body weight per dose is administered to portion Z of the brain of a human patient; and
(3) A diabetes treatment drug comprising compounds A and B at a weight ratio of 5:1 to 4:1.

These examples may possibly be patentable notwithstanding the fact that compounds A and B are already known for anti-asthma activity, anti-cancer action, and as diabetes drugs, respectively. These examples are found in Chapter 3 of Annex B of the Examination Handbook with detailed discussions on patentability requirements with respect to given background.

6. Disclosure requirements – enablement and support

In Japan, we have basically two disclosure requirements: one is enablement[7] and the other is support.[8] The enablement requirement concerns disclosure in the specification while the support requirement relates to the specification and claims.

In order to satisfy the enablement requirement in medical fields, it is generally necessary to have wet lab experimental data. Such data may come from *in vitro*, *in vivo* or animal experiments depending on the nature of the invention, but they are essential in the case of second medical uses, and reasoning as to why such data support the invention should preferably be discussed in the specification. It is generally impossible to cure the lack of enablement using later-filed experimental examples. So-called prophetic examples are not accepted to satisfy the enablement requirement.

Also, it is necessary for a skilled person to be able to produce or repeat the claimed subject matter based on the disclosure in the specification plus technical common knowledge at the time of filing. For a substance that can be produced only by a microorganism, it is necessary to have not only the name of the microorganism, but also its characteristics, growth conditions and other information that are necessary for a skilled person to produce the substance. It may be desirable to deposit the microorganism with an international authority depository. If the subject matter of the application happens to be a group of new chemical compounds, how to prepare the entire set of compounds has to be disclosed.

The support requirement may be more of a problem before the JPO. To support a given range of claims, it may be necessary to have several examples. It is always desirable to have as many examples as possible at the time of original filing. Of course, under the first-to-file system, the applicant is always under pressure to file quickly, but the lack of support can be fatal. The use of priority year may be an option, with cautionary remarks on the possibly limited availability of the benefits of priority for the added matter in the later-filed application.

7. Article 36(4)(i).
8. Article 36(6)(i).

There are other standard disclosure requirements such as clarity and conciseness, but they play a minor role when it comes to second medical use inventions.

II. Novelty

1. General definition of novelty and prior art

Article 29(1) of the Patent Act provides that novelty is lost if the claimed invention is publicly known, publicly used and described in a distributed publication or publicly available through the Internet anywhere in the world at the time of filing.[9]

Also, according to Article 29-2, an invention that is disclosed in a Japanese patent or utility model application filed prior to the application in question and published later than the filing of such application is not patentable.[10] According to Article 29-2, if the applicant or inventors are the same in the two Japanese applications, the prior-filed application is not novelty destroying against the later-filed application, so as to avoid problems of self-collision.

2. Grace period

Japan has liberal provisions for exceptions to the lack of novelty or grace period. If a Japanese or PCT application is filed within six months from the public disclosure

9. Article 29(1) provides that:
   "An inventor of an invention that is industrially applicable may be entitled to obtain a patent for the said invention, except for the following:
   (i) an invention that was publicly known in Japan or a foreign country, prior to the filing of the patent application;
   (ii) an invention that was publicly worked in Japan or a foreign country, prior to the filing of the patent application; or
   (iii) an invention that was described in a distributed publication, or an invention that was made publicly available through an electric telecommunication line in Japan or a foreign country, prior to the filing of the patent application."
10. Article 29-2 provides that: "Where an invention claimed in a patent application is identical with an invention or device (excluding an invention or device made by the inventor of the invention claimed in the said patent application) disclosed in the description, scope of claims or drawings (in the case of the foreign language written application under Article 36-2(2), foreign language documents as provided in Article 36-2(1)) originally attached to the written application of another application for a patent or for a registration of a utility model which has been filed prior to the date of filing of the said patent application and published after the filing of the said patent application in the patent gazette under Article 66(3) of the Patent Act (hereinafter referred to as 'gazette containing the patent') or in the utility model bulletin under Article 14(3) of the utility Model Act (Act No. 123 of 1959) (hereinafter referred to as 'utility model bulletin') describing matters provided for in each of the paragraphs of the respective Article or for which the publication of the patent application has been effected, a patent shall not be granted for such an invention notwithstanding Article 29(1); provided, however, that this shall not apply where, at the time of the filing of the said patent application, the applicant of the said patent application and the applicant of the other application for a patent or for registration of a utility model are the same person."

including public sales or use by the inventor, or by a person having the right to obtain a patent with a proper notice to the Patent Office as to claiming of benefits, it is possible to remove such disclosure from the prior art base. Also, if the disclosure is made against the intention of the inventor or a person having the right to obtain a patent, such disclosure may be excluded from the prior art if a Japanese or PCT application is filed within six months from the disclosure. The grace period is provided in Article 30 of the Patent Act.

3. *Definition of skilled person*

According to the statutory provisions, "a skilled person" is "a person ordinarily skilled in the art of the invention." This is generally believed to be a fictitious person who has technical common knowledge at the time of filing in the area of technology to which the claimed invention belongs and satisfies the following two requirements that:

(i) they are capable of using normal technical means for research and development (including document analysis, experiment, technical analysis, manufacture, etc.); and
(ii) they have ordinary creativity such as choice of materials and design modification (Examination Guidelines, Part II, Chapter I, Section 1 on enablement requirement).

This definition of a skilled person is somewhat different from that for the purpose of assessing inventive step.

4. *Scope of disclosure*

4.1 *General rules*

The prior art disclosure is read by a skilled person in view of technical common knowledge at the time of filing. If the prior art disclosure is not enabling, for example, if it was impossible to prepare a chemical compound identified by its name in the prior art in view of technical common knowledge at the time of filing, such chemical compound may not be prior art regarding the claimed invention.

4.2 *First medical use*

No special rules are applicable to the first medical use. General rules are applicable.

4.3 *New subject matter*

New subject matter may not be entered into a patent application by way of amendments. The current standard for new matter is that if an amendment includes an item that is not explicitly stated in the application, it should be determined whether such item is derivable for a skilled person in view of the entire application with reference to the technical common knowledge at the time of filing.

According to the Examination Guidelines (Part II, Chapter IV, Section 3.2), even if matter mentioned in amendments are not explicitly stated in the application as a whole, matter obvious from the application can be included in amendments considering the following:

The examiner shall take note of the following (i) and (ii) for determining whether amended matter is "matter obvious from the statement in the originally attached description, etc."

(i) The technology concerning amended matter cannot sufficiently be considered as "matter obvious from the statement in the originally attached description, etc." just because the technology itself is well known or commonly used.

(ii) In some cases, a person skilled in the art may understand that amended matter is obvious from several statements in the originally attached description, etc. in light of the common general knowledge as of the filing. The several statements in the originally attached description, etc. are, for example, a statement of the problem to be solved by the invention and a statement of examples of the invention, or a statement in the description or drawings.

4.4 *New data*

New data which are entered into a patent application by the applicant would become prior art as of the date on which such new data became available to the public, for example, through an entry in the patent office database.

5. ***Requirement for second medical use***

5.1 *Distinction from first medical use*

This is a difficult question to answer in general. Like the determination of inventive step, all factual circumstances have to be considered even when the scope of first medical use is determined.

5.2 *Sub-species of first medical use*

The concept of a selection invention may be applicable to second medical use. For example, a broad disclosure covering a relatively large number of compounds may not be prior art against a species included in the compounds, if no specific example matches the species. Probably, it is required that the species show unexpected behavior from the broad disclosure, in order for it to be considered new.

5.3 *Dosage regimes*

As noted above, a dosage regime may be patentable even if the subject compound or composition is already known.

III. Inventive step

1. Definition of inventive step

While Article 29(1) of the Patent Act defines the industrial applicability and novelty requirements, Article 29(2) defines the inventive step requirement as follows: "Where, prior to the filing of the patent application, a person ordinarily skilled in the art of the invention would have been able to easily make the invention based on an invention prescribed in any of the items of the preceding paragraph, a patent shall not be granted for such an invention notwithstanding the preceding paragraph."

It should be noted that the inventive step requirement has Article 29(1) as the definition of the prior art base.

2. Same scope of disclosure as for novelty?

As noted above, Article 29-2 of the Patent Act defines secret prior art and provides that the claimed invention in the patent application in question may lack novelty if the invention is disclosed in another Japanese patent or utility model application filed prior to and published later than the filing of the application. Since the provisions for the inventive step requirement have nothing to do with Article 29-2, secret prior art is not considered when the inventive step requirement is assessed.

3. Assessment of inventive step

The claimed invention does not satisfy the inventive step requirement if reasoned logic can be formed that a person skilled in the art could easily arrive at the claimed invention based on the prior art at the time of filing. For this purpose, it is necessary to assess comprehensively various facts in support of the existence or non-existence of inventive step.

According to the Examination Guidelines, "a person skilled in the art" is defined, in essence, as a hypothetical person who meets all the following conditions:

(i) they have the common knowledge in the technical field of the claimed invention at the time of filing;
(ii) they are capable of using ordinary technical means for research and development (including document analysis, experiment, technical analysis, manufacture, etc.);
(iii) they are capable of exercising ordinary creativity in selecting materials and modifying designs; and
(iv) they are capable of comprehending everything in the state of the art in the technical field of the claimed invention at the time of filing, and comprehend everything in the field relevant to problems to be solved by the invention.

It is also noted in the Examination Guidelines that it may be appropriate to consider a person skilled in the art to be a "team of experts" rather than an individual person in certain areas of technology.

Such definition of a skilled person for the purpose of assessing the inventive step requirement is not the same as that for other patentability requirements such as disclosure requirement.

IV. Amendment of claims after grant

1. Admissibility of post-grant amendments in general

It is possible to amend the patented claims after grant in Japan. Such post-grant amendments are referred to as "corrections."

Article 126(1) of the Patent Act provides that:

> "The patentee may file a request for a trial for correction with regard to the correction of the description, claims or drawings attached to the application; provided, however, that such correction shall be limited to the following:
> (i) restriction of the claims;
> (ii) correction of errors or incorrect translations; or
> (iii) clarification of an ambiguous statement."[11]

This so-called correction is possible even after the expiration of the patent or while infringement lawsuits are pending before the court.

2. Procedural issues

2.1 Independent limitation proceedings

Corrections have to be requested at the JPO. It is procedurally impossible to ask the court to allow corrections. After corrections are requested, the JPO normally issues a decision relatively quickly, within three to four months. Appeal is possible against the decision of the JPO before the IP High Court. If the correction is allowed, a patent is deemed to have been granted as corrected.

2.2 Opposition proceedings

In Japan, once-abolished opposition proceedings restarted in April 2015. The opposition proceedings are conducted before the JPO. Corrections are possible and integrated into opposition proceedings. At particular phases of the opposition proceedings, corrections can be requested.

2.3 Nullity actions

During nullity actions, which have to take place before the JPO, corrections can be requested.

11. While the JPO uses the term "trial" in English for proceedings that are considered by a panel of three appeal examiners, it is in fact a document-based proceeding that moves fairly quickly.

V. Change of patent category

The change of patent category is possible in certain limited cases.

The Supreme Court of Japan rendered two decisions[12] in June 2015 in which a product-by-process claim was found inherently ambiguous, and therefore not allowable or valid, unless the applicant or patentee can show that, with intrinsic or external evidence, it was impossible or utterly impractical to use a format other than the product-by-process claim.

In March 2016, the Appeal and Trial Department of the JPO decided to allow the change from a patented product-by-process claim into a process claim as a correction of an ambiguous statement.

Other than such exceptional cases, a change of patent category is not allowable.

C. INFRINGEMENT AND LITIGATION

I. Legal framework

1. National statutory laws

In Japan, the Code of Civil Procedure provides the basic framework of civil litigation. Currently, infringement cases involving technological issues like patent cases can be brought only before either the Tokyo or Osaka District Court, although Japan has 50 district courts throughout the country. Also, there are many patent-specific rules at the Tokyo and Osaka District Courts, and the Intellectual Property High Court, which has the only appellate jurisdiction over all patent infringement cases as well as appeals from decisions made by the Appeal and Trial Department of the JPO. Such rules are published and available, for example, on the website of the court.

2. Case law

Japan is a civil law country. All courts make decisions on the basis of statutory laws while lower courts are required to follow Supreme Court decisions. In principle,

12. *Pravastatin Sodium* case decisions, June 5, 2015, the Second Petty Bench of the Supreme Court of Japan, Case Nos. 2012(ju)1204 and 2012(ju)2658. The Court made two points clear: the scope of a product-by-process claim is not limited by the process, and the clarity requirement is satisfied only if it can be shown that a product-by-process was the only way to define the invention. To quote from the decisions:

> "Even if a patent claim concerning a product invention recites the manufacturing process of a product, the technical scope of the patented invention should be determined to cover products that have the same structure and characteristics, etc., as those of the product made in accordance with the manufacturing process."

> "When patent claims concerning a product invention recite the manufacturing process of a product, such claims would satisfy the requirement [that] 'the invention be clear' according to Article 36(6)(ii), Patent Act, only if circumstances exist under which it is impossible or utterly impractical to directly identify the structure or characteristics of the product at the time of filing."

case law should play a limited role in litigation in Japan, but as a matter of fact, all court decisions in patent infringement cases are published on the court website and through other media, and closely studied for possible guidance.

II. Claim construction

1. General rules

Article 70 of the Patent Act sets out basic rules for claim construction.

Article 70 reads as follows:

> "(1) The technical scope of a patented invention shall be determined based upon the statements in the scope of claims attached to the application.
>
> (2) In the case of the preceding paragraph, the meaning of each term used in the scope of claims shall be interpreted in consideration of the statements in the description and drawings attached to the application.
>
> (3)In the case of the preceding two paragraphs, statements in the abstract attached to the application shall not be taken into consideration."

In Japan, the all element rule is applicable. The JPO and courts alike do not make any distinction whether a feature or an element is recited in the preamble or the body of a patent claim.

2. Specific issues for use claim

Use claims are interpreted the same way as with other types of patent claims.

III. Scope of protection

1. In general

Since a second medical use should be claimed as a product in Japan, the scope of protection covers the manufacture, sale, offer for sale, importation and exportation of the claimed product for a particular claimed use.[13]

If the Swiss-type claim format is used, it would probably be considered as a process for manufacturing a product and afforded the same scope of protection as

13. Article 2(3) of the Patent Act provides the definition of working of an invention as follows:
"(3) 'Working' of an invention in this Act means the following acts:
(i) in the case of an invention of a product (including a computer program, etc., the same shall apply hereinafter), producing, using, assigning, etc. (assigning and leasing and, in the case where the product is a computer program, etc., including providing through an electric telecommunication line, the same shall apply hereinafter), exporting or importing, or offering for assignment, etc. (including displaying for the purpose of assignment, etc., the same shall apply hereinafter) thereof;
(ii) in the case of an invention of a process, the use thereof; and

a product claim which includes a use limitation. Having said that, a method claim normally encounters more problems than a product claim, partly because Japan does not have a discovery system. It is generally difficult to obtain evidence of what is done in the factories or laboratories of the other party, resulting in difficulties in enforcing method claims in general.

1.1 Prescription

The only exemptions from infringement liabilities provided in the Patent Act are found in Article 63. Article 63(3) is the only provision that is relevant to our study here and reads: "A patent right for the invention of a medicine to be manufactured by mixing two or more medicines or for the invention of a process to manufacture such a medicine shall not be effective against the act of preparation of a medicine as is written in a prescription."

This means that physicians and pharmacists are not exempt from infringement liabilities concerning a drug patent unless mixing of two or more drugs is involved.

1.2 Experimental use and testing of a patented drug by a generics maker

Under Article 69(1)[14] of the Patent Act, acts done for experimental or research purposes are excluded from the patent protection. If a product or a method is used for purely scientific testing, it would probably not infringe any patent. The purpose of Article 69(1) is to promote scientific or technological developments. Therefore, experimental manufacturing and sale for testing the market is not exempted. If testing is carried out to see whether a patented invention really works, such testing would clearly fall under the experimental use exception and does not infringe the patent. On the other hand, if a patented invention is used to see whether it is commercially viable, such testing, most probably, does not fall under the experimental use exception of Article 69(1).

A big issue here is whether or not carrying out experiments for the sole purpose of obtaining governmental approval for marketing generic drugs may be exempted under Article 69(1). On April 16, 1999, the Supreme Court handed down a decision[15] concerning the question of experimental use exemption in favor of generic drug manufacturers. The Court found that tests carried out during the patent term in an attempt to obtain governmental approvals for manufacture and sales after the expiration of patents do not constitute patent infringement under Article 69(1) of the Patent Act.

Prior to the Supreme Court decision, on July 18, 1997, the Tokyo District Court rendered three decisions in actions brought by Otsuka Pharmaceutical Co., Ltd. against several generic drug makers. In those decisions, the 29th civil division of the

---

(iii) in the case of an invention of a process for producing a product, in addition to the action as provided in the preceding item, acts of using, assigning, etc., exporting or importing, or offering for assignment, etc. the product produced by the process."

14. Article 69(1) reads as follows: "A patent right shall not be effective against the working of the patented invention for experimental or research purposes."
15. The Second Petty Bench, Case No. 1998(ju)153.

Court found no patent infringement for experiments done by generic drug makers during the patent term. This was a complete reversal of earlier decisions made by various courts. For example, in the *Synthelabo* case, the Nagoya District Court had found patent infringement because the experimental use exemption (Article 69 of the Patent Act) was not applicable to the experiments which were done for the sole purpose of obtaining governmental approval for future sale of old patented drugs and which did not lead to scientific advances. The Kanazawa branch of the Nagoya High Court and the Osaka District Court have also followed the line of reasoning set out in the *Synthelabo* case. Thus, two lines of contradicting reasoning existed in Japan, and the above Supreme Court decision put an end to the confusion.

2. Absolute product protection

2.1 Off-label use

We do not have very clear guidance from court precedent on this issue in Japan. The *Ketotifen* case, which will be discussed in connection with injunctive remedies below in some details, may shed some limited light. In this case, the Tokyo District Court granted an injunction over the sale of drugs that were labeled for specific types of asthma for specific administration (twice a day orally at breakfast and bedtime) when the patent was directed to the second medical use of Ketotifen for prevention of allergic asthma because, according to the court, the labeled indications covered, but were not limited to, the claimed use of prevention.

According to another court case which happened to relate to the issue of employee invention compensation, a generic product was found infringing when its package insert did not directly and explicitly refer to such use but the patentee proved that it was "made or supplied to be intended for such use" based on a set of specific and objective facts (*Cilostazol* case, IP High Court decision dated November 21, 2006, Case No. 2005 (ne) 10125).

Naturally, whether the fact of off-label use can preclude a finding of an infringement would most likely be a fact-intensive question.

3 Dosage regimes

As discussed above, it is possible to obtain a patent when an active compound or substance was known for a specific indication if an inventor finds a remarkable improvement with a specific dosage or a combination use with another known compound or substance. What we may say here is limited to that ordinary claim construction principles should apply.

4. Doctrine of equivalents

In Japan, the Supreme Court has approved this doctrine and provided a set of clear criteria for its application.

Initially, the Tokyo and Osaka High Courts expressed affirmative views on the doctrine. Then, on February 24, 1998, in an appeal filed by the accused infringer in the so-called *Ball Spline Bearing* case, the Supreme Court redefined the doctrine of equivalents. The Supreme Court stated that for the doctrine to be applicable the following five criteria have to be considered: Even if there exists a portion in the patent claim that is different from the alleged infringing product, an infringement may be found provided:

(1) the differing portion is not an essential part of the patented invention;
(2) the same function and results are still obtained serving the same purpose as that of the patented invention even if that portion is replaced by the corresponding element found in the allegedly infringing product;
(3) the above replacement would have been easily conceived by a person skilled in the art with reference to the time of manufacture of the infringing product;
(4) the infringing product is not the same as the art publicly known at the time of filing for the disputed patent and it could not have been easily conceived by a person skilled in the art at the time of filing for the patent based on such publicly known art; and
(5) no special circumstances exist such as the intentional exclusion of the infringing product from the scope of the patented claim during the prosecution of the patent application for the patented invention.

The Supreme Court pointed out that the Tokyo High Court failed to consider condition (4) above and remanded the case back to the original court. The case was subsequently settled. In addition to the first three conditions, the Supreme Court included the last two conditions, which are traditionally considered as defense arguments, as essential for the correct application of the doctrine.

Also, the equivalent is determined in view of the state of art at the time of infringement.

Further, the newly added last two requirements are well-known legal constructs: condition (4) is reminiscent of the *Wilson Golf Ball* case in the U.S., in which it was noted that the application of the doctrine hinges on a hypothetical patent claim crafted to be non-obvious over the prior art and to cover the alleged infringing product; and condition (5) suggests the prosecution history estoppel, which is well recognized and established as a defense in some countries including Japan.

The significance of this decision is the fact that it was rendered by the Supreme Court. In a strict sense, Supreme Court decisions alone have authoritative status in Japan. Unlike lower court decisions, Supreme Court decisions function as law and are regarded as binding on lower courts. The fact that the Supreme Court said nothing negative about the doctrine of equivalents and clarified the criteria gives legitimacy to assertions of doctrine of equivalents infringement. Lower courts have handed down a number of decisions on the application of the doctrine since this Supreme Court decision, and the above criteria have invariably been adopted in those decisions. Generally speaking, however, the percentage of decisions in which the doctrine was applied in favor of patentees remains small, or about 4-6% of all cases in which the doctrine is asserted, and it should be understood that the doctrine of equivalents is available only in very limited situations.

IV. Infringing acts

1. Direct infringement

If a product in question contains, as mentioned above, all the features and limitations recited in a patent claim or if it is considered to be an infringement under the doctrine of equivalents, it would constitute a direct infringement. The same is true for patented claims directed to methods. If the allegedly infringing product does not contain some portion of the elements or features found in a claim, no direct infringement should be found with respect to that claim.

2. Indirect infringement

Also, if a third party produces a kit which contains all the elements that form the claimed product and a consumer purchases and assembles it at home, neither the sale of such kit nor assembly would constitute direct infringement, because the kit would lack some features or elements that tie the claimed structural elements together, while the assembly cannot be considered to have been done "as a business" as required in Article 68 of the Patent Act because it is done privately or for no business purposes. This is also true if an unauthorized person sells an essential component of the claimed product by omitting a few trivial elements or features recited in a patent claim.

Such acts cannot be overlooked from the standpoint of meaningful patent protection. Therefore, the Patent Act contains some provisions[16] that regard such acts as another form of infringement, so-called "indirect infringement," thus giving the same protection as a direct infringement.

We do not have any provisions for so-called "contributory infringement" in Japan.

V. Remedies

1. Injunctions

Injunctions should be automatically available once a patent infringement is found. The basis of this is Article 100 of the Patent Act, which stipulates that:

---

16. Article 101 reads as follows:

"The following acts shall be deemed to constitute infringement of a patent right or an exclusive license:

(i) where a patent has been granted for an invention of a product, acts of producing, assigning, etc., importing or offering for assignment, etc. any product to be used exclusively for the producing of the said product as a business;

(ii) where a patent has been granted for an invention of a product, acts of producing, assigning, etc., importing or offering for assignment, etc. any product (excluding those widely distributed within Japan) to be used for the producing of the said product and indispensable for the resolution of the problem by the said invention as a business, knowing that the said invention is a patented invention and the said product is used for the working of the invention; ..." (rest omitted)

"(1) A patentee or exclusive licensee may demand a person who infringes or is likely to infringe the patent right or exclusive license to stop or prevent such infringement.

(2) In making a demand under the preceding paragraph, the patentee or exclusive licensee may demand measures necessary for the prevention of such infringement including the disposal of products constituting such act of infringement (including, in the case of a patented invention of a process of producing products, products produced by the act of infringement; the same shall apply in Article 102(1)) and the removal of facilities used for the act of infringement."

A representative court case in which an injunction was available based on a patent directed to a second medical use is the Tokyo District Court decision in the *Ketotifen* case dated October 23, 1992.[17] Claim 1 of the second medical use patent in dispute read as follows: "A preventive agent for allergic asthma containing Ketotifen or pharmaceutically acceptable acid addition salt as an active ingredient." The court did not grant an injunction against the general use of "fumarate compound (Ketotifen fumarate)" which was the active ingredient for pharmaceutical products the defendants manufactured and sold. The court, however, granted an injunction against the marketing of the pharmaceutical products for the treatment of bronchial asthma, asthma, and allergic asthma; administered orally twice a day after breakfast and at bedtime although the stated efficacies of the defendants' products were broader than that of claim 1 in the disputed patent. In this permanent injunction case, an injunction was available solely upon the "statements provided in the product packaging," or the package insert, when they referred to the patented use, which were considered as sufficient evidence on "uses of invention."

2. *Damages*

General provisions on damages awards exist in the Civil Code.[18] For intangible assets such as patents, however, it is difficult to establish a clear relationship between infringement and damages under such general provisions alone. The Patent Act therefore provides for three special ways of damages calculation.

First, the profits the infringer gained in connection with the infringing acts can be presumed equal to the damages the patentee suffered under Article 102(2) of the Patent Act.[19] It used to be believed that this presumption was available when the patentee worked the patented invention, but the Grand Panel of the IP High Court rejected this belief. Now, as the Court puts it, "the fact that the patentee works the

17. Case No. 1990(wa)12094 (Chiteki Saishu vol.24, No. 3, page 805; Hanrei Jihou No. 1469, page 139).
18. Article 709, Civil Code, which reads as follows: "A person who has intentionally or negligently infringed any right of others, or legally protected interest of others, shall be liable to compensate any damages resulting in consequence."
19. Article 102(2) of the Patent Act reads as follows: "Where a patentee or exclusive licensee claims, from a person who has intentionally or negligently infringed the patent right or exclusive license, compensation for damages caused to him by the infringement, the profits gained by the infringer through the infringement shall be presumed to be the amount of damages suffered by the patentee or exclusive licensee."

patented invention is not a requirement for the applicability of the clause," and "if the patentee could have obtained profits but for infringing acts of the infringer, Article 102(2) is applicable."[20]

Secondly, the reasonable royalty may be awarded as a minimum even if the patentee does not use the patented invention under Article 102(3).

The third way of damages calculation is relatively new and was introduced in the 1998 Patent Act amendment. According to Article 102(1), the damages award can be calculated by multiplying the number or amount of products the infringer sold by the marginal profit the patentee enjoyed.[21] This third way possibly gives rise to a large award, because the profit figure used would be a marginal profit or a profit the patentee enjoyed on the last product it sold, and it should not be difficult for the patentee to show profit figures based on its own accounting figures. In order to arrive at a figure for the marginal profit, only normal manufacturing and sales costs can be deducted from the gross profit. It is probably not allowed to deduct initial R&D costs and marketing or advertising costs.

3. *Availability of information – data exclusivity*

We have so-called reexamination of a pharmaceutical and a period for data exclusivity during which a new drug should be reexamined on its approved efficacies and safety while it is publicly used. This is provided separately from patent protection. The data exclusivity period is set by the Ministry of Health, Labor and Welfare (MHLW) and is eight years from the marketing authorization in many cases.

VI. Exception from patent protection

1. *Patent exhaustion*

No statutory provisions in the Patent Act define or codify the doctrine of patent exhaustion. However, this doctrine plays a very important role in patent infringement litigation. After a product covered by a patent has been sold by the patent owner or by others with the authorization of the patent owner, patent rights are said to have

20. Waste Disposal Device case, decided on February 1, 2013, the Grand Panel of the Intellectual Property High Court, Case No. 2012(ne)10015.
21. Article 102(1) provides that: "Where a patentee or exclusive licensee claims, from a person who has intentionally or negligently infringed the patent right or exclusive license, compensation for damages caused to him by the infringement, and the person's act is the assignment of articles by which the act of the infringement was committed, the sum of money with the profit per unit of such articles multiplied by the number of articles (hereinafter referred to in this paragraph as the 'number of assigned articles') which the patentee or exclusive licensee could have sold in the absence of the infringement may be estimated as the amount of damages suffered by the patentee or exclusive licensee within a limit not exceeding an amount attainable depending on working capability of the patentee or exclusive licensee. Where there is any circumstance that prevents the patentee or exclusive licensee from selling part or the whole of the number of assigned articles, a sum equivalent to the number of assigned articles subject to that circumstance shall be deducted."

exhausted. The patent owner can no longer enforce their patent against third parties. This limitation is also referred to as the "exhaustion doctrine" or "first sale doctrine". The applicability of this doctrine is broadly recognized at least within the context of the domestic market, but there are on-going controversies as to what extent the sale of a patented product abroad can exhaust the patent over this product in the context of domestic law. This is the question of "international exhaustion."[22]

2. Experimental use and particular exemptions

Article 69 of the Patent Act, some portions of which are discussed above, is the only provision in the Patent Act that provides for exceptions from patent infringement. It reads as follows:

> "(1) A patent right shall not be effective against the working of the patented invention for experimental or research purposes.
>
> (2) A patent right shall not be effective against the following products:
> (i) vessels or aircrafts merely passing through Japan, or machines, apparatus, equipment or other products used therefor; and
> (ii) products existing in Japan prior to the filing of the patent application.
>
> (3) A patent right for the invention of a medicine (refers to a product used for the diagnosis, therapy, treatment or prevention of human diseases, hereinafter the same shall apply in this paragraph) to be manufactured by mixing two or more medicines or for the invention of a process to manufacture a medicine by mixing two or more medicines shall not be effective against the act of preparation of a medicine as is written in a prescription from a physician or a dentist and the medicine prepared as is written in a prescription from a physician or a dentist."

VII. Procedural issues

1. Preliminary injunction cases

While cases on the merits are decided by a panel of three judges, preliminary injunction cases are decided by a single judge. Also, it should be noted that preliminary injunction proceedings are *inter partes*, and the other party is always heard. Evidential level of proof is different between preliminary and permanent injunction lawsuits according to statutory provisions, but in practice it is often difficult to find any

22. We have two notable Supreme Court decisions: one is so-called BBS Automobile Aluminum Wheels case (the Third Petty Bench, the Supreme Court, decided on July 1, 1997, Case No. 1995(o)1988) concerning international exhaustion, and the other so-called Ink Tank case (the First Petty Bench, the Supreme Court, decided on November 8, 2007, Case No. 2006(ju)826) concerning refurbishment of one-time use cameras. In the BBS Automobile Aluminum Wheels case, the court denied injunctive reliefs for a German company which had patents in Germany and Japan when a parallel importer imported its high-end automobile wheels from Germany into Japan. The court emphasized the importance of the free flow of products when no indications were given on the products regarding the intended territorial scope of such products sold in Germany.

differences. When it comes to fact-intensive patent infringement lawsuits, preliminary injunction proceedings are, in many cases, nó more quickly than cases on the merits.

2. *Cases on the merits*

Before the Tokyo or Osaka District Courts, which have sole jurisdiction over particular technology-related cases, patent infringement lawsuits are concluded within 12 to 15 months on average from the filing of a complaint to the final disposal including the determination of infringement and accounting of damages. Since the Japanese legal system does not allow for Anglo-American discovery, it is generally difficult to obtain documentary evidence or other types of evidence from the other party.

VIII. Validity

1. *Relevance to infringement cases*

Nullity or invalidation proceedings are available before the JPO even during infringement court proceedings. It is also possible to argue invalidity before an infringement court. The Tokyo or Osaka District Court may stay infringement proceedings if invalidation proceedings are pending before the JPO. In reality, however, it is more likely for the court to proceed in the infringement case without waiting for a JPO decision.

2. *Double track system*

It used to be believed that Japan had a German-style bifurcation system. With the decision of the Supreme Court of Japan in the so-called *Kilby*[23] case in which a Japanese patent - a patent directed to a fundament principle of integrated circuits - owned by Texas Instruments, having survived more than 35 years from the initial filing in Japan after repeated divisional applications, was found invalid, the Supreme Court allowed infringement courts to find the asserted patent invalid and dismiss the demand of the patentee as abusive use of rights. Such finding of invalidity is binding only with respect to the parties in the litigation.

On April 11, 2000, the Supreme Court reversed the precedent set by its predecessor court in the *Kilby* case between Fujitsu and Texas Instruments (Case No. 1998(o)364). Initially, Fujitsu sought a declaratory judgment against TI. The Supreme Court agreed with the Tokyo High Court that the divisional application that resulted in the patent in dispute was illegal and therefore the patent could not be enforced. The Supreme Court affirmed the Tokyo High Court decision. In doing so, it changed the precedent set by its predecessor court some 85 to 100 years ago, and allowed courts considering infringement disputes to find patents invalid and unenforceable. The Patent Act provides that the JPO is entitled to invalidate patents, and it used to be believed that it was not possible for the infringement court to find a patent invalid prior to the JPO's decision on that issue. The Supreme Court stated that: "it

23. Dr. Kilby was awarded a Nobel Prize in 2000 for his invention of integrated circuits.

should be possible for the court that is hearing a patent infringement case to decide whether or not it is clear that grounds for invalidity exist, and as a result of such deliberation, if grounds for the invalidity clearly exist against the disputed patent, requests for an injunctive relief and damages award based on the patent should not be allowed as an abuse of patent rights."[24]

Subsequent to this Supreme Court decision, the Patent Act was amended in 2004 to codify the decision.[25]

As a result of the Supreme Court decision and the Patent Act amendment we currently have a dual track invalidation scheme in Japan. A patent may be invalidated by the JPO, with possible reviews by courts, with legal effects as to third parties, and may also be found invalid by an infringement court with legal effects only to the parties in the litigation.

Figure 1. Dual invalidation system for patents

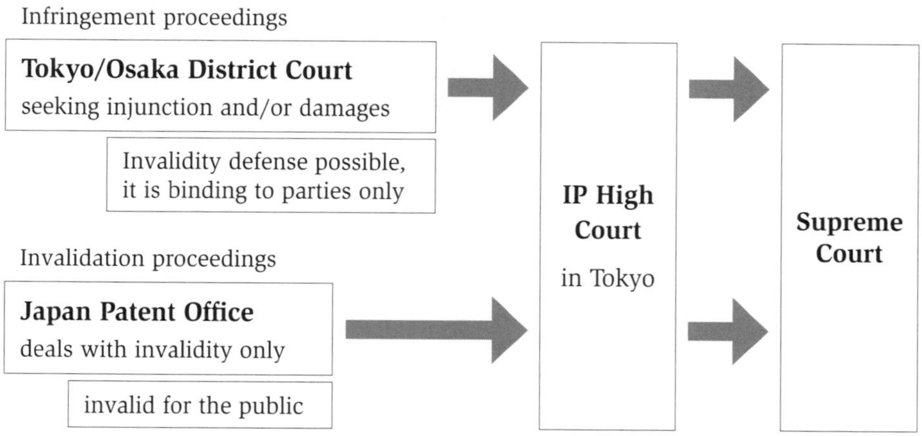

24. Article 1, Civil Code, which reads: " (1) Private rights must conform to the public welfare. (2) The exercise of rights and performance of duties must be done in good faith. (3) No abuse of rights is permitted. "

25. Article 104-3(1), Patent Act, which reads: "Where, in litigation concerning the infringement of a patent right or an exclusive license, the said patent is recognized as one that should be invalidated by a trial for patent invalidation, the rights of the patentee or exclusive licensee may not be exercised against the adverse party."

Republic of Korea

Seong-Ki Kim, Yoon Suk Shin

A. AVAILABILITY OF PROTECTION

I. Legal framework

1. National statutory laws

1.1 Pharmaceuticals

The current Patent Act of Korea (Korean Patent Act, "KPA") does not provide a specific provision on patentability of claims for pharmaceutical and (first or second) medical use inventions. Patent for pharmaceuticals and chemical compounds per se have been allowed since July 1, 1987.

The Patent Act which became effective prior to July 1, 1987 prescribed the following types of inventions as unpatentable:

(1) An invention of food or items of personal preference (since 1963);
(2) An invention of a pharmaceutical composition or a method of preparing a drug by combining at least two different drugs (since 1946);
(3) An invention of a substance that can be prepared by a chemical process (since 1963);
(4) An invention of a substance produced by a nuclear transformation method (since 1974);
(5) An invention relating to the use of a chemical substance (since 1974); and
(6) An invention that contravenes public order or morality, or an invention that may impair public health (since 1946).

The terms (2), (3), and (5) above were deleted through an amendment of the Patent Act effective July 1, 1987 to allow the protection of inventions of chemical substances and pharmaceuticals.

Further, the Korean Intellectual Property Office ("KIPO") published the Patent Examination Guidelines concerning medicinal inventions. A use invention targeted at a medicine may be defined in the form of a tangible item, i.e., a "product." The indication of a medicinal use must be described along with any medicinal effect corresponding to a disease, or to the diagnosis, treatment, relief, curing or prevention of the disease. Medicinal use claims should be in a "product" format, generally in the form of "a pharmaceutical composition for treating disease Y comprising compound X." Medicament and kit formats are also permissible.

1.2 Biologics

The Patent Act provides no specific provisions for biologics. The same provisions apply to biologics as pharmaceuticals.

2. International treaties

2.1 TRIPS

The WTO/TRIPS Agreement has been ratified and implemented fully since July 1, 1996. According to Article 27.1 of the TRIPS Agreement, Korea undertakes to provide patent protection for any invention, whether a product (such as a medicine) or a process (such as a method of producing the chemical ingredients for a medicine), while allowing certain exceptions. Patent protection should last at least 20 years from the date the patent application was filed, as prescribed in Article 88 of the Patent Act.

The restrictions under Article 31 of the TRIPS have been fully implemented in the KPA Articles 106 bis to 115.

2.2 FTAs

As of March 15, 2015/January 1, 2016, 14 free trade agreements ("FTAs") have been implemented: including Korea-US and Korea-European Union FTAs. In addition, the Korean Government is currently negotiating for FTAs with Japan and China. Under the Korea-US FTA which became effective as of March 15, 2012, the patent-marketing approval linkage system for pharmaceuticals as agreed in Article 18.9(5) allows listing medical use claims including a second medical use in the Green List. The patentee is notified of an application for a generic drug with regard to the listed patent claims in the Green List. Further, a means for preventing sales of generic products without the consent of patent owner, i.e., a nine-month stay of generic sales, is provided under the patent-marketing approval linkage system. This provision became fully effective as of March 15, 2015.

According to Article 18.9(1) and (2) of Korea-US FTA, data exclusivity is given for pharmaceuticals. In Korea, data exclusivity has been indirectly protected by a drug re-examination system, i.e., post marketing surveillance (PMS), which prohibits the filing of a generic marketing approval application referring to data filed by the original developer for (i) six years from the marketing approval date of the original developer for new drugs; or (ii) four years for new efficacy based on new clinical data.

The patent term extension for pharmaceutical patents based on approved new drugs is provided by Article 18.8(6.b) of Korea-US FTA. The patent term extension system based on a delay of marketing approval for up to five years was introduced in 1987, and medical use claims have been eligible for the patent term extension.

Under the Korea-EU FTA, patent term extension and data exclusivity are allowed. The provisions are substantially the same as for Korea-US FTA.

3. *Protection available through case law*

Regarding the second medical use defined by a new dosage regimen, the Supreme Court of Korea ruled in 2009 that claim limitations related to an administration regimen, such as dosing interval and unit dosage, must be ignored when assessing the patentability of a pharmaceutical composition invention because a new dosage regimen is not recognized as a typical medicinal use that can be protected by patent law. However, the Korean Supreme Court has overruled its previous decisions by an *en banc* decision, No. 2014 Hu 768, issued on May 21, 2015. Following the decision, a second "dosage regimen" can be considered as elements of an invention that is directed to a pharmaceutical composition when determining the novelty and inventive step of the invention. The Supreme Court opined that dosage regimen should be considered as elements of an invention because dosage regimen can give a product new significance by defining properties of a medicine as a new indication of a drug.

In 2002 Heo 4460 decision issued on July 11, 2003, the Patent Court ruled that an invention specifically limited to hepatically impaired patients is to be recognized as a second medical use invention. The invention limited to hepatically impaired patients provides a new effect in that a terfenadine acid derivative having antihistamine activity does not cause heart disease because it does not reduce action potentials and currents of various heart cell membranes. This is contrary to conventional terfenadine that may cause side effects related to heart disease in patients with impaired hepatic function. Accordingly, the subject invention is supposed to be a second medicinal use invention based on the discovery that a terfenadine acid derivative has a second new pharmacological effect as described above, which differs from the medicinal use of terfenadine, in addition to the first pharmacological effect of terfenadine.

4. *Patent term extension/SPCs*

The patent term extension scheme was introduced along with the grant of patents on chemical substances per se since July 1, 1987. Under the current patent practice, patents only relating to a first approved drug whose active pharmaceutical ingredient is a new substance are eligible for patent term extension of up to five years. Accordingly, patents relating to a second medical use are not eligible for patent term extension.

II. Policy considerations

1. Health and social issues

The policy reasons behind permitting second medical use claims would be to encourage innovation, R&D activities for making new drugs or new use of a known drug available to public, and to contribute to public health by providing an incentive for the pharmaceutical industry to invest more in developing new indications of already known pharmaceuticals, which is usually less expensive than developing a new drug.

In May 2015, the Korean Supreme Court recognized dosage regimen as a patentable element in its *en banc* decision recognizing such policy considerations.

2. Legal issues

In order to be recognized as a new medical use invention, the claim must define a medicine for treatment of a disease for which a medical effect can be demonstrated. Further, a dosage regimen, such as an administration cycle, an administration site, or an administration route, and a dose as administered to a specific patient group may be required to be defined in the claims. As for the identification of an indication or an efficacy, a dosage regimen has significance as features by which a medicine can demonstrate its efficacy.

These features of second medical use claims, in theory, might raise issues of patentability in relation to the freedom of, or exception to patent infringement liability enjoyed by, medical professionals. Although the exemptions of medical professionals from patent liability is strongly expected, patents on second medical use inventions would result in patent infringement by generic makers' follow up marketing activities of promotion for off-label use.

B. VALIDITY

I Allowable claim wording

1. Product claims

According to the KIPO Examination Guidelines, medicinal use claims may be defined in a "product" format, generally in the form of "a pharmaceutical composition for treating disease Y comprising compound X." Medicament and kit formats are also permissible.

2. Method claims

Claims defining a method of treatment of a human being are not permissible since the methods lack industrial applicability.

3. *Use claims*

Under the statutory scheme of Korean patent law, any invention is understood as one of the two categories; "product" and "method." Use claims have not been granted or construed yet. Up to now, claims commencing with the term "use" including a Swiss-type claim are not allowable. As medical use inventions have been patentable since the Supreme Court's decision issued in May 2015, it might be worthwhile trying a new claim format in the future.

4. *System claims*

System claims are generally allowable when those claims are clear on whether they define an apparatus or a process.

5. *Dosage regimes*

According to a recent Supreme Court *en banc* decision, dosage regimens are patentable elements of product claims defining a medical use invention.

6. *Patient groups*

In the Patent Court 2002 Heo 4460 decision, a specific patient group (e.g., hepatically impaired patients) is recognized as an element of a second medicinal use invention.

II. Novelty

1. *General definition of novelty and prior art*

In Korea, absolute novelty is required for patentability. Inventions publicly known or worked in or outside Korea, disclosed in a publication distributed in or outside Korea are deemed to lack novelty. The entire content of Korean patent applications as filed, whose filing dates are prior to that of the subject patent application, would also destroy the novelty once the senior applications are published.

2. *Definition of skilled person*

The KPA does not define a person of ordinary skill in the art. According to a decision of the Patent Court (2008 Heo 8150), "one of ordinary skill in the art" refers to a hypothetical person having average knowledge in the technical field to which the invention pertains prior to the filing of the application; having access and ability to understand everything in the technical field relating to the technical task of the invention prior to the filing of the application; and having a certain level of creativity, for example, the ability to perform common research or development, including experimentation, analysis, production, etc., or the ability to select proper material(s) among known materials, to optimize numerical ranges, or to substitute such material with other material(s).

3. *Scope of disclosure*

3.1 General rules

Everything made available to the public, regardless of the means of disclosure, constitutes the prior art. In case of senior patent application prior art, unclaimed details found in the patent specification as filed are considered as included in the prior art.

3.2 First medical use

An invention directed to a medical use, as well as claiming a non-medical use, was prescribed to be excluded from patent-eligible inventions prior to July 1, 1987. The 1987 amendments to the KPA allowed inventions related to medical and non-medical use to be patented. Since 1987, a known chemical composition with a new use is deemed to be a new composition. Novelty for claims to first medical use resides in the new purpose, and thus, it is a new concept of novelty found in known products.

In theory, alternative claim drafting might be available for new medical use inventions, including method of treatment. A method for medical treatment of the human body (but not the animal body) will be found to be lacking industrial applicability and thus unpatentable. Another drafting format starting with "use," for example, "use of compound X at a medicament for treatment of disease Y" is considered to be ambiguous and not clear as to whether it defines a "product" or method.

In light of the above issues, drafting a purpose-limited product claim is recommended for medical use inventions.

3.3 New subject composition matter

Since the subject composition matter of a second medical use invention is the same as that of the first medical use invention, a new subject composition matter need not be included in the disclosure of a second medical use invention.

3.4 New data

For a medicinal use invention, Korean patent practice requires that the original specification contain quantitative pharmacological data for the claimed active ingredient, unless the relevant pharmacological mechanism was established before the filing date of the patent application. New data for a second medical use invention is required in the original disclosure.

4. *Requirements for second medical use*

4.1 Distinction from first medical use

A new and inventive second medical use is patentable as long as it does not define the invention as a prohibited "method of treatment" of a human body. Though a claim directed to a method of treatment is not prohibited from being granted by a statutory provision, the Examination Guidelines of KIPO prescribe that such a claim lacks industrial applicability and to claim a second medical use, the allowable claim format must define the second use that is patentable independently from the use already known in the prior art. Distinction from the first medical use could be made in the form of "composition/substance X for use in the treatment of disease Z," for example, if use Y is already known for composition/substance X. Also available is the second use claim as a medicament defined by its function, e.g., "composition X for use as an anti-cancer medicament."

4.2 *Sub-species of first medical use*

When the second medical use is a sub-species of the first medical use, the claim format for the second medical use needs to be specific in defining the sub-species. The claim format "composition/substance X for treatment of disease Z" is allowable even when disease Z is a sub-species of disease Y. As an example, "a composition comprising compound X for treatment of Alzheimer's Disease" would be allowable over prior art showing compound X had been known for use in a treatment of brain disorders, as long as the new use is inventive.

4.3 *Dosage regimens*

Prior to the Supreme Court decision in May 2015, differences in the dosage and route of administration were not recognized to be an element of medical use inventions. Since the issuing of the 2015 decision, dosage regimes are recognized to be an element of medical use inventions. When the medical use is directed to a treatment of the same disease has been known in the prior art and a different treatment of the same disease is defined, the allowable claim format would be "composition comprising X / substance X for treatment of disease Y, wherein (as characterized in that) the composition/substance is administered 5mg per day."

4.4 *Special patient groups*

The Examination Guidelines of KIPO are silent on the allowable claim format for a second medical use invention where the distinction lies in the relevant special patient groups. No court decision has been made on the issue. Though we have to wait further developments of practice on this issue, it is expected that the same claim format as allowable in the dosage regimes will be recognized for drafting claims for an invention in which a new sub-group of patients are identified for treatment.

5. *Timing issues*

5.1 *Relevant time of development of second use*

In phase IV clinical trials for monitoring safety and efficacy of a pharmaceutical drug after it has been released on the market (post-marketing surveillance), pharmacoepidemiologic studies are performed to detect unidentified side effects or unpredicted new indications in the controlled settings of pre-marketing trials. During this period, second uses, including new indications, new patient groups, an improved dosage regimen based on enhanced efficacy and side effects, or a new dosage form for improving the product, continue to be developed.

5.2 *Role of new data*

Since new data for second medical use is required to prove the completion of a second medical use invention and to meet the requirement of the enabling disclosure at the time of filing, later addition of new data to the specification would not be allowed, nor can such data be cited in a response to an office action.

5.3 *Use of old data*

Old data can be used for the purpose of comparison with new data.

III. Inventive step/non-obviousness

1. *Definition of inventive step/non-obviousness*

According to the KPA, inventions that could have been easily conceived from the inventions which fall under either of the following subparagraphs by one of ordinary skill in the art to which the invention pertains, prior to the filing of the patent application, lack the requisite inventive step:

(i) inventions publicly known or practiced in the Republic of Korea before the filing of the patent application; or
(ii) inventions described in a publication distributed in the Republic of Korea or in a foreign country before the filing of the patent application or inventions published through telecommunication lines.

2. *Same scope of disclosure as for novelty?*

The scope of disclosure considered for determining the inventive step is narrower compared to that for novelty. The content of patent applications filed prior to the subject patent is not considered a part of prior art for the purpose of determining the inventive step.

3. *Assessment of inventive step/non-obviousness*

Inventive step is determined according to the following procedures:

(1) First step: specify the invention defined in the claims.
   - If the description of the claims is clear, an invention is specified as described in the claims.

- The terms recited in the claims are interpreted to have the meanings and scopes that are normally understood in the pertinent technical field, unless the terms are explicitly defined in the specification. Based on the technical knowledge at the time the patent application was filed and the general meaning of the term, the term should be objectively and reasonably interpreted by considering the technical significance that is intended to be represented by the term.
- If the description of the invention in the claims is clearly understandable, the technical feature of the invention should be defined based only on the description in the claims, and should not be based on the description in the specification or drawings.
- If a feature is described in the specification or drawings, but not described in the claims, the invention in the claims should be defined to exclude the feature. A feature that is described in the claims should necessarily be considered when defining the invention. Although the features in the claims may be understood by reference to the specification or drawings, a limitation that is not recited in the claims should not be introduced to specify the claims.
- If an applicant explicitly defines a term in the specification so that one of ordinary skill in the art can clearly understand the term as having a different meaning from a normal meaning in the pertinent technical field, the term is interpreted to have such a specific meaning.

(2) Second step: specify the prior art. Prior art invention should be specified from the viewpoint of one of ordinary skill in the art on the premise that the prior art invention is identical to the claimed invention in terms of the technical field and the technical problems purported to be solved.
   - A disclosed invention refers to an invention whose content is not maintained as a secret, but is disclosed or may be disclosed to the public, and is specified based on the disclosed content. In this case, a feature that is obvious to one of ordinary skill in the art in view of the disclosed content based on the technical knowledge at the time the invention was disclosed is deemed to have been disclosed when specifying the invention.
   - A practiced invention refers to an invention that was practiced in or mediated by a mechanical device or a system in a condition where the invention is or may be publicly disclosed, and thus is specified based on the fact that the invention is integrated in the mechanical device or the system. In this case, a feature that is obvious to one of ordinary skill in the art in view of the technical knowledge at the time the invention was disclosed is deemed to have been publicly worked when specifying the invention.
   - In principle, an invention distributed in a publication is specified based on what is explicitly described in the publication. However, even when a feature is not explicitly described in the publication, if it is deemed to have been substantially described in the publication, it may be considered when specifying the publication. In such case, the feature that is deemed to have been substantially described refers to the feature that is obvious

to one of ordinary skill in the art based on the technical knowledge at the time the patent application was filed.

(3) Third step: select the closest prior art. A closest prior art invention to the invention in the claims of the patent application is selected, and both inventions are compared to confirm the differences. When confirming the differences, the systematic relation between the elements of the invention should be considered. More specifically, the elements of the invention that are systematically combined should be compared to the corresponding elements in the prior art invention as a combined entity without disassembling the elements.

(4) Finally, determine the inventive step. Even if the invention in the claims of the patent application is different from the closest prior art invention, whether one of ordinary skill in the art could have easily conceived the invention in the patent application in view of the closest prior art invention should be determined based on other prior art inventions, common technical knowledge prior to the filing of the patent application and the empirical rule.

IV. Amendment of claims after grant

1. Admissibility of post-grant amendments in general

After a patent is granted, the patentee may amend granted claims by filing a petition for a correction trial to amend the claims at the Intellectual Property Tribunal ("IPT").

The allowable scope of correction to a granted patent claim is limited to (i) narrowing the claims, (ii) correcting a clerical error, or (iii) clarifying an ambiguity. The patentee is not allowed to broaden or change the scope of a claim for any reason. Further, the scope of the claims after correction should be patentable at the time the patent application was filed.

A correction trial could be initiated at any time of the patentee's choice. Also, if an invalidation trial is filed, the patentee would be allowed to file a correction request to amend the claims as a defense to the invalidity claim.

2. Procedural issues

2.1 Independent limitation proceedings

The patentee may request a trial to correct the specification, claims and/or drawings at any time after the issuance of a patent, but after a decision of patent invalidation has been final and conclusive. A trial for correction of a patent may also be requested while an infringement action involving the patent is pending. In such case, the lawsuit may be suspended at the discretion of the court until the trial for correction is completed. Nonetheless, a trial for correction of a patent should not be separately requested if an invalidation action is ongoing before the IPT. If there is any exclusive licensee or employer's non-exclusive license of the patent, it is necessary to obtain the consent of the licensee to request correction.

When a decision of granting the correction is final and conclusive, the patent application is deemed to have been filed, published, granted and registered as corrected.

2.2 Opposition proceedings

Pre-grant opposition proceedings have been incorporated into invalidation proceedings since 1996. A new ex-parte revocation of granted patents is introduced by the 2016 amendment to the KPA. Under the new ex-parte revocation system, prior art publications which were not cited by the examiner during prosecution could be cited for revocation.

2.3 Nullity actions

Once an invalidation complaint is served on the patentee, the patentee is allowed to request amendment to the patented claims, as a defense to the invalidity challenge, within the time frame allowed to file a response. The deadline for responding to the nullity complaint may be any time within one month, which may be extended upon request.

If the requested correction falls within the allowable scope of correction as discussed above, a rejection of the requested correction would be issued and the respondent would be required to respond to the rejection within a specified time period. If the response does not overcome the rejection, then the correction request is not granted.

3. Added matter

Addition of a new matter or a new claim is not allowable in post-grant corrections, even when the added matter is based on the disclosure as originally filed.

4. Sufficiency

A correction to the claims can be made within the scope of the specification or drawings of the patent application as filed. That is, the corrected claims are required to be supported by the disclosure and the specification should sufficiently describe the invention according to the corrected claims for a person of ordinary skill in the art to reproduce the invention.

5. Multiple indications

Multiple indications are permissible only when those indications are defined as a sub-set chosen from out of a "genus" claim.

V. Change of patent invention category

1. *General admissibility*

The KPA provides three categories, i.e., product, method and manufacture method of a product. A change of patent invention category is generally allowed when amending the claims during the prosecution. However, when responding to a final office action or a final rejection, the scope of claim amendment is limited to (i) narrowing the scope of claims, (ii) correcting erroneous descriptions, or (iii) clarifying unclear descriptions.

2. *Use claim as a category*

A use claims category including a Swiss-type claim is not permitted.

3. *From product to method claim*

A change from a product claim to a method claim is allowable. However, method of treatment claims are not regarded as an allowable format for lack of industrial applicability.

4. *From method to product claim*

A change from a method claim to a product claim is allowable. According to KIPO Examination Guidelines, medicinal use claims should be in a product format, generally in the form of "a pharmaceutical composition for treating disease Y comprising compound X."

5. *System claims*

System claims are allowable when it is clearly understood that they are directed to an apparatus or a method.

6. *Use claims*

The use of a product invention should be drafted as product or method claims. For non-medical use inventions, claims drafted in a form of "product", "method of using the product", "method of treating X with the product", or "agent for —ing" would be allowable.

C. INFRINGEMENT AND LITIGATION

I. Legal framework

1. National statutory laws

The patentee may file a claim for damages against the person who infringed its patent rights, moreover a patentee (or exclusive licensee) may seek a remedy of injunction against a person who infringes or is likely to infringe patent right. Further, when filing for an injunction, the patentee (or the exclusive licensee) may also seek destruction of the infringing products (including a product produced by the act of infringement), removal of equipment related to the act of infringement, and any other activity required to prevent infringement.

2. Case law

Korean courts recognize that a product or process that does not literally include exactly the same elements as defined in a patented invention may still be found to infringe if the difference between the elements of the patented invention and the accused product or process is not substantial under the doctrine of equivalents. The traditional approach adopted in Korea to understand and evaluate a patented invention is based on three aspects: structure, function and effect of the claimed invention. Since the doctrine of equivalents is invoked when the two elements, one as defined in the patented claim and the other as found in the accused product or process, are not identical (in structure), the comparison of the two elements tends to focus on the function and effect aspects, rather than structure aspect. Finding infringement by equivalents is limited by a number of rules. First, the doctrine of equivalents is not applicable to a product that was known in the prior art or that is easily conceivable thereof by a person skilled in the art. Secondly, the doctrine of equivalents does not allow reintroduction a device that has been intentionally excluded from the scope of patent claims during the patent prosecution stage.

II. Claim construction

1. General rules

Article 97 of the KPA prescribes that the scope of protection conferred by a patented invention is determined by the claims.

According to case law, the scope of protection of a patented invention or the substantial scope of protection is determined, in principle, by the subject matter defined in the claims. If the technical scope of the patented invention cannot be derived from the claims, they may be supplemented by the description of the specification. Nevertheless, the scope of patent protection cannot be expanded by the description of the specification, and if the technical scope is apparent from the claims, the claims should not be interpreted based on the description of the specification (Supreme Court Decisions in Case Nos. 96 Hu 1118 issued on May 28, 1997; 98 Hu 2856 issued on June 1, 2001; and 2004 Hu 509 issued on June 9, 2006).

2. *Specific issues for use claims*

Although the claim format "compound X for use in treating disease Y" defines the product, the scope of protection of a product defined would be limited to cover the product that is intended to be used for claimed use.

III. Scope of protection

1. *Scope of the use*

1.1 *General definition of the term "use"*

Under KIPO Patent Examination Guidelines, a use invention refers to an invention in which a product is used as a new use based on a discovered attribute of the product existing in nature, wherein such discovery is distinguishable from a simple discovery. Further, a medical use must be identified by a pharmaceutical effect for the diagnosis, cure, alleviation, or prevention of diseases.

1.2 *Manufacture of pharmaceuticals*

Since a medical use invention is claimed as a product for specific use, the manufacture of the pharmaceuticals for the claimed use is within the scope of the medical use invention. Article 2 of the KPA stipulates that, in the case of an invention of a product, manufacturing, using, assigning, leasing, importing, or offering to assign or lease including displaying for the purpose of assignment or lease of the product would all be considered as working the claimed invention.

1.3 *Sale of the product*

Sale of a drug with label instructions describing the patented use would be considered within the scope of protection of the medical use invention.

1.4 *Offer for sale*

Offer for sale of a drug with label instructions describing the patented use would be considered within the scope of protection of the medical use invention.

1.5 *Application to the patient*

Although there is no case law on the issue, the act of a physician prescribing a drug for a patented use would not be within the scope of protection of the medical use invention since prescribing is not likely considered as an act of "using" the drug under the KPA.

Under Article 96(2) of the KPA, a patent right for a combination drug manufactured by mixing two or more medicines or a method thereof does not extend to a pharmacist's act of dispensing medicines under the Pharmaceutical Affairs Act.

Although there has been no court decision addressing the issue of whether the exemption provision applies to a pharmacist's general act of dispensing under the Pharmaceutical Affairs Act, the pharmacist's act of dispensing a drug for a patented use is not likely within the scope of protection since dispensing is not likely to be regarded as an act of "using" the drug under the KPA.

A patient's use would not be considered within the scope of protection of medical use invention under the KPA since it is for personal use, not for commercial purposes.

1.6 *Combination products*

Combination products would be considered within the scope of protection of the claimed medical use invention if the combination products are used for the claimed use.

2. ***Absolute product protection***

2.1 *Limitation through the term "use"*

Claimed use would limit the scope of protection of a product claim. In Korea, there is no case law governing the interpretation of the scope of protection of a product defined by a use. However, in view of customary local practice, the scope of protection thereof would be limited to cover the product that is intended to be used for the claimed use.

2.2 *Off-label use*

In principle, if a drug is used for off-label use, the drug product would not be within the scope of the medical use invention.

However, with regard to skinny labeling, a Korean court held in a preliminary injunction case that, even though the product information leaflet of the generic product carved out the patented use, the pharmaceutical product can be within the scope of the second medical use patent (*Warner-Lambert Company LLC et al. v Samjin Pharm.*, Seoul Central District Court 2013 Kahap 1717,2014). In this case, the court decision was based on the following findings: (i) the generic company made and sold the generic product for the patented pain indication (obtaining an approval for the patented pain indication as well as non-patented indications and listing a drug price reimbursement with the relevant authorities); (ii) the generic company began manufacturing and marketing the product for the pain indication; (iii) although the generic company deleted the pain indication only from the revised leaflet without changing the approved indications of the generic product, the leaflet still contained in the general warning section that the product is effective for the pain indication; (iv) as of the court decision date, the generic product was being prescribed in significant volumes for the pain indication; (v) as of the court decision date, the generic product was listed in a number of hospitals as one of the pain indication drugs; and (vi) the sales volume of the generic product had continuously increased.

3. *Dosage regimes*

Drug products with an information leaflet describing the patented dosage regimes are considered within the scope of protection of product claim defining the dosage regimes.

4. *Patient groups*

Although there is no case law, drug products with an information leaflet describing the patented patient groups are considered within the scope of protection of product claim defining the patient groups.

5. *Extension under the doctrine of equivalents*

Korean courts recognize that the scope of a patented invention extends to a product or process that does not literally include the exact same elements as defined in a patented invention under the doctrine of equivalents, if the difference between the elements of the patented invention and the accused product or process is not substantial. Even if an accused invention contains elements which replace or change elements of the patented invention, the invention is deemed to infringe the patented invention under the doctrine of equivalents if: (i) the accused invention and the patented invention are identical in terms of the solution proposed to solve an identical technical problem; (ii) the substituted elements in the accused invention achieve the same objective and produce substantially the same effect as those of the patented invention; (iii) the substitution of elements in the accused invention is obvious to one of ordinary skill in the art ("obvious substitutability"); (iv) the accused invention was not known at the time of the filing of the patented invention or could not have been easily conceived by one of ordinary skill in the art in view of the prior art; and (v) the elements of the patented invention, which were substituted in the accused invention, were not intentionally deleted during the prosecution of the application for the patented invention (Supreme Court Decisions in Case Nos. 2004 Da 29194 issued on February 25, 2005; 2002 Hu 1102 issued on October 24, 2003; and 2001 Hu 171 issued on September 6, 2002).

Above criterion (i) indicates that the altered invention and the patented invention are identical in terms of the technical concept, or providing an identical technical solution that solves a particular technical problem that has been introduced or unsolved by prior arts, i.e., technical characteristics of an invention. If the accused invention and the patented invention are different in terms of technical solution for solving a technical problem, there is no infringement under the doctrine of equivalents (Supreme Court Case No. 2012 Hu 1132 issued on July 24, 2014).

IV. Infringing acts

1. *Infringing person or entity*

A party manufacturing or marketing the drug with label instructions which describe the patented use is liable for infringement.

A physician's prescription, a pharmacist's dispensation and a patient's use are likely to be exempt from patent infringement liability.

2. *Direct infringement*

2.1 Manufacture of the pharmaceutical

Since a medical use invention is claimed as a product for specific use, the manufacture of the pharmaceuticals for the claimed use infringes medical use invention. Article 2 of the KPA stipulates that in the case of an invention of a product, manufacturing, using, assigning, leasing, importing, or offering to assign or lease including displaying for the purpose of assignment or lease of the product is considered as working the claimed invention.

2.2 Offer for sale

Offer for sale of a drug with label instructions describing the patented use would infringe the medical use invention.

2.3 Sale

Sale of a drug with label instructions describing the patented use would infringe the medical use invention.

2.4 Export

The KPA does not include export of the patented product as an act of practicing the invention. Thus, the export of drug for claimed use does not infringe the patent.

2.5 Import

Import of a drug with label instructions describing the patented use would infringe the patented medical use invention.

2.6 Combination products

Combination products would infringe the medical use patent if the combination products are used for the claimed use.

3. *Indirect infringement*

3.1 Objective acts

The KPA provides that any of the following acts would be regarded as constituting indirect Infringement under Article 127:

(i) an act of making, assigning, leasing, importing, or offering to assign or lease articles used exclusively for the production of a patented article; or
(ii) an act of making, assigning, leasing, importing, or offering to assign or lease articles used exclusively for the practice of a patented process.

Thus, in order to establish indirect infringement under the KPA, it must be shown that an accused product has no alternative use except for use for the patented article or process. An alternative use should be commercially or economically practical in the art, and a theoretical, experimental, or temporarily feasible use is not considered as an alternative use under Korean case law. While Korean courts found indirect infringement in a few cases, there has been no court decision recognizing indirect infringement of a medicinal use claim. For a second medical use patent, it would be very unlikely that indirect infringement would be found since, by definition, the medicine has an alternative use (i.e., the first use).

3.2 Subjective conditions

The KPA does not require subjective conditions to establish indirect infringement.

3.3 Export

The KPA does not stipulate the export of articles used exclusively for the patent invention as an act of constituting indirect infringement of a patent invention. Thus, the export of drug or active pharmaceutical ingredient ("API") for claimed use would not indirectly infringe the patent.

3.4 Import

Import of a drug or API used exclusively for a patented medical use invention would indirectly infringe the patent. However, for a second medical use patent, it would be very unlikely that indirect infringement would be found since, by definition, the medicine has an alternative use (i.e., the first use).

3.5 Combination products

Combination products would not likely to infringe the medical use patent indirectly, because combination products are not exclusively used for the patented use.

4. Off-label use

4.1 General admissibility of off-label use

Off-label use is generally admissible unless it violates ethical guidelines or safety regulations. Healthcare providers may use pharmaceutical drugs for an unapproved indication or in an unapproved age group, dosage, or route of administration. Indications may depend not only upon the medical condition that is being treated, but also upon other factors, such as dose, the patient's age, size and sex, and other medical conditions. The ability to prescribe drugs for uses beyond the officially approved indications is commonly used to good effect.

4.2 Liable persons

Drug manufacturers may not be liable for infringement if the manufacturer does not market or promote off-label use. Doctors' prescription, pharmacists' dispensation and patients' use are likely to be exempt from patent infringement liability.

4.3 Objective requirements for infringement

In view of court decisions regarding skinny labeling, if drug manufacturers encourage the use of drugs for any indications that have not been approved by the government, and advises physicians that significant scientific evidence exists for the unapproved indication, or another country's drug agency has approved that indication, the court may find infringement by the drug manufacturer.

4.4 Subjective requirements for infringement

There is no subjective requirement for finding infringement under the Korean patent practice.

5. Dosage regimens

Drug products with information leaflets describing the patented dosage regimes would infringe medical use patents with the product claims defining the dosage regimens.

6. Patient groups

Although no court decisions address this issue, drug products with information leaflets describing the patented patient groups would infringe the product claim defining the patient groups.

V. Remedies

1. Injunctions

The KPA provides civil and criminal remedies for patent infringement including preliminary or permanent injunctive relief under Article 126. The provision generally applies to remedies for infringement of second medical use claims.

A patentee (or exclusive licensee) can request a preliminary or permanent injunction against a person who infringes or is likely to infringe their patent right. A patentee can seek the measures necessary to prevent the infringement.

To obtain a preliminary injunction, the patentee must show first of all a likelihood of success on the merits for patent infringement. In deciding whether to grant a preliminary injunction, the court must also take into consideration the balance of hardships between the parties, the prospects of irreparable harm to the patentee, and the public interest.

2. *Damages*

The KPA also provides civil remedies for patent infringement of damages under Article 128. Monetary damages may be awarded to a patentee (or exclusive licensee) when its patent is found to be valid and infringed and the patentee loses its profits as a result of the infringement. The damages are intended to compensate the patentee for losses suffered as a result of the infringement. A patentee is entitled to its lost profits on lost sales the patentee would have made but for the infringement. Accordingly, the patentee would bear the burden of proof to show demand for the product in the market and sufficient capacity to meet the market demand for the products.

The profits gained by the infringer as a result of the infringement are presumed to be the amount of damages suffered by the patentee.

The amount of reasonable royalty to which the patentee would normally be entitled may be claimed as the amount of lost profits of the patentee. If the amount of losses exceeds the amount of the reasonable royalty, however, the amount in excess may also be claimed as damages. In such cases, the court may take into consideration in determining the damages award whether or not there has been willfulness or gross negligence on the part of the infringer.

In addition to or instead of damages, the court may order restoration of injured business goodwill or reputation under Article 131 of the KPA.

3. *Information*

3.1 *Names of manufacturer, distributors etc.*

Prior to commercial distribution of pharmaceutical products, marketing approval by the government, the Ministry of Food and Drug Safety, is necessary, and the information on the names of the manufacturer, distributor or importer of authorized pharmaceutical products is available from publication of the government register of marketing approval.

3.2 *Names of customers*

The National Health Insurance Service (NHIS) provides health insurance services to all Korean nationals. Healthcare providers including doctors, hospitals and pharmacists get reimbursed for their prescriptions and dispensing from the NHIS for prescription drugs. Information on the names of customers for pharmaceutical products will be available from the NHIS, as most of the cases they would be prescription drugs.

3.3 *Information about infringing sales*

Under the Korean Code of Civil Procedure, pre-trial discovery is not available. To initiate a patent infringement lawsuit, the patentee usually relies on publicly available evidence at the time of filing the complaint, since evidence controlled by the opponent is difficult to obtain before a lawsuit. Once a party shows a reasonable ground for the court to believe the opponent or a third party controls relevant information, the court may order the person who controls the evidence to submit it.

The Code of Civil Procedure provides a variety of mechanisms for obtaining evidence from parties in a lawsuit. Mechanisms for collecting evidence includes live examination of witnesses, requests for production of documents and requests for inspections of premises by filing a motion to the court during a lawsuit, or even prior to filing. To facilitate the party's investigation of the opponent's written evidence, a party may file a motion asking the opponent to submit a list of related documents under their control or that are planned to be introduced as evidence by the opponent. The most common mechanism for obtaining evidence from a third-party is via a request for production of documents ordered by a court upon the motion of a party.

3.4 *Account of profits*

When the claimant's actual lost profits are not easy to prove, the amount of losses may be measured by the infringer's profit gained at the expense of the claimant's loss on principles of restitution.

In one case, Seoul District Court measured the amount of restitutional damages by multiplying the sales volume of the defendant (which is obtained from the National Health Insurance Review and Assessment Services) by the general operating profit ratio of a pharmaceutical company. At the time of determining the amount of damages in this case, the average operating profit ratio of a pharmaceutical company was 14.2% in the drug product manufacturing industry according to the National Tax Services (Seoul District Court Case No. 2014 Gahap 526972, decided on June 19, 2015).

4. *Recall and destruction of products*

At the request of the patentee, the court may issue an injunction against infringement and may issue other orders to prevent infringement.

When an injunction order is issued, the court may:

(a) prohibit the accused infringer from continuing the manufacture or sale of the goods which infringe the petitioner's right;
(b) order destruction of the infringing articles or other materials used for infringement or transfer of the infringing articles or other articles used for infringement to the custody of a court bailiff; and
(c) instruct the court bailiff to post an appropriate public notice of the order on the premises of the respondent.

5. *Recovery of legal costs*

Although the prevailing party in a patent infringement action may, in principle, recover legal costs for the litigation including court costs and attorney fees from the losing party, the recoverable attorney fees are limited to the amount calculated based on a statutory fee schedule, which represent only a small percentage of the total expenses of litigation. Litigation costs are determined in a separate proceeding.

VI. Exceptions from patent protection

1. *Exhaustion of rights*

Under the exhaustion doctrine, once an authorized sale of a patented article occurs, the patent holder's exclusive rights to control the use and sale of that article are said to be "exhausted," and the purchaser is free to use or resell that article without further restraint from patent law. "Repairing" a patented article is merely to use a patented article for which the patent rights has been exhausted, and thus, does not fall under patent infringement. However, according to some court decisions, if the repair of a patented article amounts to a new production beyond a "repair," it may constitute patent infringement. Further, providing components or supplies relating to the patented invention for repair may constitute indirect patent infringement. Generally, completely replacing the patented part or replacing important parts of the patented invention is regarded as "reconstruction," thus patent infringement, not "repair."

It is not permissible for the patentee to introduce restrictions on importation or other distribution of the patented product by means of explicit notice on the product that can override the exhaustion doctrine adopted.

A Korean court has ruled that parallel import of pharmaceuticals, which were manufactured and marketed in Italy, was allowed because patent rights were exhausted internationally (Seoul District Court Case No. 81 Kahap 466 issued on July 30, 1981). According to the international exhaustion doctrine, products marketed by the patent holder or with the patent holder's consent in one country may be imported into another country without the approval of the patent holder.

2. *Patient welfare*

Although there has been no court decision addressing this issue, the act of a licensed healthcare professional prescribing or dispensing a drug for a patented use would not infringe the medical use invention since prescribing is not likely considered as an act of "using" the drug under the KPA. Further, the pharmacist's act of dispensing a drug for a patented use would also be exempt from infringement liability.

Under Article 96(2) of the KPA, the patent right for a combination drug manufactured by mixing two or more medicines or a method therefor does not extend to a pharmacist's act of dispensing medicines under the Pharmaceutical Affairs Act.

A patient's use would not be considered as falling within the scope of protection of medical use invention under the KPA since it is for personal use, not for commercial purposes.

Article 96(1)(i) of the KPA provides includes the "Bolar exemption" by prescribing that the "research or experiment" for the purpose of obtaining a marketing approval according to the Pharmaceutical Affairs Act is exempted from patent rights.

3. *Other exhaustion issues specific to second medical use claims*

None specific to second medical use claims.

VII. Procedural issues

1. *Preliminary injunction cases*

1.1 Availability for second medical use claims

There is no limitation on the availability of preliminary injunction for second medical use claims according to statutory law or any court decision.

1.2 Specific requirements

To obtain a preliminary injunction, the patentee must show a likelihood of success on the merits in relation to validity and infringement, although a patent is presumed to be valid until it is held by the IPT to be invalid in a final decision of a patent invalidation action .

In deciding whether to grant a preliminary injunction, the court also takes into consideration the balance of hardships between the parties, the prospects of irreparable harm to the claimant and the public interest.

2. *Cases on the merits*

Effective as of January 1, 2016, a patent infringement lawsuit for damages or an injunction may be filed in one of the five specialized district courts having jurisdiction: Seoul Central District Court, Daejeon District Court, Daegu District Court, Busan District Court and Gwangju District Court. Notwithstanding the foregoing, regardless of jurisdiction, the plaintiff may elect to have the case heard at the Seoul Central District Court.

No jury trial is available for civil cases, which are tried before a panel of three judges.

The primary vehicle for introducing evidence in an infringement trial is a motion for introducing evidence. Though documentary evidence is important and believed to be reliable, live testimony of witnesses is not unusual. The presiding judge usually leads the examination of the witness. Counsel for the party producing the witness is routinely allowed to question the witness to elicit direct testimony, after which counsel for the opposing party has the opportunity to cross-examine the witness on matters within the scope of the direct testimony. Typically, the witness's party is thereafter permitted to re-conduct direct examination. The judge may additionally ask questions to clarify particular points of interest. Documents and other physical items, such as a sample of an allegedly infringing device, may also be received into evidence by a motion of a counsel.

Each party in a patent infringement case will usually present expert witnesses on technical matters. Experts are permitted to testify as to their opinions on matters within their recognized area of expertise.

Like other civil cases, court hearings for patent cases in Korea are typically held at three- or four-week intervals. The number of hearings per litigation varies, depending on the nature of the issues to be decided, from one to several. Since pre-trial discovery is not available under the Korean legal system for obtaining evidence, motion practice is widely used to obtain evidence that is not within the control of the plaintiff. Thus, the first or the second hearing date is used for filing motions to obtain evidence, as well as fixing the issues to be decided.

The party challenging the patent bears the burden of proving invalidity or unenforceability. Although the Korean Patent Act does not specifically provide a presumption of validity, a patent granted after substantive examination by the examiner is presumed to be valid. As the district court has no power to declare patent invalidity, it may simply refuse to enforce the patent when a serious doubt has been raised as to a patent's validity. A declaration of patent invalidity shall be litigated before the IPT, not a district court.

The average duration of a patent infringement suit from filing of a complaint to entry of final judgment varies depending upon the complexity of the case and the waiting list in the docket of the court in which the case is filed. The Seoul Central District Court has heard the largest number of patent cases and developed institutional expertise in patent cases, and an infringement suit before that court can be resolved within two years.

3. Enforcement of judgments

The injunction order is enforced by the bailiff at the expense of the petitioner. A preliminary injunction order is enforceable even when an appeal is pending. Judgments for damages or permanent injunction are not enforceable while an appeal is pending.

VIII. Validity

1. Relevance for infringement cases

In order to challenge the validity of a patent, an invalidation trial action must be filed with the IPT of the KIPO. However, when a patent is apparently deemed to lack novelty or inventive step, a patentee's claim for injunction or damages can be denied based on the unenforceability of the patent

2. Specifics for second medical use claims

Following the Korean Supreme Court's *en banc* Decision 2014 Hu 768, a second medical use defining "a dosage regimen" can be considered as an element of an invention that is directed to a pharmaceutical composition when determining the validity of the claims, such as the novelty and inventive step of the invention.

IX. Tactical considerations

1. Plaintiff

When potentially infringing goods are being imported into Korea, alternatively or in addition to filing an infringement suit in a district court, a patentee may request that the Korea Trade Commission ("KTC") institute an investigation of the potential infringement. The KTC proceedings differ from district court proceedings primarily as to the remedies that are available in the event that infringement is proven. The prevailing patentee in a court proceeding may be entitled to both monetary damages and an injunction against future infringement, whereas in an ITC proceeding the primary remedy is an order excluding future importation of the infringing goods into Korea and monetary damages are not available.

As another option, a scope confirmation trial, a declaratory judgment action for finding infringement or non-infringement, is available at the IPT. The IPT is an independent administrative agency under the umbrella of the Korean Intellectual Property Office. A declaratory judgment request may be initiated with or without a co-pending infringement action before a district court for damages and/or injunction. Since the panels of IPT consist of former patent examiners with technical backgrounds, it may be a good strategy to obtain a decision by the IPT wherein technical issues are well analyzed and determined before filing an infringement suit in a district court in a case of highly technical complexity.

2. Defendant

A party sued for infringement may defend itself on the grounds of non-infringement, invalidity or unenforceability or a combination of these, and typically initiates proceedings of declaratory judgment of non-infringement or invalidity before the IPT. An accused infringer can bring an action before the IPT for declaratory judgment of non-infringement without having to wait for the patentee to bring an infringement action.

China

Amy Feng, An Chen, Simon Tianle Luo

A. AVAILABILITY OF PROTECTION

I. Legal framework

1. National statutory laws

Within the territory of mainland China, Chinese patents are granted by the State Intellectual Property Office ("SIPO") under the Chinese Patent Law (promulgated in 1984, last amended in 2008). The granting of patents is further regulated by the Implementing Regulations of the Patent Law, promulgated by the State Council of China, and the Guidelines for Patent Examination, promulgated by SIPO.

The Patent Reexamination Board ("PRB") is set up in accordance with the Patent Law as a subsidiary of SIPO that has the exclusive authority to perform post-refusal reexamination of patent applications and invalidation proceedings of granted patents. The PRB's decisions, however, do not constitute case law of SIPO.

The PRB's decisions are subject to judicial review by the Beijing Intellectual Property Court as of 6 November 2014 (previously by the Beijing First Intermediate Court) for the trial instance and then the Beijing High People's Court for the appellant's instance, if appealed. On petition, the final judgment of the Beijing High People's Court may be further reviewed by the Supreme People's Court. In the review, the courts rely on the Patent Law and the Implementation Regulations as a legal basis, with reference to, but not bound by, the Guidelines for Patent Examination. Conversely, SIPO appears not to be bound by the courts' interpretations of the Patent Law in the judgments.

In the *Cubist v Patent Reexamination Board* ((2012) ZhiXingZi No. 75), the Chinese Supreme Court has for the first time affirmed the patent office's position concerning second medical use claims defined by the administration regime that the administration regime features have no definitions on the medical use invention; and construed a medical use claim as a process for manufacturing a pharmaceutical medicament.

Patent rights may be granted to inventions-creations. Article 2 of the Chinese Patent Law generally defines what inventions-creations are and what inventions are:

> "in the law, 'inventions-creations' mean inventions, utility models and designs and that '*invention*' refers to any new technical solution relating to a product, a process or an improvement thereof..."

The above definitions are also applied to patent eligibility of medical use inventions.

Article 25.1(3) of the Chinese Patent Law explicitly excludes the patentability of "methods for treatment or diagnosis of diseases" and the others.

Under this Article, no patent right will be granted to a claim directed to a method of a pharmaceutical compound or composition, either new or known, for diagnosis or for treatment of diseases.

Not until the first amendments to the Chinese Patent Law in 1993, were pharmaceutical products, and substances obtained by means of a chemical process eligible to be patented.

Consistently, the Guidelines for Patent Examination (Part II, Chapter 1, Section 4.3, the 2010 version) clearly state that "substances or materials used in the methods for diagnosis and treatment of diseases are patentable subject matter".

Moreover, the Guidelines for Patent Examination (Part II, Chapter 10, Section 4.5.2, the 2010 version) provide the guidance that *a medical use invention may be pursued either in the form of a product claim or in the form of a use claim for preparing a medicament.*

A medical use claim may be drafted in the form of "use of substance X in the manufacture of a medicament for treatment of disease Y" or similar, i.e., in the language of a Swiss-type use claim. Clearly, a claim in the form of "use of a substance for treatment of diseases" or "use of a substance as a medicament" is interpreted as a method of treatment claim under the Guidelines. In the above-mentioned *Cubist* case, the Supreme Court narrowly construed a medical use claim in the form of Swiss-type as a process for manufacturing a pharmaceutical medicament.

Under the Chinese patent practice, as shown in numerous decisions by the PRB, a claim passes the Article 25.1(3) bar so long as the preamble of the claim is in either form, even if the claim additionally recites any features of treatment, such as the method of administration. Therefore, a method of treatment claim may be converted into a Swiss-type use claim to overcome Article 25.1(3) rejection. However, such features being permitted in the claim does not mean they can contribute to patentability, as discussed later.

The next major bar to patentability for medical use inventions is novelty.

The requirement of novelty for inventions is generally set forth in Article 22(2) of the Chinese Patent Law:

> "An invention or utility model for which a patent is to be granted shall be novel, inventive and practically applicable.
>
> Novelty means that the invention or utility model is not an existing technology, and prior to the date of application, no entity or individual has filed an application heretofore with the patent administrative department of the State Council for the identical invention or utility model and recorded it in the patent application documents or patent documents released after the said date of application.

> Inventiveness means that, as compared with the technology existing before the date of application the invention has prominent substantive features and represents a notable progress and that the utility model has substantive features and represents progress.
>
> Practical applicability means that the invention or utility model can be made or used and can produce effective results.
>
> The term 'existing technology' as mentioned in this Law refers to the technologies known to the general public both at home and abroad prior to the date of application."

The Guidelines provide several rules for assessing novelty for inventions. Specifically, the Guidelines (Part II, Chapter 10, Section 5.4, the 2010 version) provides the provision concerning "novelty of use invention of a chemical product".

For medical use inventions, the Guidelines specifically provide that the following aspects shall be taken into consideration when the examination of novelty of a medical use invention is carried out.

(1) Whether or not the new use is substantially different from the known use. The use invention does not possess novelty when the difference between the new use and the known use lies merely in the form of expression, but the substance of them is the same.
(2) Whether or not the new use is disclosed directly by the mechanism of action or pharmacological action of the known use. The use does not possess novelty if it is directly equivalent to the mechanism of action or pharmacological action of the known use.
(3) Whether or not the new use belongs to generic term of the known use. The known use defined by specific term may destroy the novelty of the use defined by the generic term.
(4) Whether or not the features relating to use, such as the subject, mode, route, dosage amount, or interval of administration, can define the procedure of manufacture of a pharmaceutical. The features embodied only in the administration process cannot render the use novel.

1.1 First medical use

The first medical use invention of a new pharmaceutical compound may be pursued either in the form of a product claim or in the form of a Swiss-type use claim.

If the chemical product is new, the medical use invention of such a product is inherently new as confirmed by the Guidelines for Patent Examination (Part II, Chapter 10, Section 5.4).

The first medical use invention of a known compound which has been found to have a new therapeutic use may be protected either in the form of a pharmaceutical composition claim or in the form of a Swiss-type use claim.

SIPO interprets a purpose-limited product claim as a product claim, and the limited purpose or use is excluded from further consideration unless the use inherently limits the structure and/or composition of the product.

By this standard, a claim directed to a known chemical compound defined by a new therapeutic use is thus generally rejected as being anticipated. Whether any medical use of the chemical compound has previously been known is irrelevant in this regard.

Following the same criteria, the first medical use invention of a known compound, presented as a "pharmaceutical composition" claim, may be regarded as novel, if the compound has previously never been disclosed for pharmaceutical use or placed in a composition suitable for that use. The rationale is that the presence of pharmaceutically acceptable components in the claimed composition, as is inherently required by the pharmaceutical use, distinguishes the composition from the prior art.

1.2 Second medical use

For a known *pharmaceutical* compound, a purpose or use limited product claim is generally rejected as being anticipated. Therefore, it is difficult to obtain a patent for a second medical use invention in the form of a pharmaceutical compound or composition. Instead, the medical use invention of a known pharmaceutical compound can only be protected in the form of a Swiss-type use claim.

A close dissection of the language of a Swiss-type use claim finds that there are three decisive features in such a use claim, i.e., the substance X, the medicament and the disease Y.

If the substance X is a known pharmaceutical compound or composition, then the novelty-conferring feature has to rely on the feature "medicament" or "disease Y". In practice, novelty of a second medical use may be established if the new use, more specifically, the new disease Y, is substantially different from the known use. Under the Guidelines, the features relating to the use of the pharmaceutical substance, such as the subject to be treated, mode of administration, route of administration, dosage, or time interval of administration, may not be considered when assessing the novelty of a second medical use claim if those features have no definition on the process of manufacturing the medicament. In the *Cubist* case, the Supreme Court confirmed that the administration regimes have no definitions on the medical use invention of manufacturing a medicament for treatment of a disease. In the *Bristol-Myers Squibb v PRB* case ((2014) ZhiXingZi No. 67), the Supreme Court took into account the subject to be treated, i.e., the adult, when evaluating the inventive step of the second medical use claim, as the adult feature has been deemed as having definition on the process of manufacturing a medicament.

B. VALIDITY

I. Allowable claim wording

1. Product claims

For novelty reasons, a second medical indication of a known pharmaceutical compound cannot be patented either in the form of "compound X for treating disease Y" or in the form of "a pharmaceutical composition comprising a compound X for treating disease Y". The underlining rationale is that the requirement for a second medical indication lies in the finding of a new use of a known compound, which cannot render the compound itself novel. It has been a long-established practice in China that a product claim should be defined by the structural features of the product, such as the name, structural formula, and components of the product. It is commonly held that the use feature of a product does not define the product per se.

2. *Method claims*

A "method of treatment" claim is not allowable under the Chinese Patent Law due to the exception to patentability laid down in Article 25.1(3).

According to the Guidelines (Part II, Chapter 1, Section 4.3), "Methods for diagnosis or for treatment of diseases" refer to the processes of identifying, determining, or eliminating the cause of focus of diseases which are practised directly on living human or animal bodies.

For humanity and ethical reasons, it is acknowledged that a doctor shall be given the freedom to choose any means in the course of diagnosis or treatment of diseases. Moreover, these kinds of methods are not susceptible of industrial application because they are practised directly on living human or animal bodies, and are not inventions-creations in the context of the Patent Law. Therefore, methods for the diagnosis or treatment of diseases shall not be granted patent rights.

However, instruments or apparatus for implementing these methods of diagnosis or treatment, or substances or materials for use in such methods are subject matter for which patent right may be granted.

3. *Use claims*

Since the Chinese Patent Law does not allow "method of treatment" claims, medical use claims are a way of protecting pharmaceutical inventions. Accordingly, it is a well-established Chinese practice to grant patents for novel and inventive (second and further) medical uses. In these "use claims", novelty can only be derived from the new medical use, and in general cannot be derived from a new patient group to be treated or a novel treatment or (drug-) administration regime, etc.

The current Guidelines for Patent Examination provide some guidance on how to patent a second medical indication of a known pharmaceutical compound in China (Part II, Chapter 10, Section 4.5.2). According to the current Guidelines, a second medical indication of a known pharmaceutical compound could be patented in the form of Swiss-type use claim, which is presented as "use of compound X in the preparation of a medicament for the treatment of disease Y" or the like. The current Guidelines further provide that no patent right shall be granted to the claims directed to the medical use of a pharmaceutical compound if they are presented in such forms as "use of a compound for the treatment of diseases", "use of a compound for the diagnosis of diseases" or "use of a compound as a medicament".

Quite often, a second medical indication invention of a known compound has been initially presented either in the form of a method for the treatment of diseases or in the form of a compound for treating diseases, especially for those applications that have been drafted outside China, such as PCT applications entered into the Chinese national phase. An unpatentable subject matter issue or a novelty issue will be raised if a claim is presented in these two forms. Apparently the issues may be easily overcome by simply converting the claim into the Swiss-type use claim. However, due to the amendments, other issues such as novelty may arise that will prevent the inventions from being granted if the specifications have not been drafted in line with Chinese patent practice.

4. *System claims*

The Chinese Patent Office is sometimes faced with the question of whether medical devices and corresponding "medical systems" could be protected in a "medical use" format.

For novelty reasons, medical devices and corresponding "medical systems" cannot be protected in the form of "medical device or medical system for the treatment of disease Y", for it is generally held that the use feature of a product does not define the product per se, as discussed above for "Product claims".

5. *Dosage regimes*

The current Guidelines provide clear guidance on the determination of novelty of the medical use claim of a known chemical product. Specifically, the current Guidelines say that several factors must be considered when determining the novelty of the medical use claim of a known chemical product. In particular, the Guidelines for Patent Examination say it should be considered "whether the features involved in the use of the chemical product, such as the subjects to be administered, administration ways, administration routes, pathways, dosages and time intervals, define the preparation process of the medicament. The features embodied only in the administration process cannot render the use novel."

It is clear from the current Guidelines for Patent Examination that the dosage regimes will be ignored in determining the novelty of the Swiss-type use claims if dosage regimes do not define the preparation process of a medicament.

The Chinese Supreme Court stands on the same side as the PRB in the *Cubist v Patent Reexamination Board* case ((2012) ZhiXingZi No. 75). The Court explicitly held that the features relating to the use of the medicament, such as dosage, interval of administration and so on, do not have direct connections with the manufacturing process per se; and those features are not the features for defining the manufacturing use and cannot define the claimed manufacturing process.

6. *Patient groups*

Under the current Chinese patent practice, if the findings of new patient groups result in differences in the diseases to be treated, the Swiss-type use claims are novel. However, such differences as type, age, and gender of the patient groups cannot render the Swiss-type use claims novel.

For example, children with dementia and senile dementia are seemingly different in terms of the subjects to be treated, and are actually completely different diseases. Dementia in children is caused by the cerebral dysgenesis, leading to behaviour such as mental deficiency. In contrast, senile dementia is a degenerative brain disease, leading to behaviour such as intelligence degeneration,loss of memory and related behavioural disorders. Under such circumstances, a medical use defined by a different patient group is novel.

The Guidelines (Part II, Chapter 10, Section 5.4, the 2010 version) clearly state that the subject is related to the use of the medicament, and the features embodied only in the administration process cannot render the use novel. The Guidelines do not give an answer as to whether the subject to be treated is novelty-conferring, i.e., whether the subject to be treated is a feature embodied only in the administration process.

In the administrative disputes over patent invalidation concerning Chinese patent ZL No. 200510128719.4 (assigned to Bristol-Myers Squibb), both the administrative section (i.e., the PRB) and judicial sections (including the Beijing First Intermediate Court of first instance, the Beijing High Court of second instance, and the Supreme Court for the judicial review) acknowledged that the subject to be treated (i.e., the patient group) defines the process of manufacturing a medicament.

Specifically, Bristol-Myers Squibb amended the granted claims in response to the petitioner's request for invalidation.

The amended claim 1 is in the form of a Swiss-type use claim, directed to the use of entecavir in the manufacture of a pharmaceutical composition in the form of a tablet or capsule for once-a-day oral administration for the treatment of hepatitis B virus infection in an adult human patient.

For the purpose of evaluating the inventive step of the claimed use, the authority at each proceeding (from the PRB, the Beijing First Intermediate Court of first instance, the Beijing High Court of second instance, to the Supreme Court for the judicial review) found claim 1 is distinct from the cited reference in that claim 1 defines the subject to be treated as an adult human patient. The comparison adopted by both the administrative section and judicial sections for evaluating the inventive step suggests that the "adult human patient" feature is considered as a novelty-conferring feature in the use claim. The trial court opined that the definition of the subject to be treated as an "adult human patient" in the use claim has an influential effect on the process of manufacturing a medicament since different types of subjects require different quality control of the adjuvants and components used in the pharmaceutical medicament.

Although the Chinese Supreme Court affirmed the decision made by the previous proceedings in the Bristol-Myers Squibb's patent for lack of inventive step over the cited references, the decision or judgment concerning this case clearly show that "the subject to be treated" feature is novelty-conferring.

II. Novelty

1. General definition of novelty and prior art

Article 22(2) of the Chinese Patent Law requires "absolute novelty" and, accordingly, the prior art comprises anything that was made available to the public before the priority (or filing) date of the invention. It is irrelevant how and where the disclosure took place and even oral public disclosures and public prior uses are taken into account.

Specifically, under Article 22(2) of the Chinese Patent Law, novelty means that the invention does not form part of the prior art; nor has any entity or individual filed before the date of filing with SIPO an application relating to the identical invention disclosed in patent application documents published or patent documents announced after said date of filing.

The *prior art* here means any technology known to the public before the date of filing in China or abroad. The prior art includes publication, pubic use, and any other disclosure.

In the Guidelines for Patent Examination, it is explicitly provided that the prior art shall be the technical contents that are available to the public before the date of filing. In other words, the prior art shall be in such a state that it is available to the public before the date of filing and shall contain such contents from which the public can obtain substantial technical knowledge.

It should be noted that technical contents in a state of secrecy are not part of the prior art. The state of secrecy includes not only the situation where the obligation to keep secret arises from regulations or agreements regarding confidences but also the situation where the obligation to keep secret arises from social customs or commercial practices, that is, from implicit agreements or understandings.

However, if a person having the obligation to keep secret breaches the regulation, agreement, or implicit understanding, rendering the technical contents disclosed and making the technologies available to the public, these technologies shall form part of the prior art.

2. Definition of skilled person

Neither the Chinese Patent Law nor the Guidelines for Patent Examination defines the "person skilled in the art" in the context of the novelty assessment.

The Guidelines for Patent Examination defines the "person skilled in the art" in the context of the inventiveness assessment.

Specifically, the Guidelines for Patent Examination (Part II, Chapter 4, Section 2.4) provide that "whether or not an invention involves an inventive step shall be evaluated on the basis of the knowledge and capability of the person skilled in the art. The person skilled in the art refers to a fictional "person" who is presumed to be aware of all the common technical knowledge and have access to all the technologies existing before the filing date or the priority date in the technical field to which the invention pertains, and have capacity to apply all the routine experimental means before that date. However, they are not presumed to have creativity. If the technical problem to be solved impels that person to seek technical means in another technical field, they should also be presumed to have access to the relevant technical field and to the relevant prior art, common technical knowledge, and routine experimental means in the other technical field before the filing date or the priority date.

The purpose of establishing such a concept is to unify the standard of examination and to avoid subjectivity as far as possible.

3. *Scope of disclosure*

3.1 *General rules*

The general rule for disclosure is that the description shall set forth the invention in a manner sufficiently clear and complete so as to enable a person skilled in the relevant field of technology to carry it out; where necessary, drawings are required. In other words, the skilled person can carry out the technical solution, resolve the technical problem and achieve the expected effects according to the disclosure of the description.

3.2 *First medical use*

The first medical use of a known compound may be protected in such form as "a pharmaceutical composition comprising compound X for the treatment of disease Y", if the compound has previously never been disclosed for pharmaceutical use or placed in a composition suitable for that use.

3.3 *New subject matter*

For providing sufficient disclosure of first, second or further medical use claims, the "novel" subject matter (i.e., the therapeutic effect) must be disclosed in the application as filed.

According to the Guidelines for Patent Examination (Part II, Chapter 10, Section 3.3), for the sufficient disclosure of use for an invention of a chemical product, the description shall describe the chemical product to be used, the method for using the product and the effect to be achieved to enable a person skilled in the art to carry it out. If a person skilled in the art cannot predict the use according to the prior art, the description shall sufficiently provide data from experimental tests for a person skilled in the art to be convinced that the product is useful for said use and can solve the technical problem or achieve the technical effect as expected.

3.4 *New data*

According to the Mid-October 2013 Directive of SIPO, post-filing data can be accepted as evidence to show enablement of an invention. However, as far as we know, there are very few cases where the PRB withdrew the non-enablement rejection by relying on post-filing data.

It is still not clear whether post-filing data is acceptable to show enablement of an invention. In current practice, however, non-enablement issues or insufficient disclosure issues are seldom raised by the examiner during the prosecution, even for applications without any test data in the original specification. For older cases where a non-enablement issue is raised in previous office actions, the examiner will no longer insist on the issue in the subsequent office action if the application has not been finally rejected on the ground of non-enablement. For older cases that have been finally rejected on the ground of non-enablement, the Patent Reexamination

Board will normally withdraw the final rejections by relying on the prior art references to establish the predictability of the technical effect even if the applicants submit post-filing data to show enablement.

We note that SIPO has shifted from enablement rejection (Article 26.3) to inventiveness rejection (Article 22.2) in the past two years. If there is no test data in the original specification, the examiner would reject the application for being obvious without accepting the post-filing data. According to the cases we are currently handling, we can see that post-filing data is normally *not* acceptable to show inventive step of an invention even for the cases where (1) the data range for specific compounds is given in the original specification and (2) the applicant submits post-filing data for a specific compound for comparison with the prior art compounds.

4. *Requirements for second medical use*

4.1 Distinction from first medical use

As mentioned above, the first medical use of a known compound may be protected in such form as "a pharmaceutical composition comprising compound X for the treatment of disease Y", while the second medical use of a known compound can only be protected in the form of Swiss-type use claims, i.e., "use of compound X in the manufacture of a medicament for the treatment of disease Y."

4.2 Sub-species of second medical use

If an invention lies in the finding of novel dosage/treatment regimes of a known compound in a known disease (including dosage, time interval, route of administration or other features related to drug administration), such invention will be considered as not novel if the applicants cannot show that such features define the preparation process of medicament according to the Guidelines for Patent Examination.

If an invention lies in the finding of the sub-species of a second medical use, the sub-species is a sort of so-called "selection invention". In this case, unexpected technical effects for the sub-species are required to show inventiveness of the sub-species.

4.3 Dosage regimes

If a medical use invention lies in the finding of the features involved in the use of the medicament, such as the subjects to be administered, administration ways, administration routes, pathways, dosages and time intervals, etc. and these features do not define the preparation process of the medicament, such a medical use invention will be considered as not novel.

4.4 Special patient groups

Under current Chinese patent practice, the selection of the new patient groups to be treated can confer novelty and inventive step to a second medical use claim if the new patient groups to be treated are distinguishable from the patients to be treated in the prior art in terms of the diseases to be treated.

5. *Timing issues*

5.1 *Relevant time of development of second use*

Although second medical uses are often developed after a drug was developed, we suggest not filing the application until data such as in vitro and/or in vivo data is available. If there is no data to show the use of the second medical use in the original specification, a lack of inventive step rejection will be raised by the Chinese examiners.

5.2 *Role of new data*

As mentioned above in "New data", it is still not clear whether the post-filing new data is acceptable to show enablement of an invention. But post-filing data is normally *not* acceptable to show inventive step of an invention.

5.3 *Use of old data*

Although according to the Guidelines for Patent Examination, we can rely on the prior art knowledge such as old data to show sufficiency of the disclosure of the second medical use invention, the reliance on the prior art knowledge will, quite often, dilute the inventive step of the second medical use invention. It would be advisable to be cautious in relying on the prior art knowledge such as old data.

III. Inventive step/non-obviousness

1. *Definition of inventive step/non-obviousness*

Article 22(3) of the Chinese Patent Law stipulates that "inventiveness means that, as compared with the prior art, the invention has prominent substantive features and represents a notable progress".

Under the Guidelines for Patent Examination, to determine whether an invention has prominent substantive features is to determine, to the person skilled in the art, whether the claimed invention is non-obvious as compared with the prior art.

If the claimed invention is obvious as compared with the prior art, it does not have prominent substantive features. On the contrary, if the result of comparison shows that the claimed invention is non-obvious as compared with the prior art, it has prominent substantive features.

The Guidelines for Patent Examination provide the following "three-step" approach for assessing the non-obviousness of an invention (Part II, Chapter 4, Section 3.2.1):

(1) identifying the closest prior art;

(2) determining the distinguishing technical features and the technical problem actually solved by the invention; and
(3) determining whether the invention is non-obvious to a person skilled in the art.

With respect to the inventive step of the use invention of a chemical product, the Guidelines for Patent Examination provide some additional guidance in Part II, Chapter 10, Section 6.2, which states: "a use invention of a known product is regarded as involving an inventive step if the new use cannot be derived or expected from the structure, composition, molecular weight, known physical/chemical property and existing use of the product, but utilises a newly discovered property of the product, and produces an unexpected technical effect."

2. *Same scope of disclosure as for novelty?*

A technical solution comprising different technical features from the prior art is considered as novel. However, in order to establish inventive step, non-obviousness determined according to the above-mentioned "three-step" approach or unexpected technical features shall be established.

3. *Assessment of inventive step/non-obviousness*

Under the Guidelines for Patent Examination (Part II, Chapter 4, Section 6.3), if the technical solution of an invention is determined as non-obvious to a person skilled in the art by following the above-mentioned "three-step" approach and can produce advantageous technical effect, then the invention involves an inventive step. On the other hand, if the technical solution of an invention produces an unexpected technical effect as compared with the prior art, then the invention is determined as involving an inventive step without the need to question whether its technical solution is non-obvious.

IV. Amendment of claims after grant

1. *Admissibility of post-grant amendments in general*

Under the Guidelines for Patent Examination, it is allowed to amend the claims during the post-grant invalidation proceedings, but the amendments shall follow the following principles:

(1) the title of the subject matter of a claim cannot be changed;
(2) the protection scope of the claims cannot be broadened in comparison with the claims as granted;
(3) the amendment shall not go beyond the scope of the disclosure contained in the initial description and claims; and
(4) the addition of the technical features not included in the claims as granted is generally not allowed.

Subject to the above principles of amendments, the specific manners of amendment are generally limited to deletion of a claim, combination of claims, and deletion of a technical solution.

Deletion of a claim means one (or more) claim, either an independent claim or a dependent claim, is removed from the claims.

Combination of claims means that two or more claims dependent on the same independent claim and having no relation of dependency are combined. Under this circumstance, all the technical features of the combined dependent claims form a new claim. The new claim shall contain all the technical features of each of the dependent claims thus combined. Dependent claims that are dependent on the same independent claim shall not be combined together unless the independent claim is amended.

Deletion of a technical solution means that one or more technical solutions are removed from several parallel technical solutions defined in the same claim.

2. *Procedural issues*

2.1 Independent limitation proceedings

No independent limitation proceedings as available in Europe are available in China.

2.2 Opposition proceedings

No opposition proceedings are available in China.

3. *Added matter*

It is not allowed to add matter after grant in China.

4. *Sufficiency*

Under Rule 65 of the Implementing Regulations of the Chinese Patent Law, lack of sufficiency is a ground for invalidation.

It is assessed whether the claims under discussion are sufficiently clear and complete to enable a person skilled in the art to carry out the invention.

5. *Multiple indications*

It is possible to include multiple indications in an issued patent. Although lack of unity is a ground for final rejection, it is not a ground for patent invalidation. Even if the multiple indications that lack unity are included in the claims as granted, the claims shall not be invalidated for lack of unity.

V. Change of patent category

It is not allowed to change the patent category in accordance with the Guidelines for Patent Examination.

C. INFRINGEMENT AND LITIGATION

I. Legal framework

1. National statutory laws

In China, parallel proceedings are adopted to hear patent validity and infringement cases. Validity of an issued patent is first heard by the PRB. If either the patentee or the requester is not satisfied with the invalidation decision made by the PRB, an administrative lawsuit may be filed with the Beijing IP Court, and may be further appealed to the Beijing High Court. A patent may be enforced in China via administrative, judicial, or criminal route.

A patentee may file a request with an administrative authority for patent affairs to handle a patent infringement case. Alternatively, a patentee may file a civil lawsuit directly with a specialised court for a patent litigation in China. Counterfeiting of a patent of another person could constitute the criminal offence of infringing intellectual property. Custom protection is also available.

Generally, the Civil Procedural Law governs court proceedings for patent infringement litigation in China. The Chinese Patent Law generally defines the right of exclusion in Article 11, and protection of a patent right in Articles 59 to 74, such as the scope of a patent right in Article 59, remedy in Article 65, preliminary injection in Article 66, preservation of evidence in Article 67, and defence to patent infringement in Articles 62, 69 and 70.

Specifically, Article 11 of the Chinese Patent Law provides:

> "After the grant of the patent right for an invention or utility model, except where otherwise provided for in this Law, no entity or individual may, *without the authorisation of the patentee*, exploit the patent, that is, make, use, offer to sell, sell or import the patented product, or use the patented process, and use, offer to sell, sell or import the product directly obtained by the patented process, *for production or business purposes*." [emphasis added]

In addition to the general provisions in the Chinese Patent Law, the Supreme Court in China has released several interpretations for the purpose of appropriate adjudication of cases involving patent infringement disputes. Those interpretations include:

(1) Interpretations of the Supreme People's Court on Several Issues Concerning the Application of Law to Trial of Cases of Patent Disputes (first released in 2001, amended in 2013, and then amended in 2015, hereinafter "the 2001 Interpretations");
(2) Chinese Supreme Court's Judicial Interpretations on Several Issues Concerning Application of Law in Trial of Patent Infringement Disputes (I) (released in 2009, hereinafter "the 2009 Interpretations"); and
(3) Chinese Supreme Court's Judicial Interpretations on Several Issues Concerning Application of Law in Trial of Patent Infringement Disputes (II) (released in 2016, hereinafter "the 2016 Interpretations).

The 2001 Interpretations as well as the two subsequent amendments in view of the Third Amendments to the Chinese Patent Law provide jurisdictions for patent infringement cases in China and introduce the "All Element Rule" in the 2015 Amendment as well as the doctrine of equivalents in the 2001 version, and other provisions.

The 2009 Interpretations further provide the rules for claim construction, defence to infringement, and remedy, and for the first time introduced requirements for bringing about a lawsuit for confirmation of non-infringement.

The 2016 Interpretations further specify the rules for claim construction, introduce indirect infringement for the first time, provide defence to infringement, and others.

2. *Case law*

China is not a case law country. In practice, the Chinese Supreme Court occasionally publishes cases as guidance for the lower courts to follow.

II. Claim construction

1. *General rules*

Article 59 of the Chinese Patent Law provides the general rule for claim construction:

> "the extent of protection of the patent right for invention shall be determined by the terms of the claims. The description and the appended drawings may be used to interpret the content of the claims."

Further, Article 17 of the 2001 Interpretations, which was amended in 2015, provides the "All Element Rule" and the doctrine of equivalents:

> "The first paragraph 'the extent of protection of the patent right for invention shall be determined by the terms of the claims. The description and the appended drawings may be used to interpret the content of the claims' of Article 59 of the Patent Law means that the extent of protection of patent right should be determined by all the technical features stated in the claims, including the extent as determined by the features equivalent to the technical features.
>
> The equivalent features refer to the features which use substantially the same means, perform substantially the same function and produce substantially the same as the stated technical features and which can be contemplated by an ordinarily skilled artisan in the art at the time of infringement without inventive efforts."

The 2009 Interpretations further specify the rule for claim construction in Article 2, which provides:

> "The court shall determine the contents of the claims as provided in Article 59, paragraph 1 of the Patent Law in accordance with the statement of the claims and in connection with the understanding of the claims by those skilled in the art reading the description and accompanying drawings."

Article 3 of the 2009 Interpretations sets forth the documents which may be used to construe the claims and the order of application of those documents: first, with reference to the description and accompanying drawings, any relevant ones of the claims and prosecution history of the patent; and then with reference to any reference books, textbooks and other publicly known documents, and normal understanding of those skilled in the art.

Articles 5 and 6 of the 2009 Interpretations provide limitations to doctrine of equivalents, i.e., donation principle in Article 5 and prosecution history estoppel in Article 6.

2. *Specific issues for use claims*

The current laws and judicial interpretations do not specifically provide the principles for claim construction of a use claim for patent infringement. A use claim is generally considered as a special type of process claim. A use claim is, in essence, a process of using a product for a particular purpose or use.

In view of the essence of a use claim, a Swiss-type use claim shall be interpreted as a process of using a pharmaceutical compound for manufacturing a pharmaceutical medicament which, in turn, is used to treat a certain disease.

In contrast, the Supreme Court in the above-mentioned *Cubist* case narrowly construed a medical use claim as a process for manufacturing a pharmaceutical medicament by using a chemical compound in an administrative proceeding concerning patent validity.

From the other perspective of view, if bearing the "All Element Rule" in mind, all technical features in a second use claim shall be considered in the determination of the scope of the use claim, including those administration features which might be excluded from consideration during the patent validity proceeding.

In *Merck v the PRB* (2008), which concerned the validity of an issued patent, the Beijing High Court held that a medical use invention is essentially an invention of a process of using the medicament; and the technical features relating to how to use the medicament, e.g., the administration feature including dosage form and the dosage, should be included in the use claim. However, such judgment was not followed by the lower court, the PRB or examiners examining similar cases, as can be seen from subsequent cases.

In *Interpretation and Application of Beijing High Court's Guidelines for Determination of Patent Infringement*, edited by the IP section of the Beijing High Court and published in 2014, the scope of a use claim is limited to the particular use of the particular product recited in the claims and involves extension of the patent right for a process invention to the product (p. 458). The book also states that the scope of a medical use claim in Swiss-type form is limited by the particular purpose or use recited in the claim. That is, infringement may be established if the patentee can prove that the acts of an alleged infringer are to apply the corresponding product to the particular use (p. 459).

III. Scope of protection

1. *Scope of the use*

1.1 *General definition of the term "use"*

As discussed above, a second medical use claim is, in essence, a process of *using* a known pharmaceutical product for a particular purpose or use, i.e., for treating a particular disease. Article 11 of the Chinese Patent Law recites "use ... the patented product, or use the patented process, and use ... the product directly obtained by the patented process". However, the current laws or provisions do not provide a definition of the term "use" of a patented product, a patented process or a patented use as discussed herein.

In *Introduction to the Patent Law of China* by Mr. YIN Xintian and published in 2001, "the use of a patented product" is defined as "the utilization of the patented product so that the technical function of the patented product has been performed" (p. 152). Article 91 of the Beijing High Court's Guidelines for Determination of Patent Infringement (2013) defines the use of a patent invention in a similar way to that of Mr. YIN Xintian. Mr. YIN's book also sets forth several ways of using a patented product including using it directly to achieve the effect the product may produce; using the patented product as a means to produce other products; or using the patented products as a component or part to produce other products.

By referring to the use of a patented product as well as the essence of a medical use claim, the term "use" may be interpreted as using the particular pharmaceutical compound to the particular purpose or use, i.e., for treating the particular disease recited in the claim.

Article 104 of Beijing High Court's Guidelines for Determination of Patent Infringement (2013) confirms the above understanding, which states:

> "For a use invention patent, the patentee should prove that the alleged infringer manufactures, uses, sells, offers to sell, and imports the infringing products for the patent's particular use."

1.2 *Manufacture of the pharmaceutical*

As discussed above, manufacture of the pharmaceutical is covered by the general definition of the term "use" with the purpose of treating a particular disease.

1.3 *Sale of the product*

As discussed above, sale of the product is covered by the general definition of the term "use" with the purpose of treating a particular disease.

1.4 *Offer for sale*

As discussed above, offer for sale is covered by the general definition of the term "use" with the purpose of treating a particular disease.

1.5 Application to the patient

Under the current legal framework, it remains unclear whether application of the pharmaceutical to a particular patient by a physician infringes the use invention. However, application of the pharmaceutical to a particular patient by the patient themself should not infringe the use claim as such an act is usually interpreted as having no purpose of production or business.

2. Absolute product protection

2.1 Limitation through the term "use"

A product claim provides absolute protection and the scope of the claim is generally not limited to any particular use. Where a product claim recites a use feature, e.g., through the term "use" or the like, such a use feature will limit the scope of the product claim in applying the "All Element Rule". This is also confirmed by Article 21 of Beijing High Court's Guidelines for Determination of Patent Infringement (2013).

3. Dosage regimes

For patent validity cases, the administrative and judicial sections may not consider the dosage regimes as novelty-conferring features. For patent infringement cases, dosage regimes, when recited in the use claims, will limit the claimed use when the "All Element Rule" is applied.

4. Patient groups

Patient groups, when recited in the use claims, will limit the claimed use.

IV. Infringing acts

Within the context of Article 11, any person or entity who, without the authorisation of the patentee and for production or business purposes, makes use, offers to sell, sells or imports the particular product for the particular purpose of treating a disease as recited in the use claim, infringes the claimed use.

1. Indirect infringement

1.1 Objective acts

In Article 21(1) and (2) of the 2016 Interpretations, the Supreme Court for the first time spells out the rules for finding indirect infringement:

> "Where a party, knowing that a product is a material, equipment, part, intermediate or the like specially dedicated to practising a patent, has for production or business purposes and without authorisation of the patent holder provided the

> product to another party, who has conducted an act of infringing the patent, if the right holder claims that the act of the provider is aiding others in committing a tort under Article 9 of the Chinese Tort Law, the court shall sustain that claim.
>
> Where a party, knowing that a product or process has been patented, has for production or business purposes actively induced the act of another party of infringing the patent, if the right holder claims that the inducer's action is abetting others in committing a tort under Article 9 of the Chinese Tort Law, the court shall sustain that claim."

The first and second paragraphs effectively provide for contributory infringement and inductive infringement, respectively.

The statutory ground for the Interpretations is the aiding-and-abetting clause of Article 9(1) of the Chinese Tort Law:

> "Any who abets or aids another party in committing a tort shall be liable jointly and severally with the tortfeasor".

In both contributory and inductive infringements, the Interpretations specifically require a directly infringing act to have actually taken place. Accordingly, there cannot be indirect infringement without direct infringement, that is, there can be no indirect infringement where there is no unauthorised practising of the patent, where any unauthorised practising of the patent is not for production or business purposes, such as the practising by an individual consumer, or where any unauthorised practising of the patent falls under the exemptions provided in Article 69 of the Chinese Patent Law.

The affirmative act of a contributory infringer is "providing" a product that is specifically dedicated to practising a patent. The affirmative act of an inductive infringer is "actively inducing" others to infringe the patent.

1.2 Subjective conditions

Under Article 21 of the 2016 Interpretations, neither contributory nor inductive infringement demands a deliberate intent of the infringer to infringe on its own or cause others to infringe. The required state of mind of the contributor or inducer is to "know" that the product or process is patented or is specifically dedicated to a patented technology. Whether this includes only actual knowledge or also presumed knowledge is yet unclear. However, in the explanatory statement upon announcing the 2016 Interpretations, the Supreme Court characterises the state of mind of the indirect infringer as "obvious bad faith" that Article 21 aims to punish. This may shed light on how the subjective condition requirement will be applied by the courts.

Of the few indirect infringement cases hitherto decided, *Novartis AG. v Chongqing Xinyuanxing Co.* (2008) is a typical one related to pharmaceutical patents.

Novartis owns a patent for Imatinib. Chongqing Xinyuanxing Co. (CXYX) manufactures and sells Imatinib as well as intermediate compounds in the synthesis of Imatinib. The Imatinib CXYX manufacture is covered by Novartis' patent but the intermediate compounds are not. On its official website, CXYX specifically describes these compounds as "Imatinib intermediates". Novartis sued CXYX for direct and indirect infringements. The Chongqing First Intermediate Court found both infringements, and the Chongqing High Court affirmed these.

In the final judgment, the Chongqing High Court did not apply the aiding and abetting doctrine, but reasoned that CXYX is liable for indirect infringement because CXYX's selling of the intermediate compounds would inevitably cause direct infringement of the Novartis' patent by the purchaser, of which CXYX should be aware, given the absence of non-infringing commercial use of these compounds.

The indirect infringement case would likely come out the other way under the 2016 Interpretations, since Novartis did not sue a third party for direct infringement in connection with the CXYX's selling of the intermediates, and direct infringement should have been established so as to prove the indirect infringement.

In the following hypothetical scenarios, indirect infringement may be established under current law.

Scenario 1: A second company purchases the intermediate compounds from CXYX and makes these compounds into Imatinib.

CXYX is liable as contributory infringer, with the second company being the direct infringer.

Scenario 2: A second company synthesises the intermediate compounds by itself, and guided by the CXYX's website, manufactures Imatinib from these compounds.

In this scenario, CXYX can be liable as an inductive infringer.

V. Remedies

1. *Injunctions*

Injunctive relief is generally provided for by Article 118 of the General Principles of Civil Law of China, which states:

> "If … patent rights … of citizens or legal persons are infringed upon … they shall have the right to demand that the infringement be stopped, its ill effects be eliminated and the damages be compensated for".

1.1 Permanent injunction

Article 26 of the 2016 Interpretations provides that where a defendant has constituted infringement of a patent, the court shall generally grant the patentee's request for injunction.

There are exceptions to this general rule. First is an "innocent user" exception provided by Article 25 of the 2016 Interpretations. In accordance with the provision of this Article, if the user of an infringing product does not know that the product was made and sold without permission of the patentee, has obtained the product from a legal source, and has paid reasonable consideration for the product, the court does not have to enjoin the user from continuing to use the product.

The second is the national or public interest exception as provided in Article 26 of the 2016 Interpretations.

1.2 Preliminary injunction

According to Article 66 of the Chinese Patent Law, a patentee or party of interest may also apply to the court for preliminary injunction before lodging a suit.

A security bond must be posted along with the application. Upon receipt of the application, the court must decide whether or not to grant an injunction within 48 hours. If the preliminary injunction is granted, the patentee or party of interest must file a suit within 15 days.

2. Damages

According to Article 65 of the Chinese Patent Law, the amount of compensation for a patent infringement shall be determined on the basis of the actual losses incurred to the patentee as a result of the infringement.

If it is difficult to determine the actual losses, the amount may be determined on the basis of the gains which the infringer has obtained from the infringement.

If it is difficult to determine the losses incurred to the patentee or the gains obtained by the infringer, the amount shall be reasonably determined by reference to a multiple of the royalties for this patent.

If it is difficult to determine the losses incurred to the patentee, the gains obtained by the infringer and the royalty obtained for the patent, the People's Court may, by taking into account such factors as the type of patent, nature and particulars of the infringement, decide compensation in the sum of not less than CNY 10,000 but not more than CNY 1 million.

According to Article 28 of the 2016 Interpretations, the patent owner and the infringer may stipulate the amount of damages or the method of calculating damage for patent infringement. On request of both the patent owner and the infringer, the court shall decide the amount of damages based on the stipulation.

3. Information

3.1 Disclosure of legal source

According to Article 70 of the Chinese Patent Law, an innocent seller or user of an infringing product can be exempt from monetary damages if they can prove that the product is obtained from a legal source. This often involves production of evidence of a lawful purchase from a maker, importer or distributor. This Rule 25 of the 2016 Interpretations further spares such a user from injunction, provided that they have paid a reasonable consideration for that product. These provisions are aimed at encouraging the innocent seller or user to disclose the maker or distributor of the infringing product.

3.2 Information about infringing sales and account of profits

According to Article 27 of the 2016 Interpretations, where the actual loss of the patentee due to the infringement is difficult to determine and the patentee has provided preliminary evidence concerning the infringer's profits, and where the key evidence, such as account books, concerning the infringer's profits are under the control of the infringer, the court may shift the burden of production of such evidence to the infringer. If the infringer fails to meet the burden, the court will determine the infringer's profits based on the patentee's claim and the evidence that the patentee has furnished.

4. *Recall of products and destruction*

The Chinese laws do not provide for recall, confiscation or destruction of infringing products as remedies for infringement. Under Article 134(3) of the General Principles of Civil Law, where infringement has been found, the court may confiscate the infringing product.

However, this measure is a civil sanction to be taken by the court at its discretion, rather than a remedy granted at the plaintiff's request. In practice, the court generally would order the confiscation and destruction of tools used specially for conducting infringement, but not if the tools have a non-infringing use.

5. *Recovery of legal costs*

According to Article 65 of the Chinese Patent Law and Rules on Application of Law in Patent Dispute Cases (2015), the patentee can demand recovery of reasonable fees for investigating and stopping the infringement. Although legal costs are not specifically listed as one such expense, in many cases the court granted recovery of lawyers' fees to the winning patentee.

However, there is no legal provision for the recovery of legal costs for the defendant.

VI. Exceptions from patent protection

1. *Exhaustion of rights*

According to Article 69(1) of the Chinese Patent Law, using, offering to sell, selling or importing any patented product or product directly obtained under the patented process after the said product is sold by the patentee or by its licensed entity or individual does not constitute infringement of the patent.

2. *Bolar exemption*

According to Article 69(5) of the Chinese Patent Law, it shall not be deemed as infringement of the patent right:

Where any entity or individual manufactures, uses or imports a patented medication or a patented medical device solely for the purposes of providing the information needed for the administrative examination and approval; and any person manufactures or imports a patented medication or a patented medical device specially for such entity or individual.

3. *Compulsory license for public health purposes*

According to Article 50 of the Chinese Patent Law, for the purpose of public health, SIPO may grant a compulsory licence for a patented medicine so as to produce and export it to the country or region that conforms to the provisions of the relevant international treaty to which the People's Republic of China has acceded.

4. *Non-granting of injunction based on national or public interest considerations*

According to Article 26 of the 2016 Interpretations, where a patent has been found to be infringed, the court may choose not to enjoin the infringer from practising the patent based on national or public interest considerations, and instead order the infringer to pay a reasonable royalty.

Public health is generally regarded as a typical public interest in Chinese jurisdiction.

VII. Procedural issues

1. *Preliminary injunction cases*

Preliminary injunction is generally provided for in Article 66 of the Chinese Patent Law:

> "Where a patentee or interested party has evidence to prove that someone else is committing or is going to commit an infringement upon the patent right, and its lawful rights and interests will be damaged and are difficult to be remedied if the said infringement is not stopped in time, it may, prior to initiating a lawsuit, apply to the People's Court for taking such measures as ordering the stop of the relevant act.
>
> When an applicant files an application, they shall provide a security. If they fail to do so, the application shall be rejected."

Generally, to apply for a preliminary injunction, the patentee needs to show:

- that they have likelihood of success in the infringement litigation,
- that irreparable damages would arise but for the injunction,
- that a security bond has been put with the court, and
- that public interest would not be affected by the injunction.

In *Novartis v Chiatai Tianqing* (2014), the Beijing Second Intermediate Court granted a petition for injunction filed by Novartis, who was asserting patent infringement on the basis of the second medical use of Gleevec (imatinib mesylate) for treating GIST, ordering Chiatai Tianqing to delete the reference to GIST from the instructions for use contained in its marketed generic version of Gleevec.

While this is an interim rather than preliminary injunction, it demonstrates the availability of preliminary injunction for second medical use claims.

2. *Cases on merits*

The Civil Procedure Law governs the proceeding of a civil lawsuit for patent infringement.

2.1 Standing

Article 60 the Chinese Patent Law provides that the patentee or an interested party has the right to bring a patent infringement suit.

According to the relevant judicial interpretations of the Supreme People's Court, an interested party may be a legal successor to the patent right, an exclusive licensee of the patent, or a sole licensee of the patent. However, while a legal successor or exclusive licensee has independent right to sue, a sole licensee can bring a suit on its own only when the patentee does not sue.

2.2 Venue

A patentee or interested party or has two options to sue the suspected infringer: either suing the suspected infringer, being it a manufacturer, seller, importer, etc., in the place where it is located; or suing the manufacturer and the seller of the infringed product as co-defendants in the place where the seller is located.

The court hierarchy in China consists of four levels: the Supreme Court, the high courts, the intermediate courts, and the local basic-level courts.

According to the Supreme People's Court's rules on application of law in patent dispute cases (2015), the intermediate courts in the provincial capitals, capitals of autonomous regions, or municipalities, and other intermediate or basic People's Courts designated by the Supreme Court, have jurisdiction on patent infringement cases in the first instance. However, basic People's Courts designated by the Supreme Court generally have jurisdiction on infringement cases relating to utility model patents or design patents.

Under Article 19 of the Civil Procedure Law, if a patent infringement case has significant impact in the area of jurisdiction of a high court, the high court has jurisdiction on the case in the first instance.

2.3 Time

The statutory limitation for patent infringement action is two years, counting from the earliest date when the patentee or interested party knows or ought to have known the infringing acts.

However, if the patentee has known or ought to have known about this fact prior to the date when the patent right is granted, the statutory limitation shall be calculated from the date when the patent right is granted.

According to the Civil Procedure Law, generally, the court of first instance to hear a patent infringement case shall deliver judgment within six months from the acceptance of the case. If the parties appeal to the second instance court, the adjudication of second instance shall be made within three months. These time periods could be prolonged upon approval of the head of the court. However, these time frames do not apply to a case where a foreign party is involved. In such cases, there is no time limit for concluding a case.

2.4 *Burden of proof*

The plaintiff bears the burden of proof. Information and evidence available should be attached to/accompanied with the complaint or submitted later within the time period set by the court, which should at least include:

- evidence that the plaintiff is the holder of the issued patent;
- evidence that the defendant has infringed the issued patent, which should include the infringing goods and the sales receipt; and
- additional evidence may include the effect of infringement, and damages the infringement has caused to the plaintiff, which may be served as a basis for calculating damages.

However, if the litigation relates to a new product manufactured by a patented process, then the burden of proof is shifted to the defendant to prove that it has obtained the same product manufactured by a different process.

After trial, the court of first instance will render a judgment, which any party can, as of a right, appeal to the competent court of second instance, which is generally a high court for second medical use patents. The judgment of the court of second instance is final. Within six months upon the receipt of the final judgment, any party may file a petition for retrial with the next level of court, usually the Supreme Court, which has full discretion on the granting of a petition for retrial.

3. *Enforcement of judgments*

After a civil judgment becomes effective, the part of the judgment related to assets are enforced by the court of the first instance, or by the court of the same level as the court of the first instance in the place where the assets subject to enforcement are situated.

Other legal instruments that shall be enforced by courts are enforced by the court in the residence of the person subject to enforcement, or by the court in the place where the assets subject to enforcement are situated.

VIII. Validity

1. *Patent invalidity and stay of court proceedings*

Patent invalidity is not a defence in patent infringement litigation, nor do the courts have the authority to rule on patent validity in infringement suits. To challenge the validity of the patent, the defendant has to file a patent invalidation request with the Patent Reexamination Board of SIPO.

If the defendant has filed an invalidation request in the reply period, they may then request the court to stay the infringement proceedings, pending for the result of the invalidation proceedings. It is up to the court to decide whether or not to stay. Generally, the court tends not to stay the proceedings if the patent at issue is a patent for invention but is likely to rule to stay if it involves a utility model or design patent.

According to Article 3 of the 2016 Interpretations, the court generally should stay the proceedings when a request for invalidation is filed against the patent at issue as a result of the patent obviously violating Article 26(3) or (4) (the sufficiency of disclosure, clarity, and support requirements), to such an extent that the description cannot be used for claim construction. Note that, in this circumstance, the defendant does not have to file the request for invalidation within the reply period.

According to Article 2 of the 2016 Interpretations, once the underlying patent of an infringement suit is declared invalid by the Patent Reexamination Board, the court hearing the suit may immediately order dismissal of the case, without waiting for the result of judicial review of the Patent Reexamination Board's decision. The dismissal is of procedural nature, so the plaintiff can re-file the suit if the Board's decision is eventually overturned by the court.

India

Hari Subramaniam

A. AVAILABILITY OF PROTECTION

I. Legal framework

1. National statutory laws

The Indian patent system is governed by the Patents Act, 1970 and the Patent Rules, 2003.

1.1 Pharmaceuticals

History

India's patent system is in many ways nascent but in reality the first codified patent law was enacted on 12 January 1911 with the Indian Patents and Designs Act, 1911. When India became independent in 1947, the Indian government conducted a study on the socio-economic conditions prevailing in the country at that point of time. Several high powered committees were constituted to study most of the British legislation in force in India and make necessary changes thereto to make them conducive to the environment of new independent India. As far as the patent system was concerned it was realised that more than 95% of the patents in force in India at that point of time were held by foreign multinationals and institutions. Most of such patents were not utilized in India but merely existed as monopoly rights, which, it was generally felt, acted as impediments to the technological progress of the country. It was also felt that since India was quite weak and backward in the area of food and pharmaceuticals, immediate steps must be taken to make the country more self-reliant in these sectors. In order to achieve the above objectives, a high powered Patents Committee headed by Justice G. Ayyangar was constituted which prepared a report and submitted it to the government. The report, commonly referred to as Ayyangar's Report became the genesis for the new Indian Patents Act, 1970 which came into force on 20 April 1972.

Some of the important changes brought about by The Patents Act, 1970 are as follows:

(i) the term of the patent was reduced from 16 years from the date of filing to 14 years in all areas of technology except food, drugs and chemical substances;
(ii) food, drugs and chemical substances *per se* were held to be unpatentable;
(iii) patents were available for processes for preparing food, drugs and chemical substances but with a truncated term of seven years from the date of filing or five years from the date of grant whichever was shorter;
(iv) a negative list was introduced rendering many areas of technology including living organisms, any kind of treatment of plants, animals and humans and mere new uses of known substances unpatentable;
(v) provisions for "Licences of Right" were introduced for patents relating to pharmaceutical processes which enabled any third party to demand a licence as a matter of right.

India joined the WTO (and GATT/TRIPS Agreement as it existed then) in 1994 under which it was required to amend the patents law in a phased manner between 1 January 1995 and 31 December 2004.

The first set of reforms took place effective 1 January 1995 under which it was possible to file patent applications for pharmaceuticals and chemical products *per se* without the fear of summary rejection. These applications were kept in a "mail box" which was to be opened on 1 January 2005 for examination and patent grant. Simultaneously, India was also required to amend the patents law to grant patents for pharmaceuticals and chemical products *per se*. Effective 20 May 2002, the term of the patent was also increased to 20 years from the date of filing.

On 7 December 1998 India joined the Paris Convention and submitted its instrument of accession to the Patent Cooperation Treaty (PCT).

Between 1995 and 2005, pipeline protection was available in terms of exclusive marketing rights on patent applications for pharmaceutical products provided the applicant for patent had received a corresponding foreign patent as well as marketing approval in its country of origin. For an Indian applicant, it was necessary that it had obtained a patent for a process for preparing the pharmaceutical product.

While the above provisions were available most overseas applicants failed to take advantage of such provisions. A few applications made by some pharma majors for exclusive marketing rights were rejected by the Indian Patent Office. However, an Indian company, United Phosphorus Limited was successful in obtaining pipeline protection for an agrochemical comprising of specific proportions of carbendezem and mancozip, which it successfully enforced against seven Indian companies.

In keeping with its commitments under the TRIPS Agreement, the Indian Patents Act underwent three legislative amendments as follows:

(a) The Patents (Amendment) Act, 1999 (17 of 1999) (with effect from 1 January 1995);
(b) The Patents (Amendment) Act, 2002 (38 of 2002) (with effect from 20 May 2003 and with effect from 2 April 2007);
(c) The Patents (Amendment) Act, 2005 (15 of 2005) (with effect from 1 January 2005 and with effect from 2 April 2007)

The most important changes brought about by the above are as follows:

(1) definition of invention was changed as follows:
  (i) Section 2(1)(j): "invention" means a new product or process involving an inventive step and capable of industrial application;
  (ii) Section 2(1)(j)(a): "inventive step" means a feature of an invention that involves technical advance as compared to the existing knowledge or having economic significance or both and that makes the invention not obvious to a person skilled in the art;
  (iii) Section 2(1)(l): "new invention" means any invention or technology which has not been anticipated by publication in any document or used in the country or elsewhere in the world before the date of filing of patent application with complete specification, i.e., the subject matter has not fallen in public domain or that it does not form part of the state of the art;
  (iv) Section 2(1)(ta): "pharmaceutical substance" means any new entity involving one or more inventive steps;

(2) following negative list was reintroduced holding certain classes of inventions to be unpatentable:
Section 3: What are not inventions. – The following are not inventions within the meaning of this Act -
  (a) an invention which is frivolous or which claims anything obviously contrary to well established natural laws;
  (b) an invention the primary or intended use or commercial exploitation of which could be contrary public order or morality or which causes serious prejudice to human, animal or plant life or health or to the environment;
  (c) the mere discovery of a scientific principle or the formulation of an abstract theory [or discovery of any living thing or non-living substances occurring in nature];
  (d) the mere discovery of a new form of a known substance which does not result in the enhancement of the known efficacy of that substance or the mere discovery of any new property or new use for a known substance or of the mere use of a known process, machine or apparatus unless such known process results in a new product or employs at least one new reactant.
Explanation – For the purposes of this clause, salts, esters, ethers, polymorphs, metabolites, pure form, particle size, isomers, mixtures of isomers, complexes, combinations and other derivatives of known substance shall be considered to be the same substance, unless they differ significantly in properties with regard to efficacy;
  (e) a substance obtained by a mere admixture resulting only in the aggregation of the properties of the components thereof or a process for producing such substance;
  (f) the mere arrangement or re-arrangement or duplication of known devices each functioning independently of one another in a known way;
  (g) *** [earlier provision which held method of testing to be unpatentable was repealed]

(h) a method of agriculture or horticulture;
(i) any process for the medicinal, surgical, curative, prophylactic [diagnostic, therapeutic] or other treatment of human beings or any process for a similar treatment of animals to render them free of disease or to increase their economic value or that of their products;
(j) plants and animals in whole or any part thereof other than micro-organisms but including seeds, varieties and species and essentially biological processes for production or propagation of plants and animals;
(k) a mathematical or business method or a computer programme *per se* or algorithms;
(l) a literary, dramatic, musical, or artistic work or any other aesthetic creation whatsoever including cinematographic works and television productions;
(m) a mere scheme or rule or method of performing mental act or method of playing game;
(n) a presentation of information;
(o) topography of integrated circuits;
(p) an invention which in effect, is traditional knowledge or which is an aggregation or duplication of known properties of traditionally known component or components.

(3) Provisions for both pre and post grant oppositions were introduced. In addition, the amended Patents Act did not provide for any appeal against the decision of the Controller of Patents in a pre-grant opposition. Therefore, *prima facie*, if an application was refused in a pre-grant opposition, the refusal would be final resulting in complete loss of rights.

While the above amendments were primarily effected to render the Indian legislation TRIPS compliant and at the same time safeguard domestic interests, some of them had serious consequences on inventions relating to pharmaceutical products.

A pre-grant opposition could be filed by any person (including a person who is not an interested person, similar to "straw man" in EPO) anytime before the grant of a patent. This resulted in several Indian companies resorting to serial oppositions ensuring that a patent is never granted. However, the Hon'ble High Court of Delhi in the *UCB Farchem* case as well as *Gilead Sciences v Cipla Ltd.* put an end to serial oppositions holding that once an opposition is determined in favour of an applicant, no further oppositions could be filed. In addition, the Court held that although no appeal was provided for against the decision of the Controller of Patents in a pre-grant opposition, an applicant had a right of appeal. This was because a pre-grant opposition is only an extension of examination proceedings and an applicant had a right of appeal against any adverse order passed during examination proceedings.

While the above changes were quite important and affected the Indian patent system drastically, Section 3(d) mentioned above turned out to be a thorn in the side of the innovators, particularly in the pharmaceutical sector. Between 2009 and 2016 more patent applications were rejected during examination and opposition proceedings under Section 3(d) alone than in the previous thirty years on all grounds put together.

In 2012, the Hon'ble Supreme Court of India in *Novartis AG v Union of India & others*, passed a landmark judgement in which Section 3(d) was interpreted extensively. Section 3(d) as worded, precludes from patentability a mere new form of a known substance unless such new form exhibits a significant increase in efficacy. The explanation to Section 3(d) lays down that salts, esters, ethers, polymorphs, metabolites, pure form, particle size, isomers, mixtures of isomers, complexes, combinations and other derivatives of known substance shall be considered to be the same substance, unless they differ significantly in properties with regard to efficacy. In the *Novartis* case, the patent application in question claimed *beta* crystalline form of imatinib mesylate, an anti-cancer drug which showed excellent results in treatment of blood cancer particularly in children. The excellent result of this form of the mesylate salt was attributed to the fact that it was 30 times more orally bioavailable than the known compound. However, the Supreme Court in a detailed judgment held that a mere increase in bioavailability, although extremely useful, was only a property and not a significant increase in efficacy. In this context, the court clarified that the expression "efficacy" with respect to pharmaceutical substances could only mean "therapeutic efficacy", i.e., an efficacy at a molecular and cellular level. As a result of this judgment, several more cases relating to salts and derivatives of known compounds have been rejected by the Indian Patent Office despite the fact that most of the corresponding foreign applications proceeded to grant.

Even prior to the Supreme Court's judgment, the Indian Patent Office rejected Gilead's patent application for an anti HIV drug, bis poc PMPA which was a carbamate form of the known drug propyl methoxy adenosine phosphate. The subject molecule was several times more efficacious than PMPA in terms of kill rate of the virus. Bis poc PMPA, acting as a pro-drug cleaved through the gut wall to penetrate the infected cells and once it reached the blood, converted itself into PMPA which then killed the infection. Bis poc PMPA acted as a pro-drug and a delivery mechanism and while the Patent Office acknowledged that the invention was non-obvious, rejected the application under Section 3(d). This was despite the fact that corresponding applications had proceeded to grant in more than 50 countries and several Indian companies obtained voluntary licences from Gilead to manufacture and market the drug. The matter is currently under appeal.

However, in another recent judgment, the Patent Office granted a patent for Gilead's hepatitis C drug sobusvir, rejecting the pleas of several opponents on the ground that Section 3(d) did not apply to this case.

1.2 Biologics

Biologics and biosimilars have been making news in India ever since various Indian companies such as Zydus Cadila, Torrent Pharmaceuticals Limited and Hetero Drugs Limited launched several biosimilars in India. In fact, Zydus Cadila (Cadila Healthcare Limited) became the first company in the world to launch a biosimilar of adalimumab for treatment of arthritis in India. The law on patentability of biologics in India is a little unclear. As a molecule, a biosimilar is a much bigger molecule than a generic version and should be patentable *per se* although, it might be difficult to obtain regulatory approval. Processes for preparing biosimilars are certainly patentable in India. At this point in time, India does not have any judicial precedents with respect to biologics or biosimilars.

2. *International treaties*

2.1 *TRIPS*

India became a signatory to the TRIPS Agreement with effect from 1 January 1995 and has effected several reforms to Indian patent legislation. India also joined the Paris Convention and Patent Cooperation Treaty with effect from 7 December 1998. India is also a signatory to Budapest Treaty for deposit of micro organisms and recognises accession numbers to deposits made under the Budapest Treaty.

2.2 *FTAs*

India has Free Trade Agreements with Sri Lanka (28 December 1998) and Thailand (9 October 2003) to abolish tariffs, quotas and preferences on many goods, if not all.

India also has Trade Agreements (TAs) with Bangladesh, Bhutan, the Maldives, China, Japan, South Korea and Mongolia which involve mutually beneficial concessions.

3. *Availability through case law*

Indian jurisprudence does not have too many judicial precedents in patent law. Most of the statutory prohibitions are through legislative enactments i.e., Patents Act, 1970 and what is statutorily prohibited from patentability cannot be made patentable by judicial precedents. However, Indian courts are active in interpreting statutes and are known for laying down law in a clear and concise manner.

4. *Patent term extensions/SPCs*

None available in India.

II Policy considerations

1. *Health and social issues*

The Patents Act, 1970 has several inbuilt safeguards bearing in mind health and social issues. The Indian patent system stipulates that patents are not granted merely to provide monopoly and block technological progress but to advance development. Therefore, the law provides that if a patent is not worked within three years from the date of grant to meet the reasonable requirements of the public at a reasonable price, a third party may apply for a grant of compulsory licence. "Reasonable requirements of the public" is defined as "meeting the demands of the public at a reasonable price". "Reasonable price" does not necessarily mean the lowest price since a patented drug is expected to be more expensive, but means reasonable in the context. In *Natco Limited v Bayer AG*, the Indian Patent Office granted a compulsory licence to Natco for an anti-cancer drug "Nexvar". Natco successfully established that it could manufacture and sell the drug at a price of about USD 170 per patient per month as compared to Bayer's price of over USD 5,000. Bayer could not satisfactorily establish why its price of USD 5,000 was reasonable. In addition, it was a matter of record that Bayer catered to only about 2% of the demand, that too most by import.

The Indian courts have also been little hesitant in granting interim injunctions against defendants in patent infringement suits bearing in mind health considerations but in the last couple of years Novartis AG has successfully obtained orders of interim injunctions against several Indian companies from manufacturing its patented drug vildagliptin. Similarly, Merck has obtained preliminary injunctions restraining several Indian companies from infringing its patented drug sitagliptin.

2. *Legal issues*

The Indian government appears to be completely against any attempt at "evergreening" or extending monopoly or even timelines. Section 3(d) was enacted solely with a view to preventing evergreening and has been enforced rather strictly. File wrapper divisionals are held to be invalid and divisional applications for coverage of subject matter not held to be in disunity with the claims on the parent application are held to be void.

B. VALIDITY

I Allowable claim wording

1. *Product claims*

Claims for novel and non-obvious chemical entities whether new molecules, new derivatives exhibiting significant increase in efficacy or synergistic compositions made of two or more actives are permissible. Markush claims for a chemical compound are patentable provided the specification as originally filed discloses adequate examples for various claimed permutations and combinations in terms of their utility. Swiss-type claims or a compound or a composition defined only in terms of its medical use are strictly prohibited. Thus "use of aspirin as an anticoagulant" or "use of aspirin in preparation of a medicament to treat blood clotting" or " a method treatment... which comprises administering to a patient in need thereof an effective amount of aspirin" would all be rejected in India.

2. *Method claims*

Methods of manufacture are patentable. However, methods of treatment in any form are not patentable. However, where it is possible to convert the method of treatment claims into composition of matter claims based on original disclosure, patents have granted. In *re* 7503/DELNP/2007 (Patent No. 256057), the claims as originally filed defined a method for treatment which comprised administering to a patient an effective amount of Calcitonin (anti osteoporosis) followed by an effective amount of Glucocorticoid (anti inflammatory). Such a claim was rejected as being statutorily unpatentable under Section 3(i) of the Patents Act, 1970. However, when the claims were amended to define a synergistic composition comprising of effective amounts of Glucocorticoid and Calcitonin, a patent was granted. Similarly, in *re* Indian Patent Application No. 2293/KOLNP/2008 (Patent No. 262384) the Patent Office allowed a claim for a synergistic composition comprising a specific histone deacetylase inhibitor and a specific chemotherapeutic agent, despite the fact that the two drugs were not mixed together outside the human body and the original claims were directed towards a method of treatment of advanced cancer comprising administering two drugs into the human body one after the other. The application was allowed on the ground that there was adequate support in the description for excellent synergistic effect of the two drugs which was far superior to the efficacy of either of the individual drugs or other combination therapies.

However, in *re*: 3183/DELNP/2008 even when the original method of treatment comprising administering Milnacipran (anti fibromyalgia) and Pregabalin (anti epileptic drug) one after another was amended to a synergistic composition of Milnacipran and Pregabalin the application was rejected on the ground that there was no support for a synergistic composition in the original description. However, where a new use of a known substance envisages use of two or more substances together, it will be worthwhile to have adequate support in the description for composition claims. Similarly, where there is a method of treatment involved, it would be worthwhile to have adequate support in the description for *in vitro* assays which could then provide some kind of protection, if not complete protection.

3. *Use claims*

Use claims are not patentable in India. However, where possible, use claims may be dealt with in a manner similar to method of treatment claims described above in order to obtain some kind of patent protection.

4. *System claims*

System and device claims are patentable in India only if the novelty and the inventive step thereof reside in features of actual construction and not in the drug contained therein. Thus, an apparatus for treatment would be patentable if the novelty resided in the construction of the apparatus and not in the treatment method or protocol. A known apparatus put to a new use would be unpatentable under Section 3(d). For example, a pregnancy detection kit or blood sugar monitoring kit comprising of known devices with known medicine loaded thereon would be unpatentable.

5. *Dosage regimes*

New dosage forms, for example dual release or delayed released dosage forms, are, subject to novelty and inventive step, patentable in India. However, dosage regimes specifically relating to treatment protocol are statutorily unpatentable under Section 3(i).

6. *Patient groups*

Invention relating to new patient groups would be considered to be either second medical use or method of treatment both of which are statutorily unpatentable under Section 3(i).

II. Novelty

1. *General definition of novelty and prior art*

Section 13 of the Indian Patents Act stipulates that the subject matter of a patent application should not have been published in any patent specification in India on or after 1 January 1912 or in any document anywhere in the world. It also stipulates that it should not have been claimed in any claim of an Indian patent specification having an earlier priority date. Novelty is always assessed with respect to a single prior published document. Normally, the services of a notional person skilled in the art are not utilized in assessing novelty. A mosaic of several documents to challenge novelty is not permissible. However, novelty is deemed to have been destroyed if the subject matter of the invention was publicly used in India before the priority date of the relevant patent application.

2. *Definition of skilled person*

Until very recently the Indian courts had followed the British definition of "a person skilled in the art" and held that a person skilled in the art is a person who is capable of assimilating and understanding an enormous amount of literature relating to his field but does not have a scintilla of inventive ability. However, the Intellectual Property Appellate Board (IPAB) has in several recent decisions held that the person skilled in the art is not an automaton or an unimaginative dullard but is quite a skilled person who is not only capable of understanding technical literature but also equipped with good imagination. Thus, recent judgments in India have raised the bar for inventive step.

3. *Scope of disclosures*

3.1 General rules

Section 10(4) of the Patents Act stipulates that every complete specification shall (i) fully and particularly describe the invention and its operation or use and the method by which it is to be performed; and (ii) disclose the best method of performing the invention which is known to the applicant and for which he is entitled to claim protection. In addition, Section 25(1)(g) relating to pre-grant opposition and Section 25(2)(g) relating to post-opposition stipulate that an application or a patent may be opposed on the ground that "the complete specification does not sufficiently and clearly describe the invention or the method by which it is to be performed". Under Section 64(1)(h) a patent may be revoked on the ground that:

> "the complete specification does not sufficiently and fairly describe the invention and the method by which it is to be performed, that is to say, that the description of the method or the instructions for the working of the invention as contained in the complete specification are not by themselves sufficient to enable a person in India possessing average skill in, and average knowledge of, the art to which the invention relates, to work the invention, or that it does not disclose the best method of performing it which was known to the applicant for the patent and for which he was entitled to claim protection".

3.2 *First medical use*

3.3 *New subject matter*

3.4 *New data*

New medical uses, whether first or second, are simply not patentable in India. However, if there is sufficient data for therapeutic uses in the specification as originally filed it could form a basis for converting the claims, where possible, into composition claims.

4. *Requirements for second medical use*

Since second medical use is statutorily unpatentable in India, there are no requirements stipulated under the law for second medical use. In fact, even if all generally accepted requirements for second medical use have been complied with, the subject matter would still be unpatentable in India.

5. *Timing issues*

Timing issues are relevant only with respect to establishing efficacy of a claimed substance. Post filing data have been generally permitted in India as extrinsic evidence particularly if submitted in the form of a declaration or affidavit. Such data become particularly relevant to overcome Section 3(d) rejection when what is claimed is a new form of a known substance.

III. Inventive step/non-obviousness

For the assessment of inventive step, India follows problem-solution approach as well as the teaching-suggestion-motivation approach. However, in *Sankalp Rehabilitation Trust v F. Hoffmann La Roche*, (Order No. 250/2012 in OA/8/2009/PT/CH) followed in *Enercon v Alloys Wobben*, (Order No. 123 of 2013 in ORA/08/2009/PT/CH) and *Fresenius Kabi Oncology v Glaxo Group & Anr.*, (Order No. 161 of 2013 in ORA/22/2011/PT/KOL), the IPAB has attributed much higher skills to a person skilled in the art and has laid down that a skilled person is not an automaton or unimaginative dullard but an educated person with good levels of understanding as well as imagination.

IV. Amendment of claims after grant

1. *Admissibility of post-grant amendments in general*

Amendments are permissible throughout the life of the patent application and granted patent. However, no amendment may be made which introduces new matter or widens the scope of any claim as originally filed. Under Section 59, no amendment may be made except for the purposes of incorporation of actual fact and that too only by way of disclaimer, correction or explanation.

2. *Procedural issues*

Amendments may be made during prosecution, opposition proceedings and invalidation proceedings. However, the Patent Office will not pass any orders allowing or refusing amendments if there are any proceedings pending before the High Court or Intellectual Property Appellate Board in respect of said patent application or patent.

3. *Added matter*

India has strict rules for allowing added matter. Explanation of an existing matter may be added. However, new examples or entirely new matter is not permissible.

4. *Sufficiency*

The specification is required to be sufficient enough for a person of average skill and average knowledge to perform the invention. Claims must be sufficiently supported by description and examples and the description must disclose the best method of performing the invention known to the applicant. Failure to comply with these requirements constitutes valid grounds for pre-grant and post-grant oppositions as well as revocation proceedings.

5. *Multiple indications*

Adequate description with multiple indications would support a claim for non-obviousness as well as increased therapeutic efficacy. However, any claim for method of treatment of any indication will not be patentable.

V. Change of patent category

1. *General admissibility*

Subject to adequate support and description in the specification as originally filed, a change of patent category is permissible. It is also possible to file a voluntary amendment to include claims supported by the original description and if any objection on the ground of disunity is raised, cover them by a separate divisional application.

2. *Use claim as a category*

3. *From product to method claim*

4. *From method to product claim*

5. *System claims*

6. *Use claims*

As previously mentioned, use claims, method of treatment claims and system claims without any novel features in the construction are not patentable in India. Subject to this and subject to adequate support in the original description, a change of patent category is generally permissible.

C. INFRINGEMENT AND LITIGATION

I. Legal framework

1. *National statutory laws*

Infringement actions and litigation are normally governed by the Patents Act, 1970, the Code of Civil Procedure, 1908 and Indian Evidence Act, 1872.

2. *Case law*

India follows the principle of *stare decicis*. Judicial precedents have binding force and courts have often interpreted legislative enactments either liberally or restrictively. A judicial pronouncement by the Supreme Court of India is regarded as the law of the land unless overturned by the Supreme Court itself or a Parliamentary enactment.

II. Claim construction

1. *General rules*

India does not have too many precedents on claim construction and often follows British precedents. However, Indian courts generally follow literal interpretation and where literal interpretation does not lead to a sensible meaning, it follows purposive construction and also relies upon the description.

2. *Specific issues for use claims*

Not applicable to India.

III. Scope of protection

1. *Scope of the use*

Not applicable to India. However, under Section 48 when a patent is granted, for any product or process, the patent confers upon the patentee exclusive right to prevent any unauthorized third party from the act of making, using, offering for sale, selling or importing for that purpose that product (or as the case may be, the product obtained directly by that process) in India.

2. *Absolute product protection*

When a patent is for a product, the protection is absolute and is not limited through the claimed use or off-label use.

3. *Dosage regimes*

Not applicable in India.

4. *Patient groups*

Not applicable in India.

5. *Extension under the doctrine of equivalents*

The Indian courts do not employ the term "doctrine of equivalents" but would normally injunct any third party from performing any act using equivalents if it can be established by the patentee that such equivalents are well accepted as equivalents in the technical field to which the invention relates.

IV. Infringing acts

1. *Infringing person or entity*

Under Section 48, any person or entity who manufactures, sells, uses or offers for sale in India or imports into India a patented product or a product directly prepared by a patented process will be guilty of infringement. Export will be infringement if the manufacture takes place in India. If several persons are involved in an assembly line, every person will be guilty of contributory infringement.

2. *Direct infringement*

Where a patent is granted for either a product *per se* or a process of manufacture, Section 48 as described above will apply. However, since use and treatment claims are not patentable in India second medical use and methods of treatment will not constitute acts of infringement.

3. *Indirect infringement*

Please see 2 above.

4. *Off-label use*

Please see 2 above.

5. *Dosage regimes*

Not applicable in India.

6. *Patient groups*

Not applicable in India.

V. Remedies

1. *Injunctions*

Injunctions are governed by the Code of Civil Procedure. Both interim and permanent injunctions are available. In extreme cases, even an *ex parte* order of injunction is possible. Where there is apprehension of imminent infringement, a *qua tiamet* order may be obtained.

In order to obtain an interim injunction the plaintiff must establish (i) *prima facie* case of validity of the patent (ii) *prima facie* case of infringement (iii) absence of delay and (iv) possibility of irreparable harm if the injunction is not granted. India also follows doctrine of "clean hands" or equitable conduct. Thus, any misrepresentation of material facts could be fatal to an interim injunction.

2. *Damages*

3. *Information*

The patentee may, at its discretion, claim either an account of profits or damages. As of now, there are no infringement actions which have gone to full trial where heavy damages have been imposed.

Basically, in order to succeed at an interim stage, it will be necessary to provide details of infringers as well as infringing activities without which an injunction cannot be secured. While an interim injunction may be obtained and the court may appoint a commissioner to make an inventory of infringing products, recall and destruction of infringing products will take place only after trial on merits. It will be difficult to recover legal costs except perhaps nominal and reasonable attorney costs.

VI. Exceptions from patent protection

1. *Exhaustion of rights*

India does not have any specific provisions dealing with domestic or international exhaustion of rights.

2. *Patient welfare*

Patient welfare is not an exception to a patent protection. However, in the interest of society, a compulsory licence may be granted if reasonable requirements of the public with respect to the patented invention are not met. In addition, the government may use the invention for its own use. In exceptional cases, the Courts may decline to grant interim injunctions, particularly where the patentee itself is not adequately working the invention in India.

3. *Others specific to second medical use claims*

Not applicable to India.

VII. Procedural issues

1. *Preliminary injunction cases*

1.1 *Availability for second medical use claims*

Not applicable to India.

1.2 *Specific requirements*

Please see above.

2. *Cases on the merits*

Please see above.

3. *Enforcement of judgments*

Judgments pronounced by Indian courts are, subject to any appeals, enforceable with immediate effect.

VIII. Validity

1. *Relevance for infringement cases*

Under Section 64 of the Patents Act, any defendant in a suit for infringement may file a counterclaim for revocation of the patent. In addition, under Section 107, every ground for revocation shall be available as a ground for defence. Under Section 114, if any claim is found to be invalid the patentee may still obtain relief on the basis of valid claims.

2. *Specifics for second medical use claims*

Not applicable in India.

IX. Tactical considerations

1. *Plaintiff*

A suit for infringement may not be filed in any court inferior to the District Court. However, subject to territorial and pecuniary jurisdictions, a suit may be directly filed in a High Court which has ordinary original jurisdiction. At present, only a few High Courts have original jurisdiction.

India does not encourage forum shopping. Therefore, jurisdiction will be determined by the place where the defendant resides or where the cause of action arises. A cause of action is deemed to arise in a place where infringing products are available.

In important matters, it might be worthwhile for the patentee to institute suits for infringement without delay, well armed with *prima facie* case of validity of the patent and *prima facie* case of infringement. Sending an advance cease and desist notice may not be always advisable since it could precipitate a petition for revocation of the patent.

2. *Defendant*

It would be advisable for a defendant to take action to prevent interim injunctions against it. It could therefore, file petitions for revocations in advance if it believes that the patent is not valid. Alternatively, if it believes that its actions are non-infringing it could file a suit for declaration of non-infringement.

Brazil

Maria Carmen de Souza Brito

A. AVAILABILITY OF PROTECTION

I. Legal framework

Second or further medical uses of known substance claims are accepted by the Brazilian Patent and Trademark Office ("BPTO") and the courts, and even by ANVISA in some specific cases. ANVISA is the Brazilian Regulatory Agency in charge of the analysis and granting of market approvals for drugs in Brazil, corresponding to the U.S. Food and Drug Administration ("FDA") and the European Medicines Agency ("EMA").

It is important to note that, in Brazil, pharmaceutical patents need the prior consent from ANVISA before their granting by the BPTO, according to Brazilian Industrial Property Law No. 9,279/96 ("IP Law") of May 14, 1996 as amended by the inclusion of Article 229-C of Law No. 10.196/01:

> "Article 229-C: The granting of patents for pharmaceutical processes and products will depend on the prior consent of the National Health Surveillance Agency - ANVISA."

So, in short, a patent application claiming a second medical use which presents novelty, inventive step and industrial application might be allowed in Brazil.

1. National statutory laws

It should be initially noted that the IP Law was a major breakthrough in the pharmaceutical field since it enabled the protection of pharmaceutical products, either non-biological or biological. Previously, only pharmaceutical processes were allowable.

The IP Law does not contain any provision against second medical use inventions. However, the BPTO's Guidelines for examination of patent applications, based on Resolution 124 of December 4, 2013, foresees that the claims in the pharmaceutical field, which involve the use of chemical pharmaceuticals for the treatment of a new disease, should use the format conventionally called "Swiss-type", and it should be understood as an equivalent to a process of manufacture.

Said type of use claim provides protection for use in the manufacture of a product. It does not cover a therapeutic method which is not considered an invention according to item VIII of Article 10 of IP Law:

> "Article 10 – The following are not considered to be inventions or utility models:
> (...)
> VIII – operating or surgical techniques and therapeutic or diagnostic methods, for use on the human or animal body;"

Furthermore, the Brazilian PTO's Guidelines for examination of patent applications in biotechnology field, according to Resolution 144 of March 12, 2015, item 4.2.1.3, states that a non-natural biological process and the use of a natural product can be protected provided that the patentability requirements are met, as follows:

> "*4.2.1.3 Use of natural products*
>
> When the process claimed involves the whole or part of natural living beings and biological materials found in nature, including the genome or germoplasm, but does not consist of a natural biological process, there is no obstacle for the patentability thereof in light of that prescribed in Article 10 (IX) of the IP Law. Accordingly, the use of a natural product can be eligible for protection, provided that is in accordance with patentability requirements."

It should still be emphasized that ANVISA carries out an examination on the merits for pharmaceutical patent applications related to drugs or therapies considered as strategic to the Brazilian Health System, based on the provisions of ANVISA Resolution 21 of April 15, 2013, Article 4:

> "Article 4. After receiving the patent applications forwarded by BPTO, ANVISA will analyze such patent applications based on public health issues, through a decision consolidated in written opinion issued by the competent organizational unit within the Agency. [modified by Resolution No. 21/2013]
>
> §1 – It is considered that a patent application is contrary to public health when: [modified by Resolution No. 21/2013]
>
> I – The pharmaceutical product or process disclosed in the patent application has a health risk, or [modified by Resolution No. 21/2013]
>
> II – The patent application relating to a pharmaceutical product or process is of interest to the policies of medicines or pharmaceutical care in the Brazilian Universal Healthcare System ["SUS"], and does not comply with the patentability requirements and other criteria established by Brazilian Law No. 9.279/96. [modified by Resolution No. 21/2013]
>
> §2 – The health risk will be characterized when the pharmaceutical product contains, or the pharmaceutical process results in, a substance which use has been prohibited in the country. [included by Resolution No. 21/2013]

> §3 The patent application relating to a pharmaceutical product or process is considered of interest to the policies of medicines or pharmaceutical care in SUS when it comprises, or results in, a substance listed in the Ordinances of the Brazilian Ministry of Health that defines the strategic products within SUS, and in its updates, as well as it comprises, or results in, a substance belonging to the therapeutic destination listed in said Ordinances. [included by Resolution No. 21/2013]."

Summarily, (a) pharmaceutical patent applications related to a subject matter that represent a risk to the human health will be denied; (b) pharmaceutical patent applications related to a substance or a therapeutic destination considered strategic for the SUS will be submitted to a substantive examination regarding the patentability requirements; and (c) pharmaceutical patent applications not related to a prohibited substance, and to a substance or a strategic therapeutic destination for SUS will not be submitted to a substantive examination regarding the patentability requirements.

1.1 Pharmaceuticals

In the pharmaceutical area, claims that involve the use of chemical pharmaceutical products for the treatment of a new disease have a format that is conventionally called "Swiss-type", namely:

> "Use of a compound of formula X, characterized by being for the preparation of a medicament to treat disease Y."

It should be pointed out that this type of claim confers protection for use for the manufacture of a product, but does not confer protection for the therapeutic method, which is not considered an invention under Article 10 (VIII) of the IPL. Claims of the type "use for treatment", "process/method for treatment", "administration for treatment" or equivalents thereof correspond to therapeutic method claims and, therefore, are not considered an invention under Article 10 (VIII) of the IP Law.

1.2 Biologics

Article 10 (IX) of the IP Law states that:

> "Article 10 – The following shall not be considered as inventions or utility models:
>
> (...) IX – natural living beings and biological materials, in whole or in part, found in nature or isolated therefrom, including the genome or germplasm of any natural living being, and natural biological processes."

On the other hand, Article 18 defines that:

> "Article 18 – The following are not patentable:
>
> (...) III – living beings, in whole or in part, except for transgenic microorganisms that meet the three patentability requirements – novelty, inventive activity and industrial application – foreseen in article 8, and which are not mere discoveries;

> Sole Paragraph – For the purpose of this law, transgenic microorganisms are organisms, except for the whole or part of plants or animals, provided with features – due to direct human intervention in their genetic composition – that normally cannot be attained by the species under natural conditions."

Thus, biological material found in nature is not patentable, even if isolated.

On the other hand, any invention created by direct human intervention, i.e., that cannot normally be attained by the species under natural conditions, is acceptable for patentability, such as monoclonal antibodies, humanized antibodies, vectors of expression, recombinant proteins, or transgenic microorganisms or viruses.

Process claims are also acceptable for biological inventions since the claimed process does not occur naturally.

2. *International treaties*

2.1 *TRIPS*

Brazil has signed and implemented the TRIPS Agreement (Trade-Related Aspects of Intellectual Property Rights Agreement).

Article 27 of TRIPS states that patents must be granted for any inventions, whether products or processes, in all fields of technology, provided that they are new, involve an inventive step and are capable of industrial application. In addition, it states that patents must be granted and patent rights enjoyed without discrimination as to the field of technology.

In the same way that TRIPS provides flexibility to the Member States regarding the patentability of second medical uses, i.e., with no specific favorable or unfavorable provision, the Brazilian IP Law also does not foresee the allowance or denial of such an invention. Both TRIPS and the Brazilian IP Law do not have any provision excluding (or allowing exclusion of) second medical uses from patentability.

2.2 *FTAs*

There is no FTA in force in Brazil related to intellectual property rights.

3. *Availability through case law*

So far, the second instance Brazilian Courts (Courts of Appeal) have judged only one patent case related to second medical use.

Eli Lilly filed a lawsuit before the Federal Court of Rio de Janeiro challenging the Patent Office's decision which rejected Brazilian patent application No. PI9606903-1, claiming the second use of atomoxetine for the manufacture of a medicament for treating attention-deficit/hyperactivity disorder.

The Federal Court of Appeals confirmed that second medical use is a patentable subject matter in Brazil, since there is no statutory prohibition in this regard. However, the Court maintained the rejection of said Brazilian application, alleging that the claimed use of atomoxetine for treating attention-deficit/hyperactivity disorder would not meet the patentability requirements (novelty and inventive step).

4. *Patent term extension/SPCs*

No patent term extension or SPCs are applicable.

However, it is important to note that Article 40 of IP Law states that:

> "Article 40 – A patent of invention will have a term of 20 (twenty) years and a utility model patent a term of 15 (fifteen) years, counted from the filing date.
>
> Sole Paragraph – The term will not be less than 10 (ten) years for patents of invention and 7 (seven) years for utility model patents, counted from grant, except when INPI is prevented from proceeding with the examination as to the merit of the application, due to a proven pendente lite or for reasons of "force majeure"."

In other words, the expiry term of a patent of invention is 20 years counted from the filing date or 10 years counted from granting date, whichever is later.

The provisions of this Article enable the patentee to have the granted patent in force during a period of at least 10 years. This is very important to the patentee, since there is a huge backlog in the examination of patent applications in Brazil, so that the patentee would not be jeopardized by having a granted patent alive for a undesirably shorter period in view of the delay in the issuance of technical opinions from the BPTO and/or ANVISA.

II. Policy considerations

1. *Health and social issues*

The patentability of second medical uses is a matter of debate and therefore exemplifies the continuing challenge in patent law of balancing access against innovation. A second medical use can itself be inventive, and the development and clinical testing of a second use is no less in need of incentives than the first use, and in some cases may be more therapeutically valuable than the first use.

The granting of patent protection for second medical uses potentially provides an important incentive for the identification and development of solutions for unmet medical needs. Patent protection may permit pharmaceutical companies to generate the revenues required to fund further innovation.

Brazil, as a developing country, does not have the ideal conditions for the development of new drugs, since the development of a new drug is a very long, costly and complex process. Thus, Brazil benefits greatly from permitting second medical use claims, since the development of a new therapeutic use is a simpler process (once the safety profile of drugs known for human use has already been established), and more local companies would be encouraged to invest in research and development.

2. *Legal issues*

The IP Law does not contain any provision against the patentability of second medical use claims and the PTO's Guidelines for examination provides the wording of an acceptable medical use claim in Swiss-type format.

On the other hand, ANVISA has been adopting a contrary position in relation to the PTO, since this Agency understands that a second medical use lacks novelty.

Even though no data are available with respect to the effects on the pharmaceutical industry of allowing second medical use claims, we can state that the extent of such allowance has been limited since there is no case law for patent infringement of second medical use in Brazil so far.

B. VALIDITY

I. Allowable claim wording

Acceptable wording for claims based on the current Guidelines and PTO's and ANVISA's current practice can be found below.

1. Product claims

Examples of acceptable product claims are as follows:

As to non-biological product:

- Compound characterized by having general formula (X) (Markush formula) wherein radical X is..., Y is..., Z is...and so on.
- Compound characterized by being X.
- Composition characterized by comprising compound X and a pharmaceutically acceptable carrier.
- Combination characterized by comprising compounds X and Y and a pharmaceutically acceptable carrier.
- Kit characterized by comprising a first composition containing compound X and a second composition containing compound Y.

As to biological product:

- DNA or RNA sequence characterized by having SEQ ID No. X.
- Recombinant protein characterized by having SEQ ID No. X.
- Transgenic microorganism characterized by having expression vector X consisting in SEQ ID No. X.
- Monoclonal antibody binding to protein X characterized by being produced by hybridoma Y, filed with number Z.
- Humanized antibody against a-actin characterized by comprising the murine variable region which consists of SEQ ID No. X and human γ chain regions.
- Humanized antibody against α-actin characterized by comprising the murine complementarity determining regions (CDR1; CDR2; CDR3) which consist of SEQ ID No. X, SEQ ID No. Y and SEQ ID No. Z in the light chain and SEQ ID No. A, SEQ ID No. B and SEQ ID No. C in the heavy chain and human γ chain regions.

2. *Method claims*

Therapeutic, diagnostic and surgical methods including steps involving the human/animal body are not considered an invention so that claims covering such subject matter are not patentable. On the other hand, non-therapeutic method (involving healthy organisms) and diagnostic methods *in vitro* are patentable.

Examples of acceptable method claims are as follows:

As to non-biological method:

- Method for preparing/manufacturing a compound of general formula X (Markush formula) characterized by comprising steps Y, Z, etc.
- Method for preparing/manufacturing compound X characterized by comprising steps Y, Z, etc.

As to biological method:

- Method for inserting gene X in a plant/microorganism characterized by comprising steps of X, Y, Z.
- Method for inducing the ovulation in bovines characterized by the administration of an effective amount of hormone X.
- Method for increasing the wool production characterized by administering compound X in sheep.
- Diagnostic method characterized by comprising the step of detecting protein X in a sample by using antibody Y in an ELISA analysis.

It is relevant to highlight that both BPTO and ANVISA have been adopting a very restrict position regarding Markush formulae and they usually require the proper definition of the substituents in the claims based on the chemical classes as supported by the application as initially filed, for example, in the illustrative examples. More specifically, they require the limitation of the claimed compounds based on the compounds or classes of compounds clearly exemplified in the application. As a general rule, the patent practitioners are totally against this restrictive interpretation due to the fact that the purpose of an example is to solely illustrate how the invention works and can be reproduced, and not to limit the claims.

3. *Use claims*

The acceptable format for a second medical use claim is the classic Swiss-type use format, as follows:

> "Use of substance X, characterized by being for manufacturing/preparing a medicament for the treatment of disease/condition Y."

Claims having the following format:

> "Composition characterized by comprising the compound X for use in the treatment of disease/condition Y."

may be granted, as long as the compositions to which they relate are novel and present an inventive step.

It should be pointed out that this type of claim confers protection for the use of manufacture, but does not confer protection for the therapeutic method, which is not considered an invention under Article 10 (VIII) of the IP Law. Claims of the type "use for treatment", "process/method for treatment", "administration for treatment" or equivalents correspond to therapeutic method claims and, therefore, are not considered an invention under Article 10 (VIII) of the IP Law.

Furthermore, whenever the claim comprises the description of the treatment, for example, "Use of substance X, characterized in that it is for manufacturing/ preparing a medicament for the treatment of disease/condition Y, this treatment comprising the steps of...", the deletion of the text that describes the treatment is generally requested, not because it would be protecting the therapeutic method, but rather because it would be inconsistent with the object to be protected.

4. *System claims*

Examples of acceptable wording for system claims are as follows:

- Controlled release system characterized by comprising polymer X and compound Y to promote a sustained release by at least 12 hours.
- System for detection of compound X characterized by using antibody Y.
- Diagnostic system for condition X characterized by comprising device Y, device W and device Z, wherein device Y...

5. *Dosage regimes*

Although there are no specific considerations in the Brazilian Guidelines for this type of second use invention, claims relating to dosage regimes involving the administration of a drug in a patient are generally objected to by the BPTO and ANVISA on the grounds that these claims are in fact related to a therapeutic method.

However, it would be very important in order to encourage research into medical uses of a known substance for a known indication but with different dosage regimes that the Brazilian PTO grants patents for such an invention.

6. *Patient groups*

There are no specific considerations in the Brazilian Guidelines for this type of second use claim.

However, it would be very important in order to encourage research into medical uses of a known substance for a known indication but with different patient populations that the Brazilian PTO grants patents for such an invention.

II. Novelty

1. *General definition of novelty and prior art*

According to the IP Law, an invention is novel if not included in the state of the art:

> "Article 11: – Inventions and utility models are considered to be new when not included in the state of the art.
>
> § 1 – The state of the art comprises everything made accessible to the public before the date of filing of a patent application, by written or oral description, by use or any other means, in Brazil or abroad, without prejudice to the provisions of Articles 12, 16 and 17.
>
> § 2 – For the purpose of determining novelty, the whole contents of an application filed in Brazil, but not yet published, will be considered as state of the art from the date of filing, or from the priority claimed, provided that it is published, even though subsequently."

For reference purposes, Articles 12, 16 and 17 refer to a 12-month grace period and priority rights.

2. *Definition of skilled person*

According to the Guidelines for examination of patent applications issued by the Brazilian PTO (Resolution 124/2013), the definition of a person skilled in the art is broad and is understood as a person with average skill in the art, as follows:

> "2.14. The person skilled in the art can be one with average skill in the art in question at the time of filing of the application, with technical-scientific level, and/or one with operating working knowledge of the object.
>
> It is considered that they had at their disposal the means and the ability to work and carry out routine experimentation usual the technical field in question.
>
> There may be cases where it is most appropriate to think in terms of a group of people, as in the case of a production team or research. This may apply particularly in certain advanced technologies such as computers and nanotechnology."

3. *Scope of disclosure*

3.1 *General rules*

Inventions of use include: (i) a new use as a medicament of a product already known with an use outside the medical field (first medical use) and (ii) a new medical use of a product already known as a medicament (second medical use).

3.2 *First medical use*

The disclosure of an invention of a first medical use should include the pathology and/or clinical condition which will have the benefit of a compound. Tests showing the results of the therapy should be described.

3.3 *New subject matter*

The pathology and/or clinical condition which will have the benefit of a compound should be described, as well as tests showing the results thereof.

3.4 *New data*

There is no specific rule for presenting new data for protecting a new medical use. Data and tests should be indicated allowing the new medical use to be distinguished in relation to the previous non-medical use by indicating the pathology and/or clinical condition and benefits obtained for the patient.

4. *Requirements for second medical use*

4.1 *Distinction from first medical use*

A second medical use is considered as new when it is substantially different from the use already known in the art. The second medical use should reveal an application of a pharmaceutical product already known for treating a pathology and/or clinical condition distinct from that for which the product had already employed in the first use.

Inventive step will be recognized when unexpected results in view of the prior art are achieved.

Generally, the mechanism of the action of the drug, the correlation between therapeutic activity/chemical structure and the etiology of the target diseases are considered for evaluating inventive step of the second medical use.

4.2 *Sub-species of first medical use*

There is no specific rule for sub-species of first medical use.

4.3 *Dosage regimes*

Claims relating to dosage regimes involving the administration of a drug in a patient are generally objected to by the Brazilian PTO and ANVISA on the grounds that such claims are in fact related to a therapeutic method.

However, it would be very important in order to encourage research into medical uses of a known substance for a known indication but with different dosage regimes that the Brazilian PTO grants patents for such an invention.

4.4 *Special patient groups*

Generally, claims relating to special patient groups are objected to by the Brazilian PTO and ANVISA on the grounds that these claims would lack inventive step.

However, it would be very important in order to encourage research into medical uses of a known substance for a known indication but with different patient populations that the Brazilian PTO grants patents for such an invention.

5. *Timing issues*

5.1 Relevant time of development of second use

There is no specific rule for the relevant time of development of a second medical use, but it is a general understanding that an inventive step may be recognized when there is a technical problem whose solution was necessary and desired for many years and the invention is the answer to this need.

5.2 Role of new data

There is no specific rule for new data involving a second medical use.

5.3 Use of old data

There is no specific rule for old data involving a second medical use.

III. Inventive step/non-obviousness

1. *Definition of inventive step/non-obviousness*

According to the Article 13 of the IP Law an invention is inventive if it is not derived in an evident or obvious manner from the prior art, as follows:

> "Article 13 – An invention shall be taken to involve inventive activity when, for a person skilled in the art, it does not derive in an evident or obvious manner from the state of the art."

2. *Same scope of disclosure as for novelty?*

The scope of disclosure is not exactly the same as for the novelty since Article 11 of the IP Law, § 2, states that:

> "Article 11 – Inventions and utility models are considered to be new when not included in the state of the art. (...)
>
> § 2 – For the purpose of determining novelty, the whole contents of an application filed in Brazil, but not yet published, will be considered as state of the art from the date of filing, or from the priority claimed, provided that it is published, even though subsequently."

3. *Assessment of inventive step/non-obviousness*

Inventive step will be recognized when unexpected results in view of the prior art are achieved.

Generally, in second medical use inventions, inventive step has been evaluated taking into account the mechanism of action of the drug, the correlation between therapeutic activity/chemical structure and the etiology of the target diseases.

IV. Amendment of claims after grant

1. *Admissibility of post-grant amendments in general*

There is no formal procedure for amending a granted patent.

However, formal amendments aiming at correcting formalities, for example, a typographical error, are accepted through an annotation in an additional sheet enclosed at the end of the Letters Patent.

In case a claim or part thereof is nullified through either an administrative or a judicial instance, such annotation may also be attached to the Letters Patent.

However, this is not a usual procedure.

2. *Procedural issues*

The only manner to request amendment after grant is by requesting the nullity of the patent. The nullity may affect just some of the claims.

During the administrative proceedings, it is possible that claims are individually restricted. In this case, the amended claims will be substituted in the patent by means of an annotation.

2.1 *Independent limitation proceedings*

Independent limitation proceedings can be discussed before the court as an act of good faith. However, it should be understood to be an attempt, and success is not guaranteed.

2.2 *Opposition proceedings*

A proceeding for administrative nullity can be filed by any interested third party within six months counted from the granting date of the patent. After this period, the granted patent can only be challenged through a lawsuit before the courts at any time during the term of the patent.

Amendments in the claims can be requested during the proceeding for administrative nullity with the intention of totally or partially nullifying a claim. In these cases, in principle, the amended claim would be substituted in the patent by means of an annotation.

2.3 *Nullity actions*

After the six-month term of the opposition proceedings has expired, any lawfully interested party can file a nullity action aiming at requesting amendments or nullifying some of the patent claims. If the patent is maintained with a restricted scope of protection by means of an annotation, the patent is declared partially null.

Based on decisions in the judicial sphere, in few cases, we have noticed a more flexible position by judges and court-appointed experts concerning modifications to the granted patents, based on the argumentation that the proposed annotation would be only to narrow the scope of protection as supported by the specification, which would not be harmful to third parties' interests.

3. *Added matter*

The request for amending the claims after the granting of the patent (either in administrative or judicial instance) should not go beyond the matter of the application as filed, and it should not extend the scope of protection. Particularly, it should be limited to possible restrictions based on the matter described in the dependent claims. Any addition of matter which extends to the granted set of claims probably will not be accepted.

In the judicial sphere, it is possible to discuss amendments by adding features described in the specification, proved it is exclusively for limiting the scope of protection.

4. *Sufficiency*

Even during administrative or oral proceedings, any lawfully interested parties may require the nullity of some/all claims on the grounds that the specification does not describe the subject matter clearly and sufficiently so as to enable a person skilled in the art to execute it. Amendments can be performed provided that they are sufficiently described in the specification/examples, only with intention of narrowing the scope of protection.

5. *Multiple indications*

More than one set of claims may be proposed, however, there is no formal proceeding for doing so.

Considering the position of judges and court-appointed experts concerning modifications to the granted patents, it is not usual to see constant changes concerning amendments after grant.

V. Change of patent category

1. *General admissibility*

Voluntary amendments can be filed in Brazil for changing a category only up the request for examination, according to the Resolution No. 93/2013 (which provides an interpretation of Article 32 of IP Law), provided that such amendments are based on the matter initially disclosed.

After the request for examination, voluntary amendments are acceptable only when consisting of (i) a restriction of the scope of protection, (ii) a correction of minor typing and/or translation mistakes, and/or (iii) formal amendments to adapt the application to Brazilian practice. Particularly, the inclusion of new categories of claims or broadening the claims for which the examination has been requested are not allowable. Although such provisions have been challenged before the BPTO and Courts, no favorable jurisprudence has been affirmed so far.

In this sense, once the request for examination is submitted, any voluntary amendment extending the scope of the claim beyond the set of claims for which the examination has been requested will be considered as broadening of the scope of protection, even if it is described in the application as initially filed.

Therefore, during the administrative instance, these are the options:

a. Filing voluntary amendments until the request for examination (until 36 months after the filing date): at this stage, it is possible to amend the application with a certain degree of freedom, provided that the amendments are supported by the subject matter initially disclosed in the application;
b. Filing amendments after the request for examination but before the end of the patent application examination: in this case, amendments should fulfill the provisions of the aforementioned Resolution No. 93/2013; and
c. Amendments resulting from technical examination: amendments can be filed as a response to an office action, in accordance with aforementioned Resolution No. 93/2013.

For example, if a request for examination is submitted for a set of claims containing a therapeutic method claim, the amendment of the claims to refer to a "Swiss-type" format is currently objected to based on said Resolution.

2. *Use claim as a category*

Use claim is an acceptable category of claim in Brazil. In the pharmaceutical field, second use claims are also acceptable in a classic Swiss-type use format, as follows: "Use of compound X, characterized by being for manufacturing/preparing a medicament for the treatment of disease/condition Y".

3. *From product to method claim*

The change of a claim category through a voluntary amendment is acceptable in Brazil until the request for examination. During this phase, if a product claim is replaced by a method claim, the BPTO will accept such amendments if the method is duly supported by the application as initially filed. In addition, such method should be related to the production of this product, with the assurance that other products are not generated.

4. *From method to product claim*

A voluntary amendment in the set of claims from method to product claim can be performed until the request for examination. It should be noted that a change of category from method to product *per se* should be duly supported by the application as initially filed. In other words, the application as filed should contain all the features necessary to disclose the product.

It should be borne in mind that, for this type of change, the novelty and inventive step of the product should be evidenced in the claims, since the technical effect of this type of the invention usually relies on the features of the method.

5. *System claims*

System claims are acceptable in Brazil and are classified in the "product claim" category, provided that they refer to a system of co-operative equipment.

6. *Use claims*

Use claim and second use claims are acceptable in Brazil. Second medical use claims are acceptable in a classic Swiss-type format, as follows: "Use of compound X, characterized by being for manufacturing/preparing a medicament for the treatment of disease/condition Y".

C. INFRINGEMENT AND LITIGATION

I. Legal framework

1. *National statutory laws*

The main Brazilian laws applicable to patent lawsuits are the Brazilian Industrial Property Law (Federal Law No. 9,279/1996) and the Brazilian Code for Civil Procedure (Federal Law No. 13,105/2015).

2. *Case law*

Brazil is a civil law country. So, each lawsuit is decided on a case-by-case basis. In other words, there is no sample court decision that will fit all patent infringement litigations.

II. Claim construction

1. *General rules*

The scope of protection conferred by a patent will be determined by the content of the claims, interpreted in the light of the specification and drawings.

An application for a patent must refer to a single invention or to a group of inventions so interrelated as to make up a single inventive concept.

The claims must be based on the specification, characterizing the particularities of the application and defining clearly and precisely the subject matter to be protected.

In Brazil, there is no "Markman hearing", also known as a "claim construction hearing", which is a pretrial hearing in a court action during which a judge examines evidence from all parties on the appropriate meanings of relevant key words used in a patent claim.

2. *Specific issues for use claims*

Second use claims are acceptable in a classic Swiss-type format, as follows: "Use of compound X, characterized by being for manufacturing/preparing a medicament for the treatment of disease/condition Y".

III. Scope of protection

1. *Scope of the use*

1.1 *General definition of the term "use"*

An invention of new use of a known product refers to the invention that uses a known product for a new purpose.

A use claim should be regarded as equivalent to a "process claim", and not to a therapeutic method, which is not considered an invention according to Article 10 (VIII) of the IP Law.

1.2 *Manufacture of the pharmaceutical*

In case a third party manufactures the pharmaceutical intended for the treatment of a disease covered by the use claim, direct infringement will be recognized.

In case a third party manufactures the pharmaceutical with no knowledge of the final application, it may be accused of an infringement by contribution.

1.3 *Sale of the product*

See item 1.2 above.

1.4 *Offer for sale*

See item 1.2 above.

1.5 *Application to the patient*

There is no specific rule or jurisprudence regarding application to the patient.

1.6 *Combination products*

Combination of compounds X and Y for treating a determined disease could infringe a claim relating to the use of compound X alone for the same disease, since the potentially infringing product would fall within the scope of the use claim.

2. *Absolute product protection*

2.1 *Limitation through the term "use"*

Use claim should not be construed as relating to substance X which is itself known, but as intended for use as defined according to a Swiss-type use claim.

2.2 *Off-label use*

There is no relevant discussion on this issue in Brazil.

3. *Dosage regimes*

There is no specific rule or jurisprudence regarding the scope of protection for dosage regimes.

4. *Patient groups*

There is no specific rule or jurisprudence regarding the scope of protection for patient groups.

5. *Extension under the doctrine of equivalents*

In Brazil, infringement by equivalence is expressly provided for in the IP Law, as follows:

> "Article 186. The criminal offenses of this Chapter are committed even if the violation does not affect all the claims of the patent or if it is restricted to the use of means equivalent to the subject matter of the patent."

Accordingly, to demonstrate nonliteral infringement in Brazil, it is necessary to prove that the means or process used by the alleged infringer is equivalent to the patented subject matter. In principle, it is not necessary to compare each particular element or step defined in the claim with the respective element or step in the infringing subject matter, but rather only the whole invention with the infringing product or process. In other words, even if a specific feature defined in a claim is totally omitted from an infringing product, if this product can still be regarded as an overall equivalent to the patented product, equivalence might be argued. Nevertheless, many practitioners consider that equivalence should preferably be established on an element-by-element basis rather than by an overall comparison.

Brazilian courts apply this concept in a broad way. In a few decisions, the courts have expressly indicated the criteria used to decide in favor of nonliteral infringement. As indicated below, the Court of Appeal of São Paulo has already applied the "tripartite test" for infringement by equivalence.

In general, Brazilian courts adopt a pro-patentee position when there are "insubstantial differences" between the claimed invention and the infringing subject matter. In these cases, the courts find patent infringement on the merits of the case, in a final ruling. A possible restriction to the application of the concept of infringement by equivalence relies in consideration of the prosecution history of the case.

IV. Infringing acts

The Brazilian IP Law in Article 42 expressly specifies acts that are considered to be patent infringements:

> "Article 42 – A patent confers on its proprietor the right to prevent third parties from manufacturing, using, offering for sale, selling or importing for such purposes without his consent:
> I – a product that is the subject of a patent;
> II – a process, or product directly obtained by a patented process.
>
> § 1 – The patentee is further guaranteed the right to prevent third parties from contributing to the practice by other parties of the acts referred to in this article.
>
> § 2 – The rights in a process patent will be violated, insofar as item II is concerned, when the holder or owner of a product fails to prove, through specific judicial ruling, that it was obtained by a manufacturing process different from that protected by the patent."

1. Infringing person or entity

Anyone (person or entity) exploiting the subject matter covered by a patent without the authorization of the patentee is considered an infringer.

2. Direct infringement

Direct infringement occurs when the product or the process incorporates all elements of a claim. Literal patent infringement happens, for instance, in the following situations:

(a) the manufacturing of a pharmaceutical product (for instance, a compound, a composition or a kit) which is patented, without the authorization of the patentee;
(b) the use of a patented pharmaceutical process (for instance, a process for preparing a compound or a composition) without the authorization of the patentee;
(c) the exportation, sale, exhibition, or offering for sale, maintaining in stock, concealing, or receiving, with a view to the use of it for economic purposes, of a product manufactured in violation of a patent;
(d) the importation of a patented product without the patentee's consent, for the purposes mentioned in point (c) above, provided that the product was not placed on the market by the patentee or with their consent; or
(e) the supplying of a component of a patented invention, provided that the final application of this component necessarily leads to the exploitation of the subject matter of the patent.

2.1 Manufacture of the pharmaceutical

See point (a) of item 2 above

2.2 Offer for sale

See point (c) of item 2 above

2.3 Sale

See point (c) of item 2 above

2.4 Export

See point (c) of item 2 above

2.5 Import

See point (d) of item 2 above

2.6 Combination products

See point (e) of item 2 above

3. Indirect infringement

Indirect infringement (or contributory infringement) is expressly foreseen in aforementioned Article 42 §1, and in Article 185 of the IP Law:

> "Article 185 – Supplying a component of a patented product, or material or equipment for carrying out a patented process, provided that the final application of the component, material or equipment necessarily leads to the exploitation of the subject matter of the patent."

3.1 Objective acts

An indirect infringement is the act of supplying a component of a patented product, or material or equipment for carrying out a patented process, provided that the final application of this component, material, or equipment *necessarily leads* to the exploitation of the patented product or process.

3.2 Subjective conditions

There are none. The indirect infringement is determined through objective analysis on a case-by-case basis.

3.3 *Export*

It could be possible to interpret the provisions of aforementioned Article 42 §1, and Article 185 in a way that the exportation to another country by an unauthorized third party of a matter that contributes to an infringement in such country is an infringement of a Brazilian patent. However, due to lack of case law in this regard, it is difficult to foresee the Court's reaction to this argument.

3.4 *Import*

The importation of a matter that contributes to an infringement in Brazil is considered an infringement of a Brazilian patent.

3.5 *Combination products*

The combination of products resulting in a patented product is considered a patent infringement.

4. ***Off-label use***

There is no representative discussion on off-label use in Brazil.

4.1 *General admissibility of off-label use*

Not applicable.

4.2 *Liable persons*

Not applicable.

4.3 *Objective requirements for infringement*

Not applicable.

4.4 *Subjective requirements for infringement*

Not applicable.

5. ***Dosage regimes***

So far, there is no case law for patent infringement involving dosage regimes.

6. ***Patient groups***

So far, there is no case law for patent infringement involving patient groups.

V. Remedies

Criminal and civil remedies are available as follows:

Criminal remedies:

- search and seizure;
- criminal complaint;
- arrest and possible imprisonment of infringers; and
- costs.

Civil remedies:

- search and seizure;
- injunction;
- damages;
- destruction of seized products; and
- costs.

1. Injunctions

The Court may grant a preliminary injunction or a permanent injunction:

- preliminary injunction (or restraining order): the defendant (alleged infringer) will not be permitted to exploit the subject matter covered by the patent until a final decision on the merits is duly rendered, under the threat of a daily fine. The goal here is to prevent future violations;
- permanent injunction: the defendant (infringer) will be prohibited from exploiting the subject matter covered by the patent as long as the patent is in force.

2. Damages

According to Article 210 of the Brazilian IP Law, the amount of damages awarded to the injured party is determined according to one of the following criteria most favorable to the plaintiff: (a) the benefits that would have been gained by the injured party if the violation had not occurred; (b) the benefits gained by the infringer; or (c) licensing royalties.

3. Information

3.1 Names of manufacturer, distributors etc.

The court may order the defendant to provide names of, for instance, manufacturers and distributors.

3.2 Names of customers

The court may order the defendant to provide names of customers.

3.3 *Information about infringing sales*

The court may order the defendant to provide information about infringing sales in order to determine the amount of damages awarded to the plaintiff.

3.4 *Account of profits*

The court may order the defendant to provide information about profits in order to determine the amount of damages awarded to the plaintiff.

4. *Recall of products and destruction*

The Court may order the recall or the destruction of seized products.

5. *Recovery of legal costs*

The patent owner may recover attorneys' fees of 10–20% of the amount of damages recovered by the patent owner, as well as all the official costs connected with the litigation. "Official costs" is defined as a filing fee paid to the court by the filing party. It is reimbursed by the losing party.

VI. Exceptions from patent protection

1. *Exhaustion of rights*

Brazilian law (Article 43) expressly provides the following exceptions to the rights conferred by a patent:

- acts done privately and without commercial ends;
- acts for experimental purposes related to studies or to scientific or technological research;
- the preparation of a medicine according to a medical prescription for individual cases; and
- acts of use after domestic exhaustion of rights.

Among these exceptions is the principle of national exhaustion of rights. A patentee would still, however, be entitled to prevent third parties from carrying out the parallel importation of patented products.

2. *Patient welfare*

The leading international instrument regarding intellectual property rights nowadays is the World Trade Organization's (WTO) Trade-Related Aspects of Intellectual Property Rights Agreement – TRIPS. Regarding the objective of intellectual property rights, TRIPS Article 7 sets forth that the "protection and enforcement of intellectual property rights should contribute to the promotion of technological innovation and to the transfer and dissemination of technology, to the mutual advantage of producers and users of technological knowledge and in a manner conducive to social and economic welfare, and to a balance of rights and obligations".

In addition, Article 5 of the Brazilian Federal Constitution, which refers to fundamental rights and guarantees, states in paragraph XXIX that "the law shall ensure the authors of industrial inventions of a temporary privilege for their use, as well as protection of industrial creations, property of trademarks, names of companies and other distinctive signs, in view of the social interest and the technological and economic development of the country".

Therefore, although there is no jurisprudence specifically regarding patient welfare, the judge may take the above legal provisions into account when making a decision.

3. Others specific to second medical use claims

There is no specific requirement in order to show an infringement of a second medical use patent.

VII. Procedural issues

1. Preliminary injunction cases

In civil law, a patentee can request a preliminary injunction at any time and even before the defendant knows of the action. The judge may even grant a preliminary injunction without hearing the defendant if they consider that serving the defendant with the summons would risk the integrity of the evidence.

1.1 Availability for second medical use claims

This is possible as long as the requirements for granting a preliminary injunction are met. Please see comments in item 1 above.

1.2 Specific requirements

Before granting an injunction, the judge must be convinced that: (i) there is a likelihood of success of the plaintiff's claims (a technical expert's written opinion is usual a very powerful piece of evidence); and (ii) the plaintiff's right is threatened by the activity of the defendant and could be severely damaged if no action is taken before a final decision on the merits is rendered.

2. Cases on the merits

So far, there is no case law for patent infringement of second medical use.

3. *Enforcement of judgments*

In Brazil, judgments ordering or prohibiting acts/injunctions are enforceable. The court will order the defendant to post the amount of damages suffered by the plaintiff in a judicial account and this amount is then transferred to the plaintiff.

VIII. Validity

1. *Relevance for infringement cases*

Invalidity of a patent is expressly provided for in the law as a matter of defense in the course of an infringement action. In other words, the defendant of a patent infringement lawsuit – the alleged infringer – may state that there is no infringement under the allegation that the patent is invalid. If the invalidity defense is successful in an infringement action, the decision has a legal effect only between the parties.

Aside from arguing nullity of the patent as a matter of defense in the course of an infringement action, the accused party may also file an invalidity lawsuit before a Federal Court requesting nullity of the patent, with the BPTO as a codefendant. If there is sufficient evidence on the invalidity of the patent in the nullity action, an injunction may be granted whereby the effects of the patent are suspended until a final decision on the merits is issued. In this scenario, the infringement action will probably be suspended until the Federal Court decides on the merits of the nullity action. However, the infringement action judge has complete discretion as to whether or not to stay that action pending the Federal Court's decision.

2. *Specifics for second medical use claims*

There is no specific requirement.

IX. Tactical considerations

1. *Plaintiff*

1.1 *Requesting ex parte injunction before serving warning letter*

It is important to ascertain whether a plaintiff should serve the potential infringer with a preparatory warning letter. This opens up the risk of suffering a patent nullity action or a declaratory noninfringement action even before the filing of the patent infringement action. Instead of serving a warning letter, consider going straight for an *ex parte* injunction. Even if the alleged infringer is enjoined, it can still file a nullity action, but it will have stopped the harm – at least while the case is pending.

1.2 *Priority to obtain preliminary injunction*

Because sometimes the final ruling takes years in Brazil due to the court's huge backlog, in many cases, it is vital to obtain a preliminary injunction (or restraining order). In this case, due to fact that the state court judges often do not have technical backgrounds, it is strongly recommended to obtain as many expert opinions to support the preliminary injunction claim (preferably from local professors) as possible.

1.3 *Obtaining discovery privately and early*

There is no discovery process in Brazil. If the goal is to collect damages rather than stop the infringement, it is important to obtain as much information privately about the sales of the allegedly infringing product before starting court proceedings. For example, it is possible to use information from criminal proceedings. The patent owners usually choose to recover damages based on the profits obtained by the infringer. This amount will only be calculated at the very end of the litigation, but if the patent owner can collect all information in advance, that will minimize the risk of not being able to obtain such data at the end of the litigation.

1.4 *Suing on strong patents*

The patent owner must be very aware of any weaknesses in its patent before trying to enforce it. The potential infringer will certainly file a nullity action in the Federal Courts. If the patent is not strong and the potential infringer can show prior art that was not taken into consideration during the patent prosecution phase, for instance, there is always the chance that the BPTO, as mandatory codefendant, will review its position and request the cancellation of the patent. This would create a serious obstacle for the patent owner, should the owner choose to defend the patent in the Federal Courts by suing the BPTO.

1.5 *Reviewing the prosecution history of the patent*

Although industrial property law does not contain specific provisions related to prosecution history "estoppel," it is interesting to note that this has been applied. In fact, the courts have been applying a general legal concept called *venire contra factum proprium*, which, in a nutshell, provides that parties cannot take contradictory courses during prosecution either in the BPTO or the courts. Therefore, patentees cannot argue one way to have their patent granted, and, thereafter, enforce their rights with opposing arguments.

Hence, before starting a patent litigation, it is very important to review the prosecution history of the patents involved and carefully analyze the potentially infringing product, to check for possible inconsistency issues that might jeopardize the case.

2. *Defendant*

2.1 *Monitoring of the courts*

Monitor the state courts in attempt to detect the filing of a possible patent infringement court action. If this court action is detected on the same day on which it was filed, there is an opportunity to submit a written brief in an attempt to avoid the granting of an *ex parte* preliminary injunction.

2.2 *Non-infringement declaratory court action*

File a court action seeking a declaration stating that the product does not infringe a certain patent before a state court. In order to proceed with this lawsuit, it is necessary to submit technical comments and pieces of evidence proving the non-infringement.

2.3 *Nullity action*

File an invalidity lawsuit before a Federal Court requesting nullity of the patent. The Brazilian Patent Office will be a codefendant in this lawsuit.

If there is sufficient evidence about the invalidity of the patent (for instance, a written opinion by a Brazilian scholar attesting to this fact), a preliminary injunction may be granted whereby the effects of the patent are suspended until a final decision on the merits is issued.

In this scenario, an eventual infringement action will probably be suspended until the Federal Court decides on the merits of the nullity action. However, it is important to bear in mind that the judge handling a possible patent infringement action has complete discretion as to whether or not to stay that action pending the Federal Court's decision.

Mexico

Javier Uhthoff-Orive

A. AVAILABILITY OF PROTECTION

Surgical, therapeutic and diagnostic methods for the treatment of the human or animal body are statutorily excluded from patentability in most legislations around the world, and Mexican law is no exception.

Under the Mexican Law of Industrial Property ("MLIP"), said methods are excluded from patentability since they are not considered as inventions. The exclusion of medical treatment derives from ethical reasons based on the desirability not to put obstacles in the way of the saving of lives and the caring for the suffering by medical professionals.

However, it is feasible to obtain patent protection in Mexico for pharmaceutical methods of treatment involving a compound or composition if method of treatment claims can be amended in line with the "Swiss-style" claims and the EPC 2000 format:

> "The use of a substance X for the manufacture of a medicament for the treatment of a disease Y".
>
> "Compound (or substance) X for use as a medicament useful in the treatment of a disease or condition Y".

I. Legal framework

1. *National statutory laws*

Article 19 of the MLIP (cited below) contains various subject matter eligibility issues as it refers to subject matter which is not considered as an invention in Mexico. Among the excluded subject matter, Article 19 (VII) contains reference to surgical, therapeutic or diagnostic treatment applicable to the human body and animals.

> "Article 19. The following shall not be considered inventions for the purposes of this Law:

I. theoretical or scientific principles;

II. discoveries that consist in making known or revealing something that already existed in nature, even though it was previously unknown to man;

III. diagrams, plans, rules and methods for carrying out mental processes, playing games or doing business, and mathematical methods;

IV. computer programs;

V. methods of presenting information;

VI. aesthetic creations and artistic or literary works;

VII. methods of surgical, therapeutic or diagnostic treatment applicable to the human body and to animals; and

VIII. juxtaposition of known inventions or mixtures of known products, or alteration of the use, form, dimensions or materials thereof, except where in reality they are so combined or merged that they cannot function separately or where their particular qualities or functions have been so modified as to produce an industrial result or use not obvious to a person skilled in the art."

Derived from the above exclusion in the law, and due to widespread interest from patent applicants to protect inventions related to pharmaceutical indications of drugs, Mexican patent practice has been adapted, as in other countries, to provide availability of protection for such inventions through "use" claims. In Mexico, there are no provisions that *expressly* regulate inventions related to novel uses of known compounds or second medical uses, *per se*. Nevertheless, as with any other invention, it is imperative that it complies with the definition of invention provided in Article 15 MLIP (cited below), with the patentability requirements and that it does not fall within the exclusions of Articles 16 and 19 of the IPL. In particular, a claim under Mexican practice must not claim a method of treatment as such and it must disclose a non-obvious result or use of a known compound or a synergistic effect of known compounds. As stated, such practice is not clearly and literally provided in the MLIP, in fact, Mexican Law does not clearly provide for the protection of "uses". Several Articles in the MLIP only provide for the existence of two types of inventions, products and processes (i.e., Articles 12, 24, 25 of the MLIP). However, certain other Articles do contain references to uses. In spite of this, for many years now, patent applications have been filed and patents granted for pharmaceutical uses under the referenced "Swiss-type" use draft for claims and more recently under the purpose-limited product claims (EPC 2000 product-for-use claims).

"Article 15. Any human creation that allows matter or energy existing in nature to be transformed for use by man for the satisfaction of his specific needs shall be considered an invention."

1.1 Pharmaceuticals

In Mexico, no distinction exists nor has been made between pharmaceutical products and biologic or biotech drug products in terms of the availability for patenting their therapeutic indications as second medical uses. In light of this, many granted patents exist related to these types of inventions regardless of the nature of the drug molecule (chemical synthesis or biologic).

1.2 Biologics

As stated above, no distinction exists between pharmaceutical products and biologic or biotech drug products in terms of the availability for patenting their therapeutic indications as second medical uses.

2. International treaties

Mexico is a member state of several free trade agreements, including the North America Free Trade Agreement ("NAFTA") with the U.S. and Canada; as well as other international agreements directly or indirectly related to TRIPS. In this regard, Mexican judicial case law has established that international treaties signed by Mexico are hierarchically at the same level as the National Constitution and therefore, all legal provisions and regulations existent in international treaties are at the same level of importance and enforceability as the Mexican Constitution and are even above local laws in cases of dispute. In light of the above, many issues which may be ambiguous or discussible under national law can be addressed by enforcing international treaty provisions.

2.1 TRIPS

Mexico is a member state of TRIPS and therefore all its provisions are applicable.

Article 27(1) TRIPS states that patents shall be granted to 'any inventions, whether products or processes, in all fields of technology, provided that they are new, involve an inventive step and are capable of industrial application'. It is open to question whether TRIPS requires protection for second medical use claims, although some argue that denying patentability to second medical use claims is contrary to TRIPS, particularly Article 27(1). Moreover, Article 27(3)(a) TRIPS permits exclusions from patentability of diagnostic, therapeutic and surgical methods of treatment of humans or animals. Some member states justify denial of patent protection to second medical use claims on the basis that such claims are related to or simply another form of a method of medical treatment, and therefore permissibly excluded from patentability.

2.2 FTAs

As mentioned above, Mexico is a member state of various free trade agreements, including NAFTA and, as of recently, the Trans-Pacific Partnership Agreement ("TPP") both of which include intellectual property, and more specifically patent-related provisions.

Under NAFTA and the TPP, patents must be granted for inventions that are new, involve an inventive step, and are capable of industrial application. NAFTA and TRIPS allow member states to exclude methods of medical treatment from patent protection. In Article 1709(3)(a) of NAFTA, for example, parties are permitted to exclude from patent protection "diagnostic, therapeutic and surgical methods for the treatment of humans or animals." Similarly, the TRIPS agreement, in Article 27(3) (a), allows member states to exclude from patent protection "diagnostic, therapeutic and surgical methods for the treatment of humans and animals."

3. *Availability through case law*

Mexico has very little case law regarding patents in general, and even less when referring to substantive issues regarding subject matter eligibility. Patent litigation in Mexico is quite rare and most cases are usually resolved through formal issues, main patenting requirement issues (novelty, inventive step) or even agreed between the parties before reaching a substantive analysis stage. In spite of the above, a handful of cases are currently under litigation referring to second medical use claims. However, since a final resolution has not been reached, the outcomes are yet to be determined.

4. *Patent term extension/SPCs*

There are no provisions for patent term extensions or supplementary protection certificates in Mexican law. Normally the 20-year term for patents is quite strict in Mexico and, in practice and according to local law, cannot be extended under any circumstance.

In theory, the life term of a patent could be extended under certain international treaties (for example, NAFTA) where the Health Regulatory Authority has delayed the process of obtaining marketing authorization for a patented product. However, in practice this has not been attempted, mainly because the NAFTA provision in this regard, as written, seem an option for the signatory states and not a requisite.

The same happens with the recently signed (TPP), form which member is also a recently included member state. In the TPP, although clearer provisions regarding patent term extensions have been included, they are still provided as an option or a recommendation for signatory states.

The most apparent change for patents under the TPP is the existence of two categories of patent term extension; namely, (1) patent term extension owing to delays in prosecuting patent applications at the patent office, and (2) specifically for pharmaceutical patents, derived from delays in obtaining marketing or regulatory approval.

4.1 *Patent prosecution delays*

For patent office delays, the TPP requires that patent terms shall be extended where "unreasonable delays" happen in application processing, meaning more than five years from the filing date or more than three years after a request for examination of an application.

4.2 *Marketing approval delays for pharmaceutical patents*

The TPP also grants patent term extension to pharmaceutical patents impacted by "unreasonable curtailment" or delay in obtaining regulatory or marketing approval.

II. Policy considerations

1. Health and social issues

There are policy reasons underlying the exclusion of medical treatments from patentability. The exception for medical treatment derives from ethical reasons based on a need not to be a hurdle to saving lives, relieving suffering and healing diseases. Medicine is a profession which must be open to the sharing of knowledge and practice and the patenting of methods of treatment could result in and obstacle for medical professionals.

It can also be argued that, in a publicly funded health care system, patenting methods of treatment may also entail significant costs if doctors are required to pay royalties for the methods they use to treat patients, or if hospitals are required to obtain patent licenses for the treatments that they provide.

In spite of the above, it is also desirable to provide patent protection to inventions that deserve it, to promote further research and development of new and better medical treatments. Therefore, protection for the compounds and compositions that alleviate diseases is indeed necessary.

In this way, the patentability of medical uses, in general, through the application of claim wording such as Swiss-type and "product-for-use" provide a certain equilibrium in light of the fact that the interpretation of said claims permits a medical professional to continue applying all necessary methods of treatment but also providing exclusivity to innovators for their research and development against competitors that may dishonestly profit from the research and development efforts of others.

2. Legal issues

As noted above, although methods of medical treatment are not patentable in Mexico, patents are nonetheless allowed for drug compounds that are used or indicated in medical treatments. Although there is no specific, clear and legal provision in Mexican law for patenting compounds that are characterized by their use and/or uses of products for a specific purpose, the rationale for allowing use or compound for use patents derives from the fact that patents are available in Mexico for inventions. An invention is defined as in the referenced Article 15 MLIP as "any human creation that allows matter or energy existing in nature to be transformed for use by man for the satisfaction of his specific needs".

In this way, drug compounds are considered a "human creation that allows matter or energy existing in nature to be transformed for use by man for the satisfaction of his specific needs" and therefore, are within the legal scope for obtaining patent protection. The utility requirement (transformation of matter or energy) in this definition is important for "use" or "second medical use" patents. The utility requirement for obtaining a patent prevents the obtaining of a patent monopoly over an invention if it is not clear what useful application that invention might have as that would be contrary to public policy interests existing behind patent law: to promote the advancement of scientific knowledge and development. Every invention must therefore have a provable utility in order to be patentable.

This requirement of utility therefore means that "use" or "second medical use" drug patents are obtained, not simply for compounds as such, but for compounds having a specific and clear utility. This utility must be included in the patent specification. A patent right is then granted for that compound and limited to that particular use (or uses). However, a new use or a previously known use (in the cases of second medical use patents) would not be covered by the granted patent claim(s). In other words, "use" or "second medical use" claims permit the legal balance between the necessary freedom to operate for healthcare professionals and the necessary recompense for research and development.

B. VALIDITY

I. Allowable claim wording

1. Product claims

In Mexico, as stated above, pharmaceutical products are eligible for a patent when they are novel and inventive. Much of the normal claim drafting used around the world for product claims is normally accepted in Mexico, such as: Markush claims, compound claims, composition claims, combination claims, polymorphs, enantiomers, crystalline forms, salts, hydrates, and so on, in the case of chemical synthesis products; and for claims based on a sequence or other structural features when referring to biologic compounds. In the case of "use" or "second medical use" cases, the recently allowable compound-for-use draft in Mexico is intended to provide clarity on the correct interpretation of these claims as purpose-limited product claims. Allowable claim wording in this respect is normally "Compound X for use in the treatment of disease Y", "Composition X for use in the treatment of disease Y" or "Compound (or composition) X for use in a method of treatment of disease Y" or other similar derivations.

2. Method claims

Method or process claims are eligible for a patent in Mexico when the methods are novel, inventive and do not refer to a method for treating the human or animal body. In the biotech and pharmaceutical areas, methods of manufacture are indeed eligible for a patent, however methods for treatment are not.

3. Use claims

For a long time, Swiss-type ("use of X for the manufacture of a medicament for the treatment of disease Y") claims have been allowable in Mexico. Nevertheless, enforcement of said patent claims has proved complex since their interpretation is problematic due to the lack of a clear definition of use patents and therefore, use claims have been interpreted as process claims in some instances. In light of the above, and since the availability of compound-for-use drafting for "use" or "second medical use" patents, it may be more desirable to use said drafting instead of the Swiss-type form as it permits the correct interpretation of product and not of process.

4. *System claims*

Systems that are novel and inventive are eligible in Mexico unless the system or elements thereof involve excluded subject matter (Article 19 MLIP) or are simply a mixture of previously known inventions that may function independently.

5. *Dosage regimes*

Dosage regime "use" or "second medical use" claims are not excluded from patenting in Mexico per se. However, dosage regimes are complicated since, normally, the only novel feature of such regimes is the regime itself and not the compound or the newly claimed disease. In light of the above, dosage regime claims may be objected to due to lack of inventive step considering that developing and researching a new dose or dose regime of a previously known compound or drug for the treatment of a previously known disease could be interpreted as a normal procedure for a person skilled on the art without the necessity of an inventive step. In practice, patents have been allowed containing dosage and dosage regime claims in Mexico when the applicant is able to prove that the dose or dosage regime provides a technical effect that is surprising or not foreseeable from the existing prior art. In some of these cases, side effects problems that existed in the prior art compound or use thereof, which are corrected or solved by the new dose or dosage regime, are sufficient to prove inventive step.

6. *Patient groups*

As with dosage regimes, "use" or "second medical use" claims directed to specific patient groups are not excluded from patenting in Mexico per se. However, claims directed to a "use" or "second medical use" in a particular patient group are complicated since, as with dosage regime claims, the only novel feature of such uses is the particular patient group and not the compound or the newly claimed disease. Therefore, patient group use claims may be objected to due to lack of inventive step considering that developing and researching a use of a previously known compound or drug for the treatment of a previously known disease could be interpreted as a normal procedure for a person skilled on the art without the necessity of an inventive step. Once again, in practice, patents have been allowed containing patient group specific use claims in Mexico when the applicant is able to prove that the novel patient group provides a technical effect that is surprising or not foreseeable from the existing prior art. For example, if the prior art contained some teaching or suggestion directed to a problem derived from using that specific drug with a particular patient group and the "new" invention provides the solution to said problem, then the inventive step issue could be overcome.

II. Novelty

1. General definition of novelty and prior art

The MLIP provides the following Articles 16, 17 and 12 for providing novelty requirements as well as the general definitions of "new" and "prior art":

> "Article 16. Inventions that are new, the result of an inventive step and industrially applicable under the terms of this Law shall be patentable, with the exception of:
>
> I. essentially biological processes for obtaining, reproducing and propagating plants and animals;
>
> II. biological and genetic material as found in nature;
>
> III. animal breeds;
>
> IV. the human body and the living matter constituting it; and
>
> V. plant varieties."
>
> "Article 17. The prior art on the filing date of the patent application or, where applicable, the recognized priority date, shall be used to determine whether an invention is new and involves an inventive step. Furthermore, in order to determine whether an invention is new, the prior art shall include all patent applications filed in Mexico prior to said date and still pending, even if the publication referred to in Article 52 of this Law occurs at a later date."
>
> "Article 12. For the purposes of this Title:
>
> I. "new" means anything not found in the prior art;
>
> II. "prior art" means the body of technical knowledge that has been made public by oral or written description, by use or by any other means of dissemination or information, within the country or abroad;
>
> III. "inventive step" means the creative process the results of which are not obvious from the prior art to a person skilled in the art;
>
> IV. "industrial application" means the possibility of an invention being produced or used in any branch of economic activity;
>
> V. "claim" means the essential characteristic of a product or process for which protection is precisely and specifically claimed in the application for a patent or registration and granted, where appropriate, in the corresponding title; and
>
> VI. "filing date" means the date on which the application is filed with the Institute, or with the offices of the Ministry of Trade and Industrial Development within the country, provided that it meets the requirements specified in this Law and the Regulations thereunder."

As can be seen, the definitions of novelty and prior art in Mexico are very straightforward, defining novelty as anything which is not found in the prior art and the prior art as all technical knowledge that has been made public either in written or oral form or by the putting the invention into practice in a public manner, or through any other form of dissemination. Care should be taken regarding Article 17 MLIP that provides that all patent applications filed in Mexico (this includes internationally filed PCT patent applications) are considered, for novelty purposes, as part of the prior art regardless of whether published or not.

2. *Definition of skilled person*

The "skilled person" is not defined within the MLIP nor its regulations however, in practice, Mexican examiners apply the recognized definition provided by the European Law, i.e.: the „person skilled in the art" is a skilled practitioner in the relevant field of technology, who is possessed of average knowledge and ability and is aware of what was common general knowledge in the art at the relevant date. They should have had access to everything in the „state of the art", in particular, the documents cited, and to have had at their disposal the means and capacity for routine work and experimentation, which are normal for the field of technology in question. If the problem prompts the person skilled in the art to seek its solution in another technical field, the specialist in that field is the person qualified to solve the problem. The skilled person is involved in constant development in their technical field. They may be expected to look for suggestions in neighboring and general technical fields or even in remote technical fields, if prompted to do so. Assessment of whether the solution involves an inventive step must therefore be based on that specialist's knowledge and ability. There may be instances where it is more appropriate to think in terms of a group of persons, e.g. a research or production team, rather than a single person. It should be borne in mind that the skilled person has the same level of skill for assessing inventive step and sufficient disclosure.

3. *Scope of disclosure*

3.1 *General rules*

A patent application or patent disclosure must contain sufficient information to allow a person skilled in the art, using their common general knowledge, to perceive the technical teaching inherent in the claimed invention and to put it into effect accordingly. In other words, the disclosure of the invention must be reproducible without undue burden, and this must be true over the whole scope of the claim. This requirement must be complied with as from the date of filing. Article 55 bis of the MLIP provides that the subject matter content of a Mexican patent application as filed may not later be extended.

3.2 *First medical use*

For obtaining patent protection for a first medical use of a drug product the patent applicant must disclose at least the basic technical information and data (experiments and results thereof) that may let the person skilled in the art understand that the drug product may, with a plausible possibility, serve the stated purpose (therapeutic indication). This does not mean that the applicant must necessarily include clinical trial data or even clinical or test *in vivo* data related to humans or animals. *In vitro* experiments, for example, showing the mechanism of action of the disclosed compound or binding tests thereof may suffice to enable a medical use (first or second). In case of a second medical use, if the second indication derives from the same or a similar mechanism of action as the first one, then the applicant must indeed submit further technical proof, such as *in vivo* studies in animal models or humans, to demonstrate that the second indication (second use) would indeed be a plausible possibility and for complying with novelty and inventiveness requirements.

3.3 *New subject matter*

Under Mexican law and practice, new subject matter may not be added to a filed patent application or granted patent under any circumstance. This is clearly addressed in Article 55 bis MLIP:

> "Article 55 bis. Documents submitted either in compliance with any of the requests referred to in Articles 50 and 55 of this Law or, in the case of voluntary alterations, may not contain additional material or claims that give a scope greater than that contained in the original application considered as a whole.
>
> Voluntary alterations shall be accepted only up to before the issue of the decision on the appropriateness or otherwise of the grant of a patent referred to in Articles 56 and 57 of this Law."

3.4 *New data*

Under Mexican law and practice, new data is allowable as long as it is solely filed for purposes of demonstrating novelty, inventive step or utility of the already disclosed scope of an invention originally filed. Such new data cannot be submitted to support and enable additional or new subject matter that was not originally disclosed in the patent specification.

4. ***Requirements for second medical use***

In general, requirements for second medical use (known compound for new disease) claims are the same or similar to first medical use claims, except that the applicant must submit sufficient technical proof to demonstrate the technical effect (i.e., the new therapeutic indication), going as far as possible to establish the mechanism of action (if said mechanism is new) or demonstrating that the new disease may indeed be treated, with a plausible possibility.

4.1 *Distinction from first medical use*

A distinction between the first medical use and the second medical use must be clearly established when filing for a patent application on a second medical use, mainly to clarify the novelty and inventive step issues between the two. Normally, this is done in the description of the invention within the antecedents that already exist in the prior art as well as the advantages and differences of the disclosed invention vis-à-vis said prior art.

4.2 Sub-species of first medical use

A sub-species of the first medical use may indeed be eligible in Mexico as long as said sub-species complies with the requirements of inventive step.

"Second medical use" claims directed to a sub-species derived from the first medical use are not excluded from patenting in Mexico per se. However, claims directed to a second medical use in a particular sub-species may be complicated since, as with to dosage regime claims, the only novel feature of such use is a sub-species of the first use and not the compound or the newly claimed disease. As a result, sub-species use claims may be objected to due to lack of inventive step considering that developing and researching a use of a previously known compound or drug for the treatment of a previously known disease (or a sub-species thereof) could be interpreted as a normal procedure for a person skilled on the art without the necessity of an inventive step. In practice, patents can be allowed containing sub-species use claims in Mexico when the applicant is able to prove that the novel sub-species use contains a novel and inventive technical effect that is surprising or not foreseeable from the existing prior art. For example, if the prior art contained some teaching or suggestion directed to a problem derived from using that specific drug with a particular sub-species and the "new" invention provides the solution to said problem, then the inventive step issue could be overcome.

4.3 Dosage regimes

As stated under I.5 above, dosage regime "second medical use" claims are not excluded from patenting in Mexico per se. However, dosage regimes are complicated since the only novel feature of such regimes is the regime itself and not the compound or the newly claimed disease. In light of the above, dosage regime claims may be objected to due to lack of inventive step considering that developing and researching a new dose or dose regime of a previously known compound or drug for the treatment of a previously known disease could be interpreted as a normal procedure for a person skilled on the art without the necessity of an inventive step. In practice, patents have been allowed containing dosage and dosage regime claims in Mexico when the applicant is able to prove that the dose or dosage regime provides a technical effect that is surprising or not foreseeable from the existing prior art. In some of these cases, side effect problems that existed in the prior art compound or use thereof, which are corrected or solved by the new dose or dosage regime are sufficient to prove inventive step.

4.5 Special patient groups

As stated under I.6 above, as with dosage regimes, "second medical use" claims directed to specific patient groups are not excluded from patenting in Mexico per se. However, claims directed to a "second medical use" in a particular patient group are complicated since, as with dosage regime claims, the only novel feature of such uses is the particular patient group and not the compound or the newly claimed disease. Thus, patient group use claims may be objected to due to lack of inventive step considering that developing and researching a use of a previously known compound or drug for the treatment of a previously known disease could be interpreted as a normal procedure for a person skilled on the art without the necessity of an inventive step. In practice, patents have been allowed containing patient group specific use claims in Mexico when the applicant is able to prove that the novel patient group provides a technical effect that is surprising or not foreseeable from the existing prior art. For example, if the prior art contained some teaching or suggestion directed to a problem derived from using that specific drug with a particular patient group and the "new" invention provides the solution to said problem, then the inventive step issue could be overcome.

5. *Timing issues*

5.1 *Relevant time of development of second use*

In Mexico, there are no provisions or regulations within Mexican law and practice regarding the relevant time of development of second use.

5.2 *Role of new data*

In Mexico, new data is allowable as long as it is solely filed for purposes of demonstrating novelty, inventive step or utility of an already disclosed scope of the invention originally filed. Such new data cannot be submitted to support and enable additional or new subject matter that was not originally disclosed in the patent specification.

5.3 *Use of old data*

Old data may indeed be used in terms of support in the specification for second medical use claims. Of course, it will ultimately be necessary to comply with novelty and inventive step requirements and, in such cases, differences between the invention and the prior art have to be duly supported and specified.

III. Inventive step/non-obviousness

1. *Definition of inventive step/non-obviousness*

Under Article 12 (III) MLIP, inventive step is defined as "*the creative process the results of which are not obvious from the prior art to a person skilled in the art*":

> "Article 12. For the purposes of this Title:
>
> I. "new" means anything not found in the prior art;
>
> II. "prior art" means the body of technical knowledge that has been made public by oral or written description, by use or by any other means of dissemination or information, within the country or abroad;
>
> III. "inventive step" means the creative process the results of which are not obvious from the prior art to a person skilled in the art;

IV. "industrial application" means the possibility of an invention being produced or used in any branch of economic activity;

V. "claim" means the essential characteristic of a product or process for which protection is precisely and specifically claimed in the application for a patent or registration and granted, where appropriate, in the corresponding title; and

VI. "filing date" means the date on which the application is filed with the Institute, or with the offices of the Ministry of Trade and Industrial Development within the country, provided that it meets the requirements specified in this Law and the Regulations thereunder.

2. *Same scope of disclosure as for novelty?*

The scope of disclosure for inventive step is the same as for novelty under Mexican law and practice, i.e., a patent application or patent disclosure must contain sufficient information to allow a person skilled in the art, using their common general knowledge, to perceive the technical teaching inherent in the claimed invention and accordingly to put it into effect.

3. *Assessment of inventive step/non-obviousness*

By definition, a deductive analysis implies constructing a syllogism based on premises (from the prior art) that lead to a specific necessary conclusion in order to make such syllogism true. In order to make an inventive step analysis possible, a person skilled in the art must have a problem to solve. In order to solve such a problem, it must be assumed that the technician will refer to the prior art and its teachings for a solution. The technician will construct syllogisms based on prior art premises or statements in order to deduce a solution that is expected to work. Such solution should be compared to the solution proposed by the patent in order to verify if it is the same solution or not. If the same solution is reached, the invention would not be the result of an inventive step, but rather the result of a "deductive process".

Furthermore, this approach is consistent with the MLIP, which expressly recognizes (Article 19 (VIII)) that certain combinations of known inventions or modifications thereof might be patentable if they "cannot work separately", i.e. in a synergistic effect, or produce an "industrial result or use that is non-obvious to a technician in that subject matter" (that is, the deduction from the prior art will lead the technician to a different result than the one obtained by combining the inventions or by the novel use).

Under this "deductive" approach, if properly used, the hindsight problem is not present, since the technician will expect such a solution to work based only on premises of the prior art, without taking into account the analyzed invention.

Whereas this approach may seem at first sight as similar to the "teaching-suggestion-motivation" approach used previously in the US, the "deductive" approach does take into account the ability of reasoning by the technician, and therefore, the selection of the premises from the prior art might not necessarily (at least by statute) need express teaching or suggestion, but rather be the result of necessarily following the premises of the combined prior art by the technician.

In practice, the Mexican Institute of Industrial Property seems to apply the problem-solution approach and its officers have publicly stated that they intend to apply the same when examining patents with regard to inventive step.

In the case of second medical use claims, it is always useful to avail of technical data providing advantages and clear differences in the technical effect claimed as second use *vis-à-vis* the prior art, especially the document or documents relating to the claimed compound and its first medical use.

IV. Amendment of claims after grant

1. Admissibility of post-grant amendments in general

The MLIP provides, in Article 61 (cited below) the possibility for post-grant amendments for both patents and utility models, but such provision only allows amendments that comply with very specific requirements and in a very limited manner.

> "Article 61. Changes in the text or drawings of the patent protection title may be allowed only under the following circumstances:
>
> I. to correct any obvious errors or errors in form; and
>
> II. to limit the scope of the claims.
>
> The changes authorized shall be published in the Gazette.

2. Procedural issues

2.1 Independent limitation proceedings

As can be seen from Article 61 MLIP limitation of subject matter scope is allowable in post-grant amendments in Mexico. In such a case, the amendment must clearly limit the scope of the claims in order for it to be accepted.

2.2 Opposition proceedings

The MLIP does not provide for opposition proceedings after the granting of a patent. Ja

2.3 Nullity actions

Although not proven in practice due to the scarcity of patent nullity actions in Mexico, in theory, post-grant amendments may indeed be submitted during nullity actions. In that regard, such post-grant amendments must comply in full with the limitations provided by Article 61 MLIP.

3. Added matter

No additional matter may be introduced as previously mentioned and provided by Article 55 bis MLIP.

4. *Sufficiency*

Amendments introduced to a patent after grant must be duly supported and enabled by the patent specification as originally filed.

5. *Multiple indications*

No multiple indications are allowable after the granting of the patent.

V. Change of patent category

1. *General admissibility*

The only changes that are allowable in Mexico after grant are those provided under Article 61 MLIP, i.e., for correcting clerical errors and for limiting the scope of the granted claims. In light of the above, Mexican law and practice do not provide for any changes in patent category.

2. *Use claim as a category*

The MLIP does not provide for "uses" as a patent category, in fact, only processes and products are defined as categories under Mexican law. Nevertheless, pharmaceutical uses have been allowed for quite some time in Mexico which, in theory, should be interpreted as product claims.

C. INFRINGEMENT AND LITIGATION

I. Legal framework

1. *National statutory laws*

Infringement of a patent is considered and administrative matter as foreseen in the MLIP, which in its Article 213 (XI)-(XIV) foresees the different conducts considered as "infringement".

Patent infringement occurs only if the extension of the protection conferred by a patent (which is determined by the content of the claims) perfectly corresponds to the factual evidence that is incorporated as elements of an infringement claim. In other words, the facts have to match the provisions set forth in law. This is very important because both Mexican law and practice are extremely formalistic in nature, and patent infringements are prosecuted as administrative procedures that share the strict application of the law principle that stems from tax and criminal law.

Article 213 (XI)–(XIV) establishes the following conduct as infringements:

"Article 213. The following shall constitute administrative infringements:

...

XI. manufacturing or developing goods protected by a patent or by a utility model or industrial design registration, without the consent of the owner thereof or without the appropriate license;

XII. offering for sale or bringing into circulation goods protected by a patent or by a utility model or industrial design registration, in the knowledge that they have been manufactured or developed without the consent of the owner of the patent or registration or without the appropriate license;

XIII. using patented processes without the consent of the owner of the patent or without the appropriate license;

XIV. offering for sale or bringing into circulation goods that are the result of the use of patented processes, in the knowledge that they have been used without the consent of the owner of the patent or of the person who holds an exploitation license;

…"

2. *Case law*

Within the Mexican legal system there is no formal "case law", as it is a country with a Roman tradition legal system thus the primary and most important source of the law is what is formally enacted by the Congress with some minor effect of Administrative Regulations issued by the Executive Branch through the different government agencies.

2.1 Case law vs. "jurisprudencia"

However, there is a specific system concerning the different criteria adopted by the courts and judges, collectively called *"jurisprudencias"*, which according to the Organic Law of the Federal Judicial Power (LOPJF) can only be created by the higher Federal Courts (either the Supreme Court of the Nation or the Federal Circuit Courts) when the criteria adopted originates in the resolution of at least five different cases involving similar rights or matters, and such criteria can be invoked in subsequent matters that fall into the scope of those particular criteria. Lesser courts are obliged to follow *"jurisprudencia"*, but this does not replace the formally enacted laws nor there is much emphasis on case law, in contrast to common law systems.

II. Claim construction

1. *General rules*

Patent infringement occurs only if the extension of the protection conferred by a patent (which is determined by the content of the claims) perfectly corresponds to the factual evidence that is incorporated as elements of an infringement claim. In other words, the facts have to match the provisions set forth in law. This is very important because both Mexican law and practice are extremely formalistic in nature, and patent infringements are prosecuted as administrative procedures that share the *strict application of the law* principle that stems from tax and criminal law.

Considering the *strict application of the law* principle, under Mexican law there are no infringements other than literal infringements.

2. *Specific issues for use claims*

As stated above, there is no other infringement possible other than the literal infringement, thus concerning "use" patents the claims should protect exactly the actual utilization that the plaintiff is trying to assert.

III. Scope of protection

1. *Scope of the use*

The patent owner is obliged to clearly demonstrate the alleged infringement by comparing elements of the infringing article to the claims of the infringed patent, a principle that is equally applied in "use" patents.

An exception to this rule applies only to process patents when the patent owner has made reasonable efforts to demonstrate the infringement but was unsuccessful in doing so. In that case, the burden of proof is reversed and on the defendant. In other words, the patent will be deemed to be infringed when the holder or owner of a product fails to prove that the product was obtained by a manufacturing process different from the one protected by the patent.

1.1 *General definition of the term "use"*

Considering the strict application of the law principle, under Mexican law there are no infringements other than literal infringement, thus the term "use" refers to – as defined in Article 213 (XII) MLIP – as the utilization or exploitation of a patented product or compound ("*sale, offer for sale or brought into circulation*"), or the same conduct regarding a protected process, when they are protected in relation to a defined use.

1.2 *Manufacture of the pharmaceutical*

Considering the manufacture of a pharmaceutical product would also fall within the broad term "exploitation" (utilization), such conduct would also be considered as infringing if it is directly linked (and there is sufficient evidence to credit such a link) to the specific use that is protected.

1.3 *Sale and offer for sale of the product*

As in the previous paragraph, the sale and/or offer for sale and any other action falling within the broad term "exploitation" (utilization), such conduct would also be considered as infringing if it is directly linked (and there is sufficient evidence to credit such a link) to the specific use that is protected.

1.4 Application to the patient

The sole application to the patient (*"off-label use"*) cannot be considered "exploitation" of the patented use, as long as the manufacturer, seller, distributor, and so on advertises or explicitly indicates the use that is covered under the patent.

1.5 Combination products

As with the terms discussed in the previous paragraphs, a combination of products that is not expressly protected by a patent (i.e. the *"use"*) would not be considered to be infringing.

2. Absolute product protection

2.1 Limitation through the term "use"

The term "use" occurs only if the extension of the protection conferred by a patent (which is determined by the content of the claims) perfectly corresponds to the factual evidence that is incorporated as elements of an infringement claim. In other words, the facts have to exactly match the provisions set forth in law and even if the term "use" can be construed as the realization of different conduct, it is limited to actions involving the sale, distribution offer for sale and bringing into circulation of a product that is protected by a patent that covers exactly the manner of utilization that is the ultimate reason why said product is being sold, offered for sale, distributed, brought into circulation, and so on.

This is very important for the principle of "strict application of the law" that is applied to infringement matters under Mexican law as discussed above (see I. 1.).

2.2 Off-label use

Considering the above and while there is no specific provision under Mexican law, we consider that off-label use is allowed in Mexico.

3. Dosage regimes

Again, the *"strict application of the law"* principle is relevant here, because if the patent for an specific use covers an exact dosage, using the compound in a different dosage than the one covered by the claims could prevent the user from infringing, thus rendering the patent to be very difficult to enforce (see B.5. above).

4. Patient groups

A very similar situation and application exists here regarding the *"strict application of the law"* principle for enforcement (*i.e.* infringement) purposes, which means if the allegedly infringing conduct does not conform exactly to the claims of the patent, there is no infringement.

5. *Extension under the doctrine of equivalents*

Mexico does not have a doctrine of equivalents, and there are no specifically defined laws that provide guidelines on the handling of equivalents. Thus equivalents may fall within the provisions of the Articles of the Mexican law that refer to novelty of invention (Articles 16 and 17 MLIP) and therefore the "equivalent" cases may be handled by applying the regulations established by such Articles. "Equivalents" are usually analyzed during prosecution to establish the differences between the prior art and the invention that is being patented. It is important to mention that patent litigation in Mexico is not as abundant as in other countries, and therefore case law is scarce. However, as time passes, these kinds of cases are expected to become more common.

In the cases where claim interpretation is involved, the MLIP provides that the conferred right of a patent is determined by the allowed claims and that the specification, drawings, biologic material deposits, and so forth, must be used if interpretation is needed. Hence, before starting patent litigation, it is very important to review the prosecution history of the patents involved and carefully analyze the potentially infringing product to check for possible inconsistency issues that might jeopardize the case. When inconsistencies are found the patentee can voluntarily amend the patent at any time provided such amendments do not modify the patented matter, and only if such amendments are to limit the scope of the claims and/or to clarify an obvious mistake. In practice, it is very difficult, if not impossible, to remedy structural weaknesses of a patent via amendments.

In summary, neither Mexican law nor practice recognize "equivalents" when dealing with a patent infringement. Accordingly, the alleged infringing conduct must conform exactly to the claims contained in the patent title that is considered as being infringed.

IV. Infringing acts

Under Mexican law, the legal enforcement of a patent always involves, as a first step, filing for an administrative infringement claim before the Mexican Institute of Industrial Property ("IMPI"). Further appeals to the resolution issued by IMPI can be filed before the Specialized Chamber on Intellectual Property Matters of the Federal Court of Administrative and Taxing Affairs ("SEPI-TFJFA") and, as a last recourse, federal *amparo* appeals before Federal Circuit Courts.

As a result of a firm and definitive resolution declaring an infringement, the successful plaintiff can file an action requesting the recovery of damages and losses, although these claims are regular civil claims tried before regular civil courts.

Considering this, and although there are no 'specialized courts' concerning patent infringements, these matters are examined and tried before authorities specializing in IP affairs.

1. *Infringing person or entity*

Patent holders, authorized licensees and their representatives are entitled to lodge an infringement claim against an alleged infringer. In this regard, the alleged infringer could argue, as part of the defense strategy, the lack of sufficient legal standing.

As IMPI is obliged to examine legal standing to admit the infringement claim, the alleged infringer could file an extraordinary *amparo* federal appeal before a District Court to combat the decision of IMPI to admit the infringement claim as a result of the recognition of the legal standing of the plaintiff.

It should be mentioned that witness depositions and confessional statements are not allowed according to the MLIP.

2. *Direct infringement*

Under Mexican law there are no specific gradations concerning inducement or contributory infringement as the plaintiff is entitled to credit any and all causes of the claimed infringement committed by the infringer, which in turn are limited to the conduct described by law only, specifically Article 213 of the MLIP, which does not foresee contributory matters or inducement as infringing conduct.

Any patent owner and/or their recorded licensee is legally entitled to file diverse actions in order to stop the manufacturing, distribution, transportation, importation and/or sale of an allegedly infringing product by requesting the IMPI to issue a provisional or preliminary administrative order (similar to a preliminary injunction) intended to immobilize and secure infringing products at the place where such infringing articles are located (including customs offices in case of imported items).

Conduct considered as patent infringement is established in Article 213 of the MLIP, which include the manufacture of the pharmaceutical (2.1), offer for sale (2.2), sale (2.3) and export (2.5).

2.1 *Manufacture of the pharmaceutical*

2.2 *Offer for sale*

2.3 *Sale*

2.4 *Import*

2.5 *Export*

Following the same line of thought, any activities taking place outside Mexican territory should have a direct impact on any of the conduct foreseen by Mexican law as an infringement. For example, a clear example of a cause of patent infringement would be to import a product that is either protected by a patent or is a result of the use of a procedure that is patented.

In addition to the above, Article 25 of MLIP expressly foresees the enforceability of patent (be it for use, a process or a product) against import of either a patented product and/or a product that is the direct result of an unauthorized patented process. The import of a product intended to be used in a manner protected by a patent should fall in the same category.

3. *Indirect infringement*

There is no "indirect infringement" under Mexican Law, which adds to the "strict application of the law" principle as discussed in earlier subjects.

4. *Off-label use*

4.1 *General admissibility of off-label use*

For infringement purposes and as discussed in earlier paragraphs, there are no specific provisions in Mexican patent law concerning the admissibility of "off-label use", but considering the "strict application of the law" principle plus the fact that there is no specific provision in this subject, off-label use is generally admitted in Mexico.

V. Remedies

1. *Administrative and civil remedies are available as follows:*

Administrative remedies:

- provisional measures (injunctions); as discussed in earlier paragraphs, any patent owner and/or their recorded licensee is legally entitled to file diverse actions to stop the manufacturing, distribution, transportation, importation, and/or sale of an alleged infringing product by requesting IMPI to issue a provisional or preliminary administrative order (similar to a preliminary injunction) intended to immobilize and secure infringing products at the place where such infringing articles are located (including customs offices in case of imported items). These measures comprise
  - seizure (immobilization) of infringing products;
  - closure of infringing establishment;
  - order to withdraw from circulation all infringing products and related (advertisements) items; and
  - order to stop any and all allegedly infringing conduct.

Civil remedies:

- recovery of damages and losses;
- destruction of seized products; and
- recovery of attorneys' fees.

Mexican law does not provide any criminal remedies for patent infringement, whereas criminal law remedies are available for trademark owners.

2. *Damages*

Once the infringement procedure has terminated and, ideally, the patent owner has obtained a firm and definitive resolution of infringement (i.e. a resolution obtained after exhausting all of the available appeals and recourses, including an *"amparo"* federal appeal trial), then the patent owner is entitled to file a completely new and separate procedure before a Civil Court where only the damages and losses are to be tried.

This is due to provisions set forth in last paragraph of Article 6bis of the Commerce Code, which, roughly translated, states: "Civil actions that are the provoked by unfair competition acts [patent infringements are considered unfair competition acts] can only be initiated when there is a firm ruling in the administrative matter, when this is applicable", the same provision that has been confirmed and reinforced by multiple *jurisprudencias* issued by the Mexican Supreme Court and that, as has been shown in the foregoing, has resulted in the particular problems of the Mexican legal system.

2.1 *Practical implications of such differences*

In a typical patent infringement case, it may take between seven and ten years to obtain a definitive infringement resolution, of course depending on the complexity of the specific case, and once such a definitive infringement resolution is issued the patent owner could have a suitable basis for filing an action to recover damages and losses. Consequently not many companies or individuals have the will or the budget to be involved in such lengthy and costly litigation procedures, which is one of the main reasons for the absence of cases being tried before higher federal courts concerning this particular subject.

2.2 *Mexican law provisions concerning quantification of damages in patent matters*

While in the Mexican legal system the main law governing patent affairs is the MLIP, there are other legal bodies that are applicable concerning cases involving the relief (indemnification) for damages and losses, using provisions that, as stated in previous paragraphs, include the Commerce Code and the Federal Civil Code, as discussed later.

2.3 *Provisions set forth in the MLIP*

Notwithstanding the above, the MLIP does include specific provisions that help to roughly determine the amounts involved in a damages case, as stated in Articles 24 and 221 bis of such Law:

> "Article 24. Once the patent has been granted, the patent owner may seek damages from third parties who, prior to the grant, make use of the patented process or product without his consent, where said use is made after the date on which publication of the application in the Gazette takes effect."
>
> "Article 221 bis. Compensation for material damages or indemnification for damages and harm due to violation of the rights conferred by this Law shall in no case be less than 40 per cent of the public sale price of each product or the price of the rendering of services where infringement of any one or more of the industrial property rights provided for in this Law is involved."

As can be read from the above provisions, the law grants the right to the patent owner to pursue at least the equivalent of 40% of the public sales price of each of the products that were a result of the infringement of the patent. In this regard and as previously stated, once the patent owner obtains a firm and definitive resolution declaring an infringement to the patent, such resolution may serve as the basis of a civil claim in which the plaintiff (patent owner) may request at least 40% of the sales price of each product manufactured as a result of the infringement declared.

2.5 *Other applicable legal bodies and provisions*

Please also note that under Mexican law (Articles 2108, 2109 and 2110 of the Federal Civil Code) the concept of "damages" is strictly defined as "the reduction or decrease in the patrimony or assets of any individual or corporation that is direct result of the actions and/or omissions of another party", and the concept of "losses" is also strictly defined as the "inability to receive a lawful earning or profit, that an individual or company was both entitled and reasonably expecting to receive or obtain, as a consequence of the actions or omissions of another party".

2.6 *Restrictions concerning the concepts and application of "damages and losses"*

Taking into account the above, it is important to point out that in Mexican law there are no provisions concerning consequential, collateral or punitive damages, thus the amount of damages in litigation in Mexico are almost always considerably lower than in the U.S., due to the restriction in the definition of damages and losses and also because the plaintiff must fully credit not only the basis of its claim (i.e. an infringement to a patent) but also the direct relation (cause-effect) between the amount claimed and the action/omission of the defendant, leaving little discretion to the judge to interpret the particular situation and award an amount that is much higher than the actual damage and/or loss that was duly credited by apportioned evidence.

3. *Information*

The production of evidence is not confined to the "discovery" phase at first instance. Documentary evidence should be produced by the parties at the moment of producing (filing) their corresponding responses (briefs) – in other words, the plaintiff produces its evidence in the complaint, and the defendant in its response.

Although there are a number of allowed types of evidence foreseen in law, Mexican practice favors documental evidence and expert opinions along with IMPI's own in-house experts who are regular examiners who routinely render a "technical brief" in most infringement proceedings. It should also be noted that although these technical briefs are in essence "technical opinions" there is no available remedy or recourse to challenge the report within the administrative IMPI procedure.

It is worth mentioning that witness depositions and confessional statements are not allowed, according to the MLIP.

4. *Permanent injunction*

If the plaintiff is successful in the infringement action, the corresponding resolution will generally include a permanent injunction prohibiting the defendant from infringing the patent for the duration of the patent term, as well as prohibiting any other activity or action that may be construed as unfair competition directly related to the declared infringement. In practice, the injunction is usually granted as part of IMPI ruling declaring the infringement. However, the injunction is typically suspended when an appeal is lodged. After all appeals are exhausted the suspended injunction becomes permanent as part of the infringement declaration.

5. *Recovery of legal costs*

Administrative procedures are limited to declaring the existence or not of an infringement matter, plus the imposition of fines as one of the penalties for the infringement. Such procedures do not include the possibility to include attorneys' fees at either the administrative IMPI level or at the appellate level.

The associated costs and length of a patent infringement procedure are substantial. Accordingly, where the owner of the patent is a foreign entity without legal presence and assets in Mexico, pursuing provisional measures against an infringer will likely require the posting of a mandatory and costly guarantee bond that may never be recovered.

VI. Exceptions from patent protection

1. *Exhaustion of rights*

Mexico follows the exhaustion of rights doctrine. Thus the patent owner has no right to enforce a patent against the importer/distributor/seller of a product that is a result of a patented process or a patented product that has been put into circulation (marketed) directly by the patentee or under their consent by a third party.

The above limitation includes parallel imports – in other words, if the patented items and/or products obtained as a result of a patented process were legally put in the market and afterward imported by unauthorized channels – thus the owner of a patent would not have any right on which to base a legal action intended to detain the import of such goods.

2. *Patient welfare*

While this exception is not foreseen under Mexican law, there have been recent cases outside IP matters that have brought attention to this specific exception, which could maybe open the way to use patient welfare as an exception on a patent matter, but then again this is only a theoretical discussion and it is not supported by any precedent nor disposition in the law.

3. *Others specific to second medical use claims*

None foreseen under Mexican Law.

VII. Procedural issues

1. *Preliminary injunction cases*

As discussed above, provisional measures are set forth in Article 199 bis of MLIP and said measures include the power to secure (seize) and immobilize offending products.

In this sense, according to Article 199 bis (1) of the MLIP, in order to determine the implementation of provisional orders, IMPI will require the petitioner to:

- demonstrate the corresponding ownership of rights and any of the following conditions:
  - the existence of a violation of its trademark rights;
  - that the violation of rights is imminent;
  - the existence of the possibility of irreparable damage being suffered; and
  - the existence of a well-founded concern that evidence may be destroyed, concealed, lost or altered;
- post a bond intended to guarantee the possible damages that may be caused by the seizure; and
- provide the necessary information for the identification of the infringing goods.

Likewise, the defendant could request the release of the provisional measures by posting a counter-bond.

The party requesting the provisional measures is liable for the payment of damages caused to the person against whom they have been carried out when the final decision declares that there was no violation nor threat of violation to the complainant's rights or when the provisional measures were requested and the complaint or the trademark infringement action was not filed before the competent authority or IMPI, regarding the merits of the case, within a period of 20 days counted as from the execution of the measure, according to Article 199 bis (3) of the MLIP.

VIII. Validity

1. *Relevance for infringement cases*

Patent litigation in Mexico is a relatively unexplored field, so much so that only a handful of matters involving patent rights have arrived at the higher courts. Thus, the *jurisprudencias* (case law) concerning patent damages is virtually nonexistent.

By now it should be clear that, to pursue a civil claim to recover patent infringement damages, the patent owner must first file an administrative infringement claim that will start an infringement procedure where no damages or losses are examined. In a patent infringement matter the plaintiff is not able to request relief for damages because the law only foresees this procedure as a means of determining whether there was an infringement or not, leaving damages and losses out of the matter being tried.

It is estimated that there are about 30 to 40 patent infringement litigation complaints filed each year, thus it is quite a small universe and experience in this field is limited, let alone in the enforcement of second medical use patents.

2. Specifics for second medical use claims

Considering the information discussed in previous chapters and although there are practical implications concerning the construction of second medical use claims, the enforcement of such claims presents the same issues and challenges as "regular" use patents, with the advantage of Article 192 bis (1) of MLIP concerning the exception when the burden of proof is reversed on the defendant.

IX. Tactical considerations

1. Plaintiff

Early case patent validity analysis is extremely important in Mexico. Patent owners must be very diligent in discovering any flaws of their patent(s) before trying to actively enforce them. It is almost a rule in Mexico that any alleged infringer will surely file an invalidity counterclaim against the asserted patent.

With this in mind, if the validity of the patent is questionable due to mistakes or oversights in the prosecution of the patent, the enforcement results can be adverse. In addition, appeals will face increasing difficulty because the appeal court would have to revoke an invalidity ruling from IMPI before even considering a negative IMPI infringement declaration.

Furthermore, as discussed above, the associated costs and length of a patent infringement procedure are substantial. Accordingly, where the owner of the patent is a foreign entity without legal presence and assets in Mexico, pursuing provisional measures against an infringer will likely require the posting of a mandatory and costly guarantee bond that may never be recovered.

2. Defendant

The recurring key aspect here is using the *"strict application of the law"* principle in favor of the defendant, as the conduct should exactly conform to provisions set forth in the dispositions that establish the infringing conduct, thus the evidence should be completely flawless and conclusive of the alleged infringement.

Resolution Question Q238 – Second medical use and other second indication claims

---

Congress Toronto
Adopted resolution
September 17, 2014

AIPPI

Noting that:

1) The scope of this resolution is the permissibility of patent protection for new therapeutic uses of known compounds and substances, the protection conferred by such patents, and their interplay with regulatory frameworks governing the marketing of pharmaceuticals.
2) While requirements of patentability other than patent eligible subject matter – particularly requirements of novelty and inventive step – may be relevant to the permissibility of patent protection for new therapeutic uses of known compounds and substances, this resolution does not specifically address such requirements. Issues of patent term extension, compulsory licensing, entitlement and supplementary protection certificates are also outside the scope of this resolution.
3) AIPPI has previously studied the impact of public health issues on exclusive patent rights (Q202). That resolution focused on exceptions to exclusive patent rights applicable to medicines and other medical products.
4) AIPPI has further studied issues related to liability for contributory infringement of IPRs and in particular patents (Q204 and Q204P), the availability of injunctions in case of infringement of IPRs (Q219), and relief in IP proceedings other than injunctions or damages (Q236).
5) None of the above-mentioned resolutions is affected by the present resolution.

Considering that:

1) In this resolution, the term "second medical use(s)" refers to new therapeutic use(s) of known compounds and substances. A "second medical use" may be the second or any subsequent new therapeutic use of a known compound or substance.
2) Second medical uses may provide solutions to unmet medical needs and significant benefits to patients. They may require significant investment in research and development and represent socially, medically and economically valuable innovations.
3) Pursuant to Article 27 of the TRIPS Agreement, patents may be obtained for any inventions in all fields of technology.
4) Pursuant to Article 41 of the TRIPS Agreement, members shall ensure that enforcement procedures are available to permit effective action against any act of infringement.
5) Second medical uses qualify as patent eligible subject matter in many, but not all, jurisdictions.
6) Of those jurisdictions that permit patent protection for second medical uses, there is variation as to the types of second medical uses that may be protected, and as to permissible claim formats. Typically, one or more of the following claim formats are permissible: method of treatment claims; claims in the form "use of substance X in the manufacture of a medicament for the treatment of condition Y" (Swiss-type claim); use claims in the form "use of substance X for the treatment of condition Y"; and purpose-limited product claims in the form "substance X for use in the treatment of condition Y".
7) Even where the permissible claim format is consistent between jurisdictions, the actual protection conferred by a patent granted for a second medical use may vary, e.g. due to different claim constructions; different requirements for direct or indirect (contributory) infringement; and any exemptions from infringement or liability for infringement.
8) In some jurisdictions that permit patent protection for second medical uses, regulatory frameworks allow a generic applicant for marketing authorization to exclude from the product information (e.g. product label, package inserts etc., collectively referred to as "label instructions") references to patented second medical uses. This is often referred to as "skinny labelling", or "carving-out" patent protected indications.
9) In many jurisdictions, the regulatory framework provides incentives for generic substitution of a branded pharmaceutical without preventing such substitution if the generic pharmaceutical has not been authorized for the prescribed, patented second medical use.
10) Lack of harmonized laws relating to patent protection for second medical uses and associated regulatory frameworks create uncertainty for all stakeholders, and in particular for originator and generic pharmaceutical companies.
11) The present resolution strives to harmonize patent eligibility of second medical uses and the available protection, independent of any specific claim format.

Resolves that:

1) As a matter of principle clearly reflected in the TRIPS Agreement, patents should be granted without discrimination for any inventions in all fields of technology, including inventions relating to second medical uses.
2) A second medical use should be patentable if it meets the patentability requirements of novelty, inventive step (non-obviousness), and utility or industrial applicability.
3) Exceptions to patent eligibility for methods of medical treatment of the human or animal body should not preclude the patentability of second medical uses. Where such exceptions exist, claim formats for the protection of second medical uses that are compatible with those exceptions should be available.
4) Exclusions from patentability should not depend on the type of second medical use. Patent eligible second medical uses may include, but are not limited to, the use of a known compound or substance for the treatment of a disease or condition not previously treated by that compound or substance; the use of a known compound or substance for the treatment of a new patient class; a different mode of administration of a known compound or substance; the use of a known compound or substance in a new dosage regimen; and a new therapeutic application of a known compound or substance based on a different technical effect.
5) Second medical uses that qualify for patent protection should not be limited to uses that treat disease but should include uses directed at alleviating or preventing disease or otherwise improving health.
6) Each jurisdiction should recognize at least one claim format that provides patent protection for second medical uses, commensurate with this resolution.
7) In principle, every unauthorized act that constitutes a commercial exploitation of a patented second medical use, and acts that contribute thereto, should constitute an act of infringement and give rise to liability for infringement.
8) The unauthorized making, storing, offering, promoting, marketing, distributing, dispensing, selling, importing and exporting of a pharmaceutical with label instructions specifying the patented second medical use should constitute acts of infringement.
9) The fact that a pharmaceutical does not contain label instructions specifying the patented second medical use should not *per se* exclude the finding of infringement of a patent for the second medical use. In particular:
    a) Offering, selling, or promoting a pharmaceutical for a patented second medical use, but without label instructions for such use, as well as placing such pharmaceutical on the market with concomitant references to such second medical use by means other than the label instructions, should constitute infringement;
    b) Whether or not other acts directed to putting a pharmaceutical without label instructions for a patented second medical use to such use amount to infringement should be assessed on a case-by-case basis, taking into account factors such as:
        i) the intent of the alleged infringer;

ii) knowledge of the uses of the pharmaceutical by the alleged infringer, or whether such uses are obvious in the circumstances;
iii) the ability to identify the uses to which the pharmaceutical is put;
iv) the labelling of the pharmaceutical, including whether the label is mandated to include any reference to carved out indications;
v) any marketing or promotional activity carried out by the alleged infringer;
vi) any steps taken by the alleged infringer to discourage/encourage infringing use;
vii) economic conditions of the relevant market, including the relative sizes of the markets for the different uses and the volume of the allegedly infringing pharmaceutical;
viii) prescription practices of relevant professionals, including whether the prescribed use is conveyed to the person who chooses the particular pharmaceutical to be administered; and
ix) dispensing practices, including regulatory provisions aimed at generic substitution.

10) If there is a finding of infringement of a patent claim for a second medical use, liability should be determined in the same manner as liability is determined for infringement of any other type of patent claim, and the same relief should be available as for infringement of any other type of patent claim.
11) However, private acts for non-commercial purposes, including use by patients, should not give rise to liability for infringement of a second medical use claim, provided that such exemption should not extend to any party contributing to such use in a non-private capacity or for commercial purposes.
12) Injunctive relief for infringement of a patented second medical use should not be denied solely because such relief could prevent a pharmaceutical from being commercialized for non-patented uses. Consideration should be given to all circumstances of the case, including the interests of the involved parties.
13) The regulatory frameworks governing the importation and marketing of pharmaceuticals, their labelling, prescription, distribution, dispensing and reimbursement should facilitate transparency as to whether such pharmaceuticals are being dispensed for patented medical uses, and, while not preventing the legitimate commercialization of pharmaceuticals for non-patented medical uses, facilitate enforcement of patent protection for second medical use.
14) AIPPI urges the relevant authorities to implement the necessary measures so that effective protection of second medical uses is not jeopardized by regulatory frameworks.

AIPPI LAW SERIES

1. Sanna Wolk, Kacper Szkalej (eds.), *Employees' Intellectual Property Rights*, 2015 (ISBN 978-90-411-5972-4).
2. Jochen Bühling (ed.), *Patent Protection for Second Medical Uses*, 2016 (ISBN 978-90-411-8253-1).